HANDBOOK OF A
PSYCHOLOGY

MW00996928

The *Handbook of Arab American Psychology* is the first major publication to comprehensively discuss the Arab American ethnic group from a lens that is primarily psychological. This edited book contains a comprehensive review of the cutting-edge research related to Arab Americans and offers a critical analysis regarding the methodologies and applications of the scholarly literature. It is a landmark text for both multicultural psychology as well as for Arab American scholarship.

Considering the post-9/11 sociopolitical context, in which Arab Americans are under ongoing scrutiny and attention, as well as numerous misunderstandings and biases against this group, this text is timely and essential. Chapters in the *Handbook of Arab American Psychology* highlight the most substantial areas of psychological research with this population relevant to diverse subdisciplines, including cultural, social, developmental, counseling/clinical, health, and community psychologies. Chapters also include content that intersects with related fields such as sociology, American studies, cultural/ethnic studies, social work, psychiatry, and public health. The chapters are written by distinguished scholars who merge their expertise with a review of the empirical data in order to provide the most up-to-date presentation of scholarship about this population.

The *Handbook of Arab American Psychology* offers a noteworthy contribution to the field of multicultural psychology and joins references on other racial/ethnic minority groups, including the *Handbook of African American Psychology*, *Handbook of Asian American Psychology*, *Handbook of U.S. Latino Psychology*, and *Handbook of Chicana/o Psychology and Mental Health*.

Mona M. Amer, PhD, is an associate professor of psychology at the American University in Cairo, Egypt. Dr. Amer's primary research and policy interests are in ethnic/racial disparities in behavioral health, with a specialization in the Arab and Muslim minorities. Within that framework she is interested in immigration/acculturation and mental health, mental illness stigma and other cultural barriers to service utilization for minority groups, and the development of culturally valid research measures. Dr. Amer is the co-editor of *Counseling Muslims: Handbook of Mental Health Issues and Interventions*, and previous editor-in-chief of the *Journal of Muslim Mental Health*.

Germine H. Awad, PhD, is an associate professor of psychology in the Department of Educational Psychology at the University of Texas at Austin. Her research can be broadly categorized in the area of prejudice and discrimination as well as ethnic/racial identity and acculturation. Her research tends to focus on two ethnic groups: Arab Americans and African Americans. She has conducted research on predictors of discrimination for Arab Americans and predictors of prejudice toward the group. Dr. Awad is the co-chair of the APA Committee on Ethnic Minority Affairs (CEMA) working group on Arab/Middle Eastern Americans and has served on several journal editorial boards.

HANDBOOK OF ARAB AMERICAN PSYCHOLOGY

Edited by Mona M. Amer and Germine H. Awad

Routledge
Taylor & Francis Group
NEW YORK AND LONDON

First published 2016
by Routledge
711 Third Avenue, New York, NY 10017

and by Routledge
2 Park Square, Milton Park, Abingdon, Oxon OX14 4RN

Routledge is an imprint of the Taylor & Francis Group, an informa business

© 2016 Taylor & Francis

The right of the editors to be identified as the authors of the editorial material, and of the authors for their individual chapters, has been asserted in accordance with sections 77 and 78 of the Copyright, Designs and Patents Act 1988.

All rights reserved. No part of this book may be reprinted or reproduced or utilized in any form or by any electronic, mechanical, or other means, now known or hereafter invented, including photocopying and recording, or in any information storage or retrieval system, without permission in writing from the publishers.

Trademark notice: Product or corporate names may be trademarks or registered trademarks, and are used only for identification and explanation without intent to infringe.

Library of Congress Cataloguing in Publication Data
Handbook of Arab American psychology / edited by Mona M. Amer and Germine H. Awad.
pages cm.
Includes bibliographical references and index.
1. Arab Americans–Psychology. I. Amer, Mona M. II. Awad, Germine H.
E184.A65H365 2016
155.8′4927073–dc23 2015013941

ISBN: 978-0-415-84192-4 (hbk)
ISBN: 978-0-415-84193-1 (pbk)
ISBN: 978-0-203-76358-2 (ebk)

Typeset in Bembo
by Out of House Publishing

CONTENTS

ACKNOWLEDGMENTS

We are grateful to the many people who contributed to making this book possible. Special appreciation is due to George Zimmar, our publisher at Routledge, for believing in the vision of this project and for his unwavering support and guidance over the years. We are honored to have so many talented and exceptional pioneers of Arab American scholarship join us in this endeavor as authors. Their incredible efforts, patience, and collaborative spirit – sometimes under the rush of very tight time lines – helped us achieve an inspiring end product, and for that we are very grateful. We were also fortunate to have two undergraduate editorial assistants who helped facilitate the work: Reem Deif, who showed endless dedication and enthusiasm in numerous referencing and indexing tasks up into the final hours of the project, and Sherine Mikhail, whose detective work with theses and dissertations helped us acknowledge unpublished research that otherwise would have been overlooked in this text. Of course, none of this could have been accomplished without the support of those who are closest to us. Mona Amer thanks her family (Sabah, Magid, Sophi, and Hoda) for their extraordinary and never-ending patience, encouragement, and forgiveness throughout the process. Germine Awad would like to acknowledge her husband (Kevin) for his unwavering support, patience, and belief in this project, and her children (Asa and Isis), who served as a welcome diversion in hectic times.

EDITORS

Mona M. Amer, PhD, is an associate professor of psychology at the American University in Cairo, Egypt, where she received the university's Excellence in Teaching Award. She obtained a doctorate in clinical psychology from the University of Toledo, Ohio, and completed predoctoral and postdoctoral fellowships in the Department of Psychiatry at Yale University School of Medicine, New Haven, Connecticut. In 2006 Dr. Amer was awarded the American Psychological Association's (APA/ APAGS) Award for Distinguished Graduate Student in Professional Psychology for her pioneering work with Arab and Muslim Americans. She was also the sole recipient of the 2005–7 APA Minority Fellowship Program's postdoctoral fellowship in mental health and substance abuse services, focused on behavioral health disparities. Dr. Amer's primary research and policy interests are in ethnic/racial disparities in behavioral health, with a specialization in the Arab and Muslim minorities. Within that framework she is interested in immigration/acculturation and mental health, mental illness stigma and other cultural barriers to service utilization for diverse racial/ethnic groups, and the design of culturally valid research measures. She has, moreover, developed cultural competence training programs for practitioners working with Muslim and Arab clients, and served on the Steward Group of the National Network to Eliminate Disparities, U.S. Substance Abuse and Mental Health Services Administration. Dr. Amer is the co-editor of *Counseling Muslims: Handbook of Mental Health Issues and Interventions* and previous Editor-in-Chief of the *Journal of Muslim Mental Health*.

Germine H. Awad, PhD, is an associate professor of psychology in the Department of Educational Psychology at the University of Texas at Austin. In that capacity she is affiliated with both the Human Development, Culture and Learning Sciences as well as Counseling Psychology programs. Dr. Awad received her master's degree and doctorate in applied experimental psychology from Southern Illinois University, Carbondale. She is the recipient of two teaching awards and the Emerging Scholar-Research Contribution Award from Division 45 (Society for the Scientific Study of Culture, Ethnicity and Race) of the American Psychological Association (APA). Her research can be broadly categorized in the areas of prejudice and discrimination as well as ethnic/racial identity and acculturation. She has published in the areas of discrimination, racial and ethnic identity, affirmative action attitudes, and multicultural research methodology. Her research tends to focus on two ethnic groups: Arab Americans and African Americans. She has conducted research on predictors of perceived discrimination for Arab Americans and predictors of prejudice toward this group. Dr. Awad has served as membership chair for Division 45 of the APA and is the co-chair of the APA Committee on Ethnic Minority Affairs (CEMA) working group on Arab/Middle Eastern Americans. She has served as a member of three journal editorial boards: *Cultural Diversity and Ethnic Minority Psychology*, *Journal of Black Psychology*, and the *Journal of Multicultural Counseling and Development*.

CONTRIBUTORS

Wahiba Abu-Ras, PhD, is an associate professor at the School of Social Work, Adelphi University, New York. She received her doctorate from Columbia University School of Social Work, New York. Her research concentrates on trauma and mental health among Muslim and Arab Americans, and related issues such as domestic violence, the impact of 9/11, coping with trauma, and the role of religion and imams. She is also interested in social work curriculum development in the Middle East. She serves on the board of trustees of Muslim Mental Health Inc.

Nuha Abudabbeh, PhD, is a clinical and forensic psychologist. She is presently a consultant to the Court Services of the District of Columbia and is assistant clinical professor of psychology at The George Washington University, Washington, D.C. She is the recipient of several awards for her work with both Arab American and African American communities. She established the Naim Foundation to provide psychosocial services for Arab Americans during the 1980s and 1990s. She also established a national call-in mental health program in Arabic, which was on the air for 11 years.

Sameera Ahmed, PhD, is director of the Family & Youth Institute, Canton, Michigan, and clinical assistant professor of psychiatry at Wayne State University, Detroit, Michigan. Her research interests include risk behaviors and protective factors of Muslim adolescents and emerging adults, skills-based parenting and marital interventions to strengthen families, and promoting culturally and religiously meaningful psychotherapy. She co-edited the book *Counseling Muslims: Mental Health Issues and Interventions* and is an Associate Editor for the *Journal of Muslim Mental Health*.

Sawssan R. Ahmed, PhD, is an assistant professor in the Department of Psychology at California State University, Fullerton and a volunteer assistant professor in the Department of Family Medicine and Public Health, Division of Global Health at the University of California, San Diego. She completed her graduate work in clinical psychology and postdoctoral training in developmental issues and health disparities. Her research focuses on the role of sociocultural risk and protective factors in physical and mental health, with special interests in Arab Americans, adolescents, and refugees.

Juhayna Ajami, PsyD, is a clinical psychologist in the San Francisco Bay Area. She completed her doctorate in clinical psychology at The George Washington University, Washington, D.C. Dr. Ajami completed her predoctoral internship training at Saint Elizabeths Hospital in Washington, D.C. and her postdoctoral fellowship at the Institute on Violence, Abuse, and Trauma in San Diego, California.

She has garnered experience providing individual and group therapy as well as psychological and neuropsychological assessments to forensic and trauma populations.

Kristine J. Ajrouch, PhD, is a professor of sociology at Eastern Michigan University, Ypsilanti, and adjunct research professor in the Life Course Development Program at the Institute for Social Research, University of Michigan, Ann Arbor. She obtained her doctorate in sociology from Wayne State University, Detroit, Michigan, and completed her postdoctoral training at the University of Michigan, Ann Arbor. Her research focuses on cultural aspects of social relations across the life course. She is a co-editor for the book *Biopsychosocial Perspectives on Arab Americans: Culture, Development, and Health.*

Alean Al-Krenawi, PhD, is president of Achva Academic College and professor in the Spitzer Department of Social Work at Ben-Gurion University of the Negev, Beersheba, Israel. His research interests include multicultural mental health and social work with indigenous populations, polygamy, and political violence. He has published eight books and numerous book chapters and peer reviewed journal articles related to these topics. He conducts studies in Canada, Israel, Palestine, and other Arab countries. He obtained his doctorate from the University of Toronto, Canada.

Aisha M. Al-Qimlass, MS, is a doctoral student in counselor education at North Carolina State University in Raleigh. She received her master's degree in vocational rehabilitation in 2008 from San Diego State University, California. She is a certified rehabilitation counselor, a licensed clinical addictions specialist associate, and a licensed professional counselor associate. Her professional experience includes developing and providing individual, group, and family assessment, counseling, and rehabilitation services in the U.S. and in Kuwait.

Hala Alyan, PsyD, is a counselor in the Counseling and Wellness Center at New York University, New York City. She is a graduate of the clinical psychology program at Rutgers University, Piscataway, New Jersey. She completed her doctoral internship at Bellevue Hospital Center in New York City, specializing in trauma work with immigrant and refugee populations, and her postdoctoral fellowship at New York University. She received her Bachelors from the American University of Beirut, Lebanon, and master's degree from Columbia University, New York City.

Wafa M. Amayreh, MA, is a doctoral student of counseling psychology at the University of Texas at Austin. She earned a master's degree in cultural translation from the American University of Paris, France, where her research interests were national identity and contemporary art. She also holds a BA in critical social thought. Her current research interests include mental health issues among Arab Americans, ethnic identity development, acculturation, and discrimination. She is also interested in cross-cultural conceptualizations of subjecthood in psychology.

Nadia S. Ansary, PhD, is an associate professor of psychology at Rider University, Lawrenceville, New Jersey. She received her doctorate in developmental psychology in 2006 from Teachers College, Columbia University, New York. Her research focuses on risk and resilience among vulnerable adolescent populations with a specific focus on the mental wellbeing and bullying of Muslim youth. Her publications address community outreach to the Muslim American community, the association between ethnic identity and psychosocial outcomes, as well as bullying in schools.

Mireille Aprahamian, EdD, is a behavioral scientist currently working for Northrop Grumman Corporation in support of various U.S. Department of Defense initiatives. She is also a faculty associate at George Mason University, Fairfax, Virginia, and Johns Hopkins University, Baltimore, Maryland. Her expertise includes acculturation, identity development, and cross-cultural communication issues and their impact on mental health of Arab, Armenian, and Middle Eastern communities. She obtained her doctorate in counseling psychology from Argosy University, Washington, D.C.

Cynthia L. Arfken, PhD, is a professor in the Department of Psychiatry and Behavioral Neurosciences at Wayne State University, Detroit, Michigan. Her expertise is in alcohol and drug abuse epidemiology and health service research. Her publications have included seminal research on alcohol and drug use among Arab Americans and American Muslims. She received her doctorate in chronic disease epidemiology from Yale University, Connecticut, and completed a postdoctoral fellowship in alcohol research from the University of California, Berkeley, California.

Karen J. Aroian, PhD, is a Chatlos Endowed Professor at the University of Central Florida, Orlando, Florida. Her degree is in nursing science with a minor in anthropology and a clinical background in psychiatric-mental health nursing. She has conducted research for over 30 years with numerous immigrant groups from Eastern Europe, Latin America, Asia, and the Middle East. In addition to the U.S., countries of destination for her research with immigrants include Israel and Spain.

May H. Aydin, PhD, is the director of the Information and Technology Services Program at the National Science Foundation's National Center for Science and Engineering Statistics, Arlington, Virginia. She obtained her doctorate in gerontology from the University of Massachusetts Boston. Her research interests include early and later-life trauma exposure and impact on psychological well-being among aging populations in the Middle East and those of Middle Eastern origin in the U.S.

Amelia Ayoob, MA, has a Bachelor of Arts in political science from Humboldt State University in Arcata, California. She completed her Master of Arts in geography at the University of South Carolina, Columbia, South Carolina, in Fall of 2014. Her thesis research was a qualitative case study of the community-building and place-making practices of Arab Christians in northern ("upstate") South Carolina.

Louise Cainkar, PhD, is a sociologist and associate professor of social welfare and justice at Marquette University, Milwaukee, Wisconsin. She has published dozens of articles and book chapters in the field of Arab American studies. Her 2009 book *Homeland Insecurity: The Arab American and Muslim American Experience After 9/11* (Russell Sage Foundation) was honored by the Arab American National Museum. Her current work is on second generation Arab American teenagers living transnationally in Yemen, Palestine, and Jordan. She is the incoming president of the Arab American Studies Association.

Ayse Çiftçi, PhD, is an associate professor and training director of the counseling psychology program in the Department of Educational Studies at Purdue University, West Lafayette, Indiana. She obtained her doctoral degree from the University of Memphis, Tennessee. Her research interests focus broadly on cross-cultural psychology and diversity issues specifically related to immigrants and international students. In addition to serving as an editorial member of several journals, she co-edited a *Journal of Muslim Mental Health* thematic issue focused on mental health stigma.

Florence J. Dallo, PhD, is an associate professor in the School of Health Sciences at Oakland University, Rochester, Michigan. She obtained her doctorate in preventive medicine and community health from the Graduate School of Biomedical Sciences, Galveston, Texas. Her research focuses on health conditions, mortality patterns, health behaviors, and healthcare delivery among Arab Americans. She has over 30 peer-reviewed publications, many of which have focused on Arab Americans, and two book chapters on diabetes and maternal and child health devoted to this population.

Fatimah El-Jamil, PhD, is a clinical assistant professor and director of the graduate clinical program in the Department of Psychology at the American University of Beirut, Lebanon. She is a New York-licensed clinical psychologist, practicing and supervising at her private practice in Beirut, Lebanon. She has authored and co-authored several chapters on domestic violence in the Middle East and on cross-cultural psychotherapy, addressing the challenges faced in the practice of current psychotherapy models in the U.S. and the Arab region.

Rand Ramadan Fakih, PhD, is adjunct faculty of education at Wayne State University, Detroit, Michigan. She holds a master's degree in educational psychology from the American University of Beirut, Lebanon, and a doctorate in educational psychology from Wayne State University, Detroit. Her research interests primarily focus on identity, culture, and immigration. She has examined the potential role of ethnic identity in mitigating the negative effects of discrimination on psychological wellbeing in a sample of Arab American youth.

John R. Graham, PhD, is a professor and director of the School of Social Work at Florida Atlantic University, Boca Raton, Florida. He was previously at the University of Calgary, Alberta, Canada, for 17 years, where he served as Murray Fraser Professor of Community Economic Development, and coordinator of the Faculty of Social Work's PhD and MSW international programs. He has published nine books and over 100 journal articles, many related to social welfare among Arab communities.

Emily R. Grekin, PhD, is an associate professor of clinical psychology in the Department of Psychology at Wayne State University, Detroit, Michigan. Her research focuses on the development of substance use disorders among adolescents and young adults. She received her doctorate in clinical psychology from Emory University, Atlanta, Georgia. She completed a clinical internship at Indiana University Medical School, Indianapolis, Indiana, and a postdoctoral fellowship in alcohol research at the University of Missouri, Columbia, Missouri.

Karen L. Haboush, PsyD, is clinical associate professor and school psychology internship coordinator in the school psychology program at the Graduate School of Applied and Professional Psychology, Rutgers, The State University of New Jersey, Piscataway. She received her doctorate in school psychology from Rutgers in 1989. Her publications, presentations, and clinical work have focused on culturally competent practice with Arab American students and families, and the application of school psychology practice with Arab American students.

Linda G. Haddad, PhD, is the associate dean for academic affairs in the College of Nursing at the University of Florida in Gainesville, Florida. She has an outstanding record of scholarly contributions to nursing and public health knowledge regarding tobacco prevention. A significant amount of her research has focused on applying smoking cessation programs to Arabic-speaking immigrants in the Southern region of the U.S. She has been studying, conducting research, and disseminating her work on smoking and tobacco prevention regarding Arab and Arab American youth and young adults since 1999.

Julie Hakim-Larson, PhD, is a professor of child clinical psychology at the University of Windsor, Canada. She received her doctorate in lifespan developmental psychology from Wayne State University, Detroit, and obtained postdoctoral training in child clinical psychology. Her research interests include emotion, mental health, and culture, with an emphasis on individuals and families of Arab and Middle Eastern ethnicity. She is a co-editor of the book *Biopsychosocial Perspectives on Arab Americans: Culture, Development, and Health.*

Adnan Hammad, PhD, is the chief executive officer of the National Arab American Medical Association, and previous founder and senior director of the Arab Community Center for Economic and Social Services (ACCESS), Dearborn, Michigan. He holds a doctorate in public health policy and administration from Victoria University, Manchester, U.K. His work has focused on a holistic approach to managing the healthcare needs of the Arab American community by integrating primary and specialty medical care, public health research, and environmental and mental health.

Charles Harb, PhD, is an associate professor of social and political psychology and chair of the Department of Psychology at the American University in Beirut, Lebanon. His research interests are in identity dynamics and group relations, with a special focus on the Arab world. He has conducted research on sectarianism, social cohesion, political violence, identity motives, self-construals, values, and life satisfaction. He has also consulted on several United Nations projects on governance and social cohesion.

Emily R. Johnson, MS, is the director of the School Health Interdisciplinary Program of Alachua County, Florida and a doctoral student of health and human performance in the Department of Health Education and Behavior at the University of Florida, Gainesville, Florida. She holds a BS degree in applied physiology and kinesiology and a master's degree in health education, both from the University of Florida, Gainesville. Her research interests include adolescent risk behaviors, positive youth development, and adolescent weight control and disordered eating.

Randa A. Kayyali, PhD, is an adjunct professor of anthropology at The George Washington University, Washington, D.C., and has taught Arab World Studies at the American University in Washington, D.C. She authored *The Arab Americans* (Greenwood Press, 2006), which was translated into Arabic as *El-Amerikeun El-Arab* (Arab Institute for Research and Publishing, 2007). She currently serves on the Board and as treasurer of the Arab American Studies Association. She researches and writes on Arab and Arab American gender, race, ethnicity, and religion.

Maryam Kia-Keating, PhD, is an associate professor of clinical psychology at the University of California, Santa Barbara, and a licensed clinical psychologist. She completed her graduate training at Harvard University and Boston University, Boston, Massachusetts, and postdoctoral training at the University of California, San Diego. Her research focuses on coping and resilience in the context of traumatic and stressful experiences, with special attention to refugee and immigrant populations, including Iranian, Iraqi, Somali, and Afghan youth and families.

Ibrahim Aref Kira, PhD, is the director of the Center for Cumulative Trauma Studies, Stone Mountain, Georgia. He is the lead developer of the Developmentally-Based Trauma Framework (DBTF) and its measurement tools. His primary interests include researching the effects of cumulative trauma profiles on the health of multiply traumatized individuals, and developing more appropriate interventions for them. He is the past director of the Center for Torture and Trauma Survivors, Decatur, Georgia. Dr. Kira has authored over 45 peer-reviewed publications.

Anahid Kulwicki, PhD, is dean to the College of Nursing and Health Sciences at the University of Massachusetts, Boston. She has a distinguished career in both healthcare and higher education, has organized studies as a Fulbright Research Scholar in Jordan, and has published dozens of works on topics related to the health of Arab Americans, with a particular focus on women and adolescents. She holds a doctorate in nursing synthesis and a master's degree from Indiana University in nursing care of children, in addition to a bachelor's degree in nursing from the American University of Beirut, Lebanon.

Mark A. Lumley, PhD, is a clinical health psychologist and professor of psychology in the Department of Psychology at Wayne State University, Detroit, Michigan. He has published over 110 peer-reviewed articles, particularly on emotional stress, emotion regulation, and physical health problems such as chronic pain. He has mentored numerous students to PhD, including several Arab Americans, and has conducted research on Iraqi refugees, including a clinical trial of brief narrative exposure therapy and a longitudinal study of the mental and physical health of new Iraqi refugees.

Omar M. Mahmood, PhD, is a research scientist in the Department of Psychiatry at the University of California, San Diego, California, and a staff neuropsychologist at Executive Mental Health, Inc. in Los Angeles, California. His clinical expertise is in the psychological assessment of children and adults. He is licensed to practice psychology in California and has also worked as a consultant neuropsychologist with Arabic-speaking clients in North America as well as the Middle East (Saudi Arabia, United Arab Emirates, Egypt, and Kuwait).

Rosanne Menna, PhD, is a professor in the Department of Psychology at the University of Windsor, Ontario, Canada. She received her doctorate in applied psychology and human development from the University of Toronto. She is a clinical child psychologist active in the supervision and training of future clinicians. Her research interests include the development of competence and coping in children and adolescents, immigrant youth, parent–child interactions, and early intervention. She is a co-author of the book *Early Intervention with Multi-Risk Families: An Integrative Approach.*

Sheila Modir, MSW, is a clinical psychology doctoral student at the University of California, Santa Barbara. She holds a master's degree in social welfare from the University of California, Los Angeles, and has worked in Belgium with the Red Cross to support Middle Eastern refugees seeking asylum. Her research focuses include acculturation, trauma, immigration, and refugee youth, as well as identifying coping mechanisms and resilience factors in vulnerable populations.

Caroline Nagel, PhD, is an associate professor of geography at the University of South Carolina, Columbia, South Carolina. Her work has explored the politics of integration, "race," and multiculturalism among Arab-origin activists in the United States and Britain. More recently, she has focused on immigrant outreach efforts by evangelical churches in the U.S. South. In 2010–11 she served as a Fulbright scholar at the American University of Beirut, Lebanon, where she studied the politics of citizenship in Lebanon.

Sylvia C. Nassar-McMillan, PhD, is a professor and program coordinator of the Counselor Education program at North Carolina State University in Raleigh. She has published extensively on issues related to Arab Americans, and was lead editor for an interdisciplinary book published by Springer titled *Biopsychosocial Perspectives on Arab Americans: Culture, Development, and Health.* In 2013, she received the Extended Research Award from the American Counseling Association and an Endowed Chair appointment from Eastern Michigan University for her nationally renowned contributions on Arab Americans.

Mona D. Nour, MEd, is a doctoral student in counselor education at North Carolina State University in Raleigh. She earned her master's degree in college counseling and student development in 2005 from North Carolina State University, Raleigh. Over the last decade she has held counseling, advising, administrative, and teaching positions at universities and community colleges. Her professional interest areas include counseling international students and researching identity development of individuals of Middle Eastern and North African descent.

Sarah Rasmi, PhD, is an assistant professor of psychology at the American University in Dubai, United Arab Emirates. She completed her doctorate in applied social psychology at the University of Guelph, Ontario, Canada. Her research interests focus on acculturation and personal values theories, with an emphasis on the psychological and sociocultural adaptation of immigrant Arab youth and families. She is particularly interested in the acculturation gap and intergenerational conflict within parent-emerging adult dyads.

Sonia Salari, PhD, is an associate professor in the Department of Family and Consumer Studies at the University of Utah, Salt Lake City. She has additional affiliations with the Sociology Department and the Gerontology Center and is a member of the Center on Aging. She obtained her doctorate in sociology from State University of New York at Albany and completed her postdoctoral training at the Carolina Population Center at the University of North Carolina, Chapel Hill. Her current research interests include minority aging, family policy, mid- and later-life adult development, domestic violence, and elder mistreatment.

Raja Salloum, MSW, is a clinician for Arab American and Muslim American clients at the Mental Health Association in Passaic County, Clifton, New Jersey. She provides cultural competence training to various social service agencies with the goal of improving service delivery to Arab and Muslim communities. She collaborated with others in delivering the first Arab American disability conference in the U.S. She received her master's degree in social work with a clinical specialization from Rutgers University, Newark, New Jersey.

Rita Stephan, PhD, is a foreign affairs officer at the U.S. Department of State, a visiting researcher at the Center for Contemporary Arab Studies at Georgetown University, Washington, D.C., and a senior demographics fellow at the Arab American Institute, Washington, D.C. She was previously an analyst at the U.S. Census Bureau. She received her doctorate in sociology from the University of Texas at Austin, with a portfolio in women's and gender studies. Her publication topics include the Lebanese women's movement, social movements, social networks, and Arab Americans.

Nancy Howells Wrobel, PhD, is a professor of psychology at the University of Michigan, Dearborn, and a licensed clinical psychologist. She completed her doctoral work at Wayne State University, Detroit, Michigan. Her teaching and research interests focus on assessment, particularly assessment and diagnostic decisions across cultural groups. Her published research includes validation of Arabic versions of mental health and dementia screening instruments, as well as acculturative stress measures. She has also written about mental health risks and trauma in Arab Americans.

Aieyat Zalzala is a doctoral student in the counseling psychology program at the Department of Educational Studies, Purdue University, West Lafayette, Indiana. She holds a BA in brain, behavior, and cognitive science from the University of Michigan, Ann Arbor. Her research interests focus on intimate partner violence among Arab and Muslim populations. Her clinical experiences include assessment and counseling with diverse populations with various concerns (e.g. depression, anxiety, posttraumatic stress disorder) at community mental health and college counseling centers.

Maisa S. Ziadni, MS, is a doctoral student of clinical psychology at Wayne State University, Detroit, Michigan. She received her BA in psychology and health sciences from Guilford College, Greensboro, North Carolina, and her master's in psychology from Drexel University, Philadelphia, Pennsylvania. She studies the effects of trauma on chronic illness, and interventions for trauma. She has collaborated on a clinical trial of brief narrative exposure therapy with Iraqi refugees, and published on predictors of human insecurity among Gazans in the West Bank.

PREFACE

> We pushed our ethnicity down because we wanted dearly to be a part of this country. We changed our names, gave ourselves nicknames, to make it easier for Americans to accept us.
>
> Kaffirs, or sub-humans.
>
> Discriminated against.
>
> Victims of bias and stereotyping.
>
> Defenseless against the fears and frustrations of society.
>
> These words have meaning to us.
>
> No one can really understand the truth of their own ethnicity until they have experienced the pains and the joys of another's.
>
> In the American melting pot, Arab Americans are a small bubble, an ingredient that still floats apart from the rest of society's brew.
>
> (Hanania, 1996, p. 9)

These words were penned 20 years ago by Ray Hanania, a Christian Palestinian American journalist and stand-up comedian. Although his book, satirically titled *I'm Glad I Look Like a Terrorist: Growing Up Arab in America* (1996, Urban Strategies Group Publishing Co.), presents his experiences as an ethnic minority with a dose of humor, these words serve as a sober reminder that the pressures facing Arabs in America have not changed in essence over the years. Certainly, the backlash following the World Trade Center attacks on September 11, 2001 (henceforth referred to as "9/11"), and the ongoing hostile sociopolitical climate toward Arabs and Muslims has meant that 9/11 was a turning point for the Arab American community. It has made it harder for Arabs to be accepted as part of the country and easier for them to be a target for stereotyping and discrimination. However, although heightened post 9/11, those acculturation challenges and stressors pre-dated 9/11 by decades.

The *Handbook of Arab American Psychology* aims to capture the historical developments that impacted the cultural identity and psychological experiences of Arab Americans, as well as the rapidly shifting and nuanced characteristics of the Arab American community today. The book focuses on people from the 22 Arabic-speaking countries in North Africa and the Middle East who are living in the U.S. It is a rich and diverse population, including immigrants, refugees, and descendants of families that first built their homes in the U.S. several generations ago. Considering the heightened scrutiny of Arab Americans in the public media, pervasive misunderstandings and biases against this group, and the minimal attention toward Arab Americans even in the multicultural psychology literature, this text is both timely and essential.

While there are many books that focus on Arab Americans, this is the first major publication to discuss comprehensively the Arab American population from a lens that is primarily psychological.

Part I provides a detailed orientation to Arab American culture and community, exploring identity and acculturation within the sociopolitical context. The emphasis is on understanding the psychological processes and challenges related to racial identity, ethnic identity, and acculturation. The chapters examine the factors that affect these processes (including religious experiences and discrimination), the psychological outcomes of these processes, and the ways in which the community has collectively responded to challenges, such as through civic engagement.

Part II of the *Handbook* offers an examination of psychological issues from a lifespan development perspective. This includes salient factors affecting Arab American youth identity development, traditions and practices throughout the family life cycle, the development of gender roles and sexuality into adulthood, and common experiences faced in older adulthood. International students (who are temporary sojourners in the U.S.) and refugees (who are forced migrants) face unique migration circumstances, legal statuses in the U.S., and cultural adaptation challenges. As such, Part III of the *Handbook* discusses their experiences.

Next, the *Handbook* concentrates on behavioral health status and interventions. Part IV reviews key issues such as psychological wellbeing, trauma, intimate partner violence, substance abuse (including tobacco, alcohol, and other drugs), and health conditions. This is followed by a series of chapters that are relevant to psychological practice. This fifth section begins with an examination of the process of individual and family-level services, including Arab Americans' attitudes toward help-seeking, psychological assessment and testing upon entry to the service system, general considerations for counseling, and formal psychotherapeutic approaches. The remaining chapters in this section discuss systemic interventions and considerations in the school, healthcare, and community settings. Finally, the *Handbook* ends with a section (Part VI) that critiques the psychological scholarship on Arab Americans thus far, including reflections on research measures, study designs, sampling and data collection strategies, and overall trends in the field.

Throughout the *Handbook* there is a recurrent emphasis on documenting both risk and protective factors, with an effort to present a multidimensional view of Arab Americans that incorporates resilience and strength. This is a departure from much of the existing literature, which tends to accentuate stress, vulnerability, and victimization. Most authors also examine the topics in their chapters from an ecological perspective, appreciating the multilayered contextual factors that affect the Arab American experience. Another theme that ties the chapters together is an examination of the definition and characteristics of Arab Americans, and the importance of severing the conflation of Arabs with Muslims.

Although the *Handbook* emphasizes psychological concepts and methods, the authors represent diverse disciplines, and the chapters draw from literatures produced by different fields. As such, the subjects covered are of relevance to many other disciplines, including sociology, ethnic/cultural studies, social work, nursing, public health, and psychiatry. The chapters have been written primarily for scholars, academics, and university students, although many of the chapters also contain material that is pertinent to mental health and healthcare practitioners.

The structure of the *Handbook* chapters is designed to be useful to these diverse audiences. The core of the chapters is a thorough and cutting-edge review of the research literature. Diverging from previous publications on Arab Americans, particularly those that offer advice for culturally sensitive service provision, the authors in this handbook have taken care to situate claims within the empirical evidence. To complement this research review is a section near the beginning of the chapters that presents relevant theoretical constructs and models. These theories and concepts serve as a backdrop for the research literature and provide a richer layer of understanding to the topics. Toward the end of the chapters is a case example that brings to life the theoretical constructs and research findings, and also provides a useful illustration for didactic purposes. The chapters end with a critical examination of the existing research in that subject area, analyzing the strengths and gaps in the literature, as well as suggesting an agenda for future work in the field.

The final chapter of the book diverges from this format by focusing entirely on a critique of the literature. The chapter documents the publication trends and topics captured in the psychological literature on Arab Americans thus far, and highlights the major themes that have been interwoven throughout this book. The chapter offers suggestions for future research topics and how to improve research design and methodology. Also included is a discussion on the practical ways that the field can progress, particularly with regard to supporting graduate students, enhancing professional research networks, and facilitating funding streams. A table is presented with suggestions for future areas of inquiry that can be a resource for graduate students trying to decide on topics for dissertations and theses. With this vision for strategies to encourage the volume, quality, and relevance of Arab American psychological scholarship, it is hoped that the *Handbook* will have an impact on moving the field forward and supporting the Arab American community through empirical research and interventions. Perhaps with such efforts, in the future Arab Americans will no longer be seen as a small bubble floating apart from the rest of society's brew, but rather as an important ingredient in the diverse ethnic framework that brings strength to American society.

PART I

Identity, Culture, and Context

1

THE ARAB REGION

Cultures, Values, and Identities

Charles Harb

Misconceptions about the Arab world are pervasive, with media accounts and news headlines often portraying the Arab Middle East as a region of perpetual and often irrational violence, with radicalized religious groups that have nihilistic tendencies bent on the destruction of the "Western world" and its values. As Edward Said (1999, p. 24) observed long before the events of 9/11 and the subsequent "War on Terror:"

> Uncounted films and studies have by now permanently impressed the average consumer of TV news and movie entertainment that Arabs are terrorists, and that unlike any other people connected to monotheism, such activities as permanent war against infidels and the gratuitous abuse of women and other disadvantaged people are congenital to the Arab psyche.

The scarcity of rigorously conducted empirical research on the Arab world and the consequent paucity of reliable and valid information on its social and cultural fabric have left traditions of misconceptions guide the discourse on the Arab peoples. A Social Science Citation Index (SSCI) search conducted in December 2014 on the key words "Arab" and "psychology" for the past quarter century (1989–2014) yielded a stunningly low 73 hits, almost half of which dealt with Israeli–Arab issues or terrorism. Research by Öngel and Smith (1994), and Smith, Harb, Lonner, and van de Vijver (2001) showed that over a period of 25 years, about 1% of studies published in the *Journal of Cross-Cultural Psychology* included Arab samples or authors. The inaccessibility and scarcity of locally produced research has often permitted externally imposed propositions, distorted knowledge, and popular stereotypes to go unchallenged (Said, 1997).

Until the 1980s, scholars interested in studying the Arab world and Islam were often led toward studies in Orientalism, which were the predominant venues that informed American and European scholars about the Middle East and its people (Said, 1994, 1995/1978). Orientalist studies present the "Orient," or Eastern culture and history, through the eyes of Western values and assumptions, exaggerating the differences and distorting perceptions of the region. Extensive academic inbreeding and little concern for rigorous methodologies led Orientalism to become an externally imposed and ethnocentrically biased school of knowledge (Said, 1995).

An example of this bias is illustrated by the casual mention of "Islamic countries" whenever one refers to populations that predominantly follow Islam (Halliday, 1996, 2000; Said, 1997). Islam is a religion, and as such should be distinguished from governance models and state polity. Of the many countries around the world with majority-Muslim populations today, only Iran (which is not part of the Arab world) can be labeled an Islamic state, since it is the only country with an exclusively Islamic rule, and with Islamic Law (Sharia) as the sole basis for legislation. The Kingdom of Saudi Arabia could also be considered Islamic in that the legal system is almost entirely based on derivations from the Qur'an and sayings (hadith) of Prophet Muhammad, even if interpreted through a particular religious lens and applied to an absolute monarchy. All other countries around the world with majority-Muslim populations follow a complex set of laws and constitutions that combine, to various degrees, both secular and Qur'an-inspired legislative systems. Consequently, labeling them as "Islamic countries" is akin to labeling nations in the West as "Christian countries."

This chapter provides a brief social, economic, political, and cultural description of the Arab world, highlighting the complexity and diversity of the region. This contextual framing is then followed by a review of prominent theories on values, with a focus on those models with data collected from samples in the Arab region. A case example of a Lebanese expatriate living in Saudi Arabia is provided to illustrate some of the cultural nuances and diversity seen across the Arab world. Finally, the existing literature is critiqued, with suggestions for future advancement.

The Arab World

The Arab world consists of 22 countries spread from the Atlantic Ocean to the Persian-Arabian Gulf, with an estimated population of 363 million (Economic and Social Commission for Western Asia, 2013). The 22 countries, as defined by membership in the League of Arab States, comprise Algeria, Bahrain, Comoros, Djibouti, Egypt, Iraq, Jordan, Kuwait, Lebanon, Libya, Mauritania, Morocco, Oman, Palestine, Qatar, Saudi Arabia, Somalia, Sudan, Syria, Tunisia, United Arab Emirates (UAE), and Yemen. The population of the Arab world is similar in size to that of the U.S. or of the European Union.

The Arab world is diverse, with people from different ethnic, religious, and cultural backgrounds. Skin color ranges from white to black, with sometimes wide variations seen within the same country. While specific and rigorous estimates are difficult to find, the majority of individuals in the Arab countries are Arab and Muslim (including both Sunni and Shi`a Muslims). However, there are notable populations of ethnic and religious minorities. For example, about 20 million individuals (40% of Moroccans and 20–25% of Algerians) identify themselves as belonging to the Berber-Amazigh ethnic minority (International Crisis Group, 2003), and more than five million ethnic Kurds live in Syria and Iraq (Aziz, 2011). Furthermore, about 13 million identify themselves as Christians, and make up significant portions of nationals in some countries, including 38.3% in Lebanon, 14.5% in Bahrain and 14.3% in Kuwait (Pew Research Center, 2011). There are also sizeable groups of people who adhere to the Druze, Jewish, and Hindu faiths. While formal and semi-formal Arabic are shared across the Arab region and dominate written communication, colloquial Arabic and dialects are region specific and dominate verbal communication. Additionally, French and English languages are widely used in nations where a strong colonial past existed.

The current "modern" borders of Arab countries were artificially decreed by the infamous Sykes-Picot Agreement of 1916, through which the French and British colonial powers divided the region into their respective spheres of influence (Barakat, 2008; Hourani, 1991). While direct colonization of some Arab countries ended with the end of the Second World War, some countries did not gain their independence until 1971 (e.g. Bahrain, Qatar, UAE). The region continues to be of significant geostrategic importance as nearly half of the world's total proven oil reserves are in Arab countries, making the region "the world's single most important supplier of crude oil" (Fattouh and El-Katiri, 2012, p. 9). Although U.S. dependency on foreign oil production has decreased, other economic powers (e.g. China) continue to rely on Middle Eastern oil to meet their domestic needs. Controlling this area is of strategic importance and one reason why dozens of Western military bases continue to pepper the region. It is thus not surprising to see local populations expressing negative attitudes toward Western powers (Arab Center for Research and Policy Studies, 2013).

The Four Cultural-Geographical Divisions

Historical developments across the 22 countries shaped four main cultural divisions within the Arab world (see Barakat, 2008; Hourani, 1991): the Fertile Crescent (a crescent-shaped region capping the Arabian Desert/Arabian Peninsula), the Nile Valley (located in eastern North Africa), the Gulf states (situated in the Arabian Peninsula), and the Maghreb (situated in western North Africa).

The Fertile Crescent. This area includes Palestine, Jordan, Syria, Lebanon, and Iraq. The territory is historically rich, being the birthplace of two of the world's monotheistic religions (Judaism and Christianity), and the location of some of the oldest continuously inhabited cities in the world (see World Heritage sites identified by United Nations Educational, Scientific, and Cultural Organization, n.d.). People living in this part of the Arab region are especially diverse in ethnicities and religious sects, a diversity that is both a blessing (bringing e.g. cultural wealth) and a curse (bringing e.g. sectarian and ethnic tensions). The Fertile Crescent has been plagued by decades of conflict and wars, with the Israeli–Arab conflict (ongoing since 1948), and the U.S. invasion of Iraq in 2003 as two infamous examples. The region continues to be marred by internal and sectarian conflicts (Iraq, Lebanon, Syria), and is a stage for proxy wars (a war instigated by a major power that does not itself participate) between regional and international powers.

Nile Valley. This region contains what was once the largest country in Africa (Sudan, before its southern section split into a separate nation in 2011), and the most populous nation in the Arab world (Egypt). Egypt is distinguished by its millennia-old history, mixing both its Ancient Egyptian Pharaonic past and Arab-Islamic identity. Egypt's rich history and demographic weight give it a pivotal role in inter-Arab politics and relations, and a central role in the Israeli–Arab conflict. Egyptian politics have been dominated by rivalries between nationalist-secular and Islamic parties (e.g. the Muslim Brotherhood), and all Egyptian presidents from Egypt's independence to the uprisings of 2011 came from military backgrounds.

The Gulf States. This region includes the Kingdoms of Saudi Arabia and Bahrain, as well as Kuwait, Qatar, and the UAE. The arid Arabian Peninsula, home to Islam's holiest site Mecca, saw little development until the discovery of oil over a century ago and the socioeconomic boom that followed (Barakat, 2008). The monarchies of the Gulf have allowed few political freedoms, and have relied instead on strong family networks and ties, and a strict enforcement of perceived religious norms to enforce their rule. Some cities in the Gulf, such as Dubai (UAE) and Doha (Qatar), have witnessed massive and rapid economic development and physical expansion, and have become globalized international destinations.

The Maghreb. Nations in this region (Morocco, Algeria, Tunisia, Libya, and Mauritania) currently form an economic development union, "Union du Maghreb Arab". The large Sahara Desert and the Atlas mountain range favored the Maghreb's relations and trade with Mediterranean countries, especially with France, a former colonial power (French language is widely used in Morocco, Tunisia, and Algeria). Conflict over the Western Sahara area, as well as conflict over the civic and cultural rights of the 30-million-strong Amazigh people, continues to sour inter-Maghreb relations (Barakat, 2008). As in many Arab countries, the power struggle between nationalist/secular parties and religious ones is decades old, and varies from bloody conflict (e.g. the Algerian civil war of 1991–2002) to relatively peaceful political transitions (e.g. the Tunisian uprising of 2011).

Social Divisions

Although the four regions of the Arab world have been considered culturally and politically distinct entities, levels of similarities and differences have not been sufficiently investigated. Some sociologists proposed an alternative approach to understanding the region, based on societal diversity, and suggested distinguishing among three models: socially homogenous, socially mosaic, and socially pluralistic (Barakat, 2008). The socially homogenous category refers to societies in which the social structure is made up of one group that is completely integrated socially and culturally. This homogeneity leads to a highly centralized and dominating political system, in which consensus is easy to reach (e.g. Egypt, Tunisia, and Libya). The socially mosaic category refers to societies in which the social composition is made up of several groups, the identities of which overpower the general (or collective) identity, and which often lead to a system of differential power-sharing. In such societies, intergroup relations alternate between coexistence and conflict (e.g. Lebanon, Sudan). Finally, the socially pluralistic category refers to societies in which the social structure is made up of several groups that preserve their particular identities, but which have found a way of agreement and consensus between their individual identities and the collective/national one. The independence of their particular identity does not prevent the "need to merge;" for example, the various groups adopt one educational curriculum for all (e.g. Syria, Iraq, Algeria, and Morocco).

Social Realities

While social and geo-cultural categorizations of the region help paint a diversified Arab landscape, bleak social realities unify them. A series of in-depth United Nations reports covering the Arab region showed high levels of illiteracy, huge disparities in wealth, a majority of citizens living in poverty, gender inequities, and inadequate health and educational benefits (United Nations Development Programme, 2002, 2003, 2006). The GDP of all Arab countries combined was reported to be less than the GDP of Spain (United Nations Development Programme, 2002). A 2005 report noted widespread authoritarianism, corruption, and abuse of power by ruling elites (United Nations Development Programme, 2005). Foreign military occupation and wars only add to this bleak picture (United Nations Development Programme, 2009). These realities have a strong effect on Arab youth, and thus the future of the region.

The Youth Bulge. The Arab populations are young, with majorities in many countries under 25 years of age. Some estimate that a third of the Arab region is under 15, and a fifth are between the ages of 15 and 24 years. This "youth bulge" is thought to have peaked in 2010, and is set to decline from 20 to 17% in the coming years (Mirkin, 2013).

Unemployment is a top concern for youth in the region. With one in every three Arabs currently without a job (Urdal, 2012), employment ranks as the highest priority across polls and countries of the region (see e.g. Arab Center for Research and Policy Studies, 2013; ASDA'A Burson-Marsteller, 2014). The Arab region is the only region in the world with unemployment rates above 10%, with Arab youth hit hardest (Mirkin, 2013). These rates vary by nation, from a low of 2% youth unemployment in Qatar, to a high of 30% in Egypt and 44% in Iraq (Mirkin, 2013). United Nations analysts estimate that 92 million jobs need to be created by 2030 to absorb this growing workforce (Economic and Social Commission for Western Asia, 2014b).

It is not surprising that a quarter of Arab citizens want to emigrate from the region (Arab Center for Research and Policy Studies, 2013). A 2009 report on Arab labor migration noted a brain drain effect with 12–14% of the Arab populations' highly skilled persons (and 18.2% of Arab doctors) living abroad (League of Arab States, 2008; United Nations Department of Economic and Social Affairs, n.d.). Over a million highly skilled migrants lived and worked internationally in the more economically developed countries of the Organization for Economic Cooperation and Development (OECD), and Arab-born citizens had a "higher level of education than the native-born in OECD countries" (United Nations Department of Economic and Social Affairs, n.d., p. 3). For example, Arabs accounted for one-tenth of all physicians and 63% of foreign-born physicians working in France (United Nations Department of Economic and Social Affairs, n.d.).

Uprisings: Unity in Diversity

These bleak social realities exert tremendous amounts of stress on already strained Arab societies. The tensions between nationalists and pan-Islamists; the discourse between liberalism and traditionalism; the differential pull between loyalty to family, tribe, state, or nation; all contribute to exacerbate a truly dynamic situation. On the one hand, common cultures and languages, shared historical experiences, and geographical continuity point toward unity within the Arab world. On the other hand, sectarian, ethnic, tribal, or regional loyalties, the absence of a clear vision of the future, and the continued interference of foreign interests in this geostrategic area point toward divisiveness (Economic and Social Commission for Western Asia, 2014a).

The 2011 Arab uprisings occurred in the context of deteriorating life conditions under repressive regimes and a bulging youth population. Each of the uprisings in the Arab world took a different path and reached a different outcome, and thus reflect the uniqueness of each uprising. Country-specific outcomes ranged from the relatively peaceful and rapid political transitions (e.g. democratic elections in Tunisia) to the most brutal and protracted of repressions and social divisions (e.g. civil strife in Syria).

This diversity in social movements and outcomes does not preclude a unity of purpose and a common identity. The rapid – contagious – spread of popular uprisings across different Arab contexts shows a shared sense of future and a common identity. A survey of 20,350 participants from 14 Arab countries (Algeria, Egypt, Iraq, Jordan, Kuwait, Lebanon, Libya, Mauritania, Morocco, Palestine, Saudi Arabia, Sudan, Tunisia, and Yemen) found that 79% believed in "the integrity of a single Arab nation" or that "Arab peoples comprise one nation, notwithstanding the possible differences between Arab peoples" (Arab Center for Research and Policy Studies, 2013, p. 8). This was a reported 7% increase over the same poll conducted in 2011.

The strong endorsement of a statement on the similarity between Arab peoples does not eliminate the importance of other social identities in each country. Social identities are hierarchically organized by their level of inclusiveness (e.g. pan-national (Islamic/Arab), national, ethno-sectarian, tribal-familial, etc.), and are sampled differently across contexts and cultures (Harb, 2010). For example, in some Arab nations (such as Egypt) national identity supersedes other identities, while in others (e.g. Tunisia, Yemen, and Libya) Islamic identity ranks first (Al Jazeera Center for Studies, 2013).

Cultural Dimensions Models: Understanding Values in the Arab World

While the study of identities helps increase understanding of how Arab peoples define themselves, the study of cultural values allows for a deeper understanding of the goals that motivate them. The study of values has been essential to the understanding of cultural differences and similarities. Values are beliefs or concepts that pertain to desirable behaviors or end states; they transcend specific situations and guide the selection or evaluation of events and behavior (Schwartz, 1992, 1994). The central role values play in everyday life and the different profiles that emerge across different ecosystems has placed values at the core of cross-cultural research (Smith, Fischer, Vignoles, and Bond, 2013). Several large-scale investigations of values have taken place, the most prominent of which are the Hofstede Cultural Dimensions, the World Values Survey, and the Schwartz Value Survey. These studies have permitted the profiling of cultural values in each country, allowed for between-country comparisons, and have provided indicators of the sociocultural system in operation at a given location.

Table 1.1 Hofstede's Cultural Dimensions

Cultural Dimension	*Definition*
Individualism	The fundamental issue addressed by this dimension is the degree of interdependence a society maintains among its members: whether people's self-image is defined in terms of "I" or "we." Higher scores indicate more individualist values. In individualist societies people emphasize looking after themselves and their direct family only. In collectivist societies the needs of the group may supersede the needs of the individual, and people belong to "ingroups" that take care of them in exchange for loyalty.
Uncertainty Avoidance	The dimension Uncertainty Avoidance relates to the way that a society reacts to uncertainties and ambiguities over the future. This ambiguity brings with it anxiety, and different cultures have learned to deal with this anxiety in different ways. Higher scores indicate that members of a culture feel threatened by ambiguous or unknown situations and have therefore created beliefs and institutions to ensure conformity.
Masculinity	A high score (masculine) on this dimension indicates that the society is driven by competition, achievement, and success, with success being defined as material rewards or being the winner or best in the field. This value system begins in school and continues throughout life, as shown in organizational behavior. The other end of the dimension represents societies that emphasize cooperation, consensus, and modesty.
Power Distance	This dimension deals with the fact that not all individuals in societies are equal – it expresses the attitude of the culture toward these inequalities. Power distance is defined as the extent to which the less powerful members of institutions and organizations within a country expect and accept that power is distributed unequally. Higher scores reflect societies that are more hierarchical and in which power inequalities are not challenged.
Pragmatism*	This dimension represents the tension in society between maintaining links with the past while facing the challenges of the present and future. Societies that score low on this dimension, for example, prefer to maintain their long-standing traditions and norms while being skeptical of social change. Those that score high, on the other hand, take a more pragmatic approach: they encourage adaptation, saving, and persistence in preparation for the future.
Indulgence*	This dimension is defined as the extent to which society encourages control of desires and impulses. These values are transmitted to children through the socialization process. High scores on this dimension represent relatively weak control over gratification of human drives and needs, called "indulgence." The other side of the dimension represents relatively strong control, or "restraint," which is often supported through strict social norms.

Note: Content adapted from Hofstede et al. (2010) and the Hofstede Centre (http://geert-hofstede.com). Dimensions denoted * are new dimensions added to the Hofstede et al. (2010) revision.

Hofstede's Cultural Dimensions

The first truly cross-cultural and distinctively rigorous exploration of values to include a sample from the Arab region is Hofstede's international survey. From 1967 to 1973, Hofstede (1980) conducted a multi-national, 66-country survey of work-related values of the 117,000 employees of the international company IBM. Analyses of the data enabled Hofstede to map organizational culture along four dimensions: Individualism–Collectivism, Uncertainty Avoidance, Masculinity–Femininity, and Power Distance (see Table 1.1).

Hofstede's (1980) seminal work did not include any specific Arab country but only referred to a small sample from the "Arab Region." His ranking of national cultures indicated that the "Arab Region" ranked 26th on the Individualism dimension. In comparison, the U.S. ranked first, and Japan ranked 22nd, thus indicating that the "Arab Region" is a relatively collectivist culture, in other words more likely to put the interest of the group ahead of personal interest. Hofstede's study further ranked the "Arab Region" as 27th on Uncertainty Avoidance, indicating moderate levels of tolerance toward ambiguities. By way of comparison, Germany ranked 29th, and Japan ranked 7th (the latter indicating high levels of uncertainty avoidance and a need for predictability). The "Arab Region" ranking for Masculinity–Femininity was 23rd (i.e. showing moderate levels of competitiveness), comparable to Canada (at 24th) but significantly less competitive than Japan (ranked 1st on Masculinity). However, on the Power Distance dimension, the "Arab Region" ranked 7th (Mexico and Venezuela, 5th and 6th; Indonesia and Ecuador, 8th and 9th), indicating a highly hierarchical culture with strong power differentials between individuals. In sum, the "Arab Region" ranked high on Power Distance, and moderately on Collectivism, Masculinity–Femininity, and Uncertainty Avoidance.

Unsatisfied with Hofstede's dimensions and findings, and mirroring The Chinese Culture Connection's (1987) criticism about the lack of comprehensiveness of the Hofstede project, Ali (1988, 1992) set about exploring cultural value dimensions inspired by Islamic traditions and the Qur'an. To parallel the potential bias of Hofstede's self-declared "Protestant Work Ethic" value system, he developed an Islamic Work Ethic (IWE) scale based on values found in the Qur'an and the sayings and practices of the Prophet and the early Islamic leaders. Although he hypothesized that the IWE may have waned in modern times, he nonetheless found support for and identification with the IWE in both studies. Importantly, IWE scores were positively correlated with individualism scores in a sample of Arab students studying in the U.S. (Ali, 1988), and in a sample of Saudi Arabian managers in Saudi Arabia (Ali, 1992).

Over the years, research testing, exploring, and challenging the Hofstede dimensions led Hofstede to revise his work and add two additional dimensions (Pragmatism and Indulgence) to the original four (Hofstede, Hofstede, and Minkov, 2010). With more samples collected from more countries and including more diverse populations, the Hofstede Center now boasts data from ten Arab samples ranked on the six dimensions (see Table 1.2). While there are no specific details about the sampling used in the reported studies and data sets, the overall results seem to mimic the findings of the earlier 1980 study. All ten countries ranked high on the Power Distance and the Uncertainty Avoidance

Table 1.2 Arab Countries' Scores on the Six Hofstede Cultural Dimensions

Countries	*Individualism*	*Uncertainty Avoidance*	*Masculinity*	*Power Distance*	*Pragmatism*	*Indulgence*
Egypt	25	80	45	70	7	4
Iraq	30	85	70	95	25	17
Jordan	30	65	45	70	16	43
KSA	25	80	60	95	36	52
Kuwait	25	80	40	90	ND	ND
Lebanon	40	50	65	75	14	25
Libya	38	68	52	80	23	34
Morocco	46	68	53	70	14	25
Syria	35	60	52	80	30	ND
UAE	25	80	50	90	ND	ND

Note: Data obtained from the Hofstede Centre (http://geert-hofstede.com). Scores can range from a low of 0 to a high of 100. ND = No Data; KSA = Kingdom of Saudi Arabia; UAE = United Arab Emirates.

dimensions, indicating strong hierarchical structures and an orientation to avoid ambiguous and unknown situations. The countries scored low on the Individualism dimension and mid-scale on the Masculinity dimension, signifying collectivist yet competitive cultures. The Arab samples generally scored quite low on the two new dimensions of Pragmatism and Indulgence, indicating highly normative and restrained social systems.

More importantly, however, the samples taken from the Arab region differed substantially from one another, with a 25-point difference between samples on each of the six dimensions. This wide range of differences, and the absence of clear clusters within the scores, may reflect the "unity and diversity" of the region. However, inspection of results also shows some surprising findings. For example, Lebanon scored conservatively (25%) on the Indulgence dimension, indicating a rather restrained culture, while Saudi Arabia scored mid-scale (52%) on that same dimension, indicating indulgence by comparison. These results do appear counterintuitive, and may point to a potential sample selection bias.

World Values Survey

Started in 1981, the World Values Survey (WVS) continues to be among the more popular projects exploring value differences and similarities, with data collected from almost 100 countries. The WVS taps into a variety of concepts and explores attitudes toward democracy, gender equality, and religiosity, as well as attitudes toward the environment, work, family, national identity, and culture, to name a few (World Values Survey, 2014). WVS researchers posit that countries can be classified along two bipolar dimensions: (a) traditional versus secular/rational values, and (b) survival versus self-expression values (World Values Survey, 2014). Traditional values are thought to emphasize religion, family ties, and deference to authority, while secular-rational values stress the opposite. Survival values are characterized by low trust and concerns for physical and economic security, whereas self-expression values relate to concerns for participation in economic and political decision-making, and supposedly a growing tolerance of foreigners.

In May 2014 the sixth wave of the WVS was released, with a record number of 13 Arab states included (Algeria, Bahrain, Egypt, Iraq, Jordan, Kuwait, Lebanon, Libya, Morocco, Palestine, Qatar, Tunisia, and Yemen). Arab countries scored highest globally on both the traditional and survival value dimensions, at the conceptual opposites of the secular, rational, and self-expressive "Protestant Europe" (e.g. Sweden, Denmark, Norway) and "English Speaking" countries (e.g. Australia, New Zealand, U.S.; World Values Survey, 2014). In their summary of the main findings, the authors stated that "the social dominance of Islam [sic] and individual identification as Muslim both weaken emancipative values" (World Values Survey, 2014, Catalogue of Findings, para. 31). Such claims show obliviousness to the popular rebellions that swept through the Arab world and a prejudicial view of both religion and the region. They assume a rather static set of Arab societies, and fail to capture the popular uprisings' request for freedom, opportunity, and empowerment (emancipation) without the need to transform their value system. Furthermore, questions about the construct validity of the WVS and the problems that can plague some single-item measures (posed by e.g. Ariely & Davidov, 2011; Chiu, Chia, and Wan, 2015; Van de Vliert, 2013) may weaken confidence in the academic utility of the WVS.

Schwartz's Value Survey

Challenges to both the WVS and the Hofstede dimensions prompted Schwartz (1992, 1994) to propose a major revision of values research across cultures. Schwartz revisited the psychological theories dealing with values research, and refocused the definition more rigorously around the motivational goals these values aim to address. Schwartz proposed a universal model of ten value types along which cultures can be classified (see Table 1.3).

Table 1.3 Universal Value Types Represented in the Schwartz Value Survey

Value Type	*Motivational Goal*
Self-Direction	Independent thought and action through freedom of choice, exploration, and creativity
Stimulation	Excitement, novelty, variety, and challenge in life
Hedonism	Pleasure or gratifying organismic needs
Achievement	Personal success through demonstrating competence according to social standards
Power	Attainment of social status, prestige, and control or dominance over people and resources
Security	Safety, harmony, and stability of society, relationships, and self
Conformity	Restraint of inclinations, impulses, and actions likely to upset or harm others, and avoidance of violating social expectations or norms
Tradition	Respect, commitment, and acceptance of the customs and ideas of one's culture or religion
Benevolence	Preservation and enhancement of the welfare of people with whom one is in frequent personal contact
Universalism	Understanding, appreciation, tolerance, and protection of the welfare of all people and for nature

Note: Adapted from Schwartz (1992, 1994).

Schwartz's Value Survey contains data from over 60,000 respondents from over 200 samples in 82 nations (Schwartz, 2012). Samples are not limited to university students but often include teachers and, in 37 cases, nationally representative samples. Unfortunately, none of these studies include samples from the Arab world. The robustness of the Schwartz Value Survey led the European Union to adopt the Schwartz values as their values instrument in the Union's recurrent assessment of European societies, called the European Social Survey.

Schwartz's Value Survey, which builds upon and improves Hofstede's earlier work, provides researchers with a sensitive instrument measuring a universal set of value types, the reliability and validity of which has been confirmed in over 82 nations (Schwartz, 2012). While Schwartz posits that the ten value types are universally recognized and differentially endorsed across cultures, he does not preclude the presence of other values that would be important in specific cultures. As such, in an unpublished doctoral dissertation of value type preferences in three student samples from Jordan, Lebanon, and Syria, Harb (2003) found morality (nobility of character, high moral standards) and hospitality (welcoming to strangers or guests, generosity) to rank highest in both Syrian and Jordanian samples, and third in the Lebanese sample. Both Syrian and Jordanian samples also endorsed the benevolence, tradition, and conformity values, while the Lebanese sample's responses violated the circular properties of the values model (i.e. participants endorsed values at the opposite ends of the values spectrum). In other words, while these Arab samples showed tendencies toward more collective and conservative goals in line with values research on the region, they also showed that their most important values (e.g. hospitality and morality) were not the ones identified in the mainstream literature, and that hypothesized values structures may not even hold in some samples.

Shared Characteristics of Arab Cultures

Several polls and ethnographic studies have proposed that certain characteristics are prominently featured in the Arab world. Religion, morality, a culture of honor, generosity and hospitality values, and the central role of the family are recurrent themes, and are thus briefly described below.

Religion

Repeated polls in the Arab world report high levels of religiosity across Arab countries (e.g. Gallup, 2012; Pew Research Center, 2013). While such findings allude to potentially observant and devout populations, they do not explain the cultural practices and the role religion actually plays in the lives of Arab peoples. These global surveys, as well as single-item measures of religiosity, cannot capture the complexity of this multifaceted construct within the region.

Furthermore, some polls do show alternative social undercurrents that contrast with stereotypical descriptions of the region as monolithically religious. For example, a poll of 3,500 youth from 16 different Arab countries showed that family, friends, and religion held the most influence in shaping the youth's lives, but in divergence from these traditional values, there was also a growing number of young people embracing "modern values" (ASDA'A Burson-Marsteller, 2014). Almost half the participants endorsed the statement that "traditional values are outdated and belong in the past. I am keen to embrace modern values and beliefs" (p. 8), a three-fold increase over the 2011 poll results (17, 25, 40, and 46% for 2011, 2012, 2013, and 2014, respectively). While the survey has serious limitations (e.g. small sample sizes, questionable construct validity, etc.), this noticeable trend was consistent across data sets.

The loose and divergent definitions of religion and religiosity in the various surveys cited (e.g. defined in terms of value systems, or social norms, or intrinsic vs. extrinsic, or political) make for generally poor construct validity. Undeniably, a majority of individuals in the Arab world report that religion plays some role in their lives; delineating what role religion plays exactly may warrant significantly more research.

Morality

In a review of the predominant values in Islam, Abu-Rida (1998) highlighted a series of individual values that have come to seep into Arab culture and society. Abu-Rida remarked that the word *haq* (loosely translated as "right") appears over 200 times in the Qur'an, and can be considered its most important value. The connotations of *haq* go beyond the literal denotation that reflects the difference between right and wrong, to include conceptions of justice and associations with a certain "nobility of character." Abu-Rida's review specifically identified a set of satellite values that revolve around man as a moral being, the most salient of which are: justice, generosity, respect of the individual (privacy), fairness, and humility.

Honor

Honor is another dominant characteristic often associated with Arab cultures (Gregg, 2005). By being tightly linked to matters of reputation, honor increases group cohesiveness and serves as a conduit of social and cultural norms. Dishonorable behavior is considered disruptive and threatening to the social standing of individuals, families, and communities. "Honor culture" is of course not restricted to the Arab region, as it is found across the globe, including in the U.S. (see e.g. Vandello, Cohen, and Ransom, 2008).

Hospitality and Generosity

Hospitality is another deeply rooted value and an important cultural norm in Arab societies. Inhospitable behavior is not only a source of shame, but possibly a marginalizing factor too. As one writer stated, "Nomadic hospitality or *diyafa* dates to pre-Islamic times and emerged as a coping mechanism in the desert environment, where individuals were utterly dependent on the assistance of others during travel or for protection from avengers or oppressors" (Feghali, 1997, p. 353). Hospitality's deep roots in the Middle East are also shown in Islamic precepts forming one of its five pillars, the zakat. Counterbalancing disparities between rich and poor, the zakat requires Muslim adults to give 2.5% of their wealth every year (i.e. net savings maintained over the previous lunar year) to the poor. Hospitality and generosity, whether culturally bound or religiously inspired, are deeply entrenched in Arab cultures.

Family

The above-mentioned central values are culturally socialized and constantly reinforced through the family, the importance of which cannot be underestimated in Arab societies (Dwairy, Achoui, Abouserie, and Farah, 2006). The family, one of culture's main conduits, nurses the individual into the cultural matrix in which he or she will operate (Poortinga and Georgas, 2006). This is especially salient in Arab societies where the social position of the family (including its role, influence, and financial assets) protects its members from state power and helps them acquire jobs and positions (Barakat, 2008). The family is the primary identification unit and provider of social support in many Arab societies. Because of the emphasis on family relations, Arab adolescents are assumed to grow up with greater sensitivity to their elders than to their peers, in contrast with the more horizontal relationships of American adolescents (Dwairy et al., 2006).

In an investigation of the type of self-construals (i.e. construction of self-hood) that dominated in three Arab samples (e.g. Personal, Relational, Collective self-construals, etc.), Harb and Smith (2008) found self-construals connected to and shaped by the participant's family to be the most prominent, above both the individuated and collective self-construals. Additionally, in an exploration of identity hierarchies in a representative sample of Lebanese youth, Harb (2010) found "family" to be the most highly endorsed identity category beyond all others (e.g. self, nation, professional, sectarian, etc.).

Case Example: Between Beirut and Riyadh

Samah grew up in a middle-class family in Beirut, Lebanon. While his parents were deeply religious (his father had completed the hajj, and his mother was considered pious), they were not considered conservative, and were tolerant of his liberal choices. The family enjoyed a comfortable and active social life, with guests and visitors a recurrent feature of the household. After completing his graduate education in the U.S., Samah went on to work for a major regional consulting firm in Lebanon. His direct supervisor, a family friend, suggested Samah be temporarily relocated to the firm's offices in Riyadh, Saudi Arabia, where he would enjoy a higher salary and greater benefits. This was common practice for rising managers, with skilled labor often migrating to Gulf states for short periods.

Samah's cultural and organizational experiences in Saudi Arabia were drastically different from his experiences in Lebanon. While the firm employed mostly Lebanese nationals in Beirut, it employed a variety of Arab nationals in Riyadh. The diversity gave him firsthand experience of the wide spectrum of differences (and communalities) between Arabs, for each expatriate family had different food preferences, customs, and dialects. Furthermore, the cutthroat competition and fast-paced life he had experienced in Beirut was replaced by a more cordial and laid-back working environment in Riyadh, even if the same barriers continued to strictly separate management layers.

He grew close to his Arab colleagues, and lived, like most of them, in a gated compound especially designed for the firm's expat employees and their families. However, the compound life exacerbated Samah's sense of remoteness and added another obstacle to his encounters with the local community. Social life was different. The hot desert climate meant that people preferred spending their leisure time in confined, air-conditioned spaces, with malls a preferred destination for many. While cafés and restaurants were numerous, pubs, movie theaters, and open meeting venues were not. The strict gender segregation and conservative attitudes particular to Riyadh made for constrained social lives, and contrasted dramatically with Beirut's open-air restaurants and pubs, Mediterranean temperate climate, and less conservative attitudes.

Samah's story is not unique, and reflects the potential diversity of experiences one would have in different regions of the Arab world. The variety of geographies, climates, peoples, customs, and traditions make for a complex region that cannot be captured with one brushstroke. Family and community are quite important, and interpersonal networks are essential in people's social lives. While many consider themselves religious, differences in practices make for contrasted experiences, with religiosity operating independently from conservative values and norms.

Critique

The 2011 uprisings piqued scholarly interest in the Arab peoples, and efforts were launched to understand the dynamics that animated them. Unfortunately, the serious threats to validity affecting both polls and academic research weaken confidence in the interpretation of and generalization from reported findings. For example, many of the polls cited suffer from single-item measures of important concepts, when more items may be needed to ensure both construct validity and instrument reliability. It is also not clear how complex concepts such as values (e.g. ASDA'A Burson-Marsteller, 2014) and religiosity (e.g. World Values Survey, 2014) can be captured through single-item measures across a spectrum of culturally and socioeconomically different groups.

Furthermore, polling is notoriously difficult in many Arab countries, both in terms of sampling and in terms of content. Some countries (e.g. Lebanon) have no official census data or up-to-date information on population parameters, making sample selection a difficult task. Other countries have population segments that are difficult to survey because of challenges in accessing some participants (e.g. women in some areas) or because some segments suffer from high levels of illiteracy (e.g. rural areas in Egypt). Furthermore, countries with authoritarian regimes tend to restrict and control access to information about their populations, with censors periodically inspecting questionnaires for perceived sensitive content. In other words, polling in the Arab region can be challenging, and very few polls manage to overcome these threats to external validity.

Academic research tends to be more rigorously defined and better designed than polls, but may suffer from external validity threats. Hofstede's (1980) first sampling of the "Arab Region" included a very small sample composed of a variety of IBM employees from six different Arab nations. Hofstede's subsequent publications do report data on a substantial number of individual Arab countries, but provide negligible information on sample characteristics or sample selection processes. As such, it is not clear how representative the data is of Arab populations. Schwartz's published values research, which included samples from over 82 countries from 6 continents, did not include a single sample from Arab countries. Schwartz's Israeli identity, the absence of normalized relations between Arab states and Israel, and support for the Boycott, Divestment, and Sanctions movement may partially explain the absence of collaborative work on the Schwartz Value Survey.

These large-scale cross-cultural projects focus on universal value orientations, and overlook certain locally relevant values that may play a prominent role in the selection of individual behavior. The examples of hospitality/generosity and morality highlighted earlier are a case in point: These values, which are absent from the original value scales, were the most highly endorsed values by student samples from the region.

Some of the research published continues to suffer from subtle forms of Orientalism. The popular World Values Survey posits two underlying bipolar dimensions, one of which pits *traditional* versus *secular/rational* values. The labeling of this value dimension carries a derogative connotation, and assumes that traditional societies may possess irrational values. Furthermore, as discussed above, the authors' monolithic and condescending view of the role Islam plays in influencing Arab behavior and attitudes casts serious doubts on the merit and rigor of the WVS research.

Some scholars have challenged the monolithic and often reductionist approaches to the region (e.g. Said, 1995), while others have explored the many social and cultural differences within the region (e.g. Barakat, 2008). Scholarly explorations of the value profiles of Arab peoples tend to paint rather conservative and hierarchically organized populations. Importantly, available research shows large differences within populations and between countries, and thus caution is needed when making generalized descriptions about the region. Furthermore, values and identities are still being shaped by social upheavals and foreign interventions, and as such, have yet to crystalize into a stable form. Importantly, a systematic bottom-up (emic) approach that explores values types and structures in the Arab world is still lacking, and such a project would allow a locally relevant and culturally sensitive understanding of behavior motivators.

The role religion plays in daily life is complex and insufficiently researched. When authoritarian regimes clamp down on political freedoms and ban public protest, mosques and universities become exclusive sanctuaries where individuals can still meet and discuss public affairs. It is thus not surprising to see students and religious parties taking a prominent role in the Arab uprisings that shook the Arab world in 2011. Research investigating the normative, motivational, psychological, social, and political roles that religion and identity play in Arab daily life is sorely needed. Additionally, researching the diverse traditions within Islam and the different value profiles promoted by the various centers of religious learning (e.g. Cairo, Mecca, Najaf, Qom, etc.) are equally important to understanding the different worldviews and customs adopted by communities in the region.

Psychological research that includes Arab samples is scarce, and available peer-reviewed publications are not always held to the same standards of evidence that is expected of other publications in academia. Professional psychological associations in Arab countries are weak (or nonexistent), and lack institutional or state support. Local or regional funds are limited, as governments tend to direct their resources toward more pressing matters and social needs. On the other hand, international funds available to researchers in the area are often based on agendas determined by the donors' own interests, and are not necessarily aligned with local needs. In this context, misconceptions and Orientalist assumptions are likely to continue unabated, with self-serving biases and blind spots a common feature in many narratives.

Conclusion

In sum, the Arab world offers a culturally rich and socially complex set of dynamics that await robust and systematic exploration. In contrast to monolithic perceptions about Arabs, in actuality the region is diverse in terms of histories, ethnicities, religions, and even languages. At the same time, there is also unity in some of the sociopolitical and economic challenges affecting the region. Research has also begun to identify some of the key values that are shared across the region and how they may contrast with values in other parts of the world. Findings converge in describing the Arab peoples as rather conservative and hierarchically organized. Tradition, morality, generosity, and concern for the group seem to be primary motivators for many. However, much of this research has been marred by methodological flaws that should be remedied in future research. While the absence of substantial financial and human resources may hinder a robust program of investigation, continued interest in the region, and the graduation of a new generation of Arab psychologists from local and Western universities, is promising a more informed and better-researched future.

Acknowledgment

The author would like to acknowledge the assistance of Aya Adra in the preparation of this manuscript.

References

Abu-Rida, M. A.-H. (1998). Al-ma'yir w al-kiyam [Criteria and values]. In A. Bouhdiba & M. M. al-Dawalibi (eds.), *Mukhtalaf jawaneb al-thakafa al-islamiya: Al-fard w al-mujatam' fi al-islam* [*The different aspects of Islamic culture: The individual and society in Islam*] (vol. 2, pp. 19–59). Paris: UNESCO.

Ali, A. (1988). Scaling an Islamic work ethic. *Journal of Social Psychology* 128, 575–583. doi: 10.1080/00224545.1988.9922911

Ali, A. J. (1992). The Islamic work ethic in Arabia. *Journal of Psychology* 126, 507–519. doi: 10.1080/00223980.1992.10543384

Al Jazeera Center for Studies (2013). *The Arab Spring: Results of the Arab youth opinion poll.* Retrieved from http://studies.aljazeera.net/en/reports/2013/07/20137296337455953.htm

Arab Center for Research and Policy Studies. (2013). *The ACRPS announces the results of the 2012/2013 Arab Opinion Index*. Retrieved from http://english.dohainstitute.org/file/get/44aba9e5-3cd1-42fd-bd89-fa197b9f6d4a.pdf

Ariely, G. & Davidov, E. (2011). Can we rate public support for democracy in a comparable way? Cross-national equivalence of democratic attitudes in the World Value Survey. *Social Indicators Research* 104, 271–286. doi: 10.1007/s11205-010-9693-5

ASDA'A Burson-Marsteller. (2014). *Arab Youth Survey 2014: "We want to embrace modern values."* Retrieved from http://arabyouthsurvey.com/wp-content/themes/arabyouth-english/downloads/AYS-Whitepaper-en.pdf

Aziz, M. A. (2011). *The Kurds of Iraq: Ethnonationalism and national identity in Iraqi Kurdistan*. London: Tauris Academic Studies.

Barakat, H. (2008). *Al-mujtam' al-arabi al-mu'asir: Bahth fi taghayyor alahual waa'al'alaqat* [*The modern Arab society: Research on changing situations and relations*]. Beirut: Center for Arab Unity Studies.

Chiu, C., Chia, S. I., & Wan, W. W. N. (2015). Measures of cross-cultural values, personality and beliefs. In G. J. Boyle, D. H. Saklofske, & G. Matthews (eds.), *Measures of personality and social psychological constructs* (pp. 621–651). London: Academic Press.

Dwairy, M., Achoui, M., Abouserie, R., & Farah, A. (2006). Adolescent-family connectedness among Arabs: A second cross-regional research study. *Journal of Cross-Cultural Psychology* 37, 248–261. doi: 10.1177/0022022106286923

Economic and Social Commission for Western Asia. (2013). *Development policy implications of age-structural transitions in Arab countries* (Population and Development Reports, Issue No. 6). Retrieved from www.escwa.un.org/information/publications/edit/upload/E_ESCWA_SDD_13_2_E.pdf

Economic and Social Commission for Western Asia. (2014a). *Arab integration: A 21st century development imperative.* Retrieved from www.escwa.un.org/information/publications/edit/upload/E_ESCWA_OES_13_3_E.pdf

Economic and Social Commission for Western Asia. (2014b). *Sustainable development goals ... An Arab regional perspective.* Retrieved from http://css.escwa.org.lb/SDPD/3315/5.pdf

Fattouh, B. & El-Katiri, L. (2012). *Energy and Arab economic development* (Arab Human Development Report, Research Paper Series). New York: United Nations Development Programme. Retrieved from www.arab-hdr.org/publications/other/ahdrps/ENGFattouhKatiriV2.pdf

Feghali, E. (1997). Arab cultural communication patterns. *International Journal of Intercultural Relations* 21, 345–378. doi: 10.1016/S0147-1767(97)00005-9

Gallup. (2012). *After the Arab uprisings: Women on rights, religion, and rebuilding.* Washington, D.C.: Gallup World Headquarters. Retrieved from www.gallup.com/poll/155306/Arab-Uprisings-Women-Rights-Religion-Rebuilding.aspx

Gregg, G. S. (2005). *The Middle East: A cultural psychology.* New York: Oxford University Press.

Halliday, F. (1996). *Islam and the myth of confrontation: Religion and politics in the Middle East.* London: I. B. Tauris.

Halliday, F. (2000). *Nation and religion in the Middle East.* Boulder, CO: Lynne Rienner Publishers.

Harb, C. (2003). *Culture and self: Values, self-construals and life satisfaction in the UK, Lebanon, Jordan and Syria* (Doctoral dissertation). Available from ProQuest Theses and Dissertations database. (UMI No. U162408).

Harb, C. (2010). *Describing the Lebanese youth: A national and psycho-social survey* (Working Paper Series, No. 3). Beirut: The Issam Fares Institute for Public Policy and International Affairs (IFI), American University of Beirut. Retrieved from www.aub.edu.lb/ifi/public_policy/arab_youth/Documents/working_paper_series/ifi_wps03_ay_Harb.pdf

Harb, C. & Smith, P. B. (2008). Self-construals across cultures: Beyond independence-interdependence. *Journal of Cross-Cultural Psychology* 39, 178–197. doi: 10.1177/0022022107313861

Hofstede, G. (1980). *Culture's consequences: International differences in work-related values.* Beverly Hills, CA: Sage.

Hofstede, G., Hofstede, G. J., & Minkov, M. (2010). *Cultures and organizations: Software of the mind* (3rd edn.). New York: McGraw-Hill.

Hourani, A. (1991). *A history of the Arab peoples.* New York: Warner Books.

International Crisis Group. (2003). *Algeria: Unrest and impasse in Kabylia* (Middle East/North Africa Report No. 15). Cairo/Brussels: International Crisis Group. Retrieved from www.crisisgroup.org/en/regions/middle-east-north-africa/north-africa/algeria/015-algeria-unrest-and-impasse-in-kabylia.aspx

League of Arab States. (2008). *At-taqreer aleqleemy lehejrat al`amal al`arabeya: Hejrat alkefa'at al`arabeya, nezeef 'am foras?* [Regional report on Arab labour migration: Brain drain or brain gain?] Cairo, Egypt. Retrieved from www.poplas.org/uploads/publication/pdf/migration_2008_ar_1.pdf

Mirkin, B. (2013). *Arab Spring: Demographics in a region in transition* (Arab Human Development Report, Research Paper Series). New York: United Nations Development Program. Retrieved from www.arab-hdr.org/publications/other/ahdrps/AHDR %20ENG %20Arab %20Spring %20Mirkinv3.pdf

Öngel, Ü. & Smith, P. B. (1994). Who are we and where are we going? JCCP approaches its 100th issue. *Journal of Cross-Cultural Psychology* 25(1), 25–53. doi: 10.1177/0022022194251003

Pew Research Center. (2011). Global Christianity: A report on the size and distribution of the world's Christian population. Washington, D.C.: The Pew Forum on Religion & Public Life. Retrieved from www.pewforum.org/files/2011/12/Christianity-fullreport-web.pdf

Pew Research Center. (2013). *The world's Muslims: Religion, politics and society*. Washington, D.C.: The Pew Forum on Religion and Public Life. Retrieved from www.pewforum.org/files/2013/04/worlds-muslims-religion-politics-society-full-report.pdf

Poortinga, Y. H. & Georgas, J. (2006). Family portraits from 30 countries: An overview. In J. Georgas, J. W. Berry, F. J. R. van de Vijver, Ç. Kagitçibasi, & Y. H. Poortinga (eds.), *Families across cultures: A 30-nation psychological study*. New York: Cambridge University Press.

Said, E. W. (1994). *Culture and imperialism*. London: Vintage Books.

Said, E. W. (1995). *Orientalism*. London: Penguin Books (original work published 1978).

Said, E. W. (1997). *Covering Islam: How the media and the experts determine how we see the rest of the world* (2nd edn.). New York: Vintage Books.

Said, E. W. (1999). The Arabs and the West: The legacy of the past. *Bahithat: The West in Arab Societies: Representation and Interaction* 5, 12–35.

Schwartz, S. H. (1992). Universals in the content and structures of values: Theoretical advances and empirical tests in 20 countries. In M. P. Zanna (ed.), *Advances in experimental psychology* (vol. 25, pp. 1–65). Orlando, FL: Academic Press.

Schwartz, S. H. (1994). Cultural dimensions of values: Toward an understanding of national differences. In U. Kim, H. C. Triandis, C. Kagitcibasi, S. C. Choi, & G. Yoon (eds.), *Individualism and collectivism: Theory, method and application* (pp. 85–122). Thousand Oaks, CA: Sage.

Schwartz, S. H. (2012). An overview of the Schwartz theory of basic values. *Online Readings in Psychology and Culture* 2(1). doi: 10.9707/2307-0919.1116

Smith, P. B., Fischer R., Vignoles, V. L., & Bond, M. H. (2013). *Understanding social psychology across cultures: Engaging with others in a changing world* (2nd edn.). Thousand Oaks, CA: Sage Publications.

Smith, P. B., Harb, C., Lonner, W. J., & van de Vijver, F. J. R. (2001). The journal of cross-cultural psychology between 1993 and 2000: Looking back and looking ahead. *Journal of Cross-Cultural Psychology* 32(1), 9–17. doi: 10.1177/0022022101032001004

The Chinese Culture Connection. (1987). Chinese values and the search for culture-free dimensions of culture. *Journal of Cross-Cultural Psychology* 18, 143–164. doi: 10.1177/0022002187018002002

United Nations Department of Economic and Social Affairs. (n.d.). *International migration in the Arab region*. Retrieved from www.un.org/en/development/desa/population/events/pdf/8/P06_League_Arab_States.pdf

United Nations Development Programme. (2002). *Arab human development report 2002: Creating opportunities for future generations*. New York: United Nations. Retrieved from www.arab-hdr.org/publications/other/ahdr/ahdr2002e.pdf

United Nations Development Programme. (2003). *Arab human development report 2003: Building a knowledge society*. New York: United Nations. Retrieved from www.arab-hdr.org/publications/other/ahdr/ahdr2003e.pdf

United Nations Development Programme. (2005). *Arab human development report 2004: Towards freedom in the Arab world*. New York: United Nations. Retrieved from www.arab-hdr.org/publications/other/ahdr/ahdr2004e.pdf

United Nations Development Programme. (2006). *Arab human development report 2005: Towards the rise of women in the Arab world*. New York: United Nations. Retrieved from www.arab-hdr.org/publications/other/ahdr/ahdr2005e.pdf

United Nations Development Programme. (2009). *Arab human development report 2009: Challenges to human security in the Arab countries*. New York: United Nations. Retrieved from www.arab-hdr.org/publications/other/ahdr/ahdr2009e.pdf

United Nations Educational, Scientific and Cultural Organization. (n.d.). *World Heritage list*. Retrieved from http://whc.unesco.org/en/list/

Urdal, H. (2012). *A clash of generations? Youth bulges and political violence* (Expert Paper No. 2012/1). New York: United Nations Department of Economic and Social Affairs, Population Division. Retrieved from http://www.un.org/en/development/desa/population/publications/pdf/expert/2012-1_Urdal_Expert-Paper.pdf

Van de Vliert, E. (2013). Creating cultures between arctics and deserts. In M. J. Gelfand, C. Chiu, & Y. Hong (Eds.), *Advances in culture and psychology* (vol. 3, pp. 227–282). New York: Oxford University Press.

Vandello, J. A., Cohen, D., & Ransom, S. (2008). U.S. Southern and Northern differences in perceptions of norms about aggression: Mechanisms for the perpetuation of a culture of honor. *Journal of Cross-Cultural Psychology* 39, 162–177. doi: 10.1177/0022022107313862

World Values Survey. (2014). *Findings and insights*. Retrieved from www.worldvaluessurvey.org/WVSContents.jsp?CMSID=Findings

2

RACE AND RACIALIZATION

Demographic Trends and the Process of Reckoning Social Place

Louise Cainkar

Arab Americans are immigrant and native-born persons living in the U.S. who claim ancestry in one or more of the 22 (including Palestine) Arabic-speaking countries of North Africa and southwest Asia. They are the Arab world diaspora living in the U.S. Significant Arab migrations to the U.S. began in the 1880s and have continued in a series of waves ever since. As with other non-European immigrant groups who benefitted from the removal of racial bars (Asia) and country quotas (Arab world), post-1965 Arab immigration to the U.S. is the largest of these waves and also the most internally diverse. In 2010, the largest Arab nationality groups (native and foreign born) in the U.S. were Lebanese, Syrians, Egyptians, Palestinians, Iraqis, and Somalis; significant numbers of Moroccans, Yemenis, and Jordanians were also among the more recent immigrants (Asi & Beaulieu, 2013). There were about 1.9 million Arab Americans according to 2010 Census data, including persons with ancestries in Arab League states not included by the Census Bureau under the category Arab, such as Somalis (Arab American Institute, n.d.). Research by the Arab American Institute and Zogby International placed the actual figure at closer to 3.66 million (Arab American Institute, n.d.).

Arab Americans live all over the U.S. Historically they settled, worked, and engaged in trade in both urban and rural areas; yet they are also concentrated in certain places. Currently, about 30% of Arab Americans live in three states: California, New York, and Michigan. Some 94% of Arab Americans live in metropolitan areas (Arab American Institute, n.d.), with major hubs including Detroit, Los Angeles, New York, Chicago, Washington, D.C., and Northeastern New Jersey. Arab Americans practice a range of religious faiths, including Eastern Orthodox, Greek Orthodox, Assyrian Catholic, Coptic, and Roman Catholic Christianity, Sunni and Shi'a Islam, and Judaism. The majority of pre-1920 Arab immigrants were Christian, while the majority of post-1965 Arab immigrants are Muslim. Due to these historic patterns, the majority of fourth and fifth generation Arab Americans are Christian, while more recent native-born generations are more religiously diverse (Cainkar, 2006).

Overall, Arab Americans are more highly educated than the average American. The 2000 Census found that 41% of Arab Americans aged 25 and older and 36% of Arab American women of the same age group held a bachelor's degree or higher, compared to 24% of the American population as a whole (Read & Oselin, 2008). The 2013 American Community Survey (ACS) indicated even larger discrepancies between Arab Americans and the U.S. population as a whole: 45% of Arab American women and 49% of Arab American men had a bachelor's degree or higher, compared to 30% and 30% respectively of the U.S. population as a whole. While these patterns characterize the numerical majority of Arab Americans, lesser-educated subgroups include Iraqis, Yemenis, Moroccans, and Somalis, who tend to be more recent immigrants and are often refugees (U.S. Census Bureau, 2013).

High educational attainment is usually paired with high labor force participation rates, but Arab Americans are an exception. Census 2000 data (Read & Oselin, 2008) recorded Arab American women's labor force participation rate at 66.5%, lower than the rate for women in most other U.S. ethnic groups. However when examined more closely, the rate for U.S.-born Arab American women (78%) was nearly parallel to the overall U.S. rate for women, while the rate for immigrant Arab American women was relatively low (59%). Read and Oselin explained that many Arab American women, both Christian and Muslim, view university education as a family and parenting resource, rather than a means to a job. They concluded that the higher labor force participation rate of U.S.-born Arab American women showed that interactions with mainstream American society were causing some traditional gender "cultural schemas" to lose their force.

Although Arab Americans are engaged in many types of occupations and work in many industries, they are overrepresented in professional and entrepreneurial occupations. Census 2000 data showed that 42% of employed Arab Americans aged 16 and older worked in management, professional, and related occupations, compared with 34% of the overall U.S. population. Another 30% worked in sales and office jobs, compared with 27% of the overall U.S. population. Added together, these occupations accounted for more than 70% of Arab American workers (Brittingham & de la Cruz, 2005). More recent ACS data continue to show the same patterns. They also indicate that Arab American women have higher rates of management, professional, and related occupations than American women overall (U.S. Census Bureau, 2013).

Arab Americans overall have median household and family incomes that are fairly similar to the U.S. population as a whole, taking into account measurement error. According to 2013 ACS data (U.S. Census Bureau, 2013), the Arab American median household income was $51,634 and the median family income was $61,548, compared with $52,250 and $64,030 respectively for the U.S. population as a whole. These data differ from a decades-long trend of higher incomes for Arab Americans in both categories and may reflect the increase in refugees among Arab immigrants. There are nonetheless substantial variations among Arab Americans: men of Lebanese and Syrian ancestry earned significantly more than Iraqi, Jordanian, and "other Arab" men; among women, women of Lebanese ancestry had the highest earnings and women of Jordanian ancestry the lowest (U.S. Census Bureau, 2013).

Arab American families are also larger than the overall U.S. norm, and the lowest income earning groups among Arabs had the largest families (Asi & Beaulieu, 2013). Due to family size, as well as the low wages earned by entry level immigrant clerks in Arab American businesses, Arab Americans have a poverty rate that is higher than the overall U.S. population (Cainkar, 1999). The 2013 ACS (U.S. Census Bureau, 2013) reported a poverty rate of 21.0% for Arab American families, compared to 11.6% for the overall U.S. population. Arab Americans at the lower end of the income curve tend to be members of refugee families and recent immigrants without college educations.

These data taken as a whole point to Arabs as a largely successful group in American society when measured by income and educational attainment, measures that are historically associated with racial status in the U.S., such that Whites show higher rates than racial minority groups on both measures because of their historical racial privileges. Officially, Arabs are considered "Caucasian." Yet many Americans, including many Arab Americans, see Arabs as a U.S. racial minority because of negative portrayals about them and systematic discriminatory experiences they face in the U.S.

The paradox that Arab Americans are economically successful yet lack social privilege is explained in this chapter, where the unique and complex Arab American experience with race is examined over time. Following this exploration is an elaboration of how Arab Americans interpret their racial position in the twenty-first century in the U.S. Quotations from research with Arab American interviewees are provided to illustrate these experiences and interpretations. When race is understood less as skin color and more as a social position that corresponds to inclusion, treatment, and power – which is how many Americans and Arab Americans understand the term – then measures of prejudice, discrimination, and legal status gain in explanatory power over those of income and education.

Theoretical Constructs of Race and Racialization

Any scholarly discussion of race must begin by pointing out that "race" is a social construct; there are no biological races. There are people who look different from each other in myriads of ways, only one of which is skin color, the signifier of race as it is commonly understood in the West (Bonilla-Silva, 2006). Skin color, like eye color or ear size, has no inherent meaning; its meaning has been imputed by humans and passed on through culture, backed by the power and ideological dominance required to transmit and enforce such notions. As a social construct, race has always been about hierarchy: defining who was a "better" human being, meriting more freedom and social goods, and who as socially inferior could be denied opportunities, and be monitored and ostracized. The Social Darwinists of the turn of the twentieth century took race ideas and turned them into genetic mandates, arguing that race mixing would taint the superior genetic pool of the White American people. Contemporaneous outcomes of those ideas included racial bars to naturalization (only Whites could adopt American citizenship), immigration country quotas, urban ghettoes, and laws that criminalized interracial marriage and sometimes interracial sex. Since race is a social construct, it follows that it may be culturally bound and not universal. Indeed, race as a category of significant meaning for humans was invented in Europe and transmitted externally through its colonial ventures. In some parts of the world, including the Arab world, the concept of race had very little meaning prior to Western contact.

The process of racial formation (Omi & Winant, 1994) is the theoretical construction that best captures the Arab American experience over the past few decades. Simply put, Arab Americans, who once largely benefitted from the perquisites of whiteness, became non-White as a result of social processes taking place over an extended period of time that defined them as different from and inferior to Whites. Omi and Winant called such processes "racial projects," which emerge from the actions and power of dominant groups to define and spin narratives about social groups in order to convince others of a group's status. Scholars can document and measure the ways in which certain groups become White (Ignatiev, 1995; Roediger, 1991), as well as how groups become non-White.

Arab Americans began experiencing structural exclusion from a wide range of social institutions after the 1970s as a result of social constructions that were put forth claiming that Arabs (and later, Muslims) were essentially different in values and behaviors from Whites. They were represented as inherently more violent, less valuing of human life, and more oppressive of women than Whites, as well as technologically backward and politically treacherous. These racial formation projects appeared in the U.S. media, school curricula, and popular culture. Allegations about the inherent differences of Arabs were disseminated so extensively that these ideas came to be widely accepted, as shown in American public opinion polls (see below).

Race matters to the Arab American experience because perceptions of their racial status have defined their access to opportunities and flavored the character of their daily life experiences, at times in a mostly beneficial way (such as 100 years ago) and at other times (more recently) in a highly negative way. The position of Arabs in the U.S. racial hierarchy has changed over time, giving Arabs a unique experience with race in the U.S., in that their social status has changed from marginal White to one that is more reflective of an ethnic minority experience. Starting in the 1970s Arab Americans across the U.S. began to be perceived and experience treatment as people of color. With these changes in experience, Arab Americans came to understand differently their place in the racial hierarchy and racial identity, although again with complexities and variations. Arab Americans once fought in an organized manner to be recognized as Whites, as in the 1914 Dow naturalization case (see Jamal & Naber, 2008), and now many Arab Americans struggle to be recognized as an ethnic minority group. Racial formation, as Omi and Winant (1994) would call it, serves to highlight the socially constructed nature of race. Arab Americans did not change color; social perceptions of them changed.

Racialization and Arab Americans in the U.S. Social Hierarchy

The key distinction of the racial formation processes experienced by Arab Americans is that they differed in historical timing and pretext from that of other negatively racialized groups in the U.S. Unlike the racial superiority and inferiority arguments that commenced with European conquest and were used to buttress the establishment and development of the U.S. as a country of White privilege, the fall of Arabs from the status of marginal whiteness is related to events that occurred much later: to the emergence of the U.S. as a global superpower. Notions of the essential cultural differences and innate violence of Arabs were promoted to build popular support for U.S. foreign policies rather than to further domestic agendas. This significant difference in timing, along with some selective migration, helps to explain why Arab American socioeconomic status is generally better than that of other people of color in the U.S.: founding generations of Arab Americans did not experience the full range of systematic denial of opportunities and racial barriers faced by earlier racialized groups.

Arab American Social Status Pre 1960

Analysis of the published literature on the early Arab immigrant experience (1890–1930) shows that Arabs who migrated to the U.S. in the first decades of the twentieth century held structural statuses and faced prejudice and discrimination in ways largely similar to those of other "White ethnics": the late nineteenth-century southern and eastern European immigrant groups of Italians, Poles, Slavs, Jews, and Greeks. As persons considered marginal Whites, Arab Americans had access to a wide range of legal rights, including rights to property ownership, voting, immigration, and naturalization (these were sometimes contested), that persons of color were denied. They had freedom of movement across the country and patterns of residential settlement and employment that were similar to those of other marginal Whites and unlike those of people of color (Naff, 1985; Zogby, 1984). In Madison Grant's (1916) racial typology, which influenced U.S. immigration policies of the time, superior Whites were Nordics, while inferior Whites were Alpines and Mediterraneans, the latter including Arabs. Grant's proscriptions helped drive the movement to implement immigration quotas, which were finally passed into law in 1921.

Although the early wave of Arab immigrants and their children were excluded from a broad range of institutions controlled by mainstream (superior) Whites, they settled in diverse urban and rural areas and were not pressured into urban ghettoes (Hooglund, 1985, 1987). They worked in factories, ran businesses, built institutions, held government offices, and achieved economic success (Orfalea, 2006). Their social lives were interwoven with members of other White groups, which often resulted in intermarriage. Indeed, Census data show that the children of these Arab immigrants had high rates of marriage with Irish and German Americans. Of course, there are exceptions to this generalization of historical patterns. The marginal whiteness of Arab Americans was contested by power brokers in some places (Gualtieri, 2004). There were specific localities, such as Detroit, Buffalo, and parts of the South, where the right of Arabs to naturalize (become U.S. citizens) was challenged. Such variations correspond to the understanding that racial projects can have distinct local characteristics within the context of larger national structures. Responding to periodic challenges to Arab applications for naturalization, the Immigration and Naturalization Service officially stated in 1943 that Arabs were White persons who were part of Western civilization, and thus were eligible for naturalization (U.S. Department of Justice, 1943).

Civil Rights Era: Racial and Ethnic Minorities Fixed and Institutionalized

When the U.S. civil rights movement rose to its peak in the 1960s, Arab Americans were not considered by government agencies as a subjugated minority group, nor did Arab American groups make these claims. When the White House Office of Management and Budget (OMB) issued its *Race and Ethnic Standards for Federal Statistics and Administrative Reporting* in 1977, set forth in policy directive No. 15, the groups who would be formally defined as racial and ethnic minorities facing discrimination were established: Blacks, Asians and Pacific Islanders, Native Americans, and Hispanics. This definition of discriminated minority groups became institutionalized, ushering in social invisibility for groups not so identified under the assumption that no new racially discriminated groups would emerge. Yet if race is a social construction, then the social meaning of skin color is not fixed, and the possibility remains for new groups to face negative treatment, as well as for groups once treated negatively to "become White."

Arab Americans faced detrimental structural exclusions because of these institutionalized understandings. Arab American organizations that were established after the late 1960s to challenge the increasing prejudice and discrimination facing Arab Americans were not part of the coalitions, conferences, and mobilizations of people of color that were organized to represent, defend, and build power among members of these designated minority groups (Fay, 1984). This hurt Arab Americans because they stood alone, lacking the institutional support of these groups, when contesting hostile media representations, textbook biases, and selective policy enforcement by U.S. government agencies. Working on their own, their claims were easily ignored. Arab Americans also remained absent for decades from tolerance-promoting multicultural curricula and race and ethnic studies textbooks, despite the considerable efforts of educators, scholars, university-based Middle East Studies centers, and Arab American organizations (Barlow, 1994). Finally, since the darkening of Arabs began in earnest after the beneficiaries of the U.S. civil rights movement and the categories of "White" and "minority" had been set, Arab Americans experienced the unique double burden of being excluded from the benefits of whiteness *and* from the affirmative action benefits accruing to groups facing structural discrimination (Samhan, 1999). As Saliba (1999) noted, while Arab Americans were the victims of racist policies, their experiences were rendered invisible by dominant discourses about race.

Racialization as a Non-White "Other" Takes Hold: The 1970s to 2001

While the early Arab American experience was fairly similar to that of White ethnics, with the exceptions noted, the Arab American experience after the late 1960s was decidedly different. The U.S. was now a global superpower actively contesting communism, controlling oil supplies, supporting Israel, and intervening in the Arab world. The mainstream American media largely framed these actions in ways that built popular support for them. After the 1967 Israeli military conquest of the rest of Palestine, Israelis were widely represented in the U.S. media as virtuous heroes, while Arabs were represented as backward people undeserving of freedom. Arabs who actively asserted otherwise, including Arab Americans, were looked upon and treated as adversaries and enemies by U.S. government agencies and their First Amendment rights were curtailed (Bassiouni, 1974). From this point onwards, Arabs were consistently portrayed in the U.S. mainstream media as people who were innately barbarian, incapable of honesty, greedy, and oppressive. While conflicts with the Soviet Union, Cuba, and the Sandinistas were framed as matters of political ideology, the Arab enemy was framed as Arabnesss – an innate cultural disposition to violence and hatred that was said to characterize all Arab men and women.

A 1984 American-Arab Anti-Discrimination Committee (ADC) report argued that an anti-Arab climate had developed in the U.S. resulting from the mainstream reproduction of "images of greedy oil sheiks and bloodthirsty terrorists" that were tied to political events in the Middle East (Zogby,

1984, p. 18). It stated, "the source of today's defamation of Arab-Americans might be described as the domestic counterpart of the Arab-Israeli conflict" (Zogby, 1984, p. 22). Similarly, Abu-Laban and Suleiman (1989, p. 5) found that the source of bias against Arabs in the U.S. related "more to the original homeland and peoples than to the Arab-American community." While the goals of these images were political, they conveyed the notion of a fixed and monolithic Arab character.

In the late 1970s pollsters Lipset and Schneider (1977) found that American attitudes toward Arabs were "close to racist" (p. 22). Slade's (1981) analysis of American public opinion polls concluded: "Arabs remain one of the few ethnic groups that can still be slandered with impunity in America" (p. 143). Bassiouni (1974) detailed numerous American government actions aimed at silencing Arab American speech and activism. In response to stereotyping, discrimination, and government silencing, several important pan-Arab American organizations were founded during this period.

By the 1980s, anti-Arab racism had "permeated American mainstream cultural and political institutions" and "was tolerated in mainstream society" (Abraham, 1994, p. 159). The venues of transmission of anti-Arab stereotypes were broad – television, Hollywood films, news programs, textbooks, and popular culture. The roles these social institutions played in producing and reproducing anti-Arab racism were a primary focus of scholars of Arab America in the 1980s (e.g. Abu-Laban & Suleiman, 1989; Cainkar, 1988; Christison, 1989; Ghareeb, 1983; Michalak, 1988; Said, 1981; Shaheen, 1984; Terry, 1985; Zogby, 1984) and 1990s (e.g. McCarus, 1994; Stockton, 1994; Suleiman, 1999). Shaheen's work exposed the systematic stereotyping of Arabs on American television (1984), in comic books (1991), and in Hollywood (2001). Negative portrayals of Arab Americans were also propagated in other vehicles of American popular culture. In response to these representations, Cainkar (1988) found that young Palestinian Americans accentuated their Palestinian identities in order to resist and refuse the U.S. media's degradation of them. Moreover, Abraham (1994) found that Arab Americans lived in "an increasing state of apprehension" as negative attitudes were increasingly paired with government harassment and violent attacks, including murder (p. 161).

As Islamist challenges to American policies became more powerful than Arab nationalist challenges, these same constructions of Arabs were neatly extended more broadly to Muslims and became grander – they became civilizational. Harvard professor Samuel Huntington's (1993) "clash of civilizations" thesis made positioning Arabs and Muslims as a cultural "Other" an accepted scholarly perspective. Although the images and stories about Arabs, and later Muslims, were framed in cultural and not racial terms, and were mainly about Arabs and Muslims overseas, they were neatly transferred onto Arab (and Muslim) Americans and interpreted as race because the attributes were posited as inherent.

In sum, Arab Americans were transformed from a marginal White to a structurally subordinate status in the U.S. through racial formation processes that marketed social constructions of their essential human difference to the American public. The components of racialization were all there: the assertion of innate characteristics held by all members of a group and the use of power and culture to uphold these representations. Since race remained a concept that Americans knew and understood, these notions of essential human difference were corporealized, as if they were about color. This colorizing process was facilitated by the flexibility of "race" as a social construct and the historic and "observable" racial liminality of Arabs. In 1993, the Arab American Institute submitted testimony to the congressional subcommittee overseeing Census operations during a review of OMB Directive 15, and noted the "growing disconnect between ethnic identification among the Arab-American population and the undifferentiated white category" (Samhan, 1999, p. 222).

Because the formation of Arabs as a unique racial group was a process with timing and purpose different from historic American racism, its manifestation differed from that of traditionally subordinated groups (African Americans, Latinos, Asians, and Native Americans) and its current discriminatory impacts are not well measured by indices of income, occupation, education, and segregation. Arab American racialization intervened in the middle of the already successful trajectories of Arab American communities, augmented by the post-World War II immigration of Arabs possessing significant amounts of human capital. These facts have allowed Arabs to overcome some of the economic outcomes that usually correlate with subordinate status. Rather, the impacts of Arab American racialization are found mainly in a range of social and political targetings and exclusions, discrimination, and hate crimes.

Arab Americans After 9/11: Collective Responsibility for the Attacks

Arabs and Muslims were held collectively responsible for the 9/11 attacks, providing convincing evidence that their racialization as an Other was complete before the attacks occurred. The immediate public attribution of collective culpability for the attacks required an a priori understanding that all Arabs and Muslims could be held responsible because they were an alike-thinking monolithic group. A primary correlate of whiteness, in contrast, is the attribution of individual culpability; reprehensible acts are depicted as individual acts, bearing no reflection on the values and beliefs of other Whites. For example, the actions of Oklahoma City bomber Timothy McVeigh were not considered endemic to White or Christian culture. Arabs and Muslims were also understood as racially identifiable. Persons who looked like group members were targeted after 9/11 and scholars found that they had to use sloppy phenotypic categories such as "Arabs, Muslims, and persons assumed to be Arabs and Muslims" when describing events on the ground. The negative experiences of Arab Americans after 9/11, as well as U.S. government policies that targeted them with wide public support, amply demonstrate a racialized response. This is especially true considering that none of the immediately accused 9/11 hijackers were Arab Americans, nor were Arab Americans found to be involved after investigation (National Commission on Terrorist Attacks upon the United States, 2004).

The Role of Race in Post-9/11 Government Policies

As documented by Cainkar (2009), Arabs and Muslims were directly or indirectly targeted by 25 of 37 U.S. government security measures that were implemented during the two years after 9/11. At least 100,000 Arabs and Muslims were personally affected by these initiatives, which included FBI interviews, wiretapping, mass arrests, secret and indefinite detentions, closed hearings, secret evidence, government eavesdropping on attorney–client conversations, removal of aliens for technical visa violations, and mandatory special registration. Immediately after 9/11 some 1,200 citizens and noncitizens, most of Arab and South Asian descent, were rounded up and detained based on their physical appearance or names. Some 83,000 persons who came to the U.S. on nonimmigrant visas from an Arab or selected Muslim countries after January 1, 2000, were interviewed (Cainkar, 2009).

One of the policies targeting Arabs in the U.S. that was broadest in scope was Special Registration, which required aliens from 25 countries, most of them Arab, to report and register with the U.S. immigration authorities during a specified time frame in order to be fingerprinted, photographed, and questioned. The purpose of this policy, according to the then-named Immigration and Naturalization Service (n.d.), was to facilitate the "monitoring" of aliens residing in the U.S. "in the interest of national security" (p. 3). These arguments behind the policies revealed that the U.S. government viewed Arab Americans as a monolithic group that was a security risk. Government flyers were posted and distributed in Arab American communities announcing the registration program, which was reminiscent of the notices posted for Japanese living on the Pacific Coast during World War II. Of the more than 200,000 persons registered, less than 50 were found to have criminal records and none were accused of an association with terrorism (Cainkar, 2009).

Race Evidenced in Popular Support for Collective Federal Government Policies

The pulse of public sentiment toward Arab and Muslims can be ascertained by opinion polls that emerged post 9/11. For example, in mid-September of 2001 approximately 50% of poll respondents felt that Arabs in the U.S., including American citizens, should be required to carry special identity cards (Jones, 2001). Two late-September Gallup polls found that a majority of Americans favored profiling Arabs and subjecting them to special security checks before boarding planes (Jones, 2001). A 2002 Gallup poll found that a majority of Americans felt that there were "too many" immigrants from Arab countries (Mazzuca, 2002). These polls indicate that the essentialized representations of Arabs propagated in American society before 9/11 were extremely effective in garnering public support for treating Arabs, conflated with Muslims, as a singular, monolithic group. These views would not have emerged so quickly after 9/11 had they not been cultivated prior to the attacks.

Race Demonstrated in Prejudice, Discrimination, and Compromised Sense of Safety

A wide body of literature demonstrates the prejudice, discrimination, hate crimes, and compromised sense of safety experienced by a majority of Arab Americans after 9/11, phenomena that are historically correlated with racial subordination in the U.S. (Bakalian & Bozorgmehr, 2009; Cainkar, 2009; Detroit Arab American Study Team, 2009; Hagopian, 2004; Jamal & Naber, 2008; Naber, 2006). Negative experiences with the American public were neither gender- nor social class-specific and occurred in public areas, shopping malls, and schools, as well as at home and work. Attacks ranged from verbal assaults and vandalism to physical assaults and murder. In a post-9/11 ethnographic study, Cainkar (2009) found that the overwhelming majority of persons interviewed reported experiencing some type of negative treatment. This included being verbally insulted, listening to negative comments at work, being asked by teachers to explain the attacks to their classmates, being spat upon, having their home or car vandalized, being followed or watched, or being turned in to the police. Participants also identified places where they did not feel safe. Many changed their daily life patterns to avoid placing themselves in situations where they might experience hostility, including not traveling on airplanes. In the context of anti-Arab media messages, government targeting of Arab Americans with wide public support, security roundups, verbal assaults, hate crimes, and ongoing petty harassments, it would be difficult to imagine that Arab Americans did not understand themselves as a discriminated racialized group, differentiated from Whites.

Present-Day Identification and Racialization: Racial Identity as Process

Although Arab Americans have experienced structural processes of racialization that include highly negative representations, social experiences of discrimination, and political targeting based on group membership, research shows a diversity of opinions around racial identification among Arab Americans. Some Arab Americans describe themselves as White while many do not, and Arab American communities vary in their political alliances around race. An Arab American's racial identity may change over the course of his or her lifetime, and two members of the same family may take on different racial identities. Racial identity formation is thus an unfolding and ongoing process for Arab Americans.

In psychology, the process of identity formation is most commonly captured through racial identity development models informed by Tajfel and Turner's (1979) social identity theory, which postulated that one's self-concept is derived from membership in a personally relevant social group. For example, nigrescence theory, developed by psychologist Cross in the 1970s (1971, 1978, 1991, 1995), highlighted the stages through which African Americans passed to develop a positive Black social identity. The model, as refined, identifies four stages of racial identity development: pre-encounter, encounter, immersion-emersion, and internalization. As applied to African

Americans, in pre-encounter stages African Americans do not identify strongly with being Black but rather see themselves as individual Americans unaffiliated with blackness, as different from Blacks, or, in the worst case for mental health, exhibit self-loathing for being Black. Conversion to a strong and positive racial identity is a process; it begins with a "shocking personal or social event that temporarily dislodges the person from his old worldview, making the person receptive to a new interpretation of his identity and his condition" (Cross, 1978, p. 17). After the encounter the individual begins to "reinterpret the world" (p. 17), moving through post-encounter race-salient stages, including a period of intensity that phases into one of a number of internalized outcomes, all of which engage blackness in a positive form.

Cultural studies scholar Stuart Hall highlighted the key role of representations in the process of identity formation. He said, "we should think ... of identity as a 'production', which is never complete, always in process, and always constituted within, not outside, representation" (1990, p. 223). Like psychiatrist and philosopher Franz Fanon (1961) before him, Hall argued that distorted representations must be contested and resisted to avert the psychic damage that "cripples and deforms" (Hall, 1990, p. 226). Cross' initial model (1971) similarly embraced the notion that highly negative representations of Blacks produced self-deprecation, a condition he saw as being healed through engagement with blackness. Cross later expanded his theory to permit multiple pre-encounter orientations that did not include self-hatred; nonetheless, positive engagements with blackness remained key to a healthy racial identity.

All of these theorists agreed that adopting alternative identities and producing knowledge that opposes dominant discourses are necessary to avert psychological damage that can be caused by derogatory characterizations of one's social group. Just as Cainkar (1988) found stronger identification among Palestinian Americans with their Palestinian identities in the context of media degradation, so too some American Muslims may more strongly assert their Muslim identities in the face of highly negative representations. These theories would predict that some Arab Americans may reject identification with the producers of those derogatory representations and begin to construct counter hegemonic, non-White identities. Cross would argue that Arab Americans would need to experience a personal encounter with racism to put the process in motion.

Waters' (1990) research, on the other hand, suggests that Arab Americans may have racial options – a modification of her concept of ethnic options – that members of other racialized groups do not possess. Their liminal status as neither White nor non-White may open the doors for interpretation of race to a greater degree than available for other groups. It may allow some Arab Americans to define their identity contextually, deciding from one situation to another whether they are White or not. Liminality may produce variations in how Arab Americans are perceived and perceive themselves in very local contexts (e.g. their neighborhoods) as well as in organized affiliations around race. Liminality would thus suggest variation in Arab American understandings of their racial position. These options do not alter their grounded reality as a negatively stigmatized group.

Research on Arab American Racial Identity

Arab Americans have been socialized to check the White box on forms that ask about race (since they are officially Caucasian and there is no other option for "Arab." Many do so, whether they agree with this categorization or not, while others do not. The post-9/11 Detroit Arab American Study (DAAS) found that a majority (64%) of Arab and Chaldean Americans surveyed said Arabs were White, while 31% said Arabs were "other" (Detroit Arab American Study Team, 2009; Shryock, 2008). On the other hand, in Cainkar's (2009) post-9/11 study of Muslim Arab Americans in metropolitan Chicago, 63% of persons interviewed said that Arabs were not White, 20% said Arabs were White, and the rest gave equivocal responses. Awad's (2010) study found that over 80% of an Arab/Middle Eastern sample of 177 individuals chose the "other" category when one was available. These very different findings with regard to race show how complicated race is for Arab Americans. A variety of factors come into play, including local experiences with race and the role of race in political organizing, personal experiences, religious affiliation, skin color, and response to official categorization.

With regard to religion, the DAAS found that 73% of Christian Arab Americans identified as White compared with 50% of Muslims (Baker et al., 2004). Similarly, a survey conducted by sociologist Read (2008) found that Muslim Arab Americans (who were far more likely to be foreign-born than Christians) were significantly more likely to define themselves as a minority than Christian Arab Americans. Since Christianity is the dominant religion in the U.S. and is not vilified, the theories noted above might predict that Christian Arab Americans would be less likely than Muslims to experience psychological violence from negative representations and to seek out identities that separate them from dominant White society. If they can "pass" as White they might choose to do so. On the other hand, both Christian and Muslim Arab Americans have faced discrimination, been the subject of dehumanizing tropes, been hounded by the government, and have organized against anti-Arab racism. Furthermore, the religious affiliation of an Arab is not always known to the outsider. It is simply not known what role personal experiences – what Cross calls "encounters" – play in Arab American racial identification processes.

Case Example: Perspectives on Race Among Muslim Arab Americans in Metropolitan Chicago

> You understand that there is racism even if it is not personally inflicted on you. Being a first generation Egyptian American and Muslim is a difficult thing – to form an identity of your own and feel like an American and that you fit into this country when you feel you really don't anyway. So, there's always been this sort of racism. ... that outlook was always there, it was just exaggerated [after 9/11] making you feel like the enemy. That you're the bad one, and you're definitely a foreigner and do not belong in this country. I'm just as much American as anyone else. I feel like maybe I need to get the hell out of this country because something bad is going to happen to our people here
>
> (Cainkar, 2009, p. 96)

To understand the meaning of race to Arab Americans it is important to know what matters Arab Americans take into account when thinking about racial status. The above quotation comes from a U.S.-born woman interviewed in an ethnographic and sociological study conducted by the author in 2003–4 of Muslim Arab Americans in metropolitan Chicago. The study (see Cainkar, 2009) included interviews with 102 men and women from diverse backgrounds in terms of nativity status, socioeconomic status, and national origin. Interviewees were asked the following open-ended question: "There have been discussions about whether Arabs are white or not, with different points of view; do you think Arabs are white, not white, or what?" (p. 95). Although most persons gave one reason to explain their response to this question, a few offered multiple explanations. Quotations are presented below to illustrate the different kinds of response given (some of these quotes were published in Cainkar, 2009, whereas others are taken from the author's research notes). The data indicated that a range of matters are taken into account in determining the racial status of Arab Americans, including how one is treated, phenotype (physical features), the history that is considered one's own, and how one is officially defined.

Among the 63% of participants who said Arabs are not White, the largest number (36%) spoke about the ways Arabs are treated in American society. Arabs are not White because they do not benefit from the statuses and assumptions that are accorded to whiteness. For example, a Chicago-born man stated, "Arabs are definitely not white. That categorization comes from the treatment of a community by the institutions of American society. Arabs in the schools face the same institutional racism as [do] other students of color" (Cainkar, 2009, p. 96). The overwhelming majority of persons who gave this type of response were born in the U.S., suggesting that the relationship between race and inequality is learned as part of an American upbringing. A U.S.-born woman said, "The issue is, are you part of a privileged group of people that can dominate others, and I do not think we are part of that. Arabs are not part of the white or European ruling structure. We are politically excluded" (p. 96). These responses, in that they invoke issues that existed before 9/11, support the assertion that racial projects that exclude Arabs from the benefits of whiteness were in place before 9/11.

The second most common response among persons who said Arabs are not White (28%) was about skin color and phenotypic features. These responses were found among both U.S.-born and non-U.S.-born respondents, although immigrants frequently conveyed that they only learned about ideas and social systems organized around skin color after arriving in the U.S. A quote from a Kuwaiti-born woman illustrates both the use of skin color to assign race as well as its rejection as a concept of social organization: "We are definitely not white. But the whole idea of color makes no sense to me. My neighbor is black according to census forms but she is lighter than I am. There are Arabs that are lighter than white people. I don't think people should be classified like that, by color. I don't agree with it at all."

The third most common response (24%) among persons who said Arabs are not White was that Arabs cannot be a racial group because they encompass many geographic regions and skin colors. This type of response focuses on Arab diversity and distinctiveness. As one U.S.-born woman said: "Arabs are distinct upon themselves, and the Arab world encompasses both black and white" (Cainkar, 2009, p. 98). Finally, the fourth most common response (20%) among persons who said Arabs are not White was about culture and heritage. To these persons, being White means being Caucasian and European, and Arabs are neither. As expressed in this statement from a U.S.-born man, whiteness negates Arab heritage: "I have a culture and heritage, being white denies that."

On the other hand, most of the 20% of Cainkar's (2009) total sample who said Arabs were White said they knew this because it is what they had been told. For example, one American-born woman who said Arabs were White commented: "I was really surprised when I learned that we were Caucasian" (Cainkar, 2009, p. 99). A majority of persons who said Arabs were White and about one-third of persons who said Arabs were not White moved immediately into a discussion of official forms, especially Census forms and job and school applications. The discussion of race became a discussion of boxes, their responses to these boxes, and the American phenomenon of boxing people into groups by color. Arab Americans know well that they are supposed to check the White box on forms, and a majority of interviewees said they do check it even though they may have serious problems with the concept and whether they believe Arabs are White or not. A woman born in Jordan put it this way: "This confuses me every time I fill out an application. We are not white, black, Hispanic, or Asian. We are Arab. I put 'white.' If there is an 'other,' sometimes I put that. But I put 'white' because I know we are not 'other'" (p. 99).

However, many who said Arabs are White made a distinction between what they write on forms and what they see as their reality. For example, a Palestinian-born man distinguished between what he does on the job and what he feels: "We used to report quarterly on affirmative action and I always asked my boss, 'What should I do? Should I put myself as a minority or not?' He did not know either, so we called the company headquarters, and they said 'You will be considered white.' But of course in real life we are not. As far as statistics go, that's what they say, legally" (Cainkar, 2009, p. 99). Indeed, many interviewees said being required to check the White box on forms is yet another form of discrimination. One woman said, "I am resentful that I have to put down 'white.' I don't look white. I am not treated as white" (p. 99). Another said, "I felt I was at a disadvantage to have to check 'white.' I don't think it's fair because it is not who I am. ... I feel that I am a minority. Why should I be grouped with these people and not have a chance to obtain a scholarship?" As these data show, when Arab Americans select the "White" box it does not necessarily mean that they identify with being White.

Seventeen percent of participants gave responses that were coded as equivocal: They responded that Arabs were White and not White at the same time. This quote by a woman born in Chicago indicates the difficulty some Arab Americans have with figuring out the race question:

> I don't really know. I think, for me, it's always been white because of what I look like. I consider myself white. That's probably a personal reflection because my skin color is white. I've always thought all Arabs were white. I've never really thought of them as being nonwhite. But, again, why do we say we're white, because we're not white? Like people say, "you put 'white,'" and I think that it just doesn't make sense. I don't know what white means in terms of technical definition. Is it people who live north of the equator? I don't know how the experts have defined it. If you ask anybody, they say to put 'white' as a race. Do I think we're white? I don't think so.
>
> (Cainkar, 2009, p. 98)

Critique

The topic of Arab Americans and race has received heightened attention over the past ten years from sociologists, psychologists, anthropologists, and historians, yet many questions remain, particularly in the field of psychology. In light of the social history of Arab Americans presented above, much is known about the social contexts in which Arab Americans have lived and the ways in which they have been racialized over time. There is also substantial evidence that the racial categories used in the Census, on numerous reporting forms, and in much research, are unhelpful for learning more deeply about Arab American experiences.

Based on published scholarship, there is now a clear understanding of what factors Arab Americans take into account when they think about race. Yet there is little understanding of why some Arab Americans identify as White and some do not, or more precisely, of what the differences are between those who do and those who do not. It is evident that religion, skin color, residential location, and organizing practices have some intersecting roles to play, but none of these appear to be determinative of racial identity. Current research lacks an understanding of the processes individual Arab Americans undergo when considering their identity, especially their racial identity.

Although Cross' nigrescence theoretical model has been adapted for many groups (e.g. LGBTs, feminists, Asians, Latinos) it has not been investigated with regard to Arab Americans. In light of the highly ambiguous state of race for Arab Americans, as compared to other groups, it would be useful to understand the variables that predict individual Arab American movement along the racial continuum. Building on Sellers and colleagues' (Sellers, Smith, Shelton, Rowley, & Chavous, 1998) scholarship on Black identity, studies that examine how important race is to Arab American perceptions of self and what it means to an Arab American are needed. Moustafa Bayoumi's (2009) book on Arab American youth is titled by posing a question initially asked by W. E. B. Du Bois (1903) over one hundred years ago: *How Does it Feel to be a Problem?* It would be good to learn some of the answers to this question.

Conclusion

Racial identity is complicated for Arab Americans; their official racial status is White and they are repeatedly required to affirm this status on Census and official forms. Arab Americans overall are economically successful, a status correlated with whiteness, and when skin color is considered, some Arab Americans can "pass" as White. Yet Arab Americans have been represented in dominant American culture as a group distinct from Whites through the use of persistent harmful stereotypes, and they have been accorded significant negative treatment. U.S. public opinion polls continue to show highly negative perceptions of them. Many Arab Americans say they do not share the experiences of and privileges accorded to whiteness. In this complex context, universal agreement would not be expected among Arab Americans on the topic of racial status. Short of significant changes in the way Arab Americans experience American culture and society, it is highly likely that they will continue to feel social exclusion and that their identification with whiteness will continue to decrease.

References

Abraham, N. (1994). Anti-Arab racism and violence in the United States. In E. N. McCarus (ed.), *The development of Arab American identity* (pp. 155–214). Ann Arbor, MI: University of Michigan Press.

Abu-Laban, B. & Suleiman, M.W. M. (eds.) (1989). *Arab Americans: Continuity and change.* Belmont, MA: Association of Arab-American University Graduates Press.

Arab American Institute. (n.d.). *Demographics.* Retrieved from www.aaiusa.org/pages/demographics/

Asi, M. & Beaulieu, D. (2013). *Arab households in the US 2006–2010* (American Community Survey Briefs, ACSBR/10–20). Washington, D.C.: U.S. Census Bureau. Retrieved from www.census.gov/prod/2013pubs/acsbr10-20.pdf

Awad, G. H. (2010). The impact of acculturation and religious identification on perceived discrimination for Arab/Middle Eastern Americans. *Cultural Diversity and Ethnic Minority Psychology* 16(1), 59–67. doi: 10.1037/a0016675

Bakalian, A. & Bozorgmehr, M. (2009). *Backlash 9/11: Middle Eastern and Muslim Americans respond.* Berkeley, CA: University of California Press.

Baker, W., Howell, S., Jamal, A., Lin, A. C., Shryock, A., Stockton, R., & Tessler, M. (2004). *Preliminary findings from the Detroit Arab American study.* Ann Arbor, MI: Michigan Institute for Social Research, University of Michigan. Retrieved from http://webuser.bus.umich.edu/wayneb/pdfs/culture/DAAS_FINAL_REPORT.pdf

Barlow, E. (ed.) (1994). *Evaluation of secondary-level textbooks for coverage of the Middle East and North Africa.* Ann Arbor, MI: Center for Middle Eastern and North African Studies.

Bassiouni, M. C. (ed.) (1974). *The civil rights of Arab-Americans: The special measures.* North Dartmouth, MA: Association of Arab-American University Graduates.

Bayoumi, M. (2009). *How does it feel to be a problem?: Being young and Arab in America.* New York: Penguin Press.

Bonilla-Silva, E. (2006). *Racism without racists: Color-blind racism and the persistence of racial inequality in the United States* (2nd edn.). New York: Rowman & Littlefield.

Brittingham, A. & de la Cruz, G. P. (2005). *We the people of Arab ancestry in the United States* (Census 2000 Special Reports, CENSR-21). Washington, D.C.: U.S. Census Bureau.

Cainkar, L. (1988). *Palestinian women in the United States: Coping with tradition, change, and alienation* (Doctoral Dissertation). Available from ProQuest Dissertations and Theses database (UMI No. 8902623).

Cainkar, L. (1999). The deteriorating ethnic safety net among Arabs in Chicago. In Michael Suleiman (ed.), *Arabs in America: Building a new future* (pp. 192–206). Philadelphia, PA: Temple University Press.

Cainkar, L. (2006). Immigrants from the Arab world. In J. Koval, L. Bennett, M. Bennett, F. Demissie, R. Garner, & K. Kim (eds.), *The new Chicago: A social and cultural analysis* (pp. 182–196). Philadelphia, PA: Temple University Press.

Cainkar, L. (2009). *Homeland insecurity: The Arab American and Muslim American experience after 9/11.* New York: Russell Sage Foundation.

Christison, K. (1989). The American experience: Palestinians in the U.S. *Journal of Palestine Studies* 18(4), 18–36. doi: 10.2307/2537495

Cross, W. E. (1971). Negro-Black conversion experience: Toward a psychology of black liberation. *Black World* 20(9), 13–27.

Cross, W. E. (1978). The Thomas and Cross models of psychological nigrescence: A review. *Journal of Black Psychology* 5(1), 13–31. doi: 10.1177/009579847800500102

Cross, W. E. (1991). *Shades of black: Diversity in African American identity.* Philadelphia, PA: Temple University Press.

Cross, W. E. (1995). The psychology of nigrescence: Revising the Cross model. In J. G. Ponterotto, J. M. Casas, L. A. Suzuki, & C. M. Alexander (eds.), *Handbook of multicultural counseling* (pp. 93–122). Thousand Oaks, CA: Sage.

Detroit Arab American Study Team. (2009). *Citizenship and crisis: Arab Detroit after 9/11*. New York: Russell Sage Foundation.

Du Bois, W. E. B. (1903). *The souls of black folk*. Chicago, IL: A. C. McClurg & Co.

Fanon, F. (1961). *The wretched of the earth*. New York: Grove Press.

Fay, M. (1984). Old roots – new soil. In J. Zogby (ed.), *Taking root, bearing fruit: The Arab-American experience* (pp. 17–23). Washington, D.C.: American-Arab Anti-Discrimination Committee Research Institute.

Ghareeb, E. (ed.) (1983). *Split vision: The portrayal of Arabs in the American media*. Washington, D.C.: American-Arab Affairs Council.

Grant, M. (1916). *The passing of the great race*. New York: Charles Scribner's Sons.

Gualtieri, S. (2004). Strange fruit? Syrian immigrants, extralegal violence and racial formation in the Jim Crow South. *Arab Studies Quarterly* 26(3), 63–85.

Hagopian, E. (ed.) (2004). *Civil rights in peril: The targeting of Arabs and Muslims*. Ann Arbor, MI: Pluto Press.

Hall, S. (1990). Cultural identity and diaspora. In J. Rutherford (ed.), *Identity, community, culture, difference* (pp. 222–237). London: Lawrence & Wishart.

Hooglund, E. (ed.) (1985). *Taking root: Arab-American community studies: Vol. II*. Washington, D.C.: ADC Research Institute.

Hooglund, E. (ed.) (1987). *Crossing the waters: Arabic-speaking immigrants to the United States before 1940*. Washington, D.C.: Smithsonian Institution Press.

Huntington, S. (1993). The clash of civilizations? *Foreign Affairs* 72(3), 22–49.

Ignatiev, N. (1995). *How the Irish became white*. New York: Routledge.

Immigration and Naturalization Service. (n.d.). Memo HQINS 70/28 from Johnny Williams, Executive Associate Commissioner, Office of Field Operations.

Jamal, A. & Naber, N. (eds.) (2008). *Race and Arab Americans before and after 9/11: From invisible citizens to visible subjects*. Syracuse, NY: Syracuse University Press.

Jones, J. M. (2001). Americans felt uneasy toward Arabs even before September 11: Majority supports increased security measures even for Arabs who are United States citizens. Gallup News Service, September 28. Retrieved from www.gallup.com/poll/4939/americans-felt-uneasy-toward-arabs-even-before-september.aspx

Lipset, S. M. & Schneider, W. (1977). Carter vs. Israel: What the polls reveal. *Commentary* 64, 21–29.

Mazzuca, J. (2002). Recent immigration views: Cover the melting pot? Gallup Polls, Politics, July 2. Retrieved from www.gallup.com/poll/6319/Recent-Immigration-Views-Cover-Melting-Pot.aspx

McCarus, E. N. (ed.) (1994). *The development of Arab American identity*. Ann Arbor, MI: University of Michigan Press.

Michalak, L. O. (1988). *Cruel and unusual: Negative images of Arabs in American popular culture*. Washington, D.C.: ADC Research Institute.

Naber, N. (2006). The rules of forced engagement: Race, gender, and the culture of fear among Arab immigrants in San Francisco post-9/11. *Cultural Dynamics* 18(3), 235–267. doi: 10.1177/0921374006071614

Naff, A. (1985). *Becoming American: The early Arab immigrant experience*. Carbondale & Edwardsville, IL: Southern Illinois University Press.

National Commission on Terrorist Attacks upon the United States (2004). *The 9/11 Commission report: Final report of the National Commission on Terrorist Attacks upon the United States*. Washington, D.C.: National Commission on Terrorist Attacks upon the United States. Retrieved from http://govinfo.library.unt.edu/911/report/911Report.pdf

Omi, M. & Winant, H. (1994). *Racial formation in the United States: From the 1960s to the 1990s*. New York: Routledge.

Orfalea, G. (2006). *The Arab Americans: A history*. Northampton, MA: Olive Branch Press.

Read, J. G. (2008). Discrimination and identity formation in a post-9/11 era: A comparison of Muslim and Christian Arab Americans. In A. Jamal & N. Naber (eds.), *Race and Arab Americans before and after 9/11: From invisible citizens to visible subjects* (pp. 305–17). Syracuse, NY: Syracuse University Press.

Read, J. G. & Oselin, S. (2008). Gender and the education-employment paradox in ethnic and religious contexts: The case of Arab Americans. *American Sociological Review* 73, 296–313. doi: 10.1177/000312240807300206

Roediger, D. R. (1991). *The wages of whiteness: Race and the making of the American working class*. New York: Verso.

Said, E. (1981). *Covering Islam: How the media and the experts determine how we see the rest of the world*. New York: Pantheon.

Saliba, T. W. (1999). Resisting invisibility: Arab Americans in academia and activism. In M. Suleiman (ed.), *Arabs in America: Building a new future* (pp. 304–319). Philadelphia, PA: Temple University Press.

Samhan, H. H. (1999). Not quite White: Race classification and the Arab American experience. In M. Suleiman (ed.), *Arabs in America: Building a new future* (pp. 209–226). Philadelphia, PA: Temple University Press.
Sellers, R. M., Smith, M. A., Shelton, J. N., Rowley, S. A., & Chavous, T. M. (1998). Multidimensional model of racial identity: A reconceptualization of African American racial identity. *Personality and Social Psychology Review* 2(1), 18–39. doi: 10.1207/s15327957pspr0201_2
Shaheen, J. G. (1984). *The TV Arab.* Bowling Green, OH: Bowling Green State University Popular Press.
Shaheen, J. G. (1991). The comic book Arab. *The Link* 24(5), 1–11.
Shaheen, J. G. (2001). *Reel bad Arabs: How Hollywood vilifies a people.* New York: Olive Branch Press.
Shryock, A. (2008). The moral analogies of race: Arab American identity, color politics, and the limits of racialized citizenship. In A. Jamal & N. Naber (eds.), *Race and Arab Americans before and after 9/11: From invisible citizens to visible subjects* (pp. 81–113). Syracuse, NY: Syracuse University Press.
Slade, S. (1981). Image of the Arab in America: Analysis of a poll on American attitudes. *Middle East Journal* 35(2), 143–162.
Stockton, R. (1994). Ethnic archetypes and the Arab image. In E. McCarus (ed.), *The development of Arab American identity* (pp. 119–153). Ann Arbor, MI: University of Michigan Press.
Suleiman, M. W. (ed.) (1999). *Arabs in America: Building a new future.* Philadelphia, PA: Temple University Press.
Tajfel, H. & Turner, J. (1979). An integrative theory of intergroup conflict. In W. G. Austin & S. Worchel (eds.), *The social psychology of intergroup relations* (pp. 33–47). Monterey, CA: Brooks/Cole.
Terry, J. J. (1985). *Mistaken identity: Arab stereotypes in popular writing.* Washington, D.C.: Middle East Policy Council.
U.S. Census Bureau. (2013). *Selected population profile in the United States, 2013 American Community Survey 1-Year Estimates.* Retrieved from http://factfinder.census.gov/faces/tableservices/jsf/pages/productview.xhtml?pid=ACS_13_1YR_S0201&prodType=table
U.S. Department of Justice, Immigration and Naturalization Service. (1943). The eligibility of Arabs to naturalization. *INS Monthly Review* 1(4), 12–16.
Waters, M. C. (1990). *Ethnic options: Choosing identities in America.* Berkeley, CA: University of California Press.
Zogby, J. (ed.) (1984). *Taking root: Bearing fruit – The Arab American experience.* Washington, D.C.: American-Arab Anti-Discrimination Committee Research Institute.

3

ACCULTURATION AND ENCULTURATION

Ethnic Identity Socialization Processes

Julie Hakim-Larson and Rosanne Menna

> As often happens in people's lives, as it happened to me, members of succeeding generations of immigrant families suddenly find themselves pondering the question of who they are and how they got here. They begin to search for a co-identity, one that connects with their ancestral roots and uniquely cohabits with their American identity.
>
> *(Ellis, 2007, p. 11)*

This chapter begins with a brief review of various approaches to the study of ethnic identity, because they form the foundation for the research studies on the acculturation and enculturation processes of Arab Americans. In particular, the seminal works of John W. Berry, Jean Phinney, and their colleagues (e.g. Berry, Phinney, Sam, & Vedder, 2006) are discussed in light of research on the acculturation of Arab Americans to the U.S. Acculturation involves the variety of different ways that a person can adapt to a culture that is different from that of their family's culture(s) of origin. Enculturation, on the other hand, involves learning about one's culture of origin.

Becoming enculturated to Arab values, attitudes, and behaviors while residing in North America involves ethnic identity socialization, a process that is most likely to take place within the extended family life and local communities of Arab Americans (e.g. Ajrouch, 2000; French, Coleman, & DiLorenzo, 2013). This process includes direct and indirect teaching of Arab cultural values and practices through, for example, family stories, food, music, and holiday celebrations. As described further below, there are a variety of relevant theories and models of ethnic identity socialization among immigrants. These frameworks address how Arab immigrants within North America are affected by a number of background factors and global sociopolitical events. The acculturation, enculturation, and ethnic identity socialization processes are illustrated in the case example of the family immigration of an Arab American of Lebanese descent, Raff Ellis (2007). The chapter ends with a brief critique of the currently available literature on the acculturation, enculturation, and ethnic identity of Arab Americans.

Theoretical Approaches to Ethnic Identity Development

Although there have been many theoretical approaches to the study of ethnic identity, the viewpoint most often referenced is that of Jean Phinney, who has taken a developmental approach to the process of changes in ethnic self-understanding over time (e.g. Ong, Fuller-Rowell, & Phinney, 2010; Trimble & Dickson, 2005). Phinney bases her approach on Erikson's (1968) classic lifespan developmental theory of changes in ego identity and on Marcia's (1966) research on youth identity statuses, which represent the extent to which young people have explored options in their lives, and the extent to which they have made a commitment to any of the various options. Ethnic identity – the extent to which a person considers the subjective importance of his or her ethnic or cultural group – is multifaceted and includes multiple components as the person develops over time (Phinney & Ong, 2007). A person's national identity (where they reside) and ethnic identity (based on ethno-cultural family heritage) together comprise a person's overall cultural identity (Phinney, Berry, Vedder, & Liebkind, 2006).

As noted by Ong and colleagues (2010), early scholars who addressed ethnic identity tended to focus more on the content than the processes. This content included the adoption of behaviors and attitudes consistent with that of the ethnic group under consideration. To attain a more comprehensive process-oriented understanding, research on ego identity development using the theories of Erikson and Marcia's identity statuses has concentrated on how identity resolution occurs through the processes of exploration followed by commitment. Similarly, Phinney and her colleagues emphasized the processes of self-exploration leading to changes and consolidation in ethnic identity over time (Ong et al., 2010).

Self-exploration has the potential to lead to a committed ethnic identity in Arab immigrants. Depending on the social context and the specific immediate needs within that context, multiple identities may be renegotiated repeatedly both in the public (e.g. school or work) and private spheres (e.g. family) of the everyday life of Arab youth (Abu-Laban & Abu-Laban, 1999). Arab immigrants, for instance, may engage in code-switching by speaking Arabic and following cultural norms while at a family gathering with community elders. In some cases, they may then switch to the English language and Western norms with select peers at the same family gathering and/or in other outside settings such as at work.

It is not merely overt cultural norms and activities in these various social contexts that influence ethnic identity development. Rather, there are many implicit and automatic patterns of ethnocultural activities (such as visual symbols, metaphors, and values) that influence immigrants' inner psychological experiences (Adams & Markus, 2001). For Arab immigrants, these more subtle processes of ethnic identity influences might be especially important to understand given that there are multiple social forces in operation simultaneously. In the Arab world, for instance, there are both Christian and Islamic religious influences; Christians endorse some values that stem from the Middle East's predominant Islamic history, while Muslim Arabs have incorporated some traditions and values stemming from the Abrahamic ancestry (Old Testament of the Bible) that they share in common with Judaism and Christianity (Esposito, 2003). Interestingly, immigrants to North America are exposed to the predominant Protestant work ethic and focus on individual autonomy and independence, and thus may incorporate Western values into their identities (Adams & Markus, 2001). A comprehensive understanding of Arab immigrant ethnic identity will therefore need to take into account these complex identity issues.

The complexity of Arab immigrant ethnic identity may be understood further in terms of whether or not the immigrant has a self-perception that is primarily interdependent or relatively independent (Markus & Kitayama, 1991). Independent self-construals involve a tendency to believe in the inherent separateness of self from others and thus there is an orientation toward social goals that emphasize individual achievements. In contrast, interdependent self-construals include an orientation toward the self as it exists in relation to others, and thus relationship oriented goals are paramount. Barry (2005) found that some Arab American male immigrants had relatively higher independent self-construal, while others had relatively higher interdependent self-construal, with implications for their acculturation and ethnic identity. He noted that this research points to the importance of not merely studying global categories of cultures (e.g. individualistic, collectivistic) in trying to understand ethnic identity. Rather, it is important to consider the multiplicity of dimensions involved in acculturation, enculturation, ethnic identity, and self-construals at the psychological level of understanding. For example, Barry found that Arab males in the U.S. with a separated acculturation status (more value placed on heritage than on host culture) were more likely to have an interdependent self-construal, perhaps preferring the company of like-minded peers of the same ethnicity. In contrast, Arab males with an integrated acculturation status (value placed on both heritage and host culture) were found to have an independent self-construal, perhaps preferring to socialize with those with a similar independent self-construal from among their cross-ethnicity or mainstream peers.

In addition to psychological variables such as self-construal, there are contextual factors that need to be taken into consideration in theorizing about Arab ethnic identity. Of importance is the role of how Arabs are perceived and treated in North America, especially given the post-9/11 backlash in societal attitudes (Nassar-McMillan, Lambert, & Hakim-Larson, 2011). It has become apparent to many researchers that any comprehensive consideration of the ethnic identity of immigrant groups will need to take into account their history of experiencing discrimination and ongoing prejudicial attitudes that linger in their host cultures. While both Christian and Muslim Arabs have experienced discrimination and prejudicial attitudes in the U.S., Muslim Arabs are particularly vulnerable as a visible minority given their traditional clothing and appearance (e.g. the hijab among some women and beards among some men), and their observance of cultural or religious practices that are unfamiliar to the mainstream (Awad, 2010). Rumbaut (2008) noted that when there are real or perceived insults to aspects of one's ethnic identity, there may be heightened attention given to it and a reactive ethnic identity process may emerge resulting in an increased sensitivity and self-consciousness about one's ethnicity. Negative stereotypes about Arabs were in existence before the tragic events of 9/11 and abounded throughout the early history of the U.S., as evidenced in written records and Hollywood films (e.g. Shaheen, 2001); so the fact that discriminatory attitudes continue to prevail is not surprising. However, recent events in the Arab region and the near instantaneous transmission of images and world news via the Internet have put Arabs even more in the international spotlight.

Previous authors (Britto, 2008; Britto & Amer, 2007) emphasized that Muslim Arab American youth in particular have had to negotiate a relatively complex ethnic identity that does not necessarily fit into currently available models. Because Muslim Arab American youth are part of a cultural group that is at times in conflict with the Western world at a sociopolitical level, they are sometimes viewed with skepticism by mainstream American culture, and the consequences may spill over into their everyday interactions, complicating their adjustment at school and at home. Similarly, Ahmed, Kia-Keating, and Tsai (2011) found a link between sociocultural adversity (such as perceived racial discrimination) and psychological distress among Arab American youth. Having a strong ethnic identity was found to be negatively related to psychological distress. Thus, the healthy adaptation and acculturation of Arab immigrants is at least partially related to the extent to which ethnic identity formation is occurring in a supportive rather than a discriminatory environment.

Acculturation and Arab Ethnic Identity

Acculturation refers to the process of adapting to a host culture that is different from one's ethnic or heritage culture (e.g. Berry, 1997; Miller, 2007). The ease or difficulty of integrating one's host culture and ethnic culture is partly determined by the similarities and differences between the two cultures (e.g. Rudmin, 2003a). Also, immigrants or ethnic minorities who share a common heritage culture may not adapt to acculturation in the same way. This is because there are individual differences – such as psychosocial factors, religion, values, and attitudes – across individuals who share a common background culture of origin (Berry, 2009). The process of acculturation may be the source of significant difficulties for some and represent what has been called acculturative stress (Berry, 1997).

Arab Americans are from diverse geographic, religious, and political backgrounds. In comparison to other ethnic groups, there are very few studies that have examined the acculturation process among Arab Americans. From these few studies, a number of psychosocial factors that influence Arab Americans' acculturation, ethnic and American identities, and subsequent mental and physical health have been identified. Among these are: country of origin, religion, age at immigration, reason for immigration, gender, length of time in the U.S., generational status, educational background, and English language skills.

For Arab Americans, country of origin and religion are associated with acculturation and adaptation to American mainstream culture. For example, Ajrouch and Jamal (2007) found that Lebanese and Syrian Christian Arab Americans with a long history of immigration to the U.S. were more likely to identify themselves as White, compared to more recent Muslim immigrants from Yemen or Iraq. Faragallah, Schuman, and Webb (1997) found that Christian Arabs who immigrated to the U.S. reported higher levels of acculturation and life satisfaction as compared to Muslim Arabs. Overall, Christian Arabs have found it easier to adapt to American mainstream culture due to similar religious values. More recently, Awad (2010) found that higher levels of discrimination were reported by both Christian and Muslim Arab Americans with low levels of immersion in dominant society culture. However, among those with higher levels of immersion in the mainstream culture, Muslim participants reported higher levels of discrimination than Christian participants.

Age at immigration has also been linked to adaptation to American culture. Arabs who immigrated to the U.S. at a younger age and spent longer periods of time between visits to their home cultures reported higher levels of adaptation and life satisfaction, while Arab immigrants who were older upon entry to the U.S. reported poorer adjustment and life satisfaction (Faragallah et al., 1997). When acculturation begins at an early age, the process may be smoother and less stressful for individuals than when it starts later because young children have more personal flexibility and adaptability to adjust (Berry, 1997). However, older youth may experience difficulty adapting to the American mainstream as they need to resolve conflicts with their parents who may want them to maintain the values, beliefs, and traditions of their heritage culture (Hakim-Larson, Kamoo, Nassar-McMillan, & Porcerelli, 2007). Ajrouch (2000) interviewed Arab American adolescents in an attempt to learn about ethnic identity formation. Those whose parents tried to instill the traditions of the heritage culture and separate them from American mainstream culture reported feeling controlled and restricted by their parents.

Like age at immigration, the various economic and sociopolitical reasons for immigration have been linked to acculturative stress. When immigration is voluntary, for those who choose to assimilate, the acculturation process will be smoother with less stress and fewer psychological problems (Berry, 1997). However, when immigration is involuntary and acculturating individuals are rejected or marginalized by the mainstream culture, acculturation may be highly stressful and may lead to significant psychological difficulties (Berry, 1997). Jamil, Nassar-McMillan, and Lambert (2007) found that Iraqi refugees whose move was involuntary (due to political instability and war) experienced significant acculturative stress and mental health problems such as posttraumatic stress disorder (PTSD). However, immigrants from Iraq whose move was voluntary and primarily due to economic reasons experienced few if any psychological problems and acculturated more easily to the host culture. Immigrants who voluntarily immigrate may be more willing to learn about the host culture (Berry, 1997).

The different levels of acculturative stress resulting from the involuntary nature or otherwise of immigration may also vary according to the immigrant's gender. The gender roles of Arab Americans may be described as patriarchal and hierarchical. Men are primarily responsible for the family finances and represent the household in matters that are public and external to the household, while women are generally responsible for parenting, homemaking, and maintaining cultural traditions within the family (Hakim-Larson, Nassar-McMillan, & Paterson, 2012). Naff (1985) reported that first and second generation Arab American immigrant women in the twentieth century often adjusted to the American mainstream culture with minor acculturative stress. Many but not all of these women abandoned the traditions and customs of their heritage culture because of the economic goals of their families. Like many early immigrants, they wanted to assimilate into American life. These women were employed outside the home, participated in family businesses, adapted their clothing to Western culture, and in turn were empowered by these changes. Similarly, Amer and Hovey (2007) found no differences between second generation male and female Arab Americans on measures of acculturation and acculturative stress; however, second generation females did report more Arab ethnic practices as compared to second generation males. These outcomes may be quite different for more recent involuntary immigrants and refugees.

Length of residence in the U.S. and generational status are important considerations in understanding Arab American acculturation. Faragallah and colleagues (1997) found that longer length of residence in the U.S. was linked with greater identification with American culture. In contrast to earlier immigrants, recent female Arab immigrants who are uneducated, socially isolated, and do not speak English have been found to be at an increased risk for acculturative stress and interpersonal problems such as domestic violence (Kulwicki & Miller, 1999).

For Arab Americans, generational status has been found to be associated with the adoption of American culture and maintenance of the heritage culture; that is, those who are second generation report lower levels of engagement in Arab customs and language and higher levels of adoption of American mainstream culture (Amer, 2014). According to Kim (2007), maintaining one's heritage culture may not apply to individuals who are several generations removed from migration because they may have never been fully socialized into their heritage group's cultural norms. As described later in this chapter, for such individuals the process of enculturation and learning about one's family ethnic history either within the family or through deliberate genealogical research can be instrumental in ethnic identity resolution. These later generation Arab Americans may have a family history that extends back as far as four or even five generations in the U.S. to the American Industrial Revolution at the turn of the twentieth century. Thus, even for later generation Arab Americans, both acculturation and ethnic identity may be fostered by the family, especially parents, grandparents, and extended family members who continue to socialize children to identify with their Arab culture (Amer, 2014).

The level of education and degree of fluency in the English language are also related to the acculturation process. Arab Americans with higher levels of education are less likely to participate in ethnic practices (Amer & Hovey, 2007), and English language proficiency was found to be instrumental in adapting to American mainstream culture (Ajrouch, 2007).

Models of Acculturation: Relevance for Research on Arab Americans

While there is currently no dominant model of acculturation that incorporates the relevant psychosocial factors for Arab Americans as reviewed above, there are several models that are currently in use that guide contemporary research. In the past, acculturation was conceptualized as a unilinear process in that immigrants were viewed as gradually adapting to the host culture by acquiring the practices and values of the host culture while discarding those from their cultural heritage (Yoon et al., 2013). However, researchers and theorists began to recognize that it was possible for an individual to both adapt to the host culture and maintain the heritage culture, thus acquiring competence in more than one culture (Rumbaut, 1997).

In his seminal work on acculturation, Berry (1997) proposed a bidimensional model of acculturation that included two independent dimensions: cultural adaptation (the gradual process of adopting the practices and values of the new or host culture) and cultural maintenance (retention of the practices and values of the heritage culture). In Berry's model, these independent dimensions intersect, resulting in four alternative strategies that describe the process of acculturation: assimilation, separation, integration, and marginalization. In the assimilation strategy, a person adapts to the host culture, but no longer identifies with the heritage culture. In separation, a person rejects the host culture and maintains the heritage culture. In the integration strategy (also referred to as biculturalism), a person adapts to the practices and values of the host culture and also maintains the practices and values of the heritage culture. In the marginalization strategy, a person rejects both the host culture and the heritage culture. An individual utilizing the marginalization strategy may be at increased risk of experiencing more psychological distress due to a lack of community and contextual resources (Berry, 1997).

Berry's (1997) four-classification model has been instrumental in generating much research and it has spurred theorizing on the topics of acculturation and enculturation. Early versions of this model were critiqued with claims that the model was too structural and static rather than process-oriented (Rudmin, 2003a). However, it was later acknowledged that Berry had addressed many of the limitations of his early model in his updated publications (Rudmin, 2003b). Thus, Berry's approach to the classification and measurement of acculturation strategies has continued to remain an important contemporary contribution to the field. For example, Yoon and colleagues (2013) conducted a statistical meta-analysis on 325 studies of acculturation/enculturation strategies and mental health outcomes such as self-esteem, life satisfaction, depression, and anxiety. The participants in some studies included a small proportion of Arab Americans. They found that the integration acculturation strategy had the most favorable mental health outcomes, followed by assimilation and separation. Marginalization had the least favorable association to mental health outcomes.

Some researchers have proposed an expanded, multidimensional acculturation model that is influenced by demographic and contextual factors (Miller, 2007; Schwartz, Unger, Zamboanga, & Szapocznik, 2010; Yoon, Langrehr, & Ong, 2011). This expanded model includes cultural behaviors, values, practices, knowledge, and identity. It considers the differential rates and patterns of acculturation across the dimensions and the contextual influences across family, school, neighborhood, and community systems (Yoon et al., 2013). It suggests that acculturation for Arab Americans is a complex process.

Future research with Arab Americans would benefit from employing a multidimensional model of acculturation to better understand the development of ethnic and American identities, overall wellbeing, and various mental health outcomes. One negative outcome of the acculturation process is that some Arab Americans have chosen to hide or minimize their ethnic identities to protect against discrimination. On the positive side, others have instead increased their overt displays of ethnic pride and focused their attention on enculturation. One way that this is accomplished is through learning about Arab cultural practices (e.g. food, music; Hakim-Larson et al., 2012). Yoon and his colleagues (2013) highlighted the importance of considering enculturation as a complement to acculturation. As described next, enculturation involves activities that allow immigrants and their descendants in later generations to create or maintain ties to their family's culture of origin.

Enculturation and Arab Ethnic Identity

While acculturation focuses on the processes involved in adaptation when members of two cultural groups interact – as occurs when immigrants settle into a new life within their host culture (e.g. Berry, 1997) – enculturation includes being socialized into the language, behaviors, identity, sociopolitical historical knowledge, and values of one's ethnic group (e.g. Kim, Ahn, & Lam, 2009; Yoon et al., 2011; Yoon et al., 2013). While many aspects of Arab culture are similar across countries of origin and religions, there are also differences between them – for example, in dialect and certain traditions. The extent to which a person is immersed in learning about these specific aspects of their heritage culture may vary by the age of immigration. Those who have immigrated at an earlier age or who are second generation will have had less direct exposure to the heritage culture and thus less experience with the most direct form of the enculturation process in the country of origin (Berry, 1997). Rather, their enculturation process takes place in the host culture in which their families currently reside.

For some contemporary researchers, the process of enculturation is viewed as being more fundamental than that of acculturation because immigrants are typically embedded within families that provide the first and most immediate social context for the socialization of language, behavior, and cultural values. That context is often rich in the heritage or ethnic group culture(s) (Weinreich, 2009). Thus, even though a child is born to immigrant parents in the U.S., the child's first language might be Arabic rather than English. In this view, even before children of immigrants have entered school (where they may become relatively more acculturated), enculturation processes have already begun to lay down a foundation in their identity within the family context. According to Weinreich, immigrants are repeatedly challenged to reformulate their ethnic identities under a diversity of everyday social contexts and circumstances. At any given time, there may be a tension between acculturation and enculturation processes. For example, sometimes the values of the mainstream culture (e.g. freedom in America to choose one's partner by dating) will conflict with those of the ethnic group culture (e.g. arranged or family-sanctioned marriages).

As reviewed by Awad (2010), the goals of the Arab American family take priority over the goals of the individual, and high value is placed on respect for elders and their traditions. Thus, children must attend to what they are being taught by their elders during the enculturation process, whether this involves language (e.g. greeting elders) or other customs and traditions (such as food, music, traditional dress). Parents and extended family remain involved in the ethnic socialization processes of the children even into their adult years, many of whom continue to speak their heritage language at home.

The Arabic language itself provides a window into an understanding of Arab societies and cultures (Nydell, 2006). Thus, for many Arab Americans, a major component of socialization into their Arab ethnic identity through the enculturation process includes learning and utilizing the Arabic language. In contrast to the acculturation problems of immigrants in acquiring the language of the host culture, the enculturation process involves the retention and refining of one's Arabic language skills as a first generation immigrant or learning how to read, write, and speak Arabic as a second or later generation person residing in North America. Kim and colleagues (2009) suggested that it may be more accurate to use the term "cultural maintenance" as described by Berry (e.g. Berry, 2001, 2011) in referring to the enculturation of the first generation because they already have stored memories and a history of immersion in the heritage culture. This is not the case for second and later generation Arab Americans, who then must learn the Arabic language in other formal or informal but quite limited ways. Arab community centers, churches, and mosques may offer Arabic language classes to foster Arab ethnic identity in Arab Americans. Thus, bilingualism or multilingualism is of interest in the enculturation process and there are diverse manifestations of the linguistic outcomes.

Such diversity in Arabic language use stems primarily from geographical origins. According to Nydell (2006), there are five regions in which variations of the Arabic dialect are spoken: North African (Western dialect), Egyptian/Sudanese, Levantine, Arabian Peninsular, and Iraqi. Only the speakers of the Egyptian/Sudanese and the Levantine dialects have some ability to understand each other; otherwise, there are wide variations in the spoken vocabulary and grammatical structures. Written Arabic and technical advanced language is more likely to make use of classical/standard Arabic, and thus be more widely understood throughout the Arab region (Nydell, 2006). Such standard Arabic is used when a person wants to convey a sense of seriousness and sophistication. The regional dialect might be used more informally in emotional or intimate settings or for the purpose of joking, giving examples, or to denote the relative unimportance of a topic to the speaker (Albirini, 2011). Because the Arabic language itself is diglossic (i.e. consists of two forms: the classical/standard form (high form) and the more local regional dialect (low form), code-switching between the two forms may occur in a variety of both formal and informal settings depending on the specific practical purpose (Albirini, 2011). This is further complicated by code-switching between other languages (such as English or French) that may be part of an immigrant's linguistic background. The education of bilingual English- and Arabic-speaking immigrant children who are learning to read and write is complicated by these considerations (e.g. Farran, Bingham, & Matthews, 2012).

Many individuals who immigrate to other countries, such as the U.S., not only bring their specific native Arabic dialect and perhaps standard Arabic, but also other languages that they may have learned before arriving in their host countries. For example, because of the French and British occupation in the Levant region (e.g. Lebanon, Syria, Palestine) early in the twentieth century (Garraty & Gay, 1985; Najem, 2012) and the contemporary influence of universities in the Middle East where English or French is emphasized academically, many Lebanese learn English and/or French as a second language and thus some may speak two or even three languages (Arabic, English, and French). Code-switching can occur between the two forms of Arabic (high, low) as well as with additional languages, and these sometimes occur as a co-mixture within the same statement made by the individual. Another example here would be Catholic Christian Iraqi immigrants called Chaldeans who may speak both Arabic and a variation of the ancient language called Aramaic (Kamoo, 1999).

The enculturation process for Arab immigrants involves learning how to effectively and strategically alternate between the use of the English and Arabic (or other) languages in social settings such as within the home. Interestingly, Al-Khatib (2003) found that second generation Lebanese youth in London switched to using English during family conversations taking place in Arabic when they were clearly being defiant, thus signaling their feelings of Western autonomy and separation from family at that moment during the interaction. Some research points to the notion that similar conflicts occur in Asian immigrant families due to a gap in the values of parents and children – parents may attempt to enculturate their children into traditional ethnic values at the same time that children are attempting to acculturate to the values of the mainstream American society in which they live (Kim et al., 2009). In addition, being enculturated into Arabic traditions includes other socialization processes involving verbal communication such as learning polite conversational transitions (e.g. Ferguson, 1976).

In addition to learning the Arabic language directly through their families and local communities, various forms of media are instrumental in fostering enculturation. For example, Arab Americans have access to Arabic language radio programs and satellite television, which means that communications directly from the Middle East have become another informal means of enculturation into the Arabic language and culture. Some social scientists have now begun to research the use of Web-surfing and the Internet as alternative means of information gathering among Arab Americans (Muhtaseb & Frey, 2008; Nagel & Staeheli, 2004). They have suggested that, like many other Americans, Arab Americans are motivated to use the Internet for a multiplicity of reasons that may include learning about the values, behaviors, beliefs, and attitudes of others outside the U.S. Web-surfing and social communication over the Internet via chat rooms and LISTSERVS may be an especially important means of enculturation for contemporary Arab Americans. A good proportion of their Internet information gathering may come from sources outside the U.S., though it is not clear how this use compares to that of other ethnic groups or to mainstream Americans in the U.S. (Muhtaseb & Frey, 2008). It is also not clear whether the motivation among Arab Americans to use the Internet for such information gathering varies by psychosocial factors. One possibility in need of further research is that younger or more educated Arab Americans may be more likely than those who are older or less educated to use the Internet and computer-mediated communication as a means of socialization into their ethnic identities.

Processes Involved in the Socializing of Ethnic Identity

As noted by Phinney and Ong (2007), there are many opportunities for ethnic identity socialization as the individual encounters various relevant social contexts over time. These agents of socialization operate dynamically at the macro-level by transmitting broader cultural symbols, language, and media, and at the micro-level such as within families and communities through music, food, clothing, and psychological attitudes and beliefs (Hakim-Larson, 2014). While the content of such socialization includes being directly taught about various Arab cultural values, behaviors, and events, a process of exploration is necessary before a person can have a mature commitment to an ethnic identity (Phinney & Ong, 2007). This process of exploration involves a person actively seeking out specific information about his or her ethnicity by reading about it, communicating with others to learn more, and participating in cultural events sponsored by community organizations and religious institutions.

Organizations such as the Arab American Museum in Dearborn, Michigan, the Arab American Institute in Washington, D.C., and religious institutions have websites that are regularly updated. They frequently hold cultural events that promote cultural sensitivity, awareness, and acceptance of Arab ethnic traditions, and provide opportunities for the enculturation of Arab American immigrants and their second, third, and later generation descendants who are engaging in a process of exploration.

The case example presented below illustrates the process of exploration and commitment engaged in by second generation author Raff Ellis. His Maronite Christian Lebanese parents immigrated in the early part of the twentieth century. The culmination of this process resulted in Ellis (2007) writing a book about several generations of his family history.

Case Example: The Family Story of Raff Ellis

"Kidnapped!!" was the word that stuck in the mind of Ellis (2007) when he was a boy listening to his mother tell the story of how his maternal grandmother, who was a novice in training to become a Catholic nun, was "kidnapped" from her convent. She was taken by surprise and reluctance – but with family and community endorsement – by a wealthy Christian "sheikh" in Lebanon looking for a bride. The term "sheikh" is a pre-Islamic honorific title given to men of privileged status in Arabic-speaking countries (Esposito, 2003); the term "sheikha" refers to women from families of privileged wealth and status (Ellis, 2007). While growing up in Carthage, New York, Ellis was intrigued by this story and motivated many years later to trace his family's history after his mother's death in 1994. Thus, it was not until Ellis was in his 60s that he began his ethnic identity exploration by reading his mother's letters, writing down family stories, and travelling to Lebanon.

Ellis' mother, Angele, was the daughter of the "kidnapped" woman and the sheikh. She was considered a "sheikha" and was a well-respected teacher in Lebanon before she married Ellis' father, Toufic. Ellis learned that his mother repeatedly rejected the wealthy suitors arranged by one of his uncles. Toufic came from a lower social class and was the son of a stonemason; marrying him was considered to be beneath a sheikha. Nonetheless, Angele married him, partially because of his good looks and partially because of her anticipatory excitement about the idea of going to America with him. Toufic had recently started a business in Carthage, New York, and thus her future with him seemed promising.

Once married, however, there were problems with Angele getting a U.S. visa. She and her sister-in-law were held up in Marseilles, France. Meanwhile, Toufic returned to the U.S. in the hopes of getting their visas and arranging their passage to North America. Upon his arrival back in Carthage, New York, Toufic found out that his business partner (a cousin) had managed their dry goods store so poorly during his absence that he was now bankrupt and the store had closed. Toufic had thus lost his life savings and was quite devastated. Ellis reports that these events and the difficulties his father had in securing his mother's passage to the U.S. (it took 11 weeks) were very depressing for his father. His mother too became quite depressed after learning of her new husband's failures. She expressed regrets about giving up marriage to one of her wealthy suitors, and at times her family encouraged her to separate from her husband and return to Lebanon. Furthermore, she only spoke French and Arabic. She wrote to her family often with criticisms regarding her plight. A further insult was the fact that Toufic now had to make a living by selling tobacco and shining shoes, a state that Angele felt was quite beneath her. The news of Toufic's business setback travelled quickly in gossip networks in Lebanon.

Years later when asked about these early events, Toufic still had deep scars and feelings of resentment over the losses he suffered (Ellis, 2007), even though he did manage to once again have his own business. Angele remained generally unhappy but continued nonetheless to do her duties as a Christian (i.e. Maronite Catholic) wife and mother. She retained a stubborn independence, took private English language lessons, and learned to drive. Overall, she valued being an American and wanted to assimilate.

As part of his enculturation, Raff Ellis (2007) spent eight years exploring his family's history in the search for more information about his ancestors. He attempted wherever possible to find records that verified the family stories and legends he had heard or read about in his mother's letters. He notes that as a child in Carthage, he longed to assimilate and just be part of the celebrated American melting pot. However, this goal was more myth than reality in everyday life, because "those who came earlier or from more 'respectable' origins, didn't want us cast into that fabled pot with them, and we were not allowed to melt and fuse with them" (p. 301). He described being the victim of racial slurs. Though he felt ambivalence about his ethnic identity throughout his earlier life, he noted that "my ethnicity kept drawing me back, even though I had loudly protested that I wanted out" (p. 303). In exploring and writing about his family history, Raff Ellis was able to finally accept and commit to his Lebanese Arab American ethnic identity.

In his book Ellis (2007) now provides a means of helping to teach Arab Americans across generations about the early immigrant experiences. The Ellis family history demonstrates the nature of the acculturative stressors encountered by first generation immigrants and the impact of these stressors on later generations. It is noteworthy that Ellis' own journey toward self-exploration and eventual identity commitment was not a smooth one. Due to American pressures to assimilate while co-existing simultaneously with societal prejudice and discrimination against Arabs as he was growing up, Ellis struggled and resisted fully exploring his ethnic identity until a later point in his life. This book, and others that trace the life stories of Arab American immigrants, uses narratives as an interesting informal method of attempting to answer questions about ethnic identity development.

Critique

In general, sound methodological practices in conducting formal research begin with asking questions in such a way that further research will be able to give some tentative answers (Kazdin, 1998). Theoretical models are often helpful in structuring what is already known and pointing to gaps in what needs to be addressed further. Berry and colleagues (2006) identified three primary questions to be addressed in conducting research on acculturation, enculturation, and ethnic identity with immigrant youth. These questions are also applicable to the study of immigrants of all ages, as well as their descendants in second and later generations, and are therefore reflected here in a more generalized adapted form. The first, "intercultural," question asks: "Just how do immigrants and their descendants live in between two or more cultures?" The second, "adaptation," question asks: "Just how well do immigrants and their descendants do in terms of the academic, social, and personal arenas of their lives as they live in between cultures?" Finally, the third, "cross-cultural," question asks what differences there are across cultures in the patterns of intercultural functioning and adaptation at a broader level of analysis. In attempting to answer these questions, many studies have been conducted, including the seminal work of Berry and colleagues (2006); however, relatively few until recently have focused on Arab Americans.

Amer's (2014) review of the research on Arab American acculturation identified gaps in the literature. First, in taking a developmental psychopathology approach to address the immigrants' adaptation, Amer suggested that there is a need for research on risk and protective factors. Second, there is a need to account for the heterogeneity of Arab Americans, who have various countries of origin, religious backgrounds, beliefs, values, and traditions that defy easy generalization, especially given the typically small sample sizes of many studies. Amer reviewed literature demonstrating the complexities of how Arab Americans self-identify, which can vary by context, background, future plans for where they would like to reside, or by how they are perceived and labeled in the dominant American society. Finally, the literature on Arab Americans has focused more on mental health symptoms, such as depression and anxiety, in an effort to establish the need for culturally competent care; yet, how resilience is fostered and utilized as part of the acculturation process has received far less attention.

With respect to enculturation, in addition to the role of the family, global communication and visual media (such as news, television, and movies) from the Arab world likely impact which cultural values from the heritage society are incorporated into an individual's ethnic identity and which are not. While the digital age is upon us and there are studies beginning to address its impact, it is unclear to what extent immigrant youth in the U.S. text, Skype, email, browse the Web, and so on across cultural and social contexts, although as discussed above, some social scientists have begun to address this issue. One future direction will be to ascertain how to best go about identifying and assessing the outcomes of these influences on ethnic identity.

Another direction is to focus on socialization within families. Based on a clash of values and cultural practices, conflicts within families may occur between generations (grandparents, parents, and children) or within generations (sibling disputes). Longitudinal and multigenerational studies of families would help to tease out what is common and what is different from one generation to the next. Because there is such a high value placed on family life and cohesion among Arab Americans, resolution of family feuds and intrafamilial conflicts via the process of forgiveness has been described as an important issue in need of further research (Ajrouch & Antonucci, 2014). Given the complexity of ethnic identity structure and the fact that there are likely to be identity conflicts experienced when there are discrepancies in values and behaviors during the acculturation/enculturation process, it will be important to better understand how conflicts are resolved and how ethnic identity may become integrated so that a person experiences some continuity over the life course.

Conclusion

While good progress has been made in understanding some of the factors worthy of further study with Arab Americans, the question of just what constitutes healthy, adaptive, normative ethnic identity development for Arab Americans remains. The answers to this question are likely to vary by context, generation, and historical time. Describing the multifaceted and changing nature of ethnic identity development of Arab Americans will be a challenge for future research. In general developmental frameworks, such development would consist of an integrated and coherent sense of self and others over time, with the ramifications of ethnic identity crossing over from one generation to the next. Thus, there is a need for longitudinal studies of Arab American families across multiple generations to account for birth cohort and intergenerational transmission effects. Another promising area of future study involves the role of computer-mediated communication (via the Internet and social media websites) in the acculturation, enculturation, and ethnic identity of Arab Americans. Technological advances should make such studies increasingly feasible over time.

References

Abu-Laban, S. M. & Abu-Laban, B. (1999). Teens between: The public and private spheres of Arab-Canadian adolescents. In M. W. Suleiman (Ed.), *Arabs in America* (pp. 113–128). Philadelphia, PA: Temple University Press.

Adams, G. & Markus, H. R. (2001). Culture as patterns: An alternative approach to the problem of reification. *Culture & Psychology, 7*, 283–296. doi: 10.1177/1354067X0173002

Ahmed, S. R., Kia-Keating, M., & Tsai, K. H. (2011). A structural model of racial discrimination, acculturative stress, and cultural resources among Arab American adolescents. *American Journal of Community Psychology, 48*(3–4), 181–192. doi: 10.1007/s10464-011-9424-3

Ajrouch, K. J. (2000). Place, age, and culture: Community living and ethnic identity among Lebanese American adolescents. *Small Group Research, 31*(4), 447–469. doi: 10.1177/104649640003100404

Ajrouch, K. J. (2007). Resources and well-being among Arab-American elders. *Journal of Cross Cultural Gerontology, 22*, 167–182. doi: 10.1007/s10823-006-9033-z

Ajrouch, K. J. & Antonucci, T. C. (2014). Using convoys of social relations to understand culture and forgiveness from an Arab American perspective. In S. C. Nassar-McMillan, K. J. Ajrouch, & J. Hakim-Larson (Eds.), *Biopsychosocial perspectives on Arab Americans: Culture, development and health* (pp. 127–146). New York: Springer. doi: 10.1007/978-1-4614-8238-3_7

Ajrouch, K. J. & Jamal, A. (2007). Assimilating to a White identity: The case of Arab Americans. *International Migration Review, 41*, 860–879. doi: 10.1111/j.1747-7379.2007.00103.x

Albirini, A. (2011). The sociolinguistic functions of codeswitching between Standard Arabic and Dialectal Arabic. *Language in Society, 40*, 537–562. doi: 10.1017/S0047404511000674

Al-Khatib, H. (2003). Language alternation among Arabic and English youth bilinguals: Reflecting or constructing social realities? *International Journal of Bilingual Education and Bilingualism, 6*, 409–22. doi: 10.1080/13670050308667794

Amer, M. M. (2014). Arab American acculturation and ethnic identity across the lifespan: Sociodemographic correlates and psychological outcomes. In S. C. Nassar-McMillan, K. J. Ajrouch, & J. Hakim-Larson (Eds.), *Biopsychosocial perspectives on Arab Americans: Culture, development and health* (pp. 153–173). New York: Springer. doi: 10.1007/978-1-4614-8238-3_8

Amer, M. M. & Hovey, J. D. (2007). Socio-demographic differences in acculturation and mental health for a sample of 2nd generation/early immigrant Arab Americans. *Journal of Immigrant and Minority Health, 9*, 335–347. doi: 10.1007/s10903-007-9045-y

Awad, G. H. (2010). The impact of acculturation and religious identification on perceived discrimination for Arab/Middle Eastern Americans. *Cultural Diversity and Ethnic Minority Psychology, 16*, 59–67. doi: 10.1037/a0016675

Barry, D. T. (2005). Measuring acculturation among male Arab immigrants in the United States: An exploratory study. *Journal of Immigrant Health, 7*(3), 179–184. doi: 10.1007/s10903

Berry, J. W. (1997). Immigration, acculturation, and adaptation. *Applied Psychology: An International Review, 46*, 5–68. doi: 10.1080/026999497378467

Berry, J. W. (2001). A psychology of immigration. *Journal of Social Issues, 57*, 615–631. doi: 10.1111/0022-4537.00231

Berry, J. W. (2009). A critique of critical acculturation. *International Journal of Intercultural Relations, 33*, 361–371. doi: 10.1016/j.ijintrel.2009.06.003

Berry, J. W. (2011). Integration and multiculturalism: Ways toward social solidarity. *Papers on Social Representations, 20*, 2.1–2.21.

Berry, J. W., Phinney, J. S., Sam, D. L., & Vedder, P. (Eds.) (2006). *Immigrant youth in cultural transition: Acculturation, identity, and adaptation across national contexts.* Mahwah, NJ: Lawrence Erlbaum.

Britto, P. R. (2008). Who am I? Ethnic identity formation of Arab Muslim children in contemporary U.S. society. *Journal of the American Academy of Child & Adolescent Psychiatry, 47*, 853–857. doi: 10.1097/CHI.0b013e3181799fa6

Britto, P. R. & Amer, M. M. (2007). An exploration of cultural identity patterns and the family context among Arab Muslim young adults in America. *Applied Developmental Science, 11*, 137–150. doi: 10.1080/10888690701454633

Ellis, R. (2007). *Kisses from a distance: An immigrant family experience.* Seattle, WA: Cune.

Erikson, E. H. (1968). *Identity: Youth and crisis.* New York: Norton & Company.

Esposito, J. L. (Ed.) (2003). *The Oxford dictionary of Islam.* New York: Oxford University Press.

Faragallah, M. H., Schuman, W. R., & Webb, F. J. (1997). Acculturation of Arab-American immigrants: An exploratory study. *Journal of Comparative Family Studies, 28*, 182–203.

Farran, L. K., Bingham, G. E., & Matthews, M. W. (2012). The relationship between language and reading in bilingual English-Arabic children. *Reading and Writing, 25*(9), 2153–2181. doi: 10.1007/s11145-011-9352-5

Ferguson, C. A. (1976). The structure and use of politeness formulas. *Language in Society, 5*, 137–151.

French, S. E., Coleman, B. R., & DiLorenzo, M. L. (2013). Linking racial identity, ethnic identity, and racial-ethnic socialization: A tale of three race-ethnicities. *Identity: An International Journal of Theory and Research, 13*(1), 1–45. doi: 10.1080/15283488.2012.747438

Garraty, J. A. & Gay, P. (Eds.) (1985). *The Columbia history of the world.* New York: Harper & Row.

Hakim-Larson, J. (2014). Part II: The psychosocial development of Arab Americans. In S. C. Nassar-McMillan, K. J. Ajrouch, & J. Hakim-Larson (Eds.), *Biopsychosocial perspectives on Arab Americans: Culture, development and health* (pp. 147–151). New York: Springer.

Hakim-Larson, J., Kamoo, R., Nassar-McMillan, S. C., & Porcerelli, J. H. (2007). Counseling Arab and Chaldean American families. *Journal of Mental Health Counseling, 29*, 301–321.

Hakim-Larson, J., Nassar-McMillan, S., & Paterson, A. D. (2012). Counseling Middle Eastern Americans. In G. McAuliffe (Ed.), *Culturally alert counseling: A comprehensive introduction* (2nd edn.) (pp. 263–292). Thousand Oaks, CA: Sage.

Jamil, H., Nassar-McMillan, S. C., & Lambert, R. G. (2007). Immigration and attendant psychological sequelae: A comparison of three waves of Iraqi immigrants. *American Journal of Orthopsychiatry,* 77, 199–205. doi: 10.1037/0002-9432.77.2.199.

Kamoo, R. (1999). *Ancient and modern Chaldean history: A comprehensive bibliography of sources*. Lanham, MD: The Scarecrow Press, Inc.

Kazdin, A. E. (Ed.) (1998). *Methodological issues & strategies in clinical research* (2nd edn.). Washington, D.C.: American Psychological Association.

Kim, B. S. K. (2007). Acculturation and enculturation. In F. Leong, A. Inman, A. Ebreo, L. Yang, L. Kinoshita, & M. Fu (Eds.), *Handbook of Asian American psychology* (2nd edn.), Racial and Ethnic Minority Psychology (REMP) Series (pp. 141–158). Thousand Oaks, CA: Sage.

Kim, B. S. K., Ahn, A. J., & Lam, N. A. (2009). Theories and research on acculturation and enculturation experiences among Asian American families. In N.-H. Trinh, Y. C. Rho, F. G. Lu, & K. M. Sanders (Eds.), *Handbook of mental health and acculturation in Asian American families* (pp. 25–43). Totowa, NJ: Humana Press. doi: 10.1007/978-1-60327-437-1_2

Kulwicki, A. D. & Miller, J. (1999). Domestic violence in the Arab American population: Transforming environmental conditions through community education. *Issues in Mental Health Nursing, 20*, 199–215. doi: 10.1080/016128499248619

Marcia, J. E. (1966). Development and validation of ego-identity status. *Journal of Personality and Social Psychology, 3*, 551–558. doi: 10.1037/h0023281

Markus, H. R. & Kitayama, S. (1991). Culture and self: Implications for cognition, emotion, and motivation. *Psychological Review, 98*, 224–253. doi: 10.1037/0033-295X.98.2.224

Miller, M. J. (2007). A bilinear multidimensional measurement model of Asian American acculturation and enculturation: Implications for counseling interventions. *Journal of Counseling Psychology, 54*, 118–131. doi: 10.1037/0022-0167.54.2.118

Muhtaseb, A. & Frey, L. R. (2008). Arab Americans' motives for using the internet as a functional media alternative and their perceptions of U.S. public opinion. *Journal of Computer-Mediated Communication, 13*, 618–657. doi: 10.1111/j.1083-6101.2008.00413.x

Naff, A. (1985). *Becoming American: The early Arab immigrant experience*. Carbondale, IL: Southern Illinois University Press.

Nagel, C. R. & Staeheli, L. A. (2004). Citizenship, identity and transnational migration: Arab immigrants to the United States. *Space & Polity, 8*, 3–23. doi: 10.1080/13562570410001678860

Najem, T. (2012). *Lebanon: The politics of a penetrated society*. New York: Routledge.

Nassar-McMillan, S., Lambert, R. G., & Hakim-Larson, J. (2011). Discrimination history, backlash fear, and ethnic identity among Arab Americans: Post-9/11 snapshots. *Journal of Multicultural Counseling and Development, 39*(1), 38–47. doi: 10.1002/j.2161-1912.2011.tb00138.x

Nydell, M. K. (2006). *Understanding Arabs: A guide for modern times* (4th edn.). Boston, MA: Intercultural Press.

Ong, A. D., Fuller-Rowell, T., & Phinney, J. S. (2010). Measurement of ethnic identity: Recurrent and emergent issues. *Identity: An International Journal of Theory and Research, 10*(1), 39–49. doi: 10.1080/15283481003676226

Phinney, J. S., Berry, J. W., Vedder, P., & Liebkind, K. (2006). The acculturation experience: Attitudes, identities and behaviors of immigrant youth. In J. W. Berry, J. S. Phinney, D. L. Sam, & P. Vedder (Eds.), *Immigrant youth in cultural transition: Acculturation, identity, and adaptation across national contexts* (pp. 71–116). Mahwah, NJ: Lawrence Erlbaum Associates Publishers.

Phinney, J. S. & Ong, A. D. (2007). Conceptualization and measurement of ethnic identity: Current status and future directions. *Journal of Counseling Psychology, 54*, 271–281. doi: 10.1037/0022-0167.54.3.271

Rudmin, F. W. (2003a). Critical history of acculturation psychology of assimilation, separation, integration, and marginalization. *Review of General Psychology,* 7, 3–37. doi: 10.1037/1089-2680.7.3.250

Rudmin, F. W. (2003b). "Critical history of the acculturation psychology of assimilation, separation, integration, and marginalization": Correction to Rudmin (2003). *Review of General Psychology,* 7, 250. doi: 10.1037/1089-2680.7.3.250

Rumbaut, R. G. (1997). Assimilation and its discontents: Between rhetoric and reality. *International Migration Review, 31*, 923–960. doi: 10.2307/2547419

Rumbaut, R. G. (2008). Reaping what you sow: Immigration, youth, and reactive ethnicity. *Applied Developmental Science, 12*, 108–111. doi: 10.1080/10888690801997341

Schwartz, S. J., Unger, J. B., Zamboanga, B. L., & Szapocznik, J. (2010). Rethinking the concept of acculturation: Implications for theory and research. *American Psychologist, 65*, 237–251. doi: 10.1037/a0019330

Shaheen, J. (2001). *Reel bad Arabs: How Hollywood vilifies a people.* New York: Olive Branch Press.

Trimble, J. & Dickson, R. (2005). Ethnic identity. In C. Fisher & R. Lerner (Eds.), *Encyclopedia of applied developmental science* (pp. 416–421). Thousand Oaks, CA: Sage. doi: 10.4135/9781412950565.n160

Weinreich, P. (2009). "Enculturation", not "acculturation": Conceptualising and assessing identity processes in migrant communities. *International Journal of Intercultural Relations, 33*, 124–139. doi: 10.1016/j.ijintrel.2008.12.006

Yoon, E., Chang, C.-T., Kim, S., Clawson, A., Cleary, S. E., Hansen, M., ... and Gomes, A. M. (2013). A meta-analysis of acculturation/enculturation and mental health. *Journal of Counseling Psychology, 60*, 15–30. doi: 10.1037/a0030652

Yoon, E., Langrehr, K., & Ong, L. Z. (2011). Content analysis of acculturation research in counseling and counseling psychology: A 22-year review. *Journal of Counseling Psychology, 58*, 83–96. doi: 10.1037/a0021128

4

RELIGION AND RELIGIOSITY

Christian and Muslim Faiths, Diverse Practices, and Psychological Correlates

Mona M. Amer and Randa A. Kayyali

While writings by psychologists have long recognized that religion is an important element in the identities and culture of Arab Americans, few studies have explored the diversities of religious experiences among Arab Americans. Moreover, when religion is captured in empirical research with Arab Americans, it is usually in the form of examining differences between Christians and Muslims, without delving deeper into constructs of religious commitment or other markers of religious experiences and their psychological correlates.

This chapter summarizes the existing psychological literature on religion among Arab Americans. The chapter begins by briefly defining basic concepts in the psychology of religion and considering their applicability to Arab Americans. To better understand the diverse religious backgrounds of Arab Americans, readers are oriented to the most common Christian denominations and Muslim divisions. The role of religion in the lives of both Christian and Muslim Arab Americans is then presented, highlighting influences on ethnic identity, family life, traditions, and community organization. Further, empirical research tying religious constructs to acculturation and psychological wellbeing is presented. Finally, a case example is provided to illustrate the chapter contents, and the relevant literature is critiqued for gaps and limitations.

Basic Theoretical Constructs in the Psychology of Religion

Religion is a significant aspect in the study of any group of people. While in sociology, the most relevant concepts for religion are beliefs, organizational forms, and practices, in psychology the psychological wellbeing of the individual is of core concern. Particularly at issue is how different types of religious constructs may relate to psychological experiences and outcomes. One of the most widely accepted concepts in the psychology of religion is the presumed distinction between the constructs of religiosity and spirituality, although neither term has been precisely defined (Hood, Hill, & Spilka, 2009). Religiosity often refers to an individual's commitment to formal or institutional elements of religion; for instance, involvement with religious traditions such as prayer and service. On the other hand, spirituality is seen as a more private personal experience of beliefs and values that does not necessarily have to be manifested through a formal religious system (Hill & Pargament, 2003; Hood et al., 2009).

The distinction between religiosity and spirituality may be ambiguous for Arab Americans, especially those who are more traditional in their heritage culture. For those individuals, religion may be tightly interwoven with individual identity and daily cultural practices, and thus cannot be truly separated from spirituality. For instance, in Eid's (2003) qualitative study with Arab Canadian college students, participants used the term "spirituality" to refer to overarching guidance gained from formal religion, describing religion as a vehicle for reaching spirituality. This conflation between spirituality and religiosity was demonstrated in the collinearity between scales measuring religiousness and spirituality in a sample of Arab American youth (Goforth, 2011). Furthermore, during the process of developing a measure of religious coping, Christian and Muslim Arab Americans expressed criticism and confusion toward items that focused on "spirituality" as an experience on its own, and therefore those questions were removed from the final scale (Amer, Hovey, Fox, & Rezcallah, 2008).

Although religiosity (or religiousness) is often conceptualized and measured as a unitary construct, multidimensional theories of religiosity have become increasingly utilized in research. Such models help to more accurately understand the underpinnings of religious experience and also provide researchers with clearer understandings of which components of religious experience relate to which particular psychological outcomes. One of the oldest and most popular of these models is Gordon Allport's (1950) theory that religiosity has two main orientations: intrinsic and extrinsic. Intrinsic religiosity refers to an internalized personal motive for religion, with religion providing meaning and guidance for the person's values and behaviors. Extrinsic religiosity is the use of religious practices for instrumental needs such as relieving distress and gaining social support and social status (Allport, 1950; Allport & Ross, 1967). These orientations are orthogonal, with the possibility for people to endorse various levels of both orientations (Donahue, 1985).

Allport and Ross' (1967) Religious Orientation Scale, and its modified Age Universal I-E Scale (Gorsuch & Venable, 1983) have been utilized extensively across hundreds of studies to measure intrinsic and extrinsic religiosity. Research with Arab Americans, however, has called into question the utility of the I-E concept, with extrinsic religiosity in particular showing flaws in psychometric analysis. Amer and Hovey (2007) were unable to use the extrinsic subscale of the Age Universal measure due to poor reliability and validity. Similarly, in her unpublished doctoral dissertation, Meshreki (2007) found a low internal consistency reliability for the extrinsic subscale of the Religious Orientation Scale.

More recently, more complex multidimensional models have gained popularity in evaluating the various aspects of religious experience. For example, the Fetzer Institute (1999) operationalized religiosity in a measure with 12 domains including daily spiritual experiences, meaning, values, beliefs, forgiveness, private religious practices, religious/spiritual coping, and organizational religiousness. In her research with Arab Americans, Goforth (2011) administered four subscales from this measure. Another measure was developed by Abu Raiya, Pargament, Mahoney, and Stein (2008) to assess Islamic religiousness, based on samples from the U.S. and Palestine that included Arab participants. The measure includes subscales focused on, for example, beliefs, practices, ethical conduct, religious internalization, and religious coping.

Religious coping is a particularly useful construct in psychological research because it directly relates to the utilization of religious behaviors as a way to relieve stress. Religious coping can have numerous positive functions such as finding meaning in the situation, gaining mastery and control, gaining comfort and closeness to God, developing interpersonal intimacy through clergy or congregational members, and achieving a life transformation (Pargament, Ano, & Wachholtz, 2005). Empirical evidence has also suggested that religious coping can be not only helpful (positive) but also maladaptive (negative; Pargament, Smith, Koenig, & Perez, 1998). Negative religious coping refers to reacting to stressors, for example, by feeling disconnected from God, undergoing religious or spiritual discontent, and seeing the world in an ominous light.

The types of items that are traditionally used in measuring positive and negative religious coping may need to be re-evaluated for their cultural sensitivity with Arab Americans. In their development of the 15-item Brief Arab Religious Coping Scale for use with both Christian and Muslim Arab Americans, Amer and colleagues (2008) avoided questions that could be perceived as offensive or taboo, such as working in partnership with God (thereby placing humans at the same level as God) or negative religious coping questions.

Religion and Faith Traditions Among Arab Americans

It is not surprising that previous researchers avoided religious coping questions that were perceived to be offensive toward God, given that Arab Americans are generally respectful of religion and God. Both Christian and Muslim Arab Americans believe in one God. "Allah" is the Arabic word for God as used in Christianity, Islam, and in other religions, and it is therefore not the God for Muslims only.

Although the terms "Arab" and "Muslim" may be conflated in the popular media and even in some scholarly discourse, they represent two distinct groups. Arab Americans do not form the majority of Muslims in the U.S., constituting only 26% of the Muslim American community (Pew Research Center, 2011). Although the exact figures are unknown, estimates of the religious breakdown among Arab Americans have typically indicated a Christian majority. A survey conducted in 2002 found that 63% of Arab Americans identified as Christian (35% Roman/Eastern Catholic, 18% Eastern Orthodox, 10% Protestant), 24% were Muslim (including Sunni, Shi`a, and Druze), and 13% reported "other" or no religious affiliation (Arab American Institute Foundation, 2002). However, unlike earlier waves of Arab immigrants to the U.S. that were mostly Christian, of late there have been larger influxes of Muslim immigrants (Abdelhady, 2014), and thus growth in the proportion of Muslims to Christians within the Arab American population. Both Christian and Muslim Arab American populations are themselves heterogeneous with numerous subgroups, as discussed next.

Christians

There are three major divisions of Christianity: Orthodox, Roman Catholic, and Protestant, and within these divisions there are numerous branches called sects or denominations. Orthodox Christians can trace their religious lineage back to the Apostolic Church and the theological debates of early Christianity. The first major split in Christianity occurred in the fifth century CE over concerns about the nature of Christ. Christians who maintained that Christ was of a single divine nature were called Monophysites. Chalcedonians, so called because they agreed with the Council of Chalcedon, maintained that Christ had a dual nature that was both divine and human (Kelly, 1997). There are four main Monophysite Churches in the Middle East: Coptic Orthodox, Assyrian Church of the East, Syrian Orthodox, and the Armenian Orthodox (Atiya, 1968). They do not use Greek as a liturgical language, using Coptic, Assyrian, Syriac, and Armenian instead. Most Chalcedonian Christians followed the Greek Orthodox Patriarch in Constantinople (now Istanbul) and there are Patriarchs and patriarchates in Alexandria, Antioch, and Jerusalem. Christianity is therefore practiced by thousands of people in the Middle East and North Africa as well as in diaspora.

In 1054 there was a schism in the Church and the Eastern or Greek Orthodox took divergent paths from the Church of Rome, which used Latin in their services and became the Roman Catholic Church (Armstrong, 1994). The reason for this "Great Schism" was that the Eastern Orthodox Churches based in the Middle East and North Africa rejected the universal authority and infallibility of the Pope in Rome. In 1180, the Maronite Church became the first Eastern Church to accept papal supremacy (meaning that they became Roman Catholics), while other Eastern Churches "re-united" with the Roman Catholic Church and recognized the Pope as the supreme leader later in history. These Eastern Rite Catholics include the Greek Catholics (Melkites), Syrian Catholics, Catholic Copts, and Chaldean Catholic Churches that are present in Egypt, Lebanon, Syria, Palestine, Israel, Iraq, and Jordan (Saato, 2007).

The Protestant Reformation in the sixteenth century, which initially attempted to reform the Roman Catholic Church, led to a series of religious wars and the establishment of Protestantism as a form of Christian faith. Due to long-entwined histories, the Crusades, and missionary activity, there are Roman Catholics and Protestants as well as the Orthodox Christians, who have lived in the Middle East for centuries. Some of their followers immigrated to the U.S. and established churches as they settled. Up to the 1950s, about 90% of the immigrants who came from the Middle East to the U.S. were Christians, with the balance being Druze as well as Sunni and Shi`a Muslims (Haddad, 1994, p. 63).

In 1920, the largest number of these immigrants were Maronites, followed by Orthodox, Melkites, and Protestants (Hitti, 2005). Maronites from Mount Lebanon had established communities and churches in the northeast and Midwest U.S. when they first began arriving in the 1880s and 1890s. Collectively referred to as "Syrians" in the U.S. until the 1950s, Maronites today mostly consider themselves Americans of Lebanese heritage. As a result of the Lebanese civil war from 1975 to 1990, many Muslims and Christians emigrated from Lebanon (Labaki, 1992). These new immigrants bolstered the numbers of faithful in the established churches of New England and Pennsylvania and founded new churches in the states of California, Texas, and Florida, where they also settled.

The main Eastern Orthodox Church attended by Arab Americans is the Antiochian Orthodox Church, which has a North American Archdiocese located in New Jersey and parishes in almost every state. Many members have heritage from Syria, Lebanon, Jordan, and Palestine. The largest Antiochian Orthodox communities are in Detroit, New York, New Jersey, Los Angeles, Chicago, and Massachusetts. Melkites, or Greek Catholics, are a smaller Eastern Catholic sect in the U.S., with members from Lebanon, Syria, Palestine, and Jordan, as well as Egypt and Sudan. The Maronite, Antiochian Orthodox, and Melkite Churches have shown adaptations to the U.S. environment such as services in English, but also an expressed desire for distinct Eastern Christian customs and religious traditions based on Eastern Rites as well as in Syrian-Lebanese and/or Arab cultures (Kayal, 1973).

Protestants in the Arab world include Presbyterians in Lebanon and Syria, Episcopalians (Anglicans) in Jordan and Palestine, and Evangelicals in Egypt (not to be confused with the Coptic Orthodox Church). Missionary activity in the region correlates to the distribution of sects, and upheavals in those communities relates to immigration patterns of Arab Protestants to the U.S. Thus, there was an influx of Palestinian Episcopalians after expulsions by Israel in 1948 and 1967, Lebanese Presbyterians during the civil war, and Evangelical Protestants from Egypt in the 1970s and 1980s with the rise of the Muslim Brotherhood (Haddad, 1994). Upon arrival, individual Protestants may have joined churches of their denomination or established new ethnic Protestant churches, such as the United Arabic Evangelical Church.

Coptic Orthodox Christians from Egypt began emigrating and founding churches in the U.S. in the 1960s (Pennington, 1982). Since 2011, there has been an influx of both Muslim and Coptic immigrants to the U.S. from Egypt due to the unrest and uncertainties that followed the January 25, 2011, popular uprisings. The Coptic Orthodox are closely tied to their Egyptian roots and Christian heritage, which pre-date the Arab Islamic conquests of Egypt, so they may not identify as Arabs. The languages used in services are Coptic, English, and Arabic with minor "borrowings" from Greek. Today most Coptic churches are found in the major metropolitan areas across North America (Jones, 2000).

Since the 1970s, Syrian, Iraqi, Egyptian, and Iranian immigrants have founded Eastern churches in the U.S. that use Syriac, Assyrian, and Aramaic in their liturgies. These include parishes of the Syriac Orthodox Church, the Syriac Catholic Church, the Assyrian Church of the East, and the Chaldean Catholic Church. Assyrians and Chaldeans from Iraq, Syria, and Iran tend to self-identify as ethnic Assyrian or as Syriac and not as Arab or Iranian because of their distinct ethnic histories and mother tongues. According to 2013 Census figures, the population in the U.S. who self-identified as Assyrian/Chaldean/Syriac by ancestry was 119,283 (U.S. Census Bureau, 2014). Chaldean Americans have communities in Chicago, Detroit, and New York, as well as New England and California, that include families who have moved to the U.S. from Iraq over the last five decades. From the mid-1920s on, large numbers of Assyrian Christians from Syria, Iraq, and Iran have lived in Chicago.

Muslims

Muslims are followers of the faith of Islam. Islam means "submission" and Muslim is "the one who submits [to God]." Muslims believe that the words of God were recorded verbatim in the Qur'an in Arabic after the message was heard by the Prophet Muhammad through the angel Gabriel in the early seventh century CE. Muslims consider themselves Children of Abraham like Jews and Christians, who are called "People of the Book" in the Qur'an. Muslims consider that previous messages and revelations had been corrupted over time and that the Qur'an recorded the final testament of God (Esposito, 2010).

Islam has multiple branches. The main division is between Sunni and Shi`a – a division that occurred after the death of Prophet Muhammad in CE 632. The dispute was over who should succeed him as the leader of the community of believers. Some of the Prophet's followers believed that the new leader should be elected, while other followers claimed that Prophet Muhammad's successor should be his closest male family member and descendant. The latter group became known as Shi`at Ali (the Party of Ali) because they supported Ali, Prophet Muhammad's cousin and son-in-law, as the new leader. The term Sunni refers to those who follow the tradition, or Sunna, in which tribal elders had the right to choose the leader who wielded the most respect and power within the community (Esposito, 2010).

Today, the majority of Muslims in the Arab world are Sunni but there are Shi`a Muslims in Yemen, Bahrain, Saudi Arabia, Iraq, and Lebanon as well as other countries. Shi`a are more numerous outside the Arab world, including in Iran, Afghanistan and Pakistan. The Druze and Alawite religious communities that live in Lebanon, Syria, and Israel are considered to be offshoots of Shi`a Islam, with their own places of religious observance that are different from Shi`a and Sunni mosques (Hourani, 1991).

Before 1965, most Muslim Arab immigrants to the U.S. hailed from areas now known as Lebanon, Syria, and Palestine, but a 1965 change in immigration laws brought more Muslim Arabs from a multitude of North African and Middle Eastern nations, which diversified the religious, national, and linguistic heritages of the Arabic-speaking populations in the U.S. (Kayyali, 2006b). In line with the demographics of the Arab world, the majority of Arab American Muslims are Sunni – in a 2007 survey of American Muslims, those from the "Arab region" were 56% Sunni, 19% Shi`a, and 25% of another or an unspecified tradition (Pew Research Center, 2007). The latter group might be Sufis, Druze, or Alawites, or might have refused to comply with the question, reflecting a feeling of being "just Muslim."

The Role of Religion in the Lives of Arab Americans

Despite the remarkable diversity among Arab Americans regarding their religious affiliations, beliefs, and practices, the value of religion is generally shared across Arab American communities. The importance of religion can be seen in the distinct role religious identity plays in individual ethnic identity development as well as in family life, customs and traditions, community mores, and the central role of religious leaders in the community.

Ethnic Identity Development

Religion is a tightly interwoven component of Arab culture (Abi-Hashem, 2008), and thus religious identity development is often connected with ethnic identity development. When asked to define the core components of their ethnic identity, both Christian (Keck, 1989) and Muslim (Barry, Elliott, & Evans, 2000) Arab Americans identified religious values to be important. Studies have found religiosity and religious attachment to be associated with greater connection to ethnic heritage values, beliefs, and behaviors among Christian and Muslim Arab American youth and adults (Goforth, 2011; Poinsett, 2011). Likewise, in a sample of Christian and Muslim Arab Americans, those with higher levels of ethnic identity were more likely to use religious coping strategies when faced with stress (Amer et al., 2008).

Arab Americans may turn to ethnic culture as a way to strengthen religion, and conversely religion may be used as a resource for ethnic cultural maintenance. For example, for Muslims, religious motives (such as a desire to read the Qur'an) have been found to be a main driver behind the desire to learn the Arabic language and participate in Arab heritage (Martin, 2009; Seymour-Jorn, 2004). Among Christian Jordanian immigrant women (Hattar-Pollara & Meleis, 1995) and Egyptian Copts living in Washington, D.C. (Keck, 1989), religion was used as a main vehicle for ensuring the continuity of their ethnic culture in the face of pressures to assimilate. Similar trends were seen in a study of Muslim Lebanese in Detroit (Ajrouch, 1999).

Within the Family

It is hard to generalize about how much of a role religion plays in Arab American families. Moral foundations in religion can be underlying factors that serve as guides for behaviors and values that may be passed down from parents to children (Kayyali 2012). For some Arab Americans, religion keeps the family together; for example, through praying together and going to church or mosque as a unit. In other families religion can be a point of contention due to a certain amount of pressure placed on children and youth to behave in specific religiously and culturally appropriate ways.

In high-density Arab American locales, such as in Detroit, Chicago, and some areas of New Jersey/New York City, the interconnectedness of the community may mean that there are gossip grapevines that serve to inform the family of misbehavior by a child or an adult (Ajrouch, 1999; Cainkar, 1999). In this case, religion may be invoked to curb "bad" behavior. For example, observant Muslim families may discourage their minor and even adult children from socializing at a party or gathering where alcohol is served. Christian Arab American parents can be similarly conservative in their restrictions on their children, depending on their cultural backgrounds. As in the U.S. in general, Arab American parents often feel responsible for their children's choices and encourage them to follow cultural tenets that are often informed by religion, whether that is Christianity or Islam (Abudabbeh, 2005; Ajrouch, 2004; Read, 2003, 2008).

Celebrations and Fasting

The choices regarding which holidays and celebrations to follow depends on the religious and cultural traditions of the individual and family. Births, marriages, and deaths are considered significant markers of life and are thus celebrated with certain religious and cultural traditions (Kayyali, 2006a). In more traditional families, after the birth of a child, relatives and close friends would be expected to visit the hospital or the home of the parents with gifts such as gold coins or jewelry for the baby. Christians and Muslims alike usually circumcise the boys. Babies may be adorned with a blue bead to ward off the evil eye and/or a cross or a small gold or silver Qur'anic pendant, depending on the family's religion (Kayyali, 2012; Wehbe-Alamah, 2014).

Arab American marriages are usually officiated by religious figures, with Muslims inviting the local imam into a home with a small number of family guests to witness the signing of the marriage contract, and with Christians holding longer ceremonies in churches. Both Christians and Muslims usually celebrate marriages with family and friends in large, catered parties. Some Muslim families may not serve alcohol at these parties, but dancing would be commonplace even at alcohol-free weddings. Deaths, too, are officiated by priests or imams in funerary services at churches and mosques, attended by family and friends in all-black clothing. Traditionally, both Christians and Muslims hold an *`azza*, which is a three-day mourning reception held after a funeral, usually held at a family home of the deceased (Kayyali, 2012).

The religious holidays and feasts differ greatly depending on religion and sect. For all Christians, the two major holidays are Easter and Christmas. Orthodox Christians consider the holiest time of the year to be *pascha*, which celebrates the resurrection of Jesus Christ. For some Eastern Christians, paschal services begin on the Saturday night before Easter Sunday with a procession. Since most Eastern Christians follow the Julian calendar, *pascha* can fall one to five weeks later than Easter celebrations in the Gregorian calendar followed by other Roman Catholics and Protestants. While some Orthodox Christians celebrate Christmas on December 25, other Eastern Christians, such as Copts, consider January 7 the day that Jesus was born. Christians tend to take these days off from work and spend the holidays with their families.

Every year, Muslims celebrate Ramadan and two major religious holidays called eids (pronounced "eeds"), which are feasts with their families with special congregational prayers. Eid ul-Adha commemorates Abraham's attempted sacrifice of his son and takes place at the end of the hajj period of pilgrimage to Mecca. Since Abraham made his sacrifice to God with lamb, the feast often features lamb dishes. Eid ul-Fitr is a three-day celebration at the end of Ramadan (described below) in which children often receive money or gifts. In addition, for Shi`a Muslims Ashura is celebrated as a commemoration of the martyrdom and redemptive suffering of Prophet Muhammad's grandson, Hussein, in the first century of Islam (Shabbas & Alkhateeb, 1998).

Both Christians and Muslims fast, although not all Arab Americans adhere to the prescribed fasts. Fasting is considered to be abstaining from certain foods during specific days or periods, but it may also include refraining from sexual relations and limiting bad actions and thoughts. Although the rules of fasting for Christians are too complex to go into detail here, the main Christian fast is Lent, which is the six weeks before *pascha*. During Lent, and sometimes on Wednesdays and Fridays throughout the year, religious Orthodox Christians (including Copts, Armenians, Antiochian Orthodox, Chaldeans, and Melkites) abstain from eating meat, eggs, dairy, olive oil, and wine.

Muslims fast during Ramadan, which is considered the holiest month of the year and a month of spiritual and physical purification. During Ramadan, Muslims refrain from eating, drinking, and sexual relations from dawn to dusk. Children who have not reached puberty, women who are menstruating, and those who are traveling or are ill are exempt from fasting. At sunset, Muslims will gather together, pray, and consume a meal called *iftar* in Arabic, which literally means "breaking the fast." Within the Arab world there are different culinary traditions and so the traditional foods served at *iftar* differ, although breaking the fast with dates is common (Siddiqi, 2014). The Islamic calendar is calibrated according to 12 lunar months totaling 354 days, which means that the dates of Ramadan and Muslim holidays fall about 11 days earlier every year according to the Gregorian calendar.

Within the Community

Arab American immigrants may turn to the religious institutions of churches or mosques as a way to establish co-ethnic and coreligious social networks that bring together and even define communities. For example, the post-1965 Middle Eastern and North African immigrants to New York City created "sites" and communal structures throughout the city by establishing mosques and Islamic centers, private schools, and religious and secular businesses. In Brooklyn alone, there are several "mosque-centered" communities in several neighborhoods with concentrations of Egyptian, Lebanese, Palestinian, and Yemeni Muslims (Cristillo & Minnite, 2002). While in the Arab world mosques are generally a place of worship, in the U.S. mosques have taken on community roles and functions that are similar to churches, hosting social events such as wedding parties, picnics, family dinners, fundraisers, and holiday celebrations.

While mosques have been targets of surveillance, graffiti, and hate crimes post 9/11, they have played leading roles in community organizing. An examination of the Muslim American Public Opinion Survey found that "mosques are catalysts to social, civic and political integration" because they provide "a place of shared commonality, identity, and culture" (Dana, Barreto, & Oskooii, 2011, p. 504). Christians, too, may establish and/or participate in ethnic churches for social as well as religious reasons. For example, a qualitative study of 30 Christian Jordanian immigrant women in California revealed an importance in establishing and participating in church parishes as a way to develop social networks and recreate familiarity with their homeland (Hattar-Pollara & Meleis, 1995).

The Role of Religious Leaders

The leaders of Arab American religious institutions are not only spiritual guides, but also represent their communities to the American public. Religious leaders serve as community informants, often regulating outsiders' access to the community (Haddad, 1994). For example, researchers have suggested that it is often important to obtain the permission, advice, and endorsement of Christian and Muslim religious leaders as a key step toward recruiting research participants from Arab American communities (Aroian, Katz, & Kulwicki, 2006; Jaber, 2003; Shah, Ayash, Pharaon, & Gany, 2008). Religious leaders may express concern regarding their duty to prevent negative or stigmatizing information regarding their communities from being made public (Abu Raiya, Pargament, Stein, & Mahoney, 2007; Amer & Bagasra, 2013; Aroian et al., 2006).

This gatekeeper role is indicative of how Arab American religious leaders may act as protectors, ensuring the security of community information. Arab Americans may thus trust their priests and imams for support with private matters such as social conflicts and emotional distress (e.g. Abu-Ras & Abu-Bader, 2008; Ali, Milstein, & Marzuk, 2005). A total of 19% of Aloud and Rathur's (2009) sample of Muslim Arabs in Ohio reported seeking psychological support from an imam. An even higher percentage (40.8%) of Muslim Arab Americans in Khan's (2006) study reported "always" or "sometimes" seeking emotional support from an imam. This role as a counselor may have increased after 9/11. For example, in one study, all imams from Arab-majority congregations reported an increased need to counsel their community members for post-9/11 distress such as experiences of discrimination (Ali et al., 2005). Consultation from religious leaders such as sheikhs may also occur if symptoms of mental illness are believed to be caused by supernatural forces like possession by spirits called *jinn* (Padela & Curlin, 2013).

Yet, a strong counseling relationship between religious leaders and their congregants may not always be the case. Khan (2006) also found that 42.5% of her Arab respondents "never" engaged the support of imams, and this was a significantly higher percentage than that reported by Muslim African and Asian Americans. For both Christian and Muslim Arab Americans, the option of gaining advice from religious leaders was a much less frequently used strategy compared to other forms of religious coping (Amer et al., 2008). Moreover, research with imams and Arab American community leaders has shown that religious leaders may not have the knowledge and skills needed to effectively assess and counsel their congregants on mental health issues (Abu-Ras & Abu-Bader, 2008; Ali & Milstein, 2012).

Intersections among Religion, Acculturation, and Psychological Wellbeing

The above sections discussed the salience of religion to Arab American ethnic identity, family, and communal life. Research has further explored the links between religion and psychological outcomes such as psychological acculturation and mental health. Much of this work has focused on differences in outcomes based on religious affiliation (Christian versus Muslim), whereas fewer studies have explored the correlates of religiosity and religious coping.

Research Based on Religious Affiliation

Acculturation – the psychological adaptation to a culture that is different from one's heritage culture – can be a challenging process for Christian and Muslim Arab Americans. For the most part, Christians have shown better facility in adjusting to American society. In previous studies Christian Arab Americans reported greater adoption of American cultural practices and more satisfaction with life in the U.S. compared to their Muslim counterparts (Amer, 2005; Amer & Hovey, 2007; Awad, 2010; Faragallah, Schumm, & Webb, 1997). Christian Arabs were more likely to engage in behaviors that may be considered proxy indicators for acculturation, such as willingness to have one's children join the U.S. military (Schumm, 1996).

Research is mixed concerning differences between the religious subgroups in their maintenance of Arabic heritage cultures. On the one hand, some studies reported higher levels of Arab ethnic identity among Muslim Arab Americans compared to Christian Arab Americans (Amer & Hovey, 2007; Awad, 2010; Nassar-McMillan, Lambert, & Hakim-Larson, 2011). On the other hand, a socio-demographically diverse sample of more than 600 Arab American adults showed no difference in Arab ethnic identity based on religious affiliation (Amer, 2005). One potential explanation for these inconsistencies relates to participant recruitment strategy; for example, Amer's sample was largely drawn from religious and cultural organizations, thereby potentially skewing results toward both Christians and Muslims who had strong attachment to their ethnic culture.

Many authors have provided suggestions for why adjustment to American culture may be a less challenging process for Christian Arab Americans, even while Christians may maintain distinct ethnic churches and religious institutions that set them apart from a Protestant and Latin Rite Roman Catholic mainstream. One explanation is that Christians may experience greater social acceptance and greater ease in adopting American values and behaviors because they share the majority religion in the U.S. (Amer, 2005; Eid, 2003). Another explanation posits that their minority status in the Arab world, and the conditions of their departure (persecution or other stressors related to minority status) might make them less attached to the Arab world and more open to adopting American culture (Faragallah et al., 1997).

Muslim Arab Americans may face unique challenges in adjusting to American culture, particularly since many Islamic traditions (for example, those related to dress, diet, fasting, and courtship) may contradict common American cultural practices, may not be easily accommodated, or could make them visible targets for discrimination or social exclusion (Abi-Hashem, 2008; Amer & Hovey, 2007; Faragallah et al., 1997; McDermott-Levy, 2011). This is consistent with previous findings that both Christian and Muslim Arab Americans endorsed similar desires to integrate in American culture, but Christians reported more success in reaching this goal (Amer & Hovey, 2007).

The strain of facing challenges during the acculturation process is referred to as acculturative stress. Research is ambiguous regarding subgroup differences in acculturative stress, with one study showing higher stress among Muslim Arab Americans (Amer, 2005) and another showing no differences (Amer & Hovey, 2007). However, one important acculturation stressor – discrimination – has been reported to be higher among Muslim Arab Americans (Awad, 2010; Padela & Heisler, 2010). It is important to remember that both Christian and Muslim Arab Americans experienced heightened levels of discrimination post 9/11 (Rousseau, Hassan, Moreau, & Thombs, 2011). However, hateful rhetoric and prejudice has increasingly focused on Muslims and Islam. Moreover, Muslim Arab Americans may be more visibly targeted for being different; for example, due to differences in names or appearances, such as wearing the hijab (Amer & Hovey, 2007).

If adapting to American society may be more stressful for Muslim Arab Americans, a related question would be whether psychological wellbeing would be poorer among Muslim Arab Americans compared to Christians. However, the evidence is mixed. In one study Christians reported less anxiety and depression compared to Muslims, as well as better family functioning and social supports

(Amer, 2005). Other studies showed no differences between Christian and Muslim Arab Americans in regard to family cohesion and functioning (Amer & Hovey, 2007; Faragallah et al., 1997), life satisfaction (Ajrouch, 2007), and psychological distress such as depression or trauma (Abu-Ras & Abu-Bader, 2009; Ajrouch, 2007; Amer & Hovey, 2007; Reizian & Meleis, 1987). One study (Meshreki, 2007) even found Muslim Arab Americans to have more positive emotion and less depression compared to Christians.

Research on Religiosity and Religious Coping

Moving beyond subgroup differences, the level of religiosity (regardless of religious affiliation) may relate to psychological health. Decades of psychological research – mostly conducted in the U.S. – have suggested that religiosity and religious coping can serve as important resources when people are faced with stressors and adversities, potentially buffering negative mental health outcomes (Koenig, 2009; Seybold & Hill, 2001). This was shown in studies with Arab Americans. For example, higher levels of religiosity – particularly intrinsic religiosity – were associated with less acculturative stress (Goforth, 2011) as well as life satisfaction, positive affect, and less depression (Meshreki, 2007). Strength of attachment to a religious group was associated with positive affect and self-esteem (Poinsett, 2011).

On the other hand, other research with Arab Americans showed no relationship between religiosity and mental health (Abu-Ras & Abu-Bader, 2009) and a doctoral dissertation indicated that religiosity did not mediate the relationship between perceived religious discrimination and acculturative stress (Willems, 2012). Moreover, the patterns of relationships may be moderated by religious affiliation. For example, in one study intrinsic religiosity related to less depression and family dysfunction for Muslim Arab Americans, whereas for Christians the relationship was not significant (Amer & Hovey, 2007).

The use of religion to cope with stress has also shown mixed results in research with Arab Americans. One study found religious coping to be an important buffer against acculturative stressors and consequently psychological distress for adolescents (Ahmed, Kia-Keating, & Tsai, 2011), whereas another (Amer et al., 2008) found that religious coping was not associated with acculturative stress or mental health. The case example below indicates how religion and acculturative stress can be interrelated for a Muslim Arab American youth.

Case Example: Interconnections Between Culture and Religion in Reema's Identity Development and Marriage Choice

Reema is a second generation Palestinian American who was born and raised in New Jersey. Throughout her childhood, her family participated in events at the local Islamic cultural center. Her father attended the Friday sermons, which were held in Arabic, and he took Reema and her younger brother Sami to Qur'an and religion classes on Sundays. They attended activities organized by the center such as the monthly "family dinner," comedy shows, and excursions to parks. At home Reema and Sami learned to pray the five daily prayers and to fast during Ramadan, and their mother sometimes read them stories from the Qur'an.

Most of Reema's closest friends were Arab peers from the Islamic center. At school, Reema had a few classmates who were Arab American and Muslim. However, the majority of students were not from those backgrounds, and both her peers and her teachers had made disparaging comments about Muslims. Therefore, she learned not to bring attention to those aspects of her identity, instead chatting with classmates about innocuous topics.

After Reema graduated from high school, she enrolled at a nearby state university. There she joined the Muslim Students Association (MSA). Through the lectures and events coordinated by the MSA, as well as a weekly *halaqa* (religious discussion group) she attended, Reema began to gain a deeper understanding of the values and justifications underpinning the rituals she had participated in throughout her life. She registered for Arabic language courses to strengthen her ability to read Islamic books. She also began restricting her diet to halal foods, and decided to wear the hijab (headscarf). Her parents were alarmed by these changes, worried that she was becoming "too extreme" and that the hijab would make her a target for discrimination.

Family arguments regarding Reema's increasing religiosity intensified during her final year of college when she announced her interest in marrying Othman, one of her MSA peers. Her parents were horrified to hear that Othman was a second generation Pakistani. They told Reema that they should have had a more active role in selecting her spouse, and that she should marry a Palestinian. Her brother Sami agreed, stating that it would be an insult to their Palestinian heritage to marry someone from outside their community, and that a Pakistani could not truly understand the Islamic faith due to language barriers.

Reema argued that the Qur'an affirms that no ethnic group is superior to others, so there was no religious basis to restrict her marriage across ethnic or national lines, and that anyone could practice Islam, as shown by the fact that the most populous Muslim countries are in South Asia. She reasoned that since she was living in the U.S. and not Palestine, sharing Islamic religious values with her spouse was more important than sharing national background. She also said that according to Islamic teachings she had the right as a woman to marry whomever she chose.

Reema's parents asked the imam from the Islamic center to meet with them to solve this family crisis. The imam was born and raised in Egypt, where he had obtained his religious training at the renowned Al-Azhar University. Although he acknowledged that Islam does not prohibit cross-cultural marriages and that it guarantees that a woman must accept whom she marries, he admonished Reema for causing pain to her parents and adopting "Americanized" behaviors by choosing a spouse on her own. He cautioned that cross-cultural marriages are rife with difficulties, especially if the spouses' interpretations of religion are different.

This case example shows how the salience of religion to Reema's identity dynamically shifted across different settings (e.g. at the Islamic center versus at university) and throughout her maturation over time. As a child, religion was integrally interwoven in the culture of her family and community, and the local religious institution structured many aspects of her life including weekly activities and friendships. As she grew older, Reema explored her religion further, which fostered more deeply intrinsic religious motives. Her faith was a source of strength, as was her religious community of peers. She began to realize that many traditions were embedded in culture, not religion. The conflation between culture and religion was underscored when Reema decided to marry outside of her ethnic group. At that point, acute tensions grew between religious and cultural dictates, which even the religious leader was not able to resolve.

Critique

The literature on Arabs and Arab Americans frequently assumes that religion is a core component of Arab culture. Scholars have not adequately examined the contradictions between the values and traditions of religion versus culture and they have not attended to the diversities of religions within the Arab American community. Additionally, psychology scholars have tended to focus on individualized religious behaviors such as religiosity levels and religious coping, whereas routine group activities such as religious celebrations, traditions, and congregational activities have been overlooked. Greater research is needed to explore the exact nature of how religion and culture are interrelated, particularly for second and later generations of Arab Americans, who may learn about their religion and heritage cultures from sources other than their parents.

Most of the literature on Arab American religious issues focuses on Muslims. There is an additional emphasis on practicing Sunni Muslims, whereas Arab Americans from other Islamic branches, and those with Muslim identities and no mosque affiliation, have been overlooked. Secular or nonpracticing individuals from both Christian and Muslim faiths have been virtually ignored.

This could be an artifact of the research recruitment methods, which often draw samples from religious organizations, skewing the results toward higher levels of religiosity.

Studies comparing Christian and Muslim Arab Americans have observed differential patterns in their acculturation experiences and correlative mental health outcomes. This suggests that distinctions between Christians and Muslims may be significant, and the convention of lumping Arab Americans into one ethnic group for the sake of acculturation research may distort the realities and reactions that subgroups face. At the same time, this binary (Christian versus Muslim) is often too simplistic and generalizing, without attending to differences in religiosity as well as class, national background, and levels of traditionalism. Greater exploration is needed to tease apart different patterns shown by religious subgroups and the diversities within Muslim (e.g. Sunni, Shi`a) and Christian (e.g. Coptic, Antiochian Orthodox, Maronite) subgroups.

Because of limited relevant psychological scholarship, this chapter has integrated studies from related disciplines such as sociology and ethnic studies. These fields, however, are not grounded in the same theoretical models that guide the psychology of religion. Further work is needed to examine the applicability of psychology of religion concepts, such as intrinsic–extrinsic religiosity, and to explore whether it is feasible to establish a multidimensional model of religiosity that can apply to Arab Americans of different religious affiliations. Some concepts studied in the psychology of religion – such as tolerance, moral values, mysticism, forgiveness, and others – have not yet been explored among Arabs living in the U.S. Moreover, the relationship of religion and religiosity to other psychological constructs – such as prosocial behaviors, risk-taking, and personality – have also been virtually absent in the literature on Arab Americans.

Overall, the volume of psychological research related to religious affiliation and religiosity among Arab Americans is sparse. Most studies used small sample sizes, taken in very specific locations, using measures that were not examined for cultural sensitivity. For all these reasons, validity of the results is questionable and contradictory findings across studies have not been resolved. More extensive research using methodologically rigorous designs is needed to develop a clearer understanding of the relationships among variables of interest.

Conclusion

The Arab American community is heterogeneous in regard to religious affiliations and commitments. Not only are there differences between Christians and Muslims, but also within each religious group there are diverse branches, belief systems, and traditions. Many of these diverse Arab American groups have been virtually ignored in the scholarly discourse in the psychology of religion. Markers of diversity pose practical challenges in researching Arab American religious issues, but it is imperative that a larger volume of research be cultivated in order to develop firmer conclusions about relationships among variables. Future research can examine traditional concepts and models in the psychology of religion, as well as psychological correlates for certain types of religious constructs. This research could also have an applied purpose, such as finding ways to integrate the protective factors found in religious experiences into clinical services and community programs.

References

Abdelhady, D. (2014). The sociopolitical history of Arabs in the United States: Assimilation, ethnicity, and global citizenship. In S. C. McMillan, K. J. Ajrouch, & J. Hakim-Larson (eds.), *Biopsychosocial perspectives on Arab Americans: Culture, development, and health* (pp. 17–43). New York: Springer. doi: 10.1007/978-1-4614-8238-3_2

Abi-Hashem, N. (2008). Arab Americans: Understanding their challenges, needs and struggles. In A. J. Marsella, J. L. Johnson, P. Watson, & J. Gryczynski (eds.), *Ethnocultural perspectives on disasters and trauma: Foundations, issues, and applications* (pp. 115–173). New York: Springer.

Abudabbeh, N. (2005). Arab families: An overview. In M. McGoldrick, J. Giordano, & N. Garcia-Preto (eds.), *Ethnicity and family therapy* (3rd edn., pp. 423–436). New York: Guilford.

Abu Raiya, H., Pargament, K. I., Mahoney, A., & Stein, C. (2008). A psychological measure of Islamic religiousness: Development and evidence for reliability and validity. *The International Journal for the Psychology of Religion* 18, 291–315. doi: 10.1080/10508610802229270

Abu Raiya, H., Pargament, K. I., Stein, C., & Mahoney, A. (2007). Lessons learned and challenges faced in developing the psychological measure of Islamic religiousness. *Journal of Muslim Mental Health* 2, 133–154. doi: 10.1080/15564900701613058

Abu-Ras, W. & Abu-Bader, S. (2008). The impact of the September 11, 2001, attacks on the well-being of Arab Americans in New York City. *Journal of Muslim Mental Health* 3, 217–239. doi: 10.1080/15564900802487634

Abu-Ras, W. & Abu-Bader, S. (2009). Risk factors for depression and posttraumatic stress disorder (PTSD): The case of Arab and Muslim Americans post-9/11. *Journal of Immigrant & Refugee Studies* 7, 393–418. doi: 10.1080/15564900802487634

Ahmed, S. R., Kia-Keating, M., & Tsai, K. H. (2011). A structural model of racial discrimination, acculturative stress, and cultural resources among Arab American adolescents. *American Journal of Community Psychology* 48, 181–192. doi: 10.1007/s10464-011-9424-3

Ajrouch, K. J. (1999). Family and ethnic identity in an Arab American community. In M. Suleiman (ed.), *Arabs in America: Building a new future* (pp. 129–139). Philadelphia, PA: Temple University Press.

Ajrouch, K. J. (2004). Gender, race, and symbolic boundaries: Contested spaces of identity among Arab American adolescents. *Sociological Perspectives* 47, 371–391. doi: 10.1525/sop.2004.47.4.371

Ajrouch, K. J. (2007). Resources and well-being among Arab-American elders. *Journal of Cross-Cultural Gerontology* 22, 167–182. doi: 10.1007/s10823-006-9033-z

Ali, O. M. & Milstein, G. (2012). Mental illness recognition and referral practices among imams in the United States. *Journal of Muslim Mental Health* 6(2), 3–13. doi: 10.3998/jmmh.10381607.0006.202

Ali, O. M., Milstein, G., & Marzuk, P. M. (2005). The imam's role in meeting the counseling needs of Muslim communities in the United States. *Psychiatric Services* 56, 202–205.

Allport, G. W. (1950). *The individual and his religion*. New York: Macmillan.

Allport, G. W. & Ross, J. M. (1967). Personal religious orientation and prejudice. *Journal of Personality and Social Psychology* 5, 447–457. doi: 10.1037/h0021212

Aloud, N. & Rathur, A. (2009). Factors affecting attitudes toward seeking and using formal mental health and psychological services among Arab Muslim populations. *Journal of Muslim Mental Health* 4, 79–103. doi: 10.1080/15564900802487675

Amer, M. M. (2005). *Arab American mental health in the post September 11 era: Acculturation, stress, and coping* (Doctoral dissertation). Available from ProQuest Dissertations and Theses database (UMI No. 3171022).

Amer, M. M. & Bagasra, A. (2013). Psychological research with Muslim Americans in the age of Islamophobia: Trends, challenges, and recommendations. *American Psychologist* 68(3), 134–144. doi: 10.1037/a0032167

Amer, M. M. & Hovey, J. D. (2007). Socio-demographic differences in acculturation and mental health for a sample of 2nd generation/early immigrant Arab Americans. *Journal of Immigrant and Minority Health* 9, 335–347. doi: 10.1007/s10903-007-9045-y

Amer, M. M., Hovey, J. D., Fox, C. M., & Rezcallah, A. (2008). Initial development of the Brief Arab Religious Coping Scale (BARCS). *Journal of Muslim Mental Health* 3, 69–88. doi: 10.1080/15564900802156676

Arab American Institute Foundation. (2002). *Religious affiliations of Arab Americans.* Retrieved from www.aaiusa.org/page/file/b8bad613905570ea97_mghwmvb2d.pdf/ancestry.pdf

Armstrong, K. (1994). *A history of God: The 4,000-year quest of Judaism, Christianity and Islam*. New York: Ballantine Books.

Aroian, K. J., Katz, A., & Kulwicki, A. (2006). Recruiting and retaining Arab Muslim mothers and children for research. *Journal of Nursing Scholarship* 38, 255–261. doi: 10.1111/j.1547-5069.2006.00111.x

Atiya, A. S. (1968). *History of Eastern Christianity*. Notre Dame, IN: University of Notre Dame Press.

Awad, G. H. (2010). The impact of acculturation and religious identification on perceived discrimination for Arab/Middle Eastern Americans. *Cultural Diversity and Ethnic Minority Psychology* 16, 59–67. doi: 10.1037/a0016675

Barry, D., Elliott, R., & Evans, E. M. (2000). Foreigners in a strange land: Self-construal and ethnic identity in male Arabic immigrants. *Journal of Immigrant Health* 2(3), 133–144. doi: 10.1023/A:1009508919598

Cainkar, L. (1999). The deteriorating ethnic safety net among Arab immigrants in Chicago. In M. W. Suleiman (ed.), *Arabs in America: Building a new future* (pp. 192–206). Philadelphia, PA: Temple University Press.

Cristillo, L. A. & Minnite, L. C. (2002). The changing Arab New York community. In K. Benson & P. M. Kayal (eds.), *A community of many worlds: Arab Americans in New York City* (pp. 124–139). New York: Museum of the City of New York.

Dana, K., Barreto, M. A., & Oskooii, K. A. R. (2011). Mosques as American institutions: Mosque attendance, religiosity and integration into the political system among American Muslims. *Religions* 2, 504–524. doi: 10.3390/rel2040504

Donahue, M. J. (1985). Intrinsic and extrinsic religiousness: Review and meta-analysis. *Journal of Personality and Social Psychology* 48, 400–419. doi: 10.1037/0022-3514.48.2.400

Eid, P. (2003). The interplay between ethnicity, religion, and gender among second-generation Christian and Muslim Arabs in Montreal. *Canadian Ethnic Studies* 35(2), 30–60.

Esposito, J. L. (2010). *The future of Islam*. New York: Oxford University Press.

Faragallah, M. H., Schumm, W. R., & Webb, F. J. (1997). Acculturation of Arab-American immigrants: An exploratory study. *Journal of Comparative Family Studies* 28(3), 182–203.

Fetzer Institute. (1999). *Multidimensional measurement of religiousness/spirituality for use in health research*. Kalamazoo, MI: John E. Fetzer Institute. Retrieved from www.fetzer.org/resources/multidimensional-measurement-religiousnessspirituality-use-health-research

Goforth, A. N. (2011). *Acculturation and psychological adjustment among Arab American adolescents* (Doctoral dissertation). Available from ProQuest Dissertations and Theses Database (UMI No. 3465667).

Gorsuch, R. L, & Venable, G. D. (1983). Development of an "Age Universal" *I-E* Scale. *Journal for the Scientific Study of Religion* 22(2), 181–187. doi: 10.2307/1385677.

Haddad, Y. Y. (1994). Maintaining the faith of the fathers: Dilemmas of religious identity in the Christian and Muslim Arab-American communities. In E. N. McCarus (ed.), *The development of Arab-American identity* (pp. 61–84). Ann Arbor, MI: University of Michigan Press.

Hattar-Pollara, M. & Meleis, A. I. (1995). The stress of immigration and the lived experiences of Jordanian immigrant women in the United States. *Western Journal of Nursing Research* 17, 521–539. doi: 10.1177/019394599501700505

Hill, P. C. & Pargament, K. I. (2003). Advances in the conceptualization and measurement of religion and spirituality: Implications for physical and mental health research. *American Psychologist* 58, 64–74. doi: 10.1037/0003-066X.58.1.64

Hitti, P. K. (2005). *The Syrians in America*. Piscataway, NJ: Gorgias Press. (Original work published 1924).

Hood, R. W., Jr., Hill, P. C., & Spilka, B. (2009). *The psychology of religion: An empirical approach* (4th edn.). New York: Guilford.

Hourani, A. H. (1991). *A history of the Arab peoples*. Cambridge, MA: Belknap Press of Harvard University Press.

Jaber, L. A. (2003). Barriers and strategies for research in Arab Americans. *Diabetes Care* 26, 514–515. doi: 10.2337/diacare.26.2.514

Jones, R. (2000). Egyptian Copts in Detroit. In N. Abraham & A. Shryock (eds.), *Arab Detroit: From margin to mainstream* (pp. 219–240). Detroit, MI: Wayne State University Press.

Kayal, P. M. (1973). Religion and assimilation: Catholic "Syrians" in America. *International Migration Review* 7, 409–425. doi: 10.2307/3002554

Kayyali, R. A. (2006a). *The Arab Americans*. Westport, CT: Greenwood Press.

Kayyali, R. A. (2006b). The people perceived as a threat to security: Arab Americans since September 11. *Migration Information Source*, July 1. Retrieved from www.migrationinformation.org/Feature/display.cfm?ID=409

Kayyali, R. A. (2012). The family. In A. Ameri & H. Arida (eds.), *Daily life of Arab Americans in the 21st century* (pp. 57–85). Santa Barbara, CA: ABC-CLIO/Greenwood.

Keck, L. T. (1989). Egyptian Americans in the Washington DC area. *Arab Studies Quarterly* 11(2/3), 103–126.

Kelly, J. F. (1997). *The world of the early Christians*. Collegeville, MN: Michael Glazier.

Khan, Z. (2006). Attitudes toward counseling and alternative support among Muslims in Toledo, Ohio. *Journal of Muslim Mental Health* 1, 21–42. doi: 10.1080/15564900600654278

Koenig, H. G. (2009). Research on religion, spirituality, and mental health: A review. *The Canadian Journal of Psychiatry* 54(5), 283–291.

Labaki, B. (1992). Lebanese emigration during the War (1975–1989). In A. H. Hourani & N. Shehadi (eds.), *The Lebanese in the world: A century of emigration* (pp. 605–626). London, UK: I. B. Tauris.

Martin, N. (2009). *Arab American parents' attitudes toward their children's heritage language maintenance and language practices* (Master's thesis). Available from ProQuest Dissertations and Theses database (UMI No. 1472860).

McDermott-Levy, R. (2011). Going alone: The lived experience of female Arab-Muslim nursing students living and studying in the United States. *Nursing Outlook* 59, 266–277. doi: 10.1016/j.outlook.2011.02.006

Meshreki, L. M. (2007). *Religiosity, health, and well-being among Middle Eastern/Arab Muslims and Christians in the USA: A study of positive emotion as a mediator* (Doctoral dissertation). Available from ProQuest Dissertations and Theses database (UMI No. 3298373).

Nassar-McMillan, S. C., Lambert, R. G., & Hakim-Larson, J. (2011). Discrimination history, backlash fear, and ethnic identity among Arab Americans: Post-9/11 snapshots. *Journal of Multicultural Counseling and Development* 39, 38–47. doi: 10.1002/j.2161-1912.2011.tb00138.x

Padela, A. I. & Curlin, F. A. (2013). Religion and disparities: Considering the influences of Islam on the health of American Muslims. *Journal of Religion and Health* 52, 1333–1345. doi: 10.1007/s10943-012-9620-y

Padela, A. I. & Heisler, M. (2010). The association of perceived abuse and discrimination after September 11, 2001, with psychological distress, level of happiness, and health status among Arab Americans. *American Journal of Public Health* 100, 284–291. doi: 10.2105/AJPH.2009.164954

Pargament, K. I., Ano, G. G., & Wachholtz, A. B. (2005). The religious dimension of coping: Advances in theory, research, and practice. In R. F. Paloutzian & C. L. Park (eds.), *Handbook of the psychology of religion and spirituality* (pp. 479–495). New York: Guilford.

Pargament, K. I., Smith, B.W., Koenig, H. G., & Perez, L. (1998). Patterns of positive and negative religious coping with major life stressors. *Journal for the Scientific Study of Religion* 37, 710–24. doi: 10.2307/1388152

Pennington, J. D. (1982). The Copts in modern Egypt. *Middle Eastern Studies* 18(2), 158–179. doi: 10.1080/00263208208700503

Pew Research Center. (2007). *Muslim Americans: Middle class and mostly mainstream*. Retrieved from www.pewresearch.org/files/old-assets/pdf/muslim-americans.pdf

Pew Research Center. (2011). *Muslim Americans: No signs of growth in alienation or support for extremism*. Retrieved from www.people-press.org/2011/08/30/muslim-americans-no-signs-of-growth-in-alienation-or-support-for-extremism

Poinsett, M. K. (2011). *Collective identification in Arab American emerging adults: Does affirmation to ethnic, national, family, and religious groups predict positive adjustment?* (Doctoral dissertation). Available from ProQuest Dissertations and Theses database (UMI No. 3454278).

Read, J. G. (2003). The sources of gender role attitudes among Christian and Muslim Arab-American women. *Sociology of Religion* 64(2), 207–222. doi: 10.2307/3712371

Read, J. G. (2008). Discrimination and identity formation: A comparison of Muslim and Christian Arab Americans. In A. Jamal & N. Naber (eds.), *Race and Arab Americans before and after 9/11: From invisible citizens to visible subjects* (pp. 305–323). New York: Syracuse University Press.

Reizian, A. & Meleis, A. I. (1987). Symptoms reported by Arab-American patients on the Cornell Medical Index (CMI). *Western Journal of Nursing Research* 9, 368–384. doi: 10.1177/019394598700900308

Rousseau, C., Hassan, G., Moreau, N., & Thombs, B. D. (2011). Perceived discrimination and its association with psychological distress among newly arrived immigrants before and after September 11, 2001. *American Journal of Public Health* 101, 909–915. doi: 10.2105/AJPH.2009.173062

Saato, F. J. (2007). *American Eastern Catholics*. New Jersey: Paulist Press.

Schumm, W. R. (1996). Willingness to have one's children serve in the military: An indicator of acculturation among Arab immigrants to the United States: A brief report. *Journal of Political and Military Sociology* 24, 105–115.

Seybold, K. S. & Hill, P. C. (2001). The role of religion and spirituality in mental and physical health. *Current Directions in Psychological Science* 10, 21–4. doi: 10.1111/1467-8721.00106

Seymour-Jorn, C. (2004). Arabic language learning among Arab immigrants in Milwaukee, Wisconsin: A study of attitudes and motivations. *Journal of Muslim Minority Affairs* 24(1), 109–122. doi: 10.1080/136020004200 0212205

Shabbas, A. & Alkhateeb, S. (1998). Ramadan: The month of fasting and Muslim holidays. In A. Shabbas (ed.), *Arab world studies notebook* (pp. 45–46). Berkley, CA: AWAIR.

Shah, S. M., Ayash, C., Pharaon, N. A., & Gany, F. M. (2008). Arab American immigrants in New York: Health care and cancer knowledge, attitudes, and beliefs. *Journal of Immigrant and Minority Health* 10, 429–436. doi: 10.1007/s10903-007-9106-2

Siddiqi, M. H. (2014). Practicing Islam in the United States. In Y.Y. Haddad & J. I. Smith (eds.), *The Oxford handbook of American Islam* (pp. 159–173). New York: Oxford University Press.

U.S. Census Bureau. (2014). *American FactFinder – Results*. Retrieved from http://factfinder2.census.gov/faces/tableservices/jsf/pages/productview.xhtml?pid=ACS_13_1YR_B04003&prodType=table

Wehbe-Alamah, H. B. (2014). Folk care beliefs and practices of traditional Lebanese and Syrian Muslims in the Midwestern United States. In M. R. McFarland & H. B. Wehbe-Alamah (eds.), *Leininger's culture care diversity and universality* (3rd edn., pp. 137–181). Burlington, MA: Jones & Bartlett.

Willems, E. A. (2012). *Discrimination and acculturation among Arab Muslim immigrants in the U.S.* (Doctoral dissertation). Available from ProQuest Dissertations and Theses Database (UMI No. 3518522).

5

DISCRIMINATION

Heightened Prejudice Post 9/11 and Psychological Outcomes

Germine H. Awad and Wafa M. Amayreh

The history of prejudice and discrimination in the U.S. is well documented. Ethnic minority groups have contended with different manifestations of prejudice and discrimination (e.g. slavery, genocide, hate crimes) but all share the experience of being thought of as an "Other" or out-group member. Although there is a common belief that prejudice and discrimination toward Arab Americans started after the events of 9/11, bias toward this group can be documented as early as 1914 (Naber, 2000). Given the lack of recognition as an ethnic minority group by federal institutions, the placement of Arab Americans within the U.S. landscape is complicated. For example, Arab Americans are currently classified as White on the U.S. Census, yet report persistent ethnic discrimination (e.g. Cainkar, 2002, 2009). Unfortunately, a significant proportion of these discriminatory experiences have risen to the level of hate crimes (e.g. Disha, Cavendish, & King, 2011). Overt or explicit discrimination toward other ethnic minority groups has decreased in the past 30 years, with such displays considered politically incorrect. This has not been the case for Arabs and Muslims.

In this chapter, theoretical frameworks of prejudice and discrimination are presented. In particular, levels of discrimination, modern forms of prejudice, and ideological constructs such as right-wing authoritarianism (RWA) and social dominance orientation (SDO) are defined. Experimental and correlational studies examining prejudice and discrimination toward Arab Americans are presented. Literature on the experience of discrimination by Arab Americans is examined and psychology correlates are discussed. A case example presenting a family that experiences intergenerational discrimination is offered as an illustration of the chapter contents. The chapter ends with a critique of the current literature on Arab American prejudice and discrimination.

Theories Pertaining to the Underpinnings and Mechanisms of Prejudice and Discrimination

In his landmark text on prejudice, Gordon Allport defined ethnic prejudice as "an antipathy based on faulty and inflexible generalization. It may be felt or expressed. It may be directed toward an individual as a whole, or toward an individual because he is a member of that group" (1954, p. 10). Jones (1997) amended the definition by asserting that prejudice can be either a negative or positive attitude, judgment, or feeling about an individual because of their membership in a social group. Discrimination is the behavioral component of prejudice that occurs when one is treated differently based on his or her membership in a social group (Jones, 1997).

Building upon the definition of discrimination offered by Jones (e.g. 1997), Whitley and Kite (2010) outlined four levels of discrimination that may occur. The first type, individual discrimination, happens where one person treats another differently because of that other person's membership in a social group (Benokraitis & Feagin, 1995). Some examples of individual discrimination against Arab Americans include the usage of a racial epithet (e.g. "camel jockey," "towel head," or "sand nigger") or social exclusion (Ibish, 2001, 2003). The second level, organizational discrimination, occurs when an organization's policies and practices have a disparate impact on particular individuals based on their social group membership (Benokraitis & Feagin, 1995). An example of organizational discrimination is enacting a policy that women and men are not permitted to have any hair coverings at work. This would essentially deny Muslim women the right to wear a hijab (headscarf).

The third level, institutional discrimination, occurs when practices, policies, or norms of a social institution result in disparate impacts for members of certain social groups. Oftentimes, this type of discrimination is a result of seemingly neutral race policies. For example, police and Federal Bureau of Investigation (FBI) misconduct has been found to be a significant source of institutional discrimination for Arab and Muslim Americans, especially since the enactment of the USA PATRIOT Act (Ibish, 2001, 2003, 2008). The fourth level, cultural discrimination, occurs when one group has the power to determine or define pertinent cultural values (e.g. art, literature, language, ideology) for members from all social groups (Jones, 1997). An example of cultural discrimination is the determination that tall and thin women who have blond hair and blue eyes are the epitome of beauty. Very few people, especially people of color, can ever achieve those beauty standards. Even in the Middle East, Arab women use skin lighteners in an effort to achieve beauty ideals set by Western cultures that value light skin over dark skin (Hamed, Tayyem, Nimer, & AlKhatib, 2010). Arab American women are confronted with the same narrowly defined conceptualizations of beauty that confront women of all ethnic backgrounds in the U.S. Another example of cultural discrimination would be the valuing of parenting styles that foster independence early in infancy over parenting styles that foster familial interdependence and harmony. The former might be found in White families, while the latter might be more often the norm in Arab families.

Two ideological variables that have been shown to predict prejudice toward perceived outgroups such as ethnic and religious minorities are RWA and SDO. These ideological variables, which are sometimes conceptualized as aspects of personality, are thought to be a mechanism underlying prejudice and discrimination toward perceived outgroup members. Altemeyer (1981) introduced the concept of RWA, which consists of three interrelated concepts: authoritarian submission (i.e. deference to authority figures), authoritarian aggression (i.e. tendency to want to cause physical, psychological, and financial harm against those who are considered unconventional), and conventionalism (i.e. acceptance of traditional and authority-sanctioned social conventions). Social dominance orientation refers to the extent to which individuals organize their world into ingroups and outgroups and believe that their ingroup is superior to outgroup members (Pratto, Sidanius, Stallworth, & Malle, 1994).

Although overt prejudice and discrimination have decreased over the past few years, newer, more modern forms of prejudice have emerged. On the one hand, overt prejudice, known as old-fashioned prejudice or racism, is characterized by beliefs in the inherent inferiority of ethnic minorities and may manifest as racial epithet use, or exclusion from organizational and institutional spaces (Bobo, Kluegel, & Smith, 1997). U.S. history demonstrates that *de jure* discrimination (e.g. Jim Crow laws) sanctioned overt acts of hostility and exclusion toward ethnic minority groups. On the other hand, modern/symbolic prejudice is characterized by the notion that racism is a thing of the past. Modern/symbolic racists believe that recent gains of ethnic minorities are undeserved, minorities are pushing too hard and too fast in their fight for equal rights, and minorities seek special favors from the government to get ahead instead of working hard toward their goals. Individuals who espouse modern/symbolic prejudicial beliefs tend to highly endorse traditional American values such as individualism and the

Protestant work ethic and use them as justification for their negative views toward ethnic minorities (McConahay, 1986; Sears & Henry, 2003).

Another form of modern prejudice is called aversive prejudice, which occurs when one has sincerely egalitarian beliefs but also unacknowledged negative feelings toward ethnic minority group members (Gaertner & Dovidio, 1986). Individuals high in aversive prejudice are likely to avoid racial topics or even ethnic minorities. The negative feelings that those high in aversive prejudice experience may manifest themselves in more subtle or rationalizable ways. For example, these individuals may only discriminate against ethnic minorities if there is a rational reason to do so, such as denying admission to an ethnic minority graduate school candidate because of slightly lower standardized test scores. While those who endorse modern/symbolic prejudice tend to be politically conservative, individuals who show high levels of aversive prejudice tend to be politically liberal.

More recently, color-blind racial ideology (CBRI) has been posited as an ultramodern form of prejudice (Neville, Awad, Brooks, Flores, & Bluemel, 2013). Neville and colleagues outlined two facets of CBRI: power-evasion and color-evasion. The power-evasion perspective of CBRI is characterized by a deliberate denial of power relationships in society. The denial of power is intended to ignore the individual, organizational, institutional, and cultural instances of prejudice and discrimination. Color-evasion refers to ignoring race by emphasizing similarity among individuals. The aspirational goal for individuals who hold color-evasion views may be to reduce racism. Individuals high in color-evasion beliefs reject the notion that interracial divisions exist (Frankenberg, 1993).

Related to the color-evasion perspective of CBRI is the concept of racial microaggressions (Sue, 2009). Sue outlined three types of microaggressions in his framework: microassaults, insults, and invalidations. Microassaults refer to the type of blatant racial discrimination that was rampant in the pre-civil rights era. The concept of insults pertains to racial insensitivity to a person's heritage that may include instances such as questioning whether someone is truly American based on his or her ethnic background. Invalidations refer to the denial of racialized experiences faced by ethnic minorities (Sue, 2009). The following sections review many of the aforementioned concepts, which inform the literature on prejudice and discrimination toward Arab Americans.

Discrimination Toward Arab Americans

The discrimination narrative generally involves two parties, the perpetrator and the victim. This section reviews literature that focuses on the perpetrator's perspective. Stereotypes of Arabs and Arab Americans are first presented. Next, the correlates and predictors of discrimination are reviewed as they pertain to prejudice toward Arab Americans and Muslims (who are assumed to be Arab). Much of this research is in the form of correlational and experimental studies that examine pertinent factors and predictors involved in prejudice toward Arab Americans.

Stereotypes of Arabs and Arab Americans

The pervasive and consistent negative stereotyping of Arabs and Muslims exists in almost all forms of mass media. Arabs and Arab Americans were stereotyped as terrorists long before the events of 9/11 (El-Farra, 1996; Shaheen, 2003). In a landmark study, Shaheen (2003) examined the stereotypes of Arabs in over 900 films and found that Arab men are portrayed as "brute murderers, sleazy rapists, religious fanatics, oil-rich dimwits, and abusers of women" (p. 172). Shaheen argued that the portrayal of Arabs represents a general theme of "othering," where they are rarely seen as individuals that are similar to the average American. A couple of examples of negative television and film portrayals include Fox's TV series *24*, and the film *The Siege* (Ibish, 2001, 2003). On a brighter note, the American-Arab Anti-Discrimination Committee (ADC) has observed in its reports regarding discrimination and hate crimes that a significant number of individuals within the media have made a concerted effort to denounce anti-Arab racism, and many films and TV shows in the post-9/11 era are careful not to demonize Arab Americans and Muslims (Ibish, 2008).

The negative stereotypes of Arabs have adverse consequences on intergroup relations. In an experimental study using a sample of 12–16-year-old adolescents, those who endorsed stereotypes about Arabs were less likely to be empathetic toward and socially inclusive of an Arab American depicted in a vignette (Hitti, 2013). Stereotypes and unacknowledged prejudices toward Arabs and Muslims may also elicit anxiety and aggressive and violent responses among those who are prejudiced. For example, one study found that Arabs were perceived as threatening, and this was related to increased anxiety in the non-Arab study participants (Lyons, Kenworthy, & Popan, 2010). In another lab study, when participants were primed with Arab or Muslim categories prior to playing a shooting game, they were more likely to shoot an armed ambiguous target compared to when they were not primed (Mange, Chun, Sharvit, & Belanger, 2012). This study suggests that the negative stereotypes that individuals hold toward Arabs and Muslims may impact their level of aggression even when the target is not Arab or Muslim.

Employment and Housing Discrimination

Negative stereotypes toward Arab Americans may contribute to organizational and institutional discrimination toward this group. Several experimental studies provide evidence of potential employment discrimination toward Arab Americans. In one study, identical resumes with either a White or Arab-sounding name were sent to 265 contacts listed for job postings in the U.S. over a 15-month period (Widner & Chicoine, 2011). Results indicated that an Arab male applicant had to send out at least two resumes for every one sent by a White male applicant to get a call back for an interview. Furthermore, Arab American applicants were especially likely to be discriminated against when applying for an office manager position as opposed to a customer service manager position, suggesting that discrimination may be greater for positions that are considered higher status. Similarly, Derous, Ryan, and Nguyen (2012) found that in a Dutch context résumés with typical Dutch names were less likely to be negatively evaluated compared to résumés with Arab sounding names. Furthermore, evaluations of a résumé of a woman with an Arab name received much more negative evaluations compared to résumés with Arab male, Dutch female, or Dutch male-sounding names. This finding was accentuated when applying for high status jobs.

In addition to employment discrimination, evidence of housing discrimination is also presented in experimental studies. Carpusor and Loges (2006) sent out 1,115 inquiry emails to landlords who were advertising apartment vacancies in Los Angeles. Over a 10-week time period, researchers randomly assigned landlords to receive an email signed by a potential tenant with either an Arab, African American, or White sounding name. While the email signed by the African American-sounding name received the fewest positive responses, overall the Arab and African American-sounding names fared much worse than the email from the applicant with the White-sounding name.

Mechanisms Underlying Prejudice Toward Arab Americans

As discussed above, negative stereotypes toward Arab Americans likely lead to organizational, institutional, and other types of discrimination. It is important to understand what attitudinal or ideological variables may increase negative attitudes and discrimination toward Arab Americans. Ideological variables such as RWA and SDO can provide some insight into the mechanisms underlying prejudice and discrimination against Arab Americans. Several studies have examined the relationship between RWA and SDO on the perception of Arab and Muslim Americans. Oftentimes, these constructs are examined in the context of research that investigates the link between religiosity and prejudice. Given that in many instances Arab Americans are perceived to be Muslim, and Islam is considered an outgroup religion in the U.S., some scholars have hypothesized that religiosity (e.g. extrinsic, intrinsic religiosity, fundamentalism) would naturally predict prejudice toward Arab Americans. However, the link between religiosity and prejudice is rarely found in prejudice research, and when found can be explained by RWA.

In a study examining relationships among religious fundamentalism, RWA, and prejudice toward Arabs and African Americans, authoritarian aggression mediated the relationship between religious fundamentalism and prejudice (Johnson, Labouff, Rowatt, Patock-Peckham, & Carlisle, 2012). Specifically, those higher in authoritarian aggression tended to show more explicit and implicit discrimination toward Arabs and African Americans. Furthermore, when a more implicit measure (i.e. social distance) was used as the prejudice outcome variable, both authoritarian aggression and authoritarian submission positively predicted prejudice toward Arabs and African Americans (Johnson et al., 2012). Similarly, in another study, RWA significantly mediated the relationship between extrinsic religiosity (e.g. religiosity based on group identity and social convention) and prejudice toward Middle Easterners (Awad & Hall-Clark, 2009). In addition to studies examining the link between religiosity and prejudice, RWA also positively predicted endorsement of violent action toward the Middle East (Henry, Sidanius, Levin, & Pratto, 2005) and support of the death penalty when linked to Arabs (Dambrun, 2007).

Relatedly, the construct of SDO has predicted prejudice toward Arabs, Muslims, and Middle Easterners (e.g. Dambrun, 2007). Those high in SDO (e.g. with a tendency to think one's ingroup is superior and outgroups are inferior) were more likely to hold negative prejudices toward Arab groups (Dambrun, 2007; Henry et al., 2005; Rowatt, Franklin, & Cotton, 2005). The endorsement of SDO has been associated with offering less help to Arab students (Halabi, Dovidio, & Nadler, 2008) and less leniency toward Arab immigrant criminal offenders (Green, Thomsen, Sidanius, Staerklé, & Potanina, 2009). Oswald (2005) reported that individuals high in SDO were more likely to negatively stereotype Arabs, report greater social distance between themselves and Arabs, and endorse discrimination and more negative prejudices toward Arabs. In sum, RWA and SDO both consistently and strongly predict prejudice toward Arabs.

Arab American Experiences of Discrimination

As outlined above, evidence of negative stereotypes and discrimination toward Arab Americans that may be fueled by ideological variables such as RWA and SDO is well documented. It is therefore important to understand the experiences of discrimination from the perspective of those who are being discriminated against. This section focuses on Arab Americans' experiences of discrimination in the U.S. Information regarding anti-Arab discrimination from national reports is presented and discussed. Psychological research discussing the role of identity, religious identification, and acculturation on perceptions of discrimination is presented. In addition, mental health outcomes of discrimination are reviewed.

Reports of Discrimination

The American-Arab Anti-Discrimination Committee (ADC) is a national civil rights organization, established in 1980, that aims to protect the rights of Arab Americans in the U.S. The ADC works to educate the American public about Arab issues in order to combat stereotypes and discrimination. It produces reports that document prejudice and discrimination in several domains. An important note about ADC reports is that they only document cases reported to the organization; unfortunately there is likely a significant amount of underreporting of discrimination by Arab Americans not represented in the reports.

In 2001, the ADC released a report documenting hate crimes and discrimination against Arab Americans that occurred from 1998 to 2000 (Ibish, 2001). The ADC received complaints of discrimination or bias pertaining to employment, housing, immigration, education, and police misconduct.

Of all the discrimination incidents documented in the report, 35% involved complaints related to employment discrimination, 35% pertained to institutional issues such as immigration and racial profiling in airports, and 22% were cases that rose to the level of hate crimes. For example, the ADC reported receiving an average of 25 complaints a week from Arab Americans alleging employment discrimination during the three-year period of the report.

After the events of 9/11, the ADC recorded a tremendous increase in reported discrimination experienced by Arab Americans (Ibish, 2003). This 2003 publication documented instances of hate crimes and discrimination that occurred from September 11, 2001, to October 11, 2002. Specifically, it detailed incidents pertaining to new discriminatory immigration policies, the USA PATRIOT Act and general civil liberty violations, police and FBI misconduct, discrimination in educational institutions, and defamation by the media and public figures. Some findings included 80 cases of illegal removal of Arab Americans from planes prior to take-off and over 800 cases of employment discrimination that reflected a four-fold increase over previous years. Moreover, 700 cases of violence toward Arab Americans, or those perceived to be Arab or Muslim, occurred in the first nine weeks following 9/11. The report concluded that following 9/11 Arab Americans suffered a tremendous backlash that resulted in widespread violence and discrimination in multiple sectors (e.g. education, employment, housing, government).

In 2008, the ADC released another report, documenting hate crimes and discrimination that occurred from 2003 to 2007 toward Arab Americans (Ibish, 2008). The rate of violent crimes against Arab Americans had declined but was still higher than levels prior to 9/11. During the four years covered by the report, there continued to be widespread defamation and vilification of Arabs and Muslims in the film and television industry. Employment discrimination in both public and private sectors remained prevalent. This finding was supported by Equal Employment Opportunity Commission (EEOC) reports outlining discrimination lawsuits by Arab and Muslim Americans (Malos, 2010). Shortly after the publication of the 2008 ADC report, the conflict in Syria and other parts of the Middle East increased and therefore discrimination resulting from these events was not accounted for.

Although the ADC reports provide useful and detailed information on incidents of hate crimes and discrimination, they primarily depend on individuals who chose to contact ADC and report their discriminatory experiences. In other words, the individuals who are included in the report were not chosen at random. To address this concern, the Arab American Institute (AAI) commissioned a national study to assess the post-9/11 experiences of 505 randomly selected Arab Americans (Zogby, 2002). Approximately 30% reported personally experiencing discrimination and 40% knew someone who had been discriminated against since 9/11. Muslim Arabs, those who were not born in the U.S., and younger participants were more likely to report being discriminated against compared to Christian Arabs, U.S. born, and older participants. A noteworthy majority of the respondents (78%) believed that there was more racial profiling since 9/11. Despite the negative portrayal and views toward Arabs by the public, 73% of the Arab Americans surveyed reported pride in their heritage. Using data collected by Zogby across three different time periods, Nassar-McMillan, Lambert and Hakim-Larson (2011) found consistent levels of perceived discrimination.

Psychological Correlates of Discrimination

Although rates of discrimination toward Arab Americans are generally high, experiences of discrimination may be moderated by identity and psychological variables. One such identity variable is religious identification. Several studies have found that Muslims report more discrimination than their Christian counterparts (Abdulrahim, James, Yamout, & Baker, 2012; Awad, 2010; Nassar-McMillan et al., 2011), suggesting that Muslim Arab Americans may experience more discrimination. Similarly, ethnic identity is associated with perceptions of discrimination. Individuals who report higher levels of Arab ethnic identity are more likely to perceive discrimination compared to those who do not have a salient ethnic identity (Awad, 2010; Nassar-McMillan et al., 2011). Abdulrahim and colleagues (2012) also found that racial identity related to perceptions of discrimination, in that Arab Americans who did not identify as White were more likely to report having experienced discrimination.

Another psychological construct closely related to ethnic identity is acculturation (e.g. level of adaptation to the mainstream culture). In a study of 177 Arab/Middle Eastern Americans (Awad, 2010), the level of acculturation moderated the relationship between religious identification and perceived discrimination. Overall, individuals with higher levels of dominant society immersion (i.e. the extent to which an individual is acculturated to dominant society) tended to perceive less discrimination. However, when religious identification was taken into consideration, the pattern of results presented a more nuanced picture. Specifically, Muslim Arab Americans who were higher in dominant society immersion (e.g. acculturation) perceived the greatest amount of discrimination, whereas Christian Arab Americans high in dominant society immersion reported the least amount of discrimination.

Outcomes of Discrimination

Experiences of discrimination have also impacted psychological outcomes. In particular, Arab Americans who experience discrimination report higher levels of psychological distress (Ahmed, Kia-Keating, & Tsai, 2011; Moradi & Hasan, 2004; Padela & Heisler, 2010). In a study conducted in the Detroit area, 1,018 Arab American adults were surveyed about their discrimination experiences post 9/11 and results indicated that experiences of discrimination were related to high levels of psychological distress (Padela & Heisler, 2010). More specifically, those who believed that there was a lack of respect for Arab Americans in the U.S. and felt less security and safety due to discrimination were more likely to report greater psychological distress. Furthermore, those who experienced discrimination in the sample reported lower levels of happiness and poorer overall health. The perceived discrimination–psychological distress link has also been found in Arab American high school students. For example, in one study perceived discrimination and acculturative stress positively predicted psychological distress in a sample of Arab American adolescents (Ahmed et al., 2011).

There is evidence that the link between perceived discrimination and psychological distress may be moderated by certain demographic and psychological variables. One such demographic variable is religious identification. In one study conducted in Canada, the link between perceived discrimination and psychological distress did not emerge as significant for Christian Arab Canadians, but perceived discrimination significantly predicted psychological distress for their Muslim Arab Canadian counterparts (Rousseau, Hassan, Moreau, & Thombs, 2011). Within the U.S. context, Moradi and Hasan (2004) investigated the influence of personal control as a mediator between perceived discrimination and self-esteem, and discrimination and psychological distress. Findings indicated that perceptions of personal control fully mediated the relationship between discrimination and self-esteem. In addition, personal control partially accounted for the relationship between perceived discrimination and psychological distress (Moradi & Hasan, 2004). These results suggest that Arab Americans who do not feel control in their lives are likely to experience poorer mental health outcomes such as low self-esteem and greater psychological distress.

According to Ahmed and colleagues (2011), there are some protective factors that may mitigate the effects of discrimination and positively influence mental health. Cultural resources such as religious coping, religious support, and ethnic identity were negatively related to psychological distress. However, these cultural resources did not moderate the relationship between discrimination and psychological distress, resulting in these resources being interpreted as directly promotive of psychological wellbeing as opposed to a buffer between discrimination and psychological distress (Ahmed et al., 2011).

Case Example: Intergenerational Discrimination Experiences of the Sawalha Family

Osama and Nisreen Sawalha have lived in Houston, Texas, for nearly 30 years. They immigrated to the U.S. from Jordan in the late 1980s, a couple of years after they were married in a Greek Orthodox Christian ceremony. Osama owns rental properties in Houston, and Nisreen has worked as a nurse practitioner in a local clinic for about ten years. Their oldest child, Tamar, was born in Jordan and is a recent graduate of a prestigious Texas state university. She earned a BA degree in supply chain management and is currently finishing up her second year of employment at a large multinational technology company. Their second oldest child, Yousef, was born in Houston in the early 1990s. Yousef studied culinary arts and hopes to one day open a restaurant of his own. He is currently an apprentice chef at a well-known restaurant in Dallas. Osama and Nisreen's youngest child, Basel, is a senior in high school. He has applied to several colleges around the U.S. but is still unsure of his plans for the future.

Osama and Nisreen decided to immigrate to the U.S. after Osama was offered a job in a technology company. The company sponsored Osama and his family on a visa, and the family's naturalization process started shortly thereafter. Osama, Nisreen, and Tamar received U.S. citizenship in the mid-1990s, while Yousef and Basel are natural born citizens.

Osama and Nisreen experienced great difficulty finding housing after they immigrated to the U.S. and Osama accepted his first position in Houston. Even though Osama had proof that his position was well paid, the family found that landlords were consistently hesitant to rent to them. More than once, the Sawalhas were told by landlords that they preferred tenants who were not Middle Eastern. Osama and Nisreen were even told by one potential landlord that he preferred not to rent to people from the Middle East because they were loud and might lower property values in the neighborhood.

After the outbreak of the First Gulf War, Osama started experiencing prejudice and discrimination at his workplace. At first, he was unsure whether or not he was imagining that his supervisors and co-workers were treating him differently. Osama had started off his career as a very promising engineer who had the trust and enthusiastic support of his supervisor and colleagues. However, Osama noticed that he was being passed over for several promotions for positions for which he was by far the most well-qualified and experienced employee. When he decided to ask his supervisor whether or not there was something in his performance that was keeping him from being promoted, he was surprised by his supervisor's response. He was told by his supervisor that given the political context of the early 1990s, his supervisor was unsure if it was a good idea to put someone from Osama's background in a position where he might have more interaction with the public. Osama's supervisor went on to tell Osama that he did not think corporate management would think it appropriate to put a Muslim man in a position that would have him supervising women, ignoring the fact that Osama was Christian.

Experiencing anger, frustration, and sadness after this incident, Osama decided to start looking for other work and ways of supporting his family. Osama sent out résumés to nearly 40 technology companies for open positions in which he had the expertise, knowledge, and experience. He heard back from only two of the companies. A human resources coordinator from one of the companies called to schedule an interview, and expressed surprise to hear that Osama was fluent in English and only slightly accented. It was experiences such as housing and employment discrimination that inspired Osama and Nisreen to buy and maintain rental properties in Houston. Osama also experienced interpersonal discrimination due to his name. He had particular difficulty in the years following the rise of Al-Qaeda and the organization's leader, Osama Bin Laden. Osama is often embarrassed by his name and the negative associations he fears it might hold for those who hear it. In the past few years, he has contemplated legally changing his first name to Sam.

In an effort to protect the children, Osama did not mention to them the discrimination he faced. However, his children experienced their own challenges with prejudice. In college, Tamar applied for an internship from her university's alumni network. Tamar made it to the interview phase of the scholarship, and was interviewed by a distinguished alumna of her university for the chance to be offered summer housing for an internship in California. During the interview, Tamar disclosed that she was born in Jordan. Up until that point she had felt positive rapport with her interviewer. But after this disclosure, Tamar felt the interviewer become cold and clipped in her communication with Tamar, when she had been warm, enthusiastic, and connected up until this point. Tamar, was not offered housing by this alumna, and she has always wondered with regret and discomfort if her disclosure of national origin was the reason why.

Yousef, Osama and Nisreen's middle child, has been detained three times by U.S. Immigration and Customs Enforcement on re-entering the U.S. after business trips in Mexico. Each time, he provided officers with his Texas driver's license to prove his identity, and each time, he was held for hours and questioned about his relationships with individuals in the Middle East and his religious and political views. Yousef finds these experiences bewildering, especially since he is an aspiring chef who speaks very little Arabic and has not been to Jordan to visit his extended family since he was a child.

Basel, the youngest Sawalha, has experienced prejudice and discrimination in high school. Twice following unusually negative news reporting about incidents involving Arabs in the Middle East, Basel found derogatory names scrawled onto pieces of paper that were stuffed into his locker. While Basel and his parents have asked school administrators more than once to respond in a way that invokes school policies against hate crimes and discrimination, they have to date seen no action from administrators. While Basel belongs to a close-knit group of friends, he has often found that before getting to know him, students assume he comes from an extremely wealthy Muslim background. He has found that students who do not know him hold strong assumptions about his beliefs about women, his conservatism, his religious identity, his sympathy with terrorists, and his family life.

The Sawalha family vividly remembers when the Oklahoma City bombing happened. In particular, they remember hoping above all else that the bomber would be caught and not be an Arab. The family feels similarly any time they hear of an act of terrorism on the news. In addition to sadness for the chaos, they desperately hope that the instigators will not be Arab and dread the anticipated racist and discriminatory phrases they know they will hear in public in the aftermath of whatever the event might have been.

This case example illustrates the ways in which discrimination can be intergenerational and can impact all members of an Arab American family. The discrimination that the Sawalha's experienced began when they arrived in the U.S. in the 1990s, which demonstrates that prejudice toward Arabs did not start with 9/11. Osama experienced organizational discrimination by being denied promotions and during hiring when he sought another position. The Sawalha family also experienced barriers in finding housing due to discrimination by landlords. The repeated detainment of Yousef represents the many experiences of institutional discrimination, such as police detainment, reported by ADC. In addition, both Osama and Tamar experienced microaggressions when an employer expressed surprise at Osama's fluency in English and Tamar's interviewer changed her demeanor after Tamar disclosed having been born in Jordan. The psychological impact of discrimination is portrayed when the family experienced anxiety and dread that they would be discriminated against when negative events that might be attributed to Arab Americans or Muslims occur. A common theme of their discrimination experiences is the frequency with which they are misidentified as Muslims. None of the family members has ever reported their discrimination, which reflects the plausible reality that reports such as those produced by the ADC are likely an underestimation of discrimination experienced by Arab Americans.

Critique

The conflation of Arab and Muslim is profound in the literature on prejudice and discrimination toward Arabs. After the 9/11 terrorist attacks, it appears that Arabs were the outgroup of choice in many social psychological studies. Sometimes, the focus of the study itself was not on prejudice toward Arabs but rather on prejudice per se, where the design necessitated a perceived outgroup. This was especially true in experimental studies and those that involved the constructs of RWA and SDO.

In experimental studies that used methodologies such as name manipulations, it was unclear in publications what cues participants were using to make their evaluations. The names used may have been common for all Muslims, not just Arab Muslims. This raises the question: were individuals displaying prejudice toward Islam or Arabs? Many studies did not bother to disentangle the cues used to discriminate. However, one study did distinguish between cues such as skin tone, Middle Eastern dress, and name in the evaluations of men perceived to be Muslim (Brown et al., 2013). The study found that a target with a Muslim name in Middle Eastern dress garnered the most negative evaluations compared to a target with a White sounding name in Western dress. Future studies should work to disentangle the Arab and Muslim conflation to determine what cues people are most in tune with when they discriminate.

Furthermore, the experience of discrimination may differ within Arab American subgroups. For example, Arab Americans that can more easily assimilate into society (e.g. phenotypically indistinguishable from the majority) may be less likely to experience discrimination than those who resemble other ethnic minority groups in the U.S. As Abdulrahim and colleagues (2012) found, Muslims, those with darker skin, and individuals who identified as non-White reported more discrimination than their non-Muslim, lighter skinned, White identified counterparts. In some ways the pan-ethnic designation of Arab allows one to focus on similarities in experience. However, it is important to acknowledge that Arab Americans differ in their experiences of privilege and oppression in the U.S. Some Arabs may identify as and pass as White, while others may not be accorded that privilege due to obvious phenotypic markers that identify them as people of color.

Another issue that is salient with regard to research on discrimination against Arab Americans is the lack of recognition by federal bodies that would allow Arabs and Middle Eastern Americans to be accurately counted by the U.S. Census Bureau. The Office of Management and Budget (OMB) has yet to recognize the non-White status of most Arab and Middle Eastern Americans and as a result Arabs are currently counted as White by the U.S. Census. Given that most institutions in the U.S. follow the Census guidelines for collecting demographic information, it is unclear the extent to which discrimination toward Arab Americans occurs at every level of society. For example, comprehensive statistics are not available on educational, workplace, or health outcomes because data on Arab Americans are rarely collected. If they are collected, they tend to be reaggregated with White data when reported to government agencies. Therefore, comprehensive and accurate information about educational, workplace, and health disparities is lacking with this population, although such disparities may be due in large part to discrimination.

Conclusion

Arab Americans have experienced discrimination at the individual, organizational, institutional, and cultural levels. Although discrimination toward Arab Americans has arguably existed since Arabs first immigrated to the U.S., prejudiced portrayals and behavior appear to surge when there is a Middle Eastern conflict or terrorist attack (e.g. Oklahoma City bombing, 1993 World Trade Center bombing) with the most significant surge after 9/11. While much of the prejudice and discrimination that currently occurs toward other ethnic minority groups can be characterized as modern or ultramodern forms of prejudice, overt discrimination and prejudice toward Arab Americans is still considered acceptable. Therefore, much of the discrimination toward Arab Americans can be characterized as old-fashioned prejudice. The lack of recognition by federal entities of the ethnic minority status of Arab Americans exacerbates the problem by withholding the governmental protection accorded to ethnic minorities in the U.S. Arab Americans who are discriminated against consistently report psychological distress. Increased awareness of how stereotypes contribute to prejudice and discrimination toward Arab Americans may help decrease instances of bias against this group.

References

Abdulrahim, S., James, S. A., Yamout, R., & Baker, W. (2012). Discrimination and psychological distress: Does Whiteness matter for Arab Americans? *Social Science & Medicine* 75, 2116–2123. doi: 10.1016/j.socscimed.2012.07.030

Ahmed, S. R., Kia-Keating, M., & Tsai, K. H. (2011). A structural model of racial discrimination, acculturative stress, and cultural resources among Arab American adolescents. *American Journal of Community Psychology* 48(3–4), 181–192. doi: 10.1007/s10464-011-9424-3

Allport, G. W. (1954). *The nature of prejudice*. Reading, MA: Addison-Wesley.

Altemeyer, B. (1981). *Right-wing authoritarianism*. Winnipeg: University of Manitoba Press.

Awad, G. H. (2010). The impact of acculturation and religious identification on perceived discrimination for Arab/Middle Eastern Americans. *Cultural Diversity and Ethnic Minority Psychology* 16(1), 59–67. doi: 10.1037/a0016675

Awad, G. H. & Hall-Clark, B. N. (2009). Impact of religiosity and right-wing authoritarianism on prejudice towards Middle Easterners. *Beliefs and Values: Understanding the Global Implications of Human Nature* 1(2), 183–192.

Benokraitis, N. V. & Feagin, J. R. (1995). *Modern sexism: Blatant, subtle, and covert discrimination* (2nd edn.). Englewood Cliffs, NJ: Prentice Hall.

Bobo, L., Kluegel, J. R., & Smith, R. A. (1997). Laissez-faire racism: The crystallization of a kinder, gentler antiblack ideology. In S. A. Tuch & J. K. Martin (eds.), *Racial attitudes in the 1990s: Continuity and change* (pp. 14–42). Westport, CT: Praeger.

Brown, L. M., Awad, G. H., Preas, E. J., Allen, V., Kenney, J., Roberts, S., & Lusk, L. B. (2013). Investigating prejudice toward men perceived to be Muslim: Cues of foreignness versus phenotype. *Journal of Applied Social Psychology* 43(Suppl. 2), E237–E245. doi: 10.1111/jasp.12015

Cainkar, L. (2002). No longer invisible: Arab and Muslim exclusion after September 11. *Middle East Report* 224, 22–29.

Cainkar, L. A. (2009). *Homeland insecurity: The Arab American and Muslim American experience after 9/11*. New York: Russell Sage Foundation.

Carpusor, A. G. & Loges, W. E. (2006). Rental discrimination and ethnicity in names. *Journal of Applied Social Psychology* 36, 934–952. doi: 10.1111/j.0021-9029.2006.00050.x

Dambrun, M. (2007). Understanding the relationship between racial prejudice and support for the death penalty: The racist punitive bias hypothesis. *Social Justice Research* 20(2), 228–249. doi: 10.1007/s11211-007-0040-1

Derous, E., Ryan, A. M., & Nguyen, H.-H. D. (2012). Multiple categorization in resume screening: Examining effects on hiring discrimination against Arab applicants in field and lab settings. *Journal of Organizational Behavior* 33(4), 544–570. doi: 10.1002/job.769

Disha, I., Cavendish, J. C., & King, R. D. (2011). Historical events and spaces of hate: Hate crimes against Arabs and Muslims in post-9/11 America. *Social Problems* 58(1), 21–46. doi: 10.1525/sp.2011.58.1.21

El-Farra, N. (1996). Arabs and the media. *Journal of Media Psychology* 1(2), 1–7.

Frankenberg, R. (1993). *White women, race matters: The social construction of whiteness*. Minneapolis, MN: University of Minnesota Press.

Gaertner, S. L. & Dovidio, J. F. (1986). The aversive form of racism. In J. F. Dovidio, S. L. Gaertner (eds.), *Prejudice, discrimination, and racism* (pp. 61–89). San Diego, CA: Academic Press.

Green, G. E. T., Thomsen, L., Sidanius, J., Staerklé, C., & Potanina, P. (2009). Reactions to crime as a hierarchy regulating strategy: The moderating role of social dominance orientation. *Social Justice Research* 22, 416–436. doi: 10.1007/s11211-009-0106-3

Halabi, S., Dovidio, J. F., & Nadler, A. (2008). When and how do high status group members offer help: Effects of social dominance orientation and status threat. *Political Psychology* 29(6), 841–858. doi: 10.1111/j.1467-9221.2008.00669.x

Hamed, S. H., Tayyem, R., Nimer, N., & AlKhatib, H. S. (2010). Skin-lightening practice among women living in Jordan: Prevalence, determinants, and user's awareness. *International Journal of Dermatology* 49, 414–420. doi: 10.1111/j.1365-4632.2010.04463.x

Henry, P. J., Sidanius, J., Levin, S., & Pratto, F. (2005). Social dominance orientation, authoritarianism, and support for intergroup violence between the Middle East and America. *Political Psychology* 26, 569–584. doi: 10.1111/j.1467-9221.2005.00432.x

Hitti, A. (2013). *Social exclusion in cultural context: Group norms, fairness, and stereotypes* (Doctoral dissertation). Available from ProQuest Theses and Dissertations database (UMI No. 3590762).

Ibish, H. (ed.) (2001). *1998–2000 report on hate crimes and discrimination against Arab Americans.* Washington, D.C.: American-Arab Anti-Discrimination Committee.

Ibish, H. (ed.) (2003). *Report on hate crimes and discrimination against Arab Americans: The post-September 11th backlash, September 11, 2001–October 11, 2002.* Washington, D.C.: American-Arab Anti-Discrimination Committee.

Ibish, H. (ed.) (2008). *2003–2007 report on hate crimes and discrimination against Arab Americans.* Washington, D.C.: American-Arab Anti-Discrimination Committee. Retrieved from www.issuelab.org/resource/20032007_report_on_hate_crimes_and_discrimination_against_arab_americans

Johnson, M. K., Labouff, J. P., Rowatt, W. C., Patock-Peckham, J. A., & Carlisle, R. D. (2012). Facets of right-wing authoritarianism mediate the relationship between religious fundamentalism and attitudes toward Arabs and African Americans. *Journal for the Scientific Study of Religion* 51(1), 128–142. doi: 10.1111/j.1468-5906.2011.01622.x

Jones, J. M. (1997). *Prejudice and racism* (2nd edn.). New York: McGraw-Hill.

Lyons, P. A., Kenworthy, J. B., & Popan, J. R. (2010). Ingroup identification and group-level narcissism as predictors of U.S. citizens' attitudes and behavior toward Arab immigrants. *Personality and Social Psychology Bulletin* 36, 1267–1280. doi: 10.1177/0146167210380604

Malos, S. (2010). Post-9/11 backlash in the workplace: Employer liability for discrimination against Arab- and Muslim-Americans based on religion or national origin. *Employee Responsibilities and Rights Journal* 22, 297–310. doi: 10.1007/s10672-009-9132-4

Mange, J., Chun, W. Y., Sharvit, K., & Belanger, J. J. (2012). Thinking about Arabs and Muslims makes Americans shoot faster: Effects of category accessibility on aggressive responses in a shooter paradigm. *European Journal of Social Psychology* 42, 552–556. doi: 10.1002/ejsp.1883

McConahay, J. B. (1986). Modern racism, ambivalence, and the Modern Racism Scale. In J. F. Dovidio & S. L. Gaertner (eds.), *Prejudice, discrimination, and racism* (pp. 91–125). San Diego, CA: Academic Press.

Moradi, B. & Hasan, N. T. (2004). Arab American persons' reported experiences of discrimination and mental health: The mediating role of personal control. *Journal of Counseling Psychology* 51, 418–428. doi: 10.1037/0022-0167.51.4.418

Naber, N. (2000). Ambiguous insiders: An investigation of Arab American invisibility. *Ethnic and Racial Studies* 23, 37–61.

Nassar-McMillan, S. C., Lambert, R. G., & Hakim-Larson, J. (2011). Discrimination history, backlash fear, and ethnic identity among Arab Americans: Post-9/11 snapshots. *Journal of Multicultural Counseling and Development* 39(1), 38–47. doi: 10.1002/j.2161-1912.2011.tb00138.x

Neville, H. A., Awad, G. H., Brooks, J. E., Flores, M. P., & Bluemel, J. (2013). Color-blind racial ideology: Theory, training, and measurement implications in psychology. *American Psychologist* 68, 455–466. doi: 10.1037/a0033282

Oswald, D. L. (2005). Understanding anti-Arab reactions post-9/11: The role of threats, social categories, and personal ideologies. *Journal of Applied Social Psychology* 35, 1775–1799. doi: 10.1111/j.1559–1816.2005.tb02195.x

Padela, A. I. & Heisler, M. (2010). The association of perceived abuse and discrimination after September 11, 2001, with psychological distress, level of happiness, and health status among Arab Americans. *American Journal of Public Health* 100, 284–291. doi: 10.2105/AJPH.2009.164954

Pratto, F., Sidanius, J., Stallworth, L. M., & Malle, B. F. (1994). Social dominance orientation: A personality variable predicting social and political attitudes. *Journal of Personality and Social Psychology* 67(4), 741–763. doi: 10.1037/0022-3514.67.4.741

Rousseau, C., Hassan, G., Moreau, N., & Thombs, B. D. (2011). Perceived discrimination and its association with psychological distress among newly arrived immigrants before and after September 11, 2001. *American Journal of Public Health* 101, 909–915. doi: 10.2105/AJPH.2009.173062

Rowatt, W. C., Franklin, L. M., & Cotton, M. (2005). Patterns and personality correlates of implicit and explicit attitudes toward Christians and Muslims. *Journal for the Scientific Study of Religion* 44(1), 29–43. doi: 10.1111/j.1468-5906.2005.00263.x

Sears, D. O. & Henry, P. J. (2003). The origins of symbolic racism. *Journal of Personality and Social Psychology* 85, 259–275. doi: 10.1037/0022-3514.85.2.259

Shaheen, J. G. (2003). Reel bad Arabs: How Hollywood vilifies a people. *Annals of the American Academy of Political and Social Science* 588, 171–193. doi: 10.1177/0002716203588001011

Sue, D. W. (2009). *Microaggressions in everyday life: Race, gender, and sexual orientation*. Hoboken, NJ: John Wiley & Sons, Inc.

Whitley, B. E. & Kite, M. E. (2010). *The psychology of prejudice and discrimination* (2nd edn.). Belmont, CA: Cengage Learning/Wadsworth.

Widner, D. & Chicoine, S. (2011). It's all in the name: Employment discrimination against Arab Americans. *Sociological Forum* 26, 806–823. doi: 10.1111/j.1573-7861.2011.01285.x

Zogby, J. J. (2002). *Profiling and prejudice: Arab American attitudes and behavior since September 11*. Retrieved from http://b.3cdn.net/aai/cabef9b87ff08600d7_aum6iif4p.pdf

6
COMMUNITY ACTIVISM
Advocacy, Identity Politics, and the Formation of a Collective Consciousness

Caroline Nagel and Amelia Ayoob

The imagination and construction of ethnic or pan-ethnic categories is a key feature of American politics and the means by which immigrants and subsequent generations participate in the public sphere and become incorporated into the body politic (Conzen, Gerber, Morawska, Pozzetta, & Vecoli, 1992; Kurien, 2007). The establishment of community centers, museums and heritage centers, and other institutions and organizations tends to obscure the contested nature of community-building processes by lending an air of permanency and solidity to collective identities. This chapter explores the ways in which activists have produced the boundaries of the Arab American community and have connected certain identities, interests, and agendas to this community. This discussion highlights how the ambiguous and shifting status of "Arabness" within American racial and ethnic boundaries has shaped Arab American activism in particular ways. The focus here on the role of activists in forming a collective Arab American identity is not intended to suggest that Arab American identity is merely a figment of activists' imagination. Arab American identity has become meaningful to many people, especially in light of the discriminatory practices and prejudices of dominant groups and the dynamics in American society that encourage people to hyphenate identities (Abu el-Haj, 2007). The analysis instead emphasizes that community building is the particular business of activists, so that their relationship to identities and their investments in them may be different from those of non-activists.

Activism here refers specifically to individual and collective efforts through which people make claims for inclusion, recognition, or voice within the broader community and its institutions. While this analysis focuses on the engagement of activists within a pluralistic American political system, it is noted that Arab American activism and processes of Arab American community formation take place within a transnational social field (Glick Schiller, Basch, & Szanton Blanc, 1995). Arab American identities and activist agendas revolve at least partly around conflicts and events in the Arab world; and conflicts and events in the Arab world impinge on Arab American activism, sometimes in ways that undermine the unity that activists are keen to foster.

This chapter begins with a brief overview of common academic perspectives on immigrant activism and post-structural theory. It then delves more specifically into processes of Arab American activism, exploring the historical, social, and political contexts that galvanized the creation and subsequent evolution of Arab American activism since the mid-twentieth century. Next is a case example centered on the Arab American National Museum and its significance both to activist efforts and community-building projects. This case serves as a springboard into a discussion of the contested nature of Arab American identity and the ways in which scholars might address the diversity underlying the broad category of "Arab American."

Theoretical Frameworks: Immigrant Identity, Associational Activity, and Participation in the Public Sphere

Arab Americans are among many ethnic groups in the U.S. who have been maligned in particular historical moments as foreign "Others" and celebrated in other moments as part of America's multicultural tapestry. In this regard, the processes through which Arab Americans have been demarcated as a group and simultaneously included in and excluded from narratives of belonging are not entirely unique. Rather, they follow the broad contours of identify formation, community building, and associational activity among immigrant groups in the U.S. context.

Early in the twentieth century, American scholars observed and commented extensively on the tendency among immigrants to form community associations and institutions. Urban ecologists associated with the Chicago School of Sociology interpreted associational life as a community response to the social dislocation caused by migration to modern, urban societies. These theorists viewed immigrant incorporation and acculturation as a natural, ecological process, but one marked nonetheless by social disorganization, deviancy, and delinquency, as those from traditional, peasant backgrounds become unmoored from community norms. For many scholars, immigrant institutions and associations formed an important, if partial, buffer to the upheaval of immigration – a site where immigrants could find social stability and solidarity in the absence of intimate, meaningful relationships with dominant groups (see, for instance, Thomas & Znaniecki, 1920). Still, most scholars viewed these kinds of association as ultimately incapable of holding back the tide of social transformation. Scholars viewed the transition to the second generation as pivotal to community transformation, arguing that immigrants' clubs, religious institutions, and mutual-aid societies were constantly undermined by their children's acquisition of the habits and traits of the surrounding society.

The model of assimilation asserted by sociologists in the early twentieth century – that ethnicity-based associational activity would be replaced by other forms of association generated in the U.S. context – was challenged in the 1960s and 1970s by advocates of the "ethnic retention" position. This newer generation of scholars understood ethnic identity as remaining relevant to people's identities, social patterns, and political participation. Like the early Chicago School theorists, those advocating the ethnic retention viewpoint recognized that ethnic identities were not simply carried over from the homeland and transplanted from Old World to New; clearly, ethnic signifiers were transformed, reworked, and given new meaning in the U.S. context. This scholarship argued, though, that ethnic signifiers would not fade away through assimilatory processes, but would remain central to American society and to American politics. This view was perhaps most famously articulated in Glazer and Moynihan's 1963 book, *Beyond the Melting Pot*, which interpreted New York City politics as a field of competition between an array of ethnically and racially defined groups. From this perspective, ethnic groups were essentially interest groups that were mobilized within the rough and tumble of local electoral politics (Glazer & Moynihan, 1963; Yancey, Ericksen, & Leon, 1985).

Not all scholars, however, subscribed to this view. On the one hand, a number of scholars writing in the 1970s and 1980s postulated that ethnic identities among the descendants of European immigrants, in particular, were becoming largely symbolic and optional – something to be rolled out on special occasions (parades, holidays) rather than an integral part of everyday life (Gans, 1979; Waters, 1990). On the other hand, scholars observed that for some groups ethnicity was not an "option." This was especially true for non-White Americans, for whom ethnic and racial identities significantly affected social and economic opportunities. In a context of severe urban unrest, growing polarization between Blacks and Whites in American cities, and the emergence of new, politicized categories like "Chicano," "Latino," and "Asian American," the notion of interest-group pluralism seemed woefully inadequate as an explanation for minority political mobilization (Pulido, 2002).

In the 1990s, post-structuralist scholars provided an extensive critique of mainstream conceptualizations of race and ethnicity as bounded, static entities. Post-structuralism offered an alternative theoretical framework centered on the concept of "difference" (Anthias & Yuval-Davis, 2005).

The concept of difference focuses on the production and reproduction of social categories and the workings of power through these categories. From this perspective, social categories such as ethnicity, race, and nationality cannot be taken as given, but rather, must be understood as the products (and producers) of asymmetrical power relationships. Post-structuralist scholars emphasize that identities and group boundaries are always relational. In other words, categories like "White," "male," and "straight" do not exist a priori, but rather, become meaningful in relation to, and in tension with, an "Other" (i.e. "Black," "female," and "gay"). Dominant groups, by definition, have greater capacity to define, control, and subordinate the Other through stereotypes, discourses, and discriminatory social practices. Scholars also highlight the ability of subordinate groups to subvert and to challenge their status as Others and to negotiate membership within the boundaries of the "mainstream." Social categories, in this respect, can be characterized both by fixity and fluidity, though they must always be understood as socially constructed rather than natural or innate.

At a more normative level, post-structural theorists have generally recognized identity-based mobilization as a valid response to the persistent marginalization of groups deemed unassimilable by dominant society (Taylor, 1997; Young, 1990). The argument here is that the public sphere – often understood by political theorists to be a neutral realm of deliberation and debate – has typically excluded the voices, interests, and identities of culturally subordinated groups, compelling subordinated groups to form their own counter-publics. The political identity and solidarity generated within these counter-publics allows immigrants, racialized minorities, sexual minorities, and the like to challenge, to engage with, and/or to claim membership within the dominant public sphere (Fraser, 1990). While validating identity-based politics, however, theorists of difference also note the ambiguities that surround group mobilization. That is, in building the solidarity needed to engage with dominant publics, counter-publics often *essentialize* group identity – that is, they police the boundaries of group difference, enforcing certain moral and behavioral codes, especially on women and youth. They may, as well, participate in the othering of groups who are more abject than themselves. Mobilizations around difference typically become highly fragmented, with different organizations and individuals claiming to speak for a particular group and attempting to steer relationships with dominant groups in particular directions. Counter-publics, in this sense, should not be regarded as fully cohesive or immutable, but rather, as contested and unstable.

The following sections apply the theoretical insights of post-structuralism to the activities of Arab American organizations and activists, emphasizing the relationality and constructed nature of group categories, and calling attention to the political ambiguities that arise from identity-based mobilization and negotiations of societal membership. Long before the 9/11 terrorist attacks, Arabs and Muslims were cast as America's Other and as its chief civilizational foe. A series of events – the 1967 Arab-Israeli War, the Iranian Revolution, the 1991 invasion of Iraq, the second Gulf War in 2003 – had a profound effect on Arab American mobilization, pushing activists, in various ways and to varying degrees, to produce an Arab American public identity and to engage with dominant groups and institutions. Arab American activists have been keen to reclaim and to re-signify Arabness – to attach a different set of meanings associated not with terrorism, but with a rich, diverse, peaceful, and erudite culture that is different from American society but fully compatible with it. There are, however, significant political differences among activists, with some emphasizing resistance to dominant social narratives and solidarity with other subaltern groups, and others emphasizing accommodation and conformity (Naber, 2002). These aims generate their own tensions, as activists at times ignore or deny differences within the "community" in the quest for solidarity and political voice.

Arab American Activism in Historical Perspective

Many accounts of Arab Americans begin with a discussion of late nineteenth-century emigrants from Mount Lebanon, most of them Christian, who generally referred to themselves, and were referred to by immigration authorities, as "Syrians" (the term Syrian is used in this chapter to refer to this early immigrant cohort). The genealogy that traces a contemporary Arab American community to early Syrian communities, however, should not be taken at face value. Rather, the weaving of a historical narrative that identifies the early Syrian population as "Arab American" and that links them to post-1965 cohorts of émigrés from the Arab world must be recognized as the work of Arab American activists and scholars. This is not to say that the identities and associational activities of the early Syrian population do not merit discussion here. On the contrary, attention to this group reveals the complex dynamics of identity formation and the challenges of building an Arab American community and identity in the midst of multiple, competing political projects – including that of assimilation into the White middle class.

As Gualtieri (2009) has shown, members of the early Syrian community were highly engaged in discussion and debate concerning political developments in the Ottoman Empire in the early twentieth century. Gualtieri suggests that many Syrian intellectuals and associational leaders in the U.S., while critical of Ottoman centralization policies and desirous of greater autonomy for Syria, remained largely committed to the notion of an Ottoman polity prior to World War I because of concerns about European colonial designs on the Ottoman Empire. The dissolution of the Ottoman Empire, however, required many Syrian émigrés to rethink their political identities and loyalties. Many were deeply disillusioned by the imposition of European mandate rule in Syria and Palestine after World War I and spoke (or wrote) in support of Arab and Syrian national aspirations. Others – especially among Maronite Christians – voiced support for European mandate rule, which they viewed as a vehicle for the creation of an independent Lebanon. Regardless of their nationalist visions, those participating in diasporic politics, Gualtieri notes, often viewed themselves as the bearers of modernity for their homelands and as shaping a new political and social reality (see also Khater, 2001).

The reimagining of their national identity and of their relationship to homeland coincided with Syrians' negotiations of membership in American society. The position of Syrians in American society became increasingly precarious in the late nineteenth and early twentieth centuries as American political discourse became preoccupied with notions of racial purity. Efforts to exclude "degenerate races" focused specifically on Asian groups, and especially the Chinese, who were barred from immigration and naturalization through a series of federal statutes beginning in the 1880s. As Samhan (1999) notes, Syrians were not necessarily singled out by turn-of-the-century nativism; yet in the early 1900s, they did face a number of court challenges to their eligibility for citizenship on the grounds that they had been born in Asia. Syrian community leaders mobilized to assert their bona fide Caucasian identity, forming, in 1909, the Association for Syrian Unity, which sent a delegation to Washington, D.C., to present evidence about the Caucasian origins of Syrians (Samhan, 1999). Community activists also published rebuttals in local newspapers to claims about Syrians' non-whiteness and organized letter-writing campaigns to support the cause of whiteness. Such appeals in many cases revolved around claims of the Semitic origins of Syrians – origins that linked them to Jesus and therefore to Christianity and Western civilization (Gualtieri, 2009). Despite an important legal victory for Syrians in 1914 with *Dow v. the United States*, the issue of whether Syrians were Asian or Caucasian was not fully put to rest until the early 1920s, when Syrians were definitively placed outside the geographical limits of Asianness (Samhan, 1999).

For some commentators, the legacy of the early Syrian community's tenuous racial position, and of their eventual success in achieving whiteness, was a studied avoidance of more contentious forms of minority and immigrant politics through the remainder of the twentieth century. Perpetually insecure in their racial status, Syrians participated in the racialization of those who remained more definitively non-White. Some have suggested, as well, that their fight for whiteness ultimately dampened the Syrian community's interest in diasporic politics. Certainly, in the first half of the twentieth century there were activists who remained committed to nationalist projects in the Arab world. The period between 1917 and 1948, Davidson (1999) notes, was one of significant activism among Syrian immigrants in support of national self-determination for Arabs in Palestine. But it seems that overall, Syrians – like Italians, Irish, Jews, and other immigrant groups on the margins of whiteness in the early twentieth century – felt more inclined to preserve their racial privilege and their American citizenship than to fight for faraway causes. Organizational activity – by this point mostly labeled "Lebanese" following the creation of an independent state of Lebanon in 1943 – was mostly social and fraternal in nature rather than explicitly political (for a critical discussion of the racialized dynamics of White-ethnic assimilation in the twentieth century, see Jacobson, 1998).

Scholars often look to 1967 – the year of Israel's occupation of the West Bank and Gaza – as a decisive moment in the formation of a self-consciously political Arab American community (Suleiman, 1999). The formation and activation of an Arab American community reflected the growth and diversification of the Arab-origin population in the U.S. after 1965 – the year the U.S. government eliminated national-origins quotas and effectively reopened the U.S. to mass immigration (David, 2007). The post-1965 cohort of Arab immigrants included many highly educated professionals and was more diverse in regional origins than the early Syrian cohort; it also included a much greater proportion of Muslims. Unlike the early Syrian community, this cohort was steeped in anti-colonial and Arab nationalist politics (Naber, 2000). While not all of these immigrants subscribed to pan-Arab politics or to a more politicized sense of Arab identity, the invasion and occupation of the West Bank and Gaza did have a significant galvanizing effect on many of them, while also activating some second and third generation descendants of early Syrian communities (David, 2007). The two decades after the 1967 war saw the creation of a number of national Arab American organizations, including the Association of Arab American University Graduates, founded in 1967; the National Association of Arab Americans, formed in 1972; the American-Arab Anti-Discrimination Committee (ADC), founded in 1980 by former U.S. Senator James Abourezk; and the Arab American Institute (AAI), founded in 1985. (The National Association of Arab Americans officially merged with the ADC in 2002, while the Association of Arab American University Graduates was disbanded in 2007).

Arab American activism since the 1960s has had an important transnational element, with key organizations mobilizing in support of Palestine and, later, in opposition to U.S. military action in Iraq. But it is important to understand the ways in which homeland orientations and interests early on became intertwined with domestic political claims (Shain, 1996). To advocate the Palestinian cause, for instance, required the Arab American activists to address the rampant stereotyping of Arabs in American films and news media, as documented by Shaheen (2001), and to present an alternative narrative of Arabness to the dominant American public. The positive image of Arab society that they constructed emphasized the many contributions of Arab-Islamic culture and learning to Western civilization – in architecture, science, music, and literature – as well as the many contributions of people from the Arab world to American society. With respect to the latter, organizations claimed the socially prominent descendants of the early Syrian community as Arab Americans, regardless of whether these individuals identified themselves as such. They included, for instance, actor and philanthropist Danny Thomas, well-known radio personality Casey Kasem, journalist Helen Thomas, politician and diplomat George Mitchell, and many others. The success of these individuals came to signify the compatibility of Arab culture and values with American society.

At an organizational level, the desire to promote a more evenhanded approach to Palestine and, later, Iraq necessitated a deeper engagement with the American political process. National Arab American organizations became, in essence, lobbyists seeking to counteract the powerful pro-Israeli lobby by reaching out to legislators, foreign policy-makers, and other powerful political actors. An important discourse that emerged through these activities was that the unwavering support for Israel and military intervention in the Middle East was not in America's best interest, nor was it in line with America's democratic values. Again, the important discursive device at play in lobbying activities was the assertion of the fundamental Americanness of Arab Americans – their compatibility with American society and the alignment of their aims and interests with that of America as a whole. That their contributions to political campaigns were, in some instances, rebuffed, indicated that Arab American lobbyists faced many obstacles in making their case (Abourezk, 1984).

Engagement with the mainstream political process intensified and diversified through the 1980s and 1990s as the federal government sought to deport immigrants for espousing political beliefs thought to be at odds with America's security. Most notable was the ADC's 20-year involvement in the case of the LA-8, in which a group of noncitizens – seven Palestinians and one Kenyan – were arrested by the Federal Bureau of Investigation (FBI) for supporting the aims of the Popular Front for the Liberation of Palestine, a faction of the Palestine Liberation Organization (considered at the time to be a terrorist organization). The LA-8 were initially charged under a McCarthy-era statute, the McCarran-Walter Act, "which permitted the deportation of aliens advocating world communism" (Wing, 1999, p. 564). In the 1999 Supreme Court case *Reno v. ADC*, the ADC and its allies charged that the McCarran-Walter Act was in violation of the First Amendment and argued that the "Supreme Court had held years before that resident aliens were protected by the provisions of the First Amendment" (Bosniak, 2006, p. 71). In this instance, the Court ruled in favor of the government, though later federal court decisions struck down McCarran-Walter and blocked the Immigration and Naturalization Service (INS; now Immigration and Customs Enforcement) from deporting the LA-8. Eventually the federal government dropped all charges against the LA-8 (American-Arab Anti-Discrimination Committee, 2007). However, the enactment of new antiterrorism laws in the 1990s expanding the federal government's ability to monitor, detain, and deport those suspected of "aiding" terrorism (as discussed by Moore, 1999) required the ADC and other organizations to remain vigilant and engaged with the legislative process. Importantly, this kind of legal work brought the ADC into working relationships with organizations such as the American Civil Liberties Union and brought Arab American organizations more squarely into the civil-rights-advocacy realm.

There were other kinds of Arab American organizational activity and activism aside from these large national organizations. Arab American students, for instance, became involved in university campus politics in the 1980s and 1990s, which were oriented around identity-based claims and critiques of exclusionary social norms and narratives (Gutierrez, 1994). Arab American student organizations appeared on campuses and mobilized in support of the first Palestinian Intifada (a popular uprising against the Israeli occupation of Gaza and the West Bank that began in 1987) and against the U.S. invasion of Iraq in 1991. Student organizations, in conjunction with Arab American scholar-activists, were also instrumental in initiating Arab American studies courses within university ethnic-studies programs and, in a few instances (most notably at the University of Michigan), creating dedicated Arab American Studies programs and fellowships. In general, student organizations sought to legitimize the presence of Arabs and Arabness in American society and to draw attention to the connections between American imperialism in the Arab world and the cultural subordination of Arabs in the U.S. itself. In their growing assertiveness, Arab American student and faculty activists found themselves involved in acrimonious debates with pro-Israeli student groups and faculty who accused Arab American activists of anti-Semitism for their criticisms of Israel. Some of these debates fed into high-profile tenure and hiring disputes involving Arab American scholars accused of anti-Israel bias, anti-Semitism, and "terrorist sympathies" (e.g. Flaherty, 2013; Kramer, 2008).

Post-9/11 Arab American Activism and the Drive to Legitimate the Arab American Community

The events of September 11, 2001, did not alter the broad contours of Arab American activism as much as they reinforced and amplified existing responses to Arab American marginalization. The

9/11 attacks, to be sure, had a significant impact on Arab American communities, which faced the increasingly overt characterization of Arab and Muslim societies as inherently barbaric, violent, and foreign. The linkage between Arabs and terrorism was nothing new, but the process of racialization in the post 9/11 period – which tended to lump together Arabs, Muslims, South Asians, and others, regardless of national, ethnic, or faith backgrounds, into a single, stigmatized category of "Muslim" – was especially pernicious (Love, 2009). A stridently anti-Muslim discourse, which posited Muslims, and especially politicized Islam, as the enemy of the West, provided justification for the U.S. invasions of Afghanistan in 2001 and of Iraq in 2003. Closer to home, it legitimated state surveillance of Arab Americans and other Middle Easterners, whose loyalty to America was suspect. As Howell and Shryock (2003, p. 444) note, "In the aftermath of 9/11, Arab and Muslim Americans have been compelled, time and time again, to apologize for acts they did not commit, to condemn acts they never condoned, and to openly profess loyalties that, for most U.S. citizens, are merely assumed."

In the wake of 9/11, the most immediate problem facing Arab American activists was the targeting of Arab and Muslim immigrants in FBI and INS dragnet operations. Most alarming was the Special Registration Program that required over 80,000 individuals on nonimmigrant visas to be fingerprinted, photographed, and registered by the INS. Another 127,000 people, according to Cainkar (2006), were registered at their port of entry, and many others were subjected to "interviews" by FBI agents to probe their political beliefs and affiliations. Fewer than fifty of those registered were found to have criminal records, and none was found to have connections with terrorist organizations. Nevertheless, the specific targeting of "suspicious" groups would continue for years after 9/11, abetted by the PATRIOT Act, which greatly expanded the federal government's power to monitor citizens' personal communications, arrest and detain noncitizens, search personal records and information without a court order, and use wiretapping and other modes of surveillance without court oversight (Salaita, 2005).

Many ordinary people from Arab and/or Muslim backgrounds – especially those with insecure immigration status – responded to the unwanted attention of the post-9/11 period by keeping a low profile and by submitting quietly to what Salaita (2005) has called "imperative patriotism," manifested in the ubiquitous display of American flags in front yards and shop windows. Others, however, became more vocal, more visible, and more intent upon explaining their community in their own terms, rather than in terms set by the media and conservative commentators. Activist responses to the 9/11 events and the subsequent War on Terrorism varied. The larger national lobbying organizations, as well as some more localized organizations, continued to pursue a more conciliatory approach that emphasized the Americanness of Arab Americans – their contributions to society, their loyalty, their family values – while defining America as a country of diversity and tolerance. These groups continued to work through mainstream political channels, lobbying for or against domestic and foreign-policy legislation, and working with other, non-Arab organizations to promote civil rights. These groups also intensified their efforts to boost Arab American voter registration and electoral participation, as seen with the Yalla Vote initiative sponsored by the Arab American Institute.

For these organizations, public relations efforts – more than protest – have been the key to political empowerment and the normalization and destigmatization of Arabness in American society. A key phrase used within this sector has been "bridge building," suggesting the role of activists in developing positive connections between their community and the broader public. Activists have also deployed a discourse of the American immigrant experience that highlights the initial discrimination faced by all immigrants and their eventual inclusion in American society through hard work and civic participation (Nagel & Staeheli, 2005; Staeheli & Nagel, 2006). The growing emphasis on bridge building in the aftermath of 9/11 has led activists to encourage community members to participate in local (non-Arab) volunteering opportunities and service activities; it has also led to a flourishing of Arab cultural activities and events, including dance performances, culinary fairs, and music and arts festivals. Activists interviewed by Nagel and Staeheli in their research on Arab American activism after 9/11 suggested that these kinds of innocuous, seemingly apolitical activities were an important political strategy to reduce hostility toward Arab Americans and to build understanding in a non-threatening way. Activists, in this sense, have sought to translate Arab culture to mainstream America and to create a vocabulary "to explain Arab culture or, more casually, Arab 'behavior' to a curious public" (Salaita, 2005, p. 162).

Since 9/11, national Arab American organizations, while otherwise wary of state surveillance, have also been keen to compile demographic data about the Arab American population and to improve Census data-collection techniques. (People originating in Arab countries continue to be categorized as White/Caucasian by the U.S. Census Bureau; most data on Arab Americans come from place-of-birth data and the ancestry question on the American Community Survey). The importance of "accurate" data lies partly in the ability to dispel misperceptions about the Arab American population (for instance, by showing many of those counted as Arab American to be highly educated, well integrated into American society, and Christian) and to reveal the community's numerical strength and hence, potential political power. Additionally, Helen Samhan, former executive director of the Arab American Institute, has argued that a broad "Middle Easterner" Census category would more accurately reflect the experiences of Arab-origin immigrants and their descendants as a racialized minority, and enable more effective documentation of civil rights abuses and hate crimes (Gualtieri, 2009, p. 183). For advocates like Helen Samhan, the push for a new Census category positions the Arab American community as a legitimate member of multicultural America while affording them formal (federal) recognition as people of color (Samhan, 1999).

Some activists have been less inclined to follow the conciliatory line of larger national organizations and have criticized, in particular, efforts by national and local Arab American organizations to cooperate with law-enforcement officials in the War on Terrorism. The years after 9/11, for instance, revealed tensions between large national organizations and their local branches, with the latter in some cases taking a more oppositional stance toward the American security state and the War on Terrorism at home and abroad. Following earlier trends among campus activists, some of these individuals and groups have identified themselves as, and have sought solidarity with, people of color and have mobilized anticolonial discourse to combat the structural oppression of Arabs and other racialized groups. There has been increasing participation of Arab Americans in progressive, pro-immigrant, and antiwar coalitions – though as Naber (2002) notes, such progressive coalitions are often fraught with tensions because of the continued contentiousness of Palestinian/anti-Zionist politics. Some activists, as well, have begun to raise questions about sexism and homophobia *within* Arab and Arab American communities, while resisting Orientalist discourses about the oppressiveness and illiberalism of Arab and Muslim societies.

In the aftermath of 9/11, the issue of Palestine – once central to the coalescence of an Arab American identity – seemed to fade into the background, partly due to fears among Arab Americans that political advocacy and philanthropic efforts on behalf of Palestine would make them vulnerable to state surveillance and even terrorism charges (Howell & Shryock, 2003). To be sure, Palestine has remained a defining issue for some. Since the early 2000s, Palestine activism has flourished through new electronic media, which have allowed otherwise scattered and isolated individuals to mobilize around the rights of Palestinians and opposition to Israeli policies. An example of electronic activism is Al Awda (the Palestinian Right to Return Coalition), which describes itself as a broad-based, non-partisan, democratic, grass-roots organization of students and activists. But the deepening fragmentation of the Palestinian nationalist movement and the increasingly sectarian character of many current conflicts in the Arab world (e.g. the civil war in Syria and ongoing conflict in Iraq) has led many Arab American organizations to avoid all but the most innocuous statements about Middle East politics and to focus instead on more unifying domestic and civil rights issues (for a discussion of the relationship between transnational and domestic activism, see Nagel & Staeheli, 2010).

Case Example: Embedding Community Narratives Through the Creation of the Arab American National Museum

The case of the Arab Community Center for Economic and Social Services (ACCESS), a large social service and advocacy organization in Dearborn, Michigan, illustrates the ways in which activists have worked to create an Arab American community and to position this community as a legitimate component of the American multicultural mosaic. Immigrants from various parts of the Arab world have been settling in Dearborn since the early twentieth century, attracted by employment in Henry Ford's massive River Rouge factory (completed in 1928) and by opportunities to start small businesses. These early settlers were joined after World War II by waves of immigrants fleeing various conflicts and traumas in the Arab world: Palestinian refugees displaced by the creation of Israel in 1948 and the occupation of the West Bank and Gaza in 1967; Lebanese fleeing their country's civil war between 1975 and 1990; and Iraqis escaping the turmoil and poverty created by two U.S.-led wars in 1991 and 2003. These newer waves of immigrants settled in a city that, by the late 1960s, was reeling from the restructuring of the U.S. automotive industry. In 1971, local volunteers and activists created ACCESS to address rising levels of poverty brought about by the restructuring of the River Rouge plant and increasing numbers of layoffs. By the 1990s, ACCESS had grown from a storefront operation run by volunteers into a large, highly professionalized organization with several programs oriented around public health, citizenship education, youth, employment, and cultural sensitivity training. As ACCESS consolidated its presence in Dearborn, bringing together an array of immigrant and refugee groups under the Arab American umbrella, it also gained significant stature beyond Dearborn's Southend as a model of community-based, private-sector service provision (Rignall, 2000).

One of the major achievements of ACCESS was the establishment in 2005 of the Arab American National Museum – the first museum dedicated to Arab and Islamic heritage and culture in the U.S. That the construction of the museum took place only a few years after the trauma of the 9/11 terrorist attacks, during a period of heightened suspicion of and discrimination against Arabs and Muslims, speaks to the patience and persistence of Arab American activists in securing a place for themselves at America's "multicultural table" (Kurien, 2007). At a more fundamental level, the Arab American National Museum represents the successful construction of a public, pan-ethnic, Arab American category and a narrative of community that weaves together the experiences of turn-of-the-century Syrian settlers with those of post-1965 émigrés from Arab states. This narrative asserts a shared past, present, and future for those who trace their origins to the Arab world, despite significant differences among them based on cohort, generation, class, religion, gender, and the like.

As demonstrated by the fanfare around the opening of the museum and its subsequent affiliation with the Smithsonian Institution, there has been a measure of success for Arab American activists in terms of the community's inclusion within dominant narratives of the American immigrant experience and its participation in the mainstream political processes. Bridge building, in short, has paid off. Indeed, in some respects Arab Americans have become the minority group *du jour*, with public figures and institutions clamoring to include Arab American figures in their organizations and in public representations of diversity and multiculturalism. Arab activists have even succeeded in declaring Arab American Heritage Month, which, according to the Arab American Institute, is celebrated in several municipalities and schools in the U.S. Equally notable has been the identification of Arab Americans as a significant demographic category by professional organizations, government agencies, and trade organizations (the Public Relations Society of America, for instance, provides a list of resources for reaching a "multicultural audience" that includes a number of Arab American organizations). This kind of inclusion can easily be dismissed as tokenism or even commodification (Naber, 2002), but it does indicate the growing capacity of Arab Americans to shift the terms of group representation and to challenge more strident forms of anti-Arab and anti-Muslim discourse.

Critique

Despite the successes of Arab American activists in reframing Arabness in the U.S. context, many people who trace their origins to the Arab world continue to face obstacles to full participation in the dominant American public sphere. Most obviously, they continue to contend with an aggressive national security state that has deployed its sweeping authority to monitor organizations and individuals suspected of dangerous political sympathies. Arabs from Muslim backgrounds, in particular, have encountered extreme episodes of hostility, most notably in reaction to efforts to construct mosques. One example was the vitriolic opposition to the construction of a mosque in Murfreesboro, a suburb of Nashville with a growing population of mostly middle-class Muslims of Arab and South Asian origins. In this instance, local residents argued that Islam preached violence and terrorism and accused Muslims of trying to replace the U.S. Constitution with Sharia law. The presence of a mosque, they suggested, would be a threat to the security of their town and their country. A similar set of discourses underpinned the hostility toward the construction of Park51, a multistory Islamic community center located near the site of the Twin Towers in Lower Manhattan (DeFoster, 2015; Huq, 2011). These and other cases are indicative of the ways in which more inclusive rhetoric of American diversity and multiculturalism become intertwined with long-standing hostilities in the U.S. toward Arabs and Muslims.

As scholars explore the ways in which Arab Americans navigate the tensions in American society between multicultural inclusion and racist exclusion, they must be mindful of the contestedness of Arab American as a social category. Scholarship on Arabic-speaking immigrants and their descendants, much like Arab American activism, has tended to accept the concept of an Arab American community as a social reality. In some ways, the Arab American community has indeed become a social reality, enacted, performed, and reproduced in countless cultural festivals and community events organized by those who identify as Arab American. Yet scholars must consider the proliferation of competing identity projects among those who are often grouped as Arab Americans. The formation of Muslim American counter-publics since 9/11, for instance, signifies a fragmentation of the Arab American community-building project and the undermining of the narrative of "Arab" as an inclusive, multifaith category – a narrative that has been carefully cultivated by Arab American activists and that has its roots in liberal-secular forms of Arab nationalism.

The conflation of Arabs and Muslims in U.S. political rhetoric, moreover, has encouraged some Arab-origin groups – especially Christians – to distance themselves explicitly from stigmatized Arab/Muslim identities and to adhere to what some would consider much narrower or even parochial affiliations, such as "Lebanese", "Chaldean", or "Coptic" (Gualtieri, 2009; Shryock, 2008; Witteborn, 2007). The rejection of Arab identity among Christians has a long history that is linked to the political strategies of European imperial powers in the late nineteenth and early twentieth centuries and to feelings of marginalization within secular, but Muslim-dominated, nationalist movements (Makdisi, 1996; Robson, 2011; Sharkey, 2008). Scholars and activists alike have often sidelined these competing forms of collective identity in pursuit of a cohesive narrative of an Arab American community. The point is that there is a need to acknowledge and to explore further the competing and overlapping identities and political projects among those whose origins are traced to the Arab world.

At the same time, however, scholars should not automatically view the formation of multi-ethnic Muslim organizations or of more particularistic organizations based on religion or nationality as undermining Arab American organizations. Nagel and Staeheli (2010) highlight that Arab American activists have multiple identities and affiliate themselves with different kinds of organization. Being Muslim American or Lebanese or Chaldean, in other words, does not necessarily preclude being Arab American, though clearly, for some, these identities are incompatible. The challenge facing scholars is how to represent the perpetually unsettled and pluralistic nature of Arab American identity and of collective identities in general (Staeheli, 2008).

Conclusion

Arab American activists have, over the course of several decades, created a counter-public marked by a degree of internal cohesiveness that is capable of engaging with, challenging, and claiming membership in the mainstream public. The very notion of "Arab American" and the production of a coherent narrative about the community's formation, from the earliest migrations from the Ottoman Empire to contemporary flows from Arab states, owes a great deal to community activists. Again, this is not to say that "Arab American" is a category meaningful only to activists; on the contrary, in responding to marginalization and mainstream hostility as Arab Americans, community activists have made this identity meaningful to many who fall within this category by virtue of their place of origin. "Arab American" is, however, an actively constructed category; it is a political project that has been fostered, cultivated, and made meaningful to others through organizational practices.

As a socially constructed category, "Arab American" comes up against a variety of other community-building projects and alternative political identities. These projects and identities emerge within the fluid political landscape in the U.S., where political claims are often articulated by identity-based groups. They are also partly generated by international events and global processes. While collective indignation over the situation in Palestine continues to unite Arabs of different nationalities and backgrounds, conflicts of more recent vintage appear to be highly divisive, pitting Shi`as against Sunnis, and Christians against Muslims. It is remarkable, given the deepening political rifts in the Arab world, that secular, pan-Arab identities have remained so relevant to Arab American activists and members of Arab American organizations. It may be that the contentiousness of Arab world politics will lead Arab American organizations to orient their activities even more fully around domestic issues. The question is whether the focus on the collective experiences of Arab immigrants in the U.S. can counteract other conceptions of community that may be more relevant to newer immigrant groups.

References

Abourezk, J. G. (1984). Slighting Arab-Americans. *The New York Times*, August 28. Retrieved from www.nytimes.com/1984/08/28/opinion/slighting-arab-americans.html

Abu el-Haj, T. R. (2007). 'I was born here, but my home, it's not here': Educating for democratic citizenship in an era of transnational migration and global conflict. *Harvard Educational Review* 77(3), 285–316.

American-Arab Anti-Discrimination Committee. (2007). Victory for "L.A.8": Case dropped after 20-years. October 31. Retrieved from www.adc.org/index.php?id=3219

Anthias, F. & Yuval-Davis, N. (2005). *Racialized boundaries: Race, nation, gender, colour and class and the anti-racist struggle*. New York: Routledge.

Bosniak, L. (2006). *The citizen and the alien: Dilemmas of contemporary membership*. Princeton, NJ: Princeton University Press.

Cainkar, L. (2006). The social construction of difference and the Arab American experience. *Journal of American Ethnic History* 25(2/3), 243–278.

Conzen, K., Gerber, D., Morawska, E., Pozzetta, G., & Vecoli, R. (1992). The invention of ethnicity: A perspective from the U.S.A. *Journal of American Ethnic History* 12, 3–41.

David, G. C. (2007). The creation of Arab American: Political activism and ethnic (dis)unity (1). *Critical Sociology* 33, 833–862. doi: 10.1163/156916307X230340

Davidson, L. (1999). Debating Palestine: Arab American challenges to Zionism, 1917–1932. In M. Suleiman (ed.), *Arabs in America: Building a new future* (pp. 227–240). Philadelphia, PA: Temple University Press.

DeFoster, R. (2015). Orientalism for a new millennium: Cable news and the specter of the "Ground Zero Mosque." *Journal of Communication Inquiry* 39(1), 63–81. doi: 10.1177/0196859914536577

Flaherty, C. (2013). Judged by unfair standards? *Inside Higher Ed*, June 14. Retrieved from www.insidehighered.com/news/2013/06/14/prominent-arab-studies-scholar-challenges-georgetown-tenure-decision

Fraser, N. (1990). Rethinking the public sphere: A contribution to the critique of actually existing democracy. *Social Text* (25/26), 56–80. doi: 10.2307/466240

Gans, H. J. (1979). Symbolic ethnicity: The future ethnic groups and culture in America. *Ethnic and Racial Studies* 2(1), 1–20. doi: 10.1080/01419870.1979.9993248

Glazer, N. & Moynihan, D. P. (1963). *Beyond the melting pot: The Negroes, Puerto Ricans, Jews, Italians, and Irish of New York City*. Boston, MA: Massachusetts Institute of Technology Press.

Glick Schiller, N., Basch, L., & Szanton Blanc, C. (1995). From immigrant to transmigrant: Theorizing transnational migration. *Anthropological Quarterly* 68, 48–63. doi: 10.2307/3317464

Gualtieri, S. M. (2009). *Between Arab and White: Race and ethnicity in the early Syrian American diaspora*. Berkeley, CA: University of California Press.

Gutierrez, R. A. (1994). Ethnic studies: Its evolution in American colleges and universities. In D. T. Goldberg (ed.), *Multiculturalism: A critical reader* (pp. 157–167). Oxford: Blackwell.

Howell, S. & Shryock, A. (2003). Cracking down on diaspora: Arab Detroit and America's 'war on terror'. *Anthropological Quarterly* 76, 443–462. doi: 10.1353/anq.2003.0040

Huq, A. Z. (2011). Private religious discrimination, national security, and the First Amendment. *Harvard Law & Policy Review* 5, 347–374.

Jacobson, M. F. (1998). *Whiteness of a different color: European immigrants and the alchemy of race*. Cambridge, MA: Harvard University Press.

Khater, A. (2001). *Inventing home: Emigration, gender, and the middle class in Lebanon, 1870–1920*. Berkeley, CA: University of California Press.

Kramer, J. (2008). The Petition. *The New Yorker* 84(9), 50–59.

Kurien, P. (2007). *A place at the multicultural table: The development of an American Hinduism*. Piscataway, NJ: Rutgers University Press.

Love, E. (2009). Confronting Islamophobia in the United States: Framing civil rights activism among Middle Eastern Americans. *Patterns of Prejudice* 43(3/4), 401–425. doi: 10.1080/00313220903109367

Makdisi, U. (1996). Reconstructing the nation-state: The modernity of sectarianism in Lebanon. *Middle East Report* (200), 23–26. doi: 10.2307/3013264

Moore, K. M. (1999). A closer look at anti-terrorism law: Arab-American Anti-Discrimination Committee v. Reno and the construction of aliens' rights. In M. Suleiman (ed.), *Arabs in America: Building a new future* (pp. 84–99). Philadelphia, PA: Temple University Press.

Naber, N. (2000). Ambiguous insiders: An investigation of Arab American invisibility. *Ethnic and Racial Studies* 23, 37–61. doi: 10.1080/014198700329123

Naber, N. (2002). So our history doesn't become your future: The local and global politics of coalition building post September 11th. *Journal of Asian American Studies* 5, 217–242. doi: 10.1353/jaas.2003.0019

Nagel, C. R. & Staeheli, L. (2005). 'We're just like the Irish': Narratives of assimilation, belonging, and citizenship among Arab-American activists. *Citizenship Studies* 9(5), 485–498. doi: 10.1080/13621020500301262

Nagel, C. R. & Staeheli, L. (2010). ICT and geographies of British Arab and Arab American activism. *Global Networks* 10(2), 262–281. doi: 10.1111/j.1471-0374.2010.00285.x

Pulido, L. (2002). Race, class, and political activism: Black, Chicana/o, and Japanese-American Leftists in Southern California, 1968–1978. *Antipode* 34(4), 762–788. doi: 10.1111/1467–8330.00268

Rignall, K. (2000). Building the infrastructure of Arab American identity in Detroit. In N. Abraham & A. Shryock (eds.), *Arab Detroit: From margin to mainstream* (pp. 49–59). Detroit, MI: Wayne State University Press.

Robson, L. (2011). *Colonialism and Christianity in mandate Palestine*. Austin, TX: University of Texas Press.

Salaita, S. G. (2005). Ethnic identity and imperative patriotism: Arab Americans before and after 9/11. *College Literature* 32(2), 146–168. doi: 10.1353/lit.2005.0033

Samhan, H. (1999). Not quite white: Race classification and the Arab-American experience. In M. Suleiman (ed.), *Arabs in America: Building a new future* (pp. 209–226). Philadelphia, PA: Temple University Press.

Shaheen, J. (2001). *Reel bad Arabs: How Hollywood vilifies a people*. New York: Olive Branch Press.

Shain, Y. (1996). Arab-Americans at a crossroads. *Journal of Palestine Studies* 25(3), 46–59. doi: 10.1525/jps.1996.25.3.00p01247

Sharkey, H. J. (2008). *American Evangelicals in Egypt: Missionary encounters in an age of empire*. Princeton, NJ: Princeton University Press.

Shryock, A. (2008). The moral analogies of race: Arab American identity, color politics, and the limits of racialized citizenship. In A. Jamal & N. Naber (eds.), *Race and Arab Americans before and after 9/11: From invisible citizens to visible subjects* (pp. 81–113). Syracuse, NY: Syracuse University Press.

Staeheli, L. (2008). Citizenship and the problem of community. *Political Geography* 27, 5–21. doi: 10.1016/j.polgeo.2007.09.002

Staeheli, L. & Nagel, C. R. (2006). Topographies of home and citizenship: Arab American activists. *Environment and Planning A* 38, 1599–1614.

Suleiman, M. (1999). Introduction: The Arab immigrant experience. In M. Suleiman (ed.), *Arabs in America: Building a new future* (pp. 1–21). Philadelphia, PA: Temple University Press.

Taylor, C. (1997). The politics of recognition. In A. Heble, D. P. Pennee, & J. R. Struthers (eds.), *New contexts of Canadian criticism* (pp. 98–130). Peterborough, Ontario: Broadview Press.

Thomas, W. I. & Znaniecki, F. (1920). *The Polish peasant in Europe and America: Monograph of an immigrant group* (vol. 5). Boston, MA: Richard G. Badger.
Waters, M. C. (1990). *Ethnic options: Choosing identities in America*. Berkeley, CA: University of California Press.
Wing, A. K. (1999). Reno v. American-Arab Anti-Discrimination Committee: A critical race perspective. *Columbia Human Rights Law Review* (31), 561–596.
Witteborn, S. (2007). The situated expression of Arab collective identities in the United States. *Journal of Communication* 57, 556–575. doi: 10.1111/j.1460-2466.2007.00357.x
Yancey, W. L., Ericksen, E. P., & Leon, G. H. (1985). The structure of pluralism: "We're all Italian around here, aren't we, Mrs. O'Brien?" *Ethnic and Racial Studies* 8(1), 94–116. doi: 10.1080/01419870.1985.9993476
Young, I. M. (1990). *Justice and the politics of difference*. Princeton, NJ: Princeton University Press.

PART II

Lifespan Development

7
YOUTH DEVELOPMENT
An Ecological Approach to Identity

Kristine J. Ajrouch, Julie Hakim-Larson, and Rand Ramadan Fakih

Youth constitutes a fluid age category, generally referencing human development processes that precede adulthood. This chapter considers youth as the period that spans infancy through the age of 24, when basic educational and/or training commitments are generally completed. During this phase of development, individuals experience the process of becoming aware of and negotiating racial, ethnic, and gender identities. The salience of such identities occurs through various agents of socialization, starting at birth. Family constitutes the first influential agent of socialization, teaching children basic ideas of who they are and conveying expectations about their actions and beliefs. As children grow and begin to have contact with others beside family, through school activities and opportunities for peer interactions, they often encounter new ideas about what is expected by those outside their families, ideas that sometimes conflict with parental expectations. Community and media also play an important role in youth development, with their presence beginning at birth, but often growing as children spend increasingly more time outside the family context. The characteristics that an agent of socialization exhibits, and the effects they have on youth, likely vary depending on context.

This chapter examines the process of youth development and the impact of socialization among Arab Americans. The distinctiveness of Arab Americans as an ethnic group stems from the fact that their visibility is intimately tied to events and political instabilities in the Arab world. This reality places them in a uniquely marginal position as "not quite White" (Samhan, 1999), yet not fully accepted as a legal minority (Cainkar, 2009). This wider societal experience provides an overarching context for the study of Arab American youth development within an ecological model. This chapter explores theoretical models for understanding youth identity development, and then reviews research findings related to the ways in which family, peers/school, community, and media play a role in the identities of Arab American youth. This is followed by a case example to illustrate concepts and ideas introduced throughout the chapter. Finally, the chapter concludes with a critique of current research and suggests future directions for better understanding Arab American youth development.

Theoretical Frameworks Addressing Youth Identity Development

One of the central developmental tasks youth face on their journey to adulthood is the establishment of a stable identity (Erikson, 1968). This task is accomplished through the exploration of various roles and ideals, which ultimately leads to important identity commitment domains including occupation, religion, ideology, and gender roles (Erikson, 1968; Marcia, 1966). To Erikson, the culmination of the process of exploration and commitment leads to an achieved ego-identity, which refers to a sense of integration of the self as well as a sense of wholeness that derives from the past while including future goals. The construct of ego-identity incorporates the motivation, emotions, and attitudes that organize the life experiences of the developing young person (Lazarus, 1991).

Marcia (1980) extended Erikson's ego-identity theory by proposing a set of four identity statuses: diffuse, foreclosed, moratorium, and achieved. These statuses describe the processes through which individuals deal with the psychological task of establishing an identity. The criteria for each of these four categories or statuses are based on whether youth have explored alternative goals, values, and beliefs, and have made commitments in important life areas including occupation, ideologies (i.e. political and religious beliefs), and interpersonal values. Individuals who have not yet thought about identity issues and have failed to make commitments across life-defining areas are considered to be diffuse. Individuals who have committed to a particular identity domain but made this commitment by conforming to parental or societal values and beliefs rather than by exploring for themselves alternative options are considered to be foreclosed. On the other hand, individuals who are in the midst of actively evaluating all their options and experimenting with identities and beliefs but have not yet made a decision or commitment are classified as being in moratorium. Finally, an achieved identity represents a status in which individuals have reached a clear sense of self by undergoing identity exploration and making personal commitments to particular goals and beliefs. An achieved identity, considered the most adaptive status, is associated with various markers of psychological wellbeing (Kroger, 2003).

Although Erikson (1968) proposed multiple domains of identity (sexual, religious, political, ideological, and occupational), he emphasized that healthy development results from reconciling and integrating various identities into a single unified, consistent identity. These assumptions have led some researchers to operationalize and treat identity as a global construct (De Haan & Schulenberg, 1997; Goossens, 2001). Identity integration may be especially complex for Arab American youth because they have various intertwined and competing identities within a single domain (e.g. national identity, ethnic identity, and religious identity) that they must synthesize. In addition, even if integration is achieved, it is not clear whether a single identity, defined as an aggregate of multiple identity components, can explain domain-specific behaviors as well as individuals' adaptations to culture and society within which their lives are embedded. As such, drawing solely on Erikson's theory to conceptualize identity development of Arab American youth may obscure understanding of domain-specific identities that are particularly salient for this group, one of which is ethnic identity.

From a social psychological perspective, one important aspect of identity results from an individual's social group membership (Tajfel, 1981; Tajfel & Turner, 1986). According to social identity theory, individuals are motivated to develop positive social identities based on their group membership (Tajfel, 1978, 1981; Tajfel & Turner, 1986). A positive social identity is established when individuals evaluate their ingroup more favorably than the outgroup. In turn, ingroup favoritism leads to higher self-esteem as ingroup members claim the positive characteristics of the group as their own. As such, the group provides them with a sense of belonging to the world and acts as a central source of pride and self-esteem.

However, for members of socially devalued groups, such as Arab Americans, who are often portrayed in an unfavorable light (Sirin et al., 2008) that sometimes includes associations with terrorism (Sirin & Balsano, 2007), maintaining favorable definitions of group membership may be challenging. If Arab American youth internalize negative stereotypical beliefs and views of their own group from mainstream groups and media, they might be at risk for displaying lower self-esteem and experiencing loss of meaning and a sense of confusion in their lives. However, Tajfel and Turner (1986) proposed that in the face of devaluation of their group, individuals may reinterpret the meaning of their group membership (social identity) by rejecting external judgments and by comparing themselves to the outgroup on a new dimension to which they are superior to reestablish positive distinctiveness (e.g. Arab Americans have higher income and education than Americans, or exhibit higher moral standards). Accordingly, based on their socialization experiences and the larger social context in which they live, Arab American youth may adopt either a positive or a negative view of their own group.

Phinney (1989) drew on Tajfel's theory of social identity, Erikson's theory of ego-identity formation, and Marcia's work on ego-identity statuses to conceptualize and measure ethnic identity. Empirical work using Phinney's (1992) Multigroup Ethnic Identity Measure (MEIM) delineated two important dimensions of ethnic identity: ethnic identity affirmation and ethnic identity exploration (Roberts et al., 1999). Ethnic identity affirmation refers to an individual's sense of belonging and attachment to the group, whereas ethnic identity exploration denotes the extent to which individuals have investigated and learned about their ethnic background by reading books, talking to other people about their ethnic group, and participating in cultural practices and activities.

Ethnic identity is one of the aspects of social identity that is of particular relevance to youth, especially Arab Americans. This aspect of identity draws attention to ethnic group membership (Phinney, 1990, 2003). Beliefs regarding one's ethnicity are crucial for the psychological wellbeing of Arab American youth, whose social groups are misrepresented, misperceived, held in low esteem, and often discriminated against. Ethnic identity may be the shield through which youth can assert themselves in the face of threats to their sense of self. The centrality of ethnic identity is attested to by various research studies indicating that a positive attitude toward one's ethnic group among youth is associated with positive developmental outcomes including academic success (Supple, Ghazarian, Frabutt, Plunkett, & Sands, 2006), intrinsic motivation for learning (Okagaki, Frensch, & Dodson, 1996), and increased self-esteem (Carlson, Uppal, & Prosser, 2000; Costigan, Koryzma, Hua, & Chance 2010; Umaña-Taylor, Gonzales-Backen, & Guimond, 2009). A similar line of research has also found that ethnic identity may mitigate the negative effects of discrimination on the psychological wellbeing of various minority groups (e.g. Seaton, 2009; Sellers, Copeland-Linder, Martin, & Lewis, 2006; Umaña-Taylor, Wong, Gonzales, & Dumka, 2012), including Arab Americans (Fakih, 2014).

In relation to ethnic identity development, Phinney (1989, 1990, 1996) proposed that members of all ethnic groups progress through three stages: ethnic identity diffusion/foreclosure (also referred to as unexamined), moratorium, and achievement. In the initial, unexamined stage, adolescents may not give much thought to what their ethnicity means. Alternatively, they may adopt the values and attitudes ascribed to their group as their own; in this case, adolescents do not examine issues related to their ethnicity for themselves; rather, attitudes from their parents or the dominant group toward their ethnic group are often passively adopted. The second stage, moratorium, is marked by an increased salience of ethnicity. Adolescents explore the meaning of their ethnicity by engaging in various activities, including reading books about their culture, associating with same-ethnicity peers, participating in cultural events, and joining ethnic youth organizations. Finally, during the third stage, achievement, adolescents develop a clearer understanding of what their ethnicity means to them and build a strong sense of affiliation with and affinity toward their ethnic group.

Identity, however, does not develop in a vacuum; there is a growing consensus in the theoretical and empirical literature that identity is not only multidimensional but also highly context dependent. The ecological systems theory put forward by Bronfenbrenner (1989) conceptualizes the context in which the adolescent develops as a set of nested structures including the microsystem, the exosystem, and the macrosystem. The microsystem encompasses the relationship individuals have with their immediate environment, such as relationships with parents and peers. The exosystem involves the more distal environments that may indirectly influence development; an important exosystem may include neighborhood characteristics (i.e. living in an ethnically dense community vs. living in more ethnically diverse communities). Finally, the macrosystem encompasses the larger sociocultural context and may include public policies, laws, customs, political beliefs, and mass media. In addition, central to this theory is the recognition that individual characteristics interact with contextual factors to influence development. Of particular relevance to Arab youth is the prevalence of gender differences in parental and community socialization practices, which may differentially inform the process of identity development. As such, drawing on Bronfenbrenner's ecological systems model helps review the proximal and distal factors that may either promote or obstruct the development of a positive identity among Arab American youth.

Agents of Socialization for Arab American Youth Development

The ecological model of human development highlights four agents of socialization that influence youth identity: family, peers/school, community, and the media. Each is proposed to exert an effect on youth development for Arab Americans.

Family

The family context, as a microsystem, represents the very first point of socialization for children. Identities gleaned from interactions between and among family members are especially salient for children. In Arab culture, a child's identity is very much influenced by the parent-child relationship (Beitin & Aprahamian, 2014). One important value that children learn with regard to interpersonal relationships is to show respect for adults and to engage in hospitable, polite, and cordial behaviors when in the presence of guests (Nydell, 2006). Interactions that communicate to a child that he or she is an extension of the parent produce a feeling of intense closeness and connectedness in the Arab family (Joseph, 1999). It is common for a mother or father to refer to the child as *`eyouni* (my eyes), *mama*, or *baba*. Open and frequent affectionate displays and verbalized expressions of endearment toward children by parents, grandparents, aunts, uncles, cousins, and other extended family members are common (Simon, 1996). As such, this socialization process begets a sense of self that is tightly connected to adults and other children in the family. Family socialization fosters a collective identity in which the individual is viewed as important, yet best understood in relation to close and significant others.

Within this family connectedness, children often begin to learn identities around both gender and ethnicity. Learning male and female identities is a universal experience, regardless of ethnic group membership. In the Arab American family context, however, the concept of patrilineality renders traditional aspects of a gendered identity central (Ajrouch, 1999; Beitin & Aprahamian, 2014). Patrilineal family structure is a system of descent that entitles members to certain rights based on gender and also guarantees automatic family affiliation through the father (Aswad, 1988). This arrangement places enormous responsibility and simultaneous privilege on male members because it is men in the family who ensure security, maintain continuity of the family line, and provide a sense of belonging. Girls also learn responsibility toward the family in that their actions and behaviors have the potential to confer, or conversely challenge, family reputation and honor. As such, girls are often seen as valuable and in need of protection.

In the U.S. context, tensions sometimes arise between youth and parents, especially concerning daughters. Girls who learn to navigate between the culture of their parents and the dominant culture will undoubtedly benefit from both worlds (Ajrouch, 2005). However, situations may arise where girls embrace one culture over the other. Interestingly, these conflicting expectations often provide more opportunities for girls to choose various roles that include any combination of traditional and American opportunities (in the best of cases), while boys often get pushed into the role of economic provider (Ajrouch, 2004).

Learning what it means to be a boy and what it means to be a girl also has enormous influence on the meaning behind ethnic identity. The saliency of ethnicity becomes important as children reach adolescence. Adolescence fosters more opportunities to experience social life outside the family context. As a result, Arab American children learn that their taken-for-granted assumptions about how things are and should be do not necessarily represent the worldviews of others. Parental restrictions on girls during these years are especially indicative of factors that contribute to young people's sense of their ethnicity (Ajrouch, 1999, 2000, 2004). For instance, though dating is frowned upon generally, leniency toward boys is evident in that parents often turn a blind eye to their sons' dating activities, but directly prohibit it for their daughters. Moreover, other family members, including brothers, will actively ensure female family members do not date, often justifying their interference as a necessary part of their role as protector. It should be noted, however, that restrictions on girls' dating behaviors, thought to represent a kind of moral superiority to the dominant culture (see Espiritu, 2001), is not unique to Arab Americans, and seems to reflect the foundations of ethnic identity for many groups both today and historically (Ajrouch, 2004).

Peers/School

Interactions in school and with peers represent another key microsystem that influences various facets of identity. It should be noted that Arab Americans report relatively high academic achievement (Fakhoury, 2012; Tabbah, Miranda, & Wheaton, 2012), as well as comparatively higher education levels than the majority of Americans (Read, 2004). Yet, a positive sense of self among Arab Americans appears more threatened in high school years compared to middle school years (Tabbah et al., 2012). Arab American identity issues arise concerning curriculum engagement, boy–girl interactions (dating), and immigrant–U.S.-born conflict.

Curriculum engagement concerns the ways in which schools present material during instruction, including topics chosen for lessons as well as peer reactions to the lesson topic. For instance, partial information or misinformation related to current and recent historical events that touch on Arabs coupled with minimal factual instruction about Arabs in the classroom often lead to teacher and students promulgating stereotypical images of Arabs, especially Arab women, as uneducated and oppressed (Mango, 2012). Though multicultural education continues to invite widespread debate (Modood, 2013), experiences such as the above have led to calls for inclusion of Arab Americans in school curricula. In particular, there is a perceived need to encourage teachers to address misrepresentations, and to empower all students, regardless of race or ethnicity, with the skills to recognize when thoughts of prejudice and acts of discrimination are being circulated (Mango, 2012; Tabbah et al., 2012; Wingfield, 2006).

The way in which curriculum material is presented and discussed in the school setting represents a critical issue for identity, but gender matters also arise as central to identity in peer and school interactions. Gendered elements of school and peer interactions become more prominent with the advent of institutionally sanctioned activities such as school dances. Dating activities become prominent during high school, and therefore gender relations emerge with sexual possibilities. With these developments, ethnic attributes may become the basis by which to separate groups. For instance, referencing the notion that Arab girls are not allowed to date, but "White" girls are, signifies a symbolic boundary shaped by gender relations (Ajrouch, 2004). Symbolic boundaries represented through beliefs about dating behavior serve to form, or reinforce, racial and ethnic group belonging. Experiences regarding identity are increasingly more gendered and the realization of being "Arab" becomes quite salient as youth reach adolescence (Ajrouch, 1999).

Though gender relations emerge as important to identities, experiences vary among Arab American youth, especially comparing those who are U.S.-born to immigrants. In a study of Arab American immigrant attitudes toward education, Fakhoury (2012) found that immigrant youth often encountered negativity from U.S.-born Arab Americans, shunned and not accepted into the social circles of those who were U.S.-born. Arab immigrant youth, often referred to as "boaters," have been described negatively by U.S.-born Arab Americans within the school setting (see Ajrouch, 2004). This dynamic may reflect the acculturation process, whereby the U.S. born, especially the second generation or children of immigrants, strive for American aspects of their identity by distancing themselves from immigrant culture (Ajrouch, 2000, 2004). In sum, the peer and school settings highlight the influence of curriculum, gender, and immigrant interactions as influential microsystems on identity for Arab American youth.

Community

Arab American communities are uniquely structured to serve many of the economic and social service needs of the children, adolescents, and families who reside within them. Taking an ecological systems approach (Bronfenbrenner, 1994), services for Arab youth in local organizations and multicultural community centers can be viewed as having an interactive influence and impact on the developing child and adolescent in conjunction with the influences of parents, peers, schools, neighborhoods, and religious institutions. For Arab Americans, these community centers, which may or may not include affiliations with religious institutions, are uniquely situated within major U.S. metropolitan areas of various states, including California, Michigan, Illinois, Pennsylvania, New York, and Washington, D.C., among others.

Important to the ego-identity of youth is how they feel they are perceived within their neighborhoods and communities, as well as within the broader society in which they live. One youth-focused community center is located in Philadelphia, Pennsylvania, and is called Al Bustan: Seeds of Change; "al bustan" means "the garden" in Arabic. The mission of Al Bustan is to promote the enculturation and cultural identity of Arab American youth through exposure to the language and cultural traditions of the Arab world, including music and the visual arts. The center aims to promote a positive self-image among Arab American youth, as well as disseminate celebrated cultural aspects to non-Arab youth. To broaden education about Arab culture, Al Bustan fosters inclusion of both Arab and non-Arab youth of various racial and ethnic backgrounds into its cultural programs, which involve learning the Arabic language, summer camp activities, and various art and music workshops and events. For example, Al Bustan held a video workshop in which Arab American adolescents were among participants who were given the opportunity to use film media to explore their sense of inclusion and belonging to American society given the challenges to their identities in the contemporary exclusionary sociopolitical climate (Abu El-Haj, 2009). The resulting films, which emphasized universal human values, rights, and issues related to the human need for inclusion and belonging, are available to educators through the Al Bustan website.

Like Al Bustan in Pennsylvania, opportunities for Arab youth to engage in community and religious events exist throughout the major metropolitan regions of the U.S. In addition to Christian churches (e.g. Maronite Catholic and Chaldean Catholic) and Islamic mosques that have primarily Arab congregations, there are community agencies such as the Arab Community Center for Economic and Social Services (ACCESS) in Michigan, the Arab American and Chaldean Council in Michigan, and the Arab American Family Support Center in New York. Arab heritage festivals, music performances, and Arab film festivals are among the events across America that are sponsored by these religious institutions and community agencies.

While at the local level the need for inclusion and belonging may be met for some Arab American youth through community programs and organizations, it is also the case that feelings of being excluded from the broader American society are experienced by many Arab American youth. Some Arab American youth are sensitive to the fact that media images often portray Arabs as "enemies" of America and as "terrorists" (Wray-Lake, Syvertsen, & Flanagan, 2008). Fortunately, advocacy organizations such as the Arab American Institute in Washington, D.C., and the American-Arab Anti-Discrimination Committee promote Arab American youth understanding of issues around prejudice and discrimination through their educational campaigns, and foster youth participation in American political debates and discourse around social issues. Such organizations play a crucial role in promoting the wellbeing of first and second generation Arab American youth by counteracting the possible negative effects experienced from sociocultural adversities such as discrimination and the stress of acculturation within their neighborhoods and communities (Ahmed, Kia-Keating, & Tsai, 2011). Though community support serves as a potentially influential resource, social support in general has been found to be an essential resource for Arab American youth in North America.

Social support can be provided within family, peer, and broader community contexts. For example, in their study of Muslim Arab American youth aged 11–15 years in metropolitan Detroit, Ramaswamy, Aroian, and Templin (2009) found that perceived social support from family members, school personnel, and friends showed a negative relation with self-reports of stressful daily hassles and internalizing problems such as depression and anxiety. Other studies have shown that Arab youth in Canada show beneficial psychological effects when they perceive social support from others within their social network (Abu-Laban & Abu-Laban, 1999; Paterson & Hakim-Larson, 2012). Moreover, Arab Canadian youth had more friends who were also relatives than did youth of other Canadian ethnic groups (Daniel, 2013). It may be that extended family and community networks are more readily accessible to Arab Canadians compared to other Canadian ethnic groups. Another possibility is Arab youth have reacted by favoring the comfort of their ingroup relationships given possible feelings of being socially excluded from the mainstream culture.

It should be noted, however, that though ethnic community contexts serve as an important refuge from the negative images and exclusionary sentiments felt through contact with American society, community living also exhibits social control of youth through gossip (see Ajrouch, 2000). These experiences serve to reinforce a strong sense of ethnic identity, but also sometimes propel youth to leave community settings in search of greater anonymity and less constraint. In sum, community, as an exosystem context, plays an influential role in the socialization and identity of Arab American youth. Next, a more omnipresent agent of socialization in the macrosystem that permeates beyond the physical and emotional space of community is considered: the media.

Media

Media play a role in socialization as a macrosytem influence. Media portrayals have enormous impact on group position, often serving as the only source of information about a group when personal contact has not occurred (see Blumer, 1958). For Arab Americans, media portrayals of their cultural group are underrepresented, yet when present, are overwhelmingly negative (Shaheen, 2009). Media coverage through news reports and entertainment venues rarely shows Arabs in a positive light. Media depictions also intersect with other contexts, such as peers and school settings, to impact Arab American youth. Indeed, the pervasiveness of negative images has been found to influence peer relations as early as elementary school. Arab American youth report that media coverage of 9/11 has led to them being called "terrorists" in the school setting (Kumar, Warnke, & Karabenick, 2014). Those who have come of age in the twenty-first century face more visible and negative media portrayals in the aftermath of the attacks on the World Trade Center.

Another aspect of media that is important to consider involves consumption patterns. Rapid technological developments have led to a proliferation of media outlets. Indeed, media consumption among Arab American youth reflects habits of youth in general (Hernandez, 2012). Hernandez reported that as older Arab American youth access more media sources, including radio, online newspapers, magazines, and social networking sites, they are more likely to perceive their groups as negatively portrayed as compared to their younger counterparts. The absence of positive media portrayals poses genuine concern, as children often look to wider societal representations to emulate, especially as they increase social contact beyond the family context.

Case Example: Social Influences on the Development of Alex and Ranya

Arab American youth grow up in multiple contexts, each of which present various, sometimes conflicting expectations about their identities and sense of self. The case example that follows depicts a brother and sister, born in the late twentieth century to an immigrant father who has owned his own business since the age of 20, and a U.S.-born mother with advanced education who worked as a university researcher. Alex Aboud was the first-born child, and for the first four years of his life he was an only child. His paternal grandfather, who lived approximately 20 minutes away, bestowed special grace on Alex, as the first-born child, through visits, attention, and gifts. In the traditional patrilineally organized Arab family, Alex represented the next generation family leader. Four years later, Alex's sister, Ranya, was born. Around the time that Ranya was born, Alex asked for a toy kitchen set. Alex's father became distressed, commenting that boys do not play with kitchen sets, to which Alex's mother replied that some of the greatest chefs in the world are men! Alex's mother bought him the kitchen set.

Striving to reject the special treatments allotted to boys with which she had grown up, Alex and Ranya's mother conscientiously strived to provide each child with equal opportunities and expectations. Alex developed an interest in politics at an early age through discussions with his father, and by the age of seven could recite every U.S. president forwards and backwards. When Ranya was three, she helped her mother box-up her baby clothes, and in that process was told by her mother that she should save an infant undershirt that said "Future U.S. President," because Ranya's father had bought it for her when she was still in her mother's stomach. Ranya opened her eyes wide in disbelief and asked, "Did daddy think I was going to be a boy?"

Though the children did not live in an ethnic enclave, they regularly visited relatives and friends who lived in a densely populated Arab American community, and also were highly active in transnational activities, visiting their parent's homeland of Lebanon at least once a year during the summer months. Their early education was at a private Montessori school, located in the midst of a metro-area suburb that was increasingly attracting Arab American families, but located 20 miles east of Alex and Ranya's home. At the Montessori school, both Alex and Ranya were taught about ethnic and cultural diversity, with difference identified as something to celebrate. For instance, school activities encouraged ethnic sharing, such as "pot lucks" where students brought food representative of their culture. Such events contributed to and highlighted positive elements of diversity, and in so doing contributed to building a sense of community. The school curriculum and peer interactions stressed equality, understanding, and solidarity.

Both Alex and Ranya eventually left the Montessori school to attend the public school in their homogenously "White" neighborhood. In September 2001, Alex was in middle school and Ranya in third grade. When the terrorist attack happened, Alex discussed with his parents what he would say to friends at school given that the terrorists were Arab Muslims. He came up on his own with the response, "though the terrorists were Arab Muslims, not all Arab Muslims are terrorists." Ranya did not feel the need to address the attacks in school, but a number of years later, when she was in middle school and on the volleyball team, she lost her pendant – with the Arabic word for God written on it – at a game. She came home quite upset because she had worn the pendant since she was a young child. When her mother suggested she ask the coach if anyone had found it, she cried in response: "How would I describe what I lost? That it says God in Arabic? They will think I am a terrorist!"

Though both children developed friendships with others from diverse backgrounds throughout their childhood, as they grew into adolescence they increasingly preferred to spend time with friends from their ethnic background. Upon entering college, both became highly involved in ethnic student organizations, but differed in the extent to which they shared their social activities with their parents. While Alex brought home girlfriends, Ranya never shared that she had a boyfriend. Perceiving that her father would not approve, she chose to keep that part of her life hidden from her parents and brother. Her brother, having observed peers in the ethnic community, made a point to question her on a regular basis about whom she would be with and where she planned to be, as a means to monitor her social activities.

As this case example illustrates, a sense of group belonging for older children and adolescents is critical to an overall sense of wellbeing. The importance of group belonging to wellbeing is supported by most developmental models that incorporate ego identity (e.g. Kegan, 1982; Loevinger & Wessler, 1978). Several challenges to this feeling of group connectedness emerged for Alex, Ranya, and their family, however. Among these challenges were inconsistent expectations regarding how to fulfill gender role obligations, both as prescribed by their ethnic values as well as by the mainstream culture. Though Alex and Ranya's mother strived to practice gender equality, messages received from other systems of influence, including peers and community, played a role in shaping gender expectations concerning life goals and social relationships. Ranya, in particular, found herself negotiating cultural expectations learned through both her family and wider American society. Challenges were made, as well, regarding how to negotiate their ethnic identities while attempting to acculturate in an interpersonal climate of non-Arab peers, whom they suspected of unjust and unfair perceptions. Given these stressful circumstances, Arab American youth may retreat into the familiar territory of same ethnicity peers, where a supportive net is in place to help in shaping their identities.

Critique

The literature on Arab American youth focuses almost exclusively on middle and high school, as well as college settings. There are several possible reasons for the scant literature outside these contexts. First, the fact that the U.S. Census Bureau does not officially recognize Arab Americans as a minority group that is distinct from the majority "White" or Caucasian population (Samhan, 2014) means that Arab American youth are often classified with European American youth in research studies. This makes identifying Arab American youth in large data sets highly challenging, if not impossible. Some exceptions to this exist in Arab American ethnic enclave regions where it is possible to recruit through local community advertisements (e.g. Aroian, Templin, Hough, Ramaswamy, & Katz, 2011; Ramaswamy et al., 2009). Another possible reason for the lack of research on Arab American youth outside school settings may be the general difficulty that researchers have in recruiting both parents and their children for studies given parental time constraints, the lack of incentives to participate, and language and literacy barriers. One way around this is for researchers to go into the homes and to use oral interview methodologies in Arabic for data collection, a method that was utilized by Aroian and colleagues (2011). For Arab American families to participate in studies, some education around the purpose and value of the research, the limitations of confidentiality, informed consent and assent issues are necessary but complicating features of the research process.

The Arab American population is heterogeneous and represents racially and ethnically diverse Arabic-speaking people from all of the 22 members of the League of Arab States, spanning the Middle East to the northern coast of Africa (Nydell, 2006). Thus, rather than engaging in pan-Arab ethnic gloss in future studies addressing Arab youth issues, it may be more constructive to focus on the specific national, ethnic, and religious backgrounds of youth. This is important given the unique sociopolitical backgrounds of families by country of origin (e.g. Egyptian Coptic youth, Iraqi Muslim youth, Lebanese Maronite youth, Palestinian Muslim youth, etc.).

Recently, attention has focused on the possible protective factors and the positive development of minority American youth (Cabrera, Beeghly, & Eisenberg, 2012). Though not specific to Arab American youth, the special volume introduced by Cabrera and colleagues contains studies that identify possible relevant protective factors in need of further study. At the individual level, these include a young person's ability to self-regulate and maintain bicultural language skills that could potentially enhance their cognitive development. A strong ethnic identity has also been found to be an individual protective factor. At the family level, having positive relationships with family members, enhanced by maternal warmth and paternal involvement, were identified as potential protective factors. Finally, neighborhood and community supports that provide extra-curricular and after-school activities for youth were also suggested as potential protective factors.

Taking a biopsychosocial approach to healthy development in Arab American youth involves a consideration of which levels of analyses will yield the most fruitful results to understanding youth resilience in the face of psychosocial stressors and hardships (Hakim-Larson, Nassar-McMillan, & Ajrouch, 2014). Masten (2007) identified five areas for understanding resilience in the developing individual. These are in the domains of religion/spirituality, family life, peer relationships, schools/teachers, and community/culture. Research on prevention that is meant to optimize the wellbeing of Arab American youth will need to take a multilevel systems approach, incorporating these five domains, to gain a more comprehensive picture of Arab youth functioning (Hakim-Larson et al., 2014).

Conclusion

This chapter used an ecological theoretical framework to organize what is known about Arab American youth, highlighting the ways that family, peers, community, and media influence youth development. For Arab American youth, socialization at various levels (from the micro- to exo- to macrosystems influences development) both directly and in conjunction with one another. The potential for positive development may result from each, but in the face of possible strengths also lie challenges. Research has focused primarily on the adolescent years, leaving a dearth of information on early childhood development. Given that agents of socialization begin to influence development at birth, more systematic attention to the years before adolescence will address a gap in the field. Youth is an important point in the life course, increasingly seen as a period during which gender and ethnic identity emerge as key elements in daily interactions. Overall, this chapter has shown that Arab Americans as a group are increasingly more visible, though their diversity of experiences must be recognized in order to most effectively address developmental challenges and maximize success.

References

Abu El-Haj, T. (2009). Imagining postnationalism: Arts, citizenship education, and Arab American youth. *Anthropology & Education Quarterly* 40(1), 1–19. doi: 10.1111/j.1548-1492.2009.01025.x

Abu-Laban, S. M. & Abu-Laban, B. (1999). Teens between: The public and private spheres of Arab-Canadian adolescents. In M. W. Suleiman (ed.), *Arabs in America: Building a new future* (pp.113–128). Philadelphia, PA: Temple University Press.

Ahmed, S. R., Kia-Keating, M., & Tsai, K. H. (2011). A structural model of racial discrimination, acculturative stress, and cultural resources among Arab American adolescents. *American Journal of Community Psychology* 48(3–4), 181–192. doi: 10.1007/s10464-011-9424-3

Ajrouch, K. J. (1999). Family and ethnic identity in an Arab American community. In M. Suleiman (ed.), *Arabs in America: Building a new future* (pp. 129–139). Philadelphia, PA: Temple University Press.

Ajrouch, K. J. (2000). Place, age, and culture: Community living and ethnic identity among Lebanese American adolescents. *Small Group Research* 31, 447–469. doi: 10.1177/104649640003100404

Ajrouch, K. J. (2004). Gender, race, and symbolic boundaries: Contested spaces of identity among Arab American adolescents. *Sociological Perspectives* 47, 371–391. doi: 10.1525/sop.2004.47.4.371

Ajrouch, K. J. (2005). Women, gender and youth culture and movements: United States. In S. Joseph (ed.), *Encyclopedia of women and gender in Islam* (vol. 2, pp. 795–798). Netherlands: Brill Publishers.

Aroian, K. J., Templin, T. N., Hough, E. E., Ramaswamy, V., & Katz, A. (2011). A longitudinal family-level model of Arab Muslim adolescent behavior problems. *Journal of Youth and Adolescence* 40, 996–1011. doi: 10.1007/s10964-010-9615-5

Aswad, B. (1988). Strengths of the Arab family for mental health considerations and therapy. In I. Ahmed & N. Gray (eds.), *The Arab American family: A resource manual for human service providers* (pp. 93–101). Lansing, MI: Eastern Michigan University and ACCESS.

Beitin, B. K. & Aprahamian, M. (2014). Family values and traditions. In S. C. Nassar-McMillan, K. J. Ajrouch, & J. Hakim-Larson (eds.), *Biopsychosocial perspectives on Arab Americans: Culture, development and health* (pp. 67–88). New York: Springer. doi: 10.1007/978-1-4614-8238-3_4

Blumer, H. (1958). Race prejudice as a sense of group position. *Pacific Sociological Review* 1(1), 3–7. doi: 10.2307/1388607

Bronfenbrenner, U. (1989). Ecological systems theory. In R. Vasta (ed.), *Annals of child development* (vol. 6, pp. 187–249). Greenwich, CT: JAI Press.

Bronfenbrenner, U. (1994). Ecological models of human development. In T. N. Postlethwaite & T. Husen (eds.), *International Encyclopedia of Education* (2nd edn., vol. 3, pp. 1643–1647). Oxford: Elsevier.

Cabrera, N. J., Beeghly, M., & Eisenberg, N. (2012). Positive development of minority children: Introduction to the special issue. *Child Development Perspectives* 6, 207–209. doi: 10.1111/j.1750-8606.2012.00253.x

Cainkar, L. (2009). *Homeland insecurity: The Arab American and Muslim American experience after 9/11*. New York: Russell Sage Publications.

Carlson, C., Uppal, S., & Prosser, E. C. (2000). Ethnic differences in processes contributing to the self-esteem of early adolescent girls. *The Journal of Early Adolescence* 20, 44–67. doi: 10.1177/0272431600020001003

Costigan, C. L., Koryzma, C. M., Hua, J. M., & Chance, L. J. (2010). Ethnic identity, achievement, and psychological adjustment: Examining risk and resilience among youth from immigrant Chinese families in Canada. *Cultural Diversity and Ethnic Minority Psychology* 16, 264–273. doi: 10.1037/a0017275

Daniel, S. (2013). *Immigrant and non-immigrant youth in Canada: Cultural orientation, ethnicity of friends, and life satisfaction among four ethnic groups* (Master's thesis). Available from ProQuest Dissertations and Theses database (UMI No. MR87354).

De Haan, L. G. & Schulenberg, J. (1997). The covariation of religion and politics during the transition to young adulthood: Challenging global identity assumptions. *Journal of Adolescence* 20, 537–552. doi: 10.1006/jado.1997.0108

Erikson, E. H. (1968). *Identity: Youth and crisis* (1st edn.). New York: Norton.

Espiritu, Y. (2001). "We don't sleep around like white girls do": Family, culture, and gender in Filipina American lives. *Signs* 26(2), 415–440. doi: 10.1086/495599

Fakhoury, N. (2012). *Academic achievement and attitudes of Arab-American immigrants* (Master's thesis). Available from ProQuest Dissertations and Theses database (UMI No. 1533342).

Fakih, R. R. (2014). *Ethnic identity among Arab Americans: An examination of contextual influences and psychological well-being* (Doctoral dissertation). Available from ProQuest Dissertations and Theses database (UMI No. 3613203).

Goossens, L. (2001). Global versus domain-specific statuses in identity research: A comparison of two self-report measures. *Journal of Adolescence* 24, 681–699. doi: 10.1006/jado.2001.0438

Hakim-Larson, J., Nassar-McMillan, S. C., & Ajrouch, K. J. (2014). Health and well-being in Arab Americans: Prevention strategies using a biopsychosocial approach. In S. C. Nassar-McMillan, K. J. Ajrouch, & J. Hakim-Larson (eds.), *Biopsychosocial perspectives on Arab Americans: Culture, development, and health* (pp. 387–401). New York: Springer. doi: 10.1007/978-1-4614-8238-3_18

Hernandez, P. A. (2012). *Muslim American youth and media* (Doctoral dissertation). Available from ProQuest Dissertations and Theses database (UMI No. 3508762).

Joseph, S. (ed.) (1999). *Intimate selving in Arab families: Gender, self, and identity*. Syracuse, NY: Syracuse University Press.

Kegan, R. (1982). *The evolving self: Problem and process in human development*. Cambridge, MA: Harvard University Press.

Kroger, J. (2003). Identity development during adolescence. In G. R. Adams & M. D. Berzonsky (eds.), *Blackwell handbook of adolescence* (pp. 205–226). Malden, MA: Blackwell Publishing.

Kumar, R., Warnke, J. H., & Karabenick, S. A. (2014). Arab-American male identity negotiations: Caught in the crossroads of ethnicity, religion, nationality and current contexts. *Social Identities: Journal for the Study of Race, Nation and Culture* 20, 22–41. doi: 10.1080/13504630.2013.864464

Lazarus, R. S. (1991). *Emotion & adaptation*. New York: Oxford University Press.

Loevinger, J. & Wessler, R. (1978). *Measuring ego development*. San Francisco, CA: Jossey-Bass.

Mango, O. (2012). Arab American women negotiating identities. *International Multilingual Research Journal* 6, 83–103. doi: 10.1080/19313152.2012.665823

Marcia, J. E. (1966). Development and validation of ego-identity status. *Journal of Personality and Social Psychology* 3, 551–558. doi: 10.1037/h0023281

Marcia, J. E. (1980). Identity in adolescence. In J. Adelson (ed.), *Handbook of adolescent psychology* (pp. 159–187). New York: John Wiley.

Masten, A. S. (2007). Resilience in developing systems: Progress and promise as the fourth wave rises. *Development and Psychopathology* 19, 921–930. doi: 10.1017/S0954579407000442

Modood, T. (2013). *Multiculturalism* (2nd edn.). Malden, MA: Polity Press.

Nydell, M. K. (2006). *Understanding Arabs: A guide for modern times* (4th edn.). Boston, MA: Intercultural Press.

Okagaki, L., Frensch, P. A., & Dodson, N. E. (1996). Mexican American children's perceptions of self and school achievement. *Hispanic Journal of Behavioral Sciences* 18, 469–484. doi: 10.1177/07399863960184003

Paterson, A. D. & Hakim-Larson, J. (2012). Arab youth in Canada: Acculturation, enculturation, social support, and life satisfaction. *Journal of Multicultural Counseling and Development* 40, 206–215. doi: 10.1002/j.2161-1912.2012.00018.x

Phinney, J. S. (1989). Stages of ethnic identity development in minority group adolescents. *The Journal of Early Adolescence* 9(1–2), 34–49. doi: 10.1177/0272431689091004

Phinney, J. S. (1990). Ethnic identity in adolescents and adults: Review of research. *Psychological Bulletin* 108, 499–514. doi: 10.1037/0033-2909.108.3.499

Phinney, J. S. (1992). The Multigroup Ethnic Identity Measure: A new scale for use with diverse groups. *Journal of Adolescent Research* 7, 156–176. doi: 10.1177/074355489272003

Phinney, J. S. (1996). Understanding ethnic diversity: The role of ethnic identity. *American Behavioral Scientist* 40, 143–152. doi: 10.1177/0002764296040002005

Phinney, J. S. (2003). Ethnic identity and acculturation. In K. M. Chun, P. Balls Organista, & G. Marín (eds.), *Acculturation: Advances in theory, measurement, and applied research* (pp. 63–81). Washington, D.C.: American Psychological Association.

Ramaswamy, V., Aroian, K. J., & Templin, T. (2009). Adaptation and psychometric evaluation of the multidimensional scale of perceived social support for Arab American adolescents. *American Journal of Community Psychology* 43(1–2), 49–56. doi: 10.1007/s10464-008-9220-x

Read, J. G. (2004). *Culture, class, and work among Arab-American women*. New York: LFB Scholarly Publishing LLC.

Roberts, R. E., Phinney, J. S., Masse, L. C., Chen, Y. R., Roberts, C. R., & Romero, A. (1999). The structure of ethnic identity of young adolescents from diverse ethnocultural groups. *The Journal of Early Adolescence* 19, 301–322. doi: 10.1177/0272431699019003001

Samhan, H. H. (1999). Not quite white: Race classification and the Arab-American experience. In Michael W. Suleiman (ed.), *Arabs in America: Building a new future* (pp. 209–226). Philadelphia, PA: Temple University Press.

Samhan, H. H. (2014). Intra-ethnic diversity and religion. In S. C. Nassar-McMillan, K. J. Ajrouch, & J. Hakim-Larson (eds.), *Biopsychosocial perspectives on Arab Americans: Culture, development, and health* (pp. 45–65). New York: Springer. doi: 10.1007/978-1-4614-8238-3_3

Seaton, E. K. (2009). Perceived racial discrimination and racial identity profiles among African American adolescents. *Cultural Diversity and Ethnic Minority Psychology* 15, 137–144. doi: 10.1037/a0015506

Sellers, R. M., Copeland-Linder, N., Martin, P. P., & Lewis, R. L. H. (2006). Racial identity matters: The relationship between racial discrimination and psychological functioning in African American adolescents. *Journal of Research on Adolescence* 16, 187–216. doi: 10.1111/j.1532-7795.2006.00128.x

Shaheen, J. G. (2009). *Reel bad Arabs: How Hollywood vilifies a people*. Northampton, MA: Olive Branch Press.

Simon, J. P. (1996). Lebanese families. In M. McGoldrick, J. Giordano, & J. K. Pearce (eds.), *Ethnicity and family therapy* (2nd edn., pp. 364–375). New York: Guilford.

Sirin, S. R. & Balsano, A. B. (2007). Editor's introduction: Pathways to identity and positive development among Muslim youth in the West. *Applied Developmental Science* 11, 109–111. doi: 10.1080/10888690701454534

Sirin, S. R., Bikmen, N., Mir, M., Fine, M., Zaal, M., & Katsiaficas, D. (2008). Exploring dual identification among Muslim-American emerging adults: A mixed methods study. *Journal of Adolescence* 31, 259–279. doi: 10.1016/j.adolescence.2007.10.009

Supple, A. J., Ghazarian, S. R., Frabutt, J. M., Plunkett, S. W., & Sands, T. (2006). Contextual influences on Latino adolescent ethnic identity and academic outcomes. *Child Development* 77, 1427–1433. doi: 10.1111/j.1467-8624.2006.00945.x

Tabbah, R., Miranda, A. H., & Wheaton, J. E. (2012). Self-concept in Arab American adolescents: Implications of social support and experiences in the schools. *Psychology in the Schools* 49, 817–827. doi: 10.1002/pits.21640

Tajfel, H. (1978). *The social psychology of minorities*. London: Minority Rights Group.

Tajfel, H. (1981). *Human groups and social categories: Studies in social psychology*. Cambridge, England: Cambridge University Press.

Tajfel, H. & Turner, J. C. (1986). The social identity theory of intergroup behavior. In S. Worchel & W. G. Austin (eds.), *Psychology of intergroup relations* (pp. 7–24). Chicago, IL: Nelson-Hall Publishers.

Umaña-Taylor, A. J., Gonzales-Backen, M. A., & Guimond, A. B. (2009). Latino adolescents' ethnic identity: Is there a developmental progression and does growth in ethnic identity predict growth in self-esteem? *Child Development* 80, 391–405. doi: 10.1111/j.1467-8624.2009.01267.x

Umaña-Taylor, A. J., Wong, J. J., Gonzales, N. A., & Dumka, L. E. (2012). Ethnic identity and gender as moderators of the association between discrimination and academic adjustment among Mexican-origin adolescents. *Journal of Adolescence* 35, 773–786. doi: 10.1016/j.adolescence.2011.11.003

Wingfield, M. (2006). Arab Americans: Into the multicultural mainstream. *Equity & Excellence in Education* 39, 253–266. doi: 10.1080/10665680600788453

Wray-Lake, L., Syvertsen, A. K., & Flanagan, C. A. (2008). Contested citizenship and social exclusion: Adolescent Arab American immigrants' views of the social contract. *Applied Developmental Science* 12(2), 84–92. doi: 10.1080/10888690801997085

8
MARRIAGE AND FAMILY
Traditions and Practices Throughout the Family Life Cycle

Juhayna Ajami, Sarah Rasmi, and Nuha Abudabbeh

Although Arab migration to the U.S. has spanned over 120 years, it is marked by three distinct waves of migration. The first wave (1890–1940) consisted of predominantly Christian migrants from Lebanon and Syria. In the second wave (after World War II and the creation of Israel), immigration was dominated by Palestinians and Muslim Arabs. The third wave (after the 1967 Arab-Israeli war) included migrants from many different countries, particularly those escaping war in Lebanon and Iraq (Abudabbeh, 2005). Due to their collective characteristics, most Arabs have migrated with their families throughout these waves, as demonstrated by the low proportion of non-family Arab American households (de la Cruz & Brittingham, 2003).

Regardless of when and how Arabs arrived in the U.S., they were challenged to adapt to a new culture. Arab and American cultures differ in a number of important ways that have implications for family relationships. According to Hofstede (2001), Arab culture is marked by autocratic relationships, adherence to cultural norms, and prioritization of group over individual wants and needs. American culture, on the other hand, emphasizes democratic relationships and prioritizes individual needs over the group. Similarly, Schwartz (2006) found that Arab culture is low on autonomy, in contrast to American culture, which is high on autonomy.

In addition to these significant cultural changes, Arab American families have to adapt to an environment that is unwelcoming and at times hostile. Hostilities and anti-Arab sentiments post 9/11 have been documented by organizations such as the American-Arab Anti-Discrimination Committee (ADC; Ibish, 2008) and in the research literature (e.g. Awad, 2010; Wray-Lake, Syvertsen, & Flanagan, 2008). Discrimination has been found to negatively affect the psychological wellbeing of Arab Americans (Aprahamian, Kaplan, Windham, Sutter, & Visser, 2011). Despite these challenges, many Arab American families flourish and thrive.

This chapter examines how Arab American families navigate the acculturation process by exploring their marital and family features and dynamics, with a focus on the more common heterosexual marital structure. The first section evaluates the applicability of family systems theories to Arab Americans. Subsequently, a review of the literature on Arab American marriage and families is presented. A case example illustrates some key Arab American family dynamics regarding acculturation and intermarriage. Finally, the last section presents a critique of the existing Arab American literature regarding family.

Application of Family Systems and Attachment Theories to Arab American Families

Family systems and attachment theories are commonly used to study family dynamics, including parental, sibling, and marital relationships. These theories were modeled on the relationship dynamics of Western families, which has called into question their applicability to families from different ethnocultural backgrounds (e.g. Rothbaum, Rosen, Ujiie, & Uchida, 2002; Rothbaum, Weisz, Pott, Miyake, & Morelli, 2000). To make these theories more broadly applicable, several scholars have proposed modifications (e.g. van Ijzendoorn & Sagi, 1999). Unfortunately, no studies have examined the relevance of these theories to Arab American populations. Instead, Arabs are often lumped into more general categories such as "collectivistic cultures." While some research has explored Muslim families, it is imperative that readers do not make the mistaken assumption that Arab families are all Muslim families. In fact, most Arab families in the U.S. are Christian (Ajrouch, 2000), and as a result may deal with a variety of family dynamics different to those of their Muslim counterparts.

Ultimately, it is imperative to consider the diversity among Arab American families when attempting to understand their family dynamics. These characteristics include religion, socioeconomic status, nationality, reason for leaving their home country, and degree of acculturation. For instance, an upper-class Lebanese Christian family that has lived in the U.S. for 30 years will likely have a different family culture than a middle-class Iraqi Muslim family that was forced to leave Iraq due to war and has been in the U.S. for one year. This chapter addresses this gap in the literature by critically analyzing the applicability of family systems and attachment theories to Arab American families, while considering the salient diversity within this population.

Family Systems Theories

Family systems theories provide a basis for understanding family dynamics, including communication patterns, power roles, and general structure (Rothbaum et al., 2002). For example, Minuchin (1974) developed structural family theory. In this theory, a family is seen as divided into several coexisting subsystems, which vary with respect to how power and responsibilities are assigned. For example, an older sibling has more power in a sibling subsystem, whereas a parent would have more power in a parent-child subsystem. In contrast to Western families, a traditional Arab American family system would likely consist of many more subsystems that interact on a regular basis, including extended family members such as grandparents, aunts, uncles, cousins, and even close family friends. Given the current state of distribution of Arab families in the West due to wars and displacement, some large families have been forced to separate, leaving smaller, more nuclear families settling in the West. This further changes dynamics, as extended families may not be present to provide the support and guidance they normally do (Beitin & Aprahamian, 2013).

Regarding authority within family systems, structural family theory holds that gender and age play significant roles in the power distribution among subsystems (Minuchin, 1974). Among patriarchal Arab American families, men would hold more power than women in relationships (Joseph, 1999), whether it is a brother-sister, husband-wife, or father-child subsystem. The concept of patrilineality (which indicates that lineage and kinship is determined by the father) has been used to describe Arab and Arab American families (Beitin & Aprahamian, 2013; Joseph, 1999). Age further determines power distribution (Ajrouch, 1999), as a grandfather may hold the most authority in an Arab American family system due to his age and gender.

Structural and systems theories further differentiate between open and closed systems. Whereas an open system involves ongoing communication and interaction with the outside environment, a closed system implies the opposite (Bowen, 1978). In an open system, immigrant and ethnic minority families adopt the customs and language of the settlement country and are deemed to be healthier than those who do not (Goldenberg & Goldenberg, 2012). However, it is important to consider that Arab families are not necessarily unhealthy if they are reluctant to adopt American customs. For example, certain issues such as accepting homosexuality and engaging in premarital relationships and sex, as well as separating/individuating from the family may not be easily adopted by Arab families, no matter how assimilated they are (Abi-Hashem, 2008).

Another characteristic that may be misperceived by outsiders as unhealthy among Arab Americans is the Bowenian family systems theory concept of fusion, which occurs when individual family members are unable to intellectually and emotionally differentiate themselves from others in their family system (Titelman, 1998). Bowen (1985) suggested that families with a stronger tendency to fuse will have more difficulty adapting to stress. However, Arab family relationships may be perceived by observers as fused, given the strong emotional attachment between members and the tendency for individuals to place the demands and wishes of others – particularly elder family members – above their own. On the contrary, Arab American families may actually benefit from these interconnected relationships due to the fundamental support and guidance that their nuclear and extended family provide, which can ease the hardships of leaving their home country and adjusting to the U.S. This is particularly important given that Arabs are discouraged from confiding in outsiders and/or seeking professional help due to their emphasis on privacy and maintaining the family's honor and reputation (Abudabbeh, 2005).

Another concept discussed in Bowenian family systems theory is triangulation, which begins when a distressed dyad includes a third person to reduce the initial anxiety (Kerr & Bowen, 1988). Triangulation is commonly demonstrated in Arab and Arab American families, particularly in interactions between parents and children (Abudabbeh, 2005). In fact, mothers often mediate between the children and their father (Nasir, Abdul-haq, & Toukan, 2008). For example, if a father becomes angry with his children, he is more likely to have their mother scold or punish them, as opposed to handling the situation himself. This may be due to gender roles within the family, as mothers are seen as more responsible for childrearing than fathers. Children are also discouraged from engaging their father in arguments and are taught to obey their father's wishes (Abudabbeh, 2005). The children may be able to communicate more freely with their mother (Abudabbeh, 2005) and are therefore more likely to relay complaints about their father to her, instead of confronting him directly.

Bowenian theory also introduced the concept of the multigenerational transmission process, which states that values, beliefs, feelings, behaviors, and attitudes are transmitted from one generation to the next. Bowen further suggested that relationship patterns, including attachment styles, are often observed and repeated within generations of the same family (Kerr & Bowen, 1988). Research has consistently supported this assertion (e.g. Feng, Giarrusso, Bengtson, & Frye, 1999; Kretchmar & Jacobvitz, 2002). Bowen suggested that this occurs largely through the close relationships that family members have with one another (Kerr & Bowen, 1988). It is likely that the multigenerational transmission process may be even more pronounced in Arab and Arab American families, given the encouragement of strong attachments among family members (Abi-Hashem, 2008).

Attachment Theory

In addition to studying the transmission of attachment styles across generations, some family theorists have focused on understanding the development of attachment within the nuclear family. Attachment theory suggests that mother-child relationships can be characterized as either secure, ambivalent, or avoidant (Ainsworth, Blehar, Waters, & Wall, 1978). According to contemporary views of this theory, parenting that is too enmeshed and overinvolved can lead to insecure (ambivalent) attachment in children. However, what may be viewed as overinvolved and enmeshed parenting may not be maladaptive in different cultural contexts. In Japan, for example, it is common for mothers to assume that they know what their child is thinking, treat the child like they are younger than they actually are, and speak for the child (Rothbaum et al., 2002). Similarly, in Arab culture, mothers may assume that they know what their child wants and needs and may continue to treat them like children even when they are adults (Nasir et al., 2008).

Western theories of psychological development place a value on autonomy and independence beginning in adolescence (Soenens et al., 2007). However, this is not consistent with the norms of Arab culture and family, as individuals do not seek autonomy in the same way (Dwairy, Achoui, Abouserie, & Farah, 2006). Instead, in some Arab American families it is expected that children remain in the family home until marriage, regardless of their age. This is especially true of women, as they may bring shame to themselves and their family if they live on their own before marriage (Al-Krenawi & Jackson, 2014).

Autonomy likely underlies separation/individuation, which refers to the process of distinguishing oneself from one's family by developing one's own perspective, feelings, and ideas (Koepke & Denissen, 2012). Writers have examined the applicability of this concept to immigrant Arab families (Mann, 2004; Timmi, 1995). A number of considerations must be made when understanding separation/individuation for Arab American adolescents. Many Arab American parents may suffer from traumatic reactions due to the displacement and death of family and friends in their home country. These traumatic reactions, in turn, can limit their ability to provide their children with the comfort and emotional support that the children need to successfully navigate adolescence (Abi-Hashem, 2008). Although it is developmentally normative for adolescents to undergo identity exploration (Steinberg & Silk, 2002), it becomes more complicated when it happens alongside parental identity exploration that is triggered by trauma and acculturation challenges. Even in cases where immigration was by choice, parents and adolescents may still simultaneously struggle with issues of identity and acculturation.

Arab American Marriage and Family Relationships

In order to gain a clearer understanding of the applicability of the theoretical issues described above, it is essential to learn about the various dynamics of the Arab American family. Arab families are characterized by strong attachment and mutual dependency that begins in childhood and continues throughout the lifespan, supported by the salience and prevalence of extended families and filial piety. The family is one of the most central and influential aspects of Arab and Arab American culture (Barakat, 1993; Britto & Amer, 2007) and collectively takes precedence over its individual members (Bushfield & Fitzpatrick, 2010). The following sections unpack various aspects of Arab American marriage, including courtship and spousal selection, marriage customs and rituals, and spousal relationships, followed by a section on parent-child relationships throughout the lifespan. Literature regarding Arab Canadian families is included where appropriate given the scarcity of research on Arab American families and the similarity between American and Canadian culture (Hofstede, 2001).

Marriage

Marriage is a particularly important institution in Arab culture as it allows sexual intercourse, making it possible to procreate (Abudabbeh, 2005). The salience of marriage is reflected in recent U.S. Census statistics showing that Arab Americans are more likely to be married and less likely to be divorced or separated as compared to the general American population (Brittingham & de la Cruz, 2005). Arab Americans' challenges in balancing elements of their Arab heritage while also acquiring aspects of American culture become particularly evident when it comes to different cultural norms related to courtship and marriage. As a result, many Arab adolescents and emerging adults living in North America struggle with courtship (including being allowed to date) and finding partners who are both suitable to them and accepted by their family (Rasmi, Daly, & Chuang, 2014).

Courtship and spousal selection. Courtship is considered a prelude to marriage and typically involves the input of the bride and groom's nuclear and extended families (Haddad, Smith, & Moore, 2006). In Arab culture, marriage is viewed as an agreement between two families (Al-Krenawi & Jackson, 2014) – not just two individuals – and as such, extended families may continue to be involved in the couple's life after marriage by providing advice as well as emotional and financial support (Ahmad & Reid, 2008; Chapman & Cattaneo, 2013). Some Arab American families may continue to follow traditional forms of courtship and spousal selection; however, factors such as acculturation may cause some families to move away from these traditions. It is not uncommon for adolescents and emerging adults to desire more involvement in the decision-making process. Many will see their peers in romantic relationships and desire similar experiences, which can lead to conflicts within the family system, particularly if the desired relationship involves someone from a different ethnocultural or religious background (Ajrouch, 1999; Rasmi et al., 2014).

Marriage in Arab culture is largely a religious commitment: Religion plays a significant role in courtship, spousal selection, marital traditions, and spousal relationships. Indeed, certain interfaith marriages – such as between a Muslim woman and a non-Muslim man – are not only viewed as unfavorable but also as religiously forbidden (Keck, 1989). Although these views are often shared by Arab American parents, many youth find it increasingly difficult to adhere to their parents' endogamous ideologies as they grow up surrounded by people from different ethnocultural and religious backgrounds. Preferences for intercultural and interfaith marriage among Arab Americans have been shown to relate to higher levels of cultural assimilation (i.e. English language proficiency) and structural assimilation (i.e. education; Kulczycki & Lobo, 2002). The interfaith marriage issue is more salient for Arab Muslims compared to Christians given the constraints Islam places on intermarriage (Daneshpour, 2009) and because Christians belong to the majority religion in the U.S. Even though Muslim men are permitted to marry "people of the Book" (i.e. Christians or Jews), many parents expect their male children to marry a Muslim Arab woman, given that Islam is passed through the father. It is important to consider that within Christian Arab families, many parents expect their children to marry someone who is also Arab (Rasmi et al., 2014) and Christian.

Marriage customs and rituals. The diversity of Arab Americans is apparent in the variety of traditions, customs, and rituals that characterize their marriages. Across Arab cultures, marriage is considered a sacred union, with both religion and culture influencing the specific rituals performed at the marriage ceremony (Al-Krenawi & Jackson, 2014). Despite a number of intracultural variations, several aspects of Arab and Arab American marriage customs transcend religion and country of origin, including: an engagement period, religious ceremony, and wedding reception.

As is the case with American couples from other ethnic backgrounds, Arab American couples usually get engaged before they get married. European American couples usually become engaged as a function of their romantic love and their decision to spend the rest of their lives together. For Arab American couples from highly traditional families, however, romantic love is seldom the key factor in arranging a union. In Arab culture, engagement may be viewed as a time to get to know the potential partner prior to deciding whether or not to marry. In some cases, the families of a prospective couple will meet to discuss the compatibility of both the couple and the extended families. The length of the engagement period can be determined by the couple's cultural background, age, and financial capabilities (Killawi, Daneshpour, Elmi, Dadras, & Hamid, 2014). Although it is likely that some will adhere to these traditional processes, it is also likely that many couples – particularly those who are more oriented toward American culture – might select their own spouses and prioritize romantic love. Regardless of how a spouse is chosen, it is unlikely that Arab Americans will marry someone without their family's approval.

In Arab culture, the groom and his family are traditionally responsible for most of the wedding and marriage expenses (Rashad, Osman, & Roudi-Fahimi, 2005). The specific traditions practiced, however, are largely determined by a variety of factors, including nationality and religiosity. Once the couple are ready to be married, they usually take part in a religious ceremony that is performed by a cleric (i.e. priest, pastor, or sheikh). A Christian religious ceremony may take place on the same day as the wedding reception. It may be similar to a traditional Christian European American wedding ceremony as it takes place in a church and is performed by a priest or pastor; however, the specific practices performed in the church are likely dependent on the couple's Christian denomination and affiliation. In this case, a religious ceremony would likely be followed by a wedding reception, similar to Christian European American weddings.

With regard to Muslim Arab Americans, the religious ceremony (*nikah*) may occur on the same day or a different day as the wedding celebration. The religious ceremony may take place at a mosque or the bride's family home, with the bride often dressed more modestly than she will be on her wedding day. At the *nikah*, both families will document the *mahr*, the gift from the groom to the bride (Macfarlane, 2012), which could range from a copy of the Qur'an to a sum of money. Other rituals performed at the *nikah* may be influenced by the family's country of origin, religiosity, and personal preferences. For example, an Iraqi *nikah* may include traditions such as showering the couple with sugar over a piece of cloth and having them feed each other honey. These rituals are meant to symbolize wishes for a sweet and happy life. Another tradition that may be practiced among some Arab Americans, particularly those of Egyptian origin, is the preparation of the *gihaz* (or *jihaz*), which includes gifts to the bride such as new clothes and home furnishings (Rashad et al., 2005).

It is customary in both religions and across many Arab cultures to hold henna (herbal dye) parties for the bride and female relatives prior to the wedding reception. At these parties, women will sing, dance, and receive henna tattoos on their hands. The henna party is typically the same weekend as the wedding. Some more acculturated Arab Americans from both Christian and Muslim faiths may also hold a bachelorette party with friends and consider the henna party more of a family affair.

Typically, wedding receptions are void of religious influence and are instead heavily influenced by the family's country of origin. They are held in large ballrooms because they are considered a community affair and attended by many family and friends. Some wedding receptions begin with the bride and groom's entry (*zaffa*) behind a group of musicians and singers, who serve to introduce the new couple to the guests. The wedding reception may be similar to an American wedding: As dinner is served, the bride and groom cut the wedding cake, and guests dance until the end of the evening. Furthermore, wedding guests commonly give cash gifts to the couple by depositing them into a designated box at the wedding reception (Serhan, 2008). Wedding favors (i.e. small gifts for the wedding guests from the bride and groom) may be given out at the wedding ceremony and/or reception. It is possible that some Arab American weddings will follow other traditions, such as segregating men and women throughout the wedding or when dancing begins (El-Aswad, 2010).

The engagement period, religious marriage ceremony, and wedding reception described in this section reflect some traditions of Arab culture. Although it is likely that a portion of Arab Americans adhere to these customs, it is also likely that some will move away from them as they become more oriented to American culture and make modifications that suit their personal preferences. For example, a Muslim Arab American man marrying a Christian European American woman may incorporate traditions from both cultures into their engagement, marriage ceremony, and wedding.

Spousal relationships. Like all couples, the relationship between newly married Arab Americans is shaped by power and gender roles, sexual issues, and extended family influences. Arab and Arab American couples and families are patriarchal in nature, but husbands and wives both have duties to one another (Abudabbeh, 2005; Keck, 1989). Men are expected to be strong and to protect and provide for their wives, who in return are expected to care for and respect their husbands (Al-Krenawi & Jackson, 2014). Women are highly respected in the home and community for their role in continuing the family lineage by bearing children (Erickson & Al-Tamimi, 2001; Read, 2003). Despite this, wives are traditionally expected to defer to their husbands for major financial and family decisions (Al-Krenawi & Graham, 2006; Read, 2004). It is important to note that many factors can affect the patriarchal structure of Arab American families and their adherence to these traditions, including women's involvement in the labor force and financial independence (Beitin & Aprahamian, 2013), as well as the family's socioeconomic status, geographic location, education, generational status, and religious affiliation (Abi-Hashem, 2008; Read, 2002, 2003, 2004).

Discussing sex and sexuality openly with someone other than a spouse is considered taboo (Abudabbeh, 2005) and premarital sex is not accepted in Arab culture (Ajrouch, 1999; Al-Krenawi & Jackson, 2014; Beitin & Aprahamian, 2013). For this reason, Arab families seldom discuss sex with their children, other than to emphasize that it is forbidden to engage in any sexual activity until marriage (Nasir et al., 2008). Although this applies to males and females, parents emphasize this point more strongly with their daughters, who will bring shame to themselves and their families by engaging in premarital sex (Hattar-Pollara & Meleis, 1995). These beliefs about sex represent a departure from mainstream American society, where in many communities it is acceptable to talk about and engage in premarital sex (Finer, 2007). As a result of these cross-cultural differences, many Arab American parents feel pressured to closely monitor and regulate their children's behaviors and activities. Arab American adolescents, in turn, may feel more restricted than their non-Arab counterparts, which can lead to tension between them and their parents. This feeling is particularly pronounced for girls, who often notice that their brothers are afforded more social freedom than they are (Ajrouch, 1999).

As noted previously, the extended family plays a role in the spousal relationship in many ways. First, extended families will often express their opinions on marital and family issues, ranging from how to prepare food to how to raise children. For this reason, in-laws have been cited as a significant source of conflict for Muslim American couples (Chapman & Cattaneo, 2013; Eid, 2005). Given the interconnected nature of Arab families, it is expected that these findings will apply to both Christian and Muslim Arab Americans. Second, extended families often provide the couple with emotional and financial support (Ahmad & Reid, 2008), which can serve to alleviate some marital stressors, but can also create tension as noted in the previous section on family systems theory.

In cases of marriage conflict, some couples might consider divorce. For many Christian Arabs – particularly those who belong to Orthodox sects such as the Coptic Christians – divorce is forbidden except in cases of infidelity or abuse (Keck, 1989). In Islam, divorce is discouraged yet permitted (Alshugairi, 2010). In Muslim marriages where a husband does not agree to a divorce, the wife has the right to divorce him through a process called *al-khul'* (Al-Krenawi & Jackson, 2014; Rashad et al., 2005). Arab American couples who have a civil marriage in the U.S. would be subject to their state's laws. It is important to note, however, that many Arab American couples will remain in an unhappy marriage to maintain stability and avoid the shame associated with divorce (Abu-Ras, 2007). With regard to issues of child custody, while Islamic Sharia (law) dictates certain rules in case of divorce, U.S. family courts abide by the U.S. family law code (Dabbagh, 2011).

Parent-Child Relationships

As noted previously, families represent a core aspect of Arab culture (Cainkar & Read, 2013) and women are given status within the home and community for their role in bearing children and continuing the family lineage (Beitin & Aprahamian, 2013). The interconnectedness and centrality of the family, coupled with the respect shown to women for their role in caring for children, suggests that having children is very important in Arab culture. The following sections discuss family structure and roles, parenting practices, and extended family involvement.

Family structure and roles. Arab culture is characterized by hierarchical and interconnected family relationships (Dwairy et al., 2006; Hofstede, 2001; Schwartz, 2006) and the Arab American parent-child dyad is no exception. The father is the ultimate authority within the family, although this is accorded to the eldest male in his absence. Children are expected to treat their parents and other elders with the utmost respect (Abudabbeh, 2005).

Although mothers carry out the majority of the day-to-day caregiving, fathers are still expected to support, honor, and assume responsibility for their children (Abudabbeh, 2005). These roles become less discrete in Arab American families, as they encounter two significant changes. First, many Arab American families do not have the extended support system they would have had in their home country, which inevitably increases the childrearing burden on the parents. Second, many fathers work long hours outside the house to support the family financially, meaning that the mother has to do an even larger share of the caregiving (Hattar-Pollara & Meleis, 1995). Although Arab American women are less likely to participate in the labor force than the general American population (Read, 2004), many still do (Abi-Hashem, 2008) and it is likely that this will affect the domestic distribution of labor as it does in most families (for a review, see Pleck & Pleck, 1997).

Parenting practices. In a typical Arab or Arab American family, parents are powerful authority figures who socialize children to be obedient to their parents' demands (Kayyali, 2006). Arab Americans tend to parent in ways that are consistent with an authoritarian parenting style. Specifically, parents use vertical communication to lecture their children as opposed to engaging them in more interactive discussion. This is illustrated nicely by a quote from a 21-year-old male Arab Canadian in a recent study: "That's the thing with Arabic parents, their 'no' is unexplainable [sic] and just 'no'" (Rasmi et al., 2014, p. 1137). Children are expected to obey their parents' orders (especially their fathers') without question (Abudabbeh, 2005). Parents may also use corporal punishment to achieve their socialization goals (Kayyali, 2006).

Although these parenting practices may be considered maladaptive in Western countries, they do not necessarily lead to deleterious outcomes for Arab families in their home countries or North America. For example, less parental warmth was more strongly associated with negative youth and family outcomes for European Canadians than with Arab families in Canada, Egypt, and Lebanon (Rasmi, Chuang, & Safdar, 2012). Arab parents may be warm and caring in the treatment of their children (Abudabbeh, 2005), which, along with high levels of interconnectedness (Dwairy et al., 2006), may potentially protect children from experiencing negative individual and familial outcomes as a result of these parenting practices. Thus, perceived parental rejection may not be met as negatively among Arab families, where warmth and control are often separate, mutually exclusive constructs (Rudy & Grusec, 2006).

Arab and Arab American parents socialize their children in ways that are consistent with the gender roles of their culture, with a tendency to treat their sons and daughters differently (Abudabbeh, 2005; Ajrouch, 1999, 2004; Mikulincer, Weller, & Florian, 1993). Boys are typically granted more freedom than girls and are even afforded authority in their fathers' absence, as a way to groom them to be a patriarch in their own household when they have their own families. Girls, on the other hand, are perceived as more vulnerable; therefore, an emphasis is placed on protecting them and guarding their honor (Abi-Hashem, 2008). For example, a group of Arab American adolescent girls perceived their male counterparts to receive more social, but not material, freedom than they did (Ajrouch, 1999). Indeed, some research has shown that Arab brothers can be even stricter with their sisters than their parents are (Ajrouch, 1999).

Parenting Older Children

As they become older, children undergo numerous changes to their identity and peer relationships (Steinberg & Silk, 2002) as they develop their own belief and value systems (Arnett, 2007). These changes can affect the parent-child dyad and disrupt the family equilibrium as the child begins to desire and expect more autonomy. Arab American families are challenged to navigate this developmental process in a cultural context with values and norms that oppose the values and norms of their heritage culture. As a result, some families may experience acculturation gaps, which occur when a parent is more or less oriented to the heritage and/or settlement culture than their child.

Separation/individuation. It is developmentally normative in Western cultures for adolescents to want more autonomy (Steinberg & Silk, 2002). In Western families, this desire is typically met with changes to the family system. For example, parents may grant their children more autonomy or they might allow them to be more involved in family decision-making (Sorkhabi, 2010). Compared to European Americans, Arab adolescents in the Arab region not only desire less autonomy, but they do so at a later age, and are also more likely to conform to their parents' wishes (Dwairy et al., 2006). On the other hand, Arab youth living in Canada and the U.S. might be more likely to desire autonomy as they are socialized alongside European American peers who are taught to be independent and self-reliant. For example, Ajrouch (1999) found that female Arab American adolescents desired more social freedom and felt restricted in comparison to their European American peers. Similarly, a recent study found that a desire for greater independence and autonomy was a source of conflict in Arab Canadian families (Rasmi et al., 2014). On the other hand, some Arab American parents have expressed concern that growing up in the U.S. will allow children too much freedom (Abu Al Rub, 2013; Ajrouch, 1999).

It is important to contextualize Arab Americans' desire for more autonomy within the norms of their heritage culture. European American children are socialized to attain and maintain their independence. Generally, these families do not expect to have very close relationships as the child becomes an adult and his or her parents' age (McGill & Pearce, 1996). Arab children, on the other hand, are socialized to maintain a strong allegiance to their nuclear and extended families throughout their adult years (Abudabbeh, 2005). Arab children are also expected to care for their parents when they age (Barakat, 1993; Khalaila, 2010). Therefore, it is necessary to consider that the concept of separation/individuation assumes a unique meaning in Arab American families. Specifically, Arab American adolescents can desire more personal freedom while still cherishing the advice, support, and ongoing involvement of their parents and extended family.

Acculturation gaps. Arab American adolescents often have to negotiate conflicting demands and expectations that are placed on them by their family, peers, and other socializing agents. At school, for example, some adolescents will primarily speak English, interact with peers who are non-Arab, and learn in a secular environment. At home, however, adolescents may predominantly speak Arabic, practice their religious traditions, and be subjected to parental rules that are designed to enforce Arab cultural norms. Over time, many adolescents become more oriented to their peers and American culture than to their parents, who are more likely to retain their Arab beliefs and culture than their children are (Abudabbeh & Aseel, 1999; Chen & Sheldon, 2012; Rasmi, Chuang, & Hennig, in press). For example, and as previously discussed in this chapter, Arab American adolescents might be more open to dating and exogamous relationships, while their parents are more resistant to these ideas (Ganim, 2001), potentially contributing to intergenerational conflict (Rasmi et al., 2014; Soliman, 2008).

Parents and adolescents experience acculturation gaps when they are differently oriented to their heritage and settlement cultures. The acculturation gap-distress hypothesis (Szapocznik & Kurtines, 1993) posits that children are generally more oriented to the settlement culture, whereas parents are more oriented to the heritage culture, and that these gaps lead to poorer individual and familial outcomes. A recent study conducted with Arab Canadians found some support for this, as emerging adults perceived themselves to be more oriented to Canadian culture and values and less oriented to Arab culture and values than their parents (Rasmi et al., in press). Interestingly, this study found that in some instances, a strong parent-emerging adult relationship decreased the association between perceived acculturation gaps and ethnocultural identity conflict. This finding once again suggests that the warm and interconnected nature of parent-child relationships in Arab families may protect them from experiencing negative outcomes.

In sum, parent-child and other family relationships are best understood when nested within their cultural context (Harkness & Super, 2002). For example, an understanding of the Arab American family processes is furthered by an awareness of Arab cultural beliefs, values, norms, and expectations. As shown in this chapter and the below case example, applying European American parenting models without accounting for Arab cultural properties could result in an oversimplified and inaccurate account of Arab American families.

Case Example: Sama's Best of Both Worlds

Sama was born to first generation Syrian parents living in San Francisco, California. She was greeted at the hospital by her parents, maternal grandmother, two of her aunts, and three older brothers. In typical Arab fashion, news of her birth reached her extended family living in Syria, Palestine, and Lebanon. Raised in a first generation Arab American home, Sama was encouraged to speak Arabic with her parents and went on yearly family vacations to Syria and Lebanon.

As she grew up, Sama struggled to find a balance between Arab and American cultures. The customs and traditions she enjoyed during her childhood became a burden in adolescence. Worried that their daughter would become "too American," her parents enforced strict family rules, including a dress code and curfew. They also forbade any sleepovers and dating. These rules led to many arguments between Sama and her family, as her older brothers also felt inclined to make sure these rules were enforced.

After graduating from high school, most of Sama's friends moved out of their family homes, with some attending out-of-state universities. Sama, on the other hand, was only allowed to enroll in a nearby university, so that she could remain living at home. This caused several arguments between Sama and her family, as she had applied to and was accepted at one of the best universities on the East Coast. During these arguments, Sama felt upset and frustrated that instead of being proud of her accomplishments, her parents accused her of being selfish and disregarding her family's needs and reputation.

Shortly after joining an Arab American student association at university, Sama met Zeyad. He had recently immigrated to the U.S. from Lebanon and joined the association in an effort to meet fellow Arabs at his university. His Lebanese accent reminded her of the summers she spent with her cousins in Beirut, so she felt immediately drawn to him. They began dating shortly thereafter. Sama teased him for being a "boater," a colloquial term describing recent immigrants, and enjoyed teaching him about various aspects of American culture, all of which he seemed to happily embrace. As their relationship grew more serious, they began discussing the possibility of marriage. Although she was comfortable being his girlfriend, Sama harbored some hesitation about marrying Zeyad. The thought of raising children with him reminded her of the intercultural challenges she faced with her parents. Although she felt proud of her cultural background, she did not want her children to struggle as she did. She had always imagined she would marry someone American or Arab American; someone who understood that part of her identity. She was still drawn to Zeyad, however, and her family encouraged her to marry him.

Throughout Sama's childhood, her parents worried that she would eventually marry an "Amreeki" (the Arabic term for "American") and told her on several occasions that she would not be allowed to do so. In order to encourage her daughter to marry a "good Arab boy," Sama's mother recruited her favorite cousin to convince her of the union with Zeyad. This is an example of the triangulation that often occurs in Arab American families. Ultimately, Sama agreed to the marriage because she felt she could raise her children in the perfect balance of both worlds that she yearned for during her youth.

Sama's story illustrates common dynamics that Arab American youth and families experience. While it is not representative of all Arab Americans, it captures some of the acculturation gaps and conflicts that often occur between parents and their children. In addition, it highlights the difficulty reconciling the contradictory Arab and American norms, such as those related to attachment and personal freedom. Whereas Sama's friends were expected and encouraged to separate and individuate, Sama was expected to stay highly embedded within her family relationships even as she entered adulthood. These complex dynamics assume heightened importance when young Arab Americans are ready to marry and wish to find a partner who pleases them as well as their nuclear and extended families.

Critique

An understanding of Arab families has increased in recent years with the publication of comprehensive book chapters by psychologists (e.g. Abi-Hashem, 2008; Abudabbeh, 2005). However, a recent review of research examining Arabs and Arab families found that only 2% of the extant literature focused on immigration and acculturation issues (Beitin, Allen, & Bekheet, 2010). Most of this work has been theoretical or conceptual in nature, and more empirical work is needed. This type of scholarship is imperative in order to build an understanding of the hundreds of thousands of Arab families who are leaving their home countries to move to the U.S., in addition to the millions who have already left.

Because of the paucity of empirical and theoretical research regarding Arab Americans today, there are many gaps in the understanding of Arab American families. First, refugee families should be studied in greater depth, as they are impacted by dispossession and the direct or indirect experience of traumatic events. Many of these families struggle with issues beyond those experienced by typical immigrant families, such as debilitating posttraumatic stress symptoms, which may be transmitted between generations, further transforming gender roles and parenting. Second, the terms "Arab" and "Muslim" are often used interchangeably in the literature, despite the fact that many Arabs are not Muslim and many Muslims are not Arab. It is imperative that this distinction be made in future research in order to avoid inaccurate generalizations. Third, Arab Americans have often been treated as a homogeneous group even though there are many different subcultures within this population based on religion, nationality, socioeconomic status, acculturation, and reasons for migration. As shown in this chapter, these differences can affect family and marriage practices. Therefore, it is of importance that Arab American scholars seek to understand shared as well as nuanced characteristics of this population. Finally, given the diverse nature of families, research on Arab American families must move beyond studying the assumed typical family structure and also explore issues surrounding divorce, single parenting, and blended families.

Conclusion

Arab Americans are challenged to reconcile heritage and settlement cultures that are diametrically opposed on a number of dimensions, including autonomy and individualism-collectivism (Hofstede, 2001; Schwartz, 2006). They also frequently face post-9/11 discrimination, which can negatively affect their health and wellbeing (Ibish, 2008). Yet, many Arab Americans are able to maintain their traditions relating to marriage and family. It is crucial that the attitudes, behaviors, and characteristics of Arab American families are viewed in their unique cultural and sociopolitical context, so that academics and practitioners can better understand their strengths and challenges. Despite the growth in Arab American scholarship, it is imperative that the understanding of this population increases, both generally and with regard to various national, religious, and economic subgroups. This is especially important given the large number of Arab Americans currently living in the U.S., as well as the continued influx of migrants from Arab countries.

References

Abi-Hashem, N. (2008). Arab Americans: Understanding their challenges, needs, and struggles. In A. J. Marsella, J. L. Johnson, P. Watson, & J. Gryczynski (eds.), *Ethnocultural perspectives on disasters and trauma* (pp. 115–173). New York: Springer. doi: 10.1007/978-0-387-73285-5_5

Abu Al Rub, M. F. (2013). *Parenting styles used with preschool children among Arab immigrant parents in a U.S. context* (Doctoral dissertation). Available from ProQuest Dissertations and Theses database (UMI No. 3593350).

Abudabbeh, N. (2005). Arab families. In M. McGoldrick, J. Giordano, & N. Garcia-Preto (eds.), *Ethnicity and family therapy* (pp. 423–436). New York: Guilford Press.

Abudabbeh, N. & Aseel, H. A. (1999). Transcultural counseling and Arab Americans. In J. McFadden (ed.), *Transcultural counseling* (pp. 283–296). Alexandria, VA: American Counseling Association.

Abu-Ras, W. (2007). Cultural beliefs and service utilization by battered Arab immigrant women. *Violence Against Women* 13, 1002–1028. doi: 10.1177/1077801207306019

Ahmad, S. & Reid, D. W. (2008). Relationship satisfaction among South Asian Canadians: The role of 'complementary-equality' and listening to understand. *Interpersona* 2, 131–150. doi: 10.5964/ijpr.v2i2.23

Ainsworth, M. D. S., Blehar, M. C., Waters, E., & Wall, S. (1978). *Patterns of attachment: A psychological study of the strange situation*. Hillsdale, N.J.: Lawrence Erlbaum Associates.

Ajrouch, K. J. (1999). Family and ethnic identity in an Arab American community. In M. Suleiman (ed.), *Arabs in America: Building a new future* (pp. 129–139). Philadelphia, PA: Temple University Press.

Ajrouch, K. J. (2000). Place, age, and culture: Community living and ethnic identity among Lebanese American adolescents. *Small Group Research* 31, 447–469. doi: 10.1177/104649640003100404

Ajrouch, K. J. (2004). Gender, race, and symbolic boundaries: Contested spaces of identity among Arab American adolescents. *Sociological Perspectives* 47, 371–391. doi: 10.1525/sop.2004.47.4.371

Al-Krenawi, A. & Graham, J. R. (2006). A comparative study of family functioning, health, and mental health awareness and utilization among female Bedouin-Arabs from recognized and unrecognized villages in the Negev. *Health Care for Women International* 27, 182–196. doi: 10.1080/07399330500457978

Al-Krenawi, A. & Jackson, S. O. (2014). Arab American marriage: Culture, tradition, religion, and the social worker. *Journal of Human Behavior in the Social Environment* 24, 115–37. doi: 10.1080/10911359.2014.848679

Alshugairi, N. (2010). Marital trends in the American Muslim community: A pilot study. *Journal of Muslim Mental Health* 5, 256–277. doi: 10.1080/15564908.2010.551275

Aprahamian, M., Kaplan, D. M., Windham, A. M., Sutter, J. A., & Visser, J. (2011). The relationship between acculturation and mental health of Arab Americans. *Journal of Mental Health Counseling* 33(1), 80–92.

Arnett, J. J. (2007). Socialization in emerging adulthood: From the family to the wider world, from socialization to self-socialization. In J. E. Grusec & P. D. Hastings (eds.), *Handbook of socialization: Theory and research* (pp. 208–230). New York: Guilford.

Awad, G. H. (2010). The impact of acculturation and religious identification on perceived discrimination for Arab/Middle Eastern Americans. *Cultural Diversity and Ethnic Minority Psychology* 16, 59–67. doi: 10.1037/a0016675

Barakat, H. (1993). *The Arab world: Society, culture, and state*. Los Angeles, CA: University of California Press.

Beitin, B. K., Allen, K. R., & Bekheet, M. (2010). A critical analysis of Western perspectives on families of Arab descent. *Journal of Family Issues* 31, 211–233. doi: 10.1177/0192513X09345480

Beitin, B. K. & Aprahamian, M. (2013). Family values and traditions. In S. C. Nassar-McMillan, K. J. Ajrouch, & J. Hakim-Larson (eds.), *Biopsychosocial perspectives on Arab Americans: Culture, development and health* (pp. 89–105). New York: Springer. doi: 10.1007/978-1-4614-8238-3_4

Bowen, M. (1978). *Family therapy in clinical practice* (1st edn.). New York: Rowan & Littlefield Publishers, Inc.

Bowen, M. (1985). *Family therapy in clinical practice* (3rd edn.). Lanham, MD: J. Aronson.

Brittingham, A. & de la Cruz, G. P. (2005). *We the people of Arab ancestry in the United States* (Census 2000 Special Reports, CENSR-21). Washington, D.C.: U. S. Census Bureau. Retrieved from www.census.gov/prod/2005pubs/censr-21.pdf

Britto, P. R. & Amer, M. M. (2007). An exploration of cultural identity patterns and family context among Arab Muslim young adults in America. *Applied Development Science* 11(3), 137–150. doi: 10.1080/10888690701454633

Bushfield, S. & Fitzpatrick, T. R. (2010). Therapeutic interventions with immigrant Muslim families in the United States. *Journal of Religion and Spirituality in Social Work: Social Thought* 29, 165–179. doi: 10.1080/15426431003708311

Cainkar, L. & Read, J. G. (2013). Arab Americans and gender. In S. C. Nassar-McMillan, K. J. Ajrouch, & J. Hakim-Larson (eds.), *Biopsychosocial perspectives on Arab Americans: Culture, development and health* (pp. 89–105). New York: Springer. doi: 10.1007/978-1-4614-8238-3_5

Chapman, A. R. & Cattaneo, L. B. (2013). American Muslim marital quality: A preliminary investigation. *Journal of Muslim Mental Health* 7(2), 1–24. doi: 10.3998/jmmh.10381607.0007.201

Chen, J. & Sheldon, J. P. (2012). Arab-American emerging adults' bicultural identity, acculturative stress, and perceptions of parenting. *Journal of Immigrant and Refugee Studies* 10, 438–445. doi: 10.1080/15562948.2012.739952

Dabbagh, M. (2011). *Parental kidnapping in America: An historical and cultural analysis*. Jefferson, NC: McFarland & Company, Inc.

Daneshpour, M. (2009). Bridges crossed, paths traveled: Muslim intercultural couples. In T. A. Karis & K. D. Killian (eds.), *Intercultural couples: Exploring diversity in intimate relationships* (pp. 207–229). New York: Routledge.

de la Cruz, G. P. & Brittingham, A. (2003). *The Arab population: 2000* (Census 2000 Brief, C2KBR-23). Washington, D.C.: U.S. Census Bureau. Retrieved from www.census.gov/prod/2003pubs/c2kbr-23.pdf

Dwairy, M., Achoui, M., Abouserie, R., & Farah, A. (2006). Adolescent-family connectedness among Arabs: A second cross-regional research study. *Journal of Cross-Cultural Psychology* 37, 248–261. doi: 10.1177/0022022106286923

Eid, T. Y. (2005). *Marriage, divorce, and child custody as experienced by American Muslims: Religious, social, and legal considerations*. Cambridge, MA: Harvard Divinity School.

El-Aswad, E. (2010). Narrating the self among Arab Americans: A bridging discourse between Arab tradition and American culture. *Digest of Middle Eastern Studies* 19, 234–248. doi: 10.1111/j.1949-3606.2010.00032.x

Erickson, C. D. & Al-Tamimi, N. R. (2001). Providing mental health services to Arab Americans: Recommendations and considerations. *Cultural Diversity and Ethnic Minority Psychology* 7, 308–27. doi: 10. 1037//1099-9809.7.4.308

Feng, D., Giarrusso, R., Bengtson, V. L., & Frye, N. (1999). Intergenerational transmission of marital quality and marital instability. *Journal of Marriage and Family* 61, 451–463. doi: 10.2307/353761

Finer, L. B. (2007). Trends in premarital sex in the United States, 1954–2003. *Public Health Reports* 122(1), 73–78.

Ganim, H. E. (2001). *A resource for clinicians: Understanding Lebanese American adolescent girls and their families* (Doctoral dissertation). Available from ProQuest Dissertations and Theses database (UMI No. 3009221).

Goldenberg, I. & Goldenberg, H. (2012). *Family therapy: An overview* (8th edn.). Belmont, CA: Brooks/Cole.

Haddad, Y. Y., Smith, J. I., & Moore, K. M. (2006). *Muslim women in America: The challenge of Islamic identity today*. New York: Oxford University Press.

Harkness, S. & Super, C. M. (2002). Culture and parenting. In M. H. Bornstein (ed.), *Handbook of parenting, Vol. 4: Social conditions and applied parenting* (pp. 59–93). Mahwah, NJ: Erlbaum.

Hattar-Pollara, M. & Meleis, A. I. (1995). The stress of immigration and the daily lived experiences of Jordanian immigrant women in the United States. *Western Journal of Nursing Research* 17, 521–539. doi: 10.1177/019394599501700505

Hofstede, G. (2001). *Culture's consequences: Comparing values, behaviors, institutions, and organizations across nations*. Newbury Park, CA: Sage.

Ibish, H. (2008). *Report on hate crimes and discrimination against Arab-Americans*. Washington, D.C.: Arab-American Anti-Discrimination Committee. Retrieved from www.adc.org/index.php?id=3388

Joseph, S. (1999). *Intimate selving in Arab families: Gender, self and identity*. Syracuse, NY: University of Syracuse Press.

Kayyali, R. A. (2006). *The Arab Americans*. Westport, CT: Greenwood Press.

Keck, L. (1989). Egyptian Americans in the Washington DC area. In B. Abu-Laban & M. W. Suleiman (eds.), *Arab Americans: Continuity and change* (pp. 103–126). Belmont, CA: Association of Arab American University Graduates.

Kerr, M. E. & Bowen, M. (1988). *Family evaluation*. New York: W. W. Norton.

Khalaila, R. (2010). Development and evaluation of the Arabic Filial Piety Scale. *Research on Social Work Practice* 20, 353–367. doi: 10.1177/1049731510369495

Killawi, A., Daneshpour, M., Elmi, A., Dadras, I., & Hamid, H. (2014). *Recommendations for promoting healthy marriages & preventing divorce in the American Muslim community*. Washington, D.C.: Institute for Social Policy and Understanding. Retrieved from www.ispu.org/pdfs/ISPU_Promoting_Healthy_Marriages_and_ Preventing_Divorce_in_the_American_Muslim_Community.pdf

Koepke, S. & Denissen, J. J. A. (2012). Dynamics of identity development and separation-individuation in parent-child relationships during adolescence and emerging adulthood – A conceptual integration. *Developmental Review* 32, 67–88. doi: 10.1016/j.dr.2012.01.001

Kretchmar, M. D. & Jacobvitz, D. B. (2002). Observing mother-child relationships across generations: Boundary patterns, attachment, and the transmission of caregiving. *Family Process* 41, 351–374. doi: 10.1111/j.1545-53 00.2002.41306.x

Kulczycki, A. & Lobo, A. P. (2002). Patterns, determinants, and implications of intermarriage among Arab Americans. *Journal of Marriage and Family* 64(1), 202–210. doi: 10.1111/j.1741-3737.2002.00202.x

Macfarlane, J. (2012). *Understanding trends in American Muslim divorce and marriage: A discussion guide for families and communities*. Washington, D.C.: Institute for Social Policy and Understanding. Retrieved from www.ispu.org/ pdfs/ISPU %20Report_Marriage %t20II_Macfarlane_WEB.pdf

Mann, M. A. (2004). Immigrant parents and their emigrant adolescents: The tension of inner and outer worlds. *The American Journal of Psychoanalysis* 64, 143–153. doi: 10.1023/B:TAJP.0000027269.37516.16

McGill, D. W. & Pearce, J. K. (1996). American families with English ancestors from the colonial era: Anglo Americans. In M. McGoldrick, J. Giordano, & J. K. Pearce (eds.), *Ethnicity and family therapy* (pp. 451–466). New York: Guilford.

Mikulincer, M., Weller, A., & Florian, V. (1993). Sense of closeness to parents and family rules: A study of Arabs and Jewish youth in Israel. *International Journal of Psychology* 28, 323–335. doi: 10.1080/00207599308246925
Minuchin, S. (1974). *Families & family therapy*. Cambridge, MA: Harvard University Press.
Nasir, L. S., Abdul-haq, A. K., & Toukan, A. (2008). *Caring for Arab patients: A biopsychosocial approach*. London: Radcliffe Publishing.
Pleck, E. H. & Pleck, J. H. (1997). Fatherhood ideals in the United States: Historical dimensions. In M. E. Lamb (ed.), *The role of the father in child development* (pp. 33–48). New York: Wiley.
Rashad, H., Osman, M., & Roudi-Fahimi, F. (2005). *Marriage in the Arab world*. Washington, D.C.: Population Reference Bureau. Retrieved from www.prb.org/pdf05/marriageinarabworld_eng.pdf
Rasmi, S., Chuang, S. S., & Hennig, K. (in press). The acculturation gap-distress model: Extensions and application to Arab Canadian families. *Cultural Diversity and Ethnic Minority Psychology*. Advance online publication. doi: 10.1037/cdp0000014
Rasmi, S., Chuang, S. S., & Safdar, S. (2012). The relationship between perceived parental rejection and adjustment for Arab, Canadian, and Arab Canadian youth. *Journal of Cross-Cultural Psychology* 43, 84–90. doi: 10.1177/0022022111428172
Rasmi, S., Daly, T. M., & Chuang, S. (2014). Intergenerational conflict management in immigrant Arab Canadian families. *Journal of Cross-Cultural Psychology* 45, 1124–1144. doi: 10.1177/0022022114532358
Read, J. G. (2002). Challenging myths of Muslim women: The influence of Islam on Arab-American women's labor force participation. *Muslim World* 96, 18–39. doi: 10.1111/j.1478-1913.2002.tb03730.x
Read, J. G. (2003). The sources of gender role attitudes among Christian and Muslim Arab-American women. *Sociology of Religion* 64, 207–222. doi: 10.2307/3712371
Read, J. G. (2004). Family, religion, and work among Arab American women. *Journal of Marriage and the Family* 66, 1042–1050. doi: 10.1111/j.0022-2445.2004.00077.x
Rothbaum, F., Rosen, K., Ujiie, T., & Uchida, N. (2002). Family systems theory, attachment theory, and culture. *Family Process* 41, 328–350. doi: 10.1111/j.1545-5300.2002.41305.x
Rothbaum, F., Weisz, J., Pott, M., Miyake, K., & Morelli, G. (2000). Attachment and culture: Security in the United States and Japan. *American Psychologist* 55, 1093–1104. doi: 10.1037/0003-066X.55.10.1093
Rudy, D. & Grusec, J. E. (2006). Authoritarian parenting in individualist and collectivist groups: Associations with maternal emotion and cognition and children's self-esteem. *Journal of Family Psychology* 20, 68–78. doi: 10.1037/0893-3200.20.1.68
Schwartz, S. H. (2006). A theory of cultural value orientations: Explication and applications. *Comparative Sociology* 5, 137–182. doi: 10.1163/156913306778667357
Serhan, R. (2008). Palestinian weddings: Inventing Palestine in New Jersey. *Journal of Palestine Studies* 37(4), 21–37. doi: 10.1525/jps.2008.37.4.21
Soenens, B., Vansteenkiste, M., Lens, W., Luyckx, K., Goossens, L., Beyers, W., & Ryan, R. M. (2007). Conceptualizing parental autonomy support: Adolescent perceptions of promotion of independence versus promotion of volitional functioning. *Developmental Psychology* 43, 633–646. doi: 10.1037/0012-1649.43.3.633
Soliman, I. (2008). *Acculturation of Arab Americans: An exploratory mixed-methods study* (Doctoral dissertation). Available from ProQuest Dissertations and Theses database (UMI No. 338847).
Sorkhabi, N. (2010). Sources of parent-adolescent conflict: Content and form of parenting. *Social Behavior and Personality* 38, 761–782. doi: 10.2224/sbp.2010.38.6.761
Steinberg, L. D. & Silk, J. S. (2002). Parenting adolescents. In M. Bornstein (ed.), *Handbook of parenting* (2nd edn., vol. 1, pp. 103–134). Mahwah, NJ: Erlbaum.
Szapocznik, J. & Kurtines, W. (1993). Family psychology and cultural diversity: Opportunities for theory, research, and application. *American Psychologist* 48, 400–407. doi: 10.1037/0003-066X.48.4.400
Timmi, S. B. (1995). Adolescence in immigrant Arab families. *Psychotherapy* 32(1), 141–149. doi: 10.1037/0033-3204.32.1.141
Titelman, P. (1998). *Clinical applications of Bowen family systems theory*. New York: Haworth Press.
van IJzendoorn, M. H. & Sagi, A. (1999). Cross-cultural patterns of attachment: Universal and contextual dimensions. In J. Cassidy & P. R. Shaver (eds.), *Handbook of attachment: Theory, research, and clinical implications* (2nd edn., pp. 713–734). New York: Guilford.
Wray-Lake, L., Syvertsen, A. K., & Flanagan, C. A. (2008). Contested citizenship and social exclusion: Adolescent Arab immigrants' views of the social contract. *Applied Developmental Science* 12(2), 84–92. doi: 10.1080/10888690801997085

9
GENDER AND SEXUALITY
Treading Complex Cultural Challenges

Rita Stephan and Mireille Aprahamian

Gender and sexuality are often at the crossfire of culture, ethnicity, religion, and international politics for Arab Americans. They constantly face pressure to embrace popular norms in their American society while they try to preserve their conservative Arabic heritage. They are also subject to multiple stereotypes that are forced upon them by popular media and politicized historical narratives.

This chapter presents many complex aspects of Arab American gender and sexuality, highlighting the challenges Arabs in the U.S. face and how they overcome them. After a discussion of how ethnic identity is associated with gender identity development, the chapter focuses on three areas of Arab Americans' lives as related to gender and sexuality. First, it examines how they negotiate their complex gendered ethnic identities and roles. Second, it discusses sensitive issues such as dating, sex, body image, and sexual orientation, which diverge at the crossroads of Arab traditional values and American liberal customs. Third, it explores how Arab American women have maneuvered the public space despite experiencing discrimination. In particular, it discusses women's agency through their labor force participation and activism. A case example is provided to illustrate the challenges facing Arab women in expressing their sexuality or joining the workforce. The chapter ends with an analysis of the current research, providing suggestions for future areas of study.

Frameworks for Understanding the Intersection of Gender and Ethnicity

Social scientists have long studied immigrant identity development, including the tensions inscribed in the combination of ethnic identity and citizenship. Hussain and Bagguley (2005) argue that citizenship and identity "are counterposed to one another. The former expresses universal individual rights and duties, while the latter implies particularism and group membership" (p. 409). Generally, Americans of diverse ethnic origin have enjoyed the benefits conferred by the state to its citizens on an individual basis. However, their group identity has not attracted positive recognition from the state, and is often perceived by the public as different from the established sociocultural and normative standards.

Cultural and gender identities can have a great impact on individuals' psychological health (Vandiver, 2001). Society sets the expectation for gender roles of men and women, especially within a particular ethnic group (Deaux & Kite, 1987; Kite & Whitley, 1996). Definitions of gender roles and expectations are socially constructed to guide societal values and behaviors (Kramer, 2001). In fact, Deaux and Lafrance (1998) argue that "gender is considered a dynamic construct that draws on and impinges upon processes at the individual, interactional, group, institutional, and cultural levels" (p. 788).

Theories such as gender schema theory (Bem, 1981) and social learning theory (Bandura, 1977) explain the process of gender socialization and the development of cognitive schemas in children. These theories emphasize how children acquire various beliefs through modeling behaviors of others in the environment. As such, gender roles and expectations are socialized at an early age based on cultural contexts, and beliefs about gender are carried over throughout adulthood. For example, Arab American young girls are taught early on about performing femininity by being encouraged to wear dresses and jewelry. As gender-based expressions are modeled to children at a young age, individuals develop gender schemas and stereotypes about gender roles. These biases and gender belief systems have been shown to shape attitudes toward gender roles, sexuality, and civil rights, and are found to be different among men and women (Deaux & Kite, 1987; Kite & Whitley, 1996).

Gendered Ethnic Identity and Gender Roles

How Arab Americans negotiate and express their identities varies depending on their country of origin, age at immigration, levels of acculturation, and experiences in the U.S. To better understand patterns of Arab Americans' gender identity in the U.S., this section analyzes them within the context of minority and dominant culture interactions by accounting for the dynamics between self-perceptions, internalized perceptions, and stereotypical perceptions. Scholars such as Nagel and Staeheli (2004) posit that minority groups internalize dominant societal stereotypes and later express them in their own behaviors and identities. These interactions therefore shape the way in which Arab Americans, like other ethnic minorities, perceive themselves and their identity development.

Differentiated Gender Identities

Despite significant social and legal gains, ethnic minority women in general, and Arab American women in particular, suffer inequality due to institutional barriers and negative public stereotypes. However, their victimization is rarely discussed. In a comparative study of Hispanic and Arab women, Lopez and Hasso (1998) found that the Black–White dichotomy, which dominated the paradigm of race relation scholarship, rendered Arab and Hispanic women invisible or forced them to either the "frontlines" or "borders" – but never the center – of racial or cultural opposition. As this study posits, the dichotomous nature of racial relations in the U.S., which rarely extends to Arab, Hispanic, or even Asian minorities, furthers these groups' oppression and invisibility.

Multiplicity of identity is prevalent in two other areas in the case of Arab Americans: country of origin and length of citizenship. Shakir (1997) explains that differentiation based on country of origin further divides Arab Americans and isolates those who do not originate from the Levant (mainly Lebanon, Syria, Palestine, and Jordan). Palestinian women, according to Fleischmann (2003), tend to exhibit a higher level of activism and gender consciousness than other Arab American women as a result of the Palestinian political and national struggle. The other multiplicity of identity reflects the differentiated experiences of Arab American women based on the length of their citizenship in the U.S. Shakir (1997) examines the experiences and identities of the "Bint Arab" (or American women of Arab origin) in the U.S. since the late nineteenth century, drawing principally on the histories of second and third generation Arab women who feel a greater sense of integration and "Americanization" as compared to more recent immigrants. She points to the immigrants' bicultural identity, highlighting the unique difficulties of their experience. These difficulties are manifested in negotiating traditional Arab values and Western sexual freedoms. Arab women may also feel ambivalence toward the U.S. as a country that offers them opportunity but is often hostile to the Arab world. Meleis' (1991) study focuses on the individual lives of Arab American women in California who negotiate two cultures. She found that these women are at high risk for physical and mental distress as a product of the conflict between the expectations and values of their ethnic heritage and American culture.

Arab American women's internal struggles are not limited to ethnic-based identities. They are also often challenged with popular assumptions about their religious identity and behavior. This is particularly true for Muslim Arab American women. Read (2001) states that "a popular stereotype of Arab American women portrays them as Islamic traditionalists – veiled, submissive, and secluded within the home" (p. 1235-A). Although cultural and religious customs reinforce traditional gender roles, Arab American women have challenged the gender discourse within their cultural and religious traditions and have challenged the ethnic discourse within the overall definition of their American citizenship. Instead of emphasizing their religious identities, female respondents in Read and Bartkowski's (2000) study reported that their gender identities influenced and reshaped their Muslim gender discourses.

It is noteworthy that like women, Arab American men experience gender inequality that is differentiated by their ethnicity. Mohja Kahf's poem, "I Can Scent an Arab Man a Mile Away" (2003, p. 29), is a humorous illustration of the stereotypes attributed to Arab masculinity:

> My stubbly-chinned,
> black-haired, tawny-skinned
> Arab male kin, the white-robed
> and the black-tied of them,
> . . .
> They may be
> mustachio'd, macho, patriarchal,
> sexist, egotistical, parochial –
> They may, as men may,
> think themselves indomitable,
> being easily manipulable,
> – but they're mine, my
> sleek and swarthy, hairy-chested,
> curly-headed lovers of the Prophet
> and lovers of the Virgin,
> sons of the city street and village boys,
> wanderers tribal and global.

As the poem reveals, overly aggressive negative qualities are often attributed to Arab American men, who are characterized figuratively as macho (patriarchal, sexist, egoistical, and parochial) and physically as dark with heavy mustaches, curly hair, and stubbly chins. These characteristics often facilitate the negative sexualization and victimization of Arab American men.

Likewise, Arab American women have their share of sexual stereotypes. They are viewed as invisible, silent, and oppressed by culture, religion, and social structure, while being at the same time seductive and sensual. Subsequently, some Arab American women find themselves consciously and non-consciously ascribing to these characteristics and stereotypes. In a nutshell, Arab American men and women constantly negotiate among internalizing, adopting, or resisting the stereotypical assumptions and characterizations of their ethnic identities and gendered roles.

Gender Roles and Kinship

Historically, patriarchy – a social system in which males hold primary power by dominating political leadership, moral authority, social privilege, and control of property (Malti-Douglas, 2007) – is a foundation of Arab societies, in which men are viewed as the protectors, sole providers of the family, and carriers of kinship. Though this structure can often be interpreted as sexist or male dominant, some scholars argue that its foundation is more complex and it requires a historical understanding of the role of family survival and tribal dynamics in the region (Joseph, 1993; Tillion, 1983). They emphasize that gender roles in Arab societies are often interconnected with a hierarchical system that includes age relations and shapes family values. Nevertheless, as a result of this patriarchal system, some Arab societies view the role of men to be the dominant figure in the family and may exercise this privilege in abusive ways (Beitin & Aprahamian, 2013; Haj-Yahia, 2011).

Gender scholars who study Arab cultures posit that the family is not only a source of economic, emotional, and social support for men and women, but also the primary agent of social control and welfare (Joseph, 2000; Tucker, 1998). Thus, given their function as an essential structure within the political and social systems operating in Arab and Muslim-majority societies, kin groups have been viewed as oppressing women to the extent that the political and cultural oppression of women exists as a feature of these societies (Afkhami, 1995; Kandiyoti, 1991). In fact, Joseph (2001) attributes oppressive gender relations in the Middle East to the patriarchal, not Islamic, social structure: "Given the centrality of family, its patriarchal structure is crucial in understanding gender relationships in the Middle East. Family both supports and suppresses women. This paradox of support and suppression, love and power, and generosity and competition, compels both attachment to and struggle within families" (p. 10). As an example of the family serving as a source of support, Stephan (2010) has shown how the family in Lebanon empowers women and supports their civic engagement and political participation.

In practical terms, women are often expected to maintain family unity and privacy. Stepping outside these traditional roles places Arab American women in a difficult position among their family-centered communities. They are viewed as if they have co-opted the "American ways" and lost their cultural values and family ties. By asserting their femininity and focusing on caregiving and nurturing the family unit, Arab American women stand to gain the continuous support of their nuclear and extended family networks (Al-Huraibi & Konradi, 2012; Mostafa, 2005; Neal, Finlay, & Tansey, 2005).

Although Arab American women are well aware of the implication of this kin contract, they work within the family settings to modify, challenge, and improve the terms of this contract (Stephan, 2010). Their social lifestyle accommodates their Arab and American cultural norms, without questioning whether these choices are made to appease the dominant culture or their individual interests (Naber, 2006, 2013). They prefer this style of advocacy for women's rights over rushing to embrace a feminist identity that does not resonate with their social and political realities. Nevertheless, they do acknowledge the contributions of feminism in advancing women's rights and gender equality globally.

Finally, it is noteworthy that gender roles are not all predetermined by women, men, or the patriarchal structure for that matter. Variations are found across Arab American families based on factors such as education, income, and religion (Omair, 2009; Read, 2003). Less educated, non-working, conservative, and new immigrant women tend to devote more time to playing traditional gender roles than those who are more educated, are gainfully employed, are liberal in their religious and political views, or have been in the U.S. for a longer period of time. Similar variations are found across Arab Americans' expression of sexuality.

Sexuality and Body Image

Arab American identities are shaped by multiple variables and interacting forces and so is their sexual identity. Like other cultures, Arab and Muslim-majority societies have been fairly preoccupied with women's sexuality. How Arab Americans manifest these issues is clearly felt in their body image and attitude toward dating and sex.

Dating and Sex

Sex-related issues, including sexuality, have been a taboo subject of conversation among Arab communities, especially between parents and children. Topics such as dating, sex, and sexuality are generally discussed more openly in the wider American society than among Arab Americans. As such, many young Arab Americans find themselves caught between the two cultural views. This is a common stressor among Arab American female youth, who experience tremendous pressure to maintain traditional norms while balancing peer and popular culture (Naber, 2013).

Arab American girls and young women face the cultural impact of shame. When young men and women engage in inappropriate sexual behavior, this behavior is culturally described as *'ayb*, which means "shameful act" in Arabic. Generally, dating, premarital, and extramarital sex are frowned upon, and such behaviors are known to bring shame to the individual and family. Shame factors and consideration for family honor oppress the development of sexual identity outside the traditional model (Ikizler & Szymanski, 2014; Mousa, 2011). Many Arab American women complain that their parents have left their old cultures behind, except for their daughters' sexuality and dating behavior. Arab parents show their pride in their Arab culture through further restricting their daughters' freedom (Abdulhadi, Alsultany, & Naber, 2011). Some young Arab American women report suffering stricter parental rules in the U.S. than their female counterparts back in the homeland (Naber, 2013). It is therefore not surprising that Arab American women take on their own feminism to reject these double standards (as discussed below).

Body Image

In 2010, Rima Fakih became the first Arab American to win Miss USA Pageant, representing Michigan. She overcame the body objectification that Arab American women experience in the U.S. with their black hair, black eyes, and brown skin. Arab American women's attitudes toward their body is another issue that is at the crossfire of cultural versus societal standards. The discrepancy between standards of beauty in the U.S. and the way Arab American women view themselves varies greatly from one individual to another, but in general, this discrepancy may drive Arab American women to have poor body image or to try to measure up to societal standards of body image and beauty. This point is eloquently illustrated in Mohja Kahf's 2006 novel *The Girl in the Tangerine Scarf*. The internalization of such standards often leads to negative self-image, body surveillance, and body shame. A recent study of U.S. Muslim women, including those of Arab descent, found positive correlations between the internalization of American cultural beauty standards and eating problems (Tolaymat & Moradi, 2011).

Sexual Orientation

The topic of homosexuality remains a controversial topic in the Arab American community. Kayyali (2006) argues that the lesbian, gay, bisexual, and transgender (LGBT) Arab American community experiences double marginalization: the first is by other members of the LGBT community for being Arabs, and the second is within Arab American circles for being gay. Ikizler and Szymanski's (2014) findings support Kayyali's argument. Participants in their study reported suffering from discrimination on the basis of their multiple minority identities: ethnic, religious, and sexual orientation.

Other studies have argued that sexual identity development among Arab Americans and the broader Middle Eastern population takes on a fluid process. Similar to gender and ethnic identity development, Arab Americans negotiate their sexual identities depending on the dominant stereotypes and cultural contexts in which they live. Positive sexual identity development in women is associated with healthy coping skills, whereas negative sexual identity development is influenced by Arab cultural values of collective shame, especially about homosexuality (Mousa, 2011; Zaher, 2013). While homosexuality is not widely tolerated in the Arab American community, this is slowly changing. More families are open to accepting diversity in sexual orientation and are increasingly embracing the partners of their gay family members as part of the family.

Abdulhadi and colleagues (2011) stress that Arab American women, gay, and transgender activists express a multiplicity of experiences and identities. They argue that "gender and sexuality in the Arab American women, queer, and transgender experiences are situated within multiple overlapping and intersecting structures of power and privilege" (p. xxv). In her speech at the 2004 Dyke March in San Francisco, Happy Hyder embodied the intersection of ethnicity, homosexuality, and politics and found comfort in belly dancing, photography, and activism. Trying to fight prejudice within the LGBT movement, Hyder felt further marginalized; she claimed that "As dykes, we are hardly fooled by the stated desire of the U.S. government to help the women in Arab countries. This government has, for years, been installing right-wing fanatics in positions of power around the globe as they undermine women's rights here as well" (2011, p. 105). Hence, Hyder connects political oppression to sexual oppression and claims that the U.S. is as guilty as some of the Arab countries it criticizes.

Arab American Women in the Public Space

Sexual invisibility combined with political hypervisibility pushes Arab American women into a limited public space. Given the way Arab women become objectified in popular discourse, it is no wonder that Arab and Arab American feminists often find themselves cast into a liminal space, compelled to engage in a debate constructed by a set of false binaries about whether veiling is oppressive or liberating, for example, or whether feminism is a "Western" concept (Jarmakani, 2011, p. 233). Arab American women are often perceived by others to be subservient victims and, in some cases, without a voice. Yet, as this section shows, Arab American women step into the public sphere – despite the scrutinizing, hostile, and discriminatory atmosphere – to defend their cultural practices, join the labor force on their own terms, and challenge the perceived superiority of Western feminism.

Discrimination Experiences and Identity

Arab American women, particularly those who are Muslim, face unique stereotypes and discrimination experiences that shape their identity development (Abu-Ras & Suarez, 2009; Fine & Aziz, 2013). Similar trends have been observed in Canada and the U.K. (Khan, 2000; Ryan, 2011), where Muslim women negotiate their identities in response to social stereotypes and internalized messages. They are portrayed as submissive veiled women who are culturally abused, oppressed, or enslaved to their religion. Though domestic violence is prevalent in Arab societies, not all Arab women experience violence as perceived by popular assumptions.

Even before 9/11, Arab Americans experienced harassment, discrimination, and isolation due to world events and media-influenced stereotypes that have led to a lack of knowledge about Arab culture (Amer, 2005; Erickson & Al-Timimi, 2001; Hassoun, 1999). Stereotypes and criticism are shown to influence the quality of life and mental health of Arab American individuals and their families (Aprahamian, Kaplan, Windham, Sutter, & Visser, 2011; Salari, 2002). As a result of prejudice and discrimination experiences, Arab immigrants sometimes feel rejection and isolation and view themselves as unequal to their American counterparts (Georgeski, 1987). Some researchers suggest that Arab immigrants in the U.S. choose to confine themselves to their own communities because they are made to feel inferior in the greater American society (Ammar, 2000; Faragallah, Schumm, & Webb, 1997). Among those Arab Americans who are often mischaracterized and misrepresented are Muslim Arab American women (Haddad, Smith, & Moore, 2006).

As stereotypes and discrimination experiences are internalized, some Arab Americans tend to confirm their identities, while others reject them. Arab American identities were impacted by 9/11, as individuals of Arab and/or Muslim descent experienced more negative stereotyping and hate crimes (Ahmad, 2004; Amer, 2005). Some individuals who identified as Muslim conformed more saliently to the stereotypes. For example, some Muslim women increased their religious identity expression through wearing the hijab (headscarf). Opposite trends were also observed as Muslim

Arab American women rejected their religious identity in order to avoid ridicule or discrimination (Bakalian & Bozorgmehr, 2009).

Identity is often expressed through clothing, and humans cross-culturally wear certain attire to reflect their social identities. Wolf (1991) describes experiences of women in professional settings where business clothes are carefully selected to set a desired impression. Women often experience a dilemma in appearing too "feminine" or too "masculine" at work. Arab American women may try to balance traditionally modest or religious clothing with the demands of the modern world's professional attire. For Muslim Arab Americans, this challenge is tied to wearing the hijab. Dominant views in the U.S. see the hijab as oppressive and that wearing it is suggestive of female subjugation (Ruby, 2006). Arab American women in the workforce, and those who have higher levels of education, face greater scrutiny as they are often expected to reject the generally perceived "oppressive" veil (Omair, 2009).

Modern Muslim feminist discourse stresses women's need to learn more about the interpretations of veiling in the Qur'an and expects women to be more knowledgeable about their choice to wear the hijab (Ali, 2005; Sidani, 2005). In many cases, women find themselves justifying their intellect and presence of choice in wearing the hijab while defending their religious identity. In some cases, women prioritize their religious identity over social expectation; however, in many other instances, women adhere to the dominant dress code in order to set impressions and improve their position within their professional organizations. It is important to note, however, that in a study by Tolaymat and Moradi (2011), findings suggest that Muslim women do not necessarily wear the hijab to avoid sexual objectification – despite contrary perceptions. Hijab wearing was more associated with religious pride and expression of one's identity.

Women in the Workforce

Arab American women's experiences in the workforce vary tremendously by their income and tenure in the U.S. Arab American women who migrated during their adult years tend to be more driven by economics and education (Killian, Olmsted, & Doyle, 2012). Killian and colleagues argue that those who have escaped political conflict and persecution tend to value the pursuit of education and achievement of professional status. The majority of those born in the U.S. tend to have experiences similar to other American women, with a few exceptions.

Among the studies that have tackled the experiences of Arab American women is Read's (2001) work on Arab American women's religiosity and employment. Read found that Arab American women's level of religiosity negatively impacts their likelihood to participate in the labor force more than their religious affiliation with either Islam or Christianity. In other words, she found that women who were more religious were less likely to work, regardless of being Muslim or Christian. Read argues that unique cultural repertoires within religious communities are strong indicators of affirming traditional religious values.

Read's (2001) study emphasizes women's labor force participation as an important measure of women's personal achievements. She found that Arab American women are relatively well educated and prosperous. However, unlike other American women, Arab American women's feeling of responsibility to meet their families' daily household needs hinders their economic participation. Read concludes that foreign-born Arab American women are less likely than the native-born to participate in the paid labor force, and this variation is explained by cultural differences between the two groups rather than by religion or religiosity.

Indeed, Arab women have been less involved in the U.S. labor market than women in the rest of the U.S. According to the U.S. Census Bureau (Stephan, 2013), approximately 54% of Arab American women aged 16 and over were in the civilian labor force, compared with 60% of the total population. Although Lebanese women's participation in the U.S. labor force was exceptionally high (62%), women from other Arab origins had significantly lower labor force participation rates: Iraqis at 39%, Palestinians at 44%, and Jordanians at 50%, whereas Egyptians, Syrians, and Moroccans were around 57% (Stephan, 2013).

Poverty rates for female-headed households with no husband present and with related children under the age of 18 were highest for Iraqis (67%), Palestinians (62%), and Moroccans (56%). Percentages were similarly high for Jordanians (47%) and Egyptians (39%), compared to the overall Arab population in the U.S. at 39% and the total U.S. population at 38%. Only Syrians (21%) and Lebanese (28%) had lower poverty rates among these female households (Stephan, 2013).

Although Arab American women's labor participation in formal sectors is lower than women in the total U.S. population, those who are currently employed tend to earn higher incomes than other women in the U.S. population (Stephan, 2013). Many of these women often support and are supported by a network of other women who are members in their families or immigrants from their countries of origin. These family members and immigrant women provide assistance in household and childcare management, which allows women the opportunity to acquire demanding jobs that are well paid (Stephan, 2013).

Almost half of the working Arab women population is employed in management and professional occupations (48%), compared to 42% of Arab men and 39% of women in the total U.S. population. Jordanian women were more likely to be employed in management and professional occupations at 51%, whereas 50% of Egyptian, Lebanese, and Syrian working women were in these professions. Palestinians were at 47% but Moroccan women were at 35%. Moroccan women were similarly represented in sales and office occupations at 37% compared to the total Arab women population at 31%, women in the total U.S. population at 33% and Arab men at 27% (Stephan, 2013).

In summary, employment and earnings among Arab Americans vary tremendously according to country of origin, nativity status (native or foreign born), and length of presence in the U.S., among other factors. While Census data do not shed light on the relationship between religion and labor force participation, Read's study affirms that cultural, rather than religious, diversity explains the low labor force participation among Arab American women. Arabs tend to place high value on educational achievements but lower value on employment in general, and on women's employment in particular. They tend to value other gender roles such as motherhood and discourage trusting childrearing to strangers (Stephan, 2010).

A Transnational Feminism as an Alternative Ideology

In the last two decades, Arab American women have struggled to end discrimination against themselves as women and ethnic minorities. However, great efforts have been exerted by mainstream feminism and society to keep them invisible, according to Hyder (2011), an Arab American activist. She claims "We are more powerful than we can imagine – otherwise why has so much energy been expended to keep us invisible? Now take a look around at how visible and vibrant we are!" (p. 106). Saliba (1999) traces the history of modern Arab American feminism to 1981 at the National Women's Studies Association conference, when Arab American feminists such as Carol Haddad and Azizah al-Hibri joined forces with other minority feminists to challenge White feminists. Their experiences motivated many Lebanese American feminists to join their Arab American compatriots in establishing representative organizations that express their voice in local, national, and international politics (Kadi, 1994).

Jarmakani (2011) explores Arab Americans' feminism as mediated by the paradox of being simultaneously invisible and hypervisible. Calling this idea the "politics of invisibility (since hypervisibility also functions to obscure the creative work of Arab American feminists)" (p. 228), Jarmakani looks at the ways Arab American feminists have fought in collaboration with U.S.-based Black and Asian feminists, united as women of color to contest their marginalization by White feminists among others. Ultimately, she argues that one way to respond to the complexities of the U.S. context is to strategically mobilize the politics of invisibility, transforming it from a weakness into a useful and powerful tactic. She argues that Arab American feminisms have been circumscribed within a paradoxical framework and suggests that such a position might be put to strategic use. She argues:

> Arab feminism appears an oxymoron not only because Arab women are perceived to be silent and submissive according to the mythology of the veil. It is an oxymoron because Arab women are not afforded the subjectivity of thinking, theorizing individuals. We are not merely silenced, we are wholly displaced; and therefore, ontologically elided by sensationalized news stories and images of oppressed and exoticized Arab women. (p. 236)

While Western feminists have been occupied with topics – such as the veil, female genital mutilation, and suicide bombings – that further Arab and Arab American women's victimization, Arab American feminists have been pushing back against being stereotyped by their American counterparts. They claim that these topics are framed to hinder their ability to offer critical and thoughtful analysis of Arab and Muslim women's conditions, and are repeatedly forced to "fit the varied, rich, and complex lives of Arab and Muslim women into limited stereotypical boxes" (Abdulhadi et al., 2011, p. xxviii).

In the U.S., Arab American women have progressed in their fight for political recognition by engaging their social networks and by expressing solidarity with other Arab Americans and ethnic Americans in order to assert their cultural relevance. Today, Arab American women are engaged in efforts to construct multicultural feminism in the U.S. and the rest of the world.

Case Example: Samar's Love and Marriage Dilemma

Samar moved to the U.S. at the age of 16, when her family emigrated from the conservative southern part of Lebanon to Dearborn, Michigan. Like many young girls, her values and gender identity were influenced by Lebanese culture and Muslim religious standards. Growing up, she witnessed most of the women taking on domestic roles around the house and assuming the role of primary carers of the children. Through her early childhood experiences, she perceived males to be dominant and females as more nurturing.

Upon finishing high school and preparing to enter the local community college, she had a serious talk with her mother about dating and love. Her mother was worried that Samar would become interested in blond men of European descent and lose sight of her culture and religion. She reminded her of the principles of *'ayb* and how her actions would affect her entire family. Should Samar date or engage in premarital sex with any man, especially non-Arab, her family's reputation in the community would become tainted and her sisters would never be able to find a husband.

Despite her mother's warning, Samar developed a strong romantic attachment to a young man of Pakistani origin, Asif. Although her beau came from a similar religious heritage, he was not of Arab origin. Fearing her father's reaction to the intercultural dating, she hid her relationship from her entire family for two years. She felt ashamed and guilty by her actions to keep secrets and explore dating without her parents' permission. Samar could not hide her relationship any longer and ended up confessing to her mother. Knowing that this type of relationship would never be accepted by her family or community, Samar's mother advised her to terminate her relationship with Asif immediately. Unable to resist her mother's pressure, Samar agreed and begged her mother not to tell anyone.

After her graduation, with a degree in physical therapy, Samar was introduced by her aunt to a man who was 10 years her elder. The son of the mayor of her village in Lebanon, Ahmed was deeply respected by the Arab American community in Dearborn. Samar and Ahmed got married a year after they met, and bought a house on the same street as both of the families in Dearborn.

After marriage and having her first child, Samar wanted to work using her physical therapy degree, but her mother told her that the money she would earn working was not worth being away from her child. Additionally, her mother argued that success starts at home with raising children who are healthy, happy, and respectful; and that was Samar's primary responsibility. However, Samar's husband wanted her to pursue her dreams and supported her endeavor. He adjusted his work schedule to watch their child while she worked part-time.

This case narrative shows that although Samar tried to explore dating with a non-Arab man, she immediately felt the negative impact of living two separate lives and being torn between her two worlds. She was ashamed to be with Asif because she was taught that "good girls" do not date before marriage or keep secrets from their parents. Family pressure is also exemplified in constraints that women face when joining the workforce. Had it not been for Samar's husband's support, the family and community might not have accepted her joining the workforce and might have perceived her to be neglecting her primary responsibility of caring for her child.

Critique

Today, topics pertaining to Arab American gender and sexuality are still understudied. Consequently, professionals developing mental health and community resources lack knowledge and education in working with these issues and, therefore, suffer from not being able to adequately address such issues. An emerging body of literature is increasingly reflecting how young Arab Americans are not finding themselves in the existing literature on ethnic and gender relations in the U.S. or studies that focus on Arab societies. This field is increasingly reflecting Arab Americans' growing sense of identity and expression of sexuality.

Studies that focus on gender relations generalize the dominant culture's experiences to all minorities, but specifically ignore the unique experiences of invisible groups such as Arab Americans. Suffering inequality and marginalization, Arab American women struggle to strike a balance between incompatible Arabic cultural values and American social norms. Their struggles have been captured by some ethnographic studies, notably by Naber (2006, 2013), but more comprehensive studies are needed. To date, no national survey has been conducted to offer a general overview of the unique challenges that Arabs face in the U.S. Current initiatives, especially those by the U.S. Census Bureau, the American Psychological Association, and other professional and governmental entities, to recognize the Arab American community as a distinct population hold many promises for conducting comprehensive and meaningful studies on Arab American men and women in the future.

Recent studies such as those conducted by Abdulhadi and colleagues (2011) and Naber (2013) have revealed that non-mainstream forms of feminism, such as the transnational feminist stance and queer theory, have been espoused by Arab American feminists, while other feminisms, especially liberal and radical, have been less appealing to them. Like transnational and Third world feminists, Arab American feminists are more engaged in international politics. These studies have started the conversation on Arab notions of masculinity and femininity, yet future studies should be conducted on the social and psychological impacts of these notions.

Conclusion

This chapter has highlighted Arab Americans' various gender identity formations and experiences in the U.S. Gender, religious, ethnic, and occupational identities, as well as sexuality, were shown to be complex and interdependent in nature. Arab American women's psychological development is influenced by a number of interacting forces and contextual variables. Arab American women come from diverse cultural backgrounds and therefore the issues presented in this chapter may not represent all Arab American women. Nevertheless, as described, Arab American women's choices, decisions, and behaviors are often consciously and non-consciously governed by cultural norms, values, and beliefs. Understanding Arab American women requires an in-depth analysis of these collective variables.

Authors' Note

The views expressed in this chapter are those of the authors and do not represent the views of, and should not be attributed to, the U.S. Department of State.

References

Abdulhadi, R., Alsultany, E., & Naber, N. (eds.) (2011). *Arab and Arab American feminisms: Gender, violence and belonging.* Syracuse, NY: Syracuse University Press.

Abu-Ras, W. M. & Suarez, Z. E. (2009). Muslim men and women's perception of discrimination, hate crimes, and PTSD symptoms post 9/11. *Traumatology* 15(3), 48–63. doi: 10.1177/1534765609342281

Afkhami, M. (1995). *Faith and freedom: Women's human rights in the Muslim world.* Syracuse, NY: Syracuse University Press.

Ahmad, N. (2004). *Arab-American culture and health care.* Retrieved from www.case.edu/med/epidbio/mphp439/Arab-Americans.htm

Al-Huraibi, N. & Konradi, A. (2012). Second-generation Yemeni American women at the turn of the century: Between individual aspirations and communal commitments. *Humanity & Society* 36(2), 117–144. doi: 10.1177/0160597612442144

Ali, S. (2005). Why here why now? Young Muslim women wearing hijab. *The Muslim World* 95, 515–530. doi: 10.1111/j.1478-1913.2005.00109.x

Amer, M. M. (2005). *Arab American mental health in the post September 11 era: Acculturation, stress, and coping* (Doctoral dissertation). Available from ProQuest Dissertations and Theses database (UMI No. 3171022).

Ammar, N. H. (2000). Simplistic stereotyping and complex reality of Arab-American immigrant identity: Consequences and future strategies in policing wife battery. *Islam and Christian-Muslim Relations* 11, 51–70. doi: 10.1080/095964100111517

Aprahamian, M., Kaplan, D. M., Windham, A. M., Sutter, J. A., & Visser, J. (2011). The relationship between acculturation and mental health of Arab-Americans. *Journal of Mental Health Counseling* 33, 80–92.

Bakalian, A. & Bozorgmehr, M. (2009). *Backlash 9/11: Middle Eastern and Muslim Americans respond.* Oakland, CA: University of California Press.

Bandura, A. (1977). *Social learning theory.* New York: General Learning Press.

Beitin, B. K. & Aprahamian, M. (2013). Family values and traditions. In S. C. Nassar-McMillan, K. J. Ajrouch, & J. Hakim-Larson (eds.), *Biopsychosocial perspectives on Arab Americans: Culture, development, and health* (pp. 67–88). New York: Springer. doi: 10.1007/978-1-4614-8238-3_4

Bem, S. L. (1981). Gender schema theory: A cognitive account of sex typing. *Psychological Review* 88, 354–364. doi: 10.1037/0033-295X.88.4.354

Deaux, K. & Kite, M. E. (1987). Thinking about gender. In B. B. Hess & M. M. Ferree (eds.), *Analyzing gender: A handbook of social science research* (pp. 92–117). Beverly Hills, CA: Sage.

Deaux, K. & LaFrance, M. (1998). Gender. In D. T. Gilbert, S. T. Fiske, & G. Lindzey (eds.), *Handbook of social psychology* (4th edn., pp. 788–827). New York: Random House.

Erickson, C. D. & Al-Timimi, N. R. (2001). Providing mental health services to Arab Americans: Recommendations and considerations. *Cultural Diversity and Ethnic Minority Psychology* 7, 308–327. doi: 10.1037/1099-9809.7.4.308

Faragallah, M. H., Schumm, W. R., & Webb, F. J. (1997). Acculturation of Arab-American immigrants: An exploratory study. *Journal of Comparative Family Studies* 28, 182–203.

Fine, J. A. & Aziz, N. N. (2013). Does the political environment matter? Arab-American representation and September 11th. *Social Science Quarterly* 94, 551–568. doi: 10.1111/j.1540-6237.2012.00893.x

Fleischmann, E. (2003). *The nation and its "new" women: The Palestinian women's movement, 1920–1948.* Berkeley, CA: University of California Press.

Georgeski, J. D. (1987). *Nature of and differences in adjustment to and valuing of the American culture among refugees from Eastern Europe, the Middle East and African countries* (Doctoral dissertation). Available from ProQuest Dissertations and Theses database (UMI No. 8720628).

Haddad, Y. Y., Smith, J. I., & Moore, K. M. (2006). *Muslim women in America: The challenge of Islamic identity today.* New York: Oxford University Press.

Haj-Yahia, M. M. (2011). Contextualizing interventions with battered women in collectivist societies: Issues and controversies. *Aggression and Violent Behavior* 16, 331–339. doi: 10.1016/j.avb.2011.04.005

Hassoun, R. (1999). Arab-American health and the process of coming to America: Lessons from the metropolitan Detroit area. In M. W. Suleiman (ed.), *Arabs in America: Building a new future* (pp. 157–176). Philadelphia, PA: Temple University Press.

Hussain, Y. & Bagguley, P. (2005). Citizenship, ethnicity and identity: British Pakistanis after the 2001 "riots." *Sociology* 39, 407–425. doi: 10.1177/0038038505052493
Hyder, H. (2011). Dyke March, San Francisco 2004: I am also a belly dancer. In R. Abdulhadi, E. Alsultany, & N. Naber (eds.), *Arab and Arab American feminisms: Gender, violence and belonging* (pp. 104–110). Syracuse, NY: Syracuse University Press.
Ikizler, A. S. & Szymanski, D. M. (2014). A qualitative study of Middle Eastern/Arab American sexual minority identity development. *Journal of LGBT Issues in Counseling* 8, 206–241. doi: 10.1080/15538605.2014.897295
Jarmakani, A. (2011). Arab American feminisms: Mobilizing the politics of invisibility. In R. Abdulhadi, E. Alsultany, & N. Naber (eds.), *Arab and Arab American feminisms: Gender, violence and belonging* (pp. 227–241). Syracuse, NY: Syracuse University Press.
Joseph, S. (1993). Gender and relationality among Arab families in Lebanon. *Feminist Studies* 19, 465–486. doi: 10.2307/3178097
Joseph, S. (2000). *Gender and citizenship in the Middle East*. Syracuse, NY: Syracuse University Press.
Joseph, S. (2001). Women and politics in the Middle East. In S. Joseph & S. Slyomovics (eds.), *Women and power in the Middle East* (pp. 34–40). Philadelphia, PA: University of Pennsylvania Press.
Kadi, J. (ed.) (1994). *Food for our grandmothers: Writings by Arab-American and Arab-Canadian feminists*. Boston, MA: South End Press.
Kahf, M. (2003). I can scent an Arab man a mile away. In *E-mails from Sheherazad* (pp. 29–30). Gainesville, FL: University Press of Florida.
Kahf, M. (2006). *The girl in the tangerine scarf*. New York: Public Affairs Books.
Kandiyoti, D. (1991). *Women, Islam and the state*. Philadelphia, PA: Temple University Press.
Kayyali, R. (2006). *The Arab Americans*. Westport, CT: Greenwood.
Khan, S. (2000). *Muslim women: Crafting a North American identity*. Gainesville, FL: University Press of Florida.
Killian, C., Olmsted, J., & Doyle, A. (2012). Motivated migrants: (Re)framing Arab women's experiences. *Women's Studies International Forum* 35, 432–446. doi: 10.1016/j.wsif.2012.09.006
Kite, M. E. & Whitley, B. E., Jr. (1996). Sex differences in attitudes toward homosexual persons, behaviors and civil rights: A meta-analysis. *Personality and Social Psychology Bulletin* 22, 336–353. doi: 10.1177/0146167296224002
Kramer, L. (2001). *The sociology of gender: A brief introduction*. Los Angeles, CA: Roxbury Publishing.
Lopez, L. M. & Hasso, F. S. (1998). Frontlines and borders: Identity thresholds for Latinas and Arab American women. In J. O'Brien & J. A. Howard (eds.), *Everyday inequalities: Critical inquiries* (pp. 253–280). Malden, MA: Blackwell.
Malti-Douglas, F. (2007). *Encyclopedia of sex and gender*. Detroit, MI: Macmillan.
Meleis, A. I. (1991). Between two cultures: Identity, roles, and health. *Health Care for Women International* 12, 365–377. doi: 10.1080/07399339109515961
Mostafa, M. M. (2005). Attitudes towards women managers in the United Arab Emirates: The effects of patriarchy, age, and sex differences. *Journal of Managerial Psychology* 20, 540–552. doi: 10.1108/02683940510615451
Mousa, K. E. H. (2011). *Sexual and ethnic identity development among Arab American lesbians* (Doctoral dissertation). Available from ProQuest Dissertations and Theses database (UMI No. 3462984).
Naber, N. (2006). Arab American femininities: Beyond Arab virgin/American(ized) whore. *Feminist Studies* 32(1), 87–111. doi: 10.2307/20459071
Naber, N. (2013). *Arab America: Gender, cultural politics, and activism*. New York: New York University Press.
Nagel, C. R. & Staeheli L. A. (2004). Citizenship, identity, and transnational migration: Arab immigrants to the U.S. *Space and Polity* 8(1), 3–24. doi: 10.1080/13562570410001678860
Neal, M., Finlay, J., & Tansey, R. (2005). "My father knows the minister": A comparative study of Arab women's attitudes towards leadership authority. *Women in Management Review* 20, 478–97. doi: 10.1108/09649420510624729
Omair, K. (2009). Arab women managers and identity formation through clothing. *Gender in Management* 24, 421–431. doi: 10.1108/17542410910980397
Read, J. G. (2001). *Dressed for success: Culture, class and labor force achievement among Arab-American women* (Doctoral dissertation). Available from ProQuest Dissertations and Thesis database (UMI No. 3008426).
Read, J. G. (2003). The sources of gender role attitudes among Christian and Muslim Arab-American women. *Sociology of Religion* 64, 207–222. doi: 10.2307/3712371
Read, J. G. & Bartkowski, J. P. (2000). To veil or not to veil? A case study of identity negotiation among Muslim women in Austin, Texas. *Gender & Society* 14, 395–417. doi: 10.1177/089124300014003003
Ruby, T. F. (2006). Listening to the voices of hijab. *Women's Studies International Forum* 29, 54–66. doi: 10.1016/j.wsif.2005.10.006
Ryan, L. (2011). Muslim women negotiating collective stigmatization: 'We're just normal people'. *Sociology* 45, 1045–1060. doi: 10.1177/0038038511416170
Salari, S. (2002). Invisible in aging research: Arab Americans, Middle Eastern immigrants, and Muslims in the United States. *The Gerontologist* 42, 580–588. doi: 10.1093/geront/42.5.580

Saliba, T. (1999). Resisting invisibility: Arab Americans in academia and activism. In M. Suleiman (ed.), *Arabs in America: Building a new future* (pp. 304–319). Philadelphia, PA: Temple University Press.

Shakir, E. (1997). *Bint Arab: Arab and Arab-American women in the United States*. Westport, CT: Greenwood Publishing Group, Inc.

Sidani, Y. (2005). Women, work and Islam in Arab societies. *Women in Management Review* 20(7), 498–512. doi: 10.1108/09649420510624738

Stephan, R. (2010). Couple's activism in Lebanon: The legacy of Laure Moghaizel. *Women Studies International Forum* 33, 533–541. doi: 10.1016/j.wsif.2010.09.009

Stephan, R. (2013). Census projects: United States. In S. Joseph (ed.), *Encyclopedia of women and Islamic cultures*. Brill Online. Retrieved from http://referenceworks.brillonline.com/entries/encyclopedia-of-women-and-islamic-cultures/census-projects-united-states-EWICCOM_001451

Tillion, G. (1983). *The republic of cousins: Women's oppression in Mediterranean society*. London, UK: Al Saqi Books.

Tolaymat, L. & Moradi, B. (2011). U.S. Muslim women and body image: Links among objectification theory constructs and the hijab. *Journal of Counseling Psychology* 58, 383–392. doi: 10.1037/a0023461

Tucker, J. E. (1998). *In the house of the law: Gender and Islamic law in Ottoman Syria and Palestine*. Berkeley, CA: University of California Press.

Vandiver, B. J. (2001). Psychological nigrescence revisited: Introduction and overview. *Journal of Multicultural Counseling and Development* 29, 165–173. doi: 10.1002/j.2161-1912.2001.tb00515.x

Wolf, N. (1991). *The beauty myth: How images of female beauty are used against women*. New York: William Morrow & Company.

Zaher, M. (2013). *Experiences of Arab sexual minorities in the United States* (Doctoral dissertation). Available from ProQuest Dissertations and Theses database (UMI No. 3571528).

10

AGING AND LATER LIFE

Barriers and Adaptations Based on Immigration and Nativity Status

Sonia Salari, Kristine J. Ajrouch, and May H. Aydin

Older adults represent a growing proportion of the U.S. population, and demographic shifts will continue to influence population aging for decades to come. Moreover, the proportion of ethnically diverse older adults is increasing rapidly due to the aging of racial and ethnic minorities. Individuals aged 65 and over make up about 9% of the total Arab ancestry population in the U.S. (Brittingham & de la Cruz, 2005), resulting in 135,000 to 333,000 Arab Americans in that age range. Arab Americans, nevertheless, are relatively youthful in comparison to the general U.S. population due to immigration trends and a higher birth rate (Asi & Beaulieu, 2013).

Important within-group differences exist among Arab Americans (see Samhan, 2014) as a result of immigration waves. For example, national groups that began their immigration to the U.S. in the first part of the twentieth century (i.e. individuals of Lebanese and Syrian background) have the highest proportion of elders in their population (15.7% and 16.3% respectively; Brittingham & de la Cruz, 2005). These individuals and their predecessors typically immigrated during their youth and "aged in place" in the U.S. As a result, they are more likely to have U.S. citizenship compared to younger, more recent waves of Arab immigrants (such as Iraqis and Moroccans) who have arrived since the 1990s.

Immigrant status represents a central factor in understanding the strengths and challenges that come with the psychological aspects of aging. The influence of immigrant status is examined in this chapter using a lifespan/life course theoretical approach to aging. A review of the research literature illuminates the ways in which quality of life in advanced age is influenced by personal history, intergenerational relationships, physical and mental health, coping strategies, economic resources, and social support networks. These factors influence four areas that are important for understanding Arab American aging: patterns of immigration, stressors faced in the U.S., caregiving and formal aging services, and mortality and death. A case example is presented to illustrate these concepts. Finally, the chapter concludes with a critique of the literature and a suggested framework to better understand aging among Arab Americans.

Theoretical Frameworks for Understanding Ethnic Aging

A lifespan/life course approach has gained influence in the scientific study of aging (Settersten, 1999). Both lifespan and life course theories advance the importance of understanding aging as a process that begins with birth and ends with death. Lifespan developmental theory grew out of psychology and emphasizes adaptation (Baltes, 1987). A life course perspective emerged in the field of sociology and emphasizes intersections of inequality (e.g. sexism, racism, and ageism) that may advantage or disadvantage various subgroups (Elder, 1998). Both include a multidisciplinary perspective and emphasize that the aging experience should be understood with simultaneous consideration of age-graded dynamics (e.g. child, young adult, older adult) and historical-graded dynamics (period effects, e.g. war). Both perspectives also recognize that plasticity or individual agency plays an important role. For these reasons, a lifespan/life course perspective allows for attention to diversity in aging trajectories that may arise due to immigration.

Patterns of Immigration to the U.S.

Older Arab Americans in North America may have been born there, immigrated in their youth and aged there, or immigrated in later life (Salari, 2002). Each of these scenarios poses challenges (e.g. potential for discrimination, poor health, cognitive limitations, and disability) as well as benefits (e.g. family, traditions, and collectivist cultural norms). Using the lifespan/life course framework, multiple issues may be considered for better understanding the ways in which the aging experience varies by immigrant status.

U.S.-born. By 2000, approximately 46% of Arab Americans had been born in the U.S. (Brittingham & de la Cruz, 2005), with over 80% U.S. citizenship rates (El Aswad, 2013). U.S.-born elders are often the children of immigrants from the first wave of immigration, which occurred in the first part of the twentieth century. These elders grew up in an era when ethnicity was often hidden, and assimilation to U.S. White middle-class culture was encouraged and expected (Abdulrahim & Ajrouch, 2014). Their families often left the country of origin for economic reasons. Immigrant elders, on the other hand, entered the U.S. during a historical period of enormous change with regard to civil rights, race, and ethnicity. Reasons for their immigration also varied. In addition to economic pursuits, educational goals, political instabilities, and warfare also prompted families to leave their homeland (Orfalea, 1988). Cohort variations in reasons for immigration hold various implications for wellbeing and adaptation in later life (Ajrouch & Jamal, 2007).

Early-life immigrants. First generation Arab immigrants may settle in ethnic communities, which can serve as supportive networks due to functional use of the Arabic language and comfort through shared and familiar cultural beliefs. These "enclave" communities exist in several cities (e.g. Dearborn and Chicago), and can be of particular assistance to newcomers both financially and socially. Group identities are communicated through intergenerational socialization of shared values. A collective sense of "ethnic self" forms an identity with widely shared understandings of ethnic categories and boundaries (Perez & Hirschman, 2009). Although there can be strong community and ethnic identification, psychological wellbeing may vary based on characteristics of the individual and his or her own immigration/naturalization history (Perez & Hirschman, 2009). Those with fewer resources for coping are more dependent on a tight-knit community such as an ethnic enclave. These settings provide opportunities for employment, social interaction, and support, without a high degree of "acculturative stress" – or pressure to conform to the dominant culture (Portes & Rumbaut, 1996). The enclave may be most ideal for immigrants to thrive; however, these settings may also serve to isolate and create dependency if acculturation is completely thwarted (Wilmoth, 2004).

Not all first generation immigrants settle in ethnic enclaves. An example is the Arab immigrants who came to New York and New England between 1890 and 1915, who were studied extensively by Boosahda (2003). She conducted interviews and oral histories with nearly 200 mentally alert respondents in later life (age range: late 80s to 106 years old). Interviewees were typically naturalized Americans of Arab ancestry (from Syria, Lebanon, and Palestine). Much of the participants' recollections indicated that it took financial resources and courage to migrate, and that the journey was often fraught with hardships and setbacks. Many in this older generation reminisced about beginning their journey as sojourners who typically left family members behind, and working to settle in America and send money to their homeland. As they remained in North America, they often attempted to minimize their "foreignness" publically, while preserving ethnic heritage in the home through food, music, dancing, family record keeping, photos, holiday celebrations, and language spoken. Immigrants who decided to stay in America would eventually send for families and their aging parents in an effort to reunify.

Later-life immigrants. Later-life migration likely introduces changes to lifelong belief systems, social roles, networks, and communication patterns, which often create challenges to mental health and life satisfaction (Wilmoth, 2004). Most people do not choose to immigrate in later life. There are special circumstances among some ethnic groups that encourage later-life migration. Sponsorship from relatives would constitute a "pull" factor that could be a positive influence in uniting two generations together again after one had previously settled in the U.S. This family reunification has been found to ease transnational, long-distance caregiving concerns and can improve relationships between younger and older generations of Arab immigrants (Lin, 2012). There are challenges to this arrangement as well. Those from the Middle East who immigrate in later life experience isolation because they have left friends and extended family behind, and then face language barriers and difficulties with acculturation to the new society (Maloof & Ross-Sheriff, 2003; Sengstock, 1996). They may be isolated or "housebound" due to not speaking the predominant language or to having little access to transportation. Much of their time, therefore, is spent on household chores and waiting for children and grandchildren to return home from work and school commitments. Memories of greater self-sufficiency in the Arab world may make the elder transplants feel lonely and obsolete (Kayyali, 2006). Followers of children tend to have lower levels of life satisfaction and greater depressive symptoms (Abu-Bader, Tirmazi, & Ross-Sheriff, 2011; Sayegh, Kellough, Otilingam, & Poon, 2013).

Sengstock (1996) interviewed 98 Muslim immigrants who were mostly Lebanese "followers of children" residing in a Dearborn, Michigan, ethnic enclave. Over half had no education (53%) and others had attended only some elementary school (37%). Despite having dilapidated housing conditions, most respondents reported their housing as adequate. Yet, mental health and life satisfaction scores were poor. Lack of transportation was perceived as a significant barrier to improved wellbeing. Health and social advocates in the Dearborn area were encouraged to be assertive by seeking out those isolated, housebound seniors who were in need of available services. Similar psychological wellbeing challenges were found in a small sample of 70 Arab and non-Arab Muslim later-life immigrants, whereby there was an elevated risk of depressive symptoms, especially among those with higher attachment to their heritage culture or isolation from the dominant culture (Abu-Bader et al., 2011).

In addition to the "pull" factors that attract people toward immigration, later-life immigration may also be influenced by "push" factors, which can be defined as those that compel an individual to leave their homeland due to hazards or threats to personal or familial safety. An example would be Arab elders who must flee warfare, religious persecution, or other stressful or oppressive conditions in the country of origin (Abi-Hashem, 2006). Traumatic or life-threatening experiences during the life course are likely to have adverse psychological effects, and there is growing concern about long-term exposure to stress as the result of conflicts and wars that have often persisted over time (Jawad, Sibai, & Chaaya, 2009).

Prior to immigration, many who have fled war-torn homelands may have come from generations of families influenced by stress. Birth cohorts may have experienced long spells of trauma, where explosions, death, tragedy, lack of basic household utilities, and loss defined their daily existence. To cope in such an environment often required special psychological and emotional stability, problem-solving skills, resources, strong faith, and hope. A study of 40 West Bank Palestinian women in the 1980s found greater levels of political worry and personal helplessness (external locus of control) after conflict. Young women tended to have these reactions, but they differed from older women as they also showed "initiative" to better the situation. The author concluded that this difference reflected a greater internal locus of control among younger persons (Punamäki, 1990). One could surmise that perhaps repeated exposure to trauma had diminished the older women's optimism, internal locus of control, and initiative. Therefore, predictions would indicate that younger women who immigrated to the U.S. from traumatic situations in the Arab world may show more resilience and positive adaptation when compared to their older female counterparts.

Stressors and Protective Factors Experienced Within the U.S.

Endangerment and violence in the older immigrant's homeland may not be the only experience of stress, as older adults likely face difficulties in the host country as well. Discrimination, financial challenges, and acculturation represent potential strains Arab American elders face in the U.S., whether they were immigrants or U.S.-born. Other stressors differ by nativity status. At the same time, there are many resources and networks of support that Arab American elders can utilize to enhance their resilience when facing such stressors.

Discrimination

In the U.S., discrimination is a force Arab Americans must contend with at any age (Moradi & Hasan, 2004). The 9/11 terrorist attacks in 2001, and the annual anniversaries, have been associated with increases in prejudice and hardship for Arab Americans (Elaasar, 2004). Consequences of the terrorist attacks include increased attention paid to members of this ethnic minority, who became "hyper-visible" (Awad, Martinez, & Amer, 2013). Intolerance has included acts of vandalism and arson of businesses, as well as personal attacks. Older persons are not immune from negative attitudes and behaviors directed at them or their family members (Salari, 2002). With regard to immigration status, the perception of discrimination may be more pronounced among U.S.-born elders than among their immigrant counterparts (Ajrouch, 2005a).

Financial Challenges

Financial stressors may exist for Arab Americans, particularly among those who recently immigrated. The 2000 U.S. Census showed approximately 11% of Arab Americans aged 65 and over were living in poverty (Brittingham & de la Cruz, 2005). According to the American Community Survey, which is conducted by the Census Bureau, recent figures for poverty and near-poverty income in the Arab American community as a whole had risen to nearly 17% (Asi & Beaulieu, 2013), and elderly persons represent a population disproportionately vulnerable to economic hardship. Fakhouri's (2001) research found two-thirds of Arab elder respondents did not have enough resources for all their expenses.

Financial pressures were exacerbated by the economic downturn of 2008, which influenced certain areas in the U.S. harder than others. As an example, Detroit, which has a large Arab community, requested government stimulus programs to keep the automobile industry functioning and, on July 18, 2013, the city filed for bankruptcy. There are widespread concerns in the news media about how people living in poverty will be assisted under these harsh conditions (Jones, 2013), and retirement pensions will be cut substantially for many retirees under the largest municipal bankruptcy in U.S. history (Associated Press, 2014). These factors have no doubt influenced the Arab ethnic enclave communities. Other Arab enclaves exist in various cities, including Chicago. Conditions there have also been described as bleak, without a reliable economic safety net and migration en masse of the middle class to the suburbs (Cainkar, 2009). Typically, when there is widespread out-migration of the young, older first generation immigrants may be left behind in a weakened enclave environment. Results of this demographic shift may lead to a structural support vacuum, especially for those who are vulnerable.

Moreover, in recent years, there have been changes to the welfare policies in the U.S. These changes are relevant because immigrants were removed from many of the programs to which they had legally been entitled in the past. This has resulted in greater pressure on family sponsors for the financial, instrumental, and caregiving support of recent immigrants. The Personal Responsibility and Work Opportunity Reconciliation Act of 1996 reduced the chances that recent legal immigrants could qualify for means-tested welfare programs such as Medicaid and Supplemental Security Income (SSI). These programs have a requirement of low income and assets to qualify for enrollment. Traditionally, "followers of children" were eligible for SSI, instead of Social Security, because they had no labor force history in the U.S. Under the new rules, immigrants cannot qualify for this benefit, leaving them more dependent on family members (Wilmoth, 2004). Financial stress may keep immigrant families from sponsoring their older parents if recent immigrants have lower levels of education and fewer resources.

Acculturative Stress

Acculturative stress is thought to influence minority group health and is defined as "mental or emotional strain of the process of change that individuals or populations may undergo when they come in contact with a different culture" (El-Sayed, Tracy, Scarborough, & Galea, 2011a, p. 5). These pressures may be more relevant for first generation immigrants, and vary by age of immigration. Acculturative stress was linked to depression in a sample of 200 Arab Americans aged 60 to 92 with limited English fluency residing in the U.S. Those with refugee or temporary resident status were worse off compared to those with more permanent living arrangements. In addition, those who perceived pressure to learn English had poorer mental health outcomes (Wrobel, Farrag, & Hymes, 2009; see also Ajrouch, 2007a). The level of such stress may vary according to exposure to pressures to acculturate, with lower levels for those immigrants residing in ethnic enclaves (El-Sayed, Tracy, Scarborough, & Galea, 2011b).

Protective Factors and Resilience

Given the impact of stressors for older Arab populations, it is important to attend to the potential for resilience in the face of great hardship. Wrobel and Paterson (2014) suggested that emphasizing "acculturation" (adapting to a new culture while retaining one's own) rather than the more traditional focus on "assimilation" (relinquishing ethnic culture to adopt dominant identity) could promote better mental health. A collectivist orientation can foster interdependence and group goals, in which resilience could be part of the solution. Religious worship and affiliation may also be related to positive mental health outcomes among older persons of Arab ancestry. There may be a greater ability to cope with negative events, such as death (Wrobel & Paterson, 2014).

Resilience and Challenges to Wellbeing by Nativity Status

The lifespan/life course perspective advances the idea that human development is most usefully understood by attending to individual and societal level factors, with a focus on processes of adaptation and the ways in which various social status factors (e.g. race, ethnicity, gender, class) intersect. Immigrant status is a key social status factor that shapes challenges as well as resilience among elders within the Arab ancestry population in the U.S. (Salari, 2006). These stressors and pressures, as well as positive sources of support, may differ among those who: (a) were born in the U.S., (b) immigrated early in life, or (c) were later-life arrivals.

Table 10.1 illustrates challenges and negative influences on wellbeing for persons from Arab ancestry by nativity status. Negative influences for U.S.-born Arab elders are somewhat similar to other native-born Americans with the addition of changes in physical and cognitive health that may accompany aging. Numerous challenges arise among those who have recently migrated, particularly for those who have experienced trauma in the homeland or during the resettlement process.

Table 10.1 List of Key Factors That Negatively Influence Wellbeing

U.S. Born	*Early Immigrant*	*Later-Life Immigrant*
Poor health	Poor health	Poor health
Discrimination	Discrimination	Discrimination
	Homeland trauma	Homeland trauma
		Long-distance ties
		Isolation
		Lack of transportation
		Language barriers

Table 10.2 List of Key Factors That Positively Influence Wellbeing

U.S. Born	*Early Immigrant*	*Later-Life Immigrant*
Citizenship	Achieved citizenship	Escape from danger
Local family	Local family	Reunified family
Enclave support (if desired)	Enclave support	Enclave support
Language	Language acquisition	
Transportation	Transportation	
Diverse networks	Diverse networks	
Economic opportunity/entitlement	Economic development	
	Internal motivations to immigrate	

For later-life immigrants, there are a number of factors that could negatively influence wellbeing (Sayegh et al., 2013). Life disruption and loss may result as immigrants leave family and friends in the country of origin. Exposure to violence and loss may lead to psychological distress. For some, dislocation may occur more than once before permanent settlement. Family stress can result if new immigrants feel dependent or burdensome. Without access to a preexisting enclave community, there might be language barriers, transportation issues, blocked access to resources, and a lack of familiar foods and culture. With little or no paid employment history in the U.S., individuals may lack economic supports in later life. Finally, discrimination in the host country is another factor that has the potential to negatively influence wellbeing in later life. This affects persons in all three categories of nativity/immigration.

As shown in Table 10.2, positive influences on wellbeing also differ depending on nativity status. Those of Arab ancestry who were born and have aged in the U.S. may have developed continuous relationships with others for social support and interaction. Economically, they often have more options, as they have citizenship and access to public programs such as social security. The ethnic enclave is just one option of many resources available to those who are motivated by the benefits of ties to culture, such as food and language.

Those who immigrated in early life are likely to be more resilient compared to later-life immigrants, with sufficient time to adjust to the larger society after arrival. The ethnic enclave can provide the early-life immigrants with comforts of the homeland. There is a greater chance that immigration early in life came with an internal motivation, or a "pull," to the new country, with opportunities for schooling, economic betterment, or family reunification. Internal pulls toward migration may assist in the acculturation process and long-term sense of wellbeing once a person survives to old age. Positives of later-life migration include the ability to reunite with any adult children and grandchildren, and obtain safety from violence in the homeland. In addition to these benefits, there is a potential for later-life immigrants to develop new friendships and support networks gained in the ethnic enclave.

Psychological Health and Chronic Conditions in Advanced Age

Physical and mental health conditions are important predictors of wellbeing in later life. Survival to an advanced age is increasingly prevalent in the Arab world for both women and men, and there has been a shift from infectious to chronic disease causes of death (Mokdad et al., 2014). For ethnic communities in the U.S., the needs of those over the age of 65 will magnify in the next few decades. Persons 85 and over have the most intensive needs related to prevalent functional disability and cognitive impairment. Researchers have noted a health advantage among many immigrants (mostly Hispanics), but Arab American elders do not seem to enjoy this benefit (Abdulrahim & Baker, 2009; Dallo, Al Snih, & Ajrouch, 2009).

There is some evidence that functional disability and mortality are related to foreign birth and the conditions experienced in the country of origin. The U.S. Census shows higher disability prevalence among elderly foreign-born Arab Americans, compared to those of Arab ethnicity born in the U.S. (Dallo et al., 2009). Immigrants from specific countries, such as Iraq and Syria, reported higher rates of disability, likely due to the experiences of violence, warfare, and political strife in those countries of origin. Dallo and colleagues found that English language ability was an important mediator in the relationship between nativity and disability status. Furthermore, Arab American elders tend to exhibit a relationship between lower education and poor self-rated health, chronic illness, and functional disability (Ajrouch, 2007a). However, existence of a positive relationship with an adult child tended to moderate this relationship. As is the case with other groups, social relations with key others, especially family members, provide a potential resource that aids in buffering the deleterious effects of various stressor types.

Dementia is difficult to assess among those with Arab ancestry due to underreporting and cultural differences in measurement (Sayegh et al., 2013). Alzheimer's disease is a "progressive neurodegenerative condition characterized clinically by a gradual loss of memory and cognitive functions" (Meng et al., 2006, p. 871). However, detection using the Mini Mental State Exam (MMSE) can be a challenge for Arab ethnic populations due to the exam's potential cultural variations. In other words, older persons may differ with regard to language, education, and exposure to the dominant culture. Performance on the MMSE is a more valid indicator of cognitive decline among higher educated persons when compared to those with little or no education (Wrobel & Farrag, 2007).

There is evidence that Arab Americans may suffer greater depressive symptoms when compared to other minorities, such as African Americans (Jamil et al., 2008). There were high levels of depression, anxiety, and posttraumatic stress disorder among a sample of three waves of Iraqi refugees (Jamil, Nassar-McMillan, & Lambert, 2007). Nativity and age seem to make a difference within the Arab ancestry population in the U.S. Wrobel and associates (2009) found that among Arab American older adults, refugees and recent arrivals had the greatest risk of depressive symptoms compared to citizens or permanent residents.

Mental health concerns may be higher for later-life immigrants. Many transplants from the war-torn regions of the Middle East have immigrated to flee the daily feelings of grief, anguish, fear, and desperation. "Migratory grief" (see Sayegh et al., 2013) tends to exist for many who have fled danger in their homeland. Memories of the experiences are likely to result in some degree of lifelong psychological trauma, with possible mood disorders, difficulty functioning, depressive symptoms, and problems in relationships (Abi-Hashem, 2006; Sayegh et al., 2013). Observed outcomes may differ depending on the point in the life course when these war-related stressors are experienced by the older Arab immigrant (Jawad et al., 2009). In addition, immigrants may suffer from "secondary trauma" if they still have endangered family members who continue to live in the war-torn region (see Sayegh et al., 2013). Those with good health, social networks, and strong communities are expected to show the greatest level of resilience from the trauma-related stressor (Abi-Hashem, 2006).

Availability of family and community interaction is important to psychological wellbeing. A comparison between 101 immigrant and native-born Arab Americans aged 56 and over living in Detroit found wellbeing differences, with U.S.-born Arab Americans having less frequent feelings of depression and greater overall life satisfaction. Language proficiency and education appeared to account for these differences. Relationship with an adult child had a direct effect on wellbeing for later-life immigrants, but did not explain any of the variance. For this population, problems associated with financial need, poor health, cognitive decline, and issues of discrimination may serve to decrease life satisfaction and support (Ajrouch, 2007b).

Little is known about the attitudes toward and use of mental health services among older Arab Americans. Mental illness may be feared by Arabs who hold traditional beliefs, because psychiatric issues are often seen to have religious origins. Symptoms may be interpreted as a lack of faith in God. Older adults may assign negative meaning to the experience of mental illness, and the symptoms may often be met with deep-seated fear and a lack of understanding. Socially, mental illness may be denied or minimized in families of affected persons, leading to stigma and extreme isolation of the vulnerable person (Nobles & Sciarra, 2000; Salari & Balubaid, 2006).

Because of these barriers, the utilization of trained mental health practitioners may be uncommon among the older generation. Different from the individualistic focus of U.S. mental healthcare, Arab American families may have a greater tendency toward a collectivistic approach. Family members may play a strong role in care for those with mental health issues (Al-Krenawi & Graham, 2001). There may be barriers associated with securing culturally sensitive treatment in the U.S. (Nobles & Sciarra, 2000). For example, in Western societies, there is a greater emphasis on sharing "bad news" medical diagnoses (including Alzheimer's disease and mental health disorders) with the individual patient, the so-called "open awareness" approach to end-of-life care (Glaser & Straus, 1965). This practice can clash with cultural values of Arab American families, who may prefer to shield terminally ill or cognitively impaired persons from the hard realities of disease (Cohen, Werner, & Azaiza, 2009; Salari & Balubaid, 2006). Therefore, traditional remedies may be sought over modern pharmaceutical assistance (Salari & Balubaid, 2006). One example is the use of traditional healers, who have been employed widely in various regions of the Arab world. These methods would be more familiar to recent immigrants. The active role of the healer often incorporates religious influences of Islam and spiritual healing into the process (Al-Rawi & Fetters, 2012). Recruiting family members into the support network is an important part of this method, and the client is viewed as somewhat passive in the process.

Caregiving and Formal Aging Services

With the aging of the population in Arab American communities, there is a need to assess family caregiving potential, plan for service provision, and consider alternative care sources for the older population. In Arab culture there is a strong sense of filial obligation, with a high motivation to care for older family members in the home (Fakhouri, 2001). At the same time, one focus group study found the concept of independence emerging as a salient theme among Arab Americans aged 60 and over in the Detroit metropolitan area, as parents expressed a desire not to become burdensome to their offspring. Although there is cultural aversion to care facilities and state-sponsored support, recognition exists among many that these formal sources of support may be necessary (Ajrouch, 2005b).

Like most Americans, Arab American men are more likely than women to be married and living with a spouse until their death (Asi & Beaulieu, 2013). Therefore, during widowhood (a time that may last for decades), women are at risk for having no family support in the case of their own illness or functional disability. Relying almost exclusively on offspring for caregiving help, women may eventually need to use alternative care sources.

Kayyali (2006) described a cultural aversion toward formal service utilization. Arab Americans may consider residence in nursing homes an American solution, and may express either annoyance or anger toward the potential for this outcome. However, there are times when formal care is the only viable option; for example, when the level of functional disability of elderly parents becomes overwhelming, placing too much strain on family caregivers. Catastrophic chronic conditions such as dementia, stroke, Parkinson's Disease, injury, or other functional disability may force families to seek the necessary services to ensure appropriate care and safety for their loved ones.

Elders who live to advanced old age have an increased chance of a dwindling supply of caregivers. For instance, the emerging population of centenarians (who live to at least 100 years) have adult children who may be of advanced age themselves (e.g. 80-plus years old). Caregiving may strain the children's own health and resources, and the parent may outlive the immediate support network. Grandchildren may experience pressures of competing life demands, which may leave them struggling to care for multiple dependent generations. In the absence of another family caregiver, nursing homes may be an option of last resort. These issues point to the need for careful planning to prepare for an aging population with special cultural considerations.

There are a handful of services available in large cities where concentrations of people from Arab origin reside. Kayyali (2006) pointed to the logical utilization of mosques for serving older Muslim members; Ajrouch and Fakhoury (2013) agreed, but identified other resources beyond the mosque as important sources to consider. Residence in skilled nursing facilities may be the only way to obtain Medicaid assistance for a family member struggling with severe cognitive or functional decline. However, nursing home use may be hindered due to welfare reform policy restrictions for recent immigrants, who must reside in the U.S. for at least five years to qualify, and also due to limited access to Medicaid in some states (Wilmoth, 2004). A study by Fakhouri (2001) found nursing home use among a minority of elderly Arab Americans, where language barriers served as a severe impediment to social interaction. To adapt to the differences, staff members communicated basic needs via sign language. Nursing home administrators were urged to do a better job of providing a good quality of life for Arab American elderly persons by including social opportunities, bilingual aides, and considerations for dietary standards.

Mortality and Death

The final stage of the life course includes matters related to mortality and death. Factors that influence longevity, as well as issues to consider regarding death, may vary by immigrant status for Arab Americans. Life expectancy at birth has not been calculated for the entire Arab ancestry community, though there has been a study that investigated age-adjusted mortality among residents in Michigan 1990–2007 (El-Sayed et al., 2011a). The study found a lower life expectancy among Arab American men (72.8 years) and women (78.7) compared to non-Hispanic White men (74.8) and women (80.1). These findings were somewhat unexpected due to the higher relative rates of education and income among Arab Americans. The authors attributed this mortality disadvantage to high levels of chronic and infectious disease, as well as discrimination and acculturative stress. The association between immigrant status and mortality, however, was not tested.

In the first study of its kind, El-Sayed and colleagues (2011b) examined the suicide rate of Arab-ancestry Michigan residents. Those living in Wayne County (the highest concentrated Arab enclave) had lower rates of suicide than nonethnic White residents. Arab Americans in other Michigan counties had higher suicide rates than those in Wayne County, but still lower than the non-Hispanic White population. Reasons attributed by the authors for lower suicide risk among racial and ethnic minorities were protective factors including "ethnic density" and the benefits of the enclave economy. In addition, minority group members may benefit from family closeness, positive group identity, collectivist social orientation, and emotional expressiveness (Leong & Leach, 2008).

Death can be a sensitive subject among those in the Arab American community, and practitioners are warned to conduct outward discussion of the topic with caution (Nobles & Sciarra, 2000).

Muslim Arabs who immigrated during the 1970s and beyond may prefer to be buried in the U.S. in specialized cemeteries when available (in coffins, and facing Mecca if possible). There is a need to plan for the increased demand to accommodate wishes associated with death, dying, and hospice services over the next few decades (Kayyali, 2006).

Case Example: Mrs. Rana Farrag's Journey in Later Life

Mrs. Rana Farrag, aged 76, lived for 73 years in Egypt. In 2011, she became a widow after her husband Mohammed became ill with bone cancer and died after prolonged suffering. Rana was left with very few resources and very limited extended family in Egypt. Widespread violence broke out in her homeland at the beginning of the "Arab Spring." At the urging of her friends and family, she immigrated to the U.S. to join her eldest, 56-year-old son Tarek, his wife Leila, and their three adolescent children in Dearborn, Michigan. The family was glad to be united in the same country. Despite space concerns, all family members resided in the same household. Rana faced communication difficulties, as she only spoke Arabic and the younger, more Americanized grandchildren could not understand her conversation. Tarek spoke to her in her native language, but most of the time he spoke English with his family. This was isolating for Rana, and it required her to signal her needs in other ways, or remain quiet much of the time.

There were widespread economic problems in the automotive industry where Tarek made his living. Despite promises made to the U.S. government regarding sponsorship of his mother, he found it hard to support her along with his children, who were in need of college tuition in the coming years. Rana was limited in her ability to pay her own way. She suffered from painful arthritis, but considered herself fortunate health-wise.

Government aid was not available to Rana in the form of Medicaid, food stamps, or SSI, due to immigrant exclusion laws. When unexpected expenses arose, the family lacked enough food to eat. It would have been considered too stigmatizing to seek assistance from a local food bank. Fortunately, religious figures in the community recognized the family's need and invited them to gatherings and home-cooked meals.

When she became ill with pneumonia, Rana kept her symptoms hidden to keep the family from worrying about her. She also avoided healthcare services until her condition worsened and the situation became dire. Ultimately, she spent two days in hospital, which increased the financial pressures on the family. During the health crisis, Tarek and his family worried about her condition and feared she might die. Fortunately, she recovered enough to leave the hospital, and Leila and the grandchildren assisted her with personal tasks when she returned home. Her son provided instrumental support by handling her finances.

Socially, Rana was homesick and missed her friends in Egypt. It was difficult for her to see news footage of political strife in her homeland. She realized she would probably never return home. In Egypt, she had had a greater social life and access to a public transportation system. In the U.S., she was able to find friends her age who had been through similar experiences in her local immigrant enclave. In these social circles she could speak her native language, find supportive networks, and laugh again.

This case example illustrates the many stressors Rana experienced, influencing her quality of life in both Egypt and the U.S. Welfare reform policy changes now exclude "followers of children" from supplemental income supports that were available for previous later-life immigrants. Her family felt the negative effects of the recent economic downturn. Without medical insurance, she attempted to ration her own healthcare. This strategy may shorten her life eventually, unless she obtains coverage under the recently enacted Affordable Care Act. On the other hand, she was grateful to be reunited with her son and his family and get to know her grandchildren better. The immigrant enclave gave her solace, a place where she could relax and communicate more freely with her female peers who had been through similar situations.

Critique

Despite the increased attention to the topic of ethnic aging, there is still a great deal of need for further study and theoretical development. Current elderly immigrants have more pressures than those in past generations. Rigid immigration rules in the U.S. now require families to take on more burden and risk to sponsor an elderly parent. Means-tested programs (i.e. Medicaid, SSI, and Food Stamps) require low income and assets. These supplements were available to previous generations of elderly immigrants, but are no longer serving as a safety net for more recent legal immigrants. More research is needed, as it is unclear what effects these changes have had on the ethnic elderly.

Cognitive and emotional problems have also been understudied in the aging Arab American community. These problems are of importance because adults with Alzheimer's disease or other dementia are likely to experience a sharp decline in their social interactions. Other adults may begin to limit conversations or visits, and families may become isolated regarding required help with caregiving. More research is needed to document the experience for caregivers and vulnerable persons in the Arab American community. This focus is of importance to predict the need of assistance and plan accordingly, as large-scale population aging takes place over the next decades.

As was discussed above, little is known about the use of mental health services among older Arab Americans. The utilization of trained mental health counselors and therapists may be uncommon among the older generation. There is need for further research, with a focus on the symptoms, clinical needs, and help available to elderly persons. Trust must be developed between researcher and participants to overcome previous negative experiences and discrimination (Amer & Hovey, 2012).

Arab Americans in later life have been previously described as "invisible" in aging research (Salari, 2002). The omission of this ethnic population from mainstream discussions remains somewhat discouraging. As an example, the newly published *Handbook of Minority Aging* (2014) has only a very minimal description of studies concerning the lives of older Arab Americans (see, for example, the chapter by Ajrouch & Abdulrahim, 2014). The authors pointed to a need for representative and longitudinal studies to better understand this seriously understudied population (Whitfield & Baker, 2014). Sayegh and colleagues (2013) urged the use of large population-based studies to help determine the true incidence of dementia and mood and anxiety disorders among those of Arab ancestry in the U.S.

Despite the lack of attention to this population, there is reason for optimism as recent reviews and empirical studies have contributed information to help sort the realities from the myths and develop improved theoretical perspectives regarding social support, acculturative stress, discrimination, and psychological wellbeing (e.g. Abi-Hashem, 2006; Ajrouch, 2005a; 2005b; 2007a; 2007b; Awad, 2010; Boosahda, 2003; Sayegh et al., 2013; Wrobel et al., 2009). More research is needed in order to untangle the complex interactions between life course experiences, nativity, immigration, aging, and social mechanisms as they relate to psychological wellbeing in this population. The recent recognition of resilience and positive influences – rather than a continuation of the reliance on negative focus – to describe the conditions in the lives of older adults and their families, both native born and immigrants, is encouraging.

Conclusion

This chapter has illustrated how the experiences of Arab Americans in older life may differ depending on whether they are native-born U.S. citizens, early-life immigrants who have aged in place, or later-life immigrants. Each group has challenges (e.g. potential for discrimination, poor health, disability) and resiliencies (e.g. collectivist strategies, religious support, and family bonds) in later life. The body of evidence suggests the potential for unique adaptation challenges for later-life immigrants compared to the other groups. Living in an ethnic enclave is likely to provide the greatest comfort to older adults who have most recently arrived in the U.S. Quality of life is also related to the experiences of trauma in the homeland and discrimination in the host country, as well as to the resilience in coping with the aftermath.

Future research should consider how the economic recession, along with welfare reform changes, will continue to influence the survival and wellbeing of the individual and family in later life. Long-term planning for ethnic communities must take into account the rapid growth of the elderly population in future years. Will adult children be in a position to care for these older persons as their cognitive and functional impairments increase with age? Or will medical advances that help elders remain independent curb the need for 24-hour caregiving? Perhaps in future, families will rely on specialized assisted living or nursing facilities that attend to cultural needs. Ultimately, attention must be paid to the family as a unit as they cope with the increasing caregiving demands of the aging population. Rather than focusing only on the burden, there is a need for attention to be given to resilience and the benefits associated with increased contact with members of the older generation.

References

Abdulrahim, S. & Ajrouch, K. J. (2014). Arab Americans and the aging process. In S. C. Nassar-McMillan, K. J. Arouch, & J. Hakim-Larson (eds.), *Biopsychosocial perspectives on Arab Americans: Culture, development and health* (pp. 107–125). New York: Springer. doi: 10.1007/978-1-4614-8238-3_6

Abdulrahim, S. & Baker, W. (2009). Differences in self-rated health by immigrant status and language preference among Arab Americans in the Detroit metropolitan area. *Social Science and Medicine* 68, 2097–2103. doi: 10.1016/j.socscimed.2009.04.017

Abi-Hashem, N. (2006). The agony, silent grief, and deep frustration of many communities in the Middle East: Challenges for coping and survival. In P. T. P. Wong & L. C. J. Wong (eds.), *Handbook of multicultural perspectives on stress and coping* (pp. 457–486). New York: Springer. doi: 10.1007/0-387-26238-5_20

Abu-Bader, S. H., Tirmazi, M. T., & Ross-Sheriff, F. (2011). Impact of acculturation on depression among older Muslim immigrants in the United States. *Journal of Gerontological Social Work* 54, 425–448. doi: 10.1080/01634372.2011.560928

Ajrouch, K. J. (2005a). Arab American elders: Network structure, perceptions of relationship quality and discrimination. *Research in Human Development* 2, 213–228. doi: 10.1207/s15427617rhd0204_3

Ajrouch, K. J. (2005b). Arab American immigrant elders' views about social support. *Ageing and Society* 25, 655–673. doi: 10.1017/S0144686X04002934

Ajrouch, K. J. (2007a). Health disparities and Arab American elderly: Does intergenerational support buffer inequality-health link? *Journal of Social Issues* 63, 745–758. doi: 10.1111/j.1540-4560.2007.00534.x

Ajrouch, K. J. (2007b). Resources and well-being among Arab-American elders. *Journal of Cross Cultural Gerontology* 22, 167–82. doi: 10.1007/s10823-006-9033-z

Ajrouch, K. J. & Abdulrahim, S. (2014). Intersections among gender, race, and ethnicity: Implications for health. In K. E. Whitfield & T. A. Baker (eds.), *The handbook of minority aging* (pp. 455–470). New York: Springer.

Ajrouch, K. J. & Fakhoury, N. (2013). Assessing needs of aging Muslims: A focus on metro-Detroit faith communities. *Contemporary Islam* 7, 353–372. doi: 10.1007/s11562-013-0240-4

Ajrouch, K. J. & Jamal, A. (2007). Assimilating to a white identity: The case of Arab Americans. *International Migration Review* 41, 860–879. doi: 10.1111/j.1747-7379.2007.00103.x

Al-Krenawi, A. & Graham, J. (2001). The cultural mediator: Bridging the gap between a non-Western community and professional social work practice. *British Journal of Social Work* 31, 665–685. doi: 10.1093/bjsw/31.5.665

Al-Rawi, S. & Fetters, M. D. (2012). Traditional Arabic and Islamic medicine: A conceptual model for clinicians and researchers. *Global Journal of Health Science* 4(3), 164–169. doi: 10.5539/gjhs.v4n3p164

Amer, M. M. & Hovey, J. D. (2012). Anxiety and depression in post-September 11 sample of Arabs in the USA. *Social Psychiatry and Psychiatry Epidemiology* 47, 409–418. doi: 10.1007/s00127-011-0341-4

Asi, M. & Beaulieu, D. (2013). *Arab households in the United States: 2006–2010* (American Community Survey Brief, ACSBR/10–20). Washington, D.C.: U.S. Census Bureau. Retrieved from www.census.gov/prod/2013pubs/acsbr10-20.pdf

Associated Press. (2014). Detroit files plan of adjustment detailing eventual bankruptcy exit: Report. *CNBC*, February 21. Retrieved from www.cnbc.com/id/101435415

Awad, G. H. (2010). The impact of acculturation and religious identification on perceived discrimination for Arab/Middle Eastern Americans. *Cultural Diversity and Ethnic Minority Psychology* 16, 59–67. doi: 10.1037/a0016675

Awad, G. H., Martinez, M. S., & Amer, M. M. (2013). Considerations for psychotherapy with immigrant women of Arab/Middle Eastern descent. *Women and Therapy* 36, 163–175. doi: 10.1080/02703149.2013.797761

Baltes, P. B. (1987). Theoretical propositions of life-span developmental psychology: On the dynamics between growth and decline. *Developmental Psychology* 23, 611–626. doi: 10.1037/0012-1649.23.5.611

Boosahda, E. (2003). *Arab-American faces and voices: The origins of an immigrant community*. Austin, TX: University of Texas Press.

Brittingham, A. & de la Cruz, G. P. (2005). *We the people of Arab ancestry in the United States* (Census 2000 Special Report, CENSR-21). Washington, D.C.: U.S. Census Bureau. Retrieved from www.census.gov/prod/2005pubs/censr-21.pdf

Cainkar, L. (2009). *Homeland insecurity: The Arab American and Muslim American experience after 9/11*. New York: Russell Sage Foundation.

Cohen, M., Werner, P., & Azaiza, F. (2009). Emotional reactions of Arab lay persons to a person with Alzheimer's disease. *Aging & Mental Health* 13(1), 31–37. doi: 10.1080/13607860802154440

Dallo, F. J., Al Snih, S., & Ajrouch, K. (2009). Prevalence of disability among U.S. and foreign-born Arab Americans: Results from the 2000 US census. *Gerontology* 55, 153–161. doi: 10.1159/000151538

El Aswad, E. (2013). Arab Americans. In C. E. Cortes (ed.), *Multicultural America: A multimedia encyclopedia* (pp. 266–271). Thousand Oaks, CA: Sage.

Elaasar, A. (2004). *Silent victims: The plight of Arab and Muslim Americans in post 9/11 America*. Bloomington, IN: AuthorHouse.

Elder, G. H. (1998). The life course as developmental theory. *Child Development* 69(1), 1–12. doi: 10.2307/1132065

El-Sayed, A. M., Tracy, M., Scarborough, P., & Galea, S. (2011a). Ethnic inequalities in mortality: The case of Arab Americans. *PLoS ONE* 6(12), e29185. doi: 10.1371/journal.pone.0029185

El-Sayed, A. M., Tracy, M., Scarborough, P., & Galea, S. (2011b). Suicide among Arab-Americans. *PLoS ONE* 6(2), e14704. doi: 10.1371/journal.pone.0014704

Fakhouri, H. (2001). Growing old in an Arab American family. In L. Katz-Olson (ed.), *Age through ethnic lenses* (pp. 160–170). Lanham, MD: Rowman and Littlefield.

Glaser, B. G. & Straus, A. L. (1965). *Awareness of dying*. Chicago, IL: Aldine.

Jamil, H., Grzybowski, M., Hakim-Larson, J., Fakhouri, M., Sahutoglu, J., Khoury, R., & Fakhouri, H. (2008). Factors associated with self-reported depression in Arab, Chaldean and African Americans. *Ethnicity and Disease* 18, 464–470.

Jamil, H., Nassar-McMillan, S., & Lambert, R. (2007). Immigration and attendant psychological sequelae: A comparison of three waves of Iraqi Immigrants. *Journal of Orthopsychiatry* 77, 199–205. doi: 10.1037/0002-9432.77.2.199

Jawad, M. H., Sibai, A., & Chaaya, M. (2009). Stressful life events and depressive symptoms in a post-war context: Which informal support makes a difference? *Journal of Cross-Cultural Gerontology* 24(1), 19–32. doi: 10.1007/s10823-008-9059-5

Jones, T. (2013). Michigan safety net for Boomers frays on bankrupt Detroit. *Bloomberg News*, August 11. Retrieved from www.bloomberg.com/news/2013-08-12/michigan-safety-net-frays-as-detroit-s-bankruptcy-tests-boomers.html

Kayyali, R. (2006). *The Arab Americans*. Westport, CT: Greenwood Press.

Leong, F. T. L. & Leach, M. M. (2008). *Suicide among racial and ethnic minority groups: Theory, research and practice*. New York: Routledge.

Lin, K. (2012). *Aging Arab immigrants: Family portraits from the San Francisco Bay area* (Master's thesis). Available from ProQuest Dissertations and Theses database (UMI No. 1533087).

Maloof, P. S. & Ross-Sheriff, F. (2003). *Muslim refugees in the United States: A guide for service providers*. Washington, D.C.: Center for Applied Linguistics.

Meng, Y., Baldwin, C. T., Bowirrat, A., Waraska, K., Inzelberg, R., Friedland, R. P., & Farrer, L. A. (2006). Association of polymorphisms in the angiotension-converting enzyme gene and AD in Israeli-Arab community. *American Journal of Human Genetics* 78, 871–877. doi: 10.1086/503687

Mokdad, A. H., Jaber, S., Abdel Aziz, M., AlBuhairan, F., AlGhaithi, A., AlHamad, N. M., ... Hussein, S. S. (2014). The state of health in the Arab world 1990 to 2010: An analysis of the burden of diseases, injuries and risk factors. *Lancet* 383, 309–320. doi: 10.1016/S0140-6736(13)62189-3

Moradi, B. & Hasan, N. T. (2004). Arab American persons' reported experiences of discrimination and mental health: The mediating role of personal control. *Journal of Counseling Psychology* 51, 418–428. doi: 10.1037/0022-0167.51.4.418

Nobles, A. Y. & Sciarra, D. T. (2000). Cultural determinants in the treatment of Arab Americans: A primer for mainstream therapists. *American Journal of Orthopsychiatry* 70, 182–191. doi: 10.1037/h0087734

Orfalea, G. (1988). *Before the flames: A quest for the history of Arab Americans*. Austin, TX: University of Texas.

Perez, A. D. & Hirschman, C. (2009). The changing racial and ethnic composition of the U.S. population: Emerging American identities. *Population Development Review* 35(1), 1–51. doi: 10.1111/j.1728-4457.2009.00260.x.

Portes, A. & Rumbaut, R. G. (1996). *Immigrant America: A portrait* (2nd edn.). Berkeley, CA: University of California Press.

Punamäki, R. (1990). Impact of political change on the psychological stress process among West Bank Palestinian women. *Medicine and War* 6(3), 169–181. doi: 10.1080/07488009008408928

Salari, S. (2002). Invisible in aging research: Arab Americans, Muslims and Middle Eastern immigrants in the United States. *The Gerontologist* 42, 580–588. doi: 10.1093/geront/42.5.580

Salari, S. (2006). Aging: United States. In S. Joseph (ed.), *Encyclopedia of women and Islamic cultures*, vol. 3, pp. 14–17). Leiden, The Netherlands: Brill.

Salari, S. & Balubaid, H. (2006). Older Arab Americans. In American Geriatrics Society (ed.), *Doorway thoughts: Cross-cultural health care for older adults*, (vol. 2, pp. 20–35). Sudbury, MA: Jones & Bartlett Publishers.

Samhan, H. H. (2014). Intra-ethnic diversity and religion. In S. C. Nassar-McMillian, K. J. Ajrouch, & J. Hakim-Larson (eds.), *Biopsychosocial perspectives on Arab Americans* (pp. 45–65). New York: Springer. doi: 10.1007/978-1-4614-8238-3_3

Sayegh, P., Kellough, J., Otilingam, P. G., & Poon, C. Y. M. (2013). South Asian and Middle Eastern American older adults: Dementia, mood disorders and anxiety disorders. *Clinical Gerontologist* 36, 216–240. doi: 10.1080/07317115.2013.767873

Sengstock, M. C. (1996). Care of the elderly within Muslim families. In B. C. Aswad & B. Bilge (eds.), *Family and gender among American Muslims: Issues facing Middle Eastern immigrants and their descendants* (pp. 271–300). Philadelphia, PA: Temple University Press.

Settersten, R. A., Jr, (1999). *Lives in time and place: The problems and promises of developmental science*. Amityville, NY: Baywood Publishing Co.

Whitfield, K. & Baker, T. A. (2014). *Handbook of minority aging*. New York: Springer.

Wilmoth, J. (2004). *Social integration of older immigrants in 21st century America* (Policy Brief No. 29). Syracuse, NY: Center for Policy Research, Syracuse University.

Wrobel, N. H. & Farrag, M. F. (2007). Preliminary validation of and Arabic version of the MMSE in the elderly. *Clinical Gerontologist* 31(3), 75–93. doi: 10.1080/07317110802072223

Wrobel, N. H., Farrag, M. F., & Hymes, R. W. (2009). Acculturative stress and depression in an elderly Arabic sample. *Journal of Cross Cultural Gerontology* 24, 273–290. doi: 10.1007/s10823-009-9096-8

Wrobel, N. H. & Paterson, A. (2014). Mental health risks in Arab Americans across the lifespan. In S. C. Nassar-McMillan, K. J. Ajrouch, & J. Hakim-Larson (eds.), *Biopsychosocial perspectives on Arab Americans: Culture, development, and health* (pp.197–228). New York: Springer. doi: 10.1007/978-1-4614-8238-3_10

PART III

Special Populations

11

INTERNATIONAL STUDENTS

Understanding the Adjustment Process of Sojourners

Ayse Çiftçi and Aieyat Zalzala

The U.S. has one of the largest international student populations worldwide, with approximately 800,000 students seeking education in the U.S. during the 2012–13 academic year, a 7.2% increase from the previous year (Institute of International Education, 2013). Approximately 4% of these students are in higher-level education (i.e. education beyond high school, including bachelor's degrees). Eight percent of these international students come from one of the 22 Arab states in the Middle East and North Africa region. For example, Saudi Arabia alone sent 44,566 students for the 2012–13 academic year, followed by Kuwait with 5,115, Egypt with 2,601, and United Arab Emirates with 2,256 students. Some of the reasons for the U.S. attracting these international students are academic excellence, various educational opportunities, cutting-edge technology, long-term career prospects, and flexibility of educational programs. In addition, Arab international students may come to the U.S. for political or personal reasons, or for a degree or training that may not be available in their country of origin. Although some may stay and work after graduation, others will return home (Al-Hattami & Al-Ahdal, 2014; Norris, 2011).

Moving from one country to another is a challenging process. However, moving to the U.S. as a prospective Arab international student may involve many additional challenges. After receiving admission to an academic program in the U.S., these students need to apply for a student visa to be granted permission to study in the U.S. The basic process of applying for a student visa is to visit the U.S. embassy or consulate in the home country, make an appointment for a visa interview, pay application fees, and then bring completed visa application forms to the interview. Applicants are informed that they will be granted a visa based on the consulate officer's satisfaction with the applicant's desire to study in the U.S. The applicant needs to showcase that they are academically qualified for their program of study, have the appropriate funding, and plan on staying in the U.S. only for the duration of their program. There are several organizations (e.g. America-Mideast Educational and Training Services, known as AMIDEAST) that are involved with international education, training, and development activities in the Middle East and North Africa and provide Arab international students with tips on applying for their visa. These organizations provide consultation, application support services, college fairs, and other resources.

The challenges for Arab international students actually start before their arrival to the U.S. Applying to an academic program in the U.S., gaining admission, and moving to the U.S. is an expensive process. These international student applicants pay fees to apply to the academic programs and for the visa with no assurance of being accepted or the visa being granted. In addition, they will be expected to provide financial proof that they can afford their stay in the U.S. After being granted a visa and moving to the U.S., returning to visit their home countries can continue to be a challenge. With the constant changes in rules and regulations, students who leave may have their security clearance re-evaluated. This is especially relevant for Arab international students as the heightened laws around security post 9/11 created hardships for those students coming from such Arab countries (Daraiseh, 2012). Suicide attackers on 9/11 were reported to have entered the U.S. as international students and trained in aviation at U.S. institutions. As a result, there was an increase in hostile media rhetoric toward Arabs and Arab international students. The negative media was in parallel to the backlash against current and potential international students in the form of increased hate crimes and discriminating racial profiling by government officials. This profiling, including all the extensive security checks Arab international students need to undergo, has made it more difficult for Arab international students to receive approval to come to the U.S.

One of the specific changes made after 9/11 was the implementation of the Student and Exchange Visitor Information System (SEVIS). This system is an online database that allows institutions to upload data about each international student, including their visa type, status as a student, biographical information, class registration, and current address. The former U.S. Immigration and Naturalization Service (now U.S. Immigration and Customs Enforcement) had always required updated information about the student prior to and during their stay in the U.S. With this database the Immigration and Naturalization Service now has easier access to the information without having to follow the paper trail that they used prior to the installment of SEVIS. This increased surveillance of international students, specifically Arabs in the U.S., along with current federal regulations, negatively impacts international student enrollment (Urias & Yeakey, 2005). For example, from 2000 to 2004 there was a 65% drop in students coming from Gulf countries and a 52.7% drop in the number of Egyptians (Kayyali, 2006).

Applying to a college program, gaining an admission offer, and going through the visa application process can be challenging, exhausting, and expensive. Once Arab international students go through these steps, they move to the U.S. and go through an adjustment process. There have been a number of theoretical models that can explain cross-cultural adjustment, mostly focusing on psychological and social aspects of this transition (e.g. Berry, 1997; James, Hunsley, Navara, & Alles, 2004; Sam & Berry, 2010; Searle & Ward, 1990). This chapter reviews relevant theoretical models, followed by the research literature on international students, including unique challenges faced by Arab international students. In order to provide a better understanding of the diversity in this population and the complexity of their adjustment, three Arab international students were interviewed for this chapter in regard to their experiences in the U.S. Finally, the chapter provides recommendations for future research and university interventions.

Theoretical Models of Adjustment of International Students

The cross-cultural transition that individuals such as international students go through when they relocate to the U.S. has been the focus of much research in the last couple of decades. There have been different terminologies proposed for this transition, such as adaptation, acculturation, adjustment, and assimilation. Searle and Ward's (1990) and Berry's (1997) models have played a significant role in understanding how individuals transition to a new culture. Searle and Ward distinguished two different forms of adjustment: psychological and sociocultural. Psychological adjustment is rooted in stress and coping models, and refers to an individual's psychological wellbeing. However, sociocultural adaptation is rooted in social learning models and refers to learning culturally appropriate skills. Psychological adjustment is related to personality, life changes, coping styles, and social support; but sociocultural adaptation is influenced by social skills acquisition and culture learning (e.g. length of residence in the new culture, amount of interaction with host nationals, language fluency, and acculturation strategies). Although these two dimensions are related to each other, they should be conceptualized differently because they have different predictors. For example, cultural distance (i.e. the degree to which groups differ culturally) can contribute to sociocultural adjustment. The higher the cultural distance, the less sociocultural adaptation international students are likely to have to make. Thus, Arab international students' perception of cultural differences will impact their sociocultural adaptation to the U.S. For example, the more challenges they experience in understanding jokes and humor in U.S. culture, the more they may face difficulties in their sociocultural adaptation.

Another model that can be relevant to international students' cultural adjustment to the U.S. is John Berry's model. Berry (1997) proposed two dimensions as critical in acculturation: cultural maintenance and contact participation with the host culture. Cultural maintenance is the degree to which individuals value their own heritage culture. Contact participation with the host culture is the degree to which individuals value and become involved in the new host culture. Based on these two dimensions, Berry proposed four different acculturation strategies: assimilation, separation, integration, and marginalization. When individuals do not want to remain in contact with their cultural identity and seek greater interaction with host nationals and culture, this refers to assimilation. In contrast, when individuals avoid contact with people from the host culture and only remain in contact with people of their own cultural identity, this strategy refers to separation. In integration, individuals maintain some degree of heritage cultural integrity while at the same time they seek to participate as an integral part of the larger social network of the host society. When individuals have little interest in cultural maintenance and little interest in having relations with others in the host society, this is referred to as marginalization.

Searle and Ward's (1990) psychological and sociocultural adaptation model and Berry's (1997) acculturation model have received some criticisms. These criticisms mostly come from dialogical theorists and researchers. For example, Hermans and Kempen (1998) criticized the traditional dichotomy models of acculturation (i.e. "individualism versus collectivism," "egocentric versus sociocentric") as linear in nature. They argued that acculturation and identity issues should be considered as "moving and mixing" instead of a linear relationship from culture A to culture B (p. 1117). Bhatia and Ram (2001) criticized Berry's model because individuals moving from different countries or continents will have different acculturation processes. For instance, an individual moving to the U.S. from Europe will have a different acculturation process than an individual moving from Africa. They also criticized Berry's model for suggesting that integration seemed to be the ultimate goal; however, the model does not include guidelines for how to reach the goal of integration or address how other sociopolitical factors might play a role in the acculturation process.

Over the decades, researchers have tested Berry's (1997) model. In a recent study, Schwartz and Zamboanga (2008) used Berry's framework with a group of Hispanic college students. Their results, based on latent class analysis, suggested six clusters instead of four categories: undifferentiated, assimilated, partial bicultural, American-oriented bicultural, separated, and full bicultural. Three of the four acculturation strategies from Berry's model emerged in these clusters: separation, assimilation, and biculturalism (integration). Their findings also suggested variation among the acculturation categories and dependence over each other. In her review of Arab American acculturation and ethnic identity across the lifespan, Amer (2014) provided a critique about the application of these acculturation categories for Arab Americans. She argued that the traditional acculturation strategies do not work for Arab Americans, because most Arab countries were colonies and exposed to Western traditions. Therefore, for many international students, their acculturation starts before they move.

Based on Berry's integration strategy, LaFromboise, Coleman, and Gerton (1993) proposed a bicultural model of alternation, which assumes that a bicultural individual can identify with both cultures, as long as there is a sense of belonging without the loss of cultural identity (see LaFromboise et al. for a full review). According to the alternation model, it is possible to have a positive relationship with both cultures and there is no assumption of a hierarchical relationship between the two cultures (i.e. one culture being more dominant than the other). LaFromboise and colleagues stated that the alternation model is different from integration because of the emphasis of integration on "the relationship between the two cultural groups and its implicit assumption that they are tied together within a single social structure. The alternation model addresses this relationship and includes relationships that do not necessarily evolve within a larger multicultural framework" (p. 401). The authors proposed the following six dimensions of bicultural competence (i.e. ability to develop and maintain competence to function in both cultures):

1. knowledge of cultural beliefs and values, including cultural history and mores;
2. positive attitudes toward both heritage and host culture, without endorsing a hierarchical relation between the two cultures;
3. bicultural efficacy, or having confidence in one's ability to effectively live within two cultural groups while maintaining a sense of cultural identity;
4. effective verbal and nonverbal communication with others from a given culture;
5. role repertoire, or having a range of behaviors or roles that are suitable to the cultural contexts; and
6. a sense of social groundedness, i.e. in the form of a strong support system.

In conclusion, this bicultural model of alternation suggests the behavioral and psychological alternation between the host culture and culture of origin, while maintaining a positive relationship with both cultures (Bender & Ng, 2009).

The process of adjustment varies for each individual. Depending on the variation between the individual's heritage and host cultures, an individual may experience some level of acculturative stress. The intensity of the stress is contingent upon factors such as level of education and skills, sex, age, language, and race, as well as the political attitude of the host culture toward those from the person's cultural/national background. The fear of those who appear foreign is particularly prevalent in regard to Arab students who come to live in the U.S. in a post-9/11 community. Yakushko (2009) defined xenophobia as "a form of attitudinal, affective, and behavioral prejudice toward immigrants and those perceived as foreign" (p. 43). Although the U.S. is said to be a country that welcomes people from all parts of the world, xenophobia continues to exist. Therefore, it is important to examine what factors may be influencing the adjustment process of Arab international students.

Adjustment Issues Among Arab Students

Arab international students may encounter adjustment problems or stress in areas of language, academic performance, and social and cultural interactions. Language proficiency is an important factor in international students' adjustment to the U.S. and can potentially be a struggle for Arab international students. Although some come to the U.S. with some level of English-speaking skills, some enter U.S. colleges with little or no English proficiency. In addition to language-related difficulties, these students need to learn how to navigate simple logistics such as registration for classes. The students who do not speak English well may have a difficult time deciding which courses are best suited to them, even with the help of an advisor.

International students' language proficiency can influence their academic success and adjustment to the host country's culture. A high level of language proficiency instills a stronger sense of confidence and self-esteem among international students, making them more comfortable contributing to classroom discussions and performing better academically (Kao & Gansneder, 1995). Furthermore, this confidence assists in socializing with their American peers, further enhancing their cultural adjustment (Hayes & Lin, 1994). Researchers have found that gender can be one indicator of international students' proficiency. Oxford and Nyikos (1989) found that in learning a second language, females employ more learning techniques than their male counterparts. For instance, females may be more likely to actively seek out and converse with native speakers, giving them more opportunities to grow in their language proficiency. In a PsycINFO search conducted in October, 2014, using the keywords "Arab," "students," and "language," no research was found examining language proficiency among Arab international students in the U.S.

International students may come to the U.S. with certain expectations about the education system, such as higher standards, fair access to resources, and easy navigation of the system. Upon arriving, however, it can be difficult for them to understand the vast differences between their perceptions of academics in the U.S. and the system of their home country. For instance, a different teaching style in the U.S. can confuse Arab international students and lead to loss of confidence in their academic ability (Al-Hattami & Al-Ahdal, 2014). The misconception about American education systems extends to the lack of understanding of the different educational services available to students. Sherry, Bhat, Beaver, and Ling (2004) found that international students were less aware than their domestic student counterparts of the different services their educational institutions offered. This discrepancy has been shown to leave international students with more adjustment difficulties (Khawaja & Dempsey, 2008).

Students studying in a foreign country may begin to feel more comfortable after more time and interaction with the people of that country. The increase in exposure to a new culture may reduce any levels of fear and discomfort and increase the understanding of the host country's culture and people. Alreshoud and Koeske (1997) discovered that this increase in understanding, however, does not mean that Arab international students will have a change in attitude about their host country. Lack of intercultural communication competence among American students, negative stereotypes among peers, and fears of unfavorable attitudes toward international students may keep international students feeling as though they are better off with less interaction with Americans (Harrison, 2012; Williams & Johnson, 2011). The perceived discrimination experienced by Arab international students may create more difficulties in their acculturation process. For example, a number of studies indicated that international students with higher levels of perceived discrimination also reported higher levels of adjustment difficulties (Duru & Poyrazli, 2011; Kilinc & Granello, 2003).

International Arab students' perception of being discriminated against may influence how the students interact with their social environment. They may use organizations and religious venues as places to come together with people of similar ethnic identities. For instance, the use of college organizations based on nationality or religion (e.g. Muslim Students Associations, Egyptian Student Association) gives them a chance to explore their own culture rather than American culture. Duru and Poyrazli (2011) found that exposure to discrimination can result in negative attitudes about the host culture among international students, making adapting to that environment more difficult. Therefore, they may have fewer opportunities to increase their connection to the host country's social and academic environment, a connection that could have helped them in coping with the stress of adapting to a new environment. Overall, more friendships with American students have indicated less acculturation strain and better adjustment (Hechanova-Alampay, Beehr, Christiansen, & Van Horn, 2002).

Finally, Arab students may have a difficult time with practical issues, particularly related to financial challenges. Coming from their home countries to the U.S. means learning a different budgeting system, which may potentially cause them to have debt. With just a student visa, international students are not granted the same rights as a U.S. citizen, and therefore are not normally permitted to work. If they are granted permission to work, international students must maintain a full-time student schedule and cannot take on more than a part-time job (U.S. Citizenship and Immigration Services, 2014). They are also very limited in the loans they can have. For instance, student loans are only given to those students who attend an approved school and have a U.S. citizen or permanent resident who can cosign the loan with them. This is impossible for many of these students that have been sent to the U.S. alone. Funding becomes more difficult when international students cannot find work for nonresidents.

Case Examples of Three Arab International Students: Zena, Muna, and Sayed

Even though there are shared experiences that international students go through when they move to the U.S. for their education, there are certainly unique issues for Arab international students. In order to better understand the diverse experiences of Arab international students, interviews were conducted with three respondents from diverse academic and social backgrounds. The interviews included questions concerning the students' move to the U.S., relationships with Americans, changes in worldview and identities, feelings toward the U.S., and overall positive and negative moments while studying in the U.S. One purpose was to understand how these experiences influenced them, not only while they studied in the U.S., but also as they interacted with people from their country of origin. A summary of their experiences is described below (names and details have been modified to protect confidentiality). The interviewees highlight some of the same struggles other international students face, but also present the unique perspectives of Arab international students.

Zena: Moving From a Village in Lebanon as a Woman

Zena was a single, Lebanese woman who had been in the U.S. for four years, studying for her doctorate. Zena was the oldest of four siblings and the only family member living outside Lebanon. Zena stated that she was the first woman who had left her village to attend college. Because there were no doctoral degrees in her field at home, she decided to move abroad for her education. Even though she considered moving to Europe, the funding process seemed easier to her in the U.S. Using websites such as AMIDEAST, and knowing people in the U.S., helped in her transition from a small rural village to the U.S. While it was a difficult concept for her conservative community to understand, her family was much more receptive to the idea. Their receptiveness to her leaving was because they were under the impression that the U.S. could provide her with what she needed (i.e. a graduate degree) to excel in her field. Upon arriving in the U.S., she quickly recognized a number of career opportunities in her field and discovered the endless professional opportunities. This has left her considering finding work in the U.S. upon graduation.

Zena found comfort engaging with other international students, specifically students from Latin America. She found these interactions comforting, since she found that other international students were willing to learn about her culture and that she could notice cultural similarities. For example, her friends from Latin America shared similar values about family (e.g. importance of having a big family and spending time with extended family). The chance to interact with people from various backgrounds was an aspect of American culture she could appreciate. Zena stated that she knew, coming to this college, that there would be only a few individuals from Lebanon. However, she wanted to see how others live and learn about different lifestyles from other internationals and/or Americans.

Zena stated that it was at this college that she was called "Arab" for the first time. Back at home, she was Lebanese. Even though she knew many Arabs shared values and lifestyles, she always realized the differences because she interacted with other Arabs. For example, she realized that Lebanon is more liberal compared to other Arab nations. Zena also commented that it was a challenge to balance maintaining her identity as a Lebanese student while being a part of American culture.

While Zena was able to broaden her worldview by meeting people from different cultures, she was met with resistance when she attempted to engage with U.S. domestic students or European Americans. For instance, the Arab culture has greetings that are often filled with touches and hugs, and so she found herself confused with how to engage with Americans who found this sort of greeting to be an invasion of personal space. Although she made many connections with U.S.-born individuals through attending church, one reason she felt it was difficult to make friendships with

Americans was the difference in cultural interactions. Furthermore, she struggled with the individualistic ideology that is common in American culture. It was difficult for her to understand why some of her U.S.-born colleagues could go weeks without speaking with or visiting their families. She believed that the whole family should be involved in many of the decisions that she saw American students making on their own.

Another cause for this disconnect between the interviewee and her peers was the ignorance she saw to be present about Arabs. The assumption that all Arabs are Muslim, for instance, was just one example of the lack of knowledge her American peers had about her religious and cultural beliefs. She even felt that many of the Americans she did interact with had little interest in learning more about her viewpoints.

On a final note, Zena also shared some of the challenges she needed to manage with her country of origin. She stated that she had more access to different worldviews and conversations in the U.S. For example, people discuss liberal topics such as abortion. She would never have had these conversations back in Lebanon. Even though she decided to "stick to what she always believed in," these discussions changed her. For example, she became more aware of some of the racism and lack of knowledge or awareness about other cultures and communities found among members of her own community in Lebanon. She shared that whenever someone from her larger community in Lebanon asked during her visits to Lebanon about her marriage prospects, she told them that she would marry someone from China, which raised a lot of concerns but also gave her opportunities to educate her community and overcome stereotypes.

Muna: Being a Palestinian With an Israeli Passport

Muna is a Palestinian woman who moved to the U.S. from Israel a year ago. Coming from a family of educated parents and siblings who believe that academics are important made it easier for her to move to the U.S. to seek higher education. Furthermore, escaping the political and lifestyle difficulties of a Palestinian living in Israel was an important part of her decision to move to the U.S. She came on an international scholarship to study for her master's degree. After receiving this scholarship, she participated in a lengthy orientation program where she was able to learn about the education system and lifestyle in the U.S. Although this program made the transition easier, she still found it difficult to navigate everyday tasks such as using public transport instead of driving. Since arriving in the U.S. she has not made a clear decision as to whether or not it would be better to stay and work toward a doctorate or to return home. While she understood that the U.S. has a more "convenient" and predictable lifestyle and has an academically better atmosphere, she felt a lack of true connection to the U.S. In other words, she stated that she did not feel emotionally connected with anybody in the U.S.

Most of Muna's social interactions had been with those she met through the scholarship office, her romantic partner (who was also a sojourner in the U.S.), and other minority students (e.g. Arab Americans, Asian Americans) on campus. However, she struggled to form friendships with her European American peers. This struggle stemmed from some of the negative experiences she faced with this population. She described interactions in which people questioned her accent and expressed confusion about her atheist identity, since she was from a Christian family and had Israeli citizenship. The pressure to constantly explain her Palestinian identity, even though she was an Israeli citizen, often left her frustrated. She stated that her experience as a Palestinian living in Israel was a very salient experience. She also commented that she had many friends in Europe who knew more about what it was like to live as a "Palestinian in Israel" than an "Israeli in Israel." She described the ignorance that she observed in the U.S. about the complexities of the region as frustrating. She set forth the notion that many of her American peers are so consumed with American issues, they lack the enthusiasm to seek out information about what is happening in other countries. This was particularly difficult for her in interactions she had with people who were ignorant about the Israeli-Palestinian conflict.

On the other hand, Muna had also had positive experiences in America that altered her worldview. For instance, the individualism in America meant that she finally had a chance to focus on herself, rather than her whole family. While she found her strong family connections to be something she enjoyed, she also believed it to be overwhelming at times, and the American focus on the individual was a part of the culture she could appreciate.

In terms of her identity negotiation, although Muna believed that she had expanded her viewpoints, it seemed the ethnocentric ideology of the American (specifically European American) population left her clinging more to her Arab identity, rather than acculturating. She expressed a desire to communicate the beauty and complexity of the Arab culture to individuals living in the U.S. She believed that there was more than just the food and language that made up this identity.

Sayed: An Electronics Engineer From Egypt

Sayed came from Egypt to the U.S. for his doctoral studies in electronics engineering two years ago. He met his wife, who is also an international student from Egypt, in the U.S. and got married a year later. His primary purpose for coming to the U.S. was to seek the appropriate education he needed for a faculty position already offered to him at an Egyptian university. The faculty offer was made contingent upon his completion of his doctoral degree in a respected university in his field. He believed that the U.S. had better academic opportunities and would grant him the best knowledge in his field. Although he initially planned to move back to Egypt (he already had a job offer and he wanted to live with his parents and friends in Egypt), he was finding that there were job opportunities in the U.S. that were more appealing for him than going back to Egypt. The sociopolitical situation in Egypt, however, made him eager to return to Egypt so that he could bring with him all the knowledge he had gained during his time in the U.S. He stated that he was in Egypt when the January 25, 2011, popular uprisings started against the government, but things were also getting more confusing back home, so it was difficult for Sayed to be in the U.S. during these times.

Sayed had two older siblings who were living and working in the U.S., and his parents were living in Egypt. Sayed stated that he had visited the U.S. four times before moving for his doctoral degree (once when he was in high school; three times when he was an undergraduate student). Therefore, he had more realistic expectations about his move to the U.S. His move to the U.S. was made easier after contacting siblings and older students on campus who had come to the U.S. before him. The Egyptian Cultural Club (ECC) on campus was also a critical resource for finding housing and a roommate when he first moved to the U.S.

The ECC, his wife, and fellow graduate students in his program comprise most of his social network. Sayed stated that meeting his wife and getting married increased his social support and helped him with his homesickness. Since he had married, he felt more at home and husband and wife provide strong support for each other. The ECC has been a venue in which he is able to maintain many of the Egyptian customs (e.g. special days, celebrations) that have helped him remain strongly connected to his Egyptian identity. He has interacted with non-Egyptian friends in the U.S. through studying together and spending time at each others' homes, whereas when he was in Egypt he and his friends had engaged in "deeper" relationships.

Sayed's move to the U.S. meant learning new things but also facing new challenges. Living on his own in the U.S. introduced him to new responsibilities, such as paying bills and grocery shopping, that he used to rely on his family members to take care of in Egypt. Sayed stated that the language barrier had been the most difficult issue to overcome, preventing him from being able to accurately express himself. This difficulty with the English language made him feel embarrassed at times. He also mentioned moments of discrimination when he heard negative comments about the assumed lifestyle of Egyptians or when he was in public places (e.g. grocery stores or shopping malls) with his wife, who wears a hijab (headscarf). For example, a store retailer did not want to show different shirts to his wife.

Sayed stated that there were distinct differences between his experiences on campus, with his faculty and peers, and off campus. Students and faculty on campus were more informed about Arab international students and had had interactions with them. However, Sayed's experiences were somewhat different in the community when he was shopping or getting a haircut. For example, he was asked if they ride camels in Egypt. Sayed also indicated that the overall quality of life in the U.S. was better than in Egypt, and the individualistic ideology (e.g. "fix things on your own") he gained from American culture gave him the confidence to do more things on his own. The U.S. had also given him the chance to interact with a diverse group of people (e.g. international students on campus) to whom he was not exposed in Egypt.

Sayed still believed that although interacting with a diverse population on campus had altered his worldview on people, his American interactions had not made him any less proud of his Egyptian identity. He hoped that Americans could see the generosity and hospitality of Arabs and understand that the American media (e.g. U.S. news reporting) does not provide an accurate depiction of the Arab lifestyle. For example, he stated that sometimes bringing sweets from his visits to Egypt or sharing food may lead to mistaken assumptions that he was rich. Sayed stated that he explicitly discusses with others how generosity is important in his culture.

Reflecting on Zena, Muna, and Sayed

The three stories indicate the complexity and diversity among Arab international students. All three students were studying at a large public university with a very large international student population at the time of the interviews. All three commented on their interactions with other international students on campus, which were mostly positive and supportive. In addition, they discussed the positive aspects of being in the U.S., such as increased exposure to different worldviews and cultures, and engaging in more difficult conversations. Even though all three of them experienced some of the issues discussed in the adjustment literature (e.g. language proficiency, navigating the education system, impact of perceived discrimination), they also discussed the challenges they experienced due to the complexity of their identities. For example, Muna's frustration with the ignorance of her U.S. peers about the Middle Eastern region can be related to her U.S. peers' rigid and simplistic conceptualization of cultural identities in transition. Even though existing theories attempt to explain the adjustment process based on two cultural identities (i.e. home versus host), identities can be more complex for many Arab international students, creating more challenges to fit into a particular acculturation category.

Critique

Living in the U.S. post 9/11 creates unique experiences for Arab international students (e.g. increased discrimination, difficulties with student visa applications). A number of sociopolitical events (e.g. 9/11, Operation Enduring Freedom in Afghanistan, Operation Iraqi Freedom, increasingly biased and inaccurate media coverage on the Middle East and North Africa) has had a significant impact on Arab international students who are moving to the U.S. to pursue their career goals. Cross-cultural transition and the process international students go through has been studied for decades. However, as international students diversify and the context in which they function in the U.S. changes, these theories may not be capturing their experiences fully.

The heterogeneous makeup of Arabs diversifies their experiences, which are not captured by acculturation theories. Amer (2014) found that there are numerous factors influencing the acculturative process. She emphasized the diversity in this community and the way problems arise when researchers place all Arabs into one homogenous population. In addition to coming from 22 different nations in which their social environments vary, Arab international students differ in factors such as religious affiliation and socioeconomic status. Berry's (1997) model of acculturation classifies all migrants equally, removing any intersectionality of the Arab identity with other social identities. For example, religious affiliation does not only impact students' adjustment to the U.S. but also affects their connection with their home culture. Arab international students' experiences may also differ based on their families' social class. For example, Arab international students coming from Saudi Arabia (gross national income estimate for 2013 was US$31,300) will have more access to resources (e.g. housing, transportation) than students coming from Egypt (gross national income estimate for 2013 was US$6,600; Central Intelligence Agency, 2014).

Most acculturation research does not fully consider the attitudes of the host country toward the migrants. When considering individuals' willingness to assimilate, integrate, marginalize, or separate from the host country, researchers who utilize Berry's model do not typically study the host country's favorable or unfavorable attitude toward the migrant population. Croucher (2013) found that negative attitudes held toward a minority group led to an increase in hostility and a decrease in the number of communication opportunities between the majority and minority groups. Further, Alkharusi (2013) found that Muslim Arab students had more positive experiences in their living and integration with New Zealanders if those New Zealanders held positive attitudes toward them. With the increase in negative media coverage in the U.S. about the Arab nations, considering the attitudes of Americans toward Arabs is vital when conducting research in this area. For example, in the *Inside Higher Ed* online news publication, Redden (2012) discussed several incidents, including a student paper at Kansas State University "arguing that American tax dollars shouldn't be used to fund the education of Afghan, Chinese, Iranian, Iraqi or Turkish students 'who could, in the near future, become the enemy'" (para. 2).

Unlike immigrants or refugees who intend to remain in the U.S., international students have the intention to return to their home countries once they have completed their studies. This intention to return may impact their willingness to accept or reject values of the host country. Although international students voluntarily make the decision to attend school in the U.S., their lack of a support system and short-term exposure to the host culture can make adjustment more difficult for international students than for other voluntary migrators such as immigrants. Generally, this voluntary decision to sojourn in the U.S. for academic studies may be a result of several factors. They may have a stronger desire to leave their home country (the "push") than to stay (the "pull"; Mazzarol & Soutar, 2002). The host country's need for the individuals' skills may make them more inclined to migrate for personal success (Hondagneu-Sotelo, 2007), or they may wish to migrate due to their own country's emphasis on receiving the best possible education and a Western degree (Meleis, 1982). This added pressure of success due to financial investment or prestige of a Western degree may further alter an Arab international student's experience. Further research is needed to explore the unique experiences of sojourners and these added pressures for success. Furthermore, there is a need for acculturation models that are specifically relevant to sojourners, as most models are based on immigrants.

An acculturation model based on a universalist idea "denies historically, politically and socially situated realities facing immigrants and fails to explain varying experiences in immigrants' lives" (Ngo, 2008, p. 2). Making the claim that the acculturation process is the same for everyone minimizes difficult experiences faced by migrants (Bhatia & Ram, 2001). Some of the Arab international students may come to the U.S. from countries in which they were exposed to war and political turbulence. Although their initial intention is to stay in the U.S. on a temporary basis, hesitation about returning may occur if their country is still engaged in war, for fear of facing the loss of family and friends killed in the conflict (Arthur, 2004). This apprehension may make their experience more complex as they begin to reconsider returning to their home country. Furthermore, international students may turn to others with similar national backgrounds for support; however, religious, political, and social conflict within groups of fellow nationals can cause even more complications in their adjustment to the U.S. (Thomas & Althen, 1989). More research is needed to explore Arab international students' complex decision-making processes regarding whether or not to return. A deeper understanding is critical of what support and resources they use to make their final decision, and how it impacts their psychological wellbeing (especially if they continue in a state of indecision).

There is a need for culturally sensitive and evidence-based interventions to support Arab international students' adjustment to universities. These evidence-based interventions can be developed in collaboration with university counseling centers and international student offices. University counseling centers could offer psychoeducational or support groups focusing on adjustment issues, as well as provide practical information about the U.S. university environment. In these psychoeducational groups, students would be able to share their experiences, learn from each other's experiences, and feel that they are not alone in the process. Learning how to deal effectively with stress and anxiety could increase Arab international students' psychological wellbeing and help them to focus more effectively on their studies and family responsibilities. In addition, international student offices could offer conversational English sessions for international students to practice their language skills and increase their confidence. Mentoring programs could allow more senior Arab international students and U.S. students to help with more junior students when they arrive on campus. Lastly, educational programs can be developed for faculty, staff, and other students to inform them about Arab culture.

Conclusion

Arab international students have some shared experiences with the general international student population, explained by a number of adjustment theories. These shared experiences include challenges related to language proficiency skills and navigation of the education system. At the same time, Arab international students face unique and complex issues related to their adjustment. Most of these relate to post-9/11 discrimination and incorrect assumptions about Arab culture. For example, many Americans do not understand the diversity among Arab international students and expect a certain set of behaviors in their interactions. More research and evidence-based interventions are needed to understand and provide best practices to these students at U.S. universities.

References

Al-Hattami, A. A. & Al-Ahdal, A. A. M. H. (2014). Academic and social adjustments of Arab Fulbright students in American universities: A case study. *International Journal of Humanities and Social Science* 4(5), 216–222.

Alkharusi, M. J. (2013). The intercultural communication experiences of Arab Muslims studying in New Zealand: Academic and social perspectives (Unpublished doctoral dissertation). University of Waikato, New Zealand. Available at http://researchcommons.waikato.ac.nz/handle/10289/8309

Alreshoud, A. & Koeske, G. F. (1997). Arab students' attitudes toward and amount of social contact with Americans: A causal process analysis of cross-sectional data. *The Journal of Social Psychology* 137, 235–245. doi: 10.1080/00224549709595434

Amer, M. (2014). Arab American acculturation and ethnic identity across the lifespan: Sociodemographic correlates and psychological outcomes. In S. C. Nassar-McMIllan, K. J. Ajrouch, & J. Hakim-Larson (eds.), *Biopsychosocial perspectives on Arab Americans: Culture, development and health* (pp. 153–173). New York: Springer. doi: 10.1007/978-1-4614-8238-3_8

Arthur, N. (2004). *Counseling international students: Clients from around the world.* New York: Springer.

Bender, M. & Ng, S. H. (2009). Dynamic biculturalism: Socially connected and individuated unique selves in a globalized world. *Social and Personality Psychology Compass* 3(3), 199–210. doi: 10.1111/j.1751-9004.2009.00174.x

Berry, J. W. (1997). Immigration, acculturation, and adaptation. *Applied Psychology* 46, 5–34. doi: 10.1111/j.1464-0597.1997.tb01087.x

Bhatia, S. & Ram, A. (2001). Rethinking 'acculturation' in relation to diasporic cultures and postcolonial identities. *Human Development* 44(1), 1–18.

Central Intelligence Agency. (2014). *The world factbook.* Retrieved from www.cia.gov/library/publications/the-world-factbook/fields/2004.html

Croucher, S. M. (2013). Integrated threat theory and acceptance of immigrant assimilation: An analysis of Muslim immigration in Western Europe. *Communication Monographs* 80(1), 46–62. doi: 10.1080/03637751.2012.739704

Daraiseh, I. (2012). Effects of Arab American discrimination post 9/11 in the contexts of the workplace and education. *McNair Scholars Research Journal* 4(1) Article 3. Retrieved from http://commons.emich.edu/cgi/viewcontent.cgi?article=1037&context=mcnair

Duru, E. & Poyrazli, S. (2011). Perceived discrimination, social connectedness, and other predictors of adjustment difficulties among Turkish international students. *International Journal of Psychology* 46, 446–454. doi: 10.1080/00207594.2011.585158

Harrison, N. (2012). Investigating the impact of personality and early life experiences on intercultural interaction in internationalised universities. *International Journal of Intercultural Relations* 36, 224–237. doi: 10.1016/j.ijintrel.2011.03.007

Hayes, R. L. & Lin, H. (1994). Coming to America: Developing social support systems for international students. *Journal of Multicultural Counseling and Development* 22, 7–16. doi: 10.1002/j.2161-1912.1994.tb00238.x

Hechanova-Alampay, R., Beehr, T. A., Christiansen, N. D., & Van Horn, R. K. (2002). Adjustment and strain among domestic and international student sojourners: A longitudinal study. *School Psychology International* 23, 458–474. doi: 10.1177/0143034302234007

Hermans, H. J. M. & Kempen, H. J. G. (1998). Moving cultures: The perilous problems of cultural dichotomies in a globalizing society. *American Psychologist* 53, 1111–1120. doi: 10.1037/0003-066X.53.10.1111

Hondagneu-Sotelo, P. (2007). *Domestica: Immigrant workers cleaning and caring in the shadows of affluence*. Berkeley and Los Angeles, CA: University of California Press.

Institute of International Education. (2013). *International student enrollment trends, 1949/50–2012/13* (Data file). Retrieved from www.iie.org/en/Research-and-Publications/Open-Doors/Data/International-Students/Enrollment-Trends/1948–2014

James, S., Hunsley, J., Navara, G. S., & Alles, M. (2004). Marital, psychological, and sociocultural aspects of sojourner adjustment: Expanding the field of enquiry. *International Journal of Intercultural Relations* 28(2), 111–126. doi: 10.1016/j.ijintrel.2004.03.003

Kao, C. & Gansneder, B. (1995). An assessment of class participation by international graduate students. *Journal of College Student Development* 36(2), 132–140.

Kayyali, R. A. (2006). The people perceived as a threat to security: Arab Americans since September 11. *Migration Information Source*, July 1. Retrieved from www.migrationinformation.org/USfocus/display.cfm?ID=409

Khawaja, N. G. & Dempsey, J. (2008). A comparison of international and domestic tertiary students in Australia. *Australian Journal of Guidance and Counselling* 18(1), 30–46. doi: 10.1375/ajgc.18.1.30

Kilinc, A. & Granello, P. F. (2003). Overall life satisfaction and help-seeking attitudes of Turkish college students in the United States: Implications for college counselors. *Journal of College Counseling* 6(1), 56–68. doi: 10.1002/j.2161-1882.2003.tb00227.x

LaFromboise, T., Coleman, H. L., & Gerton, J. (1993). Psychological impact of biculturalism: Evidence and theory. *Psychological Bulletin* 114, 395–412. doi: 10.1037/0033-2909.114.3.395

Mazzarol, T. & Soutar, G. N. (2002). "Push-pull" factors influencing international student destination choice. *International Journal of Educational Management* 16(2), 82–90. doi: 10.1108/09513540210418403

Meleis, A. I. (1982). Arab students in western universities: Social properties and dilemmas. *The Journal of Higher Education* 53, 439–447.

Ngo, V. H. (2008). A critical examination of acculturation theories. *Critical Social Work* 9(1), 1–6.

Norris, K. (2011). Middle Eastern student perceptions of mattering and marginality at a large American university (Unpublished Master's thesis). Oregon State University. Retrieved from http://ir.library.oregonstate.edu/xmlui/bitstream/handle/1957/21763/Kent %20Norris %20Thesis.pdf?sequence=2

Oxford, R. & Nyikos, M. (1989). Variables affecting choice of language learning strategies by university students. *Modern Language Journal* 73(3), 291–300. doi: 10.1111/j.1540–4781.1989.tb06367.x

Redden, E. (2012). "I'm not Racist, But." *Inside Higher Ed*, October 16. Retrieved from www.insidehighered.com/news/2012/10/16/tensions-simmer-between-american-and-international-students

Sam, D. L. & Berry, J. W. (2010). Acculturation: When individuals and groups of different cultural backgrounds meet. *Perspectives on Psychological Science* 5, 472–481. doi: 10.1177/1745691610373075

Schwartz, S. J. & Zamboanga, B. L. (2008). Testing Berry's model of acculturation: A confirmatory latent class approach. *Cultural Diversity and Ethnic Minority Psychology* 14, 275–285. doi: 10.1037/a0012818

Searle, W. & Ward, C. (1990). The prediction of psychological and sociocultural adjustment during cross-cultural transitions. *International Journal of Intercultural Relations* 14, 449–464. doi: 10.1016/0147-1767(90)90030-Z

Sherry, C., Bhat, R., Beaver, B., & Ling, A. (2004). Students as customers: The expectations and perceptions of local and international students. *Proceedings of the HERDSA Conference*, July. Retrieved from www.herdsa.org.au/wp-content/uploads/conference/2004/PDF/P017-jt.pdf

Thomas, K. & Althen, G. (1989). Counseling foreign students. In P. Pedersen, J. Draguns, W. Lonner, & J. Trimble (eds.), *Counseling across cultures* (3rd edn., pp. 205–241). Honolulu, HI: University of Hawaii Press.

Urias, D. A. & Yeakey, C. C. (2005). *International students and U.S. border security*. Retrieved from www.nea.org/assets/img/PubThoughtAndAction/TAA_05_18.pdf
U.S. Citizenship and Immigration Services. (2014). *Students and employment*. Retrieved from www.uscis.gov/working-united-states/students-and-exchange-visitors/students-and-employment.
Williams, C. T. & Johnson, L. R. (2011). Why can't we be friends?: Multicultural attitudes and friendships with international students. *International Journal of Intercultural Relations* 35(1), 41–48. doi: 10.1016/j.ijintrel.2010.11.001
Yakushko, O. (2009). Xenophobia: Understanding the roots and consequences of negative attitudes toward immigrants. *The Counseling Psychologist* 37, 36–66. doi: 10.1177/0011000008316034

12

REFUGEES AND FORCED MIGRANTS

Seeking Asylum and Acceptance

Maryam Kia-Keating, Sawssan R. Ahmed, and Sheila Modir

In 2013, the United Nations High Commissioner on Refugees (UNHCR) reported that the number of people who experienced forced migration globally was unprecedented. A staggering total of over 51 million persons endure displacement from their homes, threatening life circumstances, and have few, if any, options (UNHCR, 2014). These statistics include refugees who have gained asylum in a country of resettlement, internally displaced persons who remain within their own borders, and asylum-seekers who hold a temporary status as they await resettlement opportunities while residing in new countries. In 2012, a majority of these people originated from Afghanistan and four Arab countries: Somalia, Iraq, Syrian Arab Republic, and Sudan. This chapter specifically focuses on Arab refugees resettled in the U.S. and key considerations for scholars.

Legally, a refugee, as described by the 1951 United Nations Refugee Convention is an individual experiencing a:

> well founded fear of being persecuted for reasons of race, religion, nationality, membership of a particular social group or political opinion, is outside the country of his nationality and is unable or, owing to such fear, is unwilling to avail himself of the protection of that country; or who, not having a nationality and being outside the country of his former habitual residence as a result of such events, is unable or, owing to such fear, is unwilling to return to it.
>
> (UNHCR, 2007b, p. 14)

Thus, although refugees can share many of the same concerns as other immigrant groups resettling in a new country, there are two notable ways in which their experiences are unique, based on this legal definition: (1) they experience persecution, oftentimes combined with exposure to violence, trauma, and a range of adversities, and, as a result, (2) they face significant impediments in returning to their countries of origin (Kia-Keating, 2009). Moreover, although the status of refugee is determined by pre-flight stressors, multiple traumatic events and significant adversities can occur during flight, as well as once a refugee is resettled in a new country (Lustig et al., 2004; Porterfield et al., 2010). These stressors can include limited resources, difficulty meeting basic needs, continual uncertainty, separation from loved ones, exposure to violence, discrimination, and economic stress. Taking the full picture of a refugee's experience using a socio-ecological perspective takes into account the variety of interacting factors that contribute to both physical and mental health.

This chapter provides a general overview of the literature on Arab American refugees, as well as specific descriptions of three major refugee groups: Iraqis, Palestinians, and Somalis. Three brief case examples highlight the kinds of benefit and challenge encountered by Arab refugees living in the U.S. Finally, future directions for scholarship and interventions are presented.

Arab Refugees in the U.S.

The U.S. has a long history of providing a new home to people exiled from their homelands due to war, political upheaval, oppression, and persecution. Over the last three decades, the U.S. has resettled over three million refugees, with average admissions of 81,500 refugees annually (U.S. Department of State, 2009a). These numbers take into consideration a significant decline in the annual admission rate that followed the 9/11 attacks on the World Trade Center in New York City (U.S. Department of Homeland Security (USDHS, 2010). Trends shift significantly over time, depending on international crises, political conflict, and need.

Iraqi refugees were the largest group resettled in the U.S. in both 2009 (numbering 18,838) and 2010 (18,016). However, from 2011 to 2012, refugees from Burma and Bhutan made up over half of all refugee admissions, while Iraqi refugees were the third-largest group entering the U.S. in those years, at 9,388 (in 2011) and 12,163 (in 2012) (Martin & Yankay, 2013). During the decade between 2002 and 2011, the top five refugee populations entering the U.S. originated from Burma, Iraq, Somalia, Bhutan, and Cuba. Notably, Arabic has been the leading language of refugees entering the U.S. in recent years, spoken by 26% of refugees admitted between 2008 and 2013 (U.S. Department of State, 2013).

It is helpful to also include those who obtain permanent residency status. An examination of records grouped by decade since the 1951 U.N. Convention reveals that among those originating from Arab countries, Somali, Iraqi, Sudanese, Egyptian, and Syrian refugees were the top five groups obtaining legal permanent resident status in the U.S. between 2001 and 2009. The number of Somali refugees and asylees becoming permanent residents was markedly higher (i.e. more than double) than any other Arab group, with estimates of around 55,354 entering the U.S. from 2001 to 2009 (USDHS, 2010).

Resettlement patterns are also a useful source of information to help inform policy and practice. The three most common states for general refugee entry into the U.S. are Texas, California, and New York (Martin & Yankay, 2013). Recent trends are reflective of overall patterns of resettlement for Arab refugees living in the U.S.; namely, California was the most common state of entry in 2013, followed by Michigan and Texas. New York, Arizona, and Illinois also housed significant numbers of newly arriving Arab refugees (U.S. Department of State, 2013). Secondary (and sometimes, tertiary) migration patterns can and do also take place once refugees arrive (e.g. Goza, 2007), as refugees make choices about preferences for living environments, group in enclaves, and/or seek out employment opportunities.

A Socio-Ecological Framework for Understanding Refugees' Experiences

In light of the profound experience of loss, forced displacement from home and country, indefinite sense of uncertainty, and irreparable changes in livelihood, there are multiple and interacting factors impacting refugees' experiences and outcomes. Thus, a theoretical framework that embraces a multidimensional perspective is warranted. The bioecological model as discussed by Bronfenbrenner suggests that human development is an outcome of interactions between individuals and the environmental contexts in which they are embedded (Bronfenbrenner, 1979; Bronfenbrenner & Morris, 2006). These ecological contexts, or systems, are nested within each other and include the microsystem (family, school, and peers), exosystem (community and neighborhood factors), and macrosystem (societal and cultural values and customs; Bronfenbrenner, 1979).

The use of an ecological framework is important in understanding Arab refugees because it requires that attention be paid to the various factors that go beyond ethnic heritage. The framework takes into account, for example, religion, tribal affiliation, economic status, education, family factors, exposure to armed conflict, and a host of other experiences related to forced migration, resettlement, and acculturation (Lustig et al., 2004). In this framework, refugees can be viewed as being influenced by and needing to adapt to multiple social contexts, with potentially differing cultural norms and expectations, simultaneously. These contexts may provide varying levels of risk or protective factors (Ehntholt & Yule, 2006; Elbedour, ten Bensel, & Bastien, 1993; Lustig et al., 2004).

Trauma, Stress, and Adversities Encountered by Arab American Refugees

Despite the influx of refugees from Arab countries into the U.S., and the unique challenges they face, particularly in the wake of 9/11, there is only limited empirical data on the psychosocial wellbeing of this population. However, it is helpful to consider the various factors that have been posited as important to the wellbeing of refugees (Porterfield et al., 2010). Refugees may be exposed to potentially traumatic events. For Arab American refugees, these can include the witnessing of and exposure to armed conflict and war, community violence, torture, and rape (Carlsson, Olsen, Mortensen, & Kastrup, 2006; Kira et al., 2008). For many Americans of Arab descent, such as those from countries with histories of long-standing conflicts, including Iraq, Palestine, Lebanon, and Somalia, exposure to violence in their home countries may be ongoing and pervasive (Abi-Hashem, 2008). Lack of physical safety, difficulty meeting basic needs, and exposure to violence can continue during flight, in locations such as refugee camps where refugees are forced to take up temporary residence. Numerous studies have linked exposure to violence to physical and mental health difficulties among Arab refugees, as discussed below.

Several studies also note the importance of environmental and social conditions encountered in a host country. Once resettled in the U.S., Arab American refugees can experience continued challenges and adversities, including coping with cultural bereavement, acculturation and acculturative gaps occurring between parents and children, major changes in social and economic standing, overall financial stress, isolation, and discrimination. Meta-analytic results have demonstrated that better mental health outcomes in resettlement are associated with permanent housing (versus temporary), economic opportunity, employment, and being able to maintain one's prior socioeconomic status (Porter & Haslam, 2005).

Additionally, Arab refugees placed in the U.S. must contend with possible post-displacement exposure to discrimination and what may be perceived as an unwelcome sociopolitical environment. Vulnerability to multiple levels of discrimination can take several forms. For example, an Iraqi refugee relocated to the U.S. may encounter discrimination associated with being a refugee (such as others' fears of refugees being diseased and mentally ill, or assumptions that they lack education), with being Arab (such as others' beliefs that they are terrorists), and/or with being Muslim. Although all levels may not be operating simultaneously, the chance of being targeted within any given interaction, setting, or system is increased by the multiple layers of potential discrimination. While a refugee may objectively be safer in a country of resettlement, his or her perception of danger may be high when confronted with these types of ongoing interpersonal conflict.

At the level of the macrosystem, Williams and Berry (1991) argue that whether one's group (based on aspects of one's identity such as ethnicity, race, or religion) is accepted by the greater society affects the likelihood that an acculturating refugee will experience prejudice and discrimination. Traditional explanatory models of refugee mental health may not be sufficient for understanding the mental health needs of this group due to these additional possible post-displacement sociopolitical factors, including continued U.S. military involvement in their home country and a documented rise in discrimination against U.S. Arabs (American-Arab Anti-Discrimination Committee, 2008; Council on American-Islamic Relations, 2004, 2009; Disha, Cavendish, & King, 2011). Furthermore, the availability of widespread, graphic, and pervasive media exposure of these ongoing conflicts may serve as triggers for traumatic stress reactions.

Some studies provide evidence that post-displacement factors, such as perceived discrimination, resettlement stressors such as housing, financial, and interpersonal problems, and acculturative stressors, may be more impactful than pre-displacement trauma (e.g. Ellis, MacDonald, Lincoln, & Cabral, 2008). In fact, a study of young Middle Eastern refugees in Denmark found that post-displacement factors, including discrimination, were a better predictor of psychological problems eight to nine years after their arrival in Denmark than traumatic experience before their arrival (Montgomery, 2008). This striking finding suggests that the level of discrimination in the country of resettlement may be as crucial in predicting the psychological wellbeing of refugees as initial trauma exposure, especially years after resettlement. Likewise, social relationships and socioeconomic status have been associated with increased risk for mental health problems for refugee adults after pre-resettlement trauma is accounted for (e.g. Carlsson et al., 2006; Kira, Smith, Lewandowski, & Templin, 2010).

There are also factors that may act in protective or promotive ways after resettlement. For example, various culturally determined factors, including ethnic identity, religious coping, and a sense of community after resettlement, may contribute to resilience in Iraqi refugee youth (Ahmed, Kia-Keating, & Tsai, 2011).

Physical and Mental Health of Arab American Refugees

Because of the dearth of studies on Arab refugees in the U.S., it is difficult to ascertain the physical and mental health status of Arab American refugees. The majority of the literature has focused on Iraqi and Somali refugees in the U.S., and little is known about the physical and mental health status of refugees from other Arab countries.

Research suggests that refugees, in general, are at increased risk for chronic psychological disorders, including depression, posttraumatic stress disorder (PTSD), and somatization, when compared to non-refugee populations (Ringold, Burke, & Glass, 2005). In one comparison of an Arab refugee and non-refugee sample, Jamil and colleagues (2002) found that Iraqi refugees reported a greater likelihood of PTSD and health problems when compared to non-refugee Arab American clients at a mental health clinic. Additionally, other surveys have found that Iraqi refugees in the U.S. report high rates of anxiety, depression, and PTSD (Taylor et al., 2014).

However, one meta-analysis of studies that compared outcomes for refugees versus non refugees found that refugees from the Middle East did not differ greatly from their non-refugee Arab descent counterparts (Porter & Haslam, 2005). It is possible that this finding is due to the ongoing civil unrest in these countries of origin, which affects the entire population of Arab Americans, regardless of refugee status. In other words, an official designation of refugee status may not fundamentally differentiate individuals from those who do not have that designation but have faced the same conditions of unrest, uncertainty, and exposure to trauma and stressors.

Arab refugees seem also to be at risk for physical health problems and issues related to health services access. With the exception of a few studies, the research on the physical health of Arab refugees in the U.S. is particularly lacking. Iraqi refugees in the U.S. have reported delaying or not seeking medical care, high rates of the presence of a chronic medical problem (Taylor et al., 2014), and numerous somatic complaints (Jamil et al., 2005), such as fatigue and headaches. It is clear that more research is needed in this area to identify issues related to healthcare access, cultural sensitivity in healthcare, and general health status for this population.

Subpopulations: Iraqi, Palestinian, and Somali Refugees

In order to gain a better understanding of the Arab refugee experience and the stressors that can lead to their physical and mental health problems, three Arab American refugee groups are examined further: Iraqi, Palestinian, and Somali refugees. This section demonstrates the numerous socio-ecological factors, including sociopolitical context and secondary migration, that have impacted these refugee groups' lives.

Iraqi Refugees

In the past few decades, Iraq has been involved in almost constant violent conflict and political unrest. This includes the Iran-Iraq war from 1980–88 (which led to over a million deaths), the First Gulf War with Kuwait, the Second Gulf War with the U.S. and its allies, and its own ethnic conflicts and civil war (Ellis, 2009; Mowafi, 2008; Wilkes, 2010). Civilians have often been targeted in these wars. Consequently, over four million Iraqis have sought refuge in other countries, including Jordan, Syria, Iran, Lebanon, Egypt, and Turkey (UNHCR, 2007a). A large number of Iraqi refugees have resettled in the U.S. (Hakim-Larson, Farrag, Kafaji, Jamil, & Hammad, 2005). According to the U.S. Citizenship and Immigration Services (2013), 84,902 Iraqi refugees have already been admitted, while another 119,202 have been approved to resettle in the U.S., but have not yet arrived.

Pre flight and during flight, Iraqi refugees may have experienced a number of potentially traumatic events including exposure to violence, and other adversities, including human rights violations; living in instability, uncertainty, and terror; and displacement (Miremadi, Ganesan, & McKenna, 2011). These experiences have been associated with mental health symptom severity, including depression, anxiety, and PTSD (Jamil, Ventimiglia, Makki, & Arnetz, 2010; Nickerson, Bryant, Steel, Silove, & Brooks, 2010). Separation of family members can often be a significant issue for Iraqis resettling in the U.S., as those living in the U.S. may experience significant stress related to family members who continue to live in unstable conditions in Iraq (Nickerson et al., 2010). This can be an especially distressing experience for Arab refugees who come from a collectivist culture in which family holds an especially significant presence. Other stressors have included acculturation, perceived discrimination, struggling to find employment, and language barriers (Jamil et al., 2007).

It is important to be aware of distinct subpopulations – such as Assyrians, Chaldeans, and Mandaeans – that are ethno-religious minority groups in Iraq. These groups have distinct characteristics – including languages, religions, and cultural traditions – that set them apart from the majority group in Iraq (U.S. Department of State, 2009b). Consequently, they may have been victims of violence and crime in Iraq (UNHCR, 2005). Despite only making up a small minority in Iraq (5%), a substantial proportion of the Iraqi refugee population in the U.S. (40%) is made up of these subgroups (UNHCR, 2005). Currently, those that have resettled in the U.S. primarily reside in Michigan and California (Arab American Institute, n.d.).

Palestinian Refugees

Since the late 1940s, the Israeli-Palestinian conflict has led to upwards of 85% of the Palestinian population being forced to leave their homes (Dumper, 2006). The Palestinian refugee population has grown to over 4.9 million (UNHCR, 2011). Palestinian refugees represent one of the largest and longest-standing refugee populations worldwide. They also represent one of the oldest Arab refugee communities in the U.S. since being displaced after the first Arab-Israeli war in 1948. Most recently, the ongoing conflict in Syria has led to a worsening situation for tens of thousands of Palestinian refugees who were resettled in Syria. These refugees have had to flee to Lebanon and Jordan, where they must compete for very limited resources with Syrian refugees (UNHCR, 2013).

In the U.S., the current number of Palestinian refugees is unknown. For example, when predominantly Sunni Palestinian refugees who were living in refugee camps in Iraq were admitted to the U.S. in 2009, they were categorized as Iraqi refugees (Jonsson, 2009). This group of Palestinian refugees, mostly residing in Southern California, is therefore a somewhat "hidden" subpopulation, because obvious data sources don't have information about them. Nonetheless, it is important to be aware of this specific group's history, chronicled by a detailed Human Rights Watch (2006) report that highlighted the alarming conditions for this group while they were residing in Iraq. These Palestinian refugees had faced continual threats to their lives through acts of violence, including torture, killing, and threats of harm, as well as detention, "disappearance," and closed borders giving them no means of escape. Faced with the choice of either returning to acute violence or facing the danger of not being able to meet basic needs, and living without prospects, many of these Palestinian refugees fled to stark refugee camps on the border. Approximately 1,350 were resettled in the U.S. in 2009 (Jonsson, 2009), but information about this group continues to be relatively scarce.

Somali Refugees

The Somali Civil War, begun in 1991, continues to impact the country over two decades later, with ongoing violence, fighting between rival clans, and a heavy toll on civilians (Devi, 2015; Kemp & Rasbridge, 2004). Somalia is one of the top three countries of origin for refugees worldwide, with numbers above one million (UNCHR, 2014). In the last two decades, over 72,000 Somali refugees have entered the U.S. (USDHS, 2010). Common pre-flight stressors for Somali refugees include living in refugee camps for extended periods of time, war violence, famine, poor health conditions, and separations from family members. In a study of 382 Somali refugees resettled in Massachusetts, approximately a third had no education, and another third had not completed high school (Geltman et al., 2013). After resettlement, some of the stressors include limited access to adequate and culturally competent healthcare (Pavlish, Noor, & Brandt, 2010), a decreased sense of safety in urban neighborhoods (Nilsson, Barazanji, Heintzelman, Siddiqi, & Shilla, 2012), perceived discrimination (Ellis et al., 2008), acculturative stress, family conflict (Nilsson et al., 2012), anxiety (Stutters & Ligon, 2001), and depression and suicidal ideation (Bhui et al., 2003).

Children and Adolescents

A large proportion of refugees admitted to the U.S. are children and adolescents under the age of 18, making up approximately one-third of refugee admissions to the U.S. in recent years (Martin & Yankay, 2013). It is important to consider the unique aspects of young refugees because of their developmental vulnerability, as well as their capacity for resilience and adaptation in the face of tremendous change (Porter & Haslam, 2005). Given that many of the key risk and protective factors are similar across immigrant and refugee youth (Kia-Keating, 2009), a few elements that are particularly distinct for refugees are described here.

First, the hardships that refugees endure can place children and adolescents at significant risk, given the potential for negative, and potentially lasting, effects on their developmental trajectories (Fazel, Reed, Panter-Brick, & Stein, 2012; Porterfield et al., 2010). Factors that impact development include malnutrition, inadequate healthcare, exposure to infectious diseases, and disruptions to education (Porterfield et al., 2010). Traumatic stress and adversities that take place pre flight, as well as those that occur after resettlement, contribute to PTSD symptoms (e.g. Ellis et al., 2008). For older refugee adolescents from diverse backgrounds, the risk of PTSD was decreased if they resettled along with family members, but was increased if they arrived as unaccompanied refugees (Hodes, Jagdev, Chandra, & Cunniff, 2008). It is also important to consider the range of other ways that psychological distress may be manifested among refugee children, including sleep problems, anxiety, depression, difficulty concentrating, and somatic complaints, among other possible outcomes.

Second, refugee children face stigmatization in their host country for various reasons. One reason might be that the label "refugee" may carry negative connotations, such as being perceived as "undesirable," "alien," and "inferior" (Jablensky et al., 1994). Another stigmatizing issue may result from racial and religious differences. Preexisting stigmas in the new culture may also play a role, such as stigma of local racial groups (whether or not refugees identify culturally with the racial groups with which they are associated). Also, for those refugees who experience mental health problems as a result of their severe traumatization and dislocation, being labeled mentally ill may add an additional burden. In the post-9/11 climate of the U.S., discrimination of ethnic and religious groups has become an increasingly significant and devastating reality, particularly for refugee groups from Arab and Middle Eastern countries (Ahmed et al., 2011). Youth from these groups face a notable problem, often contending with acculturation stressors and experiencing the tension between adhering to cultural traditions versus following mainstream cultural expectations in order to belong (Kia-Keating & Ellis, 2007).

Finally, acculturation is an important element related to refugee youth psychological adjustment, given the possibilities of how children and adolescents might adopt or identify with their culture of resettlement versus their culture of origin. Acculturative gaps between children and parents to the language and norms of the host culture can lead to relational distance and conflicts. For example, in one study of Somali parents, the mothers described experiencing that their children had lost respect for their elders, and parents reported struggling with retaining their disciplinary authority over their children (Nilsson et al., 2012).

Services and Specialized Interventions

Numerous studies on refugees suggest that refugees have significant mental health needs that require specialized attention (Ellis et al., 2010; Kaczorowski et al., 2011). Researchers have identified a number of therapeutic techniques that can be effective for refugees in general, including cognitive behavioral therapy, family therapy, and mindfulness-based approaches (Bemak & Chung, 2000; Schulz & Resick, 2006; van der Veer, 1998). While the number of studies investigating the efficacy of such treatment approaches with Arab refugees has been increasing as of late, the research on mental health interventions for these populations remains in its nascent stage (Ellis et al., 2010; Kira, Amer, & Wrobel, 2014).

The limited research on Arab refugees has recommended that when working directly with refugees from Arab countries it is important to understand the uniqueness of Arab subgroups, their cultural and historical roots, and the specifics of their refugee experiences. Specific interventions with this population can address acculturation, resettlement, past experiences of trauma, and current experiences of discrimination (Kira et al., 2014).

For example, in the case of Iraqi torture survivors, a wraparound approach that is designed for psychosocial rehabilitation, trauma-informed treatment, and assistance in meeting other medical, social, and legal needs is recommended (Farrag, Abdulkhaleq, Abdelkarim, Souidan, & Safo, 2007). The psychosocial rehabilitation can include social skills training focused on assertiveness, anger management, and problem solving (Farrag et al., 2007). An approach focused on forgiveness, empowerment, and resilience has also been associated with decreased PTSD symptoms (Kira et al., 2009).

There are special considerations for women and children. Gender discrimination and gender-based violence may be important issues to assess for female Arab refugees (James, 2010; Kira et al., 2014), while bearing in mind that experiences of domestic or sexual violence may be highly stigmatized in Arab culture. For young refugees, a multitiered prevention and intervention plan has been recommended in order to make a more comprehensive effort to reduce barriers and deliver services appropriate to the level of care necessary for each case (Ellis et al., 2013). This multitiered approach was used with Somali refugee middle school students and was found to be effective in providing the services they needed as they resettled in a new community. The model provided education and outreach through school-based skills groups focused on emotions and acculturative stress. For the Somali refugee students who were identified as needing specialized mental health services, Trauma Systems Therapy was recommended to address emotional dysregulation as well as social environment stressors (Ellis et al., 2013; Saxe, Ellis, & Kaplow, 2007). Overall, this model showed preliminary findings that were considered promising in terms of providing an effective approach to addressing the mental health needs of Somali refugee youth (Ellis et al., 2010).

Finally, it is important to consider the role of traditional, and perhaps more culturally accepted resources for support. These might include religious leaders (e.g. Muslim imams, Christian pastors), family and community support systems, schools, and peers. In one study, many of these were endorsed by Somali adolescent refugees as being experienced at times as more desirable pathways for assistance than standard U.S. mental health services, which were viewed as stigmatizing (Ellis et al., 2010). Further research is necessary to better understand how traditional ways of healing may function in the context of resettlement, including how they might combine with or help inform Western approaches.

Case Examples of Three Arab Refugees in the U.S.: Hamad, Inaya, and Haider

The following case examples serve as an opportunity to provide a picture of the multitude of risk and protective factors impacting Arab refugees resettled in the U.S. Although these are not comprehensive narratives, they provide a snapshot of the lives of three refugees in order to bring some key factors to life. They are not intended to represent all Arab refugees by any means, but simply serve as examples to consider the multiple and complex layers that underlie refugee experiences, and the ways that socio-ecological levels interact.

Hamad: Angry and Afraid at Age 12

Hamad is a 12-year-old male Syrian refugee who resettled in Michigan and lives with his maternal grandmother. His immediate family fled their home in Syria on foot after witnessing violence, and eventually arrived at a refugee camp in Jordan. His parents and three siblings still live in Jordan. As the eldest son, the family sent him to the U.S., with the intent of joining him as soon as they were able. For now, Hamad spends a lot of time unsupervised after school, during which he hangs out at local parks, usually with other adolescents from varied immigrant backgrounds. He has learned to speak English and often acts as a translator for his grandmother, but he is not yet fluent.

Hamad is referred to the school psychologist because of truancy, academic difficulties, and fights with peers. Others view him as threatening and unpredictable because of his angry outbursts. He reveals to the school psychologist that his grandmother's house in Syria was filled with bullet holes, his parents did not allow him or his siblings to go to school because of the dangers, and it was difficult to meet basic needs in the refugee camp. Now, in the U.S., he is afraid of the police, and finds homelessness alarming and a sign of the isolation and alienation that many feel. He fears that he himself might be homeless someday, and also worries that his close friends and family members will either leave or die. Despite these difficulties, he has a genuine interest in becoming a role model for his younger cousins in the U.S., who provide him with a sense of hope for the future.

Guided by ecological considerations, at the personal level Hamad's history of traumatic exposure is important to help conceptualize his case and understand the associations between his experience with violence and loss and his current wellbeing. Situational factors related to the school environment are particularly salient, given that the school personnel may have very little information about Hamad's refugee background, despite the fact that a variety of refugee-related factors might be impacting him academically and socially. School personnel may be more likely to assume a student like Hamad is a problem or troublemaker, rather than someone who needs additional culturally sensitive and trauma-informed support services. Furthermore, sociocultural issues play a central role in determining how best to support Hamad, both in terms of the separation from his family and his need for strong and predictable social support.

Inaya: Searching for Convergence Between Past, Present, and Future at Age 15

Inaya is an intelligent and engaging 15-year-old female from Somalia currently residing in Texas. She moved with her family to the U.S. at the age of 13. Her family fled Somalia when she was five, and she lived in Kenya during much of her childhood. Inaya's experience of loss has had a profound impact on her and she talks about having lost her homeland, treasured objects, and most of all, extended family relationships that have become disconnected because of separations. She has the sense that these losses will continue – for example, that she will only stay in Texas for a short time.

Inaya's family has planned an arranged marriage for her, and their pressure for her to drop out of high school in order to get married has been increasing. Her teacher refers her to the school counselor on noticing a difference in her, from being a vibrant and academically oriented student, to appearing withdrawn and disconsolate, and her grades beginning to slip because she is not submitting her homework. When she talks to the school counselor, Inaya expresses sadness at having to give up activities she loves, such as playing basketball, and aspirations she has, such as going to medical school. However, she stands firm in her position that she strongly embraces the importance of listening to her parents and fulfilling their expectations of her, as well as maintaining her religious devotion and staying connected to her Somali roots.

Inaya's experience with loss and displacement presents a foundation for understanding the personal level of her social ecology. In particular, she is experiencing a great sense of family isolation, given the current realities of how her once tight-knit extended family has been dispersed due to forced migration. A significant gender- and development-related factor that has arisen for Inaya is that she is receiving family pressure to get married and discontinue her education. Inaya embraces some of the new experiences and values espoused in the U.S., but also feels very connected to her culture and traditions.

Haider: Overwhelmed and Isolated at Age 27

Haider is a 27-year-old male Iraqi refugee who was resettled in San Diego. Haider served as a translator during the Second Gulf War. Prior to being resettled in the U.S., Haider spent time in Syria and Jordan. Haider was resettled in the U.S., arriving with his two nephews and niece. His brother (the father of his nephews and niece) was murdered in Iraq after a rumor in the community portrayed him as a traitor working for the U.S. government. After Haider's brother was murdered, Haider began to fear for his own life.

Haider had high hopes of a fresh start, new opportunities, and freedom when he arrived in the U.S. However, since arriving he has been looking for work earnestly but is finding that most available jobs require more education and skills than he has. Additionally, the high cost of living in California makes it difficult for him to provide for the basic needs of himself and his nephews and niece, beyond what he receives from governmental assistance. He feels anxious, knowing that this assistance will soon end and that he has still not found employment. Instead of offering support, the local Arab American community views him with some suspicion because of the work he used to do in Iraq.

Haider frequently has headaches and bouts of sadness during which he is unable to get out of bed and sees little hope in the future. His nephews and niece try to comfort him when he feels this way but they find themselves unable to help him much. Despite there being a local social service organization that provides mental health services for refugees, Haider cannot bring himself to go and ask for help. He believes that having a mental health problem is a sign of weakness and that men should not ask others for help. The main comfort he finds these days is playing soccer at the local park with other refugees from the community.

Ecological considerations for Haider include his experience of significant traumatic loss and, subsequently, a heightened vulnerability and fear for his own life. Certainly, situational factors that accompanied the major changes he faced due to resettlement – including loss of status and economic stress – are important to take into account. At the sociocultural level, community mistrust and a sense of isolation draw attention to the importance of helping Haider find a social support system. Moreover, stigma and other barriers to access are critical to overcome for refugees like Haider to receive and benefit from mental health services.

Critique

These case examples highlight the complexities of Arab refugee experiences. Given that there is such a limited body of empirical research focused on Arab American refugees, numerous directions for future research exist. This relative gap is exacerbated by the issue of how race and ethnicity are categorized in the U.S., often placing Arab populations in the overarching classification of "White" (Tehranian, 2009). This hinders specific examinations of Arab Americans' unique attributes, needs, and health and mental health concerns. Refugee groups are also sometimes hidden, or they may be difficult to access and engage in purely research endeavors. Using community-based participatory research methods can be a useful approach to addressing these challenges and conducting ethical research with vulnerable populations such as refugees (Ellis, Kia-Keating, Yusuf, Lincoln, & Nur, 2007). However, these methods are time-consuming, and thereby could be disadvantageous for researchers who have to meet certain markers to demonstrate scholarly achievement, limiting the number of investigations even further (Kia-Keating, 2012).

Nonetheless, given the extent of refugees' traumatic exposure, their history of persecution and loss, and other reasons for receiving asylum, as well as their potential to be resilient and make a positive contribution as new members of the U.S. community, there is an urgent need for psychologists and scholars from other disciplines to devote their attention to understanding better this rich and varied population. In particular, areas for future research should focus on better understanding personal factors related to mental health and interventions, including better identifying and assessing cultural idioms of distress, coping, and resilience. In addition, it is important to consider individual, family, and community preferences related to intervention and prevention acceptability and feasibility. Situational factors, including barriers to treatment access and facilitators of engagement in treatment, should be further elucidated. Sociocultural factors, including approaches to treatment that incorporate cultural beliefs, community resources, and psychoeducation efforts that are culturally congruent, would be useful to investigate.

Conclusion

The psychological literature on Arab refugees in the U.S. has focused on pre-flight factors, particularly the exposure to trauma and its link to poor mental health. Relatively little is known about the psychological, social, and community risk and protective factors in resettlement. In addition, the younger generation of Arab American refugees resettled in the U.S. have their own unique set of challenges and opportunities that warrant continued and deeper attention. Resettlement patterns in the U.S. will continue to shift, and it is important to continue to assess the distinct, multilayered, and complex factors that affect the lives of each new refugee group that is admitted. Psychologists have the potential to play an important role in guiding the effort to build on the resilience and capacity of Arab refugees not only to recover from the often unimaginable challenges they and their families have encountered, but also to benefit both themselves and their communities because of them.

References

Abi-Hashem, N. (2008). Arab Americans: Understanding their challenges, needs, and struggles. In A. J. Marsella, J. L. Johnson, P. Watson, & J. Gryczynski (eds.), *Ethnocultural perspectives on disaster and trauma* (pp. 115–173). New York: Springer. doi: 10.1007/978-0-387-73285-5_5

Ahmed, S. R., Kia-Keating, M., & Tsai, K. H. (2011). A structural model of racial discrimination, acculturative stress, and cultural resources among Arab American adolescents. *American Journal of Community Psychology* 48, 181–192. doi: 10.1007/s10464-011-9424-3

American-Arab Anti-Discrimination Committee (2008). *2003–2007 report on hate crimes and discrimination against Arab Americans.* Retrieved from www.issuelab.org/resource/20032007_report_on_hate_crimes_and_discrimination_against_arab_americans

Arab American Institute (n.d.). *Demographics*. Retrieved from www.aaiusa.org/pages/demographics/

Bemak, F. & Chung, R. C. (2000). Psychological intervention with immigrants and refugees. In J. F. Aponte & J. Wohl (eds.), *Psychological intervention and cultural diversity* (pp. 75–91). Boston, MA: Allyn and Bacon.

Bhui, K., Abdi, A., Abdi, M., Pereira, S., Dualeh, M., Robertson, D., … Ismail, H. (2003). Traumatic events, migration characteristics and psychiatric symptoms among Somali refugees: Preliminary communication. *Social Psychiatry and Psychiatric Epidemiology* 38, 35–43. doi: 10.1007/s00127-003-0596-5

Bronfenbrenner, U. (1979). *The ecology of human development: Experiments by nature and design*. Cambridge, MA: Harvard University Press.

Bronfenbrenner, U. & Morris, P. A. (2006). The bioecological model of human development. In R. M. Lerner & W. Damon (eds.), *Handbook of child psychology: Theoretical models of human development* (vol. 1, 6th edn., pp. 793–828). Hoboken, NJ: John Wiley & Sons Inc. doi: 10.1002/9780470147658.chpsy0114

Carlsson, J. M., Olsen, D. R., Mortensen, E. L., & Kastrup, M. (2006). Mental health and health-related quality of life: A 10-year follow-up of tortured refugees. *Journal of Nervous and Mental Disease* 194, 725–731. doi: 10.1097/01.nmd.0000243079.52138.b7

Council on American-Islamic Relations. (2004). *Unpatriotic acts – The status of Muslim civil rights in the United States 2004*. Washington D.C.: Council on American-Islamic Relations Research Center. Retrieved from www.cair.com/civil-rights/civil-rights-reports/2004.html

Council on American-Islamic Relations. (2009). *The status of Muslim civil rights in the United States 2009: Seeking full inclusion*. Washington, D.C.: Council on American-Islamic Relations Research Center. Retrieved from www.cair.com/civil-rights/civil-rights-reports/2009.html

Devi, S. (2015). Slowly and steadily, Somaliland builds its health system. *The Lancet* 385, 2139–2140. doi: 10.1016/S0140-6736(15)61009-1

Disha, I., Cavendish, J. C., & King, R. D. (2011). Historical events and spaces of hate: Hate crimes against Arabs and Muslims in Post-9/11 America. *Social Problems* 58, 21–46. doi: 10.1525/sp.2011.58.1.21

Dumper, M. (ed.) (2006). *Palestinian refugee repatriation: Global perspectives* (vol. 2). London: Taylor & Francis.

Ehntholt, K. & Yule, W. (2006). Practitioner review: Assessment and treatment of refugee children and adolescents who have experienced war-related trauma. *Journal of Child Psychology and Psychiatry* 47, 1197–1210. doi: 10.1111/j.1469-7610.2006.01638.x

Elbedour, S., ten Bensel, R., & Bastien, D. T. (1993). Ecological integrated model of children of war: Individual and social psychology. *Child Abuse & Neglect* 17, 805–819. doi: 10.1016/S0145-2134(08)80011-7

Ellis, B. H., Kia-Keating, M., Yusuf, S., Lincoln, A., & Nur, A. (2007). Ethical research in refugee communities and the use of community participatory methods. *Transcultural Psychiatry* 44(3), 459–481. doi: 10.1177/1363461507081642

Ellis, B. H., Lincoln, A. K., Charney, M. E., Ford-Paz, R., Benson, M., & Strunin, L. (2010). Mental health service utilization of Somali adolescents: Religion, community, and school as gateways to healing. *Transcultural Psychiatry* 47, 789–811. doi: 10.1177/1363461510379933

Ellis, B. H., MacDonald, H. Z., Lincoln, A. K., & Cabral, H. J. (2008). Mental health of Somali adolescent refugees: The role of trauma, stress, and perceived discrimination. *Journal of Consulting and Clinical Psychology* 76, 184–193. doi: 10.1037/0022-006X.76.2.184

Ellis, B. H., Miller, A. B., Abdi, S., Barrett, C., Blood, E. A., & Betancourt, T. S. (2013). Multi-tier mental health program for refugee youth. *Journal of Consulting and Clinical Psychology* 81, 129–140. doi: 10.1037/a0029844

Ellis, D. (2009). *Children of war: Voices of Iraqi refugees*. Toronto: Groundwood Books Ltd.

Farrag, M., Abdulkhaleq, H., Abdelkarim, G., Souidan, R., & Safo, H. (2007). The psychosocial rehabilitation approach in treating torture survivors. *Ethnicity and Disease* 17(Suppl. 3), 85–87.

Fazel, M., Reed, R.V., Panter-Brick, C., & Stein, A. (2012). Mental health of displaced and refugee children resettled in high-income countries: Risk and protective factors. *The Lancet* 379(9812), 266–282. doi: 10.1016/S0140-6736(11)60051–2

Geltman, P. L., Adams, J. H., Cochran, J., Doros, G., Rybin, D., Henshaw, M., … Paasche-Orlow, M. (2013). The impact of functional health literacy and acculturation on the oral health status of Somali refugees living in Massachusetts. *American Journal of Public Health* 103, 1516–1523. doi: 10.2105/AJPH.2012.300885

Goza, F. (2007). The Somali presence in the United States: A socio-economic and demographic profile. In A. M. Kusow & S. R. Bjork (eds.), *From Mogadishu to Dixon: The Somali disapora in a global context* (pp. 255–274). Trenton, NJ: The Red Sea Press, Inc.

Hakim-Larson, J., Farrag, M., Kafaji, T., Jamil, L. H., & Hammad, A. (2005). Medical complaints among Iraqi American refugees with mental disorders. *Journal of Immigrant Health* 7, 145–152. doi: 10.1007/s10903-005-3671-z

Hodes, M., Jagdev, D., Chandra, N., & Cunniff, A. (2008). Risk and resilience for psychological distress amongst unaccompanied asylum seeking adolescents. *Journal of Child Psychology and Psychiatry* 49, 723–732. doi: 10.1111/j.1469-7610.2008.01912.x

Human Rights Watch. (2006). *Nowhere to flee: The perilous situation of Palestinians in Iraq* (HRW Report No. E1804). Retrieved from www.hrw.org/sites/default/files/reports/iraq0706web.pdf

Jablensky, A., Marsella, A. J., Ekblad, S., Jansson, B., Levi, L., & Bornemann, T. (1994). Refugee mental health and well-being: Conclusions and recommendations. In J. Orley (ed.), *Amidst peril and pain: The mental health and well-being of the world's refugees* (pp. 327–339). Washington, D.C.: American Psychological Association.

James, K. (2010). Domestic violence within refugee families: Intersecting patriarchal culture and the refugee experience. *Australian and New Zealand Journal of Family Therapy* 31, 275–284. doi: 10.1375/anft.31.3.275

Jamil, H., Farrag, M., Hakim-Larson, J., Kafaji, T., Abdulkhaleq, H., & Hammad, A. (2007). Mental health symptoms in Iraqi refugees: Posttraumatic stress disorder, anxiety, and depression. *Journal of Cultural Diversity* 14(1), 19–25.

Jamil, H., Hakim-Larson, J., Farrag, M., Kafaji, T., Duqum, I., & Jamil, L. H. (2002). A retrospective study of Arab American mental health clients: Trauma and the Iraqi refugees. *American Journal of Orthopsychiatry* 72, 355–361. doi: 10.1037/0002-9432.72.3.355

Jamil, H., Hakim-Larson, J., Farrag, M., Kafaji, T., Jamil, L. H., & Hammad, A. (2005). Medical complaints among Iraqi American refugees with mental disorders. *Journal of Immigrant Health* 7, 145–152. doi: 10.1007/s10903-005-3671-z

Jamil, H., Ventimiglia, M., Makki, H., & Arnetz, B. B. (2010). Mental health and treatment response among Iraqi refugees as compared to other non-war exposed Arab immigrants: A pilot study in Southeast Michigan. *Journal of Immigrant & Refugee Studies* 8, 431–444. doi: 10.1080/15562948.2010.522470

Jonsson, P. (2009). Risking Israel's ire, U.S. takes 1,350 Palestinian refugees. *The Christian Science Monitor*, July 8. Retrieved from www.csmonitor.com/USA/2009/0708/p02s04-usgn.html

Kaczorowski, J. A., Williams, A. S., Smith, T. F., Fallah, N., Mendez, J. L., & Nelson-Gray, R. (2011). Adapting clinical services to accommodate needs of refugee populations. *Professional Psychology: Research and Practice* 42, 361–367. doi: 10.1037/a0025022

Kemp, C. & Rasbridge, L. A. (2004). Somalia. In C. Kemp & L. A. Rasbridge (eds.), *Refugee and immigrant health: A handbook for health professionals* (pp. 317–326). Cambridge: Cambridge University Press.

Kia-Keating, M. (2009). Immigrants and refugees in the U.S.: Overlaps and distinctions. American Psychological Association, *Children, Youth, and Families Office News*, Fall. Retrieved from www.apa.org/pi/families/resources/newsletter/2009/11/fall.pdf

Kia-Keating, M. (2012). Ethical issues in research with refugee communities. In U. A. Segal & D. Elliott (eds.), *Refugees worldwide: Law, policy, and programs* (vol. 4, pp. 235–257). Santa Barbara, CA: Praeger.

Kia-Keating, M. & Ellis, B. H. (2007). Belonging and connection to school in resettlement: Young refugees, school belonging, and psychosocial adjustment. *Clinical Child Psychology and Psychiatry* 12(1), 29–43. doi: 10.1177/1359104507071052

Kira, I., Amer, M. M., & Wrobel, N. H. (2014). Arab refugees: Trauma, resilience, and recovery. In S. C. Nassar-McMillan, K. J. Ajrouch, & J. Hakim-Larson (eds.), *Biopsychosocial perspectives on Arab Americans: Culture, Development, and Health* (pp. 175–195). New York: Springer. doi: 10.1007/978-1-4614-8238-3_9

Kira, I. A., Lewandowski, L. A., Templin, T. N., Ramaswamy, V., Ozkan, B., & Mohanesh, J. (2009). The effects of post-retribution inter-group forgiveness: The case of Iraqi refugees. *Peace and Conflict: Journal of Peace Psychology* 15, 385–413. doi: 10.1080/10781910903158669

Kira, I. A., Smith, I., Lewandowski, L., & Templin, T. (2010). The effects of gender discrimination on refugee torture survivors: A cross-cultural traumatology perspective. *Journal of the American Psychiatric Nurses Association* 16, 299–306. doi: 10.1177/1078390310384401

Kira, I. A., Templin, T., Lewandowski, L., Ramaswamy, V., Ozkan, B., & Mohanesh, J. (2008). The physical and mental health effects of Iraq war media exposure on Iraqi refugees. *Journal of Muslim Mental Health* 3(2), 193–215. doi: 10.1080/15564900802487592

Lustig, S., Kia-Keating, M., Knight, W. G., Geltman, P., Ellis, H., Kinzie, J. D., … Saxe, G. N. (2004). Review of child and adolescent refugee mental health. *Journal of the American Academy of Child and Adolescent Psychiatry* 43, 24–36. doi: 10.1097/00004583-200401000-00012

Martin, D. C. & Yankay, J. E. (2013). *Refugees and asylees: 2012*. Department of Homeland Security, Office of Immigration Statistics annual flow report. Washington, D.C.: DHS. Retrieved from www.dhs.gov/sites/default/files/publications/ois_rfa_fr_2012.pdf

Miremadi, S., Ganesan, S., & McKenna, M. (2011). Pilot study of the prevalence of alcohol, substance use and mental disorders in a cohort of Iraqi, Afghani, and Iranian refugees in Vancouver. *Asia-Pacific Psychiatry* 3(3), 137–144. doi: 10.1111/j.1758-5872.2011.00136.x

Montgomery, E. (2008). Long-term effects of organized violence on young Middle Eastern refugees' mental health. *Social Science & Medicine* 67, 1596–1603. doi: 10.1016/j.socscimed.2008.07.020

Mowafi, H. S. P. (2008). The Iraqi refugee crisis: Familiar problems and new challenges. *Journal of the American Medical Association* 299, 1713–1715. doi: 10.1001/jama.299.14.1713

Nickerson, A., Bryant, R. A., Steel, Z., Silove, D., & Brooks, R. (2010). The impact of fear for family on mental health in a resettled Iraqi refugee community. *Journal of Psychiatric Research* 44(4), 229–235. doi: 10.1016/j.jpsychires.2009.08.006

Nilsson, J. E., Barazanji, D. M., Heintzelman, A., Siddiqi, M., & Shilla, Y. (2012). Somali women's reflections on the adjustment of their children in the United States. *Journal of Multicultural Counseling and Development* 40, 240–252. doi: 10.1002/j.2161-1912.2012.00021.x

Pavlish, C. L., Noor, S., & Brandt, J. (2010). Somali immigrant women and the American health care system: Discordant beliefs, divergent expectations, and silent worries. *Social Science & Medicine* 71, 353–361. doi: 10.1016/j.socscimed.2010.04.010

Porter, M. & Haslam, N. (2005). Predisplacement and postdisplacement factors associated with mental health of refugees and internally displaced persons: A meta-analysis. *Journal of the American Medical Association* 294, 602–612. doi: 10.1001/jama.294.5.602

Porterfield, K., Akinsulure-Smith, A., Benson, M., Betancourt, T., Ellis, H., Kia-Keating, M., & Miller, K. (2010). *Resilience and recovery after war: Refugee children and families in the United States.* Washington, D.C.: American Psychological Association.

Ringold, S., Burke, A., & Glass, R. M. (2005). Refugee mental health. *Journal of the American Medical Association* 294(5), 646. doi: 10.1001/jama.294.5.646

Saxe, G. N., Ellis, B. H., & Kaplow, J. B. (2007). *Collaborative treatment of traumatized children and teens: The trauma systems therapy approach.* New York: Guilford Press.

Schulz, P. M. & Resick, P. A. (2006). The effectiveness of cognitive processing therapy for PTSD with refugees in a community setting. *Cognitive and Behavioral Practice* 13, 322–331. doi: 10.1016/j.cbpra.2006.04.011

Stutters, A. & Ligon, J. (2001). Differences in refugee anxiety and depression: Comparing Vietnamese, Somalian, and former Yugoslavian clients. *Journal of Ethnic & Cultural Diversity in Social Work* 10, 85–96. doi: 10.1300/J051v10n01_05

Taylor, E. M., Yanni, E. A., Pezzi, C., Guterbock, M., Rothney, E., Harton, E., … Burke, H. (2014). Physical and mental health status of Iraqi refugees resettled in the United States. *Journal of Immigrant and Minority Health* 16, 1130–1137. doi: 10.1007/s10903-013-9893-6

Tehranian, J. (2009). *Whitewashed: America's invisible Middle Eastern minority.* New York: NYU Press.

UNHCR. (2005). *Guidelines relating to the eligibility of Iraqi asylum-seekers.* Retrieved from www.refworld.org/docid/4354e3594.html

UNHCR. (2007a). *Statistics on displaced Iraqis around the world.* Retrieved from www.unhcr.org/461f7cb92.pdf

UNHCR. (2007b). *Convention and protocol relating to the status of refugees.* Retrieved from www.unhcr.org/3b66c2aa10.html

UNHCR. (2011). *Facts and figures about refugees.* Retrieved from www.unhcr.org.uk/about-us/key-facts-and-figures.html

UNHCR. (2013). *Syria regional refugee statistics*, April. Retrieved from http://data.unhcr.org/syrianrefugees/regional.php

UNHCR. (2014). *UNHCR Global Trends 2013.* Retrieved from http://unhcr.org/cgi-bin/texis/vtx/home/opendocPDFViewer.html?docid=5399a14f9&query=2013 %20refugee %20statistics

U.S. Citizenship and Immigration Services. (2013). *Iraqi refugee processing fact sheet.* Retrieved from www.uscis.gov/archive/archive-news/iraqi-refugee-processing-fact-sheet

USDHS. (2010). *Yearbook of Immigration Statistics: 2009.* Washington, D.C.: U.S. Department of Homeland Security, Office of Immigration Statistics. Retrieved from www.dhs.gov/xlibrary/assets/statistics/yearbook/2009/ois_yb_2009.pdf

U.S. Department of State. (2009a). *Cumulative summary of refugee admissions: Fiscal year 2008.* Washington, D.C.: U.S. Department of State. Retrieved from www.wrapsnet.org/LinkClick.aspx?fileticket=4KyOgCLk5Nk %3d&tabid=215&mid=655&language=en-US

U.S. Department of State. (2009b). *2008 human rights report: Iraq.* Retrieved from www.state.gov/j/drl/rls/hrrpt/2008/nea/119116.htm

U.S. Department of State. (2013). *Fiscal year 2013 arrivals sorted by state and country location by month.* Retrieved from www.wrapsnet.org/Reports/AdmissionsArrivals/tabid/211/Default.aspx

van der Veer, G. (1998). *Counseling and therapy with refugees and victims of trauma: Psychological problems of victims of war, torture and repression.* West Sussex, England: John Wiley & Sons Inc.

Wilkes, S. (2010). *Out of Iraq: Refugees' stories in words, paintings and music.* London: Evans Brothers.

Williams, C. L. & Berry, J. W. (1991). Primary prevention of acculturative stress among refugees: Application of psychological theory and practice. *American Psychologist* 46, 632–641. doi: 10.1037/0003-066X.46.6.632

PART IV

Behavioral Health

13

PSYCHOLOGICAL WELLBEING

Understanding Risk and Protective Factors

Wahiba Abu-Ras

Understanding psychological wellbeing among the general American population is a growing area of research, yet there is still a dearth of knowledge about certain minority and ethnic groups such as Arab Americans. This chapter discusses the literature on psychological wellbeing and mental health issues among Arab Americans. It begins with a review of different definitions of relevant concepts, including mental health, mental illness, and wellbeing. It next provides a brief presentation of the prevalence of major mental health conditions among Arab Americans. Risk and protective factors are then explored. The section that focuses on the risk factors that Arab Americans face mainly emphasizes the impact of immigration and acculturation stressors, discrimination after 9/11, and other sociocultural related stressors, such as stigma and barriers to utilization of services. Sources for resilience in coping with mental health issues include religion and spirituality, ethnic identity, family support, and community resources. A critique of the literature is presented alongside future directions for mental health research with this population.

A Framework for Understanding Resilience Through Vulnerability

This section focuses on definitions of the major concepts of mental health, mental illness, and psychological wellbeing as perceived and defined by various scholars. The section explores these concepts using an approach of understanding resilience through vulnerability.

Mental Health, Mental Illness, and Psychological Wellbeing

According to the constitution of the World Health Organization (WHO, 2014b), the concept of "health" is defined as "a state of complete physical, mental, and social wellbeing and not merely the absence of disease or infirmity" (p. 18). Moreover, the WHO has defined mental health as "a state of wellbeing in which every individual realizes his or her own potential, can cope with the normal stresses of life, can work productively and fruitfully, and is able to make a contribution to her or his community" (2014a, p. 12). Originally, the term "mental health" was intended to "reflect psychological wellbeing and resilience; in essence, a satisfactory if not optimal state of being" (Vega & Rumbaut, 1991, p. 355).

According to the U.S. Centers for Disease Control and Prevention (CDC), the concept of "mental illness," however, refers to "all diagnosable mental disorders and is characterized by sustained, abnormal alterations in thinking, mood, or behavior associated with distress and impaired functioning (Reeves et al., 2011, p. 1). This definition is primarily derived from literature that is predominantly rooted in a medical disease model and approach (Fabrega, 1990). Mental health and mental illness are two distinct terms that are socially constructed and are influenced by cultural beliefs and attitudes that shape people's perception of what is normal or abnormal behavior, how people express their emotional stress, and the way they react to traumatic events. It can be inferred from these definitions that: (a) mental illness focuses on diagnosable disorders or disease, (b) mental health is about an individual being able to be productive and use his or her resources to cope with everyday life stressors, and (c) mental stability is vital for the overall wellbeing of an individual.

The concept of "wellbeing" is another complex term that has several definitions. Bradburn (1969) was among the first to define the concept of wellbeing and referred to it as "happiness." Bradburn's definition focused on the distinction between positive and negative affect, in which he stated that "an individual will be high in psychological wellbeing in the degree to which he has an excess of positive over negative affect and will be low in wellbeing in the degree to which negative affect predominates over positive" (p. 9). Building on Bradburn's definition, Diener and Suh (1997) defined wellbeing as a concept that is characterized by three elements: pleasant affect, unpleasant affect, and life satisfaction. They wrote: "Affect refers to pleasant and unpleasant moods and emotions, whereas life satisfaction refers to a cognitive sense of satisfaction with life" (p. 200). Underlying these definitions is the idea that as people cope with life changes and stressors, their levels of wellbeing (including positive affect and life satisfaction) may be influenced. This particular definition complements the resilience (resources) and vulnerability (challenges) model.

Understanding Resilience Through Vulnerability

Understanding resilience through vulnerability has become an important framework in mental health theory and research. It involves recognition of positive adaptation, or resources, within the context of adversity and challenges (Luthar, Cicchetti, & Becker, 2000). In the last two decades, studies have shown that people can bounce back from adversity, even those who live in high-risk environments and under extreme conditions of stress. Unlike the suggestion of earlier research, resilience is no longer focused on personal traits. Instead, it is seen as an interplay of risk factors (i.e. challenges) and protective factors (i.e. resources) that involve the person, family, group, and surrounding sociocultural influences (Garmezy, 1991; Masten, Best, & Garmezy, 1990; Walsh, 2007). Resilience, in this context, can be defined as "the capability of individuals to cope successfully in the face of significant change, adversity, or risk. This capability changes over time and is enhanced by protective factors in the individual and the environment" (Stewart, Reid, & Mangham, 1997, p. 22).

Vulnerability, on the other hand, refers to when people are physically and emotionally exposed to stressors and hazards that may negatively affect their wellbeing. It can be influenced by several interrelated dimensions, including individual characteristics and behaviors, level of family and social support, and availability of community resources (Mechanic & Tanner, 2007). For example, the lack of social capital (or values and benefits gained from social networks) may exacerbate people's vulnerability. In the case of Arab Americans, many have experienced exclusion from social networks based on their ethnic and religious affiliations, and therefore have reduced social capital. Many Arab Americans came to the U.S. as immigrants or refugees. Coming from collectivist societies, where group goals and social interactions take priority over individual interests, many people become isolated and lonely in the U.S. because they lack the social support systems they once had. This can hinder adjustment to unfamiliar settings, increasing susceptibility to trauma related to stress (Abu-Ras & Abu-Bader, 2009). These experiences can negatively affect their identity as Arab Americans, as well as their ability to cope with the aftermath of 9/11 and daily stressors.

Several authors (e.g. Carter, 2008; Sakdapolrak et al., 2008; Ungar, 2008) examined the effects of religion, culture, and environment as resources that increase resilience and decrease vulnerability.

Sakdapolrak and colleagues (2008) suggested that any changes in resilience and vulnerability are a direct result of people's interactions with the institutions and environment in which they live and function. In other words, exclusion, discrimination, hate crimes, exploitation, segregation, and similar stressors may increase vulnerability, whereas ethics, family support, religion and spirituality, learning, and cooperation may increase resilience.

The importance of culture is another important element in understanding resilience. Ungar (2008) argued that the meaning of resilience is culturally specific, and that what contributes to it in one person's life or culture may not necessarily apply to another because each culture offers varying resources for maintaining wellbeing. Ungar further suggested that people attach cultural meaning to their challenges, which in return contributes to their resilience. For individuals to become resilient, they at least should have access to material resources and positive relationships, as well as opportunities for enhancing collective identity and advocating for social justice. For Arab Americans, lack of access to resources and experiences of social injustices are among the important factors that could challenge their resilience.

As such, the wellbeing of Arab Americans can be discussed in light of the balance found between those resources that contribute to resilience and the challenges that contribute to vulnerability. Before addressing the risk and protective factors that contribute to mental health outcomes, it is important to examine the scope and the nature of these mental health issues by addressing their prevalence and seriousness in the Arab American community.

The Scope and Nature of Mental Health Issues Among Arab Americans

Mental health issues are a serious public health problem and a concern for immigrants and racial/ethnic minorities. According to the CDC, as of 2004, about one-fourth of adults in the U.S. had some form of mental illness (Reeves et al., 2011). Mental health issues are associated with chronic health conditions such as obesity, diabetes, cardiovascular disease, and cancer (Reeves et al., 2011). One major concern is that the majority of the people living with mental illness do not seek help, and those from ethnic minority groups are even less likely to seek help due to cultural beliefs and structural barriers (Abu-Ras, 2003, 2007; Reeves et al., 2011).

Immigrants and ethnic minority groups are at a higher risk for developing mental health problems and psychological distress due to the unique stressors they tend to experience before, during, and after they migrate to the U.S. Immigrants experience stressors on a day-to-day basis that are both physical and psychological. These may include acculturation stress, feelings of being unwelcome, loss of homeland, as well as discrimination and experiences of hate crimes (Aranda, Castaneda, Lee, & Sobel, 2001). For example, the situation for political asylees and refugees often involves exposure to traumatic events such as war, violence, rape, imprisonment, torture, and other forms of trauma and prosecution in their home countries (Potocky-Tripodi, 2002). The impact of these traumatic experiences may be exacerbated by significant stressors faced in the U.S. after 9/11.

Many Arab Americans faced a backlash after 9/11. One study conducted after the 9/11 attacks suggests that as a result of these stressors, Arab Americans were treated with suspicion and antagonism, which led to them experiencing a significant increase in fear (Abu-Ras & Abu-Bader, 2008). The participants in that study also reported an increase in various social and mental health problems. Similarly, in a study by Abu-Ras, Gheith, and Cournos (2008) of Muslim Americans in New York (of which more than 50% were Arab Americans), 70% reported that 9/11 had had a negative effect on their lives and the majority felt less safe after 9/11. Participants reached out to imams five times more often post 9/11 compared to pre 9/11 regarding safety issues (including discrimination) and anxiety. Seeking help from the imam tripled post 9/11 for emotional problems and depression. Overall, it can be inferred that the events that took place on 9/11, and the subsequent surge in experiences of discrimination, played a noteworthy role in increasing Arab Americans' anxiety and psychological distress (Abu-Ras & Suárez, 2009).

Studies addressing the prevalence and incidence of post-9/11 mental health issues in the Arab American community show that the most common mental health concerns are depression, anxiety, and posttraumatic stress disorder (PTSD). Using the Center for Epidemiologic Studies Depression Scale (CES-D), Abu-Ras and Abu-Bader's (2009) study found a mean depression score of 21.90 (SD = 11.73), indicating a high level of clinical depression among this population. Participants who felt that their lives had changed for the worse after 9/11 reported higher levels of depression. In another study, Amer and Hovey (2012) showed that Arab Americans reported a higher rate of depression on the CES-D (mean = 17.26) compared to other standardized and community samples of four other ethnic minority groups.

With regard to anxiety and trauma symptoms, in one study 65% of 350 Arab and Muslim Americans reported anxiety as a major mental health issue (Abu-Ras & Abu-Bader, 2009). Moreover, 53% of females and 43% of males reported a clinical amount of PTSD symptoms. The same study indicated a positive relationship between high levels of anxiety and high levels of depression and PTSD. This was the case regardless of other demographic factors such as gender, religion, immigration status, and prior trauma. However, older participants, those married with children, and those with lower educational levels were more likely to report PTSD and depression. Abu-Ras and Suárez (2009) found that 94% of their sample of 102 male and female Muslim Americans, in which more than half identified as Arab, reported PTSD symptoms that were perceived by participants to be related to post-9/11 backlash. In a different study (Abu-Ras & Abu-Bader, 2008), the single biggest concern identified by almost all 83 Arab American participants was "feeling unsafe" after the events of 9/11. Feeling unsafe was the sole significant predictor of PTSD in the later study conducted by Abu-Ras and Suárez (2009), in which 82.4% reported feeling unsafe. Despite the negative effects of 9/11, positive changes were also reported. For example, in Abu-Ras and Suárez's (2009) study, 83.3% reported an increase in their self-confidence and 76.4% reported improvement to their self-esteem.

Mental Health Risk and Protective Factors

Emerging literature on Arab Americans and their psychological wellbeing has identified several risk and protective factors that affect or contribute to coping with mental health issues and fostering resilience. The risk factors fall into three main categories: (a) sociostructural-related factors, such as pre-immigration and immigration stressors and acculturation challenges; (b) sociopolitical-related factors, such as discrimination; and (c) sociocultural-related factors, such as stigma attached to mental health issues. Resilience factors support individuals in dealing with hardships and bouncing back from difficult experiences. Some of the protective factors among Arab Americans are religion and spirituality, ethnic identity, and the family support system.

Risk Factors

Pre-immigration, immigration, and acculturation stressors. Previous research suggests that more mental health issues are present in migrants who arrive from countries that are undergoing political turmoil or lack cultural similarities with the host country (Aroian & Norris, 2003; Khawaja, 2007). Political instability is common in many of the countries from which Arab Americans emigrate. The experiences of many political refugees, like Arabs, may have included political conflict, war, torture, and other traumas (Pew Research Center, 2007). Due to these kinds of pre-immigration stressors, many Arab immigrants may be vulnerable to PTSD, attention deficit hyperactivity disorder (ADHD), depression, and substance abuse (Nassar-McMillan & Hakim-Larson, 2003). About 30% of the reported social problems among Arab immigrants in Dearborn, Michigan, for example, were immigration-related (Abu-Ras, 2003).

Adding acculturation stressors to any pre-immigration exposure to traumatic events could negatively affect the wellbeing of Arab immigrants as well as their offspring and later generations.

Acculturation encompasses both cultural and psychological changes that are adopted when individuals from one cultural group come in contact with other cultural groups (Berry, 2005). Generally, groups adjust their own cultural practices in order to fit in with and feel accepted by the mainstream culture. Because Arab Americans are being highly profiled within the media, negative experiences such as prejudice, stereotyping, and racial and ethnic discrimination are exacerbated. This may cause feelings of isolation and inferiority in comparison to other members of the host society.

Acculturative stress and the degree of acculturation have been shown to impact the severity of depressive symptoms among minority groups (Berry, 2005). For example, a study of Arab Americans from 19 states and the District of Columbia showed that among Christians, those who retained more of their Arab religious and cultural values faced more acculturative stress and depression, whereas those who were more integrated into American culture had better family functioning (Amer & Hovey, 2007). Studies concerning the psychological wellbeing of Arab American elders showed that immigrant status, as a socio-demographic factor, was associated with lower life satisfaction and more frequent feelings of depression (Ajrouch, 2005, 2007).

Discrimination. Perceived discrimination has been defined as "a belief that one has been treated unfairly because of one's origin" (Mesch, Turjeman, & Fishman, 2007, p. 592). There has been a great body of research connecting perceived discrimination to negative physical and psychological health outcomes (Rousseau, Hassan, Moreau & Thombs, 2011). In addition, discrimination has been shown to increase the likelihood of engaging in negative behaviors like drug and alcohol use (Hunte & Barry, 2012).

Although the effects of perceived discrimination have been examined in several communities, research on the subject has been minimal with Arab Americans. The little research that exists shows that Arab Americans reported increased experiences of discrimination especially post 9/11, which negatively impacted their wellbeing. As anti-Arab sentiment grew in the 1990s, and was further fueled by discrimination after 9/11, Arab Americans felt unwelcome and experienced negative feelings related to their status as inferior citizens (Gavrilos, 2002). As a result, many reported increased anxiety and depression (Abu-Ras & Abu-Bader, 2008, 2009; Amer, 2005). For example, Padela and Heisler (2010) examined the resulting mental and physical health following 9/11. They found that Arab Americans had become more "visible," which resulted in greater instances of perceived discrimination and, subsequently, poorer health outcomes and more psychological distress. Rousseau and colleagues (2011) similarly found that there was a significant increase – from 25.8% in 1998 to 39.4% in 2007 – in discrimination and its associated psychological distress among Arab Canadians.

Various types of post-9/11 discrimination have impacted Arab Americans. Acute discrimination has been linked to psychological distress, with chronic discrimination also leading to anxiety and depression for Arab Americans (Abu-Ras & Abu-Bader, 2009). A study of Arab Americans in north central Florida found that recent discrimination, particularly in social interactions, was positively associated with psychological distress, although this relationship was mediated by a sense of personal control (Moradi & Hasan, 2004). Similarly, 77% of participants in Abu-Ras and Abu-Bader's (2009) study reported negative experiences related to post 9/11; of those, 63% reported discrimination and mistreatment in the workplace.

Institutional discrimination is another type of stressor that impacts many Arab Americans. Post-9/11 governmental policies targeting the community, such as detention and deportation based on national origin and ethnicity, have contributed to a pervasive sense of insecurity and vulnerability (Abu-Ras & Abu-Bader, 2008, 2009). Moreover, assaults against Arab Americans, especially those who are Muslim, have expanded to include "sacred violations" after 9/11, such as witnessing the physical destruction of the Qur'an or seeing negative images of the Prophet Muhammad (Abu-Raiya, Pargament, & Mahoney, 2011). Such violations can have lasting and detrimental effects on mental wellbeing.

Mental illness stigma. Although mental health concerns seem to have increased in the Arab American population due to discrimination post 9/11, Arab Americans remain less likely to reach out for professional help due to the stigma associated with mental health services. Aloud and Rathur's (2009) study of Arab Americans' attitudes toward seeking help for mental illness (and toward mental illness in general) indicated that fear of public stigma often becomes internalized as self-stigma, and cultural views and other factors play a role in whether or not this community seeks help for such issues or even acknowledges them as illnesses. In their review of the literature, Soheilian and Inman (2009) revealed that among Middle Eastern Americans, more negative attitudes toward mental health counseling were shown by those with higher levels of self-stigma.

Another related factor affecting Arab American mental illness stigma is the fear of bringing shame upon the family or community. According to Hassouneh and Kulwicki (2009), the fear of being judged by both one's family and one's culture is an important predictor of whether Muslim Arab American women will seek formal psychological help. The same study showed that those who do seek outside help for problems, especially for mental illnesses, are seen as shaming the family by airing dirty laundry or lacking commitment to their religious faiths. Abu-Ras (2003) found that 70% of Arab American women who experienced domestic abuse reported shame and 62% felt embarrassment seeking formal mental health services. In some cases, Arab American women who experience domestic violence may avoid mental health services because it could increase the possibility of divorce and harm their marital prospects (if they decided to remarry) and also those of their daughters. It may also work against them in cases of child custody, as they could be accused of being mentally unfit to care for their children (Abu-Ras, 2007). Therefore, stigma associated with the use of mental health services constitutes a very real barrier to service utilization among Arab Americans, and further puts them at a higher risk for developing other mental illness.

Resilience and Protective Factors

Religion and spirituality. Religion has been identified in psychological wellbeing research as a key protective factor for both prevention and recovery of mental health problems (Pietrzak, Johnson, Goldstein, Malley, & Southwick, 2009; Yates & Masten, 2004). Individuals who are more connected to their religion exhibit greater levels of wellbeing (Koenig, McCullough, & Larson, 2001). Religion and spirituality can help believers form rational and clear worldviews and internalize positive emotions, and can serve as psychological resources in helping them to feel more empowered (Levin & Chatters, 1998). Studies show that religiosity and spirituality enable people to overcome hardship and trauma (Masten & Coatsworth, 1998) and to thrive (Connor, Davidson, & Lee, 2003). Socially, religiosity encourages the formation of cohesive social networks, pro-social behaviors (Fabricatore, Handal, Rubio, & Gilner, 2004), and healthy lifestyles (Idler & Kasl, 1997; Strawbridge, Shema, Cohen, & Kaplan, 2001), which can buffer against stress. Moreover, religious individuals have been found to have more intact and stable families and to contribute to and participate in social or congregational activities (Koenig et al., 2001; Lewis, Maltby, & Day, 2005).

Research on religiosity and spirituality among Arab Americans is understudied; however, from the very few studies conducted, it has been shown that religiosity and religious coping can contribute as protective factors. Religiosity serves as a form of social expression and political mobilization, as well as a vehicle for community building and group identity among Muslim Arab Americans (Abu-Ras, Senzai, & Laird, 2013; Gozdziak & Shandy, 2002). Religious values are among the important factors that contribute to the psychological wellbeing of Arab Americans. For example, Amer and Hovey (2007) found that among Muslim Arab Americans, less religiosity was associated with depression. Religion and religious coping was also found to discourage Muslim college students, a large portion of whom were from Arab American backgrounds, from risky behaviors such as the use of alcohol and drugs (Abu-Ras, Ahmed, & Arfken, 2010; Ahmed, Abu-Ras, & Arfken, 2014). It has also been suggested that religious factors explain the low suicide rates among Arab Americans (El-Sayed, Tracy, Scarborough, & Galea, 2011). In times of heightened stress Arab Americans may utilize their religious teachings or seek support from religious leaders for additional resources to manage adversities (Abu-Ras et al., 2008; Abu-Ras & Hosein, 2014; Amer, Hovey, Fox, & Rezcallah, 2008). Beitin and Allen (2005) found that through strong community support and the use of religious coping, Arab Americans displayed resilience and were able to cope with the aftermath of 9/11.

On the other hand, Arab Americans may be at risk of experiencing discrimination based on their religious affiliation, and as a result their wellbeing may be adversely impacted. After 9/11, many Americans concluded that Islam, which is practiced by a number of Arab Americans, was not consistent with Western values and that it encouraged terror, violence, and war (Tiliouine, Cummins, & Davern, 2009). Studies showed that hate crimes and discrimination directed toward Muslims due to their religious affiliation increased their depression and their PTSD (e.g. Abu-Ras & Abu-Bader, 2009). Results from a study of British Muslims by Sheridan (2006) suggested that religious (namely Muslim) affiliation was a more significant predictor of receiving prejudice than was race or ethnicity. Other studies in North America suggested that Muslim Arab Americans face more stress compared to their Christian counterparts. For example, Muslim Arabs living in Canada reported more perceived discrimination than non-Muslim Arabs, and discrimination was significantly associated with psychological distress for the Muslim Arabs but not for the non-Muslim Arab participants (Rousseau et al., 2011). Similarly, Awad's (2010) study of 177 Arab Americans found that Muslim Arab Americans who were more acculturated into the main society experienced more discrimination in comparison to their less acculturated counterparts.

Ethnic identity. Ethnic identity and ethnic community ties are protective factors that can make it less likely to develop mental health problems. For example, in one study of 68 Muslim university students from South Asian and Middle Eastern backgrounds, those with strong heritage culture identification experienced fewer depressive symptoms in their lifetime (Asvat & Malcarne, 2008). Likewise, in Fakih's (2013) study of Arab Americans, strength of ethnic identity was related to higher self-esteem and less depression. In another study, Abdulrahim, James, Yamout, and Baker (2012) discovered that Arab Americans living in ethnic enclaves experienced more discrimination than those living outside ethnic enclaves, yet those living inside the enclaves experienced less psychological distress than those living outside the enclaves. For Arab Americans, like many other minority groups who experience any type of oppression or discrimination, one way of coping and changing these conditions could be to connect to their ethnic identity and community, and to a set of shared norms, beliefs, and behaviors.

Family and social support. Social support has been found to improve psychological wellbeing, while a lack of social support can be a risk factor and at times a predictor of PTSD after a traumatic event. Arab Americans gain social support from family and community. Family support is derived from the collectivist Arab cultural values, which emphasize the hierarchical family structure (including extended family). In Arab society, social support networks consist of the outer circle of friends and neighbors and the inner circle of family and kin. The extended family influences stability, providing emotional, instrumental, and tangible support. The family unit is seen as sacred and is greatly respected as a source of support, and therefore tends to play a large role in traditional Arab households (Al-Krenawi & Graham, 2000).

Abu-Ras' (2000) study of Arab American women in domestic violence relationships showed that the majority of the women perceived their family as a source of support to which they could turn for help in times of crisis. For many, lack of family support increased stress and further vulnerability to domestic violence (Abu-Ras, 2003). Arab immigrant women may not have customary support systems in the U.S., which may lead to loneliness, adding some difficulty to adjusting to a new society (Cainkar, 1996). When immigrants do not have these types of support system in the U.S., adjustment is hindered and the risk of stress reactions in traumatic situations is increased. For example, Abu-Ras and Abu-Bader's (2009) study confirmed that individuals who lacked social support from their communities experienced significantly more PTSD and depression symptoms and, similarly, depression was higher among those with less family support.

Case Example: Nariman Living the Past, Present, and Future

Nariman is a 16-year-old Palestinian Arab female student attending a high school in Dearborn, Michigan. Nariman emigrated with her family, including her parents and siblings, from the West Bank, Palestine, to the U.S. when she was 14 years old. Nariman's parents were working class, and were hardly able to meet their family's needs. They came to the U.S. to improve their economic situation and also escape the political unrest of the West Bank. Nariman has two siblings: ten-year-old sister Mona and five-year-old brother Yussef. Both of her parents are legal residents who work full-time in an Arab restaurant. The family lives in an Arab American ethnic enclave in Dearborn.

Because she did not gain fluency in English when she was living in Palestine, Nariman faced challenges writing and communicating her thoughts. She was too embarrassed to speak in class and avoided interactions with her classmates. In writing one of her essays, she expressed some of these difficulties and her desire to go back home to Palestine. Her English teacher therefore referred Nariman to the school counselor. The teacher reported to the counselor that Nariman was very quiet and did not seem to have friends. Nariman became frustrated when trying to communicate her thoughts in the classroom. When asked a question in class, she appeared tearful and sad, and showed signs of fear and anxiety.

During the intake session, Nariman was very anxious. When she was asked about her sadness, Nariman reported having a history of depressive symptoms since age eight. She had been referred to see a psychologist at her school in Palestine, but had never received counseling services due to the constant curfews and closing of her school district. She reported often having felt sad, frustrated, tearful, and tired. She also said that she had had difficulty sleeping at night: she had often had nightmares revolving around being killed by Israeli soldiers or her parents being arrested. Nariman expressed similar fears of being arrested by local police officers in the U.S.

Nariman expressed ongoing feelings of loneliness and isolation. At home, she and her mother were the ones who cared for the other family members, especially her younger siblings. She also spent a few hours daily helping her mother in cleaning the house and in preparing dinner, which left her exhausted and further affected her ability to complete homework on time and to socialize with peers after school. Although she lives in an area that is highly concentrated with Arab American residents, Nariman's social network was very limited and mainly included her parents, siblings, and two of her cousins who lived in the same building. She mentioned how much she missed her grandparents and her close friends from school in Palestine. Nariman also reported being bullied by some of the children in her neighborhood, who called her names. She feared going out alone and only occasionally spent time with other predominantly Arabic-speaking peers who live in her neighborhood.

This case example sheds some light on the process of migration and its impact on Nariman's feelings and experiences with traumatic events that occurred in Palestine during the second Intifada (Uprising). It also shows some of the challenges connected to an immigrant's ability to acculturate. The case emphasizes the importance of some risk factors, such as low socioeconomic status, young age, and language barriers, as well as previous exposure to political unrest and other traumatic events in her original country and also in the U.S. These stressors affected Nariman's ability to adjust to the new culture and cope with all the challenges at her school, at home, and in her new neighborhood. In addition, Nariman's case evokes some speculation about the impact of discrimination on an immigrant's ability to integrate into U.S. society, especially post 9/11, when many Arab Americans became a target for discrimination and hate crimes. Conversely, the case shows potential protective factors, such as family support, school support from her teacher and counselor, and living in a neighborhood where Nariman shared some of her cultural values and language that also could foster her sense of community belonging.

Critique

The major goals of this chapter were to examine the research on psychological wellbeing of Arab Americans and to highlight the major contributing risk and protective factors that affect their mental health and also foster their resilience. As this chapter presents, most studies on mental health were conducted after 9/11, exploring the impact of 9/11 on the wellbeing of Arab Americans. However, very few studies were conducted before 9/11 and, therefore, it would be difficult to measure the pre-9/11 severity or the changing nature of mental health challenges.

Studies conducted on depression, anxiety, and PTSD among Arab Americans have been limited in their methods. These studies have used small sample sizes and, convenience samples, and have mostly focused on specific populations in specific locations such as Michigan, where the largest concentration of Arab Americans resides. Additionally, most participants were defined as "Arab American," but the samples represented only small portions of the diverse Arab nationalities, which reduces the ability to generalize to other Arab Americans of different nationalities and religious groups. Another important limitation is that most current measures utilized in these studies were Western and based on U.S. norms. Many of these scales were constructed to represent the mainstream American culture and therefore do not always take into consideration Arab cultural differences. This may have affected the reliability and validity of the results, posing risks for misinterpretation of mental health issues. To avoid this problem, more measures need to be designed and developed specifically for the Arab American population.

While many of the studies found in this chapter focused on mental health issues such as depression, anxiety, PTSD, and substance abuse in Arab Americans, there is very little information about other mental illnesses such as schizophrenia, bipolar disorder, neurocognitive disorders, and personality disorders. There is a substantial need for early identification and treatment of these diagnoses, especially because exposure to traumatic experiences increases the risk for mental disorders. Future studies on Arab Americans should measure not only psychological symptoms, but also any related physical symptoms.

In addition, most studies have focused on Arab American adults, whereas little is known about mental health among children, youth, and the elderly. Not much research attention is given to the children of Arab Americans who, like their parents, may experience high rates of depression and anxiety themselves. It is important to explore the needs of families as a whole, because it is likely that children will be exposed to fewer risk factors at home and in their community if other members of the family are physically and mentally healthy. Often, elderly Arab American parents live with their children. It is therefore important to further explore mental health risk and protective factors for both the elderly and younger caregivers.

Finally, while many studies focus on women, there is limited research specific to men and the particular challenges they face as Arab Americans. For instance, Arab American men have faced deportation, heightened discrimination, and stereotyping. More studies are needed to examine the differences between the genders and their perception of mental health, as well as differences in the contributing risk and protective factors.

Conclusion

This chapter represented a critical first step in bridging the gaps in knowledge about the mental health concerns of Arab Americans. Among the contributing risk factors for vulnerability to psychological wellbeing among Arab Americans are pre- and post-immigration stressors and post-9/11 experiences with discrimination and backlash. However, coming from a collectivist cultural background where family and community supports, as well as religion, play a significant role, Arab Americans may be able to adapt successfully to trauma and to everyday life adversity and, further, become more resilient.

For those Arab Americans who do experience significant mental health problems, negative attitudes toward mental health counseling have been a barrier to accessing and utilizing mental health services. Therefore, it is important for mental health practitioners to engage in community outreach efforts and improve the cultural sensitivity of their services. This can include understanding and integrating aspects of Arab culture and religion, and supporting clients with psychosocial needs such as employment. Future research should include studies that capture mental health and psychological wellbeing perspectives and experiences from diverse Arab American individuals, special groups, and communities.

Acknowledgment

The author would like to thank her graduate assistant, Rozena Abdin, MSW student, for her support and technical help with the chapter.

References

Abdulrahim, S., James, S. A., Yamout, R., & Baker, W. (2012). Discrimination and psychological distress: Does Whiteness matter for Arab Americans? *Social Science & Medicine* 75, 2116–2123. doi: 10.1016/j.socscimed.2012.07.030

Abu-Raiya, H., Pargament, K. I., & Mahoney, A. (2011). Examining coping methods with stressful interpersonal events experienced by Muslims living in the United States following the 9/11 attacks. *Psychology of Religion and Spirituality* 3(1), 1–14. doi: 10.1037/a0020034

Abu-Ras, W. M. (2000). *Barriers to and utilization of services among Arab immigrant battered women in the United States* (Doctoral dissertation). Available from ProQuest Dissertations and Theses database (UMI No. 9970134).

Abu-Ras, W. (2003). Barriers to services for Arab immigrant battered women in a Detroit suburb. *Journal of Social Work Research and Evaluation* 4(1), 49–66.

Abu-Ras, W. (2007). Cultural beliefs and service utilization by battered Arab immigrant women. *Violence Against Women* 13, 1002–1028. doi: 10.1177/1077801207306019

Abu-Ras, W. & Abu-Bader, S. (2008). The impact of the September 11, 2001, attacks on the well-being of Arab Americans in New York City. *Journal of Muslim Mental Health* 3, 217–239. doi: 10.1080/15564900802487634

Abu-Ras, W. & Abu-Bader, S. H. (2009). Risk factors for depression and posttraumatic stress disorder (PTSD): The case of Arab and Muslim Americans post-9/11. *Journal of Immigrant & Refugee Studies* 7, 393–418. doi: 10.1080/15562940903379068

Abu-Ras, W., Ahmed, S., & Arfken, C. L. (2010). Alcohol use among U.S. Muslim college students: Risk and protective factors. *Journal of Ethnicity in Substance Abuse* 9, 206–220. doi: 10.1080/15332640.2010.500921

Abu-Ras, W., Gheith, A., & Cournos, F. (2008). The imam's role in mental health promotion: A study at 22 mosques in New York City's Muslim community. *Journal of Muslim Mental Health* 3, 155–176. doi: 10.1080/15564900802487576

Abu-Ras, W. & Hosein, S. (2014). Understanding resilience through vulnerability: Cultural meaning and religious practice among Muslim military personnel. *Psychology of Religion and Spirituality*. Advance online publication. doi: 10.1037/rel0000017

Abu-Ras, W., Senzai, F., & Laird, L. (2013). American Muslim physicians' experiences since 9/11: Cultural trauma and the formation of Islamic identity. *Traumatology* 19(1), 11–19. doi: 10.1177/1534765612441975

Abu-Ras, W. & Suárez, Z. E. (2009). Muslim men and women's perception of discrimination, hate crimes, and PTSD symptoms post 9/11. *Traumatology* 15(3), 48–63. doi: 10.1177/1534765609342281

Ahmed, S., Abu-Ras, W., & Arfken, C. (2014). Prevalence of risk behaviors among U.S. Muslim college students. *Journal of Muslim Mental Health* 8(1), 5–19. doi: 10.3998/jmmh.10381607.0008.101

Ajrouch, K. J. (2005). Arab-American immigrant elders' views about social support. *Ageing and Society* 25, 655–673. doi: 10.1017/S0144686X04002934

Ajrouch, K. J. (2007). Resources and well-being among Arab-American elders. *Journal of Cross-Cultural Gerontology* 22, 167–182. doi: 10.1007/s10823-006-9033-z

Al-Krenawi, A. & Graham J. R. (2000). Culturally sensitive social work practice with Arab clients in mental health settings. *Health & Social Work* 25, 9–22. doi: 10.1093/hsw/25.1.9

Aloud, N. & Rathur, A. (2009). Factors affecting attitudes toward seeking and using formal mental health and psychological services among Arab Muslim populations. *Journal of Muslim Mental Health*, 4, 79–103. doi: 10.1080/15564900802487675

Amer, M. M. (2005). *Arab American mental health in the post September 11 era: Acculturation, stress, and coping* (Doctoral dissertation). Available from ProQuest Dissertations and Theses database (UMI No. 3171022).

Amer, M. M. & Hovey, J. D. (2007). Socio-demographic differences in acculturation and mental health for a sample of 2nd generation/early immigrant Arab Americans. *Journal of Immigrants and Minority Health* 9, 335–347. doi: 10.1007/s10903-007-9045-y

Amer, M. M. & Hovey, J. D. (2012). Anxiety and depression in a post-September 11 sample of Arabs in the USA. *Social Psychiatry and Psychiatric Epidemiology* 47, 409–418. doi: 10.1007/s00127-011-0341-4

Amer, M. M., Hovey, J. D., Fox, C. M., & Rezcallah, A. (2008). Initial development of the Brief Arab Religious Coping Scale (BARCS). *Journal of Muslim Mental Health* 3, 69–88. doi: 10.1080/15564900802156676

Aranda, M. P., Castaneda, I., Lee, P., & Sobel, E. (2001). Stress, social support, and coping as predictors of depressive symptoms: Gender differences among Mexican Americans. *Social Work Research* 25(1), 37–48. doi: 10.1093/swr/25.1.37

Aroian, K. J. & Norris, A. E. (2003). Depression trajectories in relatively recent immigrants. *Comprehensive Psychiatry* 44, 420–427. doi: 10.1016/S0010-440X(03)00103-2

Asvat, Y. & Malcarne, V. L. (2008). Acculturation and depressive symptoms in Muslim university students: Personal–family acculturation match. *International Journal of Psychology* 43, 114–124. doi: 10.1080/00207590601126668

Awad, G. H. (2010). The impact of acculturation and religious identification on perceived discrimination for Arab/Middle Eastern Americans. *Cultural Diversity and Ethnic Minority Psychology* 16, 59–67. doi: 10.1037/a0016675

Beitin, B. K. & Allen, K. R. (2005). Resilience in Arab American couples after September 11, 2001: A systems perspective. *Journal of Marital and Family Therapy* 31, 251–267. doi: 10.1111/j.1752-0606.2005.tb01567.x

Berry, J. W. (2005). Acculturation: Living successfully in two cultures. *International Journal of Intercultural Relations* 29, 697–712. doi: 10.1016/j.ijintrel.2005.07.013

Bradburn, N. (1969). *The structure of psychological wellbeing*. Chicago, IL: Aldine.

Cainkar, L. (1996). Immigrant Palestinian women evaluate their lives. In B. C. Aswad & B. Bilge (eds.), *Family and gender among American Muslims* (pp. 41–58). Philadelphia, PA: Temple University Press.

Carter, R. L. (2008). Understanding resilience through ritual and religious practice: An expanded theoretical and ethnographic framework. In H. Bohle & K. Warner (eds.), *Megacities: Resilience and social vulnerability* (pp. 73–81). New York: United Nations University, Institute for Environment and Human Security. Retrieved from www.ehs.unu.edu/file/get/4044

Connor, K. M., Davidson, J. R. T., & Lee, L. (2003). Spirituality, resilience, and anger in survivors of violent trauma: A community survey. *Journal of Traumatic Stress* 16, 487–494. doi: 10.1023/A:1025762512279

Diener, E. & Suh, E. (1997). Measuring quality of life: Economic, social, and subjective indicators. *Social Indicators Research* 40(1–2), 189–216. doi: 10.1023/A:1006859511756

El-Sayed, A. M., Tracy, M., Scarborough, P., & Galea, S. (2011). Ethnic inequalities in mortality: The case of Arab-Americans. *PloS ONE* 6(12), 1–7. doi: 10.1371/journal.pone.0029185

Fabrega, H. (1990). Hispanic mental health research: A case for cultural psychiatry. *Hispanic Journal of Behavioral Sciences* 12, 339–365. doi: 10.1177/07399863900124001

Fabricatore, A. N., Handal, P. J., Rubio, D. M., & Gilner, F. H. (2004). Stress, religion, and mental health: Religious coping in mediating and moderating roles. *The International Journal for the Psychology of Religion* 14(2), 91–108. doi: 10.1207/s15327582ijpr1402_2

Fakih, R. R. (2013). *Ethnic identity among Arab Americans: An examination of contextual influences and psychological well-being* (Doctoral dissertation). Available from ProQuest Dissertations and Theses database (UMI No. 3613203).

Garmezy, N. (1991). Resilience and vulnerability to adverse developmental outcomes associated with poverty. *American Behavioral Scientist* 34, 416–430. doi: 10.1177/0002764291034004003

Gavrilos, D. (2002). Arab Americans in a nation's imagined community: How news constructed Arab American reactions to the Gulf War. *Journal of Communication Inquiry* 26, 426–445. doi: 10.1177/019685902236900

Gozdziak, E. M. & Shandy, D. J. (2002). Editorial introduction: Religion and spirituality in forced migration. *Journal of Refugee Studies* 15, 129–135. doi: 10.1093/jrs/15.2.129

Hassouneh, D. & Kulwicki, A. (2009). Family privacy as protection: A qualitative pilot study of mental illness in Arab-American Muslim women. In R. L. Piedmont & A. Village (eds.), *Research in the social scientific study of religion* (vol. 20, pp. 195–215). Leiden, NL: Brill.

Hunte, H. E. R. & Barry, A. E. (2012). Perceived discrimination and DSM-IV-based alcohol and illicit drug use disorders. *American Journal of Public Health* 102, e111–e117. doi: 10.2105/AJPH.2012.300780

Idler, E. L. & Kasl, S. V. (1997). Religion among disabled and nondisabled persons I: Cross-sectional patterns in health practices, social activities, and wellbeing. *The Journals of Gerontology, Series B: Psychological Sciences and Social Sciences* 52(6), S294–S305. doi: 10.1093/geronb/52B.6.S294

Khawaja, N. G. (2007). An investigation of the psychological distress of Muslim migrants in Australia. *Journal of Muslim Mental Health* 2, 39–56. doi: 10.1080/15564900701238526

Koenig, H. G., McCullough, M. E., & Larson, D. B. (2001). *Handbook of religion and health*. New York: Oxford University Press.

Levin, J. S. & Chatters, L. M. (1998). Research on religion and mental health: An overview of empirical findings and theoretical issues. In H. G. Koenig (ed.), *Handbook of religion and mental health* (pp. 70–84). San Diego, CA: Academic Press.

Lewis, C. A., Maltby, J., & Day, L. (2005). Religious orientation, religious coping and happiness among UK adults. *Personality and Individual Differences* 38, 1193–1202. doi: 10.1016/j.paid.2004.08.002

Luthar, S. S., Cicchetti, D., & Becker, B. (2000). The construct of resilience: A critical evaluation and guidelines for future work. *Child Development* 71, 543–562. doi: 10.1111/1467–8624.00164

Masten, A. S., Best, K. M., & Garmezy, N. (1990). Resilience and development: Contributions from the study of children who overcome adversity. *Development and Psychopathology* 2, 425–444. doi: 10.1017/S0954579400005812

Masten, A. S. & Coatsworth, J. D. (1998). The development of competence in favorable and unfavorable environments: Lessons from research on successful children. *American Psychologist* 53, 205–220. doi: 10.1037/0003-066X.53.2.205

Mechanic, D. & Tanner, J. (2007). Vulnerable people, groups, and populations: Societal view. *Health Affairs* 26, 1220–1230. doi: 10.1377/hlthaff.26.5.1220

Mesch, G. S., Turjeman, H., & Fishman, G. (2007). Perceived discrimination and the well-being of immigrant adolescents. *Journal of Youth and Adolescence* 37, 592–604. doi: 10.1007/s10964-007-9210-6

Moradi, B. & Hasan N. T. (2004). Arab American persons' reported experiences of discrimination and mental health: The mediating role of personal control. *Journal of Counseling Psychology* 51, 418–428. doi: 10.1037/0022-0167.51.4.418

Nassar-McMillan, S. C. & Hakim-Larson, J. (2003). Counseling considerations among Arab Americans. *Journal of Counseling & Development* 81, 150–159. doi: 10.1002/j.1556–6678.2003.tb00236.x

Padela, A. I. & Heisler, M. (2010). The association of perceived abuse and discrimination after September 11, 2001, with psychological distress, level of happiness, and health status among Arab Americans. *American Journal of Public Health* 100, 284–291. doi: 10.2105/AJPH.2009.164954

Pew Research Center. (2007). *Muslim Americans: Middle class and mostly mainstream*. Washington, D.C.: Pew Research Center. Retrieved from www.pewresearch.org/files/old-assets/pdf/muslim-americans.pdf

Pietrzak, R. H., Johnson, D. C., Goldstein, M. B., Malley, J. C., & Southwick, S. M. (2009). Psychological resilience and postdeployment social support protect against traumatic stress and depressive symptoms in soldiers returning from Operations Enduring Freedom and Iraqi Freedom. *Depression and Anxiety* 26, 745–751. doi: 10.1002/da.20558

Potocky-Tripodi, M. (2002). *Best practices for social work with refugees and immigrants*. New York: Columbia University Press.

Reeves, W. C., Strine, T. W., Pratt, L. A., Thompson, W., Ahluwalia, I., Dhingra, S. S., ... Safran, M. A. (2011). Mental illness surveillance among adults in the United States. *MMWR Surveillance Summaries* 60(Suppl. 3), 1–32.

Rousseau, C., Hassan, G., Moreau, N., & Thombs, B. D. (2011). Perceived discrimination and its association with psychological distress among newly arrived immigrants before and after September 11, 2001. *American Journal of Public Health* 101, 909–915. doi: 10.2105/AJPH.2009.173062

Sakdapolrak, P., Butsch, C., Carter, R. L., Cojocaru, M.-D., Etzold, B., Kishor, N., ... Sagala, S. (2008). The megacity resilience framework. In H. Bohle & K. Warner (eds.), *Megacities: Resilience and social vulnerability* (pp. 10–19). New York: United Nations University, Institute for Environment and Human Security. Retrieved from www.ehs.unu.edu/file/get/4044

Sheridan, L. P. (2006). Islamophobia pre- and post-September 11th, 2001. *Journal of Interpersonal Violence* 21, 317–336. doi: 10.1177/0886260505282885

Soheilian, S. S., & Inman, A. G. (2009). Middle Eastern Americans: The effects of stigma on attitudes toward counseling. *Journal of Muslim Mental Health* 4, 139–158. doi: 10.1080/15564900903245766

Stewart, M., Reid, G., & Mangham, C. (1997). Fostering children's resilience. *Journal of Pediatric Nursing* 12(1), 21–31. doi: 10.1016/S0882-5963(97)80018-8

Strawbridge, W. J., Shema, S. J., Cohen, R. D., & Kaplan, G. A. (2001). Religious attendance increases survival by improving and maintaining good health behaviors, mental health, and social relationships. *Annals of Behavioral Medicine* 23(1), 68–74. doi: 10.1207/S15324796ABM2301_10

Tiliouine, H., Cummins, R. A., & Davern, M. (2009). Islamic religiosity, subjective well-being, and health. *Mental Health, Religion & Culture* 12(1), 55–74. doi: 10.1080/13674670802118099

Ungar, M. (2008). Resilience across cultures. *British Journal of Social Work* 38, 218–235. doi: 10.1093/bjsw/bcl343

Vega, W. A. & Rumbaut, R. G. (1991). Ethnic minorities and mental health. *Annual Review of Sociology* 17, 351–383. doi: 10.1146/annurev.so.17.080191.002031
Walsh, F. (2007). Traumatic loss and major disasters: Strengthening family and community resilience. *Family Process* 46, 207–227. doi: 10.1111/j.1545-5300.2007.00205.x
World Health Organization. (2014a). *Social determinants of mental health*. Geneva, Switzerland: WHO. Retrieved from http://apps.who.int/iris/bitstream/10665/112828/1/9789241506809_eng.pdf?ua=1
World Health Organization. (2014b). *Twelfth general programme of work: Not merely the absence of disease*. Retrieved from www.who.int/about/resources_planning/twelfth-gpw/en/
Yates, T. M. & Masten, A. S. (2004). Fostering the future: Resilience theory and the practice of positive psychology. In P. A. Linley & S. Joseph (eds.), *Positive psychology in practice* (pp. 521–539). Hoboken, NJ: John Wiley and Sons, Inc.

14
TRAUMA
Stress, Coping, and Emerging Treatment Models

Ibrahim Aref Kira and Nancy Howells Wrobel

Relative to mainstream and other minority samples in the American community, levels of reported anxiety and depression are notably high in Arab American samples (Amer & Hovey, 2012). However, resilience and post-traumatic growth have been noticed in this population as well (e.g. Kira, Amer, & Wrobel, 2014; Kira, Templin, Lewandowski, et al., 2006). The etiology of Arab Americans' mental health status, as well as their post-traumatic growth, lies in great part in the stressors and traumas they have encountered and are currently encountering, and their coping strategies. This chapter critiques the existing frameworks for understanding their stress and trauma experiences and explores some of the factors that influence their current mental health and resilience. Further, it critiques and explores the appropriate interventions to help them, proposing a suitable intervention model. A case example is provided to illustrate how to treat Arab American clients.

Conceptual Frameworks Used to Analyze Trauma in Arab Americans

Current theories of trauma typically focus only on individual, past, single traumas, and the post-single traumatic stress disorder. These theories may not be appropriate for the study or treatment of multiply traumatized populations such as Arab Americans (e.g. Kira, 2001; Kira, Ashby, Lewandowski, et al., 2013; Kira, Fawzi, & Fawzi, 2012). The diagnostic category of posttraumatic stress disorder (PTSD) contributed to a view of such suffering as a medical diagnosis, rather than allowing for a broader perspective of the psychosocial and political factors that contribute to the apparent symptoms. Certainly, the nature and impact of traumatic events, including oppression, discrimination, war, occupation, and genocide, warrant attention (Afana, 2012; Giacaman et al., 2011).

Examining present-day stress and trauma theories and research, Kira, Ashby, Lewandowski, and colleagues (2013) identified potential inadequacies. The lack of interdisciplinary focus has led to different unintegrated projects. The focus on specific traumas (e.g. sexual abuse) may allow for the focused study of such specific traumas, but may ignore the whole picture of traumatic exposure that the person may endure across his or her lifespan, and its cumulative dynamics. Further, current trauma literature is more focused on past traumas, ignoring the present, ongoing, and potentially continuous traumatic experiences that may include microaggressions (e.g. insults and lost job opportunities) and macroaggressions (e.g. hate crimes). Ongoing traumatic stressors may modulate or amplify the effects of past traumas, and vice versa. Additionally, current trauma research has an individualistic bias that tends to ignore those stressors that target social identities such as the traumatogenic dynamics of intergroup conflict and of structural, institutional, cultural, and historical traumas.

Table 14.1 Typology of Traumatic Events in the DBTF According to Their Severity

Type	*Description*	*Examples*
Uncomplicated		
Type I	Single-episode trauma	Car accident
Complex traumas		
Type II	A. Repeated, similar traumatic episodes that have ceased (Terr, 1991)	Past sexual abuse
	B. Repeated, ongoing, similar traumatic episodes	Domestic violence
Type III	Chronic continuous traumatization	Racism
Cumulative trauma		
Type IV	Cumulative trauma across a lifetime	Past and present, ongoing stress and chronic traumas

A Developmentally Based Stress and Trauma Framework (DBTF), which integrates the disparate parts of current theories of stress and trauma, may be a more suitable framework for the analysis of trauma among Arab Americans. The DBTF defines traumatization as "a process that can be triggered by stressors with different levels of intensity that range from chronic hassles to severe traumatic complex stressors, such as the Hiroshima bombing and the holocaust. These identified stressors have the potential to trigger post-trauma spectrum disorders, and/or post-trauma spectrum competencies and growth" (Kira, Ashby, Lewandowski, et al., 2013, p. 397). Traumatization is a process that severely challenges the developmental assets and potentials of the individual.

The DBTF model applies two dimensions to classify stress and trauma, with one addressing the chronicity and severity of trauma and the other involving a developmental focus. As shown in Table 14.1, the DBTF distinguishes between four types of traumatic events in terms of chronicity and severity. Type I trauma is structurally simple with one event that occurred, such as a car accident. Type II trauma is more complex, with episodes of previous recurrent traumas, for example domestic abuse. Type III traumas are the chronic sequences of ongoing stress that continue and have not stopped, such as discrimination and oppression. Type IV is the dynamics of accumulation of all such trauma types across a lifespan. All of the above establish different trauma profiles for individuals and groups.

The severity of each trauma is determined by two factors: the developmental stage it affects and the complexity and chronicity inherent in its structures and dynamics. As classified by DBTF, developmentally-based traumas in early childhood include attachment traumas and maltreatment; for example, when refugee children are separated from parents or are neglected (which are complex Type II traumas). Throughout adolescence and adulthood, identity emerges to include increased self-autonomy, awareness and identification with social groups, and belonging to social networks. During these development stages, trauma may include personal identity traumas that can occur in cases of prostitution and human trafficking (also complex Type II traumas), role identity trauma (e.g. being fired or suffering major loss in business), and collective identity traumas that may occur as a result of oppression, discrimination, and severe inequalities (Type III trauma; Kira, 2010). Additionally, survival traumas may occur as a result of war, terrorism, and protracted intergroup conflict, or due to ecological disasters and epidemics. The DBTF also considers interdependence-based traumas, which are often transmitted interpersonally or intergroup through media, or perhaps through cross-generation processes that reflect individual, family, and systemic global interdependence (Kira, Templin, Lewandowski, et al., 2006).

When enough stress and trauma factors accumulate and outweigh the developmental assets or protective factors, or cross the threshold of the individuals' distress tolerance, then different profiles of post-trauma spectrum disorders develop that may involve comorbid PTSD and other psychiatric or substance abuse diagnoses. The trauma accumulation process may entail different dynamics. While a dose-response model (the change in effect caused by differing levels of exposure) describes linear traumatogenic dynamics, the cumulative trauma model proposes, additionally, different cumulative nonlinear dynamics that affect the threshold of distress tolerance. The threshold refers to one's capacity to withstand significant states of emotional and physical discomfort, coupled with the ability to perform adaptively given those stressors. Research indicates that distress tolerance tends to be stable across time, both at individual and group levels (e.g. Cummings et al., 2013). This threshold nonlinear model presumes that individuals have different breaking points. Even for people higher in distress tolerance, chronic and continuous stress and cumulative dynamics of traumatic and non-traumatic events can cause the person to "snap," or decompensate, as the case example at the end of this chapter illustrates.

Karam and associates (2014) found a greater degree of functional impairment as well as psychiatric morbidity in cases with four or more traumas, suggesting a risk threshold at that level. However, while a critical threshold of four or more traumas can be helpful in identifying mental health risk, caution must be taken as this finding may apply to the group but is not to be generalized to each individual client, who may have a different breaking point. Additionally, the trauma scale Karam and associates used did not include most systemic chronic traumas (e.g. gender discrimination, ethnic discrimination) or attachment disruptions. Thus, models based on a "dose" or "threshold" approach may not fully address the complex and chronic traumatization experienced by some Arab Americans. In order to more effectively understand such traumas among Arab Americans, the trauma typology outlined above, and its proposed dynamics, may be utilized as a heuristic device for analysis, assessment, and interpretation of their trauma profiles and post-trauma reactions.

Stress and Traumatogenic Events: The Journey of Arab American Immigrants and Refugees

Prior research on immigrant populations has suggested that the most reliable predictors of their current mental health include both pre-migration and post-migration traumas. In particular, studies found that pre-migration traumas accounted for the majority of variance in adult psychiatric symptoms. An additional 20% of the variance was related to post-immigration trauma, and current migration stressors contributed 14% of the variance in symptoms (Nicholson, 1997; Steel, Silove, Bird, McGorry, & Mohan, 1999). Other studies found post-immigration stressors, such as discrimination, to be more salient for immigrant adolescents (Thibeault, 2013), as well as for refugee adult victims of political violence (Chu, Keller, & Rasmussen, 2013) and Arab refugee women (Norris, Aroian, & Nickerson, 2011). Regardless, as discussed below, the compound effects of pre- and post-immigration traumas may have cumulative dynamics that negatively affect Arab Americans' physical and mental health (Kira, Amer, & Wrobel, 2014).

Traumatogenic Events in the Country of Origin

Before moving out of their country of origin, Arabs may suffer both at a personal and group level. On the one hand, just like people around the world, they may be exposed to individual attachment, personal, and role identity traumas. These include abandonment, child maltreatment, sexual abuse or rape, bullying, and loss of job. At the same time, they may have experienced severe collective identity and secondary traumatization, including historical traumas, oppression by dictatorships and police states, discrimination as minorities, and gender discrimination. The physical and mental health effects of such identity and non-identity traumas are mostly understudied in Arab countries.

Collective identity traumas. Collective identity traumas may include exposure to political oppression, discrimination, torture, and wars, which tend to occur with great frequency in Arab countries. Neria, Bravova, and Halper (2010) noted that such exposure places vast numbers of civilians at high risk for trauma-related psychopathology. Political oppression by corrupt dictatorships eventually brought several uprisings, such as the Arab Spring. Citizens of Arab countries have been subjected to a large number of conflicts, both within and between groups. While specific dates and details of these events are beyond the scope of this chapter, they include: full-scale regional wars in 1948, 1967, and 1973; the Israel-Lebanon wars (in 1978, 1982); the Israel-Hezbollah War (in 2006); the First and the Second (Al-Aqsa) Palestinian Intifadas during the late twentieth and early twenty-first centuries; the Palestinian Fatah-Hamas conflict (ongoing since 2006); and the three Israeli Gaza wars, including the recent one in 2014. Other wars have impacted those in the region, including the Lebanese Civil War (1976–84); the Iran-Iraq War (1980–88); the First and Second Gulf Wars (1990–91; 2003). Conflicts between Kurdish groups, as well as between the Iraqi government and the Kurds, and recent, still ongoing, Syrian and Iraqi civil wars, are significant political collective traumatic stressors.

In addition to these violent conflicts, Arab Americans may have experienced trauma in their homelands in the form of discrimination. This includes discrimination against religious groups; for example, Christian, Druze, Shi`ite, and Baha'i minorities in countries with different dominant religions. Further, other groups such as sexual minorities (e.g. gays and lesbians) may also face discrimination. Such discrimination has been well documented by human rights organizations like Human Rights Watch and Amnesty International.

Impact of collective identity traumas on pre-immigration mental health. There have been some efforts to determine how prevalent PTSD is in Arab countries. For instance, Dimitry (2012) conducted a thorough review of studies addressing the impact of political violence on Palestinian, Lebanese, and Iraqi youth. Among children and adolescents, there was evidence of PTSD in as many as 23% to 70% of Palestinian and 10% to 30% of Iraqi youth. Empirical research found that the oppression of Palestinian youth has detrimental mental health effects and that religiosity and militancy are some of the most effective ways of coping with their oppression (Kira, Alawneh, Aboumediene, Lewandowski, & Laddis, 2014).

In Arab countries, it is common for prisoners of war and victims of political conflicts to experience torture. The negative effects of torture on health, especially on neurological systems (e.g. due to closed head and physical injuries), are well documented (e.g. Kira, Templin, Lewandowski, et al., 2006). The prevalence of PTSD for those who experience torture may vary across different groups and its etiology is problematic. A recent study on 326 torture survivors/refugees from 30 different countries including Iraq, Sudan, and Somalia, found that the emphasis on PTSD re-experiencing may be misleading, as the torture survivors tended to suppress such painful experiences and to develop more complex symptoms than PTSD, such as dissociation (Kira, Ashby, Odenat, & Lewandowski, 2013).

Further, collective identity-related traumatic experiences such as political oppression and genocide can have negative mental health outcomes as they may contribute to identity-related annihilation anxieties and fear of cultural extinction. Empirical findings indicate that such previous traumas and difficulties combined with acculturation to a new cultural context may amplify such fear and anxiety in some refugee populations (Kira, Alawneh, et al., 2014; Kira, Templin, Lewandowski, et al., 2011). Past traumas and symptoms of post-trauma spectrum disorders further contribute to the fear of cultural extinction (Kira, Ashby, Lewandowski, et al., 2013; Nickerson, Bryant, Steel, Silove, & Brooks, 2010).

Gender discrimination. In addition to discrimination against religious and sexual minorities, another prevalent discrimination in some Arab cultures is gender discrimination (Kira, Amer, & Wrobel, 2014). Gender discrimination has been identified by Kira and associates as a Type III ongoing trauma for females, which mediates or moderates the effects of other life traumas (Kira, Lewandowski, Templin, Ramaswamy, et al., 2008; Kira, Smith, Lewandowski, & Templin, 2010). Discrimination against girls and women includes a range of events and experiences in most Arab subcultures. These were documented in a series of national gender equality profiles produced by the United Nations Children's Fund (UNICEF, 2011). Social forms of discriminatory behavior include sexual harassment and disparities in education, labor, and political representation. Other acts include domestic violence, early and forced marriage, female sexual exploitation, and trafficking (for labor or sexual exploitation), which are documented in some Arab communities. More extreme forms of discrimination may occur, and are geographically clustered rather than occurring universally in the Arab world. These include, especially in conflict situations, acts of aggression such as female genital mutilation, "honor" killings, and rape.

Gender discrimination is rooted in the patriarchal Arab cultures and thus built into the family and societal structure. For these reasons women may internalize and view these practices as a normal part of life. The practices may be rationalized by some selective religious interpretations (Heise, 1998). Gender discrimination relatively inflates identity and self-concepts for males, increasing their externalizing and risk-taking behavior; at the same time it deflates females' self-concepts, increasing their internalizing behavior (Kira, Ashby, Lewandowski, Smith, & Odenat, 2012). Women may submit to a second-class status, suppressing or reframing thoughts and emotions through internalization and acceptance. As a result, their sense of self may be degraded and violated (Kira, Ashby, et al., 2012; Kira, Smith, et al., 2010). In a study of female refugees (originating from African, Asian, and Arab countries) who had survived torture, gender discrimination was found to be associated with increases in dissociation, suicidality, and deficits in executive function, as well as PTSD (Kira, Smith, et al., 2010).

Traumatogenic Events Associated With Leaving the Country of Origin

Psychological motives to migrate can predict some of the psychological outcomes of the migration. For Arab American refugees and political asylees, political oppression and violent conflicts are typically the direct factors that push them involuntarily to leave their countries. For Arab American immigrants, it can be either the same factors or the pursuit of economic or educational opportunities that prompt them to immigrate voluntarily. Even in the case of voluntary movement, usually one parent, typically the male in the family, is the one who decides and becomes the voluntary agent, while the move for children, and in some cases for the other spouse, is involuntary. Scholars have long noted that the distinction between voluntary versus involuntary (or forced) migration is crucial in predicting their differential psychological impacts (Kunz, 1973). Forced relocation involves higher stress and trauma load and has been recognized as a traumatic event that can generate pathology and post-traumatic growth. For example, a study on Arab American elderly found higher rates of acculturation stress and depression among involuntary refugees compared to voluntary immigrants (Wrobel, Farrag, & Hymes, 2009).

Traumatogenic Events in the Process of Immigration or Refuge

For those Arab Americans who did not immigrate directly to their final destination, they may encounter serious adversities during transit. Some resort to engaging illegal travel brokers. This may result in long periods of exploitation before reaching their destinations, if they ever succeed. Places of displacement and host countries experienced en route to their final destinations may not have resources to support a wave of refugees and thus present an environment that may seem unwelcoming or hostile. Zones housing displaced Sudanese in Darfur (Hamid & Musa, 2010), and those housing Iraqis, Syrians, and Palestinians in Arab countries and in Turkey, are representative of the abject conditions faced by those who are displaced from their country of origin (e.g. Abo-Hilal & Hoogstad, 2013).

Upon arrival in a host country, asylum seekers face numerous stressors. Applicants may endure lengthy stays in detention centers, lasting months at a time, and this may have serious mental health ramifications (e.g. Tucci, Coffey, Kaplan, & Sampson, 2010). Tucci and associates noted that these individuals may sense a state of "limbo" as they are detained and faced with the threat of repatriation. Thus, they may re-experience a sense of persecution, isolation, and anxiety, which may cause them to be viewed as "uncooperative," as well as create high mental health risks.

Traumatogenic Events in the Land of Resettlement

The traumatogenic events that Arab families withstand after moving to North America include discrimination, acculturative stress, moving to the minority status, as well as economic and employment difficulties. Upon moving to the new environment, the uprooted immigrants and refugees face the challenge of rebuilding new social networks. The challenges related to post-immigration stressors have a notable impact, substantially increasing the likelihood of comorbid PTSD and major depressive disorder in Arab American women (Norris et al., 2011). The following sections elaborate on some of these challenges.

Uprootedness and the need to rebuild social networks. Uprootedness trauma is especially evident in those whose migration was involuntary, such as refugees, as well as in women and adolescents in general. Voluntary, and especially involuntary, uprootedness/re-rootedness of immigrants and refugees is a long-lasting traumatic state. The process is characterized by a deep loss of social and physical connectedness, exclusion, homesickness, grief, and nostalgia. Cultural bereavement, and challenges related to reconnecting, self-redefinition, and reconstruction of new personal and collective life space, may also occur. It may involve the loss of a social support network, loss of meaningful interpersonal and family relationships, and exclusion and rejection from deep collective belonging, as well as loss of a familiar physical environment. Threats of cultural extinction can also trigger identity annihilation anxiety. When conceptualized in the DBTF, uprootedness involves multiple trauma types, including collective attachment, collective and systemic betrayal, and identity and family traumas.

Acculturation stress. Chronic stress can be traumatic and have serious negative neurological, mental, and physical health consequences (e.g. Evans & Kim, 2013). Chronic stress related to the acculturation process can be prolonged and add to trauma load and its cumulative dynamics. Acculturative stress for Arab Americans may emanate from a variety of factors – such as language barriers, emerging new identities, and exposure to mores and values – that may appear at odds with their ethnic traditions. Within the family or social group, redefinitions of gender roles, reversal of parent/child roles, and the unequal acculturation pace of children compared to their parents also contribute to acculturative stress. While acculturation is not necessarily associated with stress, the process may be taxing for many individuals and groups. A strong relationship between acculturative stress and a number of mental health conditions has been noted in samples of Arab Americans. Examples found in the literature include prediction of depression among Arab American adolescents (Ahmed, Kia-Keating, & Tsai, 2011), adults (e.g. Amer & Hovey, 2005), and older adults (Wrobel et al., 2009). Higher levels of acculturative stress were also found to be positively associated with increased polysubstance abuse (e.g. Arfken, Kubiak, & Farrag, 2009).

Ongoing economic and housing hardships. Recent immigrants may be unable to obtain the level of social and economic status they had attained in their country of origin. This creates a sense of downward mobility, which can contribute to some psychological distress, including depression (e.g. Wrobel et al., 2009). Employment issues and inadequate living conditions of the new arrivals are key factors in their psychological distress. Their ability to support themselves and their families may be impacted by unemployment and, in some cases, eviction resulting in homelessness. This may have been particularly salient for recent Arab immigrants and refugees who arrived during the last recession (2008–13), when job opportunities were scarce.

Discrimination and the backlash after September 11, 2001. Discrimination is a collective identity trauma that targets individuals because of their group membership (Kira, Amer, & Wrobel, 2014). While negative stereotypical notions and images of Arab Americans were already present prior to 9/11, anti-Arab prejudice was intensified in a backlash against them following the events of that day. Such backlash included government institutions systematically interviewing and targeting Arab Americans, discrimination in employment and hiring (Cavanaugh, 2004; Dávila & Mora, 2005), and intimidation in the workplace (Malos, 2010). Hate crimes (as macroaggressions) and discrimination (mostly microaggressions) have added to ongoing identity threats, such as threats of subjugation, cultural extinction, and denigration, as well as to an ongoing sense of vulnerability (Hendricks, Ortiz, Sugie, & Miller, 2007; Kaplan, 2006). Abu-Ras and Abu-Bader (2008) elaborated on the mental health consequences of 9/11 for Arab Americans, listing outcomes such as "fear of hate crimes, anxiety about the future, threats to their safety, isolation, and stigmatization" (p. 217).

Discrimination among Arab Americans has been associated with a number of negative psychological outcomes, such as depression and psychological distress (Amer & Hovey, 2012; Moradi & Hasan, 2004; Padela & Heisler, 2010). While most prior studies did not control for previous trauma, a large-scale study of 502 Iraqi refugees by Kira, Lewandowski, and associates (2010) revealed that when previous trauma was controlled, post-9/11 backlash predicted and explained 23% of the variance in PTSD. Backlash trauma also predicted executive function deficit syndromes, other signs of psychological distress, and overall poor health. Similar findings were reported for Iraqi (Kira, Lewandowski, Chiodo, & Ibrahim, 2014) and Somali (Ellis, MacDonald, Lincoln, & Cabral, 2008) adolescents.

Traumatogenic Experiences Unique to Age Groups

Early childhood and adolescent traumas are presumed to affect development. Likewise, traumas among older adults can be modified by previous cumulative stress and traumas across the lifespan and the deteriorating level of functioning due to aging and mortality salience. The approach of end of life and emerging physical limitations, with gradual loss of functioning, is potentially traumatic. The following sections briefly analyze traumas for child and elderly Arab Americans.

Trauma Affecting Youth

Arab children and adolescents face potential trauma before and after coming to the U.S. One of the most traumatic events that child refugees may face during war, conflict, and displacement is the loss of parents and family, which may cause attachment disruptions. Separation from family is consistently associated with negative health and mental health status (Berman, 2001). Another related trauma for refugees and immigrants is uprootedness, with potential loss of family, friends, and possibly parents. For Arab American children, personal identity development – an important hallmark in adolescence – is challenged by bullying and prolonged and chronic stressors. School bullying is complicated by other forms of discrimination. Personal identity trauma resulting from bullying of the child because of personal qualities can intersect with discrimination as collective bullying of minorities. Bullying victimization, a Type II trauma, has been found to predict elevations in cumulative trauma disorders as well as PTSD symptoms in Iraqi refugee adolescents. Bullying victimization also predicted psychotic symptoms, dissociation, executive functions deficits, and suicidality (Kira, Lewandowski, Ashby, et al., 2014). Moreover, collective identity development for Arab American youth is challenged by an environment that often demeans their group and discriminates against them (e.g. Britto, 2008; Sirin & Fine, 2007). Ellis and colleagues (2008) found that perceived discrimination was associated with greater PTSD symptoms among Somali adolescents. Kira, Lewandowski, Chiodo, and Ibrahim (2014) found that discrimination predicted internalizing and externalizing disorders, in addition to PTSD, after controlling for other traumas among Iraqi refugee adolescents.

Children and adolescents may additionally experience chronic daily hassles at home as well as at school. Chronic daily hassles that most Arab refugee children encounter can have trauma-like effects. A longitudinal study (Aroian, Templin, & Hough, 2013) investigated which daily hassles (i.e. parent, school, peer, neighborhood, and resource) were perceived by Arab Muslim immigrant adolescents as most stressful. School and parent hassles were associated with greater stress than other hassles at every time point. Adolescents whose mothers are Arab refugees reported greater school and neighborhood and fewer parent hassles than those whose mothers are non refugees. Adolescents with unemployed fathers reported significantly more school and neighborhood hassles.

Additionally, parents' traumas may be transmitted cross-generationally, creating indirect secondary traumas for their children. Parental PTSD has been found, in a literature review, to negatively impact the mental and physical health of their children (Leen-Feldner et al., 2013). Further, parents' post-trauma spectrum disorders, such as depression, may also negatively affect their children's mental and physical health, and this relationship is independent of trauma and shared genetics (Lewis, Rice, Harold, Collishaw, & Thapar, 2011). When children of parents with a diagnosis of either PTSD or depression were compared to children whose parents did not have these disorders, there was three times the incidence of anxiety disorders, major depression, and substance dependence among those with a diagnosed parent.

Trauma can impact the cognitive processing of children, as well as school performance. For example, a study of Iraqi refugee adolescents in Michigan found that cumulative trauma suppresses their cognitive abilities and IQ, with notable deficiency in perceptual reasoning relative to verbal reasoning. Further, bullying victimization was also found to predict decreases in their perceptual reasoning, along with deficits in processing speed and working memory and significant increases in the discrepancy between perceptual reasoning and verbal comprehension, after controlling for other cumulative life traumas (Kira, Lewandowski, Ashby, et al., 2014). Such suppression of cognitive abilities is associated with underachievement and high drop-out rates in the newly arrived. The cognitive impacts of trauma on children can be explained by neuroanatomical changes that affect memory, attention, and other executive functions (Turley & Obrzut, 2012).

Trauma Affecting Older Adults

Research on trauma and related physical and mental health, and neuropsychological disorders among elderly Arab Americans is either sparse or lacks methodological rigor (Sayegh, Kellough, Otilingam, & Poon, 2013). Research findings on Arab American elders indicated that their composite stress levels were higher than Arab Americans from other age groups. Arab American elders aged 65 and older were found to be more likely to report having a functional limitation compared to their White, Black, Hispanic, and Asian counterparts (Dallo, Booza, & Nguyen, 2015). Some cross-sectional studies of convenience samples reported a high prevalence of depression among Arab American older adults (Ajrouch, 2008). Cummings, Sull, Davis, and Worley (2011) found that a vast majority of older Kurdish refugees were clinically depressed, with as many as one-fourth scoring in a range suggesting severe depression. These results suggest high psychological distress among older refugees from the Middle East. In both cross-sectional and longitudinal studies, negative mental health effects of cumulative, lifelong stressors on Arab older adults were compounded by acculturation stress and biological aging. Perceived pressure to learn a new language at this age contributed notably to the prediction of depression (Wrobel et al., 2009).

Resilience, Coping, and Post-Traumatic Growth

Despite stressors faced, and their cumulative effects, Arab Americans' coping, resilience, and distress tolerance capacities may be unique. Their strong collective cultures, their struggle for just personal and group causes, along with their culturally built intact families, give them additional developmental assets. There is likely to be a strong will to survive that brought them to the new land and motivates their self-advancement and economic success as well as effective coping. They tend to seek higher education and achievement for themselves and their children. They are also likely to seek and provide social support, which may serve as the inner working of new re-rooting processes. All of the above are among the factors associated with their resilience and post-traumatic growth.

The term resilience commonly refers to "successful adaptation and swift recovery after experiencing severe adversity during life" and "may also include post-traumatic growth" (Rutten et al.,

2013, p. 4). Achievements such as secure attachment, healthy individuation, healthy interdependence, and having an achieved role identity are important developmental assets that facilitate resilience. Resilience heightens the threshold of stress tolerance, which is one factor in the cumulative stress and trauma dynamics discussed above. Recent findings suggest links between genetic, epigenetic, neurobiological, neurochemical, and developmental dynamics and their interaction with environmental stressors as underpinnings of resilience and high distress tolerance threshold (e.g. Cicchetti, 2013). These factors are yet to be explored specifically in Arab Americans.

Values that place a premium on educational achievements are one potential protective factor for Arab Americans (Wrobel & Paterson, 2014). Haboush and Barakat (2014) documented the superiority of education and employment achievements of Arab Americans across generations compared to both the mainstream and other minorities. Education and employment are pathways to individual identity and community resilience. In general, Arab Americans enjoy a higher median income and higher level of education compared to the mainstream (de la Cruz & Brittingham, 2003). While this may contradict earlier descriptions of economic hardship for recent immigrants and refugees, it reflects the success of those who came during prior waves of immigration and represents the overall status of the current Arab American community.

Arab Americans predominantly came from intact families, with less attachment disruption, and this asset may have helped them to be more resilient in the face of subsequent adversities and developmental challenges (Dwairy, Achoui, Abouserie, & Farah, 2006). Beitin and Aprahamian (2014) explained how Arab American family values and traditions are sources of social support. The importance of extended family, healthy family relationships, and community engagement relies on the ability to muster connectivity and personal and social support that help the re-rooting process. Social support was found to predict less acculturation stress, and less depression and anxiety, in Arab Americans (e.g. Abu-Ras & Abu-Bader, 2009). Moreover, Ajrouch (2008) found that perceived emotional support from their children was related to positive health outcomes in elderly Arab Americans.

Both political and religious identity can be especially powerful sources of resilience for Arab Americans. Arab Americans from different religious denominations – Muslims and Christians alike – are generally religious and likely to use religious practices that solidify their religious and cultural identity as effective coping strategies for their cumulative and ongoing stress (Kira, Templin, Lewandowski, et al., 2006). Ahmed and associates (2011) found that ethnic identity and religious coping were inversely related to distress for Arab American adolescents. An example of the strengths derived from political struggle for just personal and group causes is Arab American torture survivors. In an empirical study of two Iraqi refugee samples, Kira, Templin, Lewandowski, and associates (2006) found that those who were victims of torture had a higher level of resilience and sociocultural adjustment compared to other non-tortured Iraqi refugees. In addition, the authors found higher levels of post-traumatic growth and greater practice of religion among the Iraqi torture victims compared to their non-tortured counterparts.

Individual and Ecological Models of Recovery Interventions

Mental health interventions for trauma have mostly been based on individualistic, biomedical models that typically address single past traumas that are related to individual or personal identity (e.g. Bracken, Giller, & Summerfield, 1997). The types of collective identity and ongoing continuous traumas, in addition to severe past traumas such as torture and oppression, constitute unique trauma profiles for some Arab Americans that differ from profiles that therapists encounter in mainstream counseling. Different trauma profiles may yield different profiles of symptoms and comorbid disorders and may need different models of intervention (Kira, Ashby, Lewandowski, et al., 2013; Kira, Fawzi, & Fawzi, 2012).

Adaptation of single past trauma-focused interventions to address present, continuous, and cumulative trauma along with collective identity has been suggested. Such adaptations broaden the focus of the treatment model and empower practitioners to be less constrained by the medical model (e.g. Bracken et al., 1997; Kira, Amer, & Wrobel, 2014; Kira, Ashby, Lewandowski, et al., 2013; Kira & Tummala-Narra, 2014). There is also a need to develop service and intervention models for Arab Americans that integrate the individual and ecological models of recovery and address present and continuous trauma, sequentially or concurrently with interventions focused on past trauma (Kira, 2002, 2010; Kira, Ashby, Lewandowski, et al., 2013; Kira & Tummala-Narra, 2014). The following sections discuss these issues further and suggest a sequential model to guide research and clinical practice with such trauma dynamics.

Individual Interventions

Single trauma-focused manualized treatments may provide fidelity, but limit the flexibility afforded to therapists to address current, continuous, and emerging traumatic events, as well as their cumulative dynamics when added to the past traumas (Kira, Amer, & Wrobel, 2014). Considering the comorbidity of disorders that some Arab Americans are enduring, trans-diagnostic approaches may be more appropriate for their conditions. Trans-diagnostic treatments are interventions aimed at treating multiple disorders at the same time. Thus, they must be developed through the knowledge of how comorbid disorders are related in terms of their causes, commonalities, course, and symptom maintenance (e.g. Chu, Merson, Zandberg, & Areizaga, 2012; Kira, Amer, & Wrobel, 2014).

To date, there are few empirical studies of the effectiveness of different psychotherapeutic diagnostic or trans-diagnostic modalities with Arab Americans (Kira, Amer, & Wrobel, 2014). Recent controlled studies (e.g. Crumlish and O'Rourke, 2010; Hijazi et al., 2014) found adapted narrative exposure therapy to be effective with refugees from other ethnic groups and with Iraqi refugees. Recent research on other ethnic groups also found comparable evidence for the effectiveness of group therapies focused on present and trauma-focused group therapy (Classen et al., 2011).

Kira and associates (Kira, Ashby, Lewandowski, et al., 2013; Kira & Tummala-Narra, 2014) proposed a new intervention model with continuous and present traumas as part of a packaged sequential approach that gives the therapist the flexibility to address them according to the client's priorities and time line. Continuous and present trauma-focused, cognitive behavioral interventions include multiple components (Kira & Tummala-Narra, 2014), as outlined in Table 14.2. The proposed approach starts with comprehensive assessment of all types of trauma (whether current, past, continuous, or cumulative) that the individual has endured and their differential effects (Kira, Fawzi, & Fawzi, 2012). This assessment is the foundation for a comprehensive treatment plan to address all functions affected. Different trauma profiles yield varied profiles of comorbid disorders that need different intervention plans.

Ecological Interventions

The socio-ecological framework suggests that the individual functions as part of a web of social networks that give a feeling of security (Kira, Amer, & Wrobel, 2014). Individual models of recovery treat the individual as a single system, while ecological approaches focus on the individual as a system embedded within different social and ecological systems that should be addressed in treatment. Treatment of interpersonal traumas (Types I and II) is focused on one or two systems, such as the internal processing through evidence-based interventions, and associated physiological interactions through medications. Type III traumas and Type IV cumulative trauma are more likely to result in health and mental health comorbidities that are too severe to be addressed at the same level as Type I and II traumas (Kira, Amer, & Wrobel, 2014).

Table 14.2 Components of Continuous Trauma-Focused Cognitive Behavioral Interventions

Intervention	*Basic Components*	*Detailed Components*
Prioritization of safety	Analyze situational dangers and risks	Active case management
Facilitation of addressing real dangers through training in basic skills for dealing with such threats and challenges	Distinguish real danger and identify challenges Teach behavioral skills that help address potential dangers and challenges	Problem solving Assertiveness training Mindfulness training Anger management and emotion regulation Enhancement of engagement
Psychoeducation	Educate regarding continuous, ongoing, and cumulative traumatic stress Educate regarding trauma proliferation and stress generation dynamics	Basic knowledge and awareness Metacognition
Inoculation against stress proliferation and accumulation dynamics	Train to identify and disrupt such existing dynamics	
Identity work and identity development	Redefine of identities Recognize personal and collective self-esteem and self-efficacy	Exploration in therapy Gender identity, sexual identity, racial identity, religious identity, national identity, and species identity (identity as a human)
Advocacy	Advocate for the individual (by treatment team) Encourage participation in cause – active social and political advocacy	Active and proactive empathy for self, others and for groups

Because the events leading to both Types III and IV traumas target individuals, groups, and communities, healing at the group and community level is essential. In particular, oppression, torture, and group violence that terrorize the community require collective healing. Types III and IV trauma-focused interventions include, in addition to interventions proposed for Types I and II, advocacy and coordination among all relevant institutions and systems involved in the individual's life. Interventions should be designed to help rebuild communities and restore damaged identities. Treatment of Types III and IV traumas therefore, may be better addressed through flexible and comprehensive ecological sequential interventions.

Common examples of such ecological multisystem, multicomponent, multimodal interventions are wraparound approaches for delinquent youth treatment (e.g. Bruns & Suter, 2010). The wraparound psychosocial rehabilitation approach has also been modified and utilized with adult torture survivors. It includes case management, assertive community outreach, supported housing, employment, and vocational services. Also included are English as a second language instruction, legal assistance, relationship counseling, and parenting education and support. Group therapy was modified to focus on individual and community healing, as well as on ethnic organization building (e.g. Kira, 2002, 2010; Kira, Ahmed, et al., 2012). Such interventions enhance the possibility of receiving social support during the re-rooting process. Interventions based on ecological models are therefore characterized by "flexible fidelity," with defined adjustable curricula that focus on clients' priorities.

Ecological model adaptations for Arab Americans are evolving. Some applications include: the multisystemic gateway providers model, which views community cultural, social, educational, and religious organizations as gateways to healing for Somali children (Ellis et al., 2010); and a comprehensive summer day-treatment and after-school program for Iraqi children who are cumulative trauma victims (Kira, 2010). While these models have ecological validity, there is also empirical evidence for their potential effectiveness. For example, there is some empirical evidence of the effectiveness of multisystemic wraparound torture rehabilitation (e.g. McFarlane & Kaplan, 2012; Raghavan, Rasmussen, Rosenfeld, & Keller, 2012).

Case Example: Samira's Suicide Attempt

The following is a case example that illustrates some of the traumas that Arab Americans encounter, their outcomes, and the treatment strategies used. There is a linear dose-related response to present and past traumas coupled with the nonlinear triggering effects of cumulative, continuous traumatic stressors. These stressors crossed the threshold of the young client's distress tolerance, resulting in an attempted suicide. The attempted suicide was real and a cry for help.

The Presenting Problem

Samira is a 16-year-old Palestinian American referred to therapy by the treating hospital for attempted suicide by Tylenol overdose. Samira immigrated to the U.S. with her family two years before the referral. Prior to that she had spent two years in a refugee camp in Syria. Before she came to the U.S., she was an outgoing student with no mental health complaints. During her two-year stay in a refugee camp, she did not receive a formal education, which put her two grades behind. Samira never systematically learned English before immigration and was then placed in all English classes based on her age group, rather than on acquired ability level. Due to the language barrier and lack of required previous coursework, she failed all of her classes. She was placed, accordingly, in special education classes with students who were much less bright and typically had behavioral problems. She continued to fail academically as well.

She had a hard time communicating with peers, was isolated, and was subjected to bullying and discrimination by her peers and school. Although her parents – who have four children – were supportive and tried to hire a tutor to help her, they were busy working to cover the bills. As a result, her personal and collective self-esteem and self-efficacy beliefs were severely impacted. Her developing personal and collective identity, in this adolescent age, was challenged with overwhelming existential distress that made her feel worthless. As a result of this sequence of adversities, she developed a major depressive disorder. When accumulated stressors surpassed the threshold of her distress tolerance, she attempted suicide.

Treatment Strategies With Samira

In this case, the interdisciplinary bilingual team of therapist, case manager, and psychiatrist applied the ecological multisystemic, multimodal, multicomponent interventions, utilizing Kira's model for continuous trauma-focused interventions with the client. The intervention plan was based on a full psychosocial and trauma assessment. Treatment focused both on support to help Samira improve her personal and collective self-esteem, and on interventions aimed at addressing discrimination and bullying. The approach both focused on continuous and present trauma, and involved social and educational advocacy interventions.

Specific interventions included home visits to work directly with Samira and the family system in her natural environment (to enhance feelings of safety and trust). Interventions also strengthened her access to advocacy and social support resources in the community, to reestablish meaningful social connections. This facilitated healthy acculturation, reinforcing both her cultural identity and the new emerging identities, and gradually increasing her personal and collective self-esteem. Therapy also sought to address her uprootedness and isolation. Individual treatment included psychoeducation, and focused on addressing continuous traumatic stress, past and ongoing traumas, and identity work and bicultural identity development, as well as current and ongoing identity threats and reactions. These therapeutic goals were achieved through skills training (assertiveness, problem solving, social skills, and mindfulness skills), stimulating a will to survive, facilitating coping by empowering her as a strong survivor, and supporting her engagement in advocacy efforts (see Kira, Ashby, Lewandowski, et al., 2013; Kira & Tummala-Narra, 2014). Social skills and other behavior skills training improved her social networks and got her connected to community center activities with her age-group peers. Antidepression medication addressed her low mood at a biophysiological level.

The ecological, advocacy approach to the case was particularly crucial here. The therapist sent a letter to the superintendent of the school district through a law firm, holding the school liable and responsible for the girl's attempted suicide and for any future harm to her in the school because of the school policies. Further, the therapist helped the parent to recruit a pro bono lawyer to advocate for the case. While the therapy itself was relatively short (eight weekly hour-and-a-half sessions), the intervention with the school system was very effective, as the school realized its immediate legal liability and immediately hired an English as a Second Language (ESL) teacher to provide extra educational support for the girl. Reframing the problem and shifting the blame from the person to the system was an important step. After two years, the girl started to do better in school, moved out of the special education class, and had no more attempted suicides or isolation problems. She was able to better handle bullying and discrimination, and ended up taking college preparatory courses.

Implications

This case was an eye-opener for the therapist, who had been trained in past-trauma-focused cognitive behavior therapy. The client suffered multiple forms of traumatic stress, and the most severe for the client were the ongoing challenges. Such ongoing adversities challenged traditional trauma treatment. It conveys that a multiplicity of accumulated risks can eventuate in severe disordered outcomes. The case emphasizes the relevance of systemic clinical care that assesses the whole family, as imbedded in a multisystem, multilevel ecology and looks for the linear and nonlinear dynamics of past and ongoing stress and distress tolerance. Samira's core trauma – the notably wrong placement at school – represented a continuous ongoing systemic betrayal trauma perpetrated by the school system, rather than by an individual or past trauma.

In this case, reframing the problem for the client, and allowing her to see herself as a victim of systemic ongoing trauma, rather than being deficient, provided crucial relief that shifted the blame and allowed her to reclaim her self-worth. As noted, aggressive advocacy as an ecological intervention helped change the system to provide more crucial educational support, which was especially critical in this case. The availability and utilization of a bilingual team was important in facilitating effective culturally competent, trusted interventions that minimized negative transference and counter-transference. The progress was relatively quick and significant, and the client was restored to a relatively healthy level of functioning.

Critique

There are several gaps in the literature on stress and trauma among Arab Americans. For instance, there is no research on sexual minorities in Arab Americans, who may have been oppressed in their own countries because of their sexual preferences. Although sociological and anthropological literature, as well as reports of human rights groups and United Nations agencies, have documented serious gender discrimination in Arab cultures, research on its psychological effects on Arab and Arab American girls and women is lacking. Further, literature on older adults and aging trauma in Arab

American women and men is limited. Future basic research should address the understudied areas of traumas in Arab Americans, such as attachment, sexual abuse, sexual minorities, gender discrimination, and voluntary versus forced migration. Intervention research should focus on further adapting evidence-based interventions and further developing and assessing the effectiveness of the proposed sequential models.

Current studies of stress and trauma in Arab Americans, as well as interventions to help them, have utilized the limited single trauma-based PTSD framework. Moreover, most of these studies utilized cross-sectional methodology with small sample sizes or a qualitative approach, such as focus groups. Longitudinal, controlled, and mixed methods research methodologies, and even cross-sectional designs that use advanced structural equation models, are still scarce. Future research should adopt more scientifically rigorous methodologies. While the new ecological treatment approaches hold promise, few controlled double-blind or longitudinal studies have been conducted to test their effectiveness. There is clearly a need for more controlled double-blind and longitudinal studies.

Conclusion

Current individualistic theories of stress and trauma commonly ignore present, ongoing, and chronic traumas, as well as the traumatogenic dynamics of intergroup conflict and of structural, institutional, systemic, and cultural traumas. Such trauma and stress frameworks are not appropriate for the study of multiply traumatized populations such as Arab Americans. This chapter proposed a relatively new Developmentally Based Stress and Trauma Framework (DBTF) and used it to assess the stresses and traumas of Arab Americans, as well as to understand the etiological dynamics of their mental health status. The authors utilized this new typology of trauma as a heuristic device to analyze the adversities that Arab immigrants and refugees have encountered and continue to encounter before, during, and after resettlement. There is a need to utilize more advanced methodologies to study trauma and post-trauma spectrum disorders in Arab Americans. Researchers should also seek to understand Arab Americans' resilience, distress tolerance, and post-traumatic growth. This will help advance psychology and related disciplines to be able better to help Arab Americans as well as other similarly multiply traumatized groups.

References

Abo-Hilal, M. & Hoogstad, M. (2013). Syrian mental health professionals as refugees in Jordan: Establishing mental health services for fellow refugees. *Intervention: International Journal of Mental Health, Psychosocial Work & Counselling in Areas of Armed Conflict* 11, 89–93. doi: 10.1097/WTF.0b013e32835f0d2c

Abu-Ras, W. & Abu-Bader, S. H. (2008). The impact of September 11, 2001, attacks on the well-being of Arab Americans in New York City. *Journal of Muslim Mental Health* 3, 217–239. doi: 10.1080/15564900802487634

Abu-Ras, W. & Abu-Bader, S. H. (2009). Risk factors for depression and posttraumatic stress disorder (PTSD): The case of Arab Muslim Americans post 9/11. *Journal of Immigrant and Refugee Studies* 7, 393–418. doi: 10.1080/15562940903379068

Afana, A. (2012). Problems in applying diagnostic concepts of PTSD and trauma in the Middle East. *The Arab Journal of Psychiatry* 23, 28–34.

Ahmed, S. R., Kia-Keating, M., & Tsai, K. H. (2011). A structural model of racial discrimination, acculturative stress, and cultural resources among Arab American adolescents. *American Journal of Community Psychology* 48(3–4), 181–192. doi: 10.1007/s10464-011-9424-3

Ajrouch, K. J. (2008). Social isolation and loneliness among Arab American elders: Cultural, social, and personal factors. *Research in Human Development* 5, 44–59. doi: 10.1080/15427600701853798

Amer, M. M. & Hovey, J. D. (2005). Examination of the impact of acculturation, stress, and religiosity on mental health variables for second-generation Arab Americans. *Ethnicity & Disease* 15(Suppl. 1), S111–S112.

Amer, M. M. & Hovey, J. D. (2012). Anxiety and depression in a post-September 11 sample of Arabs in the USA. *Social Psychiatry and Psychiatric Epidemiology* 47(3), 409–418. doi: 10.1007/s00127-011-0341-4

Arfken, C. L., Kubiak, S. P., & Farrag, M. (2009). Acculturation and polysubstance abuse in Arab-American treatment clients. *Transcultural Psychiatry* 46, 608–622. doi: 10.1177/1363461509351364

Aroian, K., Templin, T. N., & Hough, E. S. (2013). Longitudinal study of daily hassles in adolescents in Arab Muslim immigrant families. *Journal of Immigrant and Minority Health* 16, 831–838. doi: 10.1007/s10903-013-9795-7

Beitin, B. K. & Aprahamian, M. (2014). Family values and traditions. In S. C. Nassar-McMillan, K. J. Ajrouch, & J. Hakim-Larson (eds.), *Biopsychosocial perspectives on Arab Americans: Culture, development, and health* (pp. 67–88). New York: Springer. doi: 10.1007/978-1-4614-8238-3_4

Berman, H. (2001). Children and war: Current understandings and future directions. *Public Health Nursing* 18, 243–252. doi: 10.1046/j.1525-1446.2001.00243.x

Bracken, P., Giller, J. E., & Summerfield, D. (1997). Rethinking mental health work with survivors of wartime violence and refugees. *Journal of Refugee Studies* 10, 431–442. doi: 10.1093/jrs/10.4.431

Britto, P. R. (2008). Who am I? Ethnic identity formation of Arab Muslim children in contemporary U.S. society. *Journal of American Academy of Child and Adolescent Psychiatry* 47, 853–857. doi: 10.1097/CHI.0b013e3181799fa6

Bruns, E. J. & Suter, J. C. (2010). Summary of the wraparound evidence base: April 2010 update. In E. J. Bruns & J. S. Walker (eds.), *The resource guide to wraparound.* Portland, OR: National Wraparound Initiative, chapter 3.5. Retrieved from www.nwi.pdx.edu/NWI-book/Chapters/SECTION-3.pdf

Cavanaugh, B. P. (2004). September 11 backlash employment discrimination. *Journal of the Missouri Bar* 60, 186–194.

Chu, B. C., Merson, R. A., Zandberg, L. J., & Areizaga, M. (2012). Calibrating for comorbidity: Clinical decision-making in youth depression and anxiety. *Cognitive and Behavioral Practice* 19, 5–16. doi: 10.1016/j.cbpra.2010.10.005

Chu, T., Keller, A. S., & Rasmussen, A. (2013). Effects of post-migration factors on PTSD outcomes among immigrant survivors of political violence. *Journal of Immigrant and Minority Health* 15, 890–897. doi: 10.1007/s10903-012-9696-1

Cicchetti, D. (2013). Resilient functioning in maltreated children: Past, present, and future perspectives. *Journal of Child Psychology and Psychiatry* 54, 402–422. doi: 10.1111/j.1469-7610.2012.02608.x

Classen, C. C., Palesh, O. G., Cavanaugh, C. E., Koopman, C., Kaupp, J. W., Kraemer, H. C., … Spiegel, D. (2011). A comparison of trauma-focused and present-focused group therapy for survivors of childhood sexual abuse: A randomized controlled trial. *Psychological Trauma: Theory, Research, Practice, and Policy* 3, 84–93. doi: 10.1037/a0020096

Crumlish, N. & O'Rourke, K. (2010). A systematic review of treatments for post-traumatic stress disorder among refugees and asylum-seekers. *Journal of Nervous and Mental Disorders* 198, 237–251. doi: 10.1097/NMD.0b013e3181d61258

Cummings, J. R., Bornovalova, M. A., Ojanen, T., Hunt, E., MacPherson, L., & Lejuez, C. (2013). Time doesn't change everything: The longitudinal course of distress tolerance and its relationship with externalizing and internalizing symptoms during early adolescence. *Journal of Abnormal Child Psychology* 41, 735–748. doi: 10.1007/s10802-012-9704-x

Cummings, S., Sull, L., Davis, C., & Worley, N. (2011). Correlates of depression among older Kurdish refugees. *Social Work* 56, 159–168. doi: 10.1093/sw/56.2.159

Dallo, F. J., Booza, J., & Nguyen, N. D. (2015). Functional limitations and nativity status among older Arab, Asian, Black, Hispanic, and White Americans. *Journal of Immigrant and Minority Health* 17, 535–542. doi: 10.1007/s10903-013-9943-0

Dávila, A. & Mora, M. T. (2005). Changes in the earnings of Arab men in the US between 2000 and 2002. *Journal of Population Economics* 18, 587–601. doi: 10.1007/s00148-005-0050-y

de la Cruz, G. P. & Brittingham, A. (2003). *The Arab population: 2000* (Census 2000 Briefs, C2KBR-23). Washington, D.C.: U.S. Census Bureau. Retrieved from www.census.gov/prod/2003pubs/c2kbr-23.pdf

Dimitry, L. (2012). A systematic review on the mental health of children and adolescents in areas of armed conflict in the Middle East. *Child: Care, Health and Development* 38, 153–161. doi: 10.1111/j.1365-2214.2011.01246.x

Dwairy, M., Achoui, M., Abouserie, R., & Farah, A. (2006). Adolescent-family connectedness among Arabs: A second cross-regional research study. *Journal of Cross-Cultural Psychology* 37, 248–261. doi: 10.1177/0022022106286923

Ellis, B. H., Lincoln, A. K., Charney, M. E., Ford-Paz, R., Benson, M., & Strunin, L. (2010). Mental health service utilization of Somali adolescents: Religion, community, and school as gateways to healing. *Transcultural Psychiatry* 47, 789–811. doi: 10.1177/1363461510379933

Ellis, B. H., MacDonald, H. Z., Lincoln, A. K., & Cabral, H. J. (2008). Mental health of Somali adolescent refugees: The role of trauma, stress, and perceived discrimination. *Journal of Consulting and Clinical Psychology* 76, 184–193. doi: 10.1037/0022-006X.76.2.184

Evans, G. W. & Kim, P. (2013). Childhood poverty, chronic stress, self-regulation, and coping. *Child Development Perspective*, 7, 43–48. doi: 10.1111/cdep.12013

Giacaman, R., Rabaia, Y., Nguyen-Gillham, V., Batniji, R., Punamäki, R., & Summerfield, D. (2011). Mental health, social distress and political oppression: The case of the occupied Palestinian territory. *Global Public Health* 6, 547–559. doi: 10.1080/17441692.2010.528443

Haboush, K., L. & Barakat, N. (2014). Education and employment among Arab Americans: Pathways to individual identity and community resilience. In S. C. Nassar-McMillan, K. J. Ajrouch, & J. Hakim-Larson (eds.), *Biopsychosocial perspectives on Arab Americans: Culture, development, and health* (pp. 229–255). New York: Springer. doi: 10.1007/978-1-4614-8238-3_11

Hamid, A. A. & Musa, S. A. (2010). Mental health problems among internally displaced people in Darfur. *International Journal of Psychology* 45, 278–85. doi: 10.1080/00207591003692620

Heise, L. L. (1998). Violence against women: An integrated, ecological framework. *Violence Against Women* 4, 262–290. doi: 10.1177/1077801298004003002

Hendricks, N. J., Ortiz, C. W., Sugie, N., & Miller, J. (2007). Beyond the numbers: Hate crimes and cultural trauma within Arab American immigrant communities. *International Review of Victimology* 14, 95–113. doi: 10.1177/026975800701400106

Hijazi, A. M., Lumley, M. A., Ziadni, M. S., Haddad, L., Rapport, L. J., & Arnetz, B. B. (2014). Brief narrative exposure therapy for posttraumatic stress in Iraqi refugees: A preliminary randomized clinical trial. *Journal of Traumatic Stress* 27, 314–322. doi: 10.1002/jts.21922

Kaplan, J. (2006). Islamophobia in America? September 11 and Islamophobic hate crime. *Terrorism and Political Violence* 18, 1–33. doi: 10.1080/09546550500383209

Karam, E. G., Friedman, M. J., Hill, E. D., Kessler, R. C., McLaughlin, K. A., Petukhova, M., … Koenen, K. C. (2014). Cumulative traumas and risk thresholds: 12 month-PTSD in the World Mental Health (WMH) surveys. *Depression and Anxiety* 31, 130–142. doi: 10.1002/da.22169

Kira, I. A. (2001). Taxonomy of trauma and trauma assessment. *Traumatology* 2, 1–14. doi: 10.1177/153476560100700202

Kira, I. A. (2002). Torture assessment and treatment: The wraparound approach. *Traumatology* 8(2), 54–86. doi: 10.1177/153476560200800203

Kira, I. A. (2010). Etiology and treatments of post-cumulative traumatic stress disorders in different cultures. *Traumatology: An International Journal* 16(4), 128–141. doi: 10.1177/1534765610365914

Kira, I. A., Ahmed, A., Wassim, F., McAdams-Mahmoud, V., Clorain, J., & Rai, D. (2012). Group therapy for refugees and torture survivors: Treatment models innovations. *International Journal of Group Psychotherapy* 62(1), 69–88. doi: 10.1521/ijgp.2012.62.1.69

Kira, I. A., Alawneh, A. N., Aboumediene, S., Lewandowski, L., & Laddis, A. (2014). Dynamics of oppression and coping from traumatology perspective: The example of Palestinian youth. *Peace and Conflict: Journal of Peace Psychology* 20, 385–411. doi: 10.1037/pac0000053

Kira, I. A., Amer, M. M., & Wrobel, N. H. (2014). Arab refugees: Trauma, resilience, and recovery. In S. C. Nassar-McMillan, K. J. Ajrouch, & J. Hakim-Larson (eds.), *Biopsychosocial perspectives on Arab Americans: Culture, development, and health* (pp.175–195). New York: Springer. doi: 10.1007/978-1-4614-8238-3_9

Kira, I. A., Ashby, J. S., Lewandowski, L., Alawneh, A. N., Mohanesh, J., & Odenat, L. (2013). Advances in continuous traumatic stress theory: Traumatogenic dynamics and consequences of intergroup conflict: The Palestinian adolescents' case. *Psychology* 4, 396–409. doi: 10.4236/psych.2013.44057

Kira, I. A., Ashby, J., Lewandowski, L., Smith, I., & Odenat, L. (2012). Gender inequality and its effects in females torture survivors. *Psychology* 3, 352–363. doi: 10.4236/psych.2012.34050

Kira, I. A., Ashby, J. S., Odenat, L., & Lewandowski, L. (2013). The mental health effects of torture trauma and its severity: A replication and extension. *Psychology* 4, 472–482. doi: 10.4236/psych.2013.45067

Kira, I. A., Fawzi, M. H., & Fawzi, M. M. (2012). The dynamics of cumulative trauma and trauma types in adult patients with psychiatric disorders: Two cross-cultural studies. *Traumatology* 3,179–195. doi: 10.1177/1534765612459892

Kira, I. A., Lewandowski, L., Ashby, J. S., Somers, C., Chiodo, L., & Odenat, L. (2014). Does bullying victimization suppress IQ? The effects of bullying victimization on IQ in Iraqi and African American adolescents: A traumatology perspective. *Journal of Aggression, Maltreatment, and Trauma* 23, 431–453. doi: 10.1080/10926771.2014.904463

Kira, I. A., Lewandowski, L., Chiodo, L., & Ibrahim, A. (2014). Advances in systemic trauma theory: Traumatogenic dynamics and consequences of backlash as a multi-systemic trauma on Iraqi refugee Muslim adolescents. *Psychology* 5, 389–412. doi: 10.4236/psych.2014.55050

Kira, I. A., Lewandowski, L., Templin, T., Ramaswamy, V., Ozkan, B., & Mohanesh, J. (2008). Measuring cumulative trauma dose, types and profiles using a development-based taxonomy of trauma. *Traumatology* 14(2), 62–87. doi: 10.1177/1534765608319324

Kira, I. A., Lewandowski, L., Templin, T., Ramaswamy, V., Ozkan, B., & Mohanesh, J. (2010). The effects of perceived discrimination and backlash on Iraqi refugees' physical and mental health. *Journal of Muslim Mental Health* 5(1), 59–81. doi: 10.1080/15564901003622110

Kira, I. A., Smith, I., Lewandowski, L., & Templin, T. (2010). The effects of perceived gender discrimination on refugee torture survivors: A cross-cultural traumatology perspective. *Journal of the American Psychiatric Nurses Association* 16(5), 299–306. doi: 10.1177/1078390310384401

Kira, I. A., Templin, T., Lewandowski, L., Clifford, D., Wiencek, E., Hammad, A., … Mohanesh, J. (2006). The effects of torture: Two community studies. *Peace and Conflict: Journal of Peace Psychology* 12, 205–228. doi: 10.1207/s15327949pac1203_1

Kira, I. A., Templin, T., Lewandowski, L., Ramaswamy, V., Bulent, O., Abu-Mediene, S., … Alamia, H. (2011). Cumulative tertiary appraisal of traumatic events across cultures: Two studies. *Journal of Loss and Trauma: International Perspectives on Stress & Coping* 16, 43–66. doi: 10.1080/15325024.2010.519288

Kira, I. A. & Tummala-Narra, P. (2014). Psychotherapy with refugees: Emerging paradigms. *Journal of Loss and Trauma: International Perspectives on Stress & Coping*. Advance online publication. doi: 10.1080/15325024.2014.949145

Kunz, E. F. (1973). The refugee in flight: Kinetic models and forms of displacement. *International Migration Review* 7, 125–146. doi: 10.2307/3002424

Leen-Feldner, E. W., Feldner, M. T., Knapp, A., Bunaciu, L., Blumenthal, H., & Amstadter, A. B. (2013). Offspring psychological and biological correlates of parental posttraumatic stress: Review of the literature and research agenda. *Clinical Psychology Review* 33, 1106–1133. doi: 10.1016/j.cpr.2013.09.001

Lewis, G., Rice, F., Harold, G. T., Collishaw, S., & Thapar, A. (2011). Investigating environmental links between parent depression and child depressive/anxiety symptoms using an assisted conception design. *Journal of the American Academy of Child & Adolescent Psychiatry* 50, 451–459. doi: 10.1016/j.jaac.2011.01.015

Malos, S. (2010). Post-9/11 backlash in the workplace: Employer liability for discrimination against Arab-and Muslim-Americans based on religion or national origin. *Employee Responsibilities and Rights Journal* 22, 297–310. doi: 10.1007/s10672-009-9132-4

McFarlane, C. A. & Kaplan, I. (2012). Evidence-based psychological interventions for adult survivors of torture and trauma: A 30-year review. *Transcultural Psychiatry* 49, 539–567. doi: 10.1177/1363461512447608

Moradi, B. & Hasan, N. T. (2004). Arab American persons' reported experiences of discrimination and mental health: The mediating role of personal control. *Journal of Counseling Psychology* 51, 418–428. doi: 10.1037/0022-0167.51.4.418

Neria, Y., Bravova, M., & Halper, J. M. (2010). Trauma and PTSD among civilians in the Middle East. *PTSD Research Quarterly* 21, 1–8.

Nicholson, B. (1997). The influence of pre-emigration and post-emigration stressors on mental health: A study of Southeast Asian refugees. *Social Work Research* 21(1), 19–31. doi: 10.1093/swr/21.1.19

Nickerson, A., Bryant, R. A., Steel, Z., Silove, D., & Brooks, R. (2010). The impact of fear for family on mental health in a resettled Iraqi refugee community. *Journal of Psychiatric Research* 44, 229–235. doi: 10.1016/j.jpsychires.2009.08.006

Norris, A. E., Aroian, K. J., & Nickerson, D. M. (2011). Premigration persecution, postmigration stressors and resources, and postmigration mental health a study of severely traumatized US Arab immigrant women. *Journal of the American Psychiatric Nurses Association* 17, 283–293. doi: 10.1177/1078390311408900

Padela, A. I. & Heisler, M. (2010). The association of perceived abuse and discrimination after September 11, 2001, with psychological distress, level of happiness, and health status among Arab Americans. *American Journal of Public Health* 100, 284–291. doi: 10.2105/AJPH.2009.164954

Raghavan, S., Rasmussen, A., Rosenfeld, B., & Keller, A. S. (2012). Correlates of symptom reduction in treatment-seeking survivors of torture. *Psychological Trauma: Theory, Research, Practice, and Policy* 5, 377–383. doi: 10.1037/a0028118

Rutten, B. P. F., Hammels, C., Geschwind, N., Menne-Lothmann, C., Pishva, E., Schruers, K., … Wichers, M. (2013). Resilience in mental health: Linking psychological and neurobiological perspectives. *Acta Psychiatrica Scandinavica* 128(1), 3–20. doi: 10.1111/acps.12095

Sayegh, P., Kellough, J., Otilingam, P. G., & Poon, C. Y. M. (2013). South Asian and Middle Eastern American older adults: Dementia, mood disorders, and anxiety disorders. *Clinical Gerontologist: The Journal of Aging and Mental Health* 36, 216–240. doi: 10.1080/07317115.2013.767873

Sirin, S. R. & Fine, M. (2007). Hyphenated selves: Muslim Americans youth negotiating identities on the fault lines of global conflict. *Applied Developmental Science* 11, 151–163. doi: 10.1080/10888690701454658

Steel, Z., Silove, D., Bird, K., McGorry, P., & Mohan, P. (1999). Pathways from war trauma to posttraumatic stress symptoms among Tamil asylum seekers, refugees and immigrants. *Journal of Traumatic Stress* 12, 421–435. doi: 10.1023/A:1024710902534

Terr, L. C. (1991). Childhood traumas: An outline and overview. *American Journal of Psychiatry* 148(1), 10–20.

Thibeault, M. (2013). *Psychological adjustment and well-being in recently arriving immigrant adolescents* (Master's thesis). Available from ProQuest Dissertations and Theses database (UMI No. 1541400).

Tucci, M. M., Coffey, G. J., Kaplan, I., & Sampson, R. C. (2010). The meaning and mental health consequences of long-term immigration detention for people seeking asylum. *Social Science and Medicine* 70, 2070–2079. doi: 10.1016/j.socscimed.2010.02.042

Turley, M. R. & Obrzut, J. E. (2012). Neuropsychological effects of posttraumatic stress disorder in children and adolescents. *Canadian Journal of School Psychology* 27, 166–182. doi: 10.1177/0829573512440420

UNICEF. (2011). *MENA gender equality profile: Status of girls and women in the Middle East and North Africa.* Retrieved from www.unicef.org/gender/files/REGIONAL-Gender-Eqaulity-Profile-2011.pdf

Wrobel, N. H., Farrag, M. F., & Hymes, R. W. (2009). Acculturative stress and depression in an elderly Arabic sample. *Journal of Cross-Cultural Gerontology* 24, 273–290. doi: 10.1007/s10823-009-9096-8

Wrobel, N. H. & Paterson, A. (2014). Mental health risks in Arab Americans. In S. C. Nassar-McMillan, K. J. Ajrouch, & J. Hakim-Larson (eds.), *Biopsychosocial perspectives on Arab Americans: Culture, development, and health* (pp. 197–228). New York: Springer. doi: 10.1007/978-1-4614-8238-3_10

15

DOMESTIC VIOLENCE

Cultural Determinants, Reducing Risks, and Enhancing Resilience

Anahid Kulwicki

Violence is defined by the World Health Organization (WHO) as "the intentional use of physical force or power, threatened or actual, against oneself, another person, or against a group or community that either results in or has a high likelihood of resulting in injury, death, psychological harm, mal-development or deprivation" (WHO, 2002, p. 5). Family violence and domestic violence are forms of intentional force and harm that happen within the family unit. Intimate partner violence (IPV) is defined as physical injury to one's intimate partner (McHugh & Frieze, 2006).

WHO researchers conducted a study to estimate IPV against women in 15 sites in 10 countries: Bangladesh, Brazil, Ethiopia, Japan, Namibia, Peru, Samoa, Serbia and Montenegro, Thailand, and the United Republic of Tanzania. The organization found that of the 24,097 women interviewed, reported lifetime prevalence of IPV varied from 15% to 71% (Garcia-Moreno, Jansen, Ellsberg, Heise, & Watts, 2006). Results of the WHO report indicated that IPV against women has no geographic, cultural, religious, or economic boundaries, and is widespread all over the world. It is therefore extremely important to address this phenomenon globally and at the local community level.

Fass, Benson, and Leggett (2008) indicated that 5.3 million IPV incidents involving women aged 18 and older take place annually in the U.S. Tjaden and Thoennes (2000) conducted the National Violence against Women survey to provide comparable data on both women's and men's experiences of violence in the U.S. Through telephone surveys, 8,000 men and 8,000 women were interviewed regarding their experiences with stalking, physical assault, and rape. Of those surveyed, 2% of women reported being physically assaulted, raped, or both in the last 12 months. The authors concluded that women experience more IPV than men and they estimated the lifetime prevalence of IPV for the surveyed women to be 22.1% compared to 7.4% of the surveyed men.

IPV appears to be especially challenging among immigrant and refugee women due to the many cultural, religious, and political factors that contribute to its prevalence. Consequently, there is a need to examine domestic violence in different racial and ethnic contexts to better understand this phenomenon. Arabs are among immigrant groups living all over the U.S., constituting over 3.5 million people (Arab American Institute, n.d.); however, they are not receiving adequate attention in domestic violence research (Halabu, 2006). Kulwicki (1996) interviewed 277 Arab American women to explore the prevalence of domestic violence in a highly populated Arab American community in a city outside Detroit. Results indicated that 25% of these Arab American women reported being beaten by their partner, 20% reported being sexually abused by their partners, 18.4% reported being kicked by their partner, and 7% reported that their partner used a gun or knife on them. Moreover, this study revealed that, among the abused women, 56.6% reported being unable to carry out daily activities due to stress and depression.

Of the women surveyed by Kulwicki and Miller (1999) in Dearborn, Michigan, 18% approved of a man killing his wife if she was guilty of adultery. An additional Detroit-based study examining IPV among Iraqi immigrant women found that more than 80% of participants had been physically assaulted by their partner and over 30% had been raped by their partner (Barkho, Fakhouri, & Arnetz, 2011). In another study, it was found that 7% of the women who sought help for family crisis issues at an organization serving Arab Americans reported spousal abuse, and about 50% were referred to counselors for acute marital problems caused by general arguments (34%), discussion of separation and divorce (14%), and separation (10%; Aswad & Gray, 1996).

IPV among immigrant communities and minority groups presents a serious public health problem. IPV can lead to significant physical injury and mental health problems for women. It is frequently reported that current and past IPV can lead to the development of mental health problems such as anxiety, depression, posttraumatic stress disorder (PTSD), and suicide attempts (Golding, 1999; The National Center on Domestic Violence, Trauma & Mental Health, 2004). In 2002, Campbell examined health consequences of IPV and found that abuse experienced by women was linked to increased health problems such as chronic pain, sexually transmitted diseases, depression, and PTSD. Additional research has shown IPV drastically impacts women's bodies and psyche. Yoshihama, Hammock, and Horrocks (2006) found that women experiencing IPV reported more physical limitations and were less active. Yoshihama, Horrocks, and Kamano (2009) added that IPV victims show high levels of distress symptoms. Furthermore, Barkho and colleagues (2011) studied Iraqi immigrant women in Detroit and found 90% of women in abusive relationships reported experiencing one or more types of psychosomatic symptoms such as headaches, back pain, muscle pain, stomach aches, and breathing problems.

Violence within the family not only affects individual health and wellbeing, it also affects the family as a whole. Children who witness family violence or are victims of family abuse are adversely affected (Haj-Yahia, 2001). Furthermore, children who witness or experience family violence may be more likely to accept violence as an appropriate means of discipline and may be at risk of perpetuating violence in the future (Maker, Shah, & Agha, 2005).

In a study in Israel, Haj-Yahia (2001) found that Arab adolescents witnessed high rates of parental violence that can lead to feelings of hopelessness, psychological adjustment problems, and low self-esteem. The results provided strong support for the assumption that witnessing interparental aggression and violence can negatively impact the adolescents' psychological states. A teen health survey conducted by Kulwicki in 1989 researched the incidence of family violence among Arab American teenagers in a community with a large number of Arab immigrants. Of the 362 adolescents (between the ages of 11 and 19), 12.2% reported that they had been physically abused by a family member, and 17.7% reported that they had been emotionally or verbally abused. Black and associates (2013) studied exposure to violence among Iraqi refugee youth in America. They found that, of the Iraqi refugee adolescents studied, most experienced high levels of violence in their families and were accepting of teen dating violence, especially when perpetrated by males.

Because of the dearth of research on violence against children or men in Arab American families, the remainder of this chapter focuses solely on IPV in regards to males assaulting their female partners. The chapter first introduces the different theoretical models that can be used to explain IPV, then reviews the risk and protective factors of IPV among Arab Americans. Also discussed are different responses to this phenomenon and the major professional interventions. A case example is presented to reflect the chapter contents. Finally, there is a critique of the literature with suggestions for future research and interventions.

Theoretical Models Explaining Intimate Partner Violence

Various theories and models have been examined when trying to explain the underlying causes of IPV. There is no one theoretical approach that dominates the field; rather, there are many approaches that provide perspective and highlight the complexity of the issue (Cunningham et al., 1998). There are far too many theoretical models to include in this chapter. Thus, this section will focus on the theoretical models that are most pertinent to Arab Americans.

The family systems theory emphasizes that each family member plays an important role in the family's wellbeing. Each member reacts to violence within the family differently, and acts of violence are maintained through actions and reactions of each family member that over time become established patterns that are difficult to change (Cunningham et al., 1998). Because social norms within the Arab American community are against exposing family matters to the public, IPV may be kept as a family secret and a matter for the family alone to address (Abu-Ras, 2007). Therefore, seeking family counseling services for IPV within the Arab American community becomes extremely difficult. Patriarchal values and norms within this community support gender inequality, with power and authority ascribed to men over women. This often keeps women from seeking help (Abu-Ras, 2007).

Haj-Yahia's research conducted in Middle Eastern countries laid out cultural norms that Arab immigrants likely bring with them to America, and the research also supports the family systems theory. Haj-Yahia (2002) explained that the patriarchal structure of the Arab family promotes inequality between the sexes. Women and children are expected to respect their husband or father (Haj-Yahia, 1995, 1996, 2000). In addition to immediate family members, Haj-Yahia (2002) goes further to explain that the father, brothers, and other family members of the wife experiencing IPV will most likely pressure the female victim to continue suffering in an abusive relationship to preserve the honor of both families. The wife typically assumes responsibility for the family breakdown. Thus, as the family systems theory suggests, each member plays a role, and situations presented by Haj-Yahia (2002) show that the structure of the traditional Arab family does not place sanctions against perpetrators of IPV.

Social learning theory (Bandura, 1977) is a psychological approach that is based on the understanding that behavior is learned. Through social learning theory, Bandura (1977) demonstrated that children learn and imitate behaviors they observe, especially behaviors that elicit reinforcement. So, if a child observes his or her parents being abusive and aggressive toward one another, the child is more likely to internalize that behavior and be abusive in his or her relationships with others (Cunningham et al., 1998). In 1998, Haj-Yahia and Dawud-Noursi conducted research based on social learning theory by studying 832 Arab adolescents from Israel. The purpose of the study was to examine if they could predict conflict resolution tactics used among siblings based on their family or parental conflict resolution tactics. Results revealed that Arab youth utilized conflict resolution tactics similar to those they had observed from their parents. Youth who had witnessed more parental verbal abuse and physical violence were themselves more likely to use verbal and physical abuse against their siblings. Although this study did not take place in the U.S., it shows how cultural norms in the Arab community play a role in the continued cycle of domestic violence. Such cultural norms are likely to still be intact in many Arab American communities.

Mourad and Carolan (2010) use the ecological model to describe why Arab American women remain in abusive relationships and have difficulty seeking outside help. The model considers individual, interpersonal, organizational, community, and public policy factors in human relationships and their relative contributions to the individual's ability to address personal or family conflicts. According to this model, it can be concluded that Arab American women face many hardships in dealing with IPV. The first hardship is at the individual level: many women have experienced trauma in their country of origin or while immigrating to the U.S. Second, some Arab women, particularly immigrants, tend to limit their relationships to those within their family and within the Arab American community, at the expense of their interpersonal relationships outside the family. They may have difficulty initiating or maintaining relationships with individuals outside their immediate family or outside their culture due to a lack of English language skills or differences in cultural expectations. These women, therefore, remain isolated from the society they live in and do not understand how to navigate the social services they may need.

Third, there are organizational barriers that many Arab American women experience while seeking help. In this context, there may be limited social service agencies that provide culturally appropriate services to Arab American women, especially in cases of IPV. Moreover, there may be a lack of awareness of the services available, and Arab American women may not want to utilize existing services for fear of discrimination or hostility, especially after the 9/11 terrorist attacks (Amer & Hovey, 2007; Halabu, 2006; Ibish, 2003; Kulwicki, Aswad, Carmona, & Ballout, 2010). Fourth, Arab American community members usually frown upon or criticize women who make their family matters known to the public. In many instances community members, including members of religious institutions, encourage women to remain in abusive relationships and find ways to resolve their conflicts within the family for the sake of preserving family unity (Kulwicki, Aswad, et al., 2010). Finally, although laws are in place to protect women from abuse, many Arab American women who are new to the country are unfamiliar with such laws, do not have adequate English language skills to access support from law enforcement, and fear the implications of seeking outside help.

The previously highlighted theories and supporting research show the factors influencing and sustaining IPV within the Arab American community. Each model provides a rationale as to why IPV exists within this community. There are other risk factors that Arab American families experience that may contribute to domestic violence and IPV, which are laid out in the next section.

Risk and Protective Factors Contributing to IPV Among Arab Americans

Understanding the previously discussed theoretical models helps researchers and service providers predict the occurrence of IPV and the risk factors that may increase the susceptibility of Arab American women to IPV and its perpetuation. Language and cultural factors, lack of knowledge of existing services, lack of financial resources, and lack of legal resources have been found to prevent women who are victims of IPV from seeking services (Kulwicki, Hymes, Hammad, Killawi, & Farrag, 2010). IPV within the Arab American community remains a silent crisis (Kulwicki, Hymes, et al., 2010). Most Arab Americans shy away from open discussion of IPV for fear that it may reflect negatively on the community or its religion. In the Arab American community, cultural, religious, and legal norms converge to provide, in the interest of family harmony and continuity, tolerance toward perpetrators of domestic violence and a simultaneous lack of support to the victims.

Importance of Family Honor

The family unit continues to be the most sacred unit in Arab society. Within the Arab American community, family honor is deeply rooted in everyday life and cultural values (Nassar-McMillan, 2007). Individuals are expected to place family interest over individual interest, and each member of the family works to maintain the status of the family (Erickson & Al-Timimi, 2001). Family responsibilities are usually divided along gender lines, whereby men are the main breadwinners and heads of households, and women are responsible for providing physical and emotional care for the children. Males are usually responsible for preserving the family's honor through courage, honesty, economic support, and protection of their kinswomen. The honor for female family members is based on personal purity and chastity, as well as on roles and duties related to caregiving, motherhood, and maintaining the family's unity (Aswad, 1999). The family unit carries a sacred moral value, with the concepts of honor (*sharaf*) and shame (*'ayb*) underlying the family system.

Although Arab culture, like others, has undergone cultural transformations throughout history, the cultural norms of gender-specific roles persist, and immigrants may remain faithful to these values and traditions even in the U.S. Part of the patriarchal system according to which some Arab American families live is that a woman might be viewed as property or someone who needs protecting by her husband (Hamza, 2010), which can be a risk factor for IPV. Because culture usually determines the social construction of the roles of its members, it is logical then to assume that within the Arab

American family, the wife is expected to meet the needs of her family, safeguard honor, and achieve her traditional roles as mother and housewife. Women are expected sometimes not only to endure abuse, but also to be lively and productive. This ideology of family honor and gender roles can therefore provide justification for IPV (Hamza, 2010).

Cultural Norms

Cultural and religious norms have significant impact on the behaviors of the abusers and the abused members of Arab families. Most traditional Arab American women are raised in patriarchal and patrilineal households, which may contribute to staying in abusive relationships. In leaving an abusive relationship, an Arab woman risks bringing shame to her family, losing the support of her family, being separated from her children, and becoming financially unstable in a foreign country (Kulwicki, Aswad, et al., 2010). In addition to these barriers to seeking help, a woman cannot leave her children with an abusive husband for fear of being blamed for the family's demise. Moreover, talking about being abused to others or seeking help is considered shameful in the sense that it can expose family problems to the public; therefore, the victims of abuse, and not the abusers, are usually blamed for family breakdown (Kulwicki, Aswad, et al., 2010).

Another risk factor of domestic violence for immigrant women is acculturation, which is the process of adapting to a host culture. In adapting to a new language, customs, and social norms, for example, it was found that Korean immigrant women who failed to acculturate (i.e. those who were marginalized) experienced higher personal and family stress, which might be explained by the fact that they did not receive the appropriate support from their families – especially spouses – to interact with other people in the host culture (Choi, Miller, & Wilbur, 2009). In terms of seeking help, immigrant women experiencing IPV who have lived in the U.S. longer and have engaged in the acculturation process may be more likely to shift from speaking with family members to speaking with authorities about IPV (Ammar, Orloff, Dutton, & Hass, 2012). Although Arab American women who adapt to their host country's norms may face resentment from their spouses, they may be more comfortable in building social supports and speaking out about their experience.

Other instrumental factors have been documented that prevent women from seeking help outside of the family when being abused. Immigration status may be used by Arab American men to control their wives. This includes threatening deportation and refusing to process their wives' immigration papers. In conducting National Institute of Justice research, Erez, Ammar, and Orloff (2003) found that of the 157 immigrant women experiencing IPV interviewed, 65% reported that their abuser had threatened deportation as a means of punishment. Arab American women's fear of deportation and separation from their children often prevent them from seeking outside help. Finally, socioeconomic barriers, such as a lack of financial and legal resources, along with limited English proficiency, may trap women in abusive relationships (Kulwicki, 1996).

Protective Factors and Resilience

Although women living with IPV face many hardships, there are protective factors that can shield them from mental health outcomes often associated with abuse (Carlson, McNutt, Choi, & Rose, 2002). Carlson and colleagues (2002) explained that having more protective factors, such as social support, positive self-regard, self-esteem, positive outlook, and good health, is associated with less anxiety and depression. Protective factors such as having positive self-regard, higher education, and social support may help Arab American women seek help for IPV. In a study conducted by Hamza (2010), ten Arab women immigrants were interviewed to assess how trauma resulting from IPV is expressed by Arab women. Although women in this study feared for their health and wellbeing, they had great determination to leave their abusive relationships. Hamza found that women sought social support from other women who had survived similar situations. The author also found that women, in seeking help for IPV, must have shelter and financial resources, as women will not seek help if they feel they are a burden.

Arab Americans have overcome great obstacles together, such as war and terrorism in their country of origin, difficulty in immigrating to the U.S., arduous struggles as foreigners, and discrimination due to terrorist attacks such as 9/11. In surviving such hardships, Arab American families have developed various coping skills that can be used in facing future adversity (Beitin & Allen, 2005). It is important that service providers helping Arab American families escape violence understand the difficulties they face and understand their capacity to cope (Nassar-McMillan & Hakim-Larson, 2003).

Individual, Family, and Community Responses

Little attention is given to crimes committed against women in Arab communities because domestic violence is viewed as a family issue and not as a legal concern or serious public health threat. Because domestic violence is treated as a family issue, it often goes unreported or underreported. Sociocultural norms and religious practices create obstacles in seeking help and investigating crimes related to domestic violence. Arab immigrants to the U.S. bring these norms with them, creating barriers for victims seeking help outside the family and hindering efforts by law enforcement agencies and health professionals to combat this threat within the Arab American community (Kulwicki & Miller, 1999).

Because of cultural barriers in seeking help for abuse, Arab American women are more likely to speak with religious leaders, relatives, or friends rather than with formal authorities like police and social workers. In 2010, Kulwicki, Aswad, and colleagues observed that rather than helping women escape abusive situations, many religious leaders advised women to be patient and respect the sanctity of family unity by enduring abuse. Religious leaders directed women to stay with their husbands rather than seek divorce. In studying 67 immigrant women experiencing IPV in Dearborn, Michigan, Abu-Ras (2003) found that 70.1% reported a lack of encouragement by their social networks to seek outside help. Additionally, 74.6% reported barriers based on fear of what relatives and friends may think of them.

In 2007, Abu-Ras conducted a study examining the relationship between cultural beliefs and service utilization in Arab American women. She found significant positive correlations between Arab American women's traditional attitudes toward gender and IPV, and their utilization of formal mental health, social, and legal services. The more traditional the women were, the less they used these services. Arab American women may also fear racism and discrimination in seeking help as they do not wish to perpetuate the stereotypes of immigrant men being violent and immigrant women being submissive (Kulwicki, Aswad, et al., 2010). Additional barriers in seeking help faced by Arab American women in abusive relationships include limited transportation to services and lack of culturally appropriate shelters.

Professional Interventions

In 2010 Kulwicki, Aswad, and colleagues conducted focus groups with community and religious leaders, social services workers, nurses, physicians, and law enforcement officials to examine the barriers that keep Arab American women who endure IPV from seeking services. Participants laid out multiple barriers that prevent women from seeking assistance such as: (a) inadequate continuum of domestic violence prevention and intervention services, (b) conflicting opinions between traditional/religious advice and that of social service providers, (c) breaches of confidentiality or fear of them, (d) lack of services for batterers, (e) victims' economic level and immigration status, and (f) cultural norms toward family honor and shame. Issues related to economic level and immigration status were the lack of support and assistance for victims who were poor, the inability of poorer women to afford lawyers' fees and transportation costs when seeking services, and women's fears that their husbands might lose their immigration status (e.g. green card) if women reported being abused.

Victims of IPV experiencing mental health problems can benefit from interventions that are both sensitive and appropriate. Traditional interventions for IPV in the U.S. include education on causes and consequences of IPV, attention to ongoing safety, cognitive and emotional skills development, and a focus on survivors' strengths. Arab American women engaged in Kulwicki, Aswad, and associates' (2010) study suggested increasing awareness and enhancing delivery of domestic violence services. An additional suggestion was to train religious leaders, lawyers, and Arab American service providers, including physicians, in relevant issues, such as Arab family systems, rights of women, and lifestyle changes that result from immigration processes, while interacting with and accommodating the American culture. Lastly, participants believed in the importance of educating both Arab and American service providers that the maintenance of confidentiality should be both mandatory and critical to the missions of organizations that provide community services for the victims of violence. Haj-Yahia (2000) also emphasized the importance and urgency of providing Arab Americans with services such as 24-hour hotlines and counseling shelters.

Kulwicki and Miller (1999) attempted to change the environmental conditions of the Arab American community that influence IPV and keep women from seeking help. The researchers examined societal norms, religious beliefs, cultural patterns, economic status, and English language fluency of Arab American women. They worked to: (a) assess Arab Americans' attitudes and behaviors toward domestic violence, (b) develop and implement a mass media campaign that provided linguistically relevant domestic violence educational materials, and (c) educate community members on domestic violence through a community outreach campaign. Attitudes, beliefs, and behaviors of 202 Arab American respondents were studied to assess IPV in the community and determine best methods in assisting families. The authors found these approaches to be successful in domestic violence education, prevention, and intervention. They found it also imperative to maintain confidentiality in a very close-knit community. Lastly, based on the experiences with the previously developed community interventions, the authors highlighted the crucial role of the community leaders, who are usually trusted and consulted by people, and who as a result should be encouraged to engage in any effort to inform community members about the seriousness of domestic violence and its implications to the wellbeing of families.

Through Kulwicki and Miller's (1999) efforts, several programs – such as the Domestic Violence Prevention Project, the Arab Domestic Violence Coalition, and the Muslim Women's Empowerment Program – were developed and implemented to address the unique needs of Arab Americans utilizing services. These programs employed members of the Arab American community, such as religious leaders, community leaders, representatives from local schools and universities, and local health and human services representatives. Moreover, the local police department hired several Arab American officers in response to the study, and the Arab Community Center for Economic and Social Services (ACCESS), an organization that provides health and human services to the Arab community in Dearborn, Michigan, developed an Arab Batterers Intervention Program to serve Arab American domestic violence offenders who were referred by the local court system.

However, when developing IPV interventions, it is important to address the challenges in understanding the Arab American cultural identity. Arab American identity has been a topic of controversy due to the heterogeneity in terms of language and religion (Amer & Hovey, 2007). Accordingly, Arabs are not well presented and are usually invisible to many of the law enforcement agencies in the U.S. (Ammar, 2000). It is extremely important that Arab Americans should be included and understood in American society's diverse portrait in order to have successful policing for domestic violence crimes (Ammar, 2000).

Case Example: Zeinab's Experience as a Pregnant Arab American Immigrant

This case example examines a 23-year-old Arab American woman, Zeinab, who is pregnant and experiencing IPV. Zeinab's story highlights the difficulty Arab American women face when coming to a new country and enduring abuse from their partners. Family and community responses to her situation are examined, along with risk and protective factors.

Zeinab, a 23-year-old pregnant woman, visited her obstetrician, Dr. Jean Smith, for her prenatal checkup. She came as a bride from Yemen and had no family in the U.S. except her husband. She had very limited English conversational skills. Zeinab and her husband, Yousef, are both Muslim. Yousef was an immigrant himself, and worked as a dishwasher in one of the local restaurants.

Yousef accompanied Zeinab to the clinic and asked to be present, being concerned that Zeinab would not be able to communicate in English. During her visit, Dr. Smith noticed that Zeinab had a bruise on her right arm. She asked Zeinab how she got the bruise. Zeinab appeared reluctant to respond. Yousef quickly responded by stating that she fell when she was taking the laundry to the basement. Dr. Smith became concerned and, after she had completed the physical exam, asked Zeinab to have her blood tests done and come back in three days to discuss them with her.

In the meantime, Dr. Smith called the international services and asked that a translator be present during Zeinab's next visit. Zeinab returned to the clinic with Yousef and, as he was entering the exam room with his wife, Dr. Smith asked him to wait in the waiting room until he was called. Dr. Smith then asked Zeinab's permission to have a translator join them. Although hesitant to have a translator join, Zeinab felt better that the translator, Fatima, was not from her own community. Dr. Smith asked Fatima to ask Zeinab where she got the bruise on her arm. Zeinab, embarrassed and cautious, told Fatima that she did not want to discuss her personal issues with the doctor for fear that she may make her husband upset. Fatima explained to Zeinab that whatever she said would be held confidential. Zeinab started crying and said that her husband had recently been under a lot of stress and, during an argument over money, he had become upset, grabbed her by the arm, and told her that he would throw her out of the apartment if she questioned him about money.

Dr. Smith asked if Zeinab felt unsafe at home alone with her husband. Zeinab, through the translator, said "no." Dr. Smith asked that Zeinab return in two weeks with her husband because she wanted them to see an Arabic-speaking counselor. Zeinab agreed. Dr. Smith arranged for an Arabic-speaking counselor to be present during Zeinab's next visit. She also spent some time reading about Yemeni cultural norms regarding marital relationships. She learned that Yemen was a highly patriarchal society with strictly defined gender roles. Men were expected to be breadwinners and women rarely worked outside the home. She also learned that it was not uncommon within the society for men to "correct" their wives by physical coercion and that some thought that some level of corporal discipline had a religious sanction.

During the next clinic visit, Dr. Smith introduced Zeinab and Yousef to Lama, an Arabic-speaking counselor from a local Arab community center. Dr. Smith explained to Zeinab and Yousef that the difficult issues that married couples go through are more difficult when they lack the family and social support system that they may have had in Yemen. She explained that there was a local Arab community center, with counselors like Lama to assist people with their problems and to help them sort through their concerns. Dr. Smith then excused herself from the room, knowing that the couple were more likely to communicate with Lama once she had left.

Lama explained her role and tried to put the couple, especially Yousef, at ease. Knowing that confidentiality is a major concern in her community, Lama held up a privacy form to say that it was a legal document and that she could lose her job if she violated it. She also mentioned that she worked with many other members of the community and that the imams at the local mosques often referred couples to her for help. Yousef asked from which mosque people were referred and Lama declined to answer, saying that that would violate confidentiality. Even though he did not get the name of a religious authority he respected, Lama's words seemed to relax Yousef. In a gentle and non-accusatory way, she conveyed that things differ in this country from the home country, and that people from the community sometimes get into trouble with the law if they do not understand the differences.

Lama then began to inquire about the family circumstances, including living situation, support structure, children, education and language skills, and employment. She learned that Yousef was from a small village in a rural area of Yemen. He had had an education through sixth grade and could read "the Holy Book and not hard things" in Arabic, but he could not read English. He had learned enough English on the job to do it, but there were many things he did not understand and he relied on Arab friends who were better educated or who had better English to explain things. Zeinab had had no formal education, but had learned a few words of English from a friendly Arab neighbor and from her son, who had just entered kindergarten. Zeinab had almost no contact outside the home and was completely reliant on Yousef for transportation. Yousef sometimes took Zeinab to the store for grocery shopping, but he preferred to do it himself because Zeinab insisted on buying "silly things" when she went with him.

Then, Lama inquired about the problems they were facing. Yousef angrily expressed that Zeinab had been extremely demanding; so much so, that he had not been able to control his anger and that he had resorted to hitting Zeinab once. Zeinab complained that Yousef brought very little food home and that when he did, it was canned goods, not fresh vegetables, and almost no meat. At this point, Yousef admitted that he had lost his main job as a dishwasher and that his hours as a part-time busboy had been reduced. He said he was embarrassed to tell Zeinab about the job loss for fear that Zeinab would blame him for not being man enough to provide the basic family needs. He therefore pretended to go to work every day and spent some time looking for a job. Much of the food he brought home came from a local food bank his friends told him about.

Lama explained that she understood the cultural norms about a man being expected to provide for his family but, under the circumstances, he needed to be honest with Zeinab and explain how he felt about not being the provider for his family. She also explained to Zeinab that she needed to be patient with her husband. Many people were without jobs because of the local economy and therefore Zeinab should not look negatively on her husband for it. Lama referred the couple to the Special Supplemental Nutrition Program for Women, Infants, and Children, which provides access to supplemental foods, healthcare services, and nutrition education for low-income pregnant and postpartum women, and to infants and children up to five years of age. Lama explained that the couple may qualify for food stamps through this program until Yousef was able to find full-time work. In addition, she informed them about a community organization that provides job training and placement services, as well as English language classes that might be useful for both of them. Finally, Lama asked that Yousef and Zeinab both visit her every two weeks to discuss progress.

This case example presents a picture of an Arab American couple who brought the cultural norms of their host country with them to the U.S. They were experiencing IPV, but were able to find resources to help them to address their problem; however, they needed to be followed up and reached out to by counselors and other service providers based on their needs. Couples like Zeinab and Yousef are afraid to disappoint their family and community, and tend not to seek help when dealing with IPV. Because of cultural norms and risk factors, healthcare providers like Dr. Smith need to assess their patients' needs, be culturally competent, and find resources to best assist their patients.

As shown throughout this chapter, Arab American couples face difficulties in immigrating to the U.S. It is difficult to learn English, find employment, provide for a family, and adapt to American norms. The financial dependency of immigrant women upon their male partners can aggravate the situation and make women more vulnerable to being locked in an abusive relationship (Hass, Ammar, & Orloff, 2006). Yousef's low socioeconomic status and lack of resources were very prominent risk factors for IPV in this case example, which can be explained by the stress that Yousef was experiencing (Jewkes, 2002).

Moreover, it is important to consider what the cultural meaning of being a man is, and what constitutes successful manhood. Living in poverty can be perceived as a disabling factor that made Yousef unable to live up to his own ideas of "successful" manhood, and this was the source of stress that led him to abuse his wife. In other words, violence against women is thus seen not just as an expression of male power and dominance over women, but also as being rooted in male vulnerability implied by the social expectations of manhood that are unattainable due to poverty experienced by men. An inability to meet social expectations of successful manhood can trigger a crisis of male identity, which is often infused with ideas about honor and respect (Jewkes, 2002). Violence against women is seen as a means of resolving this crisis because it allows an expression of power that is otherwise denied. Consequently, in preventing IPV there is a need not only to understand the cultural meanings of masculinity, but also to recognize the effects of poverty and unemployment on men (Jewkes, 2002).

Critique

As highlighted in the case example above and throughout the chapter, IPV is a significant problem in the Arab American community that needs to be addressed. However, the research on IPV is still limited. Much research has been dedicated to understanding patterns of Arab culture and the continuation of cultural norms and patterns after immigration to America. Literature on IPV among Arab Americans is lacking national prevalence rates, empirical evidence on which factors are associated with risk for IPV, and detailed research on risk and protective factors. Although there is noteworthy research on hardships faced by Arab American women and the obstacles faced in seeking help for IPV, there is a dearth of information on interventions with Arab American women experiencing IPV.

Research in this area focuses mainly on the risks and obstacles faced by Arab American women, with limited research focusing on strengths and resilience. Evidence-based research is needed to address factors that impact the male partner as well as the female. Moreover, both protective as well as risk factors need to be addressed by research in order to develop effective anti-violence interventions designed to avoid risk factors and enhance protective factors for this phenomenon.

Future research focusing on effective interventions for Arab American women and families would be beneficial to add to this body of research. More specifically, interventions in other areas of the U.S., building on Kulwicki and Miller's (1999) work in Dearborn, Michigan, could have an impact on Arab American women nationally by providing information, outlets, counseling, and protective factors on maintaining healthy relationships with family members. Theoretically speaking, as previously explained, Arab American women face many barriers in dealing with IPV at many different ecological levels namely, individual, interpersonal, organizational, community, and policy levels. Consequently, the best interventions are those that address family conflicts and IPV at all levels, and thus can contribute to sustainable and comprehensive solutions involving all these societal parts.

Lastly, research and interventions on Arab American children experiencing family violence is imperative. Although the Arab population in the U.S. is increasing, there is limited research on the abuse of Arab American children. Because of the association of abuse witnessed as a child and future IPV, it is important to better understand youth in these situations and determine interventions to stop the cycle of abuse. Furthermore, in order to best inform service providers, it is important to understand how immigrant groups such as Arab Americans react to IPV and experience barriers in accessing services (Keller & Brennan, 2007). Research on IPV in the Arab American community has helped, and will continue to help, service providers develop and implement culturally competent, sustainable, impactful, and realistic interventions for those seeking help for IPV.

Conclusion

This chapter has examined IPV within the Arab American community. Cultural, socio-demographic, and psychological factors all play a role in domestic violence against Arab American women. Arab American women experience multiple risk factors such as a lack of support from their family and community, cultural and religious factors, and fear of economic loss or deportation that may keep them within abusive relationships. Family members, religious leaders, and the Arab community tend to encourage women to make their relationships work, and thus have acted as potential barriers to women seeking professional services. A lack of English language proficiency and a lack of culturally sensitive services are also believed to be institutional factors that can prevent women from seeking services. On the other hand, there are certain protective factors such as self-esteem, good health, and family and social support; and the availability of culturally and linguistically sensitive services. All these protective factors can help women as they seek help for themselves and their families. It is recommended that future research examine family violence faced by children, the effective intervention of Arab American IPV victims, and the resilience of Arab American women.

References

Abu-Ras, W. (2007). Cultural beliefs and service utilization by battered Arab immigrant women. *Violence Against Women* 13, 1002–1028. doi: 10.1177/1077801207306019

Abu-Ras, W. M. (2003). Barriers to services for Arab immigrant battered women in a Detroit suburb. *Journal of Social Work Research and Evaluation* 4(1), 49–66.

Amer, M. M. & Hovey, J. D. (2007). Socio-demographic differences in acculturation and mental health for a sample of 2nd generation/early immigrant Arab Americans. *Journal of Immigrant and Minority Health* 9, 335–347. doi: 10.1007/s10903-007-9045-y

Ammar, N. H. (2000). Simplistic stereotyping and complex reality of Arab-American immigrant identity: Consequences and future strategies in policing wife battery. *Islam and Christian-Muslim Relations* 11, 51–70. doi: 10.1080/095964100111517

Ammar, N. H., Orloff, L. E., Dutton, M. A., & Hass, G. A. (2012). Battered immigrant women in the United States and protection orders: An exploratory research. *Criminal Justice Review* 37, 337–359. doi: 10.1177/0734016812454660

Arab American Institute. (n.d.). *Demographics*. Retrieved from www.aaiusa.org/pages/demographics/

Aswad, B. C. (1999). Attitudes of Arab immigrants toward welfare. In M. W. Suleiman (ed.), *Arabs in America: Building a new future* (pp.177–191). Philadelphia, PA: Temple University Press.

Aswad, B. C. & Gray, N. A. (1996). Challenges to the Arab-American family and ACCESS. In B. C. Aswad & B. Bilgé (eds.), *Family and gender among American Muslims: Issues facing Middle Eastern immigrants and their descendants* (pp. 223–240). Philadelphia, PA: Temple University Press.

Bandura, A. (1977). *Social learning theory*. New Jersey: Prentice Hall.

Barkho, E., Fakhouri, M., & Arnetz, J. E. (2011). Intimate partner violence among Iraqi immigrant women in Metro Detroit: A pilot study. *Journal of Immigrant and Minority Health* 13, 725–731. doi: 10.1007/s10903-010-9399-4

Beitin, B. K. & Allen, K. R. (2005). Resilience in Arab American couples after September 11, 2001: A systems perspective. *Journal of Marital and Family Therapy* 31, 251–267. doi: 10.1111/j.1752-0606.2005.tb01567.x

Black, B. M., Chiodo, L. M., Weisz, A. N., Elias-Lambert, N., Kernsmith, P. D., Yoon, J. S., & Lewandowski, L. A. (2013). Iraqi American refugee youths' exposure to violence relationship to attitudes and peers' perpetration of dating violence. *Violence Against Women* 19, 202–221. doi: 10.1177/1077801213476456

Campbell, J. (2002). Health consequences of intimate partner violence. *The Lancet* 359(9314), 1331–1336. doi: 10.1016/S0140-6736(02)08336-8

Carlson, B. E., McNutt, L. A., Choi, D. Y., & Rose, I. M. (2002). Intimate partner abuse and mental health: The role of social support and other protective factors. *Violence Against Women* 8, 720–745. doi: 10.1177/10778010222183251

Choi, J., Miller, A., & Wilbur, J. (2009). Acculturation and depression symptoms in Korean immigrant women. *Journal of Immigrant and Minority Health* 11, 13–19. doi: 10.1007/s10903-007-9080-8

Cunningham, A., Jaffe, P. G., Baker, L., Dick, T., Malla, S., Mazaheri, N., & Poisson, S. (1998). *Theory-derived explanations of male violence against female partners: Literature updated and related implications for treatment and evaluation.* London, Ontario: London Family Court Clinic. Retrieved from www.lfcc.on.ca/maleviolence.pdf

Erez, E., Ammar, N., & Orloff, L. E. (2003). *Violence against immigrant women and systemic responses: An exploratory study.* (National Institute of Justice Report grant # 98-WT-VX-0030). Retrieved from www.ncjrs.gov/pdffiles1/nij/grants/202561.pdf

Erickson, C. D. & Al-Timimi, N. R. (2001). Providing mental health services to Arab Americans: Recommendations and considerations. *Cultural Diversity and Ethnic Minority Psychology* 7, 308–327. doi: 10.1037/1099-9809.7.4.308

Fass, D. F., Benson, R. I., & Leggett, D. G. (2008). Assessing prevalence and awareness of violent behaviors in the intimate partner relationships of college students using Internet sampling. *Journal of College Student Psychotherapy* 22(4), 66–75. doi: 10.1080/87568220801952248

Garcia-Moreno, C., Jansen, H. A., Ellsberg, M., Heise, L., & Watts, C. H. (2006). Prevalence of intimate partner violence: Findings from the WHO multi-country study on women's health and domestic violence. *The Lancet* 368(9543), 1260–1269. doi: 10.1016/S0140-6736(06)69523-8

Golding, J. M. (1999). Intimate partner violence as a risk factor for mental disorders: A meta-analysis. *Journal of Family Violence* 14, 99–132. doi: 10.1023/A:1022079418229

Haj-Yahia, M. M. (1995). Toward culturally sensitive intervention with Arab families in Israel. *Contemporary Family Therapy* 17, 429–447. doi: 10.1007/BF02249355

Haj-Yahia, M. M. (1996). Wife abuse in the Arab society in Israel: Challenges for future change. In J. L. Edleson & Z. C. Eisikovits (eds.), *Future interventions with battered women and their families* (pp. 87–101). Thousand Oaks, CA: Sage.

Haj-Yahia, M. M. (2000). Wife abuse and battering in the sociocultural context of Arab society. *Family Process* 39, 237–255. doi: 10.1111/j.1545-5300.2000.39207.x

Haj-Yahia, M. M. (2001). The incidence of witnessing interparental violence and some of its psychological consequences among Arab adolescents. *Child Abuse & Neglect* 25, 885–907. doi: 10.1016/S0145-2134(01)00245-9

Haj-Yahia, M. M. (2002). Attitudes of Arab women toward different patterns of coping with wife abuse. *Journal of Interpersonal Violence* 17, 721–745. doi: 10.1177/0886260502017007002

Haj-Yahia, M. M. & Dawud-Noursi, S. (1998). Predicting the use of different conflict tactics among Arab siblings in Israel: A study based on social learning theory. *Journal of Family Violence* 13, 81–103. doi: 10.1023/A:1022864801027

Halabu, H. M. (2006). *Domestic violence in the Arab American community: Culturally relevant features and intervention considerations* (Doctoral dissertation). Available from ProQuest Dissertations and Theses database (UMI No. 3208461).

Hamza, M. (2010). *A phenomenological study of the symptoms of expression of Intimate Partner Violence in Arab Women* (Doctoral dissertation). Available from ProQuest Dissertations and Theses database (UMI No. 3455033).

Hass, G. A., Ammar, N., & Orloff, L. (2006). Battered immigrants and US citizen spouses. *Legal Momentum*, April 24. Retrieved from http://iwp.legalmomentum.org/reference/additional-materials/research-reports-and-data/research-US-VAIW/copy_of_BB_RSRCH_ImmVictims_Battered_Imm.pdf

Ibish, I. (2003). *Report on hate crimes and discrimination against Arab Americans: The post-September 11 backlash, September 11, 2001–October 11, 2002.* Washington, D.C.: American-Arab Anti-Discrimination Committee.

Jewkes, R. (2002). Intimate partner violence: Causes and prevention. *The Lancet* 359(9315), 1423–1429. doi: 10.1016/S0140-6736(02)08357-5

Keller, E. M. & Brennan, P. K. (2007). Cultural considerations and challenges to service delivery for Sudanese victims of domestic violence: Insights from service providers and actors in the criminal justice system. *International Review of Victimology* 14(1), 115–141. doi: 10.1177/026975800701400107

Kulwicki, A. (1989). *Executive summary: Arab teen health survey. Final report.* Lansing, MI: Michigan Department of Public Health, Bureau of Community Services.

Kulwicki, A. (1996). *Arab domestic violence education project: Executive report.* Michigan: Dearborn Arab Community Center for Economic and Social Services (ACCESS).

Kulwicki, A., Aswad, B., Carmona, T., & Ballout, S. (2010). Barriers in the utilization of domestic violence services among Arab immigrant women: Perceptions of professionals, service providers & community leaders. *Journal of Family Violence* 25, 727–735. doi: 10.1007/s10896-010-9330-8

Kulwicki, A., Hymes, R., Hammad, A., Killawi, A., & Farrag, M. (2010). Development of a domestic violence risk assessment tool for Arab American clients. *Access Health*, preliminary issue, April, 12–22.

Kulwicki, A. & Miller, J. (1999). Domestic violence in the Arab American population: Transformation environmental conditions through community education. *Issues in Mental Health Nursing* 20(3), 199–215. doi: 10.1080/016128499248619

Maker, A. H., Shah, P. V., & Agha, Z. (2005). Child physical abuse prevalence, characteristics, predictors, and beliefs about parent-child violence in South Asian, Middle Eastern, East Asian, and Latina women in the United States. *Journal of Interpersonal Violence* 20, 1406–1428. doi: 10.1177/0886260505278713

McHugh, M. C. & Frieze, I. H. (2006). Intimate partner violence. *Annals of the New York Academy of Sciences* 1087(1), 121–141. doi: 10.1196/annals.1385.011

Mourad, M. R. & Carolan, M. T. A. (2010). An ecological approach to culturally sensitive intervention for Arab American women and their families. *The Family Journal* 18(2), 178–183. doi: 10.1177/1066480710364474

Nassar-McMillan, S. C. (2007). Arab American populations. In M. G. Constantine (ed.), *Clinical practice with people of color: A guide to becoming culturally competent* (pp. 85–103). New York: Teachers College Press.

Nassar-McMillan, S. C. & Hakim-Larson, J. (2003). Counseling considerations among Arab Americans. *Journal of Counseling & Development* 81, 150–159. doi: 10.1002/j.1556–6678.2003.tb00236.x

National Center on Domestic Violence, Trauma & Mental Health. (2004). *Responding to domestic violence: Tools for mental health providers.* Domestic Violence and Mental Health Policy Initiative. Retrieved from http://ocadvsa.org/wp-content/uploads/2014/04/Responding-to-DV-Tools-for-MH-Providers.pdf

Tjaden, P. G. & Thoennes, N. (2000). *Prevalence, incidence, and consequences of violence against women: Findings from the National Violence Against Women Survey.* Washington, D.C.: National Institute of Justice. Retrieved from www.ncjrs.gov/pdffiles1/nij/183781.pdf

World Health Organization. (2002). *World report on violence and health*. Geneva: WHO. Retrieved from www.who.int/violence_injury_prevention/violence/world_report/en/

Yoshihama, M., Hammock, A. C., & Horrocks, J. (2006). Intimate partner violence, welfare receipt, and health status of low-income African American women: A lifecourse analysis. *American Journal of Community Psychology* 37(1–2), 95–109. doi: 10.1007/s10464-005-9009-0

Yoshihama, M., Horrocks, J., & Kamano, S. (2009). The role of emotional abuse in intimate partner violence and health among women in Yokohama, Japan. *American Journal of Public Health* 99, 647–653. doi: 10.2105/AJPH.2007.118976

16

TOBACCO USE

Cultural Influences on Consumption and Considerations for Intervention

Linda G. Haddad, Mona M. Amer, and Emily R. Johnson

Over the next two decades, it is anticipated that tobacco use will be the cause of death for more than eight million people annually, 80% from low- and middle-income nations (World Health Organization [WHO], 2012). Five million annual deaths are attributed to direct smoking, and another 600,000 people die as a result of second-hand smoke inhalation (WHO, 2012). Third-hand smoke, which is the accumulation of second-hand smoke on surfaces that become more toxic with time (Martins-Green et al., 2014), may also possibly cause health risks to people who are exposed (Matt et al., 2011). As a primary risk factor for a broad range of diseases, including certain cancers and respiratory and cerebrovascular diseases (U.S. Department of Health and Human Services, 2014), smoking is one of the most addictive habits and the leading preventable risk factor for disease morbidity and mortality (Bullen, 2008).

Smoking prevalence in the U.S. varies noticeably among different ethnicities (Centers for Disease Control and Prevention, 2007). Despite having limited amounts of accurate national data, studies have raised concerns regarding high rates of smoking prevalence among Arab Americans. For example, a randomly selected sample of Arab immigrants living in Michigan showed that the prevalence among this group, at 38.9%, was significantly higher than the U.S. average at that time, which was 28.9% (Rice & Kulwicki, 1992). The researchers found that 40.6% of the men and 38.2% of the women surveyed were current smokers (Rice & Kulwicki, 1992). Likewise, Haddad and colleagues sampled 221 Arab immigrants living in the Richmond, Virginia area and also found high results: 67.6% of men and 32.2% of women reported being current smokers (Haddad, El-Shahawy, Shishani, Madanat, & Alzyoud, 2012).

The Arab population in the U.S. has steadily increased over the last few decades according to U.S. Census statistics, growing from 850,000 people with Arab ancestry in 1990 to 1.2 million in 2000 (Asi & Beaulieu, 2013). Out of 304 million people in the U.S. population captured by the 2010 Census (Asi & Beaulieu, 2013), approximately 1.9 million were of Arab ancestry (Arab American Institute Foundation, 2012). Since Arab immigrants are a rapidly growing immigrant group, and factors related to race and ethnicity are important to consider in the likelihood of developing addictions (Potenza, 2013), examining the health behaviors of this specific racial/ethnic minority is essential.

This chapter addresses tobacco use among Arab Americans, beginning with theoretical frameworks and models used to understand tobacco use. A summary of the trends and correlates for youth and adult tobacco use is provided, including information on the rising popularity of waterpipe use. The chapter includes a review of recent prevention and intervention efforts that are specific to this population, and details a case example of a smoking cessation program in Virginia. Finally, the chapter concludes with a critique of strengths and limitations of current literature surrounding this topic and identifies future trends for intervention literature.

Frameworks for Understanding Tobacco Use and Addiction

The pathways for tobacco use are complex. There is no one single causal explanation for why some people experiment with tobacco, or become dependent on it, and others do not. It appears that biological, psychological, and cultural factors can all influence tobacco consumption. Because the models for understanding tobacco use and addiction are too numerous to review in this chapter, only select models that are most relevant to Arab Americans are discussed.

Biological Factors

There are more than 7,000 chemicals found in tobacco smoke, and of these, nicotine is the primary reason tobacco is addictive (National Institute on Drug Abuse, 2012). Addiction, which comes from the Latin verb meaning "bound to" or "enslaved by," is characterized by compulsive drug-seeking and use (National Institute on Drug Abuse, 2012; Potenza, 2013). For the smoker, it is a behavior that is difficult to control. According to the biological model of addiction, the development and maintenance of nicotine addiction is a result of activation of reward centers in the brain, which produce pleasure-causing neurotransmitters such as dopamine. These neurotransmitters contribute to structural changes in the brain that over time alter the person's tobacco use from being voluntary to involuntary (Brower, 2006; Dingel, Karkazis, & Koenig, 2011).

When a person uses tobacco, the effects of the nicotine can be felt almost immediately. Nicotine releases adrenaline, causing increases in heart rate and respiration. However, the acute effects of nicotine only last for a short period of time, as do the pleasurable reward feelings, which causes the user to continue use in order to maintain the satisfying effects and prevent withdrawal (National Institute on Drug Abuse, 2012). Cravings for nicotine are related to acute psychological stress, and stress-induced cravings have been associated with smoking relapse in those who have previously abstained from tobacco (Gökbayrak, Paiva, Blissmer, & Prochaska, 2015). Withdrawal from nicotine appears to produce significant distress and impairment, resulting in anger, irritability, depression, difficulty concentrating on and completing tasks, impatience, and restlessness. Physiologically, nicotine withdrawal can be marked with decreased heart and metabolic rate and cortisol levels (Hughes, 2007). The general mechanisms represented in the biological model are not ethnic-specific and therefore would be expected to function similarly for Arab Americans.

Psychological Factors

Once physiologically addicted, a major consideration for understanding and promoting quitting efforts is the need to take into account the psychological readiness of the smoker to change his or her behavior (Fava, Velicer, & Prochaska, 1995). Smokers may be at different stages of readiness to quit, which can be represented by stages of change, a key construct of the transtheoretical model of change (TTM). The TTM provides a framework for understanding the process of making health-related behavior changes and has been shown to be applicable to a broad range of behaviors and interventions (e.g. Daniels et al., 2014). For tobacco cessation, the stages of change model describes five stages: precontemplation, contemplation, preparation, action, and maintenance (Fava et al., 1995). In addition, TTM acknowledges the concept of self-efficacy (i.e. belief in one's ability to resist smoking), which has been shown to be positively associated with stages of change (Haddad & Petro-Nustas, 2006). Developing an understanding of the factors that bring about movement toward smoking cessation may help design stage-matched smoking interventions (DiClemente et al., 1991).

Research on the TTM as it relates to understanding Arab Americans' decisions to quit smoking has been minimal. In a study of Arab immigrants residing in Virginia, the average perceived readiness to quit smoking was 5.0 on a scale ranging from 0 (low) to 10 (high; Haddad et al., 2012). However, the authors did not report correlates of readiness to quit with other behaviors such as actual quit attempts. Another study conducted in the Middle East did document such relationships. Haddad and Petro-Nustas (2006) studied the TTM as it related to intentions to quit smoking among 800 Jordanian college students (90% male). Their results showed that the students in the contemplation stage of change had more intention to quit smoking. Aside from individual quit behaviors, the TTM model has also been shown to be a useful framework for a smoking cessation program that was piloted for Arab Americans (see case example below). Participants in the program demonstrated progress in moving through the stages of change during the intervention process (Haddad & Corcoran, 2013).

Cultural Factors

Cultural factors can influence the experience of tobacco use, including the decision whether or not to experiment with tobacco and the decision or readiness to quit once addicted. In essence, culture plays a major role in a person's ideas about illness, disease, and health (Jadalla & Lee, 2012) and has been linked to health behaviors and health outcomes among immigrants (Byrd, Peterson, Chavez, & Heckert, 2004; Lim, Gonzalez, Wang-Letzkus, & Ashing-Giwa, 2009; Rodríguez-Reimann, Nicassio, Reimann, Gallegos, & Olmedo, 2004). Immigrants and ethnic minority groups are at the intersections of at least two cultures (ethnic heritage and the host culture), and thus may be exposed to different messages and norms regarding health behaviors such as smoking (Unger et al., 2003). Therefore, investigating the acculturation process aids in understanding smoking trends of immigrant and ethnic minority populations.

Acculturation is the complex and continuous process of the interactions between two or more cultural groups that results in cultural and psychological changes among members of those groups (Berry, 2005). Berry (1997, 2001, 2005) described four acculturation strategies: marginalization, separation, assimilation, and integration. Marginalization occurs when the individual gives up his or her original culture and faces rejection or alienation from the new culture. As a result, the acculturating individual no longer identifies with either of the two cultures (ethnic heritage and host culture). Separation refers to when the individual resists adopting the new culture and retains their original ethnic identification. Assimilation denotes when the person loses his or her original cultural identity as a result of acquiring the identity of the new host culture. Integration indicates a level of acculturation when the individual develops a bicultural position with successful identification and integration of both the old and new cultures.

In order to understand immigration transitions, it is important to examine the personal, community, and societal conditions that facilitate or hinder progress toward positive adaptation (Berry, 2001). Different individual and contextual factors influence acculturation, and therefore groups and individuals experience the acculturation process in various ways (Berry, 1997, 2001, 2005). Berry's acculturation model suggests that the interaction between the traditional culture and the host culture plays a significant role in health-related decision-making, symptoms, and attitudes toward treatments, with more acculturated individuals approximating the host society's norms (Berry, 1998). Such processes would be expected to apply to smoking behaviors.

Because acculturation can influence health-related behaviors, acculturation may play a significant role in moderating tobacco use among Arab Americans. Although tobacco use is discouraged by Islam (Islam & Johnson, 2003) – the majority religion across North Africa and the Middle East – smoking is nevertheless a socially acceptable behavior within the Arab culture, particularly among males (Al-Omari & Scheibmeir, 2009). Tobacco consumption is widespread across the Arab region and prevalence rates have escalated significantly over the past few decades (Maziak et al., 2014). The average daily smoking prevalence in Arab populations ranges from 5% in Oman to 31% in Lebanon (WHO, 2013). Among males, the rates are higher, in many Arab countries reaching or surpassing half of the adult male population (Maziak et al., 2014).

The norms regarding smoking in the Arab region are interwoven with cultural values. Sharing cigarettes with others may be seen as a sign of hospitality and respect within the Arab culture (Al-Faouri et al., 2005; Al-Omari & Scheibmeir, 2009). For males, tobacco use may be viewed as a sign of maturity and manhood (Baker & Rice, 2008). Moreover, waterpipe smoking is practiced as a leisurely social and family activity (Baker & Rice, 2008). These cultural values and practices may be imported by Arab immigrants and maintained by Arab communities in the U.S. through enculturation and socialization processes.

Therefore, it would not be surprising to find that greater attachment to Arab culture is associated with greater tobacco use. Indeed, a study that measured self-reported acculturation among 96 Arab Americans based on Berry's model found that participants who were more separated showed higher rates of nicotine dependence compared to those who were assimilated into American culture (Al-Omari & Scheibmeir, 2009). Similarly, a dissertation study of 132 Arab Americans in California found that current smokers were more oriented toward the Arab culture or a bicultural strategy of balancing Arab and American cultures, whereas participants who had never smoked were oriented more toward the European American culture (Azar, 2008).

However, studies that have used proxy variables to indicate acculturation have shown more mixed results. For example, research conducted with 221 Arab Americans in Virginia found that smoking frequency decreased with increased proportion of years lived in the U.S. only for exclusively waterpipe users; these results did not hold up for those who used both waterpipe and cigarettes (Alzyoud et al., 2014). Other proxy indicators for acculturation, such as language preference and first language learned, were not significantly associated with smoking behaviors. In another study, generation status and number of years living in the U.S. were not significant in predicting smoking (Azar, 2008). Some research has shown a different trend, linking increased tobacco use with greater exposure to the U.S. culture. Being born in the U.S. (Abou-Mediene et al., 2005; Rice et al., 2007), younger age at time of immigration (Haddad et al., 2012), and lengthier residence in the U.S. (Haddad et al., 2012) were associated with higher rates of tobacco use. Therefore, the exact links between acculturation and smoking trends need further examination.

Trends and Correlates of Tobacco Use Among Arab Americans

Although the influence of acculturation on Arab Americans' tobacco use is not entirely understood, it is evident from previous research that tobacco use continues to be a serious concern for Arab Americans. Most of the research on Arab Americans' tobacco use has focused on youth, including the growing popularity of waterpipe use. The following sections discuss these trends, including demographic and psychosocial predictors of tobacco use for youth and adults.

Tobacco Use Among Arab American Youth

Studies have shown alarming rates of tobacco use among Arab American adolescents. For example, in their research on 480 Muslim Arab middle and high school students in Virginia, Islam and Johnson (2003) found that 50% reported susceptibility to smoking (i.e. a willingness to try smoking in the future), 45% had ever experimented with cigarette smoking, 18% had smoked cigarettes during the past month, and 12% were daily smokers. These rates are similar to another study of Arab American adolescents conducted in Michigan that found 34% had ever smoked and 17% had smoked at least one cigarette over the past month (Rice, Templin, & Kulwicki, 2003). A much larger study, of 1,671

Arab American adolescents, reported a 26% rate of ever smoking and a 6.9% rate of smoking at least once over the previous month (Rice et al., 2006). These rates significantly increased with age: among the 18-year-olds, 44% had ever smoked and 14% had smoked during the past month.

Despite the relatively high rates of tobacco use among Arab American adolescents, how these rates compare to youth from other racial/ethnic groups is unclear. When compared against existing national data on adolescent smoking trends, the 30-day smoking rate for Arab Americans in Islam and Johnson's (2003) study was lower than that for White Americans and higher than that for Black Americans. Research conducted in Michigan found that rates of cigarette use were lower among Arab American adolescents compared to their non-Arab counterparts (Rice, Weglicki, Templin, Jamil, & Hammad, 2010; Weglicki, Templin, Rice, Jamil, & Hammad, 2008) and compared to national rates (Rice et al., 2006). Rice and colleagues (2006) suggested the lower rates may have been the result of underreporting, as well as increased cigarette taxes, which may have challenged access to tobacco products by lower-income persons.

One of the important considerations related to youth tobacco use is age of first experimentation. A younger age of initiation is associated with subsequent heavier or more regular tobacco use among Arab Americans (Daffa, 2010). National data show that in 2010, 60% of new smokers were below the age of 18, and from current daily smokers, 90% began smoking and developed the addiction during adolescence (National Cancer Institute, 2012). Consistent with these national statistics, research with Arab Americans has shown that age at first trial with tobacco was typically during mid-adolescence, ranging from 13 to 15 years (Haddad et al., 2012; Kulwicki & Rice, 2003). Regarding earliest age of use within the Arab American community, one study had participants who experimented with cigarette smoking at less than 10 years of age (Haddad et al., 2012). Earliest age of experimentation with waterpipe smoking was found to be as young as 12 years (Alzyoud et al., 2014) or even less than 10 years (Rice et al., 2006).

Waterpipe Smoking

Waterpipe smoking has long been popular within the Arab culture, including Arab communities in the West (Akl et al., 2013). Over the past decade it has also grown in popularity in American culture, particularly among young adults (Jarrett, Blosnich, Tworek, & Horn, 2012; Knishkowy & Amitai, 2005; Salloum, Thrasher, Kates, & Maziak, 2014), leading some scholars to refer to it as a public health crisis (Cobb, Ward, Maziak, Shihadeh, & Eissenberg, 2010). Different names are used for the waterpipe across the Arab world, including hookah, shisha, goza, nargile, and arghile. A waterpipe is a smoking device that uses flavored tobacco, that is placed in a bowl connected to a glass base filled with water. As the smoker inhales through a hose that is connected to this glass base, the tobacco is drawn through the water, where it is cooled, and exits through the hose. This process does not remove toxins from the tobacco (Shamo, Robinson, Kiley, & Boynton, 2010). Rather, the exposure to toxins, and thus health risks, is comparable to or worse than cigarettes (Fakhreddine, Kanj, & Kanj, 2014; Knishkowy & Amitai, 2005). One waterpipe smoking session can even have the effects equivalent to up to 50 cigarettes (Cobb et al., 2010).

Although waterpipe smoking is a visible trend among youth across America, research has shown that waterpipe smoking is particularly salient for Arab Americans compared to persons from other ethnicities (Grekin & Ayna, 2012). For example, in a study of about 600 university students, more than 15% of the sample had smoked waterpipe at least once in their lives, and Arab ethnicity was the most significant predictor of waterpipe use (Grekin & Ayna, 2008). Other studies have shown immigrants of Arab ethnicity to have higher rates of waterpipe smoking compared to non-Arab Whites (Jamil et al., 2009; Weglicki et al., 2008). In a study of Arab American high school students in Michigan, by the time the students had reached the age of 18, 40% had tried the waterpipe (Rice et al., 2006). Even higher rates of current waterpipe use (58%) were found in a study of 313 Arab American youth in Michigan (Shamo et al., 2010).

Several factors can explain the popularity of waterpipe use among Arab Americans, particularly youth. Waterpipe smoking may be viewed among Arab American parents and their children as being less harmful and more socially acceptable than cigarette use (Baker & Rice, 2008). Many people have the misconception that the harmful substances in tobacco are filtered out through the water (Shamo et al., 2010). Moreover, the diverse styles and colors of the waterpipes, as well as the flavors and tastes of the tobacco, can be attractive (Shamo et al., 2010).

Demographic and Psychosocial Predictors of Tobacco Use

The correlates and predictors for tobacco use among youth and adult Arab Americans are similar for both cigarette and waterpipe smoking. Comparable to research conducted in the Arab world, results in previous studies across diverse U.S. states have shown higher rates of tobacco use among male compared to female Arab Americans (Alzyoud et al., 2014; Azar, 2008; Haddad et al., 2012; Islam & Johnson, 2003; Jamil, Geeso, Arnetz, & Arnetz, 2014). Older age has also been associated with higher rates of tobacco experimentation and use (Baker, 2005; Baker & Rice, 2008; Jamil et al., 2009). However, some studies on waterpipe use in particular have documented higher rates among younger participants, perhaps as a result of its recently rising popularity among youth. In one unpublished thesis of Arab American women, regular waterpipe smokers were more likely to be younger compared to those who smoked waterpipe occasionally (Daffa, 2010). Another study of adults in Michigan found higher rates of waterpipe smoking among those younger than 25 years of age (Jamil et al., 2014).

Socioeconomic factors – specifically education and income – may also relate to tobacco use among Arab Americans. Among Arab American adults, lower educational attainment, such as not having a college degree, was found to be associated with higher rates of tobacco use (Daffa, 2010; Mehta, 2011; Shamo et al., 2010). This was also found in studies of adolescents, in which smokers were more likely to report lower educational performance (Baker, 2005; Kulwicki & Rice, 2003; Rice et al., 2006), and their parents had generally low levels of education attainment (Kulwicki & Rice, 2003). The high cost of cigarettes in the U.S. has also been shown to be a barrier to smoking among Arab immigrants facing economic challenges (Jamil et al., 2009). Nearly 50% of the nonsmokers in a study of Arab immigrants reported wanting to save money as a factor for their decision to not smoke (Haddad et al., 2012). In a study of 801 Arab and Chaldean Americans in Michigan, higher annual income (specifically, above $40,000) was predictive of current and lifetime waterpipe use (Jamil et al., 2014).

Because tobacco rates differ across Arab countries, it may be anticipated that smoking rates could differ among Arab Americans based on national background. In Haddad and colleagues' (2012) study of Arab immigrants in Virginia, those of Iraqi background demonstrated higher tobacco use compared to those from other national heritages. In a sample of Muslim Arab American adolescents, the highest rate of cigarette use was among persons of Saudi Arabian background, whereas Yemeni Americans had the lowest (Islam & Johnson, 2003). In another study, of 1,271 Arab American adolescents, those of Lebanese background were significantly more likely to have ever used tobacco compared to Yemeni and Iraqi participants (Rice et al., 2005). Given that few studies have reported on such national differences, clear trends have not yet emerged in the literature.

In contrast, trends regarding social influences on initiating and maintaining tobacco use are evident in the literature on Arab Americans, particularly in relation to peers and family. For example, 17% of a sample of 1,671 high school students had been offered a cigarette by a friend or family member over the past week (Rice et al., 2006), and these kinds of offering were associated with an increased risk for tobacco use (Rice et al., 2005). Current Arab American waterpipe smokers were likely to have a significant portion of their friends and peers who were also smokers (Baker & Rice, 2008). Having peers that smoke cigarettes and viewing smoking as a peer norm increased the likelihood for Arab American adolescents to use cigarettes (Islam & Johnson, 2003; Rice et al., 2005;

Rice et al., 2006). Likewise, adult Arab American women in California were more likely to be regular (compared to occasional) waterpipe users if they smoked with at least one close friend (Daffa, 2010).

Research with Arab Americans has shown that tobacco use is common among family members. For example, in a study of 1,872 adolescents in Michigan, more than half of the participants reported that family members smoked waterpipe at home (Weglicki et al., 2008), and in another study, parental smoking was common among a majority of adult cigarette smokers (Haddad et al., 2012). Accepting attitudes toward tobacco use among family members and having siblings, parents, or relatives who smoked encouraged Arab American adolescents to smoke cigarettes (Baker, 2005; Kulwicki & Rice, 2003; Rice et al., 2005; Rice et al., 2006). Smoking a waterpipe at home (Daffa, 2010), especially if smoking it with family members (Mehta, 2011), was also found to be related to higher rates of tobacco use for adults. Similarly, Arab American adolescents were more likely to smoke a waterpipe if members of their family were waterpipe smokers (Shamo et al., 2010; Weglicki et al., 2008). However, one study found that among Yemeni American adolescents, parental smoking was not significantly associated with their waterpipe smoking (Baker & Rice, 2008), and another study of adolescents found that the father's tobacco use was not a predictor of cigarette use (Rice et al., 2006).

Fewer studies have examined personality or psychological characteristics associated with waterpipe use. In her dissertation research of 609 students at a university in Michigan, Ayna (2013) found that a self-reported impulsive personality trait was a moderator for lifetime waterpipe smoking, with impulsivity predicting use among non-Arab participants but not for Arab Americans. Higher self-reported depression was associated with higher odds for smoking in a sample of 1,271 adolescents (Rice et al., 2005). Another study, which explored the role of self-esteem in waterpipe smoking use among Yemeni American adolescents, found that the relationship was not significant (Baker & Rice, 2008). The authors speculated that given the collectivist Arab culture, the decision to use a waterpipe may have been influenced by social image, whereas individual self-esteem was not a salient factor. This is consistent with research from the Middle East that showed self-esteem not to be a significant factor in intentions to quit smoking among university students (Haddad & Petro-Nustas, 2006). These findings shed light on potential considerations for smoking interventions, as discussed below.

Smoking Prevention and Intervention Programs for Arab Americans

High rates of tobacco use among Arab Americans contribute to increased risk for serious health conditions (Jamil et al., 2009), and therefore efforts to prevent and reduce tobacco use are vital. To develop culturally sensitive and effective programs for Arab Americans, there needs to be a solid understanding of attitudes toward and barriers to smoking use and cessation.

Attitudes and Barriers Toward Smoking Cessation

The health belief model (Becker, 1974; Janz & Becker, 1984) suggests that peoples' health-related behaviors, such as the decision to quit smoking, are the outcome of their: (a) perceptions of their susceptibility of contracting disease, (b) perceived seriousness of the disease, (c) perceived benefits of adopting the health behavior, and (d) perceived barriers to implementing the behavior. One study showed that the majority of Arab American smokers did not believe that their smoking behaviors carried health risks, and only about 25% perceived health concerns as related to their tobacco consumption (Haddad et al., 2012). Arab American adolescents reported little concern about the future health risks of their tobacco use, and only became concerned if they began to experience negative effects (such as not being able to play sports as effectively) in the present moment (Kulwicki & Rice, 2003).

Even when health risks are perceived, Arab Americans may continue to use tobacco (Shamo et al., 2010). In a dissertation study of 132 Arab Americans in California, tobacco use was high despite self-reported health concerns. Participants who were current smokers revealed numerous perceived barriers to quitting smoking, such as financial expenses, time commitment, and investing effort that outweighed the potential benefits (Azar, 2008). Barriers to smoking cessation that were reported by adolescents in Michigan included social pressures and norms to smoking with peers or at home (Kulwicki & Rice, 2003). The barriers may differ based on the type of tobacco product. For example, Haddad, El-Shahawy, and Ghadban (2014) found that dual cigarette and waterpipe smokers appeared to have less concern about their own health and more barriers to cessation compared to exclusively cigarette or exclusively waterpipe smokers.

In addition to barriers, there are numerous factors that facilitate tobacco use among Arab Americans. Some of the potential benefits and motivators include elevating one's prestige and public image (Haddad et al., 2012; Kulwicki & Rice, 2003), using smoking as a social activity with friends (Kulwicki & Rice, 2003; Shamo et al., 2010), and wanting to be socially accepted in the mainstream culture (Haddad et al., 2012). Moreover, holding positive beliefs about smoking raised the risk for experimentation with cigarettes (Islam & Johnson, 2003), and perceived positive effects of smoking (such as experiencing it as tasting good, relaxing, and a useful distractor) encouraged cigarette use among adolescents (Kulwicki & Rice, 2003).

Given the cultural norms that condone tobacco use, barriers against quitting, and motivators for continuing to smoke, it is not surprising that many studies have found low levels of motivation to quit, indicating that many Arab American smokers are in the precontemplation stage of the TTM. A study of Arab immigrant adults residing in Virginia reported that nearly half of the participants had no intention of quitting waterpipe smoking in the future (Alzyoud et al., 2014). Previous quit attempts were likewise found to be low in a study of Arab immigrants, with an average of just one quit attempt over the past two years (Haddad et al., 2012). In another sample, from California, 26% of participants did not see any potential benefits from quitting, and 30% planned to continue smoking (Azar, 2008). On the other hand, more promising results were found in a study of 119 Arab American high school students, in which 68% of the smokers reported that they had previously tried to quit smoking (Rice et al., 2003).

Culturally Sensitive Tobacco Prevention and Intervention Programs

Despite the complex attitudes toward tobacco cessation, numerous barriers to quitting, and the powerful influence of social and cultural norms in maintaining tobacco use, there are many opportunities for tobacco prevention and intervention programs in the Arab American community. Awareness messages and formal programs can be delivered at central meeting places such as religious institutions (churches and mosques), community centers, and local health centers (Baker & Rice, 2008). School-based interventions also have the potential to be effective, particularly if implemented early on (Kulwicki & Rice, 2003). Information and pro-cessation messages can be disseminated in Arabic and English through community publications (e.g. ethnic magazines and newspapers) and via pamphlets and brochures (Baker & Rice, 2008). It is important to note that awareness of available resources for smoking cessation seems to be low among Arab Americans (Haddad et al., 2012), so providing that information and facilitating access to resources is important.

Several smoking prevention and cessation programs have been tailored specifically for Arab American communities across the U.S., particularly for youth, including the program that is described in the case example below. However, most community-based programs have not been documented in the literature. One example of a program that is described in the literature was an adaptation of the Project Toward No Tobacco Use (Project TNT) that targeted Arab American high school students (Al-Faouri et al., 2005). In addition to providing information about tobacco use, the program integrated components related to enhancing self-esteem, developing skills to resist family and peer pressure, avoiding tobacco marketing, and resisting overall tobacco use. The program content was adapted to the population and delivered by trained bilingual health educators over more than four weeks in 40-minute group sessions of up to 20 students. Audiovisual material and action learning strategies (such as role play) were integrated.

Project TNT distinguished itself by embedding research components throughout the process. The program modifications were informed by an initial pilot study (Kulwicki & Rice, 2003). Further pilot studies were conducted to determine the cultural sensitivity of the program content, test the intervention on a small sample, examine the psychometric properties of the assessment measures, and inform the design of the longitudinal data collection methodology (Rice et al., 2003). Assessments of initial responses to the program were positive, as reported by the student participants and health educators (Al-Faouri et al., 2005). A quasi-experimental post-test only design was used to compare 616 high school students who completed the intervention with 700 tenth grade students who comprised a control group, and with a second control group of 781 tenth grade students that was assessed two academic years after the intervention to control for historical threats to validity. Students who participated in the intervention reported lower rates of ever using tobacco and using tobacco over the previous 30 days compared to the control groups (Rice et al., 2010).

When designing future tobacco prevention and cessation programs for Arab Americans, several elements have been suggested by previous authors as being essential to consider in the program design. The importance of targeting the entire family (and not just the individual smoker or potential smoker) was recommended in light of the influence and centrality of family among Arab Americans (Baker & Rice, 2008). Targeting the peer group is also important (Baker & Rice, 2008; Kulwicki & Rice, 2003). Powerful community leaders and gatekeepers can moreover positively influence the success of prevention and intervention efforts with their endorsement of the tobacco-related programs (Baker & Rice, 2008). These key persons include religious leaders (e.g. priests, imams), politicians, and influential businessmen.

Moreover, cultural values, norms, and worldviews should be considered when tailoring a program for Arab Americans. For example, fatalism and belief that one must rely on God's will are shared within the Arab culture. Therefore, the emphasis on individual self-determination that commonly underlies prevention programs in the U.S. may not be appropriately aligned to the culture of Arab American participants (Azar, 2008). Moreover, Baker and Rice (2008) argued that self-esteem may not be an important component of tobacco prevention initiatives for Arab American adolescents, whereas cultural influences such as family and peers may be more essential. Additionally, because religious motives were the most common explanation for why some Arab Americans chose not to use tobacco (Haddad et al., 2012), the use of religious messages can be explored as a potential ingredient in prevention and intervention programs.

Finally, when designing programs, culturally shared misconceptions about tobacco use should be countered, including beliefs that waterpipe smoking is relatively harmless compared to cigarettes (Baker & Rice, 2008). This belief was common among 234 waterpipe smokers in a recent study of Arab and Chaldean Americans in Michigan: 71% believed that waterpipe smoking was less harmful than cigarette smoking (Jamil et al., 2014). Similarly, 79% of current waterpipe smokers in a study of Arab Americans in Michigan believed that waterpipe use carried fewer risks compared to cigarettes (Shamo et al., 2010). Other misconceptions documented in the literature include the belief that waterpipe second-hand smoke is not harmful (Shamo et al., 2010). Nonsmokers in a study of adult Arab immigrants were more likely to believe that smoking is harmful to health compared to those who were current smokers (Haddad et al., 2012), which suggests that such knowledge may be preventative.

Case Example: A Linguistically Sensitive Smoking Cessation Program for Arab Americans

Haddad and Corcoran (2013) developed a culturally tailored and linguistically-sensitive smoking cessation program for Arab Americans. The program was piloted on 11 male Arab Americans who were recruited from the Islamic Center of Virginia, located in Richmond, Virginia. The initial recruitment and orientation interviews and subsequent 12-week group intervention sessions took place at the Islamic Center and were conducted by two native Arabic speakers. All program materials were in Arabic, and participants had the opportunity to provide feedback on the cultural and linguistic suitability of these materials.

After the informed consent process, researchers helped participants determine the "when" and "how" to quit smoking. Following these decisions, researchers implemented the How to Quit Smoking in Arabic intervention protocol, which was designed based on the transtheoretical model (TTM). According to the TTM framework, current smokers can be at the stages of precontemplation, contemplation, or preparation (Prochaska & DiClemente, 1983) in regard to smoking cessation.

The cessation-counseling portion of the intervention consisted of five stages, beginning at the precontemplation stage of quitting smoking. Each stage had a workbook containing key information and interactive assignments, such as goal-setting exercises and relapse prevention strategies. The five stages lasted a maximum of six to nine weeks. Weekly group meetings were conducted to obtain the participants' thoughts about the workbooks provided, which served as a process evaluation. Participants offered suggestions for integrating or considering Islamic religious practices in the program, and they also pointed out how Arabic colloquial terms differed by nation of origin.

Of the 11 participants, 8 decided they were ready to quit smoking and completed all 5 stages, and at the conclusion of the 3-month program, these 8 participants had reduced their smoking by 45%. Moreover, the motivation to quit among participants matched the stages of the TTM, indicating that this model may be a useful framework for designing smoking cessation programs for Arab Americans.

Overall, the results of this pilot study suggest that a culturally tailored Arabic-language smoking cessation program may be successful in eliciting change in smoking behaviors for adult immigrants. The experience highlighted that religion and language dialects may be important factors to consider when designing programs. Larger-scale quantitative research is needed to explore fully the validity of this program and test how effective the intervention is in helping people to quit smoking.

Critique

As reviewed in this chapter, the literature on Arab Americans' tobacco use is rich and nuanced, and provides a foundation for understanding tobacco trends and correlates for this population. At the same time, there are opportunities for many further areas of investigation. Although studies on socio-demographic predictor variables have been conducted in many U.S. states, most utilized convenience samples, and many had small sample sizes. This could explain some of the contradictory findings discussed above, which may be resolved through larger probability samples. Basic research can further explore the role of acculturation, acculturation stress, and psychological predictors for tobacco use, which can provide valuable evidence to inform more effective programming.

Further applied research focused on developing and evaluating prevention and cessation programs is important in order to design culturally sensitive interventions. While attention has been given to investigating different interventions to reduce smoking among White Americans, less attention has been given to members of other ethnic groups living in the U.S. Because each ethnic group experiences immigration and acculturation differently, examining the smoking behaviors of each group is essential (Jadalla & Lee, 2012). Thus, there is a need to develop prevention strategies that consider the acculturation process when trying to control the spread of cigarette and waterpipe use among Arab Americans. There is a great need for the identification of culturally appropriate intervention tools to aid in reducing tobacco use and encouraging smoking cessation among Arab Americans. The integration of pharmacotherapy interventions (e.g. nicotine patch or gum, opioid antagonists) can be evaluated. Furthermore, research regarding interventions would be more effective if developed with a grounding in theoretical models such as the TTM or health belief model.

In addition to formal programs, community-based efforts may also be an important strategy in addressing tobacco-related concerns. Prevention materials can be disseminated in order to educate Arab Americans about smoking, its health-compromising effects, and resources for smoking cessation. Aside from cultural, religious, and educational venues, these materials can also be distributed through various ethnic media channels that can reach wider audiences, such as newspapers, television, and radio programs. They can moreover be shared in scholarly journals to be of use to different healthcare professionals. Social media (e.g. Facebook, Twitter) and websites can be other means of disseminating knowledge around smoking cessation in the Arab American population.

Recognizing the need for more comprehensive, culturally grounded, and participatory approaches to research and interventions targeting complex health issues such as smoking, a community-based participatory research (CBPR) approach should be considered. CBPR (Minkler & Wallerstein, 2008) emphasizes empowerment of community members, who are true partners throughout the process of the applied research project. The aim of CBPR is to "increase knowledge and understanding of a given phenomenon and integrate the knowledge gained with interventions and policy and social change to improve the health and quality of life of community members" (Israel, Eng, Schulz, & Parker, 2013, p. 6). Using a CBPR methodology will ensure that the interventions developed are culturally appropriate to Arab Americans, as participation of community stakeholders is integrated in the design and implementation of the interventions to better address the needs of the population.

Conclusion

Arab Americans report high rates of tobacco use, which places them at risk for health-related concerns. The prevalence of waterpipe use is particularly alarming, and disproportionately affects youth. As such, greater efforts are needed to investigate socio-demographic, cultural, and psychological factors that predict tobacco use, as well as factors that may be protective against experimenting with tobacco. A better understanding of these factors can inform the development of effective prevention and cessation programs that are culturally tailored to Arab Americans. Using more culturally sensitive approaches to interventions, such as CBPR, may enhance ownership and partnership among community stakeholders in combating smoking. This may have a greater impact on transforming cultural beliefs and norms toward a healthier smoke-free vision of the future.

References

Abou-Mediene, S., Rice, V. H., Jamil, H., Templin, T., Hammad, A., Weglicki, L., ... Thompson, F. (2005). A comparison of psychosocial factors and tobacco use among Arab and Arab-American adolescents: Preliminary findings. *Ethnicity & Disease* 15(Suppl. 1), 60–61.

Akl, E. A., Jawad, M., Lam, W. Y., Co, C. N., Obeid, R., & Irani, J. (2013). Motives, beliefs and attitudes towards waterpipe tobacco smoking: A systematic review. *Harm Reduction Journal* 10(12). doi: 10.1186/1477-7517-10-12

Al-Faouri, I., Rice, V. H., Weglicki, L., Kulwicki, A., Jamil, H., Baker, O., ... Dakroub, M. (2005). Culturally sensitive smoking cessation intervention program redesign for Arab American youth. *Ethnicity & Disease* 15(Suppl. 1), 62–64.

Al-Omari, H. & Scheibmeir, M. (2009). Arab Americans' acculturation and tobacco smoking. *Journal of Transcultural Nursing* 20, 227–233. doi: 10.1177/1043659608330353

Alzyoud, S., Haddad, L., El Shahawy, O., Ghadban, R., Kheirallah, K., Alhawamdeh, K. A., & Jin, Y. (2014). Patterns of waterpipe use among Arab immigrants in the USA: A pilot study. *British Journal of Medicine & Medical Research* 4, 816–827. doi: 10.9734/BJMMR/2014/6220

Arab American Institute Foundation. (2012). *Demographics*. Retrieved from http://b.3cdn.net/aai/44b17815d8b386bf16_v0m6iv4b5.pdf

Asi, M. & Beaulieu, D. (2013). *Arab households in the United States: 2006–2010* (American Community Survey Briefs, ACSBR/10–20). Retrieved from www.census.gov/prod/2013pubs/acsbr10-20.pdf

Ayna, D. (2013). *Impulsivity as a correlate of waterpipe tobacco smoking* (Master's thesis). Available from ProQuest Dissertations and Theses database (UMI No. 1542678).

Azar, N. G. (2008). *Health beliefs, acculturation and tobacco use among Arab-Americans living in California* (Doctoral dissertation). Available from ProQuest Dissertations and Theses database (UMI No. 3346500).

Baker, O. (2005). Relationship of parental tobacco use, peer influence, self-esteem, and tobacco use among Yemeni-American adolescents: Mid-range theory testing. *Ethnicity & Diseas*, 15(Suppl. 1), 69–71.

Baker, O. G. & Rice, V. (2008). Predictors of narghile (water-pipe) smoking in a sample of American Arab Yemeni adolescents. *Journal of Transcultural Nursing* 19(1), 24–32. doi: 10.1177/1043659607309141

Becker, M. H. (ed.) (1974). The health belief model and personal health behavior. *Health Education Monographs* 2, 324–508.

Berry, J. W. (1997). Immigration, acculturation, and adaptation. *Applied Psychology* 46(1), 5–34. doi: 10.1111/j.1464-0597.1997.tb01087.x

Berry, J. W. (1998). Acculturation and health: Theory and research. In S. S. Kazarian & D. R. Evans (eds.), *Cultural clinical psychology: Theory, research, and practice* (pp. 39–57). New York: Oxford University Press.

Berry, J. W. (2001). A psychology of immigration. *Journal of Social Issues* 57, 615–631. doi: 10.1111/0022-4537.00231

Berry, J. W. (2005). Acculturation: Living successfully in two cultures. *International Journal of Intercultural Relations* 29, 697–712. doi: 10.1016/j.ijintrel.2005.07.013

Brower, V. (2006). Loosening addiction's deadly grip. *EMBO Reports* 7, 140–142. doi: 10.1038/sj.embor.7400635

Bullen, C. (2008). Impact of tobacco smoking and smoking cessation on cardiovascular risk and disease. *Expert Review of Cardiovascular Therapy* 6, 883–895. doi: 10.1586/14779072.6.6.883

Byrd, T. L., Peterson, S. K., Chavez, R., & Heckert, A. (2004). Cervical cancer screening beliefs among young Hispanic women. *Preventive Medicine* 38, 192–197. doi: 10.1016/j.ypmed.2003.09.017

Centers for Disease Control and Prevention. (2007). State-specific prevalence of cigarette smoking among adults and quitting among persons aged 18–35 years – United States, 2006. *MMWR* 56(38), 993–996. Retrieved from www.cdc.gov/mmwr/preview/mmwrhtml/mm5638a2.htm

Cobb, C., Ward, K. D., Maziak, W., Shihadeh, A. L., & Eissenberg, T. (2010). Waterpipe tobacco smoking: An emerging health crisis in the United States. *American Journal of Health Behavior* 34, 275–285. doi: 10.5993/AJHB.34.3.3

Daffa, R. M. (2010). Waterpipe smoking among Arab American women in San Diego, California (unpublished Master's thesis). San Diego State University, California.

Daniels, J., Farquhar, C., Nathanson, N., Mashalla, Y., Petracca, F., Desmond, M., ... Afya Bora Consortium Working Group Members. (2014). Training tomorrow's global health leaders: Applying a transtheoretical model to identify behavior change stages within an intervention for health leadership development. *Global Health Promotion* 21(4), 24–34. doi: 10.1177/1757975914528726

DiClemente, C. C., Prochaska, J. O., Fairhurst, S. K., Velicer, W. F., Velasquez, M. M., & Rossi, J. S. (1991). The process of smoking cessation: An analysis of precontemplation, contemplation, and preparation stages of change. *Journal of Consulting and Clinical Psychology* 59, 295–304. doi: 10.1037/0022-006X.59.2.295

Dingel, M. J., Karkazis, K., & Koenig, B. A. (2011). Framing nicotine addiction as a "disease of the brain": Social and ethical consequences. *Social Science Quarterly* 92, 1363–1388. doi: 10.1111/j.1540-6237.2011.00822.x

Fakhreddine, H. M. B., Kanj, A. N., & Kanj, N. A. (2014). The growing epidemic of water pipe smoking: Health effects and future needs. *Respiratory Medicine* 108, 1241–1253. doi: 10.1016/j.rmed.2014.07.014

Fava, J. L., Velicer, W. F., & Prochaska, J. (1995). Applying the transtheoretical model to a representative sample of smokers. *Addictive Behaviors* 20, 189–203. doi: 10.1016/0306-4603(94)00062-X

Gökbayrak, N. S., Paiva, A. L., Blissmer, B. J., & Prochaska, J. O. (2015). Predictors of relapse among smokers: Transtheoretical effort variables, demographics, and smoking severity. *Addictive Behaviors* 42, 176–179. doi: 10.1016/j.addbeh.2014.11.022

Grekin, E. R. & Ayna, D. (2008). Argileh use among college students in the United States: An emerging trend. *Journal of Studies on Alcohol and Drugs* 69, 472–475.

Grekin, E. R. & Ayna, D. (2012). Waterpipe smoking among college students in the United States: A review of the literature. *Journal of American College Health* 60, 244–249. doi: 10.1080/07448481.2011.589419

Haddad, L. & Corcoran, J. (2013). Culturally tailored smoking cessation for Arab American male smokers in community settings: A pilot study. *Tobacco Use Insights* 6, 17–23. doi: 10.4137/TUI.S11837

Haddad, L., El-Shahawy, O., & Ghadban, R. (2014). Comparison of barriers to cessation among Arab American smokers of cigarettes and waterpipe. *International Journal of Environmental Research and Public Health* 11, 9522–9531. doi: 10.3390/ijerph110909522

Haddad, L., El-Shahawy, O., Shishani, K., Madanat, H., & Alzyoud, S. (2012). Cigarette use attitudes and effects of acculturation among Arab immigrants in USA: A preliminary study. *Health* 4, 785–793. doi: 10.4236/health.2012.410122

Haddad, L. & Petro-Nustas, W. (2006). Predictors of intention to quit smoking among Jordanian University students. *Canadian Journal of Public Health* 97(1), 9–13.

Hughes, J. R. (2007). Effects of abstinence from tobacco: Valid symptoms and time course. *Nicotine and Tobacco Research* 9, 315–327. doi: 10.1080/14622200701188919

Islam, S. M. S. & Johnson, C. A. (2003). Correlates of smoking behavior among Muslim Arab-American adolescents. *Ethnicity & Health* 8, 319–337. doi: 10.1080/13557850310001631722

Israel, B. A., Eng, E., Schulz, A. J., & Parker, E. A. (2013). *Methods for community-based participatory research for health* (2nd edn.). San Francisco, CA: Jossey-Bass.

Jadalla, A. & Lee, J. (2012). The relationship between acculturation and general health of Arab Americans. *Journal of Transcultural Nursing* 23, 159–165. doi: 10.1177/1043659611434058

Jamil, H., Geeso, S. G., Arnetz, B. B., & Arnetz, J. E. (2014). Risk factors for hookah smoking among Arabs and Chaldeans. *Journal of Immigrant and Minority Health* 16, 501–507. doi: 10.1007/s10903-013-9772-1

Jamil, H., Templin, T., Fakhouri, M., Rice, V. H., Khouri, R., Fakhouri, H., … Baker, O. (2009). Comparison of personal characteristics, tobacco use, and health states in Chaldean, Arab American, and non-Middle Eastern White adults. *Journal of Immigrant and Minority Health* 11, 310–317. doi: 10.1007/s10903-008-9125-7

Janz, N. K. & Becker, M. H. (1984). The health belief model: A decade later. *Health Education & Behavior* 11(1), 1–47. doi: 10.1177/109019818401100101

Jarrett, T., Blosnich, J., Tworek, C., & Horn, K. (2012). Hookah use among U.S. college students: Results from the National College Health Assessment II. *Nicotine & Tobacco Research* 14, 1145–1153. doi: 10.1093/ntr/nts003

Knishkowy, B. & Amitai, Y. (2005). Water-pipe (narghile) smoking: An emerging health risk behavior. *Pediatrics*, 116, e113–e119. doi: 10.1542/peds.2004–2173

Kulwicki, A. & Rice, V. H. (2003). Arab American adolescent perceptions and experiences with smoking. *Public Health Nursing* 20, 177–183. doi: 10.1046/j.0737-1209.2003.20304.x

Lim, J., Gonzalez, P., Wang-Letzkus, M. F., & Ashing-Giwa, K. T. (2009). Understanding the cultural health belief model influencing health behaviors and health-related quality of life between Latina and Asian-American breast cancer survivors. *Supportive Care in Cancer* 17, 1137–1147. doi: 10.1007/s00520-008-0547-5

Martins-Green, M., Adhami, N., Frankos, M., Valdez, M., Goodwin, B., Lyubovitsky, J., … Curras-Collazo, M. (2014). Cigarette smoke toxins deposited on surfaces: Implications for human health. *Public Library of Science ONE Journal* 9(1), e86391. doi: 10.1371/journal.pone.0086391

Matt, G. E., Quintana, P. J. E., Destaillats, H., Gundel, L. A., Sleiman, M., Singer, B. C., … Hovell, M. F. (2011). Thirdhand tobacco smoke: Emerging evidence and arguments for a multidisciplinary research agenda. *Environmental Health Perspectives* 119, 1218–1226. doi: 10.1289/ehp.1103500

Maziak, W., Nakkash, R., Bahelah, R. Husseini, A., Fanous, N., & Eissenberg, T. (2014). Tobacco in the Arab world: Old and new epidemics amidst policy paralysis. *Health Policy and Planning* 29, 784–794. doi: 10.1093/heapol/czt055

Mehta, S. M. (2011). An exploratory study on the impact of acculturation on waterpipe smoking practices among Arab Americans in San Diego, California (unpublished Master's thesis). San Diego, CA: San Diego State University.

Minkler, M. & Wallerstein, N. (2008). *Community-based participatory research for health: From process to outcomes* (2nd edn.). San Francisco, CA: Jossey-Bass.

National Cancer Institute. (2012). *Cancer trends progress report: 2011/2012 update*. Bethesda, MD: National Institutes of Health, U.S. Department of Health and Human Services. Retrieved from http://progressreport.cancer.gov/doc_detail.asp?pid=1&did=2007&chid=71&coid=703&mid

National Institute on Drug Abuse. (2012). *Research report series: Tobacco/nicotine* (NIH Publication No. 12–4342). Retrieved from www.drugabuse.gov/sites/default/files/tobaccorrsv3.pdf

Potenza, M. N. (2013). Biological contributions to addiction in adolescents and adults: Prevention, treatment, and policy implications. *Journal of Adolescent Health* 52(Suppl. 2), 22–32. doi: 10.1016/j.jadohealth.2012.05.007

Prochaska, J. O. & DiClemente, C. C. (1983). Stages and processes of self-change of smoking: Toward an integrative model of change. *Journal of Consulting and Clinical Psychology* 51, 390–395. doi: 10.1037/0022-006X.51.3.390

Rice, V. H. & Kulwicki, A. (1992). Cigarette use among Arab immigrants in the Detroit metropolitan area. *Public Health Reports* 107, 589–594.

Rice, V. H., Templin, T., Hammad, A., Weglicki, L., Jamil, H., & Abou-Mediene, S. (2007). Collaborative research of tobacco use and its predictors in Arab and non-Arab American 9th graders. *Ethnicity & Disease* 17(Suppl. 3), 19–21.

Rice, V. H., Templin, T., & Kulwicki, A. (2003). Arab-American adolescent tobacco use: Four pilot studies. *Preventive Medicine* 37, 492–498. doi: 10.1016/S0091-7435(03)00175-0

Rice, V. H., Templin, T., Weglicki, L., Jamil, H., Hammad, A., Baker, O., … Abou-Mediene, S. (2005). Predictors of tobacco use among Lebanese, Yemeni, and Iraqi adolescents, 14–18 years of age. *Ethnicity & Disease* 15(Suppl. 1), 57–59.

Rice, V. H., Weglicki, L. S., Templin, T., Hammad, A., Jamil, H., & Kulwicki, A. (2006). Predictors of Arab American adolescent tobacco use. *Merrill-Palmer Quarterly* 52, 327–342. doi: 10.1353/mpq.2006.0020

Rice, V. H., Weglicki, L. S., Templin, T., Jamil, H., & Hammad, A. (2010). Intervention effects on tobacco use in Arab and non-Arab American adolescents. *Addictive Behaviors* 35, 46–48. doi: 10.1016/j.addbeh.2009.07.005

Rodríguez-Reimann, D. I., Nicassio, P., Reimann, J. O. F., Gallegos, P. I., & Olmedo, E. L. (2004). Acculturation and health beliefs of Mexican Americans regarding tuberculosis prevention. *Journal of Immigrant Health* 6(2), 51–62. doi: 10.1023/B:JOIH.0000019165.09266.71

Salloum, R. G., Thrasher, J. F., Kates, F. R., & Maziak, W. (2014). Water pipe tobacco smoking in the United States: Findings from the National Adult Tobacco Survey. *Preventive Medicine* 71, 88–93. doi: 10.1016/j.ypmed.2014.12.012

Shamo, F., Robinson, M., Kiley, J., & Boynton, K. (2010). Trends in hookah smoking among Arab Americans in Metro Detroit Michigan and implications for all young adults. *Access Health*, preliminary issue, 51–61.

Unger, J. B., Cruz, T., Shakib, S., Mock, J., Shields, A., Baezconde-Garbanati, L., … Johnson, C. A. (2003). Exploring the cultural context of tobacco use: A transdisciplinary framework. *Nicotine & Tobacco Research* 5(Suppl. 1), S101–S117. doi: 10.1080/14622200310001625546

U.S. Department of Health and Human Services (2014). *The health consequences of smoking – 50 years of progress: A report of the Surgeon General*. Rockville, MD: U.S. Department of Health and Human Services. Retrieved from www.surgeongeneral.gov/library/reports/50-years-of-progress/full-report.pdf

Weglicki, L. S., Templin, T. N., Rice, V. H., Jamil, H., & Hammad, A. (2008). Comparison of cigarette and water-pipe smoking by Arab and non–Arab-American youth. *American Journal of Preventive Medicine* 35, 334–339. doi: 10.1016/j.amepre.2008.06.037

World Health Organization. (2012). *WHO global report: Mortality attributable to tobacco*. Geneva, Switzerland: WHO. Retrieved from www.who.int/tobacco/publications/surveillance/rep_mortality_attributable/en/

World Health Organization. (2013). *WHO report on the global tobacco epidemic, 2013: Enforcing bans on tobacco advertising, promotion and sponsorship*. Geneva, Switzerland: WHO. Retrieved from www.who.int/tobacco/global_report/2013/en/

17

ALCOHOL AND DRUG USE

Prevalence, Predictors, and Interventions

Cynthia L. Arfken and Emily R. Grekin

This chapter addresses alcohol and other drug use among Arab Americans. The problematic use of these substances, whether it is alcohol, illegal drugs, prescription drugs, or over-the-counter drugs, is a major public health and medical problem in the U.S. (Horgan, 2001). Importantly, it exists among every racial and ethnic group examined to date, including Arab Americans. Estimates vary of the costs of alcohol and drug misuse, covering health- and crime-related costs as well as losses in productivity, but one estimate from 1995 was $110 billion for illicit drugs and $167 billion for alcohol (Harwood, 2000). Since then, deaths from prescription drugs have increased (Paulozzi, Budnitz, & Xi, 2006).

Potential consequences of drug and alcohol use for the individual include the development of chronic diseases such as cirrhosis, development of psychiatric disorders, acute injury such as involvement in a motor vehicle accident, social problems, legal complications, and death. Although drinking and taking drugs at any age can cause acute problems, earlier use is more likely to progress to problems than use initiated later (Grant, Stinson, & Harford, 2001). Because adolescents' brains are still biologically developing in the areas of judgment and self-control, they are especially likely to try something risky and be more susceptible to pressure from their peers to drink and use drugs (U.S. Department of Health and Human Services, 2007). Thus, prevention programs need to start young.

To prevent and reduce access to substances, researchers and policy makers have looked at environmental interventions such as banning the substance (e.g. heroin), restricting sales by place or time (e.g. alcohol), requiring prescription by authorized physician (e.g. opioid pain reliever), taxation (e.g. alcohol), and point of sales interventions (e.g. verifying age before purchase). To target interventions to the individual, researchers have investigated psychological and social risk and protective factors guided by different theoretical models (discussed below). Importantly, the risk and protective factors can theoretically differ at different stages along the continuum of use, from first experimentation with the substance to continued use and development of a substance use disorder. Additionally, there may be unique risk and protective factors for relapse after successful attempts to quit.

Addiction is a chronic disease characterized by a loss of control over substance use and continued use despite harmful consequences. It can be relapsing, similar to other chronic diseases, but like other chronic diseases it can be managed successfully (McLellan, Lewis, O'Brien, & Kleber, 2000). Research has repeatedly shown that medication for alcohol and opiate dependence, and therapy for all substances, are effective for most patients (Anton, et al., 2006; National Institute on Drug Abuse, 2009). Treatment approaches should be tailored to the substance abuse patterns of the individual and any co-occurring medical, psychiatric, and social problems. Importantly, treatment approaches should also be tailored to the culture of the affected person.

Before discussing alcohol and drug use among Arab Americans, it is useful to consider the alcohol and drug picture in Arab countries. Arab Americans trace their ancestry to an area with one of the lowest per capita consumption of alcohol in the world (World Health Organization, 2011). Consequently, Arab Americans may believe that alcohol and drugs are not a problem in their community. The low consumption per capita is directly attributable to the majority religion of the Arab countries, Islam, which prohibits the consumption and trafficking of alcohol (Michalak & Trocki, 2006). However, the low per capita consumption does not mean that alcohol use is absent. There are documented alcohol, heroin, cocaine, stimulant, and marijuana problems in Arab countries, as attested to by hospital admissions among both male and female Arabs (AbuMadini, Rahim, Al-Zahrani, & Al-Johi, 2008; Hasan et al., 2009). Moreover, reports point to alcohol and drug use increasing in Arab countries (Karam, Maalouf, & Ghandour, 2004), possibly due to changing economic and social environments. In the U.S., the easy accessibility of alcohol and drugs, as well as social expectations, would be expected to impact Arab Americans' use of alcohol and drugs.

Two additional points are important for understanding alcohol and drug use among Arab Americans. First, the misuse of alcohol and drugs is highly stigmatized in Arab countries, regardless of religious affiliation. The stigmatization is consistent with the emphasis placed upon family honor among Arabs; such stigmatization is common among racial/ethnic groups with a collectivist (as compared to individualistic) perspective. The stigmatization has resulted in pathways to alcohol and drug treatment dominated by external pressures such as family and the criminal justice system (Al-Krenawi, 2005). The second point is the level of conflict within Arab countries. These conflicts include civil wars (i.e. Lebanon, Iraq, Yemen, and Syria) as well as the ongoing Israeli-Palestinian conflict. The conflicts may result in people using alcohol or other substances to cope with traumatic symptoms. The trauma thus may influence use and misuse among Arab Americans. If trauma exposure history is present among an Arab American, it certainly complicates alcohol and drug treatment.

For all the above reasons, alcohol and drug use among Arab Americans is an understudied but important area. The stereotype that there is no alcohol or drug use among Arab Americans undervalues needed research to develop culturally appropriate and focused programs for prevention and treatment of alcohol and drug problems in this community. It also robs psychologists of research to inform them of the extent of the problem and tested approaches.

This chapter is divided into a description of relevant causal models for substance abuse, followed by a discussion of research on substance abuse among Arab Americans. The chapter concludes with a case example and a critique of existing research. The emphasis in the chapter is on people who can trace their ancestry to Arab countries and live in the U.S. There is a sizable population in Canada of people with Arab ancestry, but research on substance abuse among them is in the nascent stage. Finally, the chapter uses the term "abuse" to encompass a range of problematic behaviors from misuse (e.g. nonmedical use of opioid pain reliever for psychic effect) to substance use disorder as defined by the *DSM-5* (American Psychiatric Association, 2013).

Causal Models of Substance Abuse Relevant to Arab Americans

A variety of causal models has been put forth to describe the motivating factors underlying substance abuse. While older models tend to focus solely on biological (e.g. the disease model) or environmental (e.g. peer influence models) risk factors, more recent models take an integrative approach. These integrative models emphasize that risk for substance abuse is influenced by a combination of genes, biology (e.g. individual differences in alcohol metabolism), environment (e.g. peer influence), and culture (e.g. cultural attitudes toward substance use). Notably, some risk factors for substance abuse appear to be universal. For example, peer drinking and a family history of substance use are variables that increase the risk for substance use across virtually all races/ethnicities (Elliott, Carey, & Bonafide, 2012; Hawkins, Catalano, & Miller, 1992; Schuckit, 2009). Other risk factors, however, may be more culturally specific or may affect certain groups differently than others. The following sections present four causal models of substance use that are particularly relevant to Arab American populations: acculturation, positive affect regulation, self-medication, and deviance proneness.

Acculturation

For immigrant Arab Americans, psychological acculturation may impact both substance use and abuse. Berry (1997) delineated four potential acculturation pathways including: (1) assimilation, or identification and behaviors consistent with the culture of the new country; (2) integration, which is identification and behaviors consistent with both the culture of the new country and the country of origin; (3) separation, defined as identification and behavior consistent with the culture of the country of origin; and (4) marginalization, or not identifying or behaving consistently with the culture of either the new country or the country of origin. Portes and Zhou (1993) presented a theory of "segmented assimilation," which described several assimilation paths, including: (a) "straight line assimilation," or gradual assimilation into the American middle class; (b) "downward assimilation," or gradual assimilation into the lower class/urban underclass; and (c) "selective acculturation," or the desire to preserve one's ethnic culture.

Recent studies indicate that full integration into American culture (i.e. Berry's assimilation) may be associated with risky behaviors such as substance use. For example, using data from the National Longitudinal Study of Adolescent Health, Xie and Greenman (2011) found that, among immigrant adolescents living in nonpoor neighborhoods, assimilation was associated with higher educational achievement and better psychological wellbeing but also with more substance use, delinquency, and risky sexual behavior. Similarly Masel, Rudkin, and Peek (2006) using data from the Hispanic Established Populations for the Epidemiologic Studies of the Elderly, found that, among a large sample of older Mexican-Americans, proficiency in English and greater contact with European Americans predicted a higher likelihood of smoking and drinking.

Acculturation has also been associated with greater substance use among Arab Americans. For example Arfken, Kubiak, and Farrag (2009), using a sample of Arab Americans seeking treatment for substance abuse, found that rates of polysubstance abuse were highest among clients who had lived in the U.S. for more than 10 years and who were fluent in English. Although the explanation for these findings is not entirely clear, it is possible that as immigrants acculturate into American culture, protective factors associated with their native culture (e.g. religiosity, connection to family) are weakened. Support for this hypothesis comes from a study by Harker (2001) who found that, in comparison to U.S.-born adolescents, adolescents who immigrated to the U.S. reported higher levels of parental supervision, religiosity, and social support, and lower levels of parent-child conflict. This theory points to the need to examine alcohol and drug use among second generation Arab Americans.

Positive Affect Regulation

Another causal model of substance use is that of positive affect regulation. While some individuals use substances to self-medicate or relieve distress, others do so to enhance positive emotions. This positive affect model has been particularly well established across racial/ethnic groups in the alcohol use literature. Self-reported enhancement motives for drinking (i.e. drinking to get high or because "it feels good") have been associated with binge drinking (Kuntsche, Knibbe, Gmel, & Engels, 2005), getting drunk (Cooper, 1994; Kuntsche et al., 2005) and alcohol-related problems (though often indirectly, through the influence of heavy drinking; Cooper, 1994). Enhancement motives for drinking have also been associated with the personality traits of extraversion and sensation seeking (Stewart & Devine, 2000) and appear to be particularly common among adolescents who drink as a means of socializing (going to parties, bars, etc.; Cooper, 1994).

Although few studies have examined drinking motives among Arab Americans, recent focus group data (Arfken, Owens, & Said, 2012) suggest that celebration and positive affect enhancement are primary reasons for drinking among young Arab Americans. As one focus group participant noted, "How can you have fun without getting drunk?" (p. 283). It should also be noted that, although rates of past-month alcohol use are lower among Arab Americans than among non-Hispanic Whites, rates of binge drinking – defined as five drinks for a man and four drinks for a woman consumed over approximately two hours – have been found to be virtually identical across the two groups (Arfken, Arnetz, Fakhouri, Ventimiglia, & Jamil, 2011). These results suggest that researchers should investigate if Arab Americans tend to consume alcohol at parties and celebrations rather than in the home (as a daily affair).

Self-Medication

Perhaps the most enduring causal model of substance abuse is the self-medication theory (SMT; Khantzian, 2003). In its simplest form, the SMT states that individuals use substances in order to reduce stress or negative affect. Support for this hypothesis comes from the fact that large-scale, population-based studies have found strong associations between affective (mood and anxiety) disorders and substance dependence, even after controlling for demographic variables (Grant, Stinson, Dawson, Chou, Dufuor, et al., 2004; Kessler et al., 1997). Additional support comes from the fact that many substances (e.g. alcohol, opiates) have well established anxiolytic properties. Despite these findings, it is important to note that support for the SMT has been inconsistent. In particular, studies examining associations between nonclinical negative affect (e.g. everyday sadness, rather than clinical depression) and substance use have yielded small or null results (Greeley & Oei, 1999; Sher & Grekin, 2007). Moreover, evidence suggests that the use of substances to self-medicate is highly dependent on situational (e.g. the availability of alternative coping strategies) and individual difference (e.g. motives for use, severity of negative affect) variables. This has led researchers to conclude that the SMT may only apply to some individuals in some situations (Greeley & Oei, 1999; Sher & Grekin, 2007).

Self-medication models of substance abuse may be particularly relevant for Arab Americans for two reasons. First, many Arab Americans have emigrated from war-torn countries and have been exposed to war-related trauma such as violence, displacement, and loss of family. Research shows that both trauma exposure (Del Gaizo, Elhai, & Weaver, 2011) and associated posttraumatic stress disorder (Del Gaizo et al., 2011; Gootzeit & Markon, 2011) predict substance misuse, with more severe trauma predicting higher rates of substance-related consequences (Read et al., 2012). Second, many Arab Americans face ongoing prejudice and discrimination (Baker et al., 2009). Perceived discrimination is a pernicious stressor associated with substance use in other minority groups (e.g. Borrell et al., 2007; McLaughlin, Hatzenbuehler, & Keyes, 2010). While few studies have examined mechanisms underlying the relationship between discrimination and substance use, those that have support a self-medication framework. Specifically, they suggest that distress mediates the relationship between discrimination and substance use (Gibbons, Gerrard, Cleveland, Wills, & Brody, 2004). The discrimination-alcohol use relationship is stronger for those who drink to cope with negative emotions (Gibbons, Pomery, & Gerrard, 2010). Support for this causal model for substance abuse among Arab Americans has not been empirically investigated.

Deviance Proneness

The deviance proneness model (Sher, Walitzer, Wood, & Brent, 1991) conceptualizes substance abuse as one manifestation of a broad, persistent tendency toward deviance or antisocial behavior. Supporting this model is a large literature demonstrating robust associations between antisocial behavior and multiple types of substance abuse across different racial/ethnic groups (Grant, Stinson, Dawson, Chou, Ruan, et al., 2004; Markon & Krueger, 2005). Moreover, longitudinal studies indicate that childhood conduct problems, childhood academic problems, and early interpersonal problems all predict the development of future substance abuse (Conner & Lochman, 2010; Sher, Grekin, & Williams, 2005; Zucker, Fitzgerald, & Moses, 1995). Genetic studies also lend support to the deviance proneness model by suggesting that antisocial behavior and substance abuse share a common genetic vulnerability (Slutske et al., 1998). For example, Hicks, Krueger, Iacono, McGue, and Patrick (2004) examined the familial transmission of externalizing pathology among 542 families participating in the Minnesota Twin Family Study and found both a broad genetic vulnerability to externalizing pathology, as well as a more specific genetic vulnerability to conduct disorder, alcohol use disorder, and drug use disorder.

Deviance proneness may be a particularly strong risk factor for alcohol and drug use in cultures where substance use is highly stigmatized. More specifically, if individuals engage in substance use as a way to rebel against societal norms, they may be particularly likely to do so when anti-substance use norms are strong, as is the case in the Arab American community.

Prevalence of Substance Abuse Among Arab Americans

Information is limited on substance abuse among Arab Americans. Developing targeted prevention and intervention services requires community-based estimates on the prevalence of lifetime use (ever used), past month use (current use), misuse (e.g. heavy drinking, binge drinking), and abuse. Ideally, incidence of substance use disorder and age of onset would also be available. This information is currently available for major racial/ethnic groups in the U.S. through national and state level population-based surveys.

In the U.S., the only national survey that provides ongoing detailed information on alcohol and drug use is the National Survey of Drug Use and Health, an annual population-based survey of alcohol and drug use among community-dwelling people in the U.S. aged 12 years or older. This survey has one question on place of birth that can be used to identify immigrant Arab Americans. However, the answer to this question would not identify Arab Americans born in the U.S. or other countries (e.g. born in Canada but both parents are from Arab countries and the person self-identifies as Arab American). Using this survey, Arfken and colleagues (2011) found Arab immigrants had lower rates of lifetime alcohol use (50.8%), past month use (26.4%), and binge drinking (10%) than non-Hispanic U.S.-born White Americans. The study does not address why alcohol use is lower among Arab immigrants. Alternative explanations could include stigmatizing substance misuse, as discussed at the beginning of the chapter, or characteristics of the immigrants.

To address alternative reasons for substance abuse among Arab immigrants, marijuana and prescription medications misuse/dependence were examined (Arfken, Jamil, & Arnetz, 2012). The analysis used Canadian immigrants to control for immigration effects and other Middle Eastern immigrants (i.e. Iran, Afghanistan, and Pakistan) to control for being born in a country with high stigmatization of substance use. Again, Arab immigrants were less likely to have ever used marijuana (18.3%) and prescription drugs (10.3%) for nonmedical reasons than the White non-Hispanic U.S.-born group or the Canadian immigrants, suggesting that general immigrant effects did not explain the difference. The pattern of low drug use among Arab immigrants was similar to that of other Middle Eastern immigrants consistently across gender, age, education, and religiosity levels, suggesting that a stigmatizing attitude in the country of origin is important. Thus, it appears that the lower prevalence of marijuana and nonmedical prescription drug use among Arab immigrants appears to be more influenced by stigmatizing and the collectivist environment of their country of origin as opposed to general immigration factors.

However, there was no statistically detected difference in prevalence of either marijuana or prescription drug use disorder among Arab immigrants, the White non-Hispanic U.S.-born group, Canadian immigrants, and other Middle Eastern immigrants (Arfken, Jamil, & Arnetz, 2012). This suggests that the prevalence of current drug use disorder among immigrant Arab Americans (1.5% for marijuana use disorder and 0.6% for prescription drug disorder) may be just as high as rates among the White non-Hispanic U.S.-born group, and underscores the need for more research on prevention and treatment of substance use disorder.

Survey information on alcohol and drug use among Arab Americans at the state level is likewise scarce. Currently, the only state-level ongoing survey with substance use data for Arab Americans is the Michigan Behavioral Risk Factor Surveillance System, a population-based telephone survey of Michigan adults 18 years or older. In 2007, the Michigan survey added a question about self-reported Arab or Chaldean origin; thus, the survey captures both immigrants and later generations of Arab Americans as long as they answer the phone, speak English, and self-identify as Arab American. The statewide survey found lower rates of past month alcohol use among Arab Americans (45.6%) than among non-Hispanic Whites. However, there was no difference for binge drinking (17.0% among Arab/Chaldean Americans) compared to non-Hispanic Whites, supporting positive affect regulation theory. In analyses limited to those who reported drinking in the past month, the rate of binge drinking was 38.2% among Arab Americans who drank (Arfken et al., 2011).

The above research has examined commonly abused drugs, such as alcohol, marijuana, and prescription medications, among Arab Americans. However, no discussion of substance abuse among Arab Americans would be complete without discussing khat (or qat). Khat is a plant grown in the Horn of Africa and the Arabian Peninsula with leaves that are chewed. It is used predominately by Yemeni and Somali Americans. Fresh khat contains cathinone, a Schedule I psychostimulant (no medical use and high abuse potential). Over time, the cathinone degrades to cathine, a Schedule IV drug (medical use with little abuse potential). Although street dealers may say they have reyhdrated khat, the forensic laboratories of the U.S. Drug Enforcement Administration have found degradation is only minimized through rapid drying (Chappell & Lee, 2010). Cathinone has been associated with psychosis, dependency, and medical problems (Balint, Falkay, & Balint, 2009; Kroll, Yusuf, & Fujiwara, 2011). Unfortunately, little epidemiologic research on khat use has been conducted in the U.S.

Risk and Protective Factors for Substance Abuse Among Arab Americans

Identifying predictors of substance abuse among Arab Americans is in its early stages. In the general population, risk factors include: (a) demographic factors, such as being male and attending college (Slutske, 2005; Wallace et al., 2003); (b) biological factors, such as having a family history of substance use disorder or being impulsive (Grekin & Sher, 2006; Schuckit, 2009); and (c) environmental factors, such as trauma exposure and low parental monitoring and involvement (Brady, Back, & Coffey, 2004; Fallu, Brière, & Janosz, 2014). These risk factors reflect the different causal models investigated with surveys, cohort studies, and experimental studies. Importantly, the risk factors may differ for different substances and different points from experimentation to substance use disorder.

Although there is minimal information from community-based surveys on Arab Americans and a lack of cohort studies, data from substance abuse treatment and qualitative studies can suggest possible risk and protective factors for substance abuse among Arab Americans. In Michigan, studies using treatment samples are possible because the alcohol and drug use disorder treatment admission forms contain Arab American both as a race and as an ethnicity option. In one analysis using only the admission forms, Arab Americans showed male predominance (like the general population) and high geographic clustering in the metropolitan area (Arfken, Kubiak, & Farrag, 2008).

More information on risk and protective factors may be obtained from chart review of Arab American treatment clients. Arfken, Kubiak, and Farrag (2009) examined acculturation and religious affiliation using medical charts at one Arab-centric substance abuse clinic in a predominately Muslim geographic area. The charts had information on country of birth and origin, length of time in the U.S., English language proficiency, and religious affiliation. Of Arab American male clients who had been in the U.S. for fewer than 10 years and were not proficient in English, 73.2% had alcohol use disorders. However, the prevalence increased to 90.5% for those who had lived more than 10 years in the U.S. and were fluent in English. Among the male Arab American clients, 91.9% of the Muslim clients had a history of drinking and 94.4% of the Christian clients had a history of drinking. These findings support acculturation as a risk factor for alcohol use disorder. Moreover, the findings support the view that alcohol use transcends religious affiliation. The findings are limited to males, as very few Arab American females entered the Arab-centric treatment clinic, although the statewide administrative database documents that there were Arab American females who entered treatment elsewhere.

Qualitative studies can also inform analysis of risk and protective factors. Building upon survey data showing high levels of binge drinking among Arab Americans in Michigan (Arfken et al., 2011) and the chart review suggesting acculturation was a risk factor (Arfken, Kubiak, & Farrag, 2009), Arfken, Owens, and Said (2012) conducted a qualitative study among young (18–29-year-old) Arab Americans. Binge drinking is especially prevalent among young people. Treatment is usually counseling in primary care or with a therapist outside formal substance abuse treatment, and as such cannot be investigated using administrative data or chart reviews. Using purposive sampling, 12 focus groups of young men and women were conducted in the metropolitan Detroit area with separate focus groups for Muslims from Lebanon, Syria, and Palestine; Muslims from Yemen; Orthodox Christians; and Chaldeans (Arfken, Owens, & Said, 2012). Although there were some differences by religion and country of origin, social influences were preeminent, consistent with the positive affect regulation causal model. The young Arab Americans wanted to belong to a group, and if that meant binge drinking, then they would binge drink. Among the young Chaldeans, drinking among men was a status symbol; drinking among women was not permitted. These gender-based prohibitions, while still respected, appeared to be loosening with time in the U.S. and among second generation Chaldeans. These results are consistent with acculturation as a risk factor, but more definitive studies are needed.

Formal and Informal Substance Use Disorder Treatment for Arab Americans

There is limited information on effective formal substance abuse treatment among Arab Americans. Although unpublished data suggest that Arab Americans may have similar treatment completion as other racial/ethnic groups (as mentioned in Hammad, Arfken, Rice, & Said, 2014), there may be specific barriers to Arab Americans completing treatment. For example, a qualitative study of Arab American clients found a perception of stigma toward alcohol and drug use within the Arab American community. Language barriers and therapists' lack of understanding of the Arab culture also acted as obstacles to completing treatment (Arfken, Berry, & Owens, 2009).

Factors associated with Arab Americans entering treatment may differ from the general population. To examine possible pathways to treatment, the descriptions of presenting problems, or chief complaints, for people seeking substance abuse treatment in the predominately Muslim area of metropolitan Detroit were reviewed (Arfken, Kubiak, & Farrag, 2009; Arfken, Said, & Owens, 2012). It was hypothesized that Arab Americans would be more likely than other ethnicities to report external forces (e.g. criminal justice system or family) as presenting problems. The results confirmed that 43.2% of Arab Americans did mention criminal justice involvement as a reason for seeking treatment. This figure was consistent among both female and male Arab Americans and higher than that for the other racial/ethnic groups in the region. To put this percentage in perspective, Arfken, Said, and Owens (2012) examined criminal justice involvement as the reason for substance abuse treatment across major racial/ethnic groups using national data. The percentage of Native Americans, Asian Americans, and Latinos (with the exception of Puerto Ricans) citing criminal justice as a pathway to treatment was higher than that of African Americans and Whites, suggesting that people from collectivist cultures share criminal justice as a main pathway to treatment. Unfortunately, data on Arab Americans as an ethnic group is not collected nationally.

Treatment, whether formal or informal, needs to reflect substance use disorder as a chronic disease. One step in that direction was the development of a bilingual self-help group for Arab Americans. Self-help or 12-step programs are considered informal treatment. The programs are based upon active participation by people to accept and work on their alcohol and/or drug problems, with each person encouraged to speak and be heard by others at meetings. As 12-step programs have been shown to promote recovery from addiction (Fiorentine & Hillhouse, 2000) and court judges can order Arabic-speaking defendants (and others) to attend them, there was a need for one in Arabic. To address this gap, Alec Berry created the first (to the authors' knowledge) Arabic-English bilingual 12-step program in Michigan. Alec Berry, an American-born Arab American, is a Muslim American in recovery from alcohol use disorder. He served both as the group translator, liaising with the larger recovery community, and as a role model for Arab Americans to accept and work on their personal recovery. He utilized a bilingual approach in order to include non-Arab Americans in the 12-step meetings for additional modeling and assistance. With his retirement, the group discontinued, and as of this writing, there is a gap in treatment services available.

Community-Based Interventions

Community-based interventions also play an important role in addressing substance use disorder. The Arab Community Center for Economic and Social Services (ACCESS) in Dearborn, Michigan, has demonstrated leadership in this area. For example, ACCESS staff has provided prevention programs at local schools with high proportions of Arab American students. The curriculum builds upon the cultural values of family involvement and parental monitoring to enhance protective factors. Unfortunately, to date, it has not been evaluated for effectiveness or for the extent to which it is acceptable to the Arab American community. Other efforts by ACCESS have included efforts to establish a community coalition with law enforcement personnel, youth, school officials, and parents to reduce youth substance use. At the beginning, people were willing to participate, especially following publicity given to driving while intoxicated after a prominent Muslim Arab American was charged with manslaughter. However, over time the coalition disintegrated. Based on comments of community members, the first author of this chapter observed that one of the main barriers to continued participation was resistance from the Arab American community to the idea that there was a problem with alcohol and drug use.

Case Example: Ali Hussein, Businessman with Problematic Alcohol Use

Ali Hussein is a recently divorced middle-aged, successful businessman who immigrated to Michigan in the 1980s as a child with his extended family to escape the civil war in Lebanon. He has some college education, is fluent in both Arabic and English, and lives in a predominately Muslim Arab American community. He has a history of bipolar disorder for which he is currently receiving medication. The medical care was only initiated after his cousin, a social worker, convinced him that he should seek care.

Mr. Hussein also receives individual therapy for alcohol use disorder because of a court order. He explained that one evening, after he and his wife were drinking, he threatened to hit her. She called her father, who called the police. As part of his probation for battery, he agreed to seek alcohol use disorder treatment. He attends treatment sessions in accordance with the probation terms. However, he insists that all treatment be individual therapy and refuses to attend group therapy or 12-step programs. As mentioned above, he lives in a predominately Muslim community where drinking alcohol is stigmatized. Thus, he believes that public knowledge of his alcohol use disorder treatment would destroy his business. Even though he attends therapy, Mr. Hussein categorically denies any drinking problems and says that his now former wife "parties" just as much as he did.

Mr. Hussein's divorce has caused a split in the extended family (he and his ex-wife are second cousins), which is very stressful to him. Although on medication for bipolar disorder, he reports continued problems with depression, which he attributes to his arranged marriage (to his now ex-wife) as opposed to being allowed to marry the woman he loved. In therapy, he reports exposure to traumatic events (e.g. witnessing people killed in Lebanon) and meets criteria for posttraumatic stress disorder (PTSD). He also reports that family members in the U.S. and Lebanon have mood swings and problems following heavy alcohol use, but states that no one has ever had treatment for either of these issues.

This case example illustrates multiple points about alcohol and drug problems among Arab Americans. Substance use disorder exists among diverse Arab Americans, including successful and educated ones. Arab Americans with substance use disorders can have strong identification and ties to their family, culture, and community (i.e. they are not necessarily assimilated in the U.S. culture or marginalized from the Arab culture). Mr. Hussein had an arranged marriage to a second cousin, an indicator of traditional Arab customs. He is also a Muslim and aware of the strong community stigma against substance abuse and – in the Muslim Arab community – against alcohol use. Similar to the research findings of pathways to treatment, he entered treatment through the criminal justice system

The case also illustrates the critical importance of outreach by family for behavioral health issues; his cousin was the one who convinced him to seek treatment for bipolar disorder. Similar to other U.S. clients, Mr. Hussein has a family history of substance use disorder and psychiatric comorbidity. Although it has been debated if psychiatric comorbidity reflects self-medication or other causal pathways (e.g. common neuronal processes), psychiatric comorbidity must be assessed in substance use disorder treatment. The case example also illustrates challenges to treatment when the patient is coping with social consequences of alcohol problems (divorce and the split in the extended family), on top of being afraid of being seen in treatment and having limited insight. For people who experience these challenges, it may be easier to integrate substance use disorder treatment into primary care through, for example, co-location of psychologists and addiction specialists in primary care clinics.

Critique

As described throughout this chapter, few studies examine substance abuse among Arab Americans, and those that do are limited in a number of important ways. First, existing studies are almost exclusively cross-sectional. As a result, it is difficult to make causal inferences about factors associated with substance use. For example, it is not clear whether being religious predicts lowered substance use, or whether using substances predicts lowered religiosity. Similarly, it is not clear whether a preexisting tendency toward deviance predicts substance use, or whether using substances causes individuals to act in deviant ways. Second, existing studies rely heavily on a small number of data sets that are not nationally representative (most are from Michigan) and are not designed specifically to assess Arab American substance use. Thus, there is a need for additional studies that are specifically designed to test a priori hypotheses about Arab American substance use.

Third, existing studies have not addressed attempts among Arab Americans to quit using either alcohol or other drugs. Moreover, nothing has been published in the scholarly literature about tailoring substance abuse treatment approaches or prevention efforts to Arab Americans. Additionally, there are no well-validated, culturally competent substance use disorder therapies specifically targeted to the Arab American community. Future studies are needed to explore these treatment-related issues. Finally, little epidemiologic research has been conducted in the U.S. on khat, a drug used by many Yemeni and Somali Americans. Thus, it is not clear to what extent this drug is being used or what, if any, consequences it causes.

Conclusion

The research presented in this chapter has important implications for scholars as well as clinicians working with Arab American clients, especially immigrants. First, the potential for stigma surrounding alcohol and drug use in the Arab American community may be high, and therefore many Arab Americans enter treatment only under pressure from the criminal justice system.

Stigma and forced treatment may result in challenges to the treatment process, as well as decreased self-efficacy and motivation to change among clients. As such, using nonconfrontational, client-centered approaches, such as motivational interviewing, may help build rapport and readiness to change. Moreover, it is important to recognize and appreciate the often daunting barriers that some Arab Americans face when seeking treatment (e.g. finding an Arabic-speaking therapist, lack of transportation, lack of financial resources). Future research should further examine the factors that may exacerbate the prevalence, severity, and persistence of substance use among Arab Americans, including trauma, chronic discrimination, and high levels of shame and secrecy surrounding alcohol and drug use.

References

AbuMadini, M., Rahim, S., Al-Zahrani, M., & Al-Johi, A. (2008). Two decades of treatment seeking for substance use disorders in Saudi Arabia: Trends and patterns in a rehabilitation facility in Dammam. *Drug and Alcohol Dependence* 97, 231–236. doi: 10.1016/j.drugalcdep.2008.03.034

Al-Krenawi, A. (2005). Mental health practice in Arab countries. *Current Opinion in Psychiatry* 18(5), 560–565.

American Psychiatric Association. (2013). *Diagnostic and statistical manual of mental disorders* (5th edn.). doi: 10.1176/appi.books.9780890425596.910646

Anton, R. F., O'Malley, S. S., Ciraulo, D. A., Cisler, R. A., Couper, D., Donovan, D. M., ... Zweben, A. (2006). Combined pharmacotherapies and behavioral interventions for alcohol dependence. The COMBINE study: a randomized controlled trial. *Journal of the American Medical Association* 295, 2003–2017. doi: 10.1001/jama.295.17.2003

Arfken, C., Arnetz, B. B., Fakhouri, M., Ventimiglia, M. J., & Jamil, H. (2011). Alcohol use among Arab Americans: What is the prevalence? *Journal of Immigrant and Minority Health* 13, 713–718. doi: 10.1007/s10903-011-9447-8

Arfken, C., Berry, A., & Owens, D. (2009). Pathways for Arab Americans to substance abuse treatment in Southeastern Michigan. *Journal of Muslim Mental Health* 4, 31–46. doi: 10.1080/15564900902785457

Arfken, C. L., Jamil, H., Arnetz, B. B. (2012). Marijuana and non-medical prescription drug use among immigrant Arab Americans. *New Iraqi Journal of Medicine* 8, 7–13.

Arfken, C., Kubiak, S., & Farrag, M. (2008). Arab Americans in publicly financed alcohol/other drug abuse treatment. *Alcoholism Treatment Quarterly* 26(3), 229–240. doi: 10.1080/07347320802071547

Arfken, C., Kubiak, S., & Farrag, M. (2009). Acculturation and polysubstance abuse in Arab-American treatment clients. *Transcultural Psychiatry* 46, 608–622. doi: 10.1177/1363461509351364

Arfken, C. L., Owens, D., and Said, M. (2012). Binge drinking among Arab/Chaldeans: An exploratory study. *Journal of Ethnicity in Substance Abuse* 11, 277–293. doi: 10.1080/15332640.2012.735163

Arfken, C. L., Said, M., and Owens, D. (2012). Racial and ethnic differences in reported criminal justice referral at treatment admission. *Journal of Psychoactive Drug* 44, 428–433. doi: 10.1080/02791072.2012.736847

Baker, W., Howell, S., Jamal, A., Lin, A., Shryock, A., Stockton, R., & Tessler, M. (2009). *Citizenship and crisis: Arab Detroit after 9/11*. New York: Russell Sage Foundation.

Balint, E. E., Falkay, G., & Balint, G. A. (2009). Khat – a controversial plant. *Wiener Klinische Wochenschrift* 121(19–20), 604–614. doi: 10.1007/s00508-009-1259-7

Berry, J. W. (1997). Immigration, acculturation, and adaptation. *Applied Psychology* 46, 5–34. doi: 10.1111/j.1464-0597.1997.tb01087

Borrell, L. N., Jacobs, D. R., Williams, D. R., Pletcher, M. J., Houston T. K., & Liefe, C. I. (2007). Self-reported racial discrimination and substance use in the coronary artery risk development in adults study. *American Journal of Epidemiology* 166, 1068–1079. doi: 10.1093/aje/kwm180

Brady, K. T., Back, S. E., & Coffey, S. F. (2004). Substance abuse and post-traumatic stress disorder. *Current Directions in Psychological Science* 13, 206–209. doi: 10.1111/j.0963-7214.2004.00309.x

Chappell, J. S. & Lee, M. M. (2010). Cathinone preservation in khat evidence via drying. *Forensic Science International* 195(1), 108–120. doi: 10.1016/j.forsciint.2009.12.002

Conner B. T. & Lochman, J. E. (2010). Comorbid conduct disorder and substance use disorders. *Clinical Psychology: Science and Practice* 17, 337–349. doi: 10.1111/j.1468-2850.2010.01225.x

Cooper, M. L. (1994). Motivations for alcohol use among adolescents: Development and validation of a four-factor-model. *Psychological Assessment* 6, 117–128. doi: 10.1037/1040-3590.6.2.117

Del Gaizo, A. L., Elhai, J. D., & Weaver, T. L. (2011). Posttraumatic stress disorder, poor physical health and substance use behaviors in a national trauma-exposed sample. *Psychiatry Research* 188, 390–395. doi: 10.1016/j.psychres.2011.03.016

Elliott, J. C., Carey, K. B., & Bonafide, K. E. (2012). Does family history of alcohol problems influence college and university drinking or substance use? A meta-analytical review. *Addiction* 107, 1774–1785. doi: 10.1016/j.1360-0443.2012.03903

Fallu, J., Brière, F. N., & Janosz, M. (2014). Latent classes of substance use in adolescent cannabis users: Predictors and subsequent substance-related harm. *Frontiers in Psychiatry* 5(9). doi: 10.3389/fpsyt.2014.00009

Fiorentine, R. & Hillhouse, M. P. (2000). Drug treatment and 12-step program participation: The additive effects of integrated recovery activities. *Journal of Substance Abuse Treatment* 18(1), 65–74. doi: 10.1016/S0740-5472(99)00020-3

Gibbons, F. X., Gerrard, M., Cleveland, M. J., Wills, T. A., & Brody, G. (2004). Perceived discrimination and substance use in African American parents and their children: A panel study. *Journal of Personality and Social Psychology* 84, 517–529. doi: 10.1037/0022-3514.86.4.517

Gibbons, F. X., Pomery, E. A., & Gerrard, M. (2010). Racial discrimination and substance abuse: Risk and protective factors in African American adolescents. In L. Scheier (ed.), *Handbook of drug use etiology: Theory, methods, and empirical findings* (pp. 341–361). Washington, D.C.: American Psychological Association.

Gootzeit, J. & Markon, K. (2011). Factors of PTSD: Differential specificity and external correlates. *Clinical Psychology Review* 31, 993–1003. doi: 10.1016/j.cpr.2011.06.005

Grant, B. F., Stinson, F. S., Dawson, D. A., Chou, S. P., Dufuor, M. C., Compton, W., … Kaplan, K. (2004). Prevalence and co-occurrence of substance use disorders and independent mood and anxiety disorders: Results from the National Epidemiologic Survey on Alcohol and Related Conditions. *Archives of General Psychiatry* 61, 807–816. doi: 10.1001/archpsyc.61.8.807

Grant, B. F., Stinson, F. S., Dawson, D. A., Chou, S., Ruan, W., & Pickering, R. P. (2004). Co-occurrence of 12-month alcohol and drug use disorders and personality disorders in the United States: Results from the National Epidemiologic Survey on Alcohol and Related Conditions. *Archives of General Psychiatry* 61, 361–368. doi: 10.1001/archpsyc.61.4.361

Grant, B. F., Stinson, F. S., & Harford, T. C. (2001). Age at onset of alcohol use and DSM-IV alcohol abuse and dependence: A 12-year follow-up. *Journal of Substance Abuse* 13, 493–504. doi: 10.1016/S0899-3289(01)00096-7

Greeley, J. & Oei, T. (1999). Alcohol and tension reduction. In K. E. Leonard & H. T. Blane (eds.), *Psychological theories of drinking and alcoholism* (2nd edn., pp. 14–53). New York: Guilford Press.

Grekin, E. R. & Sher, K. J. (2006). Alcohol dependence symptoms among college freshmen: Prevalence, stability and person-environment interactions. *Experimental and Clinical Psychopharmacology* 14, 329–338. doi: 10.1037/1064-1297.14.3.329

Hammad, A., Arfken, C. L., Rice, V. H., & Said, M. (2014). Substance abuse. In S. C. Nassar-McMillan, K. J. Ajrouch, & J. Hakim-Larson (eds.), *Biopsychosocial perspectives on Arab Americans: Culture, Development, and Health* (pp. 287–305). New York: Springer. doi: 10.1007/978-1-4614-8238-3_13

Harker, K. (2001). Immigrant generation, assimilation, and adolescent psychological wellbeing. *Social Forces* 79, 969–1004. doi: 10.1353/sof.2001.0010

Harwood, H. (2000). *Updating estimates of the economic costs of alcohol abuse in the United States: Estimates, update methods, and data.* National Institute on Alcohol Abuse and Alcoholism. Retrieved from http://pubs.niaaa.nih.gov/publications/economic-2000/alcoholcost.PDF

Hasan, N. M., Loza, N., El-Dosoky, A., Hamdi, N., Rawson, R., Hasson, A. L., and Shawky, M. M. (2009). Characteristics of clients with substance abuse disorders in a private hospital in Cairo, Egypt. *Journal of Muslim Mental Health* 4, 9–15. doi: 10.1080/15564900902777827

Hawkins, J. D., Catalano, R. F., & Miller, J. Y. (1992). Risk and protective factors for alcohol and other drug problems in adolescence and early adulthood: Implications for substance abuse prevention. *Psychological Bulletin* 112, 64–105. doi: 10.1037//0033-2909.112.1.64

Hicks, B. M., Krueger, R. F., Iacono, W. G., McGue, M., & Patrick, C. J. (2004). Family transmission and heritability of externalizing disorders. *Archives of General Psychiatry* 69, 922–928. doi: 10.1001/archpsyc.61.9.922

Horgan, C. (2001). *Substance abuse: The nation's number one health problem: Key indicators for policy update.* Princeton, NJ: The Robert Wood Johnson Foundation.

Karam, E., Maalouf, W., & Ghandour, L. (2004). Alcohol use among university students in Lebanon: Prevalence, trends and covariates. The IDRAC University Substance Use Monitoring Study (1991 and 1999). *Drug and Alcohol Dependence* 76, 273–286. doi: 10.1016/j.drugalcdep.2004.06.003

Kessler, R. C., Crum, R. M., Warner, L. A., Nelson, C. B., Schulenberg, J., & Anthony, J. C. (1997). Lifetime co-occurrence of DSM-III-R alcohol abuse and dependence with other psychiatric disorders in the National Comorbidity Survey. *Archives of General Psychiatry* 54, 313–321. doi: 10.1001/archpsyc.1997.01830160031005

Khantzian, E. J. (2003). The self-medication hypothesis revisited: The dually diagnosed patient. *Primary Psychiatry* 10, 47–48, 53–54.

Kroll, J., Yusuf, A., & Fujiwara, K. (2011). Psychoses, PTSD, and depression in Somali refugees in Minnesota. *Social Psychiatry and Psychiatric Epidemiology* 10, 481–93. doi: 10.1007/s00127-010-0216-0

Kuntsche, E. N., Knibbe, R., Gmel, G., & Engels, R. (2005). Why do young people drink? A review of drinking motives. *Clinical Psychology Review* 25, 841–861. doi: 10.1016/j.cpr.2005.06.002

Markon, K. E. & Krueger, R. F. (2005). Categorical and continuous models of liability to externalizing disorders: A direct comparison in NESARC. *Archives of General Psychiatry* 62, 1352–1359. doi: 10.1001/archpsyc.62.12.1352

Masel, M. C., Rudkin, L. L., & Peek, M. K. (2006). Examining the role of acculturation in health behaviors of older Mexican Americans. *American Journal of Health Behavior* 30, 684–699. doi: 10.5993/AJHB.30.6.14

McLaughlin, K. A., Hatzenbuehler, M. L., & Keyes, K. M. (2010). Responses to discrimination and psychiatric disorders among black, Hispanic, female, and lesbian, gay and bisexual individuals. *American Journal of Public Health* 100, 1477–1484. doi: 10.2105/AJPH.2009.181586

McLellan, A. T., Lewis, D. C., O'Brien, C. P., & Kleber, H. (2000). Drug dependence, a chronic medical illness: Implications for treatment, insurance, and outcomes evaluation. *Journal of the American Medical Association* 284, 1689–1695. doi: 10.1001/jama.284.13.1689

Michalak, L. & Trocki, K. (2006). Alcohol and Islam: An overview. *Contemporary Drug Problems* 33, 523–562.

National Institute on Drug Abuse. (2009). *Principles of drug addiction treatment: A research-based guide* (2nd edn., NIH Publication No. 09-4180). Bethesda, MD: National Institutes of Health. Retrieved from www.drugsandalcohol.ie/12848/

Paulozzi, L. J., Budnitz, D. S., & Xi, Y. (2006). Increasing deaths from opioid analgesics in the United States. *Pharmacoepidemiology and Drug Safety* 15(9), 618–627. doi: 10.1002/pds.1276

Portes, A. & Zhou, M. (1993). The new second generation: Segmented assimilation and its variants. *Annals of the American Academy of Political and Social Science* 530, 74–96.

Read, J. P., Colder, C. R., Merrill, J. E., Ouimette, P., White, J., & Swartout, A. (2012). Trauma and posttraumatic stress symptoms influence alcohol and other drug problem trajectories in the first year of college. *Journal of Consulting and Clinical Psychology* 80, 426–439. doi: 10.1037/a0028210

Schuckit, M. A. (2009). An overview of genetic influences in alcoholism. *Journal of Substance Abuse Treatment* 36, S5–S14. doi: 10.1016/j.jsat.2008.10.010

Sher, K. J. & Grekin, E. R. (2007). Alcohol and affect regulation. In J. J. Gross (ed.), *Handbook of emotion regulation* (pp. 560–580). New York: Guilford Press.

Sher, K. J., Grekin, E. R., & Williams, N. A. (2005). The development of alcohol use disorders. *Annual Review of Clinical Psychology* 1, 493–523. doi: 10.1146/annurev.clinpsy.1.102803.144107

Sher, K. J., Walitzer, K. S., Wood, P. K., & Brent, E. E. (1991). Characteristics of children of alcoholics: Putative risk factors, substance use and abuse, and psychopathology. *Journal of Abnormal Psychology* 100, 427–448. doi: 10.1037/0021-843X.100.4.427

Slutske, W. S. (2005). Alcohol use disorders among U.S. college students and their non-college attending peers. *Archives of General Psychiatry* 62, 321–327. doi: 10.1001/archpsyc.62.3.321

Slutske, W. S., Heath, A. C., Dinwiddie, S. H., Madden, P. A. F., Bucholz, K. K., Dunne, M. P., … Martin, N. G. (1998). Common genetic risk factors for conduct disorder and alcohol dependence. *Journal of Abnormal Psychology* 107(3), 363–374. doi: 10.1037/0021-843X.107.3.363

Stewart, S. H. & Devine, H. (2000). Relations between personality and drinking motives in young adults. *Personality and Individual Differences* 29, 495–511. doi: 10.1016/S0191-8869(99)00210-X

U.S. Department of Health and Human Services. (2007). *The Surgeon General's call to action to prevent and reduce underage drinking.* Rockville, MD: Office of the Surgeon General. Retrieved from www.surgeongeneral.gov/library/calls/underagedrinking/index.html

Wallace, J. M., Bachman, J. G., O'Malley, P. M., Schulenberg, J. E., Cooper, S. M., & Johnston, L. D. (2003). Gender and ethnic differences in smoking, drinking and illicit drug use among American 8th, 10th and 12th grade students, 1976–2000. *Addiction* 98, 225–234. doi: 10.1046/j.1360-0443.2003.00282

World Health Organization. (2011). *Global status on alcohol and health.* Geneva, Switzerland: World Health Organization. Retrieved from www.who.int/substance_abuse/publications/global_alcohol_report/en/

Xie, Y. & Greenman, E. (2011). The social context of assimilation: Testing implications of segmented assimilation theory. *Social Science Research* 40, 965–984. doi: 10.1016/j.ssresearch.2011.01.004

Zucker, R. A, Fitzgerald, H. E., & Moses, H. D. (1995). Emergence of alcohol problems and the several alcoholisms: A developmental perspective on etiologic theory and life course trajectory. In D. Cicchetti & D. J. Cohen (eds.), *Developmental psychopathology. Vol. 2: Risk, disorder, and adaptation* (pp. 677–711). New York: Wiley.

18

HEALTH DISPARITIES

Using a Framework to Understand the Correlates of Health and Disease Status

Florence J. Dallo

The term "health disparity" was first coined around 1990 (Braveman, 2014) and refers to "a particular type of health difference that is closely linked with social or economic disadvantage" (U.S. Department of Health and Human Services, 2008, p. 28). Health disparities adversely affect groups of people who have systematically experienced greater obstacles to health based on their race/ethnicity, religion, socioeconomic status, and similar factors. While it is clear that health disparities in the U.S. exist (Centers for Disease Control and Prevention, 2013), pinpointing the underlying reasons has been debated by social scientists, geneticists, bioethicists, and others. Since the early 1990s, and based on published literature, the essential variables of many of the health disparities models have included race/ethnicity, socioeconomic status, age, and sex as underlying factors that help explain differences in morbidity and mortality outcomes (Williams, 1997).

This chapter reviews the important factors that affect morbidity and mortality trends among Arab Americans. A health disparities model is presented as a modification of previously published models (see Figure 18.1). Moving from left to right, this model is used as a guide to help explain why Arab Americans exhibit particular profiles of morbidity and mortality for key health conditions, and to identify health disparities that exist when comparing Arab Americans to Whites and other racial/ethnic minority groups. A case study is presented to illustrate the complex factors that interact in explaining poor health status for some Arab Americans. The chapter then describes gaps in the literature, and outlines a set of recommendations that would increase the understanding of health conditions and improve the provision of healthcare for the Arab American population.

Conceptual Framework for Understanding Arab American Health Disparities

The conceptual framework shown in Figure 18.1 showcases the various demographic (i.e. age, sex), historical (i.e. wave of immigration), socioeconomic, health behaviors, stressors, and biological processes that influence morbidity and mortality among Arab Americans. The left side of the model includes unmodifiable risk factors such as age, sex, wave of immigration, country of origin, and others. Some of these factors, such as wave of immigration, have a bidirectional relationship with socioeconomic status. For example, an older Arab who recently entered the U.S. as a refugee may have lower socioeconomic status compared to an Arab American who has lived in the U.S. for 30 years and is a U.S. citizen. Conversely, socioeconomic status can influence the individual's English language ability and ethnic identity.

Socioeconomic status then influences place of residence, discrimination, health behaviors, and access to and utilization of healthcare. Compared to those with higher socioeconomic status,

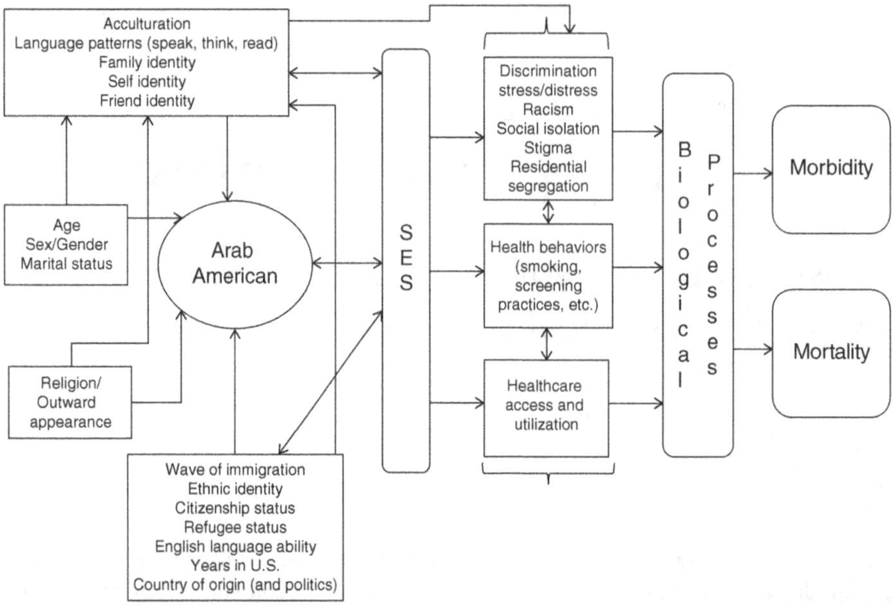

Figure 18.1 A Framework for Understanding Factors That Influence Health Outcomes of Arab Americans
Note: Modified from work by Borrell (2005); King & Williams (1995); Williams (1997).

individuals who have lower socioeconomic status are more likely to live in low-income neighborhoods and to encounter discrimination based on appearance (i.e. skin color, English language ability, and dress). They are also more likely to engage in risky health behaviors such as smoking and poor dietary practices; not have health insurance; and not visit a healthcare provider on a regular basis, which may delay certain screening and diagnostic testing for various conditions.

Taken together, the unmodifiable factors, such as age and immigration status, and the modifiable factors of socioeconomic status, acculturation, discrimination, health behaviors, and healthcare utilization all work together in shaping the underlying biological processes of elevated cortisol secretions, blood pressure, and heart rate. Over time, these heightened physiological responses can increase the risk of disease and lead to premature mortality. While the model includes many concepts, this chapter explores mainly the modifiable variables that affect morbidity and mortality among Arab Americans, such as acculturation, socioeconomic status, discrimination, health beliefs and behaviors, and healthcare access and utilization.

Acculturation

Acculturation is defined as a "dynamic and multidimensional process of adaptation that occurs when distinct cultures come into sustained contact. It involves different degrees and instances of culture learning and maintenance that are contingent upon individual, group, and environmental factors" (Organista, Marin, & Chun, 2010, p. 105). As displayed in the health disparities framework, acculturation directly affects socioeconomic status and discrimination, health behaviors, and healthcare. Furthermore, acculturation has an indirect effect on morbidity and mortality. The interconnectedness of the elements in the framework is evidenced in the available research on acculturation, specifically with regard to discrimination, health behaviors, and morbidity.

Measures of acculturation are often included in Arab American research focused on discrimination. The most striking finding is the influence of acculturation on discrimination when comparing Christian to Muslim Arab Americans. Among Christians, higher acculturation was related to lower levels of perceived discrimination (Amer & Hovey, 2007; Awad, 2010). However, among Muslims, higher acculturation was related to higher levels of perceived discrimination (Awad, 2010). These results suggest that acculturation moderates the relationship between religion and discrimination or mental health. This relationship is displayed in the model included in this chapter, which includes arrows between acculturation and religion, and acculturation and discrimination. These patterns by religion may contribute to the disparities observed in health when comparing Muslim to Christian Arab Americans.

Arab Americans who were more acculturated exhibited certain health behaviors compared to those who were less acculturated. For example, Arab Americans who were more acculturated were more likely to use alcohol (Jadalla & Lee, 2012) and drugs (Arfken, Kubiak, & Farrag, 2009). However, Arab Americans who were less acculturated were more likely to smoke cigarettes (Al-Omari & Scheibmeir, 2009; Jadalla & Lee, 2012). Moderate identification with both the American and Arab cultures was associated with better physical health, whereas strong identification with both cultures was associated with worse physical wellbeing (Jadalla & Lee, 2012). The model in the chapter showcases the importance of acculturation on health behaviors.

The results of studies associating acculturation with disease status are mixed. Dallo and James (2000) showed that blood pressure was not associated with acculturation among Chaldean (Catholic Iraqi) American women. Abdulrahim and Ajrouch (2010) showed that self-rated health, a powerful predictor of morbidity and mortality, improves with acculturation to U.S. society. Higher acculturation was associated with a lower diabetes risk (Al-Dahir et al., 2013; Jaber, Brown, Hammad, Zhu, & Herman, 2003). The stress of acculturating can also affect mental health. For example, among Christian Arabs, acculturation stress was a strong predictor for depression (Amer & Hovey, 2007).

Socioeconomic Status

Socioeconomic status is generally measured based on occupation, education, and income level. Studies have shown that individuals living in poverty have worse health outcomes than individuals not in poverty (Adler, Clark, DeMaio, Miller, & Saluter, 1999). Arab Americans generally have high rates of white-collar employment and median incomes. In addition, while Arab Americans have a high school completion rate that is higher than the national average, the level of high school completion varied from 93.5% for Egyptians to 72.5% for Iraqis (Brittingham & de la Cruz, 2005; de la Cruz & Brittingham, 2003). Despite their overall high income, the poverty rate is high for Arab Americans (16.7% compared to 11.8% in the total population). The Arab American national subgroups with the lowest rates of poverty (approximately 11% for Syrians and Lebanese) have a higher level of poverty than Whites (7.5%). The group with the highest poverty rate (26.4% among Iraqis) shows a poverty level that is higher than that of Blacks (22.1%) and Hispanics (21.2%; Brittingham & de la Cruz, 2005; Dalaker, 2001; de la Cruz & Brittingham, 2003).

In general, the estimates presented above suggest that Arab Americans may fall at opposite extremes of the spectrum with regard to income, employment, and education levels based on factors such as country of origin and sex. These differences may lead to the health disparities observed within Arab American groups and between Arab Americans and Whites or other minority groups. While the pattern observed for the general U.S. population is a wealth-health gradient (as socioeconomic status increases, health improves), the pattern may not be as straightforward for Arab Americans. As will be discussed below, factors such as discrimination, healthcare, and health behaviors serve as mediating variables in this wealth-health gradient.

Discrimination

Studies that assessed the burden of both personal experiences of discrimination and healthcare institutional discrimination showed that Arab Americans who reported more discrimination were more likely to: (a) be Muslim (Read, 2008); (b) be acculturated (Awad, 2010); (c) exhibit distance from whiteness (Padela & Heisler, 2010; Rousseau, Hassan, Moreau, & Thombs, 2010); (d) be psychologically distressed (Abdulrahim, James, Yamout, & Baker, 2012); (e) have low self-esteem (Hassan, Rousseau, & Moreau, 2013); and (f) be a refugee or have temporary resident status compared to those with permanent status (Arnetz, Rofa, Arnetz, Ventimiglia, & Jamil, 2013; Wrobel, Farrag, & Hymes, 2009). Researchers have found that living in ethnic enclaves and having cultural resources buffered the discrimination-distress association for Arab Americans (Abdulrahim et al., 2012; Ahmed, Kia-Keating, & Tsai, 2011). Political events also have affected the discrimination perceived by Arab Americans. Read (2008) found that among Arab Americans, 3.3% of Christians and 2.8% of Muslims reported they had "very often" been discriminated against prior to 9/11. In stark contrast, after 9/11, 4.0% of Christians and 11.9% of Muslims reported that they had "very often" been discriminated against.

Discrimination has been found to relate to health status among Arab Americans. For example, one study provided a striking example for birth weight of Arab Americans. Lauderdale (2006) used a surname list to identify Arab American women's birth records in California, and compared their levels of birth weight pre and post 9/11. The data showed that prior to 9/11, Arab American women had a risk of low birth weight similar to White women. In the six months after 9/11, Arab American women were 34% more likely to have a low birth weight infant compared to White women. The authors suggested that experiences of harassment and discrimination could be a key explanation for this increased risk of low birth weight post 9/11. Post-911 discrimination has also been linked to more psychological distress among Arab Americans (Padela & Heisler, 2010).

These findings suggest that the further an ethnic group's characteristics are from the mainstream U.S. culture, the greater chance of discrimination, which affects health, including mental health. From this, it can be implied that Arab American groups who stand out from the cultural mainstream may have worse mental health.

Health Beliefs and Behaviors

The extent to which Arab Americans engage in positive health behaviors, such as being physically active, eating healthily, and using preventive and screening practices, has shown mixed results in the literature. Arab Americans reporting any physical activity ranged from 20% to approximately 61% in different studies (Aswad, 2001; Dallo & Borrell, 2006; Genesee County Health Department, 2003; Jaber, Pinelli, et al., 2011; Jamil, Templin, et al., 2009). Robust studies focused on diet among Arab Americans are rare (Abou El Hassan & Hekmat, 2012).

The literature on screening and prevention has focused mainly on cancer (Al-Omran, 2005; Arshad, Williams, Mabiso, Dey, & Soliman, 2011; Schwartz, Fakhouri, Bartoces, Monsur, & Younis, 2008; Yassine, 2006). Arab Americans had lower estimates for colorectal screening and Pap smears, but higher mammography use compared to other minority groups or Whites (Yassine, 2006). Some researchers reported that barriers to cancer screening were embarrassment, fatalism, citizenship issues and language, transportation concerns, and a low understanding of the need for screening (Kawar, 2013; Saadi, Bond, & Percac-Lima, 2012; Salman, 2012). The literature on behaviors and barriers to cancer screening has come further compared to the literature on other chronic conditions. For example, some research is now focused on conducting interventions and randomized controlled trials to impact cancer knowledge and screening among Arab Americans (Ford et al., 2014).

Healthcare Access, Utilization, and Quality

Among minorities, low access to, utilization of, and quality of healthcare have been shown to be barriers in preventing disease and promoting health (Ertel et al., 2012; Moore et al., 2013; Paek & Lim,

2012; Riley, 2012). This is also true for Arab Americans. As shown in the health disparities model, and as evidenced by several studies summarized in this chapter, there are several factors that negatively affect healthcare access, utilization, and quality, such as patient and physician concordance and discordance; linguistic and cultural barriers, health insurance, and financial constraints; not requesting or receiving preventive care; and difficulty in navigating the healthcare system (Aboul-Enein & Aboul-Enein, 2010; Hammad, Kysia, Rabah, Hassoun, & Connelly, 1999; Inhorn & Fakih, 2006; Lipson & Meleis, 1983; Shah, Ayash, Pharaon, & Gany, 2008; Yosef, 2008). This, in turn, may affect underlying biological processes and ultimately increase the risk for disease morbidity and premature mortality.

Morbidity Among Arab Americans

Perceptions of discrimination, low healthcare use, and negative health behaviors are some of the factors that have been shown to adversely affect a broad range of physical and mental health outcomes for stigmatized groups in the U.S. (Padela & Heisler, 2010; Paradies, 2006; Williams, 2002). Arab Americans are no exception. This section summarizes the burden and health disparities of various physical and mental health conditions among Arab Americans.

Overweight and Obese

Obese, defined as a body mass index of 30 kg/m^2 or higher, is an important public health problem in the U.S. Approximately 36% of the U.S. population is obese and 33.1% is overweight, defined as a body mass index between 25 kg/m^2 and 30 kg/m^2. Furthermore, 78.8% of Hispanics and 76.7% of Blacks are overweight or obese compared to 66.7% of Whites (National Institute of Diabetes and Digestive and Kidney Diseases, 2014).

While studies of Arab Americans have not focused primarily on assessing overweight or obesity, many studies included overweight/obesity in their measurements. A community study in Michigan using a probability sample design, reported that 33.9% of Arab Americans were obese (Jaber, Brown, Hammad, Nowak, et al., 2003). Across different convenience sample studies with Arab Americans, estimates for overweight ranged from 28% to 56% and for obese from 28% to 34% (Al-Dahir et al., 2013; Genesee County Health Department, 2003; Hatahet, Khosla, & Fungwe, 2002; Jamil, Rajan, Grzybowski, Fakhouri, & Arnetz, 2014; Yanni et al., 2013). An analysis of national data revealed that 51% of Arab Americans were overweight or obese compared to 57% of non-Hispanic Whites (Dallo & Borrell, 2006). The estimates on overweight and obesity are challenging to compare to other ethnic groups because a majority of the data is gleaned from convenience community samples. Overall, the national study demonstrated that Arab Americans may be less likely to be overweight or obese compared to Whites.

Diabetes Mellitus

Diabetes refers to a group of diseases that affect how the body uses blood sugar (glucose). People with diabetes have high blood glucose because the body's production of insulin (which breaks down glucose) is too low, or because the body's cells do not respond properly to the available insulin. The prevalence of self-reported diabetes is 6.5% for the total U.S. population and for Mexican Americans, but is 10.0% for Blacks compared to 5.6% for Whites (Cowie et al., 2006). Among community-based studies on Arab Americans, diabetes prevalence estimates ranged from 6.0% to 19.3% (Aswad, 2001; Genesee County Health Department, 2003; Jaber, Brown, Hammad, Nowak, et al., 2003; Jamil, Fakhouri, et al., 2008; Sarsour, Tong, Jaber, Talbi, & Julliard, 2010).

Self-reported data underestimate the prevalence of diabetes, given that approximately one-third of diabetes cases in the U.S. is not diagnosed (Cowie et al., 2006). Some researchers measured glucose levels among Arab American individuals who indicated they did not have diabetes (Jaber, Brown, Hammad, Zhu, & Herman, 2003; Jaber, Slaughter, & Grunberger, 1995). They found that 10% had undiagnosed diabetes, and an additional 23% had a prior diagnosis of diabetes. Using national data, Dallo and Borrell (2006) showed that 4.8% of Arab Americans and 6.9% of non-Hispanic Whites reported that they were told by a physician they have diabetes.

From convenience community samples, it appears that Arab Americans show higher estimates of diabetes compared to other ethnic or White groups. However, the national study conducted by Dallo and Borrell (2006) demonstrated that Arab Americans are less likely to have diabetes compared to Whites. This may be because community samples often capture Arab Americans who have lower socioeconomic status, may have come as refugees, experience institutional discrimination, and have other factors that place them at higher risk for developing diabetes. The national sample of Arab Americans may have had higher socioeconomic status and other protective factors that prevented or delayed the onset of diabetes.

Hypertension

Hypertension, or elevated blood pressure, is a major modifiable risk factor for cardiovascular disease (Padwal, Straus, & McAlister, 2001). The prevalence of measured hypertension is 29.6% for the overall U.S. population and 39.1% among Blacks (Ong, Cheung, Man, Lau, & Lam, 2007). Three community-based studies focused on measuring blood pressure among Arab Americans (Dallo & James, 2000; Jaber et al., 2004; Jaber et al., 1995). These studies demonstrated that hypertension estimates ranged from 16% to 25%. National data suggested that 13.4% of Arab Americans self-reported a hypertension diagnosis compared to 24.5% of non-Hispanic Whites (Dallo & Borrell, 2006). The national data showed that Arab Americans fare better than non-Hispanic Whites as regards hypertension. However, similar to estimates for chronic conditions from community studies, it is challenging to make any generalizations because the samples and study designs greatly varied.

Hypercholesterolemia

Hypercholesterolemia is defined as elevated cholesterol levels and is a risk factor for heart disease (Fernandez & Webb, 2008). In the U.S., over half (50.4%) of individuals have high cholesterol. Blacks (37.3%) report lower levels compared to Whites (51.0%), who in turn are lower than Mexican Americans (54.3%; Ford, Mokdad, Giles, & Mensah, 2003). Four community convenience studies of Arab Americans found that self-reported hypercholesterolemia ranged from 23.1% to 46.8% (Al-Dahir et al., 2013; Aswad, 2001; Genesee County Health Department, 2003; Jamil, Dallo, et al., 2009). While it is difficult to draw any conclusions from these data because of the paucity of valid and reliable research, the wide range of estimates may illustrate the heterogeneity among Arab Americans in socioeconomic status and more specifically the wealth-health gradient. That is, are the lower estimates for hypercholesterolemia representative of the Arab Americans who have high socioeconomic status, whereas the higher estimates characterize Arab Americans with low socioeconomic status? This question remains elusive because the researchers did not present their findings in such a nuanced manner.

Heart Disease

Heart disease, used interchangeably with the term "cardiovascular disease," describes a range of conditions that affect the heart. These include heart rhythm problems, coronary artery disease, heart defects at birth, and others (Longo et al., 2011). Heart disease is the number-one cause of death in the U.S., and 6.4% of adults have had heart disease (Lethbridge-Çejku, Rose, & Vickerie, 2006). Among Arab Americans, between 6.0% and 11.5% reported having heart disease in previous studies (Aswad, 2001; Jadalla & Lee, 2012; Jamil, Dallo, et al., 2009; Jamil, Fakhouri, et al., 2008); Jamil, Hakim-Larson, et al., 2002). These estimates need to be interpreted with caution because they were convenience samples with varying study designs, which may have affected the reliability and validity of the findings.

Asthma

Asthma is a disease that affects the lungs. It causes repeated episodes of wheezing, breathlessness, and chest tightness (Centers for Disease Control and Prevention, n.d.). According to 2005–9 data from the National Health Interview Survey, 8.2% of U.S. adults reported currently having asthma, with lower estimates for Hispanics (6.3%) compared to Hispanic Whites (8.2%) and Blacks (11.1%; Akinbami, Moorman, & Liu, 2011). Asthma estimates across studies of Arab samples ranged from 5.4% to 9.4% with an outlier of 16% (Jamil et al., 2002; Jamil et al., 2011; Johnson, Nriagu, Hammad, Savoie, & Jamil, 2010). The latter estimate included only Iraqi immigrants who had arrived after the First Gulf War (Jamil et al., 2002). These immigrants may display a different health profile in general compared to other Arab/Chaldean immigrants, because those who arrived after the First Gulf War lived in a more toxic environment, experienced more traumatic events and daily stressors, and may not have seen a physician in Iraq. All of these factors may have contributed to the development of asthma, which was diagnosed when they arrived in the U.S.

Maternal and Child Health

A few studies have examined maternal and child health among Arab Americans. The prevalence of preterm birth was slightly lower for foreign-born Arab American women (7.5%) compared to U.S.-born Arab American women (8.0%) or U.S.-born White women (8.5%; El Reda, Grigorescu, Posner, & Davis-Harrier, 2007). Arab Americans had a lower infant mortality rate (4.7 per 1,000 live births) than non-Arab Whites (5.6 per 1,000 live births; Finkton, El-Sayed, & Galea, 2013). One of the theories potentially to explain this is the healthy migrant effect, which posits that immigrants are healthier than the U.S. born. One reason for this is those who are able to make the stressful migration would have to be healthy in the first place, so they arrive in the new country in better health. Other reasons for these differences between Arab American and White women may be that Arab American women are more likely to have familial support, less likely to smoke and use alcohol, more likely to be married, and more likely to depend on public insurance, all of which have been shown to reduce the risk of adverse birth outcomes.

Cancer

In 2012, 8.1% (age-adjusted) of U.S. adults 18 years of age or older reported having some type of cancer (Blackwell, Lucas, & Clarke, 2014). Published articles, many using data from National Cancer Institute's Surveillance, Epidemiology, and End Results program found that cancer was higher among Arab and Chaldean Americans for bladder, kidney, leukemia, liver, and multiple myeloma cancers compared to non-Hispanic Whites in Michigan (Schwartz et al., 2008). A similar study, but conducted in California, reported that rates for skin melanoma and colon, female breast, lung, and prostate cancer were lower for Middle Easterners compared to non-Hispanic Whites (Nasseri, Mills, & Allan, 2007). However, rates for Middle Easterners were higher for breast (male), leukemia, liver, stomach, and thyroid cancers (Nasseri et al., 2007). One explanation for these discrepancies could be policy differences between Michigan and California related to health insurance, healthcare delivery and access, and screening practices for cancer.

Mental Health

The mental health literature surrounding Arab Americans varies by conditions examined, sample characteristics, and other factors. Most studies showed that Arab Americans have higher levels of anxiety, depression, and serious psychological distress compared to the general population and other racial/ethnic minority groups (Amer & Hovey, 2012; Dallo, Kindratt, & Snell, 2013). For example, the estimates for depressive symptoms or depression ranged from 13.3% to 58% among Iraqi refugees (Jamil, Grzybowski, et al., 2008; Jamil et al., 2002) compared to 6.9% for the U.S. population (U.S. Department of Health and Human Services, 2013). For PTSD, estimates ranged from 8% to 23% among Iraqi immigrants and refugees (Jamil et al., 2002; Jamil et al., 2005; Jamil, Nassar-McMillan, & Lambert, 2007) compared to 3.5% for the U.S. population (Kessler, Chiu, Demler, & Walters, 2005).

Despite the disproportionately high estimates of mental health issues, suicide rates among Arab Americans appear very low: Arab American men had a 51% lower suicide rate and Arab American women had a 33% lower suicide rate than non-Hispanic White men and women (El-Sayed, Tracy, Scarborough, & Galea, 2011). This may be due to religious prohibitions against suicide among Muslim Arab Americans and cultural shame surrounding suicide among Arab Americans in general. Despite the stigma around mental health problems, family social support and communalism may alleviate the risk for suicidality.

Disability

According to 2000 Census data, 41.9% of individuals 65 years of age and older reported at least one of the following types of disability: sensory, physical, mental, self-care, difficulty going outside the home, or employment. The prevalence of disability was higher among Blacks (52.8%) compared to Hispanics (48.5%) or non-Hispanic Whites (40.4%; Waldrop & Stern, 2003). Studies using Census data showed that among those 65 years of age or older, the prevalence of having a functional limitation (i.e. mental, self-care, physical disability) was higher among foreign-born (~38%) compared to U.S.-born (~ 25%) Arab Americans (Dallo, Al Snih, & Ajrouch, 2009; Dallo, Booza, & Nguyen, 2015). When adjusting for factors that could affect the relationship between the prevalence of having a functional limitation and nativity status (i.e. U.S.- versus foreign-born), Dallo and colleagues found that foreign-born Arab Americans were more likely to report having a functional limitation compared to foreign-born non-Hispanic Whites (Dallo et al., 2009; Dallo, Booza, et al., 2015). However, among U.S.-born individuals, Arab Americans were less likely than non-Hispanic Whites to report having a functional limitation. These findings suggest that the burden of functional limitations varies between Arab Americans and non-Hispanic Whites and by nativity status.

Mortality Among Arab Americans

Mortality rates are important and widely used indicators of the health of a population. The first study published on mortality among Arab Americans showed that Arab American immigrants – compared to U.S.-born non-Hispanic Whites – were more likely to die from coronary heart disease, suicide, and diabetes (Nasseri, 2008). However, Arab American immigrants were less likely to die from chronic obstructive pulmonary disease, HIV/AIDS, and homicide (Nasseri, 2008). Reporting on cancer-specific mortality, one study suggested that Arab American women with breast cancer had better survival rates than European American women (Alford et al., 2009). An interesting study by Nasseri and Moulton (2011) examined patterns of death among first and second generation immigrants from the Middle East in California. They found that the first generation had higher odds of dying from colorectal cancers, diabetes, and diseases of the heart compared to non-Hispanic Whites. The first generation had lower odds of chronic obstructive pulmonary disease and suicide. Second generation Arab American men had higher odds of dying for all cancers combined as well as diseases of the heart. Second generation Arab American women had lower odds of dying from lung cancer and cerebrovascular accidents compared to non-Hispanic Whites.

In a recent study, Dallo and colleagues found that Arab Americans of 75 years of age or older had higher mortality rates when compared to Whites or Blacks (Dallo, Schwartz, Ruterbusch, Booza, & Williams, 2012). However, Arab American men had lower mortality from cancer and chronic lower respiratory disease. Arab American women had lower mortality from heart disease, cancer, stroke, and diabetes than Whites and Blacks. In a different study, El-Sayed and colleagues (2011) showed that life expectancies were 2.0 (men) and 1.4 (women) years lower for Arab Americans compared to non-Arab non-Hispanic Whites.

It is challenging to summarize mortality patterns among Arab Americans because authors compared mortality between different subgroups within their samples: Arab American immigrants vs. U.S.-born non-Hispanic Whites (Nasseri, 2008); first vs. second generation Arab immigrants (Nasseri & Moulton, 2011); and those 75 years of age or older (Dallo et al., 2012). The other studies reported on breast cancer survival rates for Arab American women (Alford et al., 2009) or estimated life expectancy (El-Sayed et al., 2011). While it is challenging to summarize mortality patterns among Arab Americans, the evidence shows that there are mortality disparities between Arab Americans and Whites. These disparities may be related to circumstances around the disease, including risk factors for and knowledge of the disease, in addition to healthcare and family factors.

Case Example: Omar and His Poorly Controlled Type 2 Diabetes

Omar Al-Hassan is a 57-year-old, married, male Arab American refugee. He is a smoker and has poorly controlled type 2 diabetes. He immigrated to the state of Michigan from Iraq two years ago, along with over 2,000 other refugees from Iraq. According to guidelines from the Centers for Disease Control and Prevention (CDC), he was required to obtain a full medical exam upon arrival. That was when the healthcare provider detected his positive diabetes status.

As a refugee with limited English language ability and having been in the U.S. for only a couple of years, he does not have consistent transportation, he is financially strained, and he feels depressed on many days. When he does visit a healthcare professional, he feels he is discriminated against because the healthcare provider does not take his questions seriously, does not spend enough time with him, and does not properly explain medication usage. When Omar asked about the side effects of Metformin (one of his medications), the healthcare professional said, "I would tell you, but you may not understand because of your limited English." In Omar's culture, a finger stick is seen as invasive and indicates that the person's condition is in dire straits. Therefore, he is not comfortable testing his blood sugar levels, and the healthcare provider chastises him for being noncompliant even though the provider did not take the time to understand Omar's own beliefs about the meaning of a finger stick.

Additionally, while he has medications that are paid for by the state for a limited period of time, he does not always have the means to refill or obtain his prescriptions because he does not have consistent transportation and does not see his physician as often as he should. His wife and five children do not completely understand his disease and do not know how to be supportive with respect to cooking the right foods, reducing stress, helping him to quit smoking, and encouraging him to begin exercising. In addition, because he attends a community health clinic, his physician does not always provide comprehensive medical exams to check for eye, foot, heart, and circulation complications that affect many people with uncontrolled diabetes.

This case demonstrates that the reasons for poor health outcomes among Arab Americans are complex and multidimensional. There are several intersecting factors that affect Omar's condition, such as older age, refugee status, positive smoking status, lack of acculturation, discrimination, and difficulty in negotiating the healthcare system even though he has access to medical care as a refugee.

Furthermore, his family does not quite know how to support him in caring for his diabetes. All of these factors may lead to the development of diabetes complications and premature mortality.

Critique

The objective of this chapter was to critically review health studies focused on Arab Americans. The attempt to describe any consistent patterns in health and disease status was thwarted because most of the research on Arab Americans was conducted using convenience samples in communities of lower socioeconomic status (and consequently poorer health). This is a serious methodological weakness, which skews the findings of these studies, because it prevents the reporting of accurate prevalence or incidence estimates. At best, the results from convenience samples represent percentages or proportions, but not prevalence or incidence.

In addition, a majority of the convenience sample studies did not report their response rates, information on those who refused to participate, their inclusion and exclusion criteria, or important explanatory variables such as socioeconomic status. Of the articles synthesized, less than 20% reported their response rates. Response rates help determine the validity and reliability of the studies. Having low response rates or reporting no response rates questions the credibility of the findings, because the Arab American sample may have been less likely to represent the target population. This may be one reason there were discrepancies in diabetes and hypertension estimates between the local community samples and national studies.

Moreover, the factors that contribute to health disparities also showed mixed results in the literature. For example, it was challenging to directly compare the studies on acculturation summarized above. This was because they used different strategies to select the sample, measure acculturation and discrimination, and collect the data. One suggestion is that more studies on Arab Americans should use the same standardized and validated instruments, such as the acculturation scale that was translated and adapted for Arab Americans from the Acculturation Rating Scale for Mexican Americas-II (Jadalla and Lee, 2015).

Despite these limitations in previous research, this chapter suggests that the health and disease status of Arab Americans can no longer be ignored. The classification of Arab Americans as "White" is not useful for health research because it masks the health of Arab Americans under that of Whites. Defining Arab Americans as Whites makes it difficult to formulate and test robust evidence-based research questions and hypotheses, which in turn dilutes the health policy implications for this group. This chapter provides clear evidence that adding a separate category for Arab Americans, or at least a label under the White category, will allow researchers to design and initiate more rigorous separate analyses for this population. This effort also would allow subgroup comparisons, given that Arab Americans are heterogeneous. Using medical records, one study found that healthcare professionals were highly likely to record inaccurately the national and cultural heritage of their Arab American patients (Lipson, Reizian, & Meleis, 1987). To truly capture the diversity of the U.S. nation, advocates of the Arab American community need to give voice and form to their ever-increasing and visible population.

Keeping these important issues in mind, this review suggests that diabetes, certain types of cancer, and psychological distress may be higher for Arab Americans compared to other minority groups and Whites. Although Arab Americans appear to fare better for conditions such as heart disease (although the evidence is mixed on this), they had higher heart-disease specific mortality rates compared to U.S.-born Whites. It is important to note the National Health Interview Survey included only first generation immigrant Arab Americans (and not second generation or beyond), which undoubtedly biased the results. Given the continued growth of this population, and to decrease the currently high risk of bias observed in these studies, it is important to explore these health conditions using more rigorous methodology, with probability sampling and standardized questionnaires.

Conclusion

Health disparities in the U.S. are pervasive. A majority of the research elucidates health disparities between Blacks, Asians, Hispanics, and Whites. This approach misses the fact that Arab Americans are masked under the White category, so the health disparities that were uncovered in this chapter between Whites and Arab Americans have been invisible in the health disparities research. This chapter has demonstrated that acculturation, socioeconomic status, discrimination, and healthcare access and utilization all affect health outcomes. In addition, this review has shown that the majority of the studies available on Arab American health are small-scale convenience sample studies conducted in lower socioeconomic status communities, which may inflate or deflate actual rates of disease morbidity and mortality. There is a need for national, regional, or state-specific research that focuses on Arab Americans as an ethnic group. Large, national epidemiological studies with a robust sampling methodology should be incorporated into the research agenda of the nation if the health of Arab Americans is to be understood and improved.

References

Abdulrahim, S. & Ajrouch, K. (2010). Social and cultural meanings of self-rated health: Arab immigrants in the United States. *Qualitative Health Research* 20, 1229–1240. doi: 10.1177/1049732310371104

Abdulrahim, S., James, S. A., Yamout, R., & Baker, W. (2012). Discrimination and psychological distress: Does whiteness matter for Arab Americans? *Social Science & Medicine* 75, 2116–2123. doi: 10.1016/j.socscimed.2012.07.030

Abou El Hassan, D. & Hekmat, S. (2012). Dietary acculturation of Arab immigrants: In the Greater Toronto area. *Canadian Journal of Dietetic Practice and Research* 73, 143–146. doi: 10.3148/73.3.2012.143

Aboul-Enein, B. H. & Aboul-Enein, F. H. (2010). The cultural gap delivering health care services to Arab American populations in the United States. *Journal of Cultural Diversity* 17(1), 20–23.

Adler, M. C., Clark, R. F., DeMaio, T. J., Miller, L. F., & Saluter, A. F. (1999). Collecting information on disability in the 2000 census: An example of interagency cooperation. *Social Security Bulletin* 62(4), 21–30.

Ahmed, S. R., Kia-Keating, M., & Tsai, K. H. (2011). A structural model of racial discrimination, acculturative stress, and cultural resources among Arab American adolescents. *American Journal of Community Psychology* 48(3–4), 181–192. doi: 10.1007/s10464-011-9424-3

Akinbami, L. J., Moorman, J. E., & Liu, X. (2011). *Asthma prevalence, health care use, and mortality: United States, 2005–2009* (Report No. 32). Hyattsville, MD: National Center for Health Statistics. Retrieved from www.cdc.gov/nchs/data/nhsr/nhsr032.pdf

Al-Dahir, S., Brakta, F., Khalil, A., Benrahla, M., Jack, L., Jr, & Kennedy, K. (2013). The impact of acculturation on diabetes risk among Arab Americans in Southeastern Louisiana. *Journal of Health Care for the Poor and Underserved* 24(Suppl.), 47–63. doi: 10.1353/hpu.2013.0038

Alford, H. S., Schwartz, K., Soliman, A., Johnson, C. C., Gruber, S. B., & Merajver, S. D. (2009). Breast cancer characteristics at diagnosis and survival among Arab-American women compared to European- and African-American women. *Breast Cancer Research and Treatment* 114, 339–346. doi: 10.1007/s10549-008-9999-z

Al-Omari, H. & Scheibmeir, M. (2009). Arab Americans' acculturation and tobacco smoking. *Journal of Transcultural Nursing* 20, 227–233. doi: 10.1177/1043659608330353

Al-Omran, H. (2005). Measurement of the knowledge, attitudes, and beliefs of Arab-American adults toward cancer screening and early detection: Development of a survey instrument. *Ethnicity & Disease* 15(Suppl. 1), 15–16.

Amer, M. M. & Hovey, J. D. (2007). Socio-demographic differences in acculturation and mental health for a sample of 2nd generation/early immigrant Arab Americans. *Journal of Immigrant and Minority Health* 9, 335–347. doi: 10.1007/s10903-007-9045-y

Amer, M. M. & Hovey, J. D. (2012). Anxiety and depression in a post-September 11 sample of Arabs in the USA. *Social Psychiatry and Psychiatric Epidemiology* 47, 409–418. doi: 10.1007/s00127-011-0341-4

Arfken, C. L., Kubiak, S. P., & Farrag, M. (2009). Acculturation and polysubstance abuse in Arab-American treatment clients. *Transcultural Psychiatry* 46, 608–622. doi: 10.1177/1363461509351364

Arnetz, J., Rofa, Y., Arnetz, B., Ventimiglia, M., & Jamil, H. (2013). Resilience as a protective factor against the development of psychopathology among refugees. *Journal of Nervous and Mental Disease* 201(3), 167–172. doi: 10.1097/NMD.0b013e3182848afe

Arshad, S., Williams, K. P., Mabiso, A., Dey, S., & Soliman, A. S. (2011). Evaluating the knowledge of breast cancer screening and prevention among Arab-American women in Michigan. *Journal of Cancer Education* 26(1), 135–138. doi: 10.1007/s13187-010-0130-x

Aswad, M. (2001). *Health survey of the Arab, Muslim, and Chaldean American communities in Michigan*. Dearborn, MI: ACCESS. Retrieved from www.accesscommunity.org/sites/default/files/documents/health_and_research_cente_19.pdf

Awad, G. H. (2010). The impact of acculturation and religious identification on perceived discrimination for Arab/Middle Eastern Americans. *Cultural Diversity & Ethnic Minority Psychology* 16(1), 59–67. doi: 10.1037/a0016675

Blackwell, D. L., Lucas, J. W., & Clarke, T. C. (2014). *Summary health statistics for U.S. adults: National Health Interview Survey, 2012*. Washington, D.C.: National Center for Health Statistics. Retrieved from www.cdc.gov/nchs/data/series/sr_10/sr10_260.pdf

Borrell, L. N. (2005). Racial identity among Hispanics: Implications for health and well-being. *American Journal of Public Health* 95, 379–381. doi:10.2105/AJPH.2004.058172

Braveman, P. (2014). What are health disparities and health equity? We need to be clear. *Public Health Reports*, 129(Suppl. 2), 5–8.

Brittingham, A. & de la Cruz, G. P. (2005). *We the people of Arab ancestry in the United States* (Census 2000 Special Reports, CENSR-21). Washington, D.C.: U.S. Census Bureau. Retrieved from www.census.gov/prod/2005pubs/censr-21.pdf

Centers for Disease Control and Prevention. (n.d.). *Asthma*. Retrieved from www.cdc.gov/asthma/default.htm

Centers for Disease Control and Prevention. (2013). CDC health disparities and inequalities report – United States, 2013. *Morbidity and Mortality Weekly Report* 62(Suppl. 3), 1–189.

Cowie, C. C., Rust, K. F., Byrd-Holt, D. D., Eberhardt, M. S., Flegal, K. M., Engelgau, M. M., ... Gregg, E. W. (2006). Prevalence of diabetes and impaired fasting glucose in adults in the U.S. population: National health and nutrition examination survey 1999–2002. *Diabetes Care* 29, 1263–1268. doi: 10.2337/dc06-0062

Dalaker, J. (2001). *Poverty in the United States: 2000* (Current Population Reports, P60-214). Washington, D.C.: U.S. Census Bureau. Retrieved from www.census.gov/prod/2001pubs/p60-214.pdf

Dallo, F. J., Al Snih, S., & Ajrouch, K. J. (2009). Prevalence of disability among US- and foreign-born Arab Americans: Results from the 2000 US census. *Gerontology* 55(2), 153–161. doi: 10.1159/000151538

Dallo, F. J., Booza, J., & Nguyen, N. D. (2015). Functional limitations and nativity status among older Arab, Asian, black, Hispanic, and white Americans. *Journal of Immigrant and Minority Health* 17, 535–542. doi: 10.1007/s10903-013-9943-0

Dallo, F. J. & Borrell, L. N. (2006). Self-reported diabetes and hypertension among Arab Americans in the United States. *Ethnicity & Disease* 16(3), 699–705.

Dallo, F. J. & James, S. A. (2000). Acculturation and blood pressure in a community-based sample of Chaldean-American women. *Journal of Immigrant Health* 2(3), 145–153. doi: 10.1023/A:1009560903668

Dallo, F. J., Kindratt, T. B., & Snell, T. (2013). Serious psychological distress among non-Hispanic whites in the United States: The importance of nativity status and region of birth. *Social Psychiatry and Psychiatric Epidemiology* 48, 1923–1930. doi: 10.1007/s00127-013-0703-1

Dallo, F. J., Schwartz, K., Ruterbusch, J. J., Booza, J., & Williams, D. R. (2012). Mortality rates among Arab Americans in Michigan. *Journal of Immigrant and Minority Health* 14, 236–241. doi: 10.1007/s10903-011-9441-1

de la Cruz, G. P. & Brittingham, A. (2003). *The Arab population: 2000* (Census 2000 Brief, C2KBR-23). Washington, D.C.: U.S. Census Bureau. Retrieved from www.census.gov/prod/2003pubs/c2kbr-23.pdf

El Reda, D. K., Grigorescu, V., Posner, S. F., & Davis-Harrier, A. (2007). Lower rates of preterm birth in women of Arab ancestry: An epidemiologic paradox – Michigan, 1993–2002. *Maternal and Child Health Journal*, 11, 622–627. doi: 10.1007/s10995-007-0199-y

El-Sayed, A. M., Tracy, M., Scarborough, P., & Galea, S. (2011). Ethnic inequalities in mortality: The case of Arab-Americans. *PloS ONE* 6(12), 1–7. doi: 10.1371/journal.pone.0029185

Ertel, K. A., James-Todd, T., Kleinman, K., Krieger, N., Gillman, M., Wright, R., & Rich-Edwards, J. (2012). Racial discrimination, response to unfair treatment, and depressive symptoms among pregnant black and African American women in the United States. *Annals of Epidemiology* 22, 840–846. doi: 10.1016/j.annepidem.2012.10.001

Fernandez, M. L. & Webb, D. (2008). The LDL to HDL cholesterol ratio as a valuable tool to evaluate coronary heart disease risk. *Journal of the American College of Nutrition* 27(1), 1–5. doi: 10.1080/07315724.2008.10719668

Finkton, D. W., Jr, El-Sayed, A. M., & Galea, S. (2013). Infant mortality among Arab-Americans: Findings from the Arab-American birth outcomes study. *Maternal and Child Health Journal* 17, 732–745. doi: 10.1007/s10995-012-1049-0

Ford, E. S., Mokdad, A. H., Giles, W. H., & Mensah, G. A. (2003). Serum total cholesterol concentrations and awareness, treatment, and control of hypercholesterolemia among US adults: Findings from the National Health and Nutrition Examination Survey, 1999 to 2000. *Circulation* 107, 2185–2189. doi: 10.1161/01.CIR.0000066320.27195.B4

Ford, S., Meghea, C., Estes, T., Hamade, H., Lockett, M., & Williams, K. P. (2014). Assessing the fidelity of the Kin Keeper[SM] prevention intervention in African American, Latina and Arab women. *Health Education Research* 29(1), 158–165. doi: 10.1093/her/cyt100

Genesee County Health Department (2003). *Arab American health survey*. Flint, MI: Genesee County Health Department. Retrieved from www.gchd.net/pdf/AAHS.pdf

Hammad, A., Kysia, R., Rabah, R., Hassoun, R., & Connelly, M. (1999). *Guide to Arab culture: Health care delivery to the Arab American community*. Dearborn, MI: ACCESS Community Health Center, Public Health Education and Research Department. Retrieved from www.naama.com/pdf/arab-american-culture-health-care.pdf

Hassan, G., Rousseau, C., & Moreau, N. (2013). Ethnic and religious discrimination: The multifaceted role of religiosity and collective self-esteem. *Transcultural Psychiatry* 50, 475–492. doi: 10.1177/1363461513495586

Hatahet, W., Khosla, P., & Fungwe, T. V. (2002). Prevalence of risk factors to coronary heart disease in an Arab-American population in Southeast Michigan. *International Journal of Food Sciences & Nutrition* 53, 325–335. doi: 10.1080/09637480220138124

Inhorn, M. C. & Fakih, M. H. (2006). Arab Americans, African Americans, and infertility: Barriers to reproduction and medical care. *Fertility and Sterility* 85, 844–852. doi: 10.1016/j.fertnstert.2005.10.029

Jaber, L. A., Brown, M. B., Hammad, A., Nowak, S. N., Zhu, Q., Ghafoor, A., & Herman, W. H. (2003). Epidemiology of diabetes among Arab Americans. *Diabetes Care* 26, 308–313. doi: 10.2337/diacare.26.2.308

Jaber, L. A., Brown, M. B., Hammad, A., Zhu, Q., & Herman, W. H. (2003). Lack of acculturation is a risk factor for diabetes in Arab immigrants in the US. *Diabetes Care* 26, 2010–2014. doi: 10.2337/diacare.26.7.2010

Jaber, L. A., Brown, M. B., Hammad, A., Zhu, Q., & Herman, W. H. (2004). The prevalence of the metabolic syndrome among Arab Americans. *Diabetes Care* 27(1), 234–238. doi: 10.2337/diacare.27.1.234

Jaber, L. A., Pinelli, N. R., Brown, M. B., Funnell, M. M., Anderson, R., Hammad, A., & Herman, W. H. (2011). Feasibility of group lifestyle intervention for diabetes prevention in Arab Americans. *Diabetes Research and Clinical Practice* 91, 307–315. doi: 10.1016/j.diabres.2010.11.032

Jaber, L. A., Slaughter, R. L., & Grunberger, G. (1995). Diabetes and related metabolic risk factors among Arab Americans. *The Annals of Pharmacotherapy* 29, 573–576

Jadalla, A. & Lee, J. (2012). The relationship between acculturation and general health of Arab Americans. *Journal of Transcultural Nursing* 23, 159–165. doi: 10.1177/1043659611434058

Jadalla, A. & Lee, J. (2015). Validation of Arabic and English versions of the ARSMA-II Acculturation Rating Scale. *Journal of Immigrant and Minority Health* 17, 208–216. doi: 10.1007/s10903-013-9889-2

Jamil, H., Dallo, F., Fakhouri, M., Templin, T., Khoury, R., & Fakhouri, H. (2009). The prevalence of self-reported chronic conditions among Arab, Chaldean, and African Americans in Southeast Michigan. *Ethnicity & Disease* 19, 293–300.

Jamil, H., Fakhouri, M., Dallo, F., Templin, T., Khoury, R., & Fakhouri, H. (2008). Self-reported heart disease among Arab and Chaldean American women residing in Southeast Michigan. *Ethnicity & Disease* 18, 19–25.

Jamil, H., Grzybowski, M., Hakim-Larson, J., Fakhouri, M., Sahutoglu, J., Khoury, R., & Fakhouri, H. (2008). Factors associated with self-reported depression in Arab, Chaldean, and African Americans. *Ethnicity & Disease* 18, 464–470.

Jamil, H., Hakim-Larson, J., Farrag, M., Kafaji, T., Duqum, I., & Jamil, L. H. (2002). A retrospective study of Arab American mental health clients: Trauma and the Iraqi refugees. *The American Journal of Orthopsychiatry* 72, 355–361. doi: 10.1037/0002-9432.72.3.355

Jamil, H., Hakim-Larson, J., Farrag, M., Kafaji, T., Jamil, L. H., & Hammad, A. (2005). Medical complaints among Iraqi American refugees with mental disorders. *Journal of Immigrant Health* 7(3), 145–152. doi: 10.1007/s10903-005-3671-z

Jamil, H., Nassar-McMillan, S. C., & Lambert, R. (2007). Immigration and attendant psychological sequelae: A comparison of three waves of Iraqi immigrants. *American Journal of Orthopsychiatry* 77, 199–205. doi: 10.1037/0002-9432.77.2.199

Jamil, H. J., Rajan, A. K., Grzybowski, M., Fakhouri, M., & Arnetz, B. (2014). Obesity and overweight in ethnic minorities of the Detroit metropolitan area of Michigan. *Journal of Community Health* 39, 301–309. doi: 10.1007/s10900-013-9760-3

Jamil, H., Raymond, D., Fakhouri, M., Templin, T., Khoury, R., Fakhouri, H., & Arnetz, B. B. (2011). Self-reported asthma in Chaldeans, Arabs, and African Americans: Factors associated with asthma. *Journal of Immigrant and Minority Health* 13, 568–575. doi: 10.1007/s10903-010-9390-0

Jamil, H., Templin, T., Fakhouri, M., Rice, V. H., Khouri, R., Fakhouri, H., … Baker, A. (2009). Comparison of personal characteristics, tobacco use, and health states in Chaldean, Arab American, and non-Middle Eastern White adults. *Journal of Immigrant and Minority Health* 11, 310–317. doi: 10.1007/s10903-008-9125-7

Johnson, M., Nriagu, J., Hammad, A., Savoie, K., & Jamil, H. (2010). Asthma, environmental risk factors, and hypertension among Arab Americans in metro Detroit. *Journal of Immigrant and Minority Health* 12, 640–651. doi: 10.1007/s10903-008-9205-8

Kawar, L. N. (2013). Barriers to breast cancer screening participation among Jordanian and Palestinian American women. *European Journal of Oncology Nursing* 17(1), 88–94. doi: 10.1016/j.ejon.2012.02.004

Kessler, R. C., Chiu, W. T., Demler, O., & Walters, E. E. (2005). Prevalence, severity, and comorbidity of 12-month DSM-IV disorders in the National Comorbidity Survey Replication (NCS-R). *Archives of General Psychiatry* 62, 617–627. doi: 10.1001/archpsyc.62.6.617

King, G. and Williams, D. R. (1995). Race and health: A multidimensional approach to African American health. In B. C. Amick, S. Levine, A. R. Tarlov, and D. C. Walsh (eds.), *Society & health* (pp. 93–130). Oxford: Oxford University Press.

Lauderdale, D. S. (2006). Birth outcomes for Arabic-named women in California before and after September 11. *Demography* 43(1), 185–201. doi: 10.1353/dem.2006.0008

Lethbridge-Çejku, M., Rose, D., & Vickerie, J. (2006). *Summary health statistics for U.S. adults: National Health Interview Survey, 2004.* Washington, D.C.: National Center for Health Statistics. Retrieved from www.cdc.gov/nchs/data/series/sr_10/sr10_228.pdf

Lipson, J. G. & Meleis, A. I. (1983). Issues in health care of Middle Eastern patients. *Western Journal of Medicine* 139, 854–861.

Lipson, J. G., Reizian, A. E., & Meleis, A. I. (1987). Arab-American patients: A medical record review. *Social Science & Medicine* 24, 101–107. doi: 10.1016/0277-9536(87)90242-5

Longo, D., Fauci, A., Kasper, D., Hauser, S., Jameson, J., & Loscalzo, J. (2011). *Harrison's principles of internal medicine* (vols. 1 and 2, 18th edn.). New York: McGraw-Hill Professional.

Moore, A. D., Hamilton, J. B., Knafl G. J., Godley P. A., Carpenter, W. R., Bensen, J. T., … Mishel, M. (2013). The influence of mistrust, racism, religious participation, and access to care on patient satisfaction for African American men: The North Carolina-Louisiana Prostate Cancer Project. *Journal of the National Medical Association* 105(1), 59–68.

Nasseri, K. (2008). Mortality in first generation white immigrants in California, 1989–1999. *Journal of Immigrant and Minority Health* 10(3), 197–205. doi: 10.1007/s10903-007-9070-x

Nasseri, K., Mills, P. K., & Allan, M. (2007). Cancer incidence in the Middle Eastern population of California, 1988–2004. *Asian Pacific Journal of Cancer Prevention* 8(3), 405–411.

Nasseri, K. & Moulton, L. H. (2011). Patterns of death in the first and second generation immigrants from selected Middle Eastern countries in California. *Journal of Immigrant and Minority Health* 13, 361–370. doi: 10.1007/s10903-009-9270-7

National Institute of Diabetes and Digestive and Kidney Diseases. (2014). *Weight control information network.* Bethesda, MD: National Institute of Diabetes and Digestive and Kidney Diseases. Retrieved from http://win.niddk.nih.gov/

Ong, K. L., Cheung, B. M. Y., Man, Y. B., Lau, C. P., & Lam, K. S. L. (2007). Prevalence, awareness, treatment, and control of hypertension among United States adults 1999–2004. *Hypertension* 49(1), 69–75. doi: 10.1161/01.HYP.0000252676.46043.18

Organista, P. B., Marin, G., & Chun, K. M. (2010). Acculturation. In P. B. Organista, G. Marin, and K. M. Chun, *The psychology of ethnic groups in the United States* (pp. 99–135). Thousand Oaks, CA: SAGE Publications.

Padela, A. I. & Heisler, M. (2010). The association of perceived abuse and discrimination after September 11, 2001, with psychological distress, level of happiness, and health status among Arab Americans. *American Journal of Public Health* 100, 284–291. doi: 10.2105/AJPH.2009.164954

Padwal, R., Straus, S. E., & McAlister, F. A. (2001). Cardiovascular risk factors and their effects on the decision to treat hypertension: Evidence based review. *BMJ* 322(7292), 977–980. doi: 10.1136/bmj.322.7292.977

Paek, M. & Lim, J. (2012). Factors associated with health care access and outcome. *Social Work in Health Care* 51, 506–530. doi: 10.1080/00981389.2012.671244

Paradies, Y. (2006). A systematic review of empirical research on self-reported racism and health. *International Journal of Epidemiology* 35, 888–901. doi: 10.1093/ije/dyl056

Read, J. G. (2008). Discrimination and identity formation in a post-9/11 era: A comparison of Muslim and Christian Arab Americans. In A. Jamal, & N. Naber (eds.), *Race and Arab Americans before and after 9/11: From invisible citizens to visible subjects* (pp. 305–317). New York: Syracuse University Press.

Riley, W. J. (2012). Health disparities: Gaps in access, quality and affordability of medical care. *Transactions of the American Clinical and Climatological Association* 123, 167–174.

Rousseau, C., Hassan, G., Moreau, N., & Thombs, B. D. (2010). Perceived discrimination and its association with psychological distress among newly arrived immigrants before and after September 11, 2001. *American Journal of Public Health* 101, 909–915. doi: 10.2105/AJPH.2009.173062

Saadi, A., Bond, B., & Percac-Lima, S. (2012). Perspectives on preventive health care and barriers to breast cancer screening among Iraqi women refugees. *Journal of Immigrant and Minority Health* 14, 633–639. doi: 10.1007/s10903-011-9520-3

Salman, K. F. (2012). Health beliefs and practices related to cancer screening among Arab Muslim women in an urban community. *Health Care for Women International* 33(1), 45–74. doi: 10.1080/07399332.2011.610536

Sarsour, L., Tong, V. S., Jaber, O., Talbi, M., & Julliard, K. (2010). Health assessment of the Arab American community in Southwest Brooklyn. *Journal of Community Health* 35, 653–659. doi: 10.1007/s10900-010-9260-7

Schwartz, K., Fakhouri, M., Bartoces, M., Monsur, J., & Younis, A. (2008). Mammography screening among Arab American women in metropolitan Detroit. *Journal of Immigrant and Minority Health* 10, 541–549. doi: 10.1007/s10903-008-9140-8

Shah, S. M., Ayash, C., Pharaon, N. A., & Gany, F. M. (2008). Arab American immigrants in New York: Health care and cancer knowledge, attitudes, and beliefs. *Journal of Immigrant and Minority Health* 10, 429–436. doi: 10.1007/s10903-007-9106-2

U.S. Department of Health and Human Services. (2008). *Phase I report: Recommendations for the framework and format of Healthy People 2020.* Washington, D.C.: U.S. Department of Health and Human Services. Retrieved from www.healthypeople.gov/sites/default/files/PhaseI_0.pdf

U.S. Department of Health and Human Services. (2013). *Results from the 2012 national survey on drug use and health: Mental health findings.* Rockville, MD: Substance Abuse and Mental Health Services Administration. Retrieved from www.samhsa.gov/data/sites/default/files/2k12MH_Findings/2k12MH_Findings/NSDUHmhfr2012.htm

Waldrop, J. & Stern, S. M. (2003). *Disability status: 2000* (Census 2000 Brief, C2KBR-17). Washington, D.C.: U.S. Census Bureau. Retrieved from www.census.gov/prod/2003pubs/c2kbr-17.pdf

Williams, D. R. (1997). Race and health: Basic questions, emerging directions. *Annals of Epidemiology* 7, 322–333. doi: 10.1016/S1047-2797(97)00051-3

Williams, D. R. (2002). Racial/ethnic variations in women's health: The social embeddedness of health. *American Journal of Public Health* 92(4), 588–597. doi: 10.2105/AJPH.92.4.588

Wrobel, N. H., Farrag, M. F., & Hymes, R. W. (2009). Acculturative stress and depression in an elderly Arabic sample. *Journal of Cross-Cultural Gerontology* 24, 273–290. doi: 10.1007/s10823-009-9096-8

Yanni, E. A., Naoum, M., Odeh, N., Han, P., Coleman, M., & Burke, H. (2013). The health profile and chronic diseases comorbidities of US-bound Iraqi refugees screened by the International Organization for Migration in Jordan: 2007–2009. *Journal of Immigrant and Minority Health* 15(1), 1–9. doi: 10.1007/s10903-012-9578-6

Yassine, M. (2006). *Special cancer behavioral risk factor survey 2006.* Okemos, MI: Michigan Public Health Institute, Cancer Epidemiology and Program Evaluation Project.

Yosef, A. R. O. (2008). Health beliefs, practice, and priorities for health care of Arab Muslims in the United States: Implications for nursing care. *Journal of Transcultural Nursing* 19, 284–291. doi: 10.1177/1043659608317450

PART V

Applied Practice and Interventions

19

HELP-SEEKING

Traditional and Modern Ways of Knowing, and Insights for Mental Health Practice

Alean Al-Krenawi and John R. Graham

The present chapter is about mental health practices among Arab Americans. Like any construct, the notion of "Arab American" obscures and neglects as much as it explains and illuminates. There is tremendous diversity within either concept of "Arab" or "American" – to say nothing of "Arab American." People understand themselves, and others, on the basis of various intersecting factors such as age, gender, degree of religious conviction, geography, range of ability, sexual orientation, and socioeconomic status. People intermarry; they move; they change and grow over time. Therefore, loosely defined categories such as "Arab American," "Arab Muslim," or "Arab Christian" are oversimplified and marked by reductionism. At the same time, they can be useful in identifying group trends in the existing scholarship. Thus, the generalizations presented in this chapter regarding culture and its intersections with mental health practice are intended as a starting point for further reflection and clarification.

Research has delved into a broad array of issues relating to mental health practices in general, among Arab peoples, and among Arab Americans in particular. Immigrants leave much behind in their country of origin, but for many, their cultural norms may be packed for transport with care. Attitudes toward mental health are no exception to that rule. Arab Americans, with familial roots that may extend deep into the soil of the Middle East and North Africa, may share many cultural expectations with Arabs from their homelands. Whether immigrant or native-born, Christian or Muslim, Arab Americans – like all people – are influenced by the mores of their ethnic culture. These mores loom large in their perceptions, utilizations, and conceptualizations of mental health healing practices.

Formal mental health services developed out of the healing rituals of myriad traditions (Bilu & Witztum, 1994; Popper-Giveon, 2009; Prince, 1976, 1981). The overlap between these two approaches – the formal and the traditional – includes the use of psychopharmacological agents, psychodrama, catharsis, abreaction, environmental manipulation, suggestion, and direct ego support (Kiev, 1964). Psychotherapeutic treatments contain specific elements of ritual (Serlin, 1993). Traditional healing, for its part, employs a number of psychotherapeutic elements, which serve on the personal, familial, and group levels to integrate parts of the self and to connect individuals to their communities and heritage (Hoch-Smith & Spring, 1978). Nonetheless, notable differences exist between formal and traditional healing systems. Perhaps the most salient are the explanations of the etiology of illness. Formal healing systems concentrate on biochemical, psychological, and environmental sources of emotional distress. By way of contrast, traditional healing practices often make etiological reference to spiritual and religious forces.

This chapter provides an overview of how Arab Americans arrive at traditional and formal treatments, and the cultural issues to be considered in those processes. First, specific theoretical models of help-seeking are presented. Next, mental health healing practices among Arab Americans are discussed, namely family and religion as the first line of defense, characteristics of ethnic Arab traditional healing, and the utilization of religious healers and underutilization of mental health services. Next, issues that affect help-seeking in the formal mental healthcare system are explored. These include traditional social norms for Arabs, stigmas and disclosure, and mistrust in multicultural competency of formal mental health systems. Next, a possible solution through a collaborative approach between the formal and traditional systems is offered, along with a case example in which a collaborative approach is used. Lastly, a critique of the current literature is presented, along with suggestions for possible future directions. The terms "client" and "treatment" are used throughout the chapter in comparing traditional healers and biomedical practitioners. By doing so, it is not meant to apply biomedical assumptions to the traditional healers discussed, nor to project biomedical ideas on traditional healing practices. Rather, common terminology is used in order to have sentences that can compare the two traditions.

Theoretical Models of Help-Seeking for Arab Americans

It is a known problem that for many reasons – cultural, religious, social – minority populations do not seek out treatment as much as young, female, educated, or middle-class populations (Gourash, 1978). Different minorities also have diverse pathways of reaching out and arriving at treatment (Cauce et al., 2002). Two different models of help-seeking are presented here. Both were based on studies conducted with Muslim Arab Americans, but their points can likely be generalized across the Arab American spectrum. Arab Americans experience a large range of challenges, including social, political, and cultural; these issues "indicate levels of social stressors and suggest the need to ensure the availability of affordable, accessible, and culturally acceptable health and mental health services" (Aloud & Rathur, 2009, p. 80).

Aloud and Rathur (2009) developed a model of mental health help-seeking pathways for Muslim Arab Americans that strived to identify "the role of Arab and Islamic cultures (including beliefs, values, and norms) on the Arab Muslim tendency toward the seeking and using of mental health and psychological services" (pp. 86–87). This exploratory model was based on the Arab and Muslim mental health literatures, as well as on empirical data. The authors stated that Muslim Arab Americans go through three stages upon understanding that they are experiencing some sort of mental or psychological distress: (1) problem awareness and recognition, (2) the decision to seek help, and (3) services selection. The individual is susceptible to various obstacles from professional and personal sources, as well as cultural and religious perceptions, which can interfere with the progression of these stages. Muslim Arab attitudes and potential help-seeking behaviors are best predicted by "cultural beliefs about mental health and psychological problems, knowledge and familiarity with formal mental health services, perceived societal stigma, and help-seeking preferences" (p. 97). Again, the authors believed that this model can be generalized to the Arab American population, although the influence of culture also has to do with how close the individual identifies and is associated with the Arab culture.

Abu-Ras, Gheith, and Cournos (2008) proposed a model of help-seeking titled "Islamic model of mental health counseling" (p. 159). This model takes into account the intersection between Islamic spirituality and conceptions of counseling and Western ideas of mental healthcare. The authors' survey of imams in New York City found that 95% used a "multifaceted model of psychotherapy and unstructured intervention approach" to support congregants who turned to them for help (p. 168). In both models, there is a fine intertwining of cultural, religious, and professional knowledge in order to assist those seeking mental health help.

Mental Health Healing Practices Among Arab Americans

Family and Religion: First-Line Defense

Arab Americans who experience emotional distress may turn for help first to their religion, family, and friends. Very telling statistics from Khan's (2006) research on Muslim Americans paint the picture: about 61.3% of the Arab subsample reported that they "always" sought comfort from prayer, 43.8% always sought comfort from the Qur'an, and 44.6% always turned to family members. From the previously discussed model of Aloud and Rather (2009), Muslim Arab American help-seeking behaviors are often influenced by indigenous family and religious sources, known collectively as *ruqia*.

If relief from the distress is not obtained, the individual may decide to contact an expert within the formal system; this will often take place within a primary healthcare context. Religious institutions and religious healers in Western cultures may be more open to new ideas, and their congregants may pursue help from healthcare professionals (Abu-Ras et al., 2008). However, the distressed individual and his or her family may seek traditional assistance before, after, or concurrently with seeking formal healing care. As discussed below, perhaps partially because Arab Americans do not have access in North America to shrines and other healing mechanisms that are common in Arab states, this population has been turning to religious leaders for spiritually based mental health treatment. For Arab Americans, their mental health needs may be to a great extent unmet, indicating a need to better understand and serve this population (Khan, 2006). While there are many Arab Americans of Christian background, the following pages focus, in particular, on those who follow Islam – with comparatively less discussion of their Christian counterparts.

Characteristics of Ethnic Arab Traditional Healing

As noted above, the etiological stance of traditional healing systems differentiates it from formal healing. Some traditional healers believe that spiritual entities (such as the *jinn* mentioned in the Qur'an) are able to enter the body and disturb its functioning. These traditional notions among Muslim Arab Americans are well reviewed in Smith's (2011) doctoral thesis. A question has been raised in the literature about whether such beliefs hinder distressed individuals from recognizing psychological disorders (El-Islam, 1982).

Traditional healing leverages the power of positive thinking. In a variety of ways, it supports the belief that an indomitable force (usually that of God) will make it possible for the healer to help persons who are suffering to overcome their distress. Several factors figure in developing client trust in the abilities of healer: the healer may relate stories of healthy outcomes, and he or she may suggest that the client confer with a cured individual.

In traditional healing systems, the healer typically takes an active role, while the client assumes a relatively passive stance. The healer guides, instructs, and suggests practical courses of treatment (Al-Krenawi & Graham, 1996; El-Islam, 1982). Traditional healers often develop a good relationship with the client, which bolsters the therapeutic alliance (Al-Krenawi & Graham, 1996, 1997; El-Islam, 1982). Further, they may harness the family's help to improve treatment compliance (Al-Krenawi & Graham, 1997). Indeed, traditional healers are skilled in identifying and engaging the dominant familial figure in the change process. By way of contrast, formal mental health systems are typically characterized by detachment, and many highly regarded approaches call for maintaining a strict separation between the client's family and the clinician (Al-Krenawi & Graham, 1999).

Traditional healing systems offer a number of distinct advantages over formal mental health services. Traditional treatment makes use of non-stigmatizing modes of culturally acceptable rituals and practices (Al-Krenawi & Graham, 1996, 1999; Aloud & Rathur, 2009; El-Islam, 1982; Gorkin & Othman, 1994). Ethnic Arab traditional healers may be adept at managing transferential and counter-transferential issues arising with clients of both sexes, using such terms as "my brother" or "my sister" in order to desexualize the clinical relationship. (The case example described further on in this chapter provides a look at an effective use of this technique.) Traditional healers may be experienced in collaborating with community and familial supports, and they are familiar with culturally based idioms of distress (Al-Krenawi & Graham, 2000).

Symptoms of emotional distress are highly context dependent. Ethnic Arab clients may express psychological issues through somatic metaphors and proverbial expressions that reflect the clients' subjective feelings (Nguyen, Foulks, & Carlin, 1991). For instance, a client might report that the pain swims through his or her body, and it is up to the person providing care to be aware of the meaning of this syntax (Al-Krenawi, 1999). Idioms of distress such as these can easily be overlooked or misinterpreted by all parties: the client, the therapist, the spiritual leader, and others (Al-Krenawi & Graham, 2000; Gearing et al., 2013). The potential for this to occur in the North American context is quite real; as such, Erickson and Al-Timimi (2001) cautioned the healthcare provider against pathologizing somatic complaints.

Utilization of Religious Healers and Underutilization of Mental Health Services

Some Arab Americans tend to avoid seeking formal mental health services. Instead, many have been turning in greater numbers to their religious leaders for psychological assistance. Thus, Abu-Ras and colleagues (2008) reported that while only one of the 22 imams in New York City they contacted had any formal training in mental health, most of the participants in this post-9/11 study had seen congregational members turn to them for religiously based psychological assistance. Herzig (2011) reported that his American-born Muslim college student participants used religious coping strategies prior to seeking formal mental healthcare; while these participants were Muslims from different backgrounds, because of their shared Islamic beliefs these findings may be relevant to the Muslim Arab American population as a whole. In their study of Muslim Arabs in the Midwestern U.S., Aloud and Rathur (2009) noted that their participants had utilized to the fullest all community resources, including religious resources, before turning for help to the formal mental healthcare system.

Similarly, Muslim Arab American participants in Smith's (2011) study reported formal psychotherapy to be "an unnecessary resource" (p. 77), maintaining that they could generally manage emotional distress by seeking assistance from family, friends, and religious leaders. This perspective supports Khan's (2006) study on Muslim Americans, the majority of whom reported that they always sought relief for emotional distress through prayer, family, and the Qur'an. The Christian Arab Americans studied by Boulos (2011) for her doctoral dissertation sought mental health assistance first through the auspices of religious and communal leaders. Ali, Milstein, and Marzuk (2005) determined that 80% of 62 imams reported spending a significant amount of time each week in providing counseling to their congregants. Of these imams, 100% of those who were imams of Arab American congregations reported the need for increased counseling for congregants since 9/11; this is compared to the 60% of imams of South Asian American communities who reported this need, and the 50% of imams of African American communities. Meanwhile, Smith (2011) reported that her Muslim Arab American study participants were not aware of a single Muslim or Arab American who had been treated in the formal mental health system. The phenomenon seems quite similar in other Western contexts: the Australian Arabic-speaking community also underutilizes the available formal mental health services (Youssef & Deane, 2006). Thus, Arab Americans often use the modern mental health systems less compared to traditional resources, and in many cases they refer to religious leaders or use both systems concurrently (Al-Krenawi & Graham, 1999).

The glitch, however, is that the congregational leaders to whom Arab Americans have been turning for psychological assistance may not be qualified to provide this service. Of the imams surveyed by Abu-Ras and colleagues (2008), 91% were foreign-born and -educated, and, as noted above, almost none had any formal training in mental health service provision. Indeed, 91% of these respondents stated that they were unfamiliar with the formal mental health services available in their respective communities. English-language fluency, mental health service training, and awareness of referral options were significant problems in this context. How then, do Arab Americans make their choices when experiencing emotional distress? Several factors that are involved in Arab American decision-making for mental healthcare are considered below.

Issues Affecting Help-Seeking in the Formal Mental Healthcare System

Arab Americans who consider seeking mental health assistance must navigate through several pressing concerns. These elements include traditional Arab social norms, social stigma and disclosure challenges, and lack of trust in the cultural competency of formal mental health systems.

Traditional Social Norms

Two powerful social norms in Arab society serve to impact the help-seeking processes: family orientation and fatalism. The Arab cultural construct of collectivism, beginning with the family, strongly colors the decision-making process made by some Arab American clients for psychological care. For some, traditional Arab family influence on the individual family member is significant and fundamental. Thus, Arab American families may, at times, provide a natural form of social support, which to some extent serves as a proxy for professional intervention. In these instances, the Arab client would be accompanied by a family member to a mental health consultation. The family would, in turn, be a major stakeholder in determining the treatment pathway (Al-Krenawi and Graham, 1999; Dwairy & Jagelman, 1998; Okasha, 1993; Qureshi, Al-Armi, & Abdelgader, 1998). This situation, in which the family has functioned as the yardstick by which decisions are made regarding healthcare choices, may be changing with the times. For instance, college-aged Muslim Arab Americans may not view practitioners who are known to their families as especially desirable providers of psychological services (Herzig, 2011). Nonetheless, the traditional ethnic Arab social norm of collectivism is deeply embedded and, as seen below, intersects with the issues of stigma and disclosure in the Arab American community.

A strong sense of fatalism is a second, and similarly powerful, factor in the mental health decision-making process for some in this population. Hamdan (2009) has written on the belief among traditional Arab communities throughout the world that emotional and physical illness emanates from supernatural forces, or from "God's will." This notion was mentioned by Aloud and Rathur (2009) in their study of Muslim Arab Americans. The authors further noted that this belief may lead to toleration of symptomology, as a kind of acquiescence to divine will. Boulos (2011) found religious fatalism to be a core issue for her first and second generation Coptic study participants, and maintained that understanding the issue is central to clinical work with this subpopulation of Arab Americans. Widening the geographic lens, Hamid and Furnham (2013) reported an inverse relationship among British Arabs between espousal of a subset of causal beliefs in the supernatural regarding psychological distress and attitudes toward seeking professional psychological help.

Stigma and Disclosure

Social stigma associated with the search for mental health treatment has been conceptualized as one of the most significant obstacles to successful outcomes across populations (Sibicky & Dovidio, 1986; Stefl & Prosperi, 1985). The use of formal mental health services in Arab populations globally has been traditionally considered a reflection of an inability to cope with weakness or to resolve emotional problems within the confines of the family (Al-Krenawi, Graham, Dean, & Eltaiba, 2004).

This help-seeking behavior may be perceived by the ethnic Arab client as a threat to group honor or as an act of disloyalty to the family (Abudabbeh & Nydell, 1993).

There is a rich literature on stigma (and the highly related issue of disclosure) for Arab Americans. In her study on psychotherapy with this sector, Martin (2014) highlighted a pervasive and persistent reluctance to turn to those outside the family for emotional help. Nassar-McMillan and Hakim-Larson (2003) found that a group of psychotherapists who work with the Arab American population viewed stigma as one of the greatest barriers to therapeutic treatment. One of Erickson and Al-Timimi's (2001) 12 recommendations for working with Arab American clients in a healing context was to use psychoeducation and empowerment techniques to help them manage their sense of stigma pertaining to mental health issues. The desire to "save face for the family" was suggested by Soheilian and Inman (2009, p. 150) as a possible reason for avoidance of counseling among a segment of Arab Americans. This finding is in line with those of Boghosian's (2011) doctoral dissertation, which described that possible avoidance of formal systems is caused by the stigma and the misunderstanding of mental health issues within the Middle Eastern American community and family.

These views on stigma can be even more complex. Ciftci, Jones, and Corrigan (2013) recommended that sensitive research be conducted to address double stigma and intersectionality, looking particularly at race, class, gender, and post-9/11 discrimination. A recent study among Australian Arabic-speaking individuals further underscores the magnitude of this issue for ethnic Arabs in the West. Youssef and Deane (2006) wrote that shame and stigma pertaining to help-seeking behavior from outside the family constituted an "overwhelming hindrance" (p. 43) to this population's accessing of formal mental health services.

Mistrust in Multicultural Competency of Formal Mental Health Systems

While Arab Americans as a group express varying degrees of openness toward formal mental healthcare, there is a broad consensus of mistrust in the multicultural competency of clinicians in this system. Strikingly, this mistrust was noted even among second and third generation Arab Americans, as well as in research on ethnically diverse Muslim Americans that is likely to hold true for Muslim Arab Americans. The American-born Muslim college students whom Herzig (2011) studied (including more than 20% of Arab ethnicity) valued multicultural competency above all other qualities in a mental health clinician. They expressed serious doubts as to the formal treatment providers' familiarity with the tenets of Islam. Smith (2011), who sampled a non-college-age population of Muslim Arab Americans, found that there was a lack of awareness among her study participants that therapists may undergo cultural competency training. Her respondents voiced concern regarding potential values conflicts with mental health clinicians in the formal system. Importantly, this mistrust of clinician multicultural competency seems to hold across religious affiliation: Boulos (2011) reported that Christian Arab Americans tend to be skeptical of the formal mental health system and prefer to seek help from their familial and religious systems.

For Muslim Arab Americans, these concerns are supported by recent research that has found mental health practitioner knowledge of Muslim Americans' religious orientation to be weak (Padela & Curlin 2012). Because Islam is the world's second-largest religion, and in light of the events of 9/11, dealings with clients demand a high level of cultural competency and sensitivity (Graham, Bradshaw, & Trew, 2009). As Khan (2006) accurately stated, "To work effectively with Muslims, counselors need to recognize not only the diversity of Muslims in America, but what diversity means with regard to inclinations to help-seeking among the predominate Muslim subgroups" (p. 22). These issues can also be generalized to the Arab American population. As Sabbah, Dinsmore, and Hof (2009) found, mental health practitioners felt less competent to work with Arab Americans compared to other ethnic groups because of a lack of knowledge about Arab worldview and culture. Al-Krenawi and Jackson (2014) urged the consideration of how cultural contexts such as marriage, family, and religious relationships can greatly influence the cultural competency of mental health practitioners working with Arab Americans.

Toward a Solution: A Collaborative Approach

What can be done in a situation in which two distinct healing systems exist, each endowed with unique strengths but neither independently able to fully meet the needs of its constituency? The stakeholders in the systems can learn to work together. Creative and exciting possibilities are emerging from the literature for collaboration between traditional-religious ethnic Arab and formal healing systems. As early as several decades ago, Rappaport and Rappaport (1981) suggested a combined-modality model in which both formal and traditional healing systems would be utilized. In this model, the medical professional would be attuned to underlying difficulties and support a client's search for a traditional healer/religious guide to complement treatment. Such a guide would treat the spiritual aspects of the distress, and the professional mental health clinician would treat the organic symptoms.

Al-Krenawi (2000) examined Rappaport and Rappaport's (1981) model. He showed that among Arab clients, the formal system was perceived as helpful in alleviating somatic complaints, while the traditional system was viewed as helpful in addressing emotional distress. This is a common outcome in societies in which traditional and Western healing systems coexist. In these contexts, individuals typically hold different expectations of the two systems and they either choose between them for different types of problem or utilize them simultaneously to deal with different aspects of the same problem (Al-Krenawi & Graham, 1999, 2000; Asuni, 1979; Jahoda, 1961; Marsella & White, 1982).

The two systems, then, may function in a synergistic manner. Toward this goal, Al-Krenawi and Graham (2003) advocated the use of a cultural mediator to broker contact between the formal mental health system and Arab American clients with traditional perspectives of mental health. Possibilities include a mental health service professional familiar with the client's culture, and a member of that culture who could help to make the available mental health treatment more culturally relevant. This suggestion is in line with a number of others that have been made in recent work on Arab Americans. Ali and colleagues (2005), for instance, suggested direct mental health professional support of imams, who have reported a widespread need to counsel persons who have been discriminated against since 9/11. This idea was highlighted by Abu-Ras and colleagues (2008), whose study participants – New York City imams – expressed a willingness to learn professional psychological techniques to better assist their congregants. Herzig (2011) supported the idea of religious leaders adding formal mental health training to their therapeutic arsenal, adding that imams might help to alleviate the stigma associated with emotional distress by spending time during sermons discussing such issues. Concrete treatment collaboration between religious leaders and mental health practitioners was also urged by Erickson and Al-Timimi (2001).

A collaborative approach might take its cue from traditional healers to therapeutically harness the strength of the Arab family. Importantly, Erickson and Al-Timimi (2001) cautioned against counseling for individuation from the ethnic Arab family as a central therapeutic goal; rather, these scholars suggested a psychoeducational approach in which the family would be helped to recognize the benefits that are accrued to the family as a whole when the distress of the individual with the presenting problem is alleviated. Along these lines, Martin (2014) recommended that the mental health professional enlist ethnic Arab family support for the treatment and involve them to whatever extent is appropriate. Youssef and Deane (2006) advised highly flexible provision of services, even to the point of interviewing ethnic Arab clients in the client's own home, where, of course, the client's family might be situated and thus engaged.

Many other possibilities for the integration of traditional and formal systems exist. Enhanced referral information should be provided to schools serving Arab American students, according to

Martin (2014). General medical practitioners in Arab American areas, to whom Arab Americans might turn for help, could also be better educated about these referral options. Youssef and Deane (2006) suggested that outreach be conducted especially with Arabic-speaking general medical practitioners, and that mental health services should be provided in the Arabic language. In short, the wealth of ideas and energy in this area of integration between the cultural and the professional is quite substantial. This is shown next in a brief case example of a therapeutic intervention that highlights the potential of a collaborative approach to mental healthcare for Arab Americans.

Case Example: Nadia's Conflict in the Context of Culture

Nadia was a 23-year-old ethnic Arab woman who came to the clinic for mental health treatment following a suicide attempt. She came from a family with a strong Arab ethnic identity and she identified with the Arab culture. She was married to an Arab man but was having an affair with another man that had become sexual in nature, and she was discovered while leaving his house one day by a member of her family. Her husband promptly returned her to her parents, and she feared that her parents would punish her harshly for disgracing the family. There was also a noted tension in her relationship with her mother. She attempted suicide and, after her stay at a local hospital, she was referred to the local community mental health center to receive outpatient mental health counseling with a male clinician.

As treatment progressed, Nadia's behavior during sessions became more and more sexualized. Her manner of dress grew provocative, and she began suggestively to touch the hand of her male therapist. Nadia's therapist, also an ethnic Arab, decided to manage her transference-based sexual overtures by the adoption, and regular reiteration, of the traditional Arabic brother role. He began to refer to Nadia as "my sister," taking care to clarify this role and emphasizing its desexualized nature. Nadia responded with a curtailing of her overtures, and the treatment was able to move forward.

In order to arrive at this solution, Nadia's therapist spent considerable time consulting with elders and religious leaders of the local community to discuss how best to use religious and culturally normative themes in his dealings with the client, an illustrative example of the collaborative approach. This allowed him to blend his personal, modern healing techniques with the appropriate traditional healing techniques that would most effectively help Nadia's course of treatment.

The therapist also explored the possibility of Nadia's family becoming involved in the treatment due to the importance placed on families in Arab culture. He began to introduce Nadia's mother to the sessions through guided imagery exercises, allowing her to "be" in the room and allowing Nadia to converse with her in a safe setting. Gradually, the therapist was able to facilitate joint sessions with Nadia and her mother, greatly improving the relationship between the two. His recognition of the ethnic importance of family in this particular case significantly helped to push forward the treatment of this client. Nadia's situation improved, and she continued with a fairly normal life after about two years of therapy.

This case example provides a glimpse into the power of multicultural competency and the use of the collaborative approach. The client's transferential behavior could have been managed therapeutically, of course, in a variety of ways. Insight-oriented work, for example, might well have called for a very different approach. However, Nadia's therapist determined that this client, at this phase of her therapeutic process, was best served by recourse to traditional Arab modes of cultural expression. The treatment provider's multicultural competency strengthened in a meaningful way his ability to help the client.

Critique

In light of a demonstrable need in the Arab American community for highly skilled and culturally sensitive mental healthcare, and the abundance of creative solutions found in the current literature, it is appropriate to ask: "What is the next step?" The answer was put forth by Erickson and Al-Timimi (2001) and, more recently, by Amri and Bemak (2013): evidence-based interventions should be implemented, and these require shoring up the store of empirically derived data. A good example of this is the recommendation made by Herzig, Roysircar, Kosyluk, and Corrigan (2013) to consider religion a core theme in the mental health treatment of Muslim Americans. These researchers based their practical suggestion on a structural equation modeling examination of their research-driven data. State-of-the-art doctoral-level research was also conducted by Amer (2005), who rigorously evaluated extant theories of Arab American acculturation and mental health with careful attention to measure development, sample size, hypothesis testing, and modeling approaches.

Perhaps it is important, too, to call attention to the stigma that Arab Americans encounter seeking mental health help. The potential stigma associated with mental health issues can be damaging, including toward marital prospects. For example, it can increase the likelihood of divorce or separation, or among Muslim Arabs, being used by a husband or his family as leverage for taking an additional wife (Al-Krenawi & Graham, 2000). Working toward the destigmatization of mental health practices among Arab Americans can be invaluable.

It is also important to echo the call in the literature for strengthening the collaborative effort between formal and traditional methods of treatment. Treatment and training programs must be developed to incorporate a strong sense of cultural competency and sensitivity. One place to start is within the literature and research *not* in English. Perhaps one of the shortcomings of research up until now is the focus on what is written in English, as opposed to what could be done in the native language of the population in question. It would be valuable to conduct studies in Arabic or other relevant languages in order to reach a larger cross-section of people and to reach a deeper understanding of what barriers are encountered by Arab Americans who seek services. It would also be helpful to search the Arabic-language literature in more depth.

The literature is also extremely limited when looking at the population of Christian Arab Americans, and even more so with regard to other minority subsets. The specific needs of these Christian subpopulations could differ because of cultural differences between Muslim Arabs and Christian Arabs, so further research on these particular subgroups would be infinitely useful for the improvement of care for Arab Americans as a whole.

As scholars and mental health providers know, successful helping behavior demands appropriate interventions at appropriate times, in appropriate venues, and with the appropriate tools. The project of providing Arab Americans with this type of service is still in its infancy and opens many doors for future study.

Conclusion

Despite a sometimes desperate need for mental health assistance, Arab Americans who experience psychological distress may hesitate to consult with mental health professionals. In some instances, collaboration between the traditional (specifically, religious) and formal healing systems is the key to enhancing the helping process for this population. Flexible strategies of psychoeducation and community outreach are urgently needed. In line with the ethical dictates of a broad swath of professional codes, practitioners are urged to educate themselves regarding traditional Arab beliefs and mores – of which there is great diversity based on religious, regional, and other grounds. In so doing, it is important to assume a stance that is continuously open to learning from the client. Essentialism – the view that there is a set range of characteristics for any cultural group – must always be avoided. One of the best ways of doing this is by being open to learning from the clients, who in their own right are "experts" on their own norms, values, opinions, and beliefs as mediated by their culture, gender, age, and other intersecting areas of positionality. Further, it is imperative that clinicians make direct and creative use of this knowledge and approach to reach out to the large, and rapidly growing, population of both Muslim and Christian Arab Americans.

While religious leaders and traditional healers have in the past constituted distinct sectors in the global Arab population, the Arab American experience depends on access to these healers and leaders. Perhaps it is even possible to suggest that the current multifaceted and highly complex set of tasks now facing Arab American religious leaders derives, at least in part, from the roles of the traditional healers that originate from Arab homelands in the Middle East and Northern Africa. What is certain is that the Arab American population, old and young, immigrant and native-born, is in need of knowledge about and access to highly skilled and culturally knowledgeable mental health providers. These can be professional clinicians or trained religious leaders. To the extent that interpenetration takes place between the wisdom of the two systems, Arab Americans will only benefit.

References

Abudabbeh, N. & Nydell, M. K. (1993). Transcultural counselling and Arab Americans. In J. McFadden (ed.), *Transcultural counselling: Bilateral and international perspectives* (pp. 261–284). Alexandria, VA: American Counselling Association.

Abu-Ras, W., Gheith, A., & Cournos, F. (2008). The imam's role in mental health promotion: A study at 22 mosques in New York City's Muslim community. *Journal of Muslim Mental Health* 3(2), 155–176. doi: 10.1080/15564900802487576

Al-Krenawi, A. (1999). Explanations of mental health symptoms by the Bedouin-Arabs of the Negev. *International Journal of Social Psychiatry* 45(1), 56–64. doi: 10.1177/002076409904500107

Al-Krenawi, A. (2000). Bedouin-Arab clients' use of proverbs in the therapeutic setting. *International Journal for the Advancement of Counselling* 22(2), 91–102. doi: 10.1023/A:1005583920356

Al-Krenawi, A. & Graham, J. R. (1996). Social work practice and traditional healing rituals among the Bedouin of the Negev. *International Social Work* 39, 177–188. doi: 10.1177/002087289603900206

Al-Krenawi, A. & Graham, J. R. (1997). Spirit possession and exorcism: The integration of modern and traditional mental health care systems in the treatment of a Bedouin patient. *Clinical Social Work Journal* 25, 211–222. doi: 10.1023/A:1025714626136

Ali, O. M., Milstein, G., & Marzuk, P. M. (2005). The imam's role in meeting the counseling needs of Muslim communities in the United States. *Psychiatric Services* 56(2), 202–205.

Al-Krenawi, A. & Graham, J. R. (1999). Gender and modern mental health services/traditional mental health utilization among the Bedouin-Arab of the Negev. *Culture, Medicine, and Psychiatry* 23, 219–243.

Al-Krenawi, A. & Graham, J. R. (2000). Culturally sensitive social work practice with Arab clients in mental health settings. *Health & Social Work* 25(1), 9–22. doi: 10.1093/hsw/25.1.9

Al-Krenawi, A. & Graham, J. R. (2003). Introduction. In A. Al-Krenawi & J. R. Graham (eds.), *Multicultural social work in Canada: Working with diverse ethno-racial communities* (pp. 1–20). Don Mills, Ontario, Canada: Oxford University Press.

Al-Krenawi, A., Graham, J. R., Dean, Y. Z., & Eltaiba, N. (2004). Cross-national study of attitudes towards seeking professional help: Jordan, United Arab Emirates (UAE) and Arabs in Israel. *International Journal of Social Psychiatry* 50(2), 102–114. doi: 10.1177/0020764004040957

Al-Krenawi, A. & Jackson, S. O. (2014). Arab American marriage: Culture, tradition, religion, and the social worker. *Journal of Human Behavior in the Social Environment* 24(2), 115–137. doi: 10.1080/10911359.2014.848679

Aloud, N. & Rathur, A. (2009). Factors affecting attitudes toward seeking and using formal mental health and psychological services among Arab Muslim populations. *Journal of Muslim Mental Health* 4(2), 79–103. doi: 10.1080/15564900802487675

Amer, M. M. (2005). *Arab American mental health in the post September 11 era: Acculturation, stress, and coping* (Doctoral dissertation). Available from ProQuest Dissertations and Theses database (UMI No. 3171022).

Amri, A. & Bemak, F. (2013). Mental health help-seeking behaviors of Muslim immigrants in the United States: Overcoming social stigma and cultural mistrust. *Journal of Muslim Mental Health* 7(1), 43–63. doi: 10.3998/jmmh.10381607.0007.104

Asuni, T. (1979). The dilemma of traditional healing with special reference to Nigeria. *Social Science and Medicine. Part B: Medical Anthropology* 13(1), 33–39. doi: 10.1016/0160-7987(79)90016-4

Bilu, Y. & Witztum, E. (1994). Injured while peeling: On beliefs and mystical practices among health patients, and their implementation in treatment. *Alpayim: A Multidisciplinary Publication for Contemporary Thought and Literature* 9(1), 21–42.

Boghosian, S. (2011). *Counseling and psychotherapy of clients of Middle Eastern descent* (Doctoral dissertation). Available from ProQuest Dissertations and Theses database (UMI No. 3453570).

Boulos, S. A. (2011). *The role of acculturation, ethnic identity, and religious fatalism on attitudes towards seeking psychological help among Coptic Americans* (Doctoral dissertation). Available from ProQuest Dissertations and Theses database (UMI No. 3471196).

Cauce, A. N., Domenech-Rodriguez, M., Paradise, M., Cochran, B. N., Shea, J. M., Srebnik, D., & Baydar, N. (2002). Cultural and contextual influences in mental health help seeking: A focus on ethnic minority youth. *Journal of Consulting and Clinical Psychology* 70(1), 44–55.

Ciftci, A., Jones, N., and Corrigan, P. W. (2013). Mental health stigma in the Muslim community. *Journal of Muslim Mental Health* 7(1), 17–32. doi: 10.3998/jmmh.10381607.0007.102

Dwairy, M. A. & Jagelman, J. (1998). *Cross-cultural counseling: The Arab Palestinian case.* New York: Haworth Press.

El-Islam, M. F. (1982). Arabic cultural psychiatry. *Transcultural Psychiatric Research Review* 19(1), 5–24. doi: 10.1177/136346158201900101

Erickson, C. D. & Al-Timimi, N. R. (2001). Providing mental health services to Arab Americans: Recommendations and considerations. *Cultural Diversity and Ethnic Minority Psychology* 7(4), 308–327. doi: 10.1037/1099-9809.7.4.308

Gearing, R. E., Schwalbe, C. S., MacKenzie, M. J., Brewer, K. B., Ibrahim, R. W., Olimat, H. S., ... Al-Krenawi, A. (2013). Adaptation and translation of mental health interventions in Middle Eastern Arab countries: A systematic review of barriers to and strategies for effective treatment implementation. *International Journal of Social Psychiatry* 59, 671–681. doi: 10.1177/0020764012452349

Gorkin, M. & Othman, R. (1994). Traditional psychotherapeutic healing and healers in the Palestinian community. *Israel Journal of Psychiatry and Related Sciences* 31, 221–231.

Gourash, N. (1978). Help-seeking: A review of the literature. *American Journal of Community Psychology* 6, 413–423. doi: 10.1007/BF00941418

Graham, J. R., Bradshaw, C., & Trew, J. L. (2009). Addressing cultural barriers with Muslim clients: An agency perspective. *Administration in Social Work* 33, 387–406. doi: 10.1080/03643100903172950

Hamdan, A. (2009). Mental health needs of Arab women. *Health Care for Women International* 30, 593–611. doi: 10.1080/07399330902928808

Hamid, A. & Furnham, A. (2013). Factors affecting attitude towards seeking professional help for mental illness: A UK Arab perspective. *Mental Health, Religion & Culture* 16, 741–758. doi: 10.1080/13674676.2012.718753

Herzig, B. A. (2011). *An examination of American-born Muslim college students' attitudes toward mental health* (Doctoral dissertation). Available from ProQuest Dissertations and Theses database (UMI No. 3467009).

Herzig, B. A., Roysircar, G., Kosyluk, K. A., & Corrigan, P. W. (2013). American Muslim college students: The impact of religiousness and stigma on active coping. *Journal of Muslim Mental Health* 7(1), 33–42. doi: 10.3998/jmmh.10381607.0007.103

Hoch-Smith, J. & Spring, A. (1978). *Women in ritual and symbolic roles.* New York: Plenum Pub Corporation.

Jahoda, G. (1961). Traditional healers and other institutions concerned with mental illness in Ghana. *International Journal of Social Psychiatry* 7(4), 245–268. doi: 10.1177/002076406100700401

Khan, Z. (2006). Attitudes toward counseling and alternative support among Muslims in Toledo, Ohio. *Journal of Muslim Mental Health* 1(1), 21–42. doi: 10.1080/15564900600654278

Kiev, A. (ed.) (1964). *Magic, faith and healing: Studies in primitive psychiatry today.* New York: The Free Press.

Marsella, A. J. & White, G. (eds.) (1982). *Cultural conceptions of mental health and therapy* (vol. 4). Hingham, MA: Kluwer.

Martin, U. (2014). Psychotherapy with Arab Americans: An exploration of therapy-seeking and termination behaviors. *International Journal of Culture and Mental Health* 7, 162–167. doi: 10.1080/17542863.2012.742121

Nassar-McMillan, S. C. & Hakim-Larson, J. (2003). Counseling considerations among Arab Americans. *Journal of Counseling and Development* 81, 150–159. doi: 10.1002/j.1556–6678.2003.tb00236.x

Nguyen, N., Foulks, E. F., & Carlin, K. (1991). Proverbs as psychological interpretations among Vietnamese. *Asian Folklore Studies* 50(2), 311–318. doi: 10.2307/1178388

Okasha, A. (1993). Psychiatry in Egypt. *Psychiatric Bulletin* 17(9), 548–551. doi: 10.1192/pb.17.9.548

Padela, A. I. & Curlin, F. A. (2012). Religion and disparities: Considering the influences of Islam on the health of American Muslims. *Journal of Religion and Health* 52, 1333–1345. doi: 10.1007/s10943-012-9620-y

Popper-Giveon, A. (2009). Adapted traditions: The case of traditional Palestinian women healers in Israel. *Forum: Qualitative Social Research* 10(2), 1–23.

Prince, R. (1976). Psychotherapy as the manipulation of indigenous healing mechanisms: A transcultural survey. *Transcultural Psychiatric Research Review* 13, 115–133.

Prince, R. (1981). The psychiatrist and the folk healer: Interface and partnership. In G. Meyer & J. Cull (eds.), *Folk medicine and herbal healing* (pp. 57–69). Illinois: Charles C Thomas Publisher.

Qureshi, N. A., Al-Armi, A. H., & Abdelgader, H. (1998). Traditional cautery among psychiatric patients in Saudi Arabia. *Transcultural Psychiatry* 35(1), 75–83. doi: 10.1177/136346159803500103

Rappaport, H. & Rappaport, M. (1981). The integration of scientific and traditional healing: A proposed model. *American Psychologist* 36(7), 774–781. doi: 10.1037/0003-066X.36.7.774

Sabbah, M. F., Dinsmore, J. A., & Hof, D. D. (2009). A comparative study of the competence of counselors in the United States in counseling Arab Americans and other racial/ethnic groups. *International Journal of Psychology: A Biopsychosocial Approach* 4, 29–45.

Serlin, I. A. (1993). Root images of healing in dance therapy. *American Journal of Dance Therapy* 15, 65–76. doi: 10.1007/BF00844028

Sibicky, M. & Dovidio, J. F. (1986). Stigma of psychological therapy: Stereotypes, interpersonal reactions, and the self-fulfilling prophecy. *Journal of Counseling Psychology* 33, 148–154. doi: 10.1037/0022-0167.33.2.148

Smith, J. (2011). *Removing barriers to therapy with Muslim-Arab-American clients* (Doctoral dissertation). Available from ProQuest Dissertations and Theses database (UMI No. 3493088).

Soheilian, S. S. & Inman, A. G. (2009). Middle Eastern Americans: The effects of stigma on attitudes toward counseling. *Journal of Muslim Mental Health* 4, 139–158. doi: 10.1080/15564900903245766

Stefl, M. E. & Prosperi, D. C. (1985). Barriers to mental health service utilization. *Community Mental Health Journal* 21(3), 167–178. doi: 10.1007/BF00754732

Youssef, J. & Deane, F. P. (2006). Factors influencing mental-health help-seeking in Arabic-speaking communities in Sydney, Australia. *Mental Health, Religion and Culture* 9(1), 43–66. doi: 10.1080/1367467051 2331335686

20
PSYCHOLOGICAL ASSESSMENT
Distinguishing the Clinically Relevant From the Culturally Unique

Omar M. Mahmood and Sawssan R. Ahmed

Psychological assessment is a cornerstone of clinical psychology, focusing on the evaluation of behavior, emotion, and cognition in order to characterize a client's level of functioning. Accurate and rigorous assessment is a necessary precursor to any psychological interventions. Although this applied science is frequently used to identify dysfunction (e.g. psychopathology, maladjustment, or neurocognitive disorders) the assessment tools available to clinicians can also be used to simply describe an individual's baseline level or even to identify individuals functioning at exceptionally high levels (e.g. giftedness). For practitioners in North America, the field of psychological assessment has developed in a predominantly Eurocentric linguistic and cultural context, making it challenging at times to conduct an accurate evaluation of individuals outside the mainstream. Factors such as language fluency, cultural expression of psychological distress, and differences in acculturation must be considered when conducting clinically useful assessments for diverse populations.

Assessment of psychological states for Arab Americans shares many similarities with psychological assessment for other ethnic minority groups. This chapter provides an overview of considerations related to the pursuit of culturally competent evaluations with Arab American examinees. Specific elements of the assessment process are discussed, with attention toward strategies for accurate evaluation of psychological constructs. The conceptual framework and methodology focuses primarily on what is needed to formulate clinical impressions of a client, particularly related to psychopathology. Other types of assessment that are meant to examine specialized domains (e.g. developmental delay, academic skills, occupational functioning) will not be explicitly expounded upon, although many of the concepts in this chapter are applicable and relevant to the fields of developmental, school, and industrial/organizational psychology. Two case examples are presented: one focusing on an adult forensic evaluation, and the other on the psychoeducational evaluation of a child. Finally, the chapter concludes with a brief critique of the current state of clinical assessment of Arab Americans along with suggested studies for future development of this budding area of culturally relevant psychology.

The Etic-Emic Conceptual Spectrum

The use of standard data-gathering methods, psychometric instruments, and diagnostic techniques inevitably leads to challenges when working with ethnic minority populations. Dana (1993) proposed that there is an inherent tension between emic and etic perspectives when it comes to testing for psychological constructs in an individual from an ethnic minority group. The etic perspective assumes there are universal indicators of certain psychological realities, found in all people, that can be evaluated during the course of an assessment. The emic approach, on the other hand, maintains that there are unique, culture-specific factors that must be investigated during a psychological assessment and interpreted within the context of each culture's norms. Overemphasizing the etic approach would mean that a clinician compares an examinee's responses, behavior, and test performances to a single standard of psychological findings and conclusions while attributing any deviations from that criterion to the presence of pathology. To favor the emic approach unilaterally would result in a very specific description of the examinee with limited clinical value due to the failure to understand how the individual compares to the population and to what extent the symptoms affect his or her ability to function in the context of the greater society.

While some assessment measures are more suitable for etic purposes (e.g. criterion-based tests that compare responses to normative samples) and others are more useful in emic assessments (e.g. open-ended self-report measures or tests designed to assess implicit or unique psychological states), many assessment tools could be used potentially for either approach. This would depend on the data gathered, how they are interpreted, and the context in which the psychologist chooses to characterize the findings. For example, a standardized memory test could be used during a cognitive evaluation, but the examiner may decide to look only at raw scores on consecutive learning trials in order to identify the client's relative strengths and weaknesses, rather than use standard scores that would compare the client's performance to a standardization sample that may not be culturally representative. Similarly, a clinician with extensive experience in assessing members of a specific minority group may choose to use responses on a projective test to assess how a client's expression of symptoms compares to a subset of individuals from the same ethnolinguistic group who have previously been seen in the clinician's practice. In reality, the etic and emic viewpoints are not simply dichotomous; rather, they are two ends of a dynamic continuum.

When undergoing a psychological evaluation, many Arab Americans will benefit most from a combination of etic and emic methods of assessment. This would entail a balance between, on the one hand, placing individuals in broad population-based diagnostic categories and, on the other hand, contextualizing their behavior, emotions, and cognitions within the cultural paradigms specific to Arab Americans. Depending on some of the variables discussed in this chapter and the way they manifest within an individual Arab American, certain domains of functioning will be more accurately assessed using etic tools, while other domains will simultaneously require an emic tool in order to be measured properly. At each step in the assessment process, the challenge for a clinician is to decide what point along the etic-emic spectrum they will use as a basis for engaging the examinee.

When preparing for an assessment, a clinician may encounter a number of issues that may pull more toward one end or the other of the etic-emic spectrum. The ability to make sound decisions in this regard is a reflection of the clinician's cultural competence. Assessing an ethnic minority client in a competent manner entails knowing when to generalize the individual's data to a large comparison group, knowing when to individualize the interpretation exclusively to the client, and having the requisite knowledge of the client's cultural group in order to make these kinds of decisions (Sue, 1998). Stereotypes and misconceptions of Arab Americans can potentially influence any clinician during an assessment. Thus, the assessment process requires clinician self-awareness and an understanding of how sociocultural factors influence the design of a culturally competent assessment.

Factors Influencing Assessment of Arab Americans

Various sociocultural factors may play a role in the assessment of Arab Americans by influencing what tools are used to gather data and how information should be interpreted. Three of the main factors include language, acculturation, and symptom expression.

Language

Language use during an evaluation, and its relationship to assessment and diagnosis, has long been studied by multicultural psychologists. For example, an early study offered some evidence to suggest that bilingual individuals are diagnosed with greater cognitive difficulties when speaking their nondominant language, while they appear to exhibit greater emotional difficulties when responding in their dominant language (Grand, Marcos, Freedman, & Barroso, 1977). Wrobel, Farrag, and Hymes (2009) found that poor English skills (and the perceived stress due to the belief that one's English is poor) were predictive of depression in Arab Americans. Therefore, the client's linguistic ability or comfort is likely to influence assessment results, and the influence of language in the expression of emotional symptoms is a potential confound that could hinder the adequate and accurate assessment of mood. Clinicians who understand and speak the language of their ethnic minority clients may have an added advantage in detecting variations in thought and expression (Malgady, Rogler, & Costantino, 1987).

Failure to account for the language preferences of Arab Americans can pose a challenge when choosing interview questions, selecting tools for an assessment, interpreting responses, and deciding whether to conduct all or parts of the evaluation in Arabic. According to the Detroit Arab American Study (Baker et al., 2003), a large majority of their sample (80%) reported that they speak English very well or well. However, an even higher percentage (86%) also reported that they speak a second language at home (mostly Arabic), compared to only 12% of the general population who reported they speak a language other than English at home. Thus, a clinician encountering an Arab American client who is fluent in English may not realize that the client is better equipped to express deep, personal, and emotional states in their native tongue.

An interesting dilemma is presented when an individual primarily speaks Arabic at home and in most social and day-to-day situations, but received formal education in American curriculum schools and is employed in an English-dominant work environment. This may be particularly relevant to Arab American sojourners whose early life experiences are predominantly based in the Arabic-speaking world, but then after moving to North America for education and work their default professional language has become English. For them it is likely that the ability to express core emotional experiences is more easily accomplished in Arabic, whereas their academic achievement, fund of knowledge, and premorbid intelligence may be more accurately assessed with the use of tests that are administered in English and normed on individuals who were educated in North America.

For bilingual Arab Americans who were born and raised in the U.S. or Canada, the language in which the assessment is conducted may not have as dramatic an effect on symptom manifestation. For such individuals, their skill in describing behaviors or expressing emotions may be somewhat equivalent in English and Arabic. In his seminal paper on bilingualism, Cummins (1979) hypothesized that there is an interdependence between languages that are learned simultaneously. That is, children who exhibit learning difficulties in one language will show similar problems in the second language and, by the same principle, children who acquire academic skills in one language will be able to transfer those skills to the second language. Indeed, evidence has shown that bilingual Arabic-English children demonstrate a significant relationship between their two languages in the areas of reading working memory and syntactic awareness. This suggests that bilingualism does not impair their skills in either Arabic or English, and children with similar rates of deficits in both languages may exhibit a general language impairment (Abu-Rabia & Siegel, 2002). Therefore, in addition to knowing which language is currently dominant, an awareness of the developmental linguistic history (which language was acquired early on and which one was learned later) can be relevant to the assessment process. Furthermore, assessing the same construct in both languages may be helpful in clarifying what role, if any, language plays in the data collected and whether there is an underlying psychological or neurocognitive factor that impairs functioning independent of language.

Acculturation

Similar to issues of language, in order to determine how applicable measures designed for North American samples are to ethnic minority clients, it is important for psychologists to evaluate acculturation as another moderator of clinical presentation and test performance (Cuéllar, 2000; Dana, 1998). For the Arab American who is highly acculturated to the dominant culture, there may be very little adjustment for the clinician to make when preparing for the interview and testing session. However, some tests may be deemed less appropriate for an Arab American client who is less familiar with cultural concepts that are implied in certain test items (e.g. idioms or proverbs, or questions with nonliteral or figurative wording). Cuéllar, Siles, and Bracamontes (2004) suggest that a clinician would be justified in using the measurement of acculturation as a gauge in deciding how much to alter a test battery (e.g. removing items that unfairly disadvantage an ethnic minority client) to ensure a culturally competent assessment.

The client's acculturation level is not only relevant to gauging the cultural suitability of test items, it is also important because the level of acculturation can affect the expression (and thereby the detection) of symptoms during an assessment. However, fluency in English (particularly when spoken with an American accent) may mask an individual's actual level of acculturation during a clinical interview. With the international proliferation of American schools and American/Western mass media, it is quite common for individuals from various parts of the world to be well versed in American linguistic and cultural standards. Therefore, without specifically assessing for it, a clinician would not know how integrated or assimilated into mainstream culture an Arab American client is. As such, administering an acculturation questionnaire or assessing for acculturation specifically during a clinical interview may be warranted when conducting assessments with Arab American clients. Many in professional psychology have long recognized the need for incorporating acculturation measures in the clinical assessment and diagnosis of ethnic minorities (Roysircar & Maestas, 2002).

Expression of Symptoms

The manner in which psychopathology manifests among Arab Americans is another important consideration that can ultimately define the method of interviewing, the questions asked, and the type of data upon which a clinician focuses the assessment. A number of researchers have documented the trend for individuals from Arab cultures to emphasize somatic symptoms when self-reporting psychological distress (Al-Krenawi, 2005; El-Rufaie, Al-Sabosy, Bener, & Abuzeid, 1999; Hamdi, Amin, & Abou-Saleh, 1997). This phenomenon is not limited to Arabs; the process of focusing on and amplifying somatic symptoms when describing emotional distress is quite common in cultures throughout the world, including the West (Kirmayer & Young, 1998). Somatization can have the potential effect of distracting the clinician, whereby reports or observations of physical symptoms may be misinterpreted as behavioral agitation. Alternatively, the tendency to express emotional turmoil in physiological terms may be overlooked if interview questions or items on a questionnaire fail to ask adequately about somatic manifestations of distress.

Multiple explanations have been posited to explain why persons from different cultures, particularly from the Global South, may express symptoms somatically. It has been argued that the cultural stigma toward mental health problems can be somehow mitigated by shifting the focus to physical symptoms, thereby allowing clients to interpret their psychopathology as medical disorders. It has also been suggested that reporting somatic symptoms for emotional conditions is the result of a holistic understanding and experiencing of the connection between psyche and body such that concepts and vocabulary used to express mental states overlap greatly with those used to express physical symptoms (Meleis, 1981; Racy, 1980). However, a cross-cultural World Health Organization study found that increased rates of somatization were not related to Eastern vs. Western or developed vs.

underdeveloped countries of origin, but rather related to lower levels of formal education (Gureje, Simon, Ustun, & Goldberg, 1997).

Just as the explanation for symptom somatization has not been resolved in the literature, another debate relates to the extent to which this style of symptom expression is affected by acculturation. Some authors suggest that the same styles of expression found among Arab clients in the Middle East will apply to Arab Americans or Arabs living in Western countries (e.g. Al-Krenawi & Graham, 2000; Erickson & Al-Timimi, 2001). However, it is unclear whether this cultural conceptualization of symptomatology transfers invariably to the Arab diaspora and their descendants living outside the Arabic-speaking world. Whatever its prevalence among Arab Americans of different acculturation levels and generational statuses, the clinical significance of expressing psychological distress in physical terms is also elusive. Even if an Arab American client possesses the tendency to over-report somatic complaints in place of emotional symptoms, focusing exclusively on this style of symptom expression during an assessment may ignore the fact that it is only one aspect of the client's overall clinical picture.

Cultural Considerations for the Assessment Process

As with any assessment process, a series of steps is necessary to ensure a thorough and complete assessment. These steps include the clinical interview, psychological testing, and behavioral observations. The following sections explore how culture may play a role in the various stages of the assessment process, culminating in making a diagnosis.

The Clinical Interview

Dana (1993) mentions that the major stages of a conventional clinical interview (e.g. establishing rapport, clarifying purposes, asking the intake questions, identifying the problem(s), providing a summary of the session, offering reassurance to alleviate anxiety) should all be analyzed for cultural suitability when assessing an ethnic minority client. Knowledge of Arab American etiquette, social interaction rules, and cultural expectations of privacy are essential for clinicians to tailor the interview to minimize negative reactions to questions and to maximize the client's investment in the assessment process.

One of the initial goals of the clinical interview is to understand the primary complaints that initially brought the client in for an assessment and the individual's and/or family's perspective on these presenting problems. A barrier to seeking mental health services for ethnic minority clients is the perceived mismatch between their beliefs and the clinician's beliefs about what is causing their psychological symptoms (Hoberman, 1992; Leong & Lau, 2001). As such, Arab American clients may be more likely to return for subsequent assessment sessions (and later, treatment) if their conceptualizations of presenting problems (e.g. spiritual explanations, family dynamics, perceived trauma) are articulated and discussed with the clinician.

Clinicians who work with Arab Americans report that a number of additional people could potentially be interviewed as informants regarding the client's presenting complaints. Examples are the male head of the household speaking on behalf of the client, or children of the client whose English is more fluent and who have a better knowledge of healthcare procedures (Nassar-McMillan & Hakim-Larson, 2003). With the possibility of multiple informants, it is important that the clinician and the client are in agreement regarding the perceived causes, descriptions, and consequences of symptoms or complaints.

Psychological Testing

In order to better understand the symptoms or complaints of a client, in many cases psychological tests may be administered as part of the assessment process. Tests of cognitive functioning, in their most common usage, are essentially etic instruments, because an examinee's test scores are based on comparisons to large standardization samples. As previously mentioned, for the acculturated Arab American whose primary language is English, the clinician may not need to alter the test selection and administration process. As an Arab American examinee gets culturally and linguistically further away from the European American groups that most U.S.-based instruments were designed for, the cross-cultural construct validity of the test decreases or may vanish altogether. Even nonverbal measures of cognitive functioning that are supposedly culture-free (e.g. Raven's Progressive Matrices, the Seashore Rhythm Test, or the Rey-Osterrieth Complex Figure Test) require perceptual skills and cultural knowledge that are typically acquired through mainstream experiences (Rosselli & Ardila, 2003). Thus, any verbal or nonverbal test may pose limitations when interpreting scores produced by individuals who do not fall in the normative group for which the test was standardized.

Notably, a number of tests in various cognitive domains have been developed in the Arabic-speaking world and normed on local samples. This includes tests of general intellectual functioning such as the Wechsler intelligence scales (e.g. Meleika, 1996) and the Stanford–Binet (e.g. Hanoura, 2002; Mohamed & Abdel Samee, 2011), as well as tests of nonverbal intelligence including Raven's Standard Progressive Matrices (Abdel-Khalek & Raven, 2006) and the Test of Nonverbal Intelligence (Al-Ghatani, Obonsawin, Binshaig, & Al-Moutaery, 2011). Other examples are tests of verbal learning and memory such as the Rey Auditory Verbal Learning Test (Poreh, Sultan, & Levin, 2012), and tests of executive functioning such as the verbal fluency test (Khalil, 2010) and the Wisconsin Card Sorting Test (Al-Ghatani et al., 2011). Although these Arabic-language tests are generally not available for use in the U.S., the adaptation of these tests to Arab populations may lend some credence to their cross-cultural applicability.

Personality measures are another category of tests that are typically used as etic instruments. Examinees complete inventories based on their specific pattern of attitudes and behaviors, and these responses are converted into personality profiles based on norms established from large samples of clinical and/or nonclinical populations. The most widely used personality test is the Minnesota Multiphasic Personality Inventory (MMPI), which has been translated into over 150 languages and used in over 50 countries (Butcher, 1985; Dana, 1993). The MMPI has been translated into Arabic and used in multiple Arab countries (Meleika, 1998; Soliman, 1996; Taher, 2007; Torki, 1980). The second edition (MMPI-2) has also been translated into Arabic (Askar & AbdelKader, 2008; Soliman, 1996) and was developed using a set of guidelines that were meant to increase within-culture relevance and cross-cultural equivalence (Butcher, Lim, & Nezami, 1998). However, the use of a translated version of the MMPI is not without challenges. Many translations have not been validated for linguistic equivalence or back-translated for accuracy, which, even if implemented, does not address the issue of literal translations that are cross-culturally meaningless (Dana, 1993; Guthrie & Lonner, 1986).

Beyond the issues of literal translation, there are some items on the MMPI and other self-report measures that may be culturally problematic for Arab Americans due to a lack of familiarity with the emotional connotation of colloquial expressions. For example, Soliman (1996) encountered difficulty reproducing MMPI-2 items that used "slang" terms in ways that would retain the same meaning in Arabic (e.g. translating "raw deal from life" to "unfair treatment," or "I feel blue" to "feel gloomy"). It is unclear whether an item that has been linguistically distilled in this manner can elicit the same emotional valence as the original colloquial phrase would. Butcher and colleagues (1998) note that item equivalency is crucial in determining the specificity of a psychological concept and whether it is possible to interpret cross-cultural differences between different versions of the MMPI. This is an example of the delicate balance between assessing an Arab American client with culturally inappropriate questions, while at the same time attempting to gather cross-culturally relevant clinical data.

The use of projective tests may be consistent with both emic and etic sides of assessment. Instead of matching what examinees say to criterion responses to be scored in a binary fashion (e.g. correct/

incorrect, absent/present), projective measures rely upon the client to provide the "answers" based on their own interpretation of the question or stimuli. One of the most well-known projective tests, the Rorschach Inkblot Test, is ambiguous enough in its instructions yet structured in its specific stimuli to produce a testing experience that is potentially equivalent across most cultures (Ritzler, 2004). The fact that the Rorschach's task items require no translation and are simply visual forms suggests that the test has "transportability" that may lend itself to cross-cultural assessment (Dana, Hinman, & Bolton, 1977; Lindzey, 1961).

Although no validation study of the Rorschach exists for the Arab American population, studies have used the Rorschach in Arabic-speaking samples (Dwairy, 2006; Miner & De Vos, 1960; Sayed, 2003; Tibon, Handelzalts, & Weinberger, 2005). Rorschach responses produced by a sample of French Algerians contained expressions of psychological distress that varied in terms of self-identification with French culture and Arab culture and combinations thereof (De Vos & Miner, 1989). That is, the respondents' descriptions of Rorschach stimuli reflected concepts of the self that ranged from a primary affinity with an Arab heritage, to a combined Franco-Arab notion of self, to a mainly French cultural identity. Given the aforementioned importance of acculturation in the assessment of Arab Americans, even the use of presumably culture-free projective tests may result in open-ended expressions of mental or emotional states that need to be interpreted within the context of the individual's cultural background.

Apperception projective tests, which depict ambiguous scenes for which examinees are asked to provide a story, may have more limited use for Arab Americans than the Rorschach due to the static elements of culture, race, and ethnicity portrayed in the specific images of people and settings. As Dwairy (2006) points out when discussing a response to a Thematic Apperception Test (TAT) picture depicting a scene that was designed and normed for American respondents, an Arab who is not acculturated to dominant culture in the West may produce responses that convey more about his or her perception of stereotypical American culture than actual and current psychological functioning.

As previously mentioned, language plays a major role in the content and severity of psychological symptoms expressed during an assessment. This applies for projective measures as well: The language respondents use may influence the extent of psychopathology detected. For example, when comparing English and Arabic responses from the same participants on the TAT and Rorschach Inkblot tests, Sayed (2003) found evidence for greater emotional expression in the Arabic responses.

Behavioral Observations

The recording of behavioral observations is in some ways the quintessential method of assessing an individual from an emic perspective. The purpose is to characterize the specific and idiosyncratic external manifestations of the internal states that are relevant to the client's current emotional and neurocognitive functioning. However, not all perceived unconventional behaviors can be assumed to be attributed to a psychological disorder. Clinicians have been noted to overpathologize ethnic minority clients when misinterpreting unfamiliar behavioral presentations as symptoms of mental illness (Baker & Bell, 1999; Snowden, 2003).

Behaviors that are sometimes associated with Arab Americans that are culturally normative but can be misinterpreted include animated hand and face gestures when describing symptoms (Safadi & Valentine, 1990), speaking with a loud voice (Samovar & Porter, 1991), indirect communicative styles (Feghali, 1997), or attributing negative experiences to supernatural or unseen causes (Nydell, 1987). Collateral interviews with other healthcare workers who may have had opportunities to observe a client over longer periods of time (e.g. nurses, social workers), as well as interviews with (and observations of the client's behavior in the presence of) family members, could be useful in establishing a premorbid picture of the individual with respect to their normative behavioral presentation.

Diagnostic Determinations

Making a final diagnosis requires the integration of the clinical interview, test data, and behavioral observations. For ethnic minority clients, interpretations of the assessment findings often need to strike a balance between etic and emic data points. Too much diagnostic emphasis on deviations from mainstream norms can be misleading, but at the same time pathology can be underestimated if nonnormative behaviors or cognitions are solely attributed to cultural factors. As such, an accurate diagnostic assessment will entail knowledge of clinical psychology, Arab American culture, and the specific psychosocial history of the client. Based on these factors, clinicians can determine where the clinical picture of the client lies within the spectrum of normative population-wide symptoms, within the client's specific cultural context, and within the client's individual pattern of emotions and behaviors.

Case Example 1: A Forensic Evaluation of Mr. Younis

Mr. Younis is a 24-year-old male who was born in Jordan, where he spent his early childhood. When he was 11 years old, he and his family immigrated to the U.S., where he attended junior high and high school. Five years ago, while he was still a first-year university student, he was stopped by police due to erratic driving. At the scene, he was aggressive and appeared to be quite agitated. A search of his vehicle revealed a gun that was later matched by ballistic experts to a bullet that killed one of Mr. Younis' classmates a few weeks prior. He was charged with first degree murder. From the time of his arrest and throughout his court appearances, Mr. Younis spoke very little. He never admitted to any crime but also never said much to defend himself or to help his case. He was observed to be quite paranoid and showed very little trust toward anyone involved in the case, including both the prosecution and the defense teams. His public defender at the time tried to argue that Mr. Younis did not have the mental capacity to stand trial. However, a court-appointed psychologist found inconclusive evidence for this after conducting an assessment of Mr. Younis. The psychologist was not well versed in Arab culture and had minimal resources and time to conduct a comprehensive and culturally appropriate assessment.

In his initial evaluation, the psychologist concluded that Mr. Younis exhibited low average intelligence and diagnosed him with an unspecified anxiety disorder. He reviewed statements from classmates and peers indicating that Mr. Younis was very religious and liked to discuss spirituality frequently. He noted that during the evaluation, Mr. Younis made exaggerated hand gestures, spoke in a loud voice, and occasionally talked about "speaking with God and angels." The psychologist attributed these behaviors and statements to anxiety and a high degree of religiosity. In his testimony before the court, the psychologist stated that Mr. Younis had enough cognitive capacity to understand the nature of his crime and the wherewithal to plan it. Due to the fact that he never denied the crime, his general apathy during the trial and lack of interest in helping his defense, and the overwhelming amount of physical and circumstantial evidence, Mr. Younis was convicted and sentenced to death.

In the years that followed, his case was taken up by lawyers at the State's Habeas Corpus office, who gathered evidence for an appeal. As part of their appeal, the lawyers argued that Mr. Younis never received a culturally competent psychological evaluation. They believed that in his initial trial, Mr. Younis was portrayed as a "religiously fanatic Arab" who planned and executed a crime, albeit with a low average intelligence. The defense lawyers stated that this portrayal was supported by the psychologist's conclusions that were quick to stereotype Mr. Younis and overlooked symptoms of psychosis. His current lawyers gathered additional information to support their appeal. In particular, they interviewed family and friends who had known him for a number of years prior to the incident. Their interviews revealed that Mr. Younis had undergone a profound change in functioning in the last few months of high school, before he left for university. He became increasingly suspicious of others and began to talk excessively about conspiracy theories and his fears of mind control. At the time of his initial assessment, Mr. Younis did not speak much, so these delusional symptoms were not apparent. In addition, the hyper-religious content of his speech was also relatively new, as Mr. Younis did not grow up in a religious family and was not known among his friends to speak about spiritual matters.

During his last few years in prison, Mr. Younis finally received the appropriate psychiatric treatment he had needed all along. He responded well to antipsychotic medication and eventually reached a point where he was a more "testable" examinee. His defense team brought in a psychologist who was sensitive to cultural differences to conduct a re-evaluation in light of a more detailed history. The new assessment revealed that the first evaluation likely underestimated Mr. Younis' intellectual functioning due to psychosis interfering with his ability to properly engage in testing. The new assessment found that while most of his cognitive abilities were intact, Mr. Younis exhibited a significant deficit in executive functioning, suggesting an impaired ability to make decisions and anticipate consequences. This, combined with the psychotic episode that apparently precipitated a violent outburst, suggested that Mr. Younis had transitioned from a prodromal phase to an active phase of schizophrenia some time during the stressful period between graduating high school and moving away to college. His delusions were not some expression of cultural and religious fervor, but instead represented an active psychotic episode during which Mr. Younis did not have mental capacity. After this new interpretation was presented during the appeal, Mr. Younis was removed from death row and sentenced instead to life imprisonment with the possibility of parole, as long as he complied with psychiatric treatment.

As shown in this case example, a forensic evaluation entails an interesting juxtaposition between etic and emic approaches to assessment. In a court of law, it may be assumed that the examinee is viewed with a more universal lens, implying that there are certain standards of psychological health that are applicable to all people (e.g. the criteria for competency, legal standards for mental disability). However, in cases involving ethnic minority clients, it is important for psychologists working in forensic settings to have an awareness of the American Psychological Association's (2003) *Guidelines on Multicultural Education, Training, Research, Practice, and Organizational Change for Psychologists* to ensure that assessments of their clients are fair and meaningful, taking into consideration the individual's cultural norms (Heilbrun, DeMatteo, Marczyk, & Goldstein, 2008). In the case of Mr. Younis, the first psychologist overemphasized what were assumed to be cultural and religious expressions and thus ignored signs of a disease process. During the appeal, his defense lawyers realized that an accurate evaluation would have to rely on various sources of data in addition to what was gathered from Mr. Younis himself. Statements from family and friends, academic records, and medical documentation during his imprisonment were all useful in characterizing Mr. Younis' level of functioning.

Case Example 2: A Psychoeducational Evaluation of Karim

Karim is a 12-year-old boy who recently moved from Syria to the U.S. with his family. Due to the political unrest in their country of origin, Karim's family was able to enter under refugee status. Karim started attending public school in the Los Angeles area and was enrolled as an English Language Learner student while taking regular classes in the fifth grade. After a few months, his teachers began to suspect that Karim was having difficulties in school beyond the challenges typically associated with learning English. He was not progressing as well as his peers, including other English Language Learner students in his classes. After holding meetings with Karim's teachers and his parents, the school psychologist realized that she would need to consult with a psychologist familiar with Arab culture who could aid in assessing for cognitive, emotional, and developmental factors that may be influencing Karim's academic achievement. The consultant psychologist was provided with all available records and arrangements were made for her to assess Karim at school.

When Karim's parents first had enrolled him in the school, they had informed the administrative staff that he had attended a French-language school in Syria from kindergarten until the fourth grade. He never repeated any grades and was successfully promoted to the next level each year. However, no academic transcripts or teachers' reports were ever submitted. According to his current school records, Karim's English language level was rated at the "beginner" level. Teacher feedback forms indicated that his academic skills were well below his grade level and that he frequently stated in class that the material was "too hard."

Prior to meeting Karim, the consultant psychologist met with Karim's parents and conducted an interview in Arabic to obtain educational and developmental history. A number of issues that were previously unclear or not known to the school were clarified. Firstly, Karim's parents reported that at the age of seven, he had experienced a fall and head injury. There was no loss of consciousness, but he was observably shaken up by the experience and later began to develop seizures. He was prescribed Keppra, an antiepileptic medication. Karim's mother reported that Karim had not experienced a seizure in the last three years and so she had decided to stop giving him the medication about a year ago, around the time when they left Syria. When asked about early school experiences, Karim's father stated "we are not a learned family."

Upon meeting the consultant psychologist, Karim presented as polite and reserved. He initially tried to answer questions in English, even when spoken to in Arabic. However, he eventually realized the assessment would go much more smoothly if he continued in his native language. The majority of the clinical interview, covering life history, academic experiences, and social and emotional functioning, was conducted in Arabic. When assessing for diagnostic criteria for various disorders during the interview, both Karim and the examiner encountered some difficulty in arriving at mutual understandings of the questions and answers. There were times when the examiner had to ascertain whether linguistic differences made it challenging for her to convey symptoms defined in English and translated to Arabic, or whether Karim's difficulty understanding the material and expressing himself simply reflected the limited familiarity with psychological terminology that many 12-year-olds would struggle with.

During the administration of tests, Karim sometimes had to be oriented to test-taking procedures in greater detail than the consultant psychologist would typically use. For example, sample items were occasionally repeated multiple times to ensure Karim understood what the task required. Also, timed subtests were sometimes restarted when Karim would not wait for the examiner to say "go" before beginning. With the exception of occasional reminders needed to keep him on the task at hand, Karim was generally motivated during testing and appeared to put forth his best effort once he understood what was required of him.

The Raven's Standard Progressive Matrices were administered to assess Karim's general intellectual functioning, which was placed in the low average range. The nonverbal subtests of the Wechsler Intelligence Scale for Children (4th edition), comprising the Perceptual Reasoning and Processing Speed index scores, were also administered. Karim's performances on these non-language-based tests corroborated a low average intellectual ability. A number of neuropsychological tests were also administered, with particular attention to those measures that have been normed in Arabic-speaking populations. His overall cognitive profile was generally intact, with some marked deficits in visuospatial ability and executive functioning. In addition, an assessment of Karim's current academic skill set in relation to his new school environment was needed, so he was given subtests of the Woodcock Johnson Tests of Achievement (3rd edition). His performance suggested that although he was able to grasp some of the academic material he was exposed to in his new English-language environment, he was still functioning well below his grade level. The responses from Karim's parents on an Arabic version of the Child Behavior Checklist indicated that he had some problems with attention and concentration and that he could be oversensitive when he feared he had done something wrong. On an Arabic version of the Child Depression Inventory, Karim endorsed mild to moderate symptoms of depression characterized by negative self-esteem, low confidence in his functional abilities, and interpersonal problems.

In this case example, teachers, the school psychologist, and the consultant psychologist all collaborated to provide the most culturally sensitive and relevant description of Karim's psychoeducational functioning. Consideration for the emic approach meant that Karim had to be evaluated in a way that accounted for his language and cultural background and did not penalize him for being new to the U.S. That being said, an etic approach to assessing his academic skills was also necessary in order to compare Karim's progress in school to peers within the same class and to help educators formulate interventions that would aid Karim in eventually achieving grade-level performances in his new environment. In this case, a careful and culturally sensitive assessment yielded information that would help educators design an appropriate, individualized plan for Karim. The assessment found that a combination of his beginner-level English proficiency, some circumscribed deficits in neuropsychological functioning, his overall low average intellectual ability, and his challenges with emotional adjustment were all likely contributing to his academic difficulties; and thus, should each be addressed accordingly.

Critique

One of the greatest limiting factors to the current knowledge base of psychological assessment in the Arab American community is simply the lack of empirical research with this population. As Haboush (2007) mentions when discussing cultural factors relevant to school psychologists who conduct assessments and interventions with Arab Americans, most literature on the topic "is either descriptive or drawn from case examples and lacks empirical support" (p. 184). Anecdotal evidence and single or small-sample case studies are helpful in highlighting cultural factors that may be diagnostically relevant, and providing clinical lore. However, without the appropriate statistical power afforded by larger samples and controlling for confounding variables, it is difficult to make definitive conclusions of how well a particular interviewing technique, questionnaire, or other test consistently performs when used to detect psychiatric or neurocognitive disorders among Arab Americans.

While research studies have focused on psychological phenomena among Arab Americans, the samples used almost always consist of students or individuals recruited from the community. Very rarely, if ever, does a research study focus on a clinical sample of Arab Americans recruited from an outpatient clinic, a healthcare center, or a hospital setting. Thus, while researchers may learn something about the utility and psychometric properties of various assessment methods and tools, it remains to be seen how effective these practices and measures are for Arab American individuals who present with clinically significant psychopathology.

In addition to research on assessment tools, the assessment tools themselves are lacking for this population. To help expand the cache of culturally relevant assessment tools available to clinicians, two complementary approaches would be to: (1) focus on developing new, Arab American-specific measures, and (2) revise and revalidate existing tests and questionnaires to correct for any test bias for Arab Americans (i.e. distortions in detecting or failing to detect symptoms). Okazaki (1998) points out that the development of some ethnic-specific measures has resulted in incremental validity in predicting psychopathology above and beyond existing assessment tools. In particular, there is some theoretical justification in constructing new measures for immigrant refugee populations, whose unique set of experiences and immediate circumstances may differ significantly from their ethnic minority peers who emigrated from similar regions of the world.

Efforts to develop completely new measures would assume that Arab Americans require entirely unique tests because they do not simply lie on a cultural continuum between Arabs in the Middle East and European Americans in North America. In contrast, using existing measures by making alterations and/or re-norming for Arab Americans would suggest that the current tools available to clinicians are largely sufficient as long as adjustments are made to account for cultural factors. In such cases psychologists should first identify and assess possible cultural mediators and moderators that may alter how an existing test measures a particular construct (e.g. language, acculturation, and cultural relevance of test items). If a construct is found to be mediated or moderated by such cultural factors, then it is possible that statistical adjustments could be made in order to make test results more applicable to Arab American clients.

Another useful research effort would be to explore what individual or contextual factors (e.g. English language fluency, years of education in U.S. schools, generational status) are most strongly associated with variations in test scores for Arab Americans. The approach of adapting existing psychological assessment tools for use in ethnic minority populations has shown some success in other cultural groups and could be implemented for Arab Americans. The approach of developing brand new tools would be more intensive (and likely more expensive); however, this may be necessary at times in order to accurately assess certain psychological constructs or detect specific psychopathological symptoms in Arab Americans. Given the paucity of research in this area, the field would appear to be wide open for both endeavors.

Conclusion

While the state of the assessment tools that have been validated on Arab Americans remains extremely limited, it is important to note that Arab Americans do not belong to a monolithic group; there is no one identifying social or cultural marker for members of this population. As such, an assessment may be most effective when clinicians can dynamically scale their choice of assessment methods between etic and emic approaches in order to appropriately capture the nuanced clinical presentation of each individual Arab American client they assess. Utilizing this cultural lens, which recognizes the limitations of the current body of knowledge and is able to shift between etic and emic approaches, will help ensure that a culturally appropriate assessment process is undertaken when working with Arab Americans. Future scholarship in this area has the opportunity to increase the tools available to clinicians interested in the valid psychological assessment of Arab Americans.

Acknowledgment

The authors would like to express gratitude to Pashtana Omar for her valuable assistance with this chapter.

References

Abdel-Khalek, A. M. & Raven, J. (2006). Normative data from the standardization of Raven's Standard Progressive Matrices in Kuwait in an international context. *Social Behavior and Personality: An International Journal* 34, 169–80. doi: 10.2224/sbp.2006.34.2.169

Abu-Rabia, S. & Siegel, L. S. (2002). Reading, syntactic, orthographic, and working memory skills of bilingual Arabic-English speaking Canadian children. *Journal of Psycholinguistic Research* 31, 661–678. doi: 10.1023/A:1021221206119

Al-Ghatani, A. M., Obonsawin, M. C., Binshaig, B. A., & Al-Moutaery, K. R. (2011). Saudi normative data for the Wisconsin Card Sorting Test, Stroop Test, Test of Non-Verbal Intelligence-3, Picture Completion and Vocabulary (subtest of the Wechsler Adult Intelligence Scale-Revised). *Neurosciences (Riyadh)* 16(1), 29–41.

Al-Krenawi, A. (2005). Mental health practice in Arab countries. *Current Opinion in Psychiatry* 18, 560–564.

Al-Krenawi, A. & Graham, J. R. (2000). Culturally sensitive social work practice with Arab clients in mental health settings. *Health & Social Work* 25(1), 9–22. doi: 10.1093/hsw/25.1.9

American Psychological Association. (2003). Guidelines on multicultural education, training, research, practice, and organizational change for psychologists. *American Psychologist* 58, 377–402. doi: 10.1037/0003-066X.58.5.377

Askar, A. & AbdelKader, H. (2008). *Ekhtebar Al-Shakhseyya al Mota`aded Al-Awgoh- MPI2* [Minnesota Multiphasic Personality Inventory- 2 (MMPI-2)]. Cairo, Egypt: Anglo-Egyptian.

Baker, F. M. & Bell, C. C. (1999). Issues in the psychiatric treatment of African Americans. *Psychiatric Services* 50, 362–368. doi: 10.1176/ps.50.3.362

Baker, W., Stockton, R., Howell, S., Jamal, A., Lin, A. C., Shryock, A., & Tessler, M. (2003). Detroit Arab American Study (DAAS), 2003. Detroit Area Studies Series. Ann Arbor, MI: Inter-University Consortium for Political and Social Research. doi: 10.3886/ICPSR04413.v2

Butcher, J. N. (1985). Current developments in MMPI use: An international perspective. In C. D. Speilberger & J. N. Butcher (eds.), *Advancements in personality assessment* (vol. 4, pp. 83–94). Hillsdale, NJ: Lawrence Erlbaum.

Butcher, J. N., Lim, J., & Nezami, E. (1998). Objective study of abnormal personality in cross-cultural settings: The Minnesota Multiphasic Personality Inventory (MMPI-2). *Journal of Cross-Cultural Psychology* 29(1), 189–211. doi: 10.1177/0022022198291010

Cuéllar, I. (2000). Acculturation as a moderator of personality and psychological assessment. In R. H. Dana (ed.), *Handbook of cross-cultural and multicultural personality assessment* (pp. 113–129). Mahwah, NJ: Lawrence Erlbaum.

Cuéllar, I., Siles, R. I., & Bracamontes, E. (2004). Acculturation: A psychological construct of continuing relevance for Chicana/o psychology. In R. J. Velasquez, L. M. Arellano, & B. W. McNeill (eds.), *The handbook of Chicana/o psychology and mental health* (pp. 23–42). Mahwah, NJ: Lawrence Erlbaum.

Cummins, J. (1979). Linguistic interdependence and the educational development of bilingual children. *Review of Educational Research* 49, 222–251. doi: 10.3102/00346543049002222

Dana, R. H. (1993). *Multicultural assessment perspectives for professional psychology*. Boston, MA: Allyn & Bacon.

Dana, R. H. (1998). *Understanding cultural identity in intervention and assessment*. Thousand Oaks, CA: Sage.

Dana, R. H., Hinman, S., & Bolton, B. (1977). Dimensions of examinees' response to the Rorschach: An empirical synthesis. *Psychological Reports* 40, 1147–1153. doi: 10.2466/pr0.1977.40.3c.1147

De Vos, G. A. & Miner, H. (1989). Oasis and Casbah: Acculturative stress. In G. A. De Vos & L. B. Boyer (eds.), *Symbolic analysis cross-culturally: The Rorschach test* (pp. 201–245). Berkeley, CA: University of California Press.

Dwairy, M. A. (2006). *Counseling and psychotherapy with Arabs and Muslims: A culturally sensitive approach*. New York: Teachers College Press.

El-Rufaie, O. E. F., Al-Sabosy, M. M. A., Bener, A., & Abuzeid, M. S. O. (1999). Somatized mental disorder among primary care Arab patients: I. Prevalence and clinical and sociodemographic characteristics. *Journal of Psychosomatic Research* 46, 549–555. doi: 10.1016/S0022-3999(98)00101-9

Erickson, C. D. & Al-Timimi, N. R. (2001). Providing mental health services to Arab Americans: Recommendations and considerations. *Cultural Diversity and Ethnic Minority Psychology* 7, 308–327. doi: 10.1037/1099-9809.7.4.308

Feghali, E. (1997). Arab cultural communication patterns. *International Journal of Intercultural Relations* 21, 345–378. doi: 10.1016/S0147-1767(97)00005-9

Grand, S., Marcos, L. R., Freedman, N., & Barroso, F. (1977). Relation of psychopathology and bilingualism to kinesic aspects of interview behavior in schizophrenia. *Journal of Abnormal Psychology* 86, 492–500. doi: 10.1037/0021-843X.86.5.492

Gureje, O., Simon, G. E., Ustun, T. B., & Goldberg, D. P. (1997). Somatization in cross-cultural perspective: A World Health Organization study in primary care. *American Journal of Psychiatry* 154, 989–995. doi: 10.1176/ajp.154.7.989

Guthrie, G. M. & Lonner, W. J. (1986). Assessment of personality and psychopathology. In W. J. Lonner & J. W. Berry (eds.), *Field methods in cross-cultural research* (vol. 8, pp. 231–264). Beverly Hills, CA: Sage.

Haboush, K. L. (2007). Working with Arab American families: Culturally competent practice for school psychologists. *Psychology in the Schools* 44, 183–198. doi: 10.1002/pits.20215

Hamdi, E., Amin, Y., & Abou-Saleh, M. T. (1997). Performance of the Hamilton Depression Rating Scale in depressed patients in the United Arab Emirates. *Acta Psychiatrica Scandinavica* 96, 416–423. doi: 10.1111/j.1600-0447.1997.tb09942.x

Hanoura, M. A.-H. (2002). *Maqayees Stanford-Binet Lil-Zakaa': As-surah al-rabi`a* [Stanford-Binet Intelligence Test: 4th edn]. Cairo, Egypt: Anglo-Egyptian.

Heilbrun, K., DeMatteo, D., Marczyk, G., & Goldstein, A. M. (2008). Standards of practice and care in forensic mental health assessment: Legal, professional, and principles-based consideration. *Psychology, Public Policy, and Law*, 14(1), 1–26. doi: 10.1037/1076-8971.14.1.1

Hoberman, H. M. (1992). Ethnic minority status and adolescent mental health services utilization. *The Journal of Mental Health Administration* 19, 246–267. doi: 10.1007/BF02518990

Khalil, M. S. (2010). Preliminary Arabic normative data of neuropsychological tests: The verbal and design fluency. *Journal of Clinical and Experimental Neuropsychology* 32, 1028–1035. doi: 10.1080/13803391003672305

Kirmayer, L. J. & Young, A. (1998). Culture and somatization: Clinical, epidemiological, and ethnographic perspectives. *Psychosomatic Medicine* 60, 420–430.

Leong, F. T. L. & Lau, A. S. L. (2001). Barriers to providing effective mental health services to Asian Americans. *Mental Health Services Research* 3, 201–214. doi: 10.1023/A:1013177014788

Lindzey, G. (1961). *Projective techniques and cross-cultural research*. New York: Ardent Media.

Malgady, R. G., Rogler, L. H., & Costantino, G. (1987). Ethnocultural and linguistic bias in mental health evaluation of Hispanics. *American Psychologist* 42, 228–234. doi: 10.1037/0003-066X.42.3.228

Meleika, L. K. (1996). *Meqias Wechsler-Bellevue Lezakaa' al Rashedeen wal Moraheken: Daleel al meqias* [Wechsler-Bellevue Intelligence Scale: Test manual]. Cairo, Egypt: Anglo-Egyptian.

Meleika L. K. (1998). *Ekhtebar al-Shakhseyya Mota`aded Al-awgoh* [Minnesota Multiphasic Personality Inventory (MMPI)]. Cairo, Egypt: L. K. Meleika.

Meleis, A. I. (1981). The Arab American in the health care system. *The American Journal of Nursing* 81, 1180–1183.

Miner, H. M. & DeVos, G. A. (1960). *Oasis and Casbah: Algerian culture and personality in change* (Anthropological papers, No. 15). Ann Arbor, MI: University of Michigan.

Mohamed, M. T. & Abdel Samee, A. M. (2011). *Maqayees Stanford-Binet Lil-Zakaa': As-surah al-khaamisah* [Stanford-Binet Intelligence Test: 5th edn]. Cairo, Egypt: Arab Corporation for Psychological Tests.

Nassar-McMillan, S. C. & Hakim-Larson, J. (2003). Counseling considerations among Arab Americans. *Journal of Counseling & Development* 81, 150–159. doi: 10.1002/j.1556-6678.2003.tb00236.x

Nydell, M. (1987). *Understanding Arabs: A guide for westerners*. Yarmouth, ME: Intercultural Press.

Okazaki, S. (1998). Psychological assessment of Asian Americans: Research agenda for cultural competency. *Journal of Personality Assessment* 70(1), 54–70. doi: 10.1207/s15327752jpa7001_4

Poreh, A., Sultan, A., & Levin, J. (2012). The Rey Auditory Verbal Learning Test: Normative data for the Arabic-speaking population and analysis of the differential influence of demographic variables. *Psychology & Neuroscience* 5(1), 57–61. doi: 10.3922/j.psns.2012.1.08

Racy, J. (1980). Somatization in Saudi women: A therapeutic challenge. *The British Journal of Psychiatry* 137, 212–216. doi: 10.1192/bjp.137.3.212

Ritzler, B. (2004). Cultural applications of the Rorschach, apperception tests, and figure drawings. In M. J. Hilsenroth & D. L. Segal (eds.), *Comprehensive handbook of psychological assessment* (vol. 2, pp. 573–585). New York: Wiley.

Rosselli, M. & Ardila, A. (2003). The impact of culture and education on non-verbal neuropsychological measurements: A critical review. *Brain and Cognition* 52(3), 326–333. doi: 10.1016/S0278-2626(03)00170-2

Roysircar, G. & Maestas, M. L. (2002). Assessing acculturation and cultural variables. In K. Kurasaki, S. Okazaki, & S. Sue (eds.), *Asian American mental health* (pp. 77–94). New York: Kluwer Academic/Plenum.

Safadi, M. & Valentine, C. A. (1990). Contrastive analyses of American and Arab nonverbal and paralinguistic communication. *Semiotica* 82(3/4), 269–292. doi: 10.1515/semi.1990.82.3-4.269

Samovar, L. A. & Porter, R. E. (1991). *Communication between cultures*. Belmont, CA: Wadsworth.

Sayed, M. A. (2003). Psychotherapy of Arab patients in the West: Uniqueness, empathy, and "otherness." *American Journal of Psychotherapy* 57, 445–460.

Snowden, L. R. (2003). Bias in mental health assessment and intervention: Theory and evidence. *American Journal of Public Health* 93, 239–243. doi: 10.2105/AJPH.93.2.239

Soliman, A. M. (1996). Development of an Arabic translation of the MMPI-2: With clinical applications. In J. Butcher (ed.), *International adaptations of the MMPI-2: Research and clinical applications* (pp. 463–486). Minneapolis, MN: University of Minnesota Press.

Sue, S. (1998). In search of cultural competence in psychotherapy and counseling. *American Psychologist* 53, 440–448. doi: 10.1037/0003-066X.53.4.440

Taher, N. S. (2007). Self-concept and masculinity/femininity among normal male individuals and males with Gender Identity Disorder. *Social Behavior and Personality* 35, 469–478. doi: 10.2224/sbp.2007.35.4.469

Tibon, S., Handelzalts, J. E., & Weinberger, Y. (2005). Using the Rorschach for exploring the concept of transitional space within the political context of the Middle East. *International Journal of Applied Psychoanalytic Studies* 2(1), 40–57. doi: 10.1002/aps.30

Torki, M. A. (1980). Validation of the MMPI MF Scale in Kuwait. *Psychological Reports* 47(3f), 1152–1154. doi: 10.2466/pr0.1980.47.3f.1152

Wrobel, N. H., Farrag, M. F., & Hymes, R. W. (2009). Acculturative stress and depression in an elderly Arabic sample. *Journal of Cross-Cultural Gerontology* 24, 273–290. doi: 10.1007/s10823-009-9096-8

21
COUNSELING
Settings, Clinical Considerations, and Counselor Cultural Competence

Sylvia C. Nassar-McMillan, Mona D. Nour, and Aisha M. Al-Qimlass

Counseling psychology, along with related helping professions, has realized the tremendous impact of culture on the development of individuals and families. Correspondingly, models for culturally competent psychological practices and interventions, ethical codes, and the like have emerged on the landscapes of both professional best practice and empirical literature. These models have expanded initial examinations of multicultural issues within counseling and psychology practice into broader systemic arenas as well as within the realms of advocacy and social justice.

This chapter discusses counseling considerations for Arab Americans. It begins with a review of key theoretical models of counselor multicultural competence. Next is an overview of counseling issues among Arab Americans that may arise across various counseling practice settings. Culturally based values and behaviors and their associated influences within the counseling process are described. Subsequently, the chapter discusses considerations for counselor development and cultural competence. A case example is provided for illustrative purposes. Finally, the chapter critiques current counseling research and practice related to Arab Americans, and provides recommendations for improvement.

Theoretical Model of Counselor Multicultural Competence

Among the earliest frameworks of multicultural competence in the counseling literature was the American Counseling Association's (ACA) Multicultural Counseling Competencies (Arredondo et al., 1996). The competencies advocated that counseling professionals developed enhanced awareness of themselves, their clients, and culturally specific counseling interventions. As such, counselors were encouraged to gain awareness of their own attitudes and beliefs about specific client populations, knowledge about specific client populations, and their own skills as counselors in providing services to diverse clients.

Subsequently, Sue (2001) established a "cube" model connecting the three dimensions of counselors' awareness of their attitudes and beliefs, knowledge, and skills, with four foci or levels of analysis, which are: (1) individual, (2) professional, (3) organizational, and (4) societal. Sue's model essentially expanded the culturally specific counseling components of the ACA model to apply them beyond the individual intervention level, to the levels of the profession of psychology, organizations, and societal levels or systems. At the individual level, in terms of self-awareness, counseling psychologists need to assess any relevant internally held biases toward one's own culture (e.g. privileges), recognizing that any new knowledge gained about the client's culture will interact with long-standing bias. For example, counselors need to identify their own values about: career choice; marriage and family;

to what extent they themselves are individualistically versus collectively oriented; the ways in which they may be similar to or different from their clients; and so on. Counselors need to determine the ways in which this array of dynamics might impact counseling delivery, and gain knowledge about the cultures and lived experiences of their clients. Moreover, it is important for counselors to anticipate how their typical counseling style might be perceived by their clients, and to be open to learning and applying new skills.

One of the common ways that counselors may gain knowledge about diverse clients such as Arab Americans is from the academic literature. As such, a scholarly review of the literature, such as that presented in this chapter, can be useful to practicing counselors. Some skills-based information and recommendations are also provided below, potentially enhancing readers' ability to better utilize skills and develop appropriate counseling interventions and research strategies for Arab Americans.

Counseling Settings and Issues

Counseling psychologists and counselors provide services across myriad settings in contemporary U.S. society. Arab Americans are present in every facet of society and thus may present in any number of these counseling settings. Their presenting issues may be quite generalized, such as depression or anxiety related to life stress. These issues may be directly or indirectly linked to clients' culture of origin. In this section, potential presenting issues within a range of settings are discussed, from school counseling, college counseling, career counseling, and marriage and family counseling, to clinical mental health counseling.

School Counseling

Arab American youth come from diverse cultural backgrounds and can undergo a vast range of psychological transformations during their school-age years. Because the school arena represents a highly valued component in Arab American culture, academic achievement is a crucial aspect of healthy psychosocial development for Arab American youth (Haboush & Barakat, 2014). The interplay of normal child and adolescent development, with the added aspect of integrating potentially multiple cultures, can present various levels of challenge for Arab American youth, such as bullying and social exclusion at school (Haboush, 2007), intercultural and intergenerational gaps with their parents at home (Rasmi, Chuang, & Hennig, 2014), and identity navigation challenges in general (Britto, 2008).

The stressors facing Arab American youth can impact their mental health, social relationships, and academic performance, any of which may lead them to seek school counseling services. For example, a study of Arab American high school students revealed that adolescents who perceived greater levels of racism and discrimination were at significantly higher levels of risk for acculturative stress, depression, anxiety, and internalizing and externalizing symptoms (Ahmed, Kia-Keating, & Tsai, 2011). Moreover, school-aged children who are recent refugees may exhibit posttraumatic stress disorder (PTSD; Abu-Ras & Abu-Bader, 2008), thus potentially disrupting both academic performance and peer relationships (Saigh, Yasik, Oberfield, Halamandaris, & Bremner, 2006). The effects of trauma on the structure of the brain may result in impairments in memory, concentration, attention, fluid reasoning, and verbal reasoning (Haboush, Selman, & Sievering, 2008), potentially compounding academic performance and social relationships even further. However, as with mainstream American children and adolescents, parental support for younger children (Kira, Lewandowski, Somers, Yoon, & Chiodo, 2012) and peer support for older adolescents and young adults (Sheikh, 2009) can provide protective factors, thus supporting the development of resilience among these young people in the face of stressors. Also, a study showed that Arab American adolescents who had successfully integrated their ethnic identities into mainstream culture, as well as those who used higher levels of religious coping, experienced decreased levels of psychological distress (Ahmed et al., 2011).

College Settings

Typical developmental tasks for college students worldwide involve preparation for post-college employment and career development. For mainstream westernized American college students, developmental theorists such as Erikson (1956) and Marcia (1966) have discussed identity development as key for this late adolescent to emerging adult population, with Marcia applying these tasks to areas such as occupation, religion, and peer relationships, among others. These westernized theories may or may not apply to Arab American college-aged youth, depending on their respective levels of acculturation and a host of other variables. Thus, it is important to apply Western-based theories and assessment with caution in considering Arab American youth, for whom interdependent relationships with parents and other family members may continue to be highly valued.

During college, Arab American students face similar clinical issues as mainstream or other ethnic minority groups, yet may continue to experience particularly high levels of discrimination. For example, one study of college students revealed that participants who were non-Arab college students, having limited understanding of Arab culture, indicated negative attitudes toward Arab Americans along with decreased positive regard (Abouchedid & Nasser, 2006). Other scholars, too, have reported alarmingly high percentages of Arab American college-aged students experiencing anti-Arab discrimination (Britto, 2008; Shammas, 2009). Negative stereotypes toward any population can have an adverse impact on mental health and wellbeing (Haboush & Barakat, 2014). This dynamic can be especially salient at the college level while students are just beginning to develop a strong self-identity, which includes their cultural identity.

Moreover, intergenerational and acculturation differences between Arab American youth and their parents and older family members (i.e. grandparents, aunts, uncles) can create added tension at home (Nassar-McMillan, Rezcallah, & Nour, 2014; Rasmi et al., 2014). Arab American college students show a wide array of acculturation differences among their family members, and parental restrictions ranging from high levels of control by parents over their offspring to more individualistic, autonomous expectations from parents. College students of Arab descent might present in college counseling settings with identity issues related to navigating aspects of college social life in line with core family values and expectations. Nassar-McMillan, Rezcallah, and Nour (2014) noted that in a healthy developmental process individuals ideally learn to balance selected aspects of their native culture with a connection to the newer, or host, culture.

Career Counseling

Career counseling and the professionals who provide it can be found in schools, colleges, and community settings. The focus of this type of counseling is on providing career development interventions at developmentally appropriate levels. For example, with younger-aged populations the focus might be on career interest and career exploration, while with high school and college-aged populations, it might shift to career goal setting and identification of relevant training options. For adults in the workplace, career counseling provided either within the workplace, such as by an Employee Assistance Program, or externally within a private practice setting, may focus on acquiring and retaining meaningful employment.

The value placed on education by Arab Americans has a corresponding impact on career choice and subsequent employment (Haboush & Barakat, 2014). Arab Americans, on the whole, fare better than their non-Arab American counterparts in both educational and career aspirations (Arab American Institute, 2014). Despite this trend, individuals perceived as Arab or Muslim have faced particular scrutiny and mistrust in the U.S. in the post-911 era (e.g. Nassar-McMillan, Lambert, & Hakim-Larson, 2011; Padela & Heisler, 2010). Over 800 cases of employment discrimination against Arab Americans were reported in the year following 9/11 (American-Arab Anti-Discrimination

Committee, 2003). In one study using two fictitious résumés with similar credentials and employment experience, Widner and Chicoine (2011) exposed blatant signs of employment discrimination against Arab Americans, yielding the finding that an applicant with an Arab-sounding name had to apply to twice as many jobs as an applicant with a White-sounding name for the same end result (i.e. callbacks for interviews). Further, Dávila and Mora (2005) found a decrease in earnings of Arab males compared to non-Hispanic Whites that was inexplicable based on any observable characteristics beyond ethnicity.

In addition to discrimination, other potential issues may be raised by Arab Americans during career counseling. For those who are Muslim, challenges may arise related to their religion, particularly if certain practices, such as fasting or daily prayer, are perceived by employers or work colleagues as interfering with clients' work requirements in some way (Nassar-McMillan & Tovar, 2012). Finally, the collectivist nature of Arab American culture might influence decision-making about job offers and promotions, and the role of family in career determination, particularly for women (Read & Oselin, 2008). These factors may also come into play when exploring career development decisions and concerns with Arab American clients.

Marriage and Family Counseling

The intraethnic diversity among Arab Americans, spanning multiple Arab countries and generations, is reflected in the interconnections between Arab American couples and family members. Partners might come from differing Arab countries, family backgrounds and expectations, acculturation levels, and education levels. In interviews with 18 Arab American couples, Beitin and Allen (2005) found several complex themes: discrimination, identity, immigration, and acculturation. Couples said they felt forced to identify as either Arab or American with little room for integrating the two cultures. Thus, the continued themes of identity, discrimination, and intergenerational or intercultural differences within the household or extended family are likely to be central foci within couples and family counseling settings. Counseling professionals often need to discern the relationship dynamics, communication styles, and negotiation patterns within the family unit in order to best foster mutual support and resilience.

Clinical Mental Health Settings

Clinical mental health settings can range from inpatient facilities such as residential substance abuse treatment centers or psychiatric hospitals, to agencies providing outpatient services such as those dealing with sexual assault or other crisis-based agencies. Arab Americans may also seek counseling at private practice facilities providing individual or group counseling, or more traditional community mental health centers. These diverse settings may serve any of the issues already discussed from other settings, as well as often the more severe array of mental health disorders presented within a community, such as anxiety, depression, bipolar disorder, and schizophrenia.

Mental health concerns among Arab Americans vary depending on multiple factors, such as immigration status, impetus for migrating, experiences with political turmoil, intergenerational relations, psychosocial development, and more (Abdelhady, 2014; Abudabbeh, 2005; Amer & Hovey, 2007; Nassar-McMillan, Gonzalez, & Mohamed, 2014). In particular, acculturative stress related to immigration and resettlement processes may be linked to higher incidences of anxiety and depression (Jamil, Farrag, et al., 2007; Jamil, Nassar-McMillan, & Lambert, 2007; Kira, Amer, & Wrobel, 2014; Kira et al., 2007). Moreover, traumatic events experienced prior to or during immigration can be linked to PTSD as well (Jamil, Nassar-McMillan, and Lambert, 2007; Kira et al., 2007; Kira et al., 2014; Wrobel & Paterson, 2014). These issues, while possibly identified or even diagnosed within another setting, are most likely to be presented ultimately within a clinical mental health setting.

Cultural Values and Behaviors: Implications for Counseling

Arab Americans represent a diverse population with variations across language, religion, customs, and the like (Samhan, 2014). For example, there is a large population of various Arab Christian sects as well as several divisions of Islam (Nassar-McMillan, 2010; Samhan, 2014). Despite this diversity, there are some cultural commonalities that can inform a variety of considerations for better assessing and treating Arab American clients. These considerations relate to personal space and nonverbal communication styles, emotional expression and somatization of emotion, the locus of control and the roles of honor and shame, the role of the family, respect for elders and authority, and religion and religiosity. Exploring these issues with individuals, couples, or families can facilitate counselors' understanding of clients' worldview.

Nonverbal Communication and Personal Space

Cultural values may influence communication styles among Arab Americans during the counseling process. Through a review of recent literature and research, Al-Krenawi and Graham (2000) highlighted Arab Americans' use of many nonverbal behaviors when interacting with one another that represent respect and intimacy, or other personal relationship characteristics. For example, nonverbal behaviors that may signify respect within the Arab culture include not showing the bottom of one's foot to any individual in the room while seated, not putting one's back to any individual in the room while seated, offering items with the right hand, and typically avoiding eye contact with strangers. Arab Americans may also maintain more personal space with individuals with whom they are not yet "close."

Personal space, including hand shaking and kissing on the cheeks (in the form of a social greeting), poses an important consideration when interacting with Arab Americans due to their possible religious affiliation and adherence to their religious principles. For example, a relatively devout Muslim man or woman will keep added space between them and members of the opposite sex and may refrain from shaking hands with the opposite sex as well (Al-Krenawi & Graham, 2000; Graham, Bradshaw, & Trew, 2010; Nassar-McMillan, 2010). It may be difficult initially to determine a client's religious affiliation or level of devoutness. Therefore, assessment of cultural and religious background, and consulting with clients regarding their preferred level of space and the meanings behind their behaviors, may be essential to effective communication with clients.

Emotional Expression and Somatization of Emotion

Another main point regarding communication styles involves the use of verbal communication. As a whole, Arab Americans may be more emotionally guarded when interacting with strangers, which may be observed in counseling sessions (Graham et al., 2010). Moreover, women within the Arab American community and culture also tend to be less intense and less direct in their communication styles than men (Al-Krenawi & Graham, 2000; Graham et al., 2010; Nassar-McMillan, Gonzalez, & Mohamed, 2014); however, this may not be a clear indication of their communication style with family and friends.

The Arab American population tends to express emotion in a more complex way than may be common to mainstream Americans. In particular, studies have indicated that Arab Americans tend to express emotions indirectly through physical symptoms or ailments (Al-Krenawi & Graham, 2000; Graham et al., 2010), known as somatization of emotion. For example, compared to European Americans, Arab Americans may express more symptoms of fatigue and lack of energy when reporting issues of depression (Al-Krenawi & Graham, 2000). Arab Americans experiencing anxiety or depression may complain of frequent stomachaches and headaches instead of the actual emotional distress. In many cases clients may first have sought medical attention (Aloud & Rathur, 2009) and subsequently been referred to counseling. For these reasons, accurate diagnoses will depend on awareness of the ways emotions may be expressed within the Arab American culture.

Honor and Shame

As a collectivist culture rooted in tradition and family, Arab Americans may experience subtle or sometimes blatant indicators of what would bring honor or shame to the family and community at large. For example, if a youth gets in trouble at school for truancy, the family's response may be concern about how that could impact the family's reputation. This principle of honor and shame tends to affect many of the decisions and goals individuals set for themselves, as well as their behaviors (Abudabbeh, 2005; Graham et al., 2010; Scull, Khullar, Al-Awadhi, & Erheim, 2014; Youssef and Deane, 2006).

Another main point regarding shame and honor that may be seen within the counseling session would be clients' or families' hesitation to seek professional help, as this may be viewed as bringing shame on the family (Aboul-Enein & Aboul-Enein, 2010; El-Islam, 2008; Graham et al., 2010; Hassouneh & Kulwicki, 2009). This may be displayed as clients setting appointments but failing to keep them, and being guarded in the information they share for fear that it becomes "public" knowledge and consequently affects their family. There may also be a reluctance to discuss the underlying issues in favor of focusing on more superficial ones that may be perceived as less shaming to the family.

Role of Family

The family unit within the Arab American culture encompasses the nuclear family as well as members of the extended family, through either blood or marriage. In North America, this extended family can include members of the larger Arab American community within their geographic area of residence. This then tends to create close knowledge of one another, complicating privacy issues and, correspondingly, leading to potential issues of shame when family members are privy to private information about others in the family. At the same time, the family is typically one of the individual's main sources of emotional, mental, physical, spiritual, and economic support (Aboul-Enein & Aboul-Enein, 2010; Ajrouch, 2004; Aloud & Rathur, 2009; Hassouneh & Kulwicki, 2009; Khan, 2006).

Respect for Elders and Authorities

Respect, especially toward elders and other perceived authority figures, is a common and foundational cultural value that Arab Americans are taught at a very early age (Beitin & Aprahamian, 2014; Nassar-McMillan, 2010). This respect for authority and elders stems from a patriarchal family system. When working with Arab Americans, the client and family may look to the counselor or psychologist as the authority figure and therefore may tend to want concrete answers or a quick "fix," rather than working the process themselves (Al-Krenawi & Graham, 2000).

Religion and Religiosity

Determining clients' relative level of observation and adherence may be important in counseling Arab Americans (Graham et al., 2010). Clients' religiosity may impact issues they raise within the counseling session, such as frustration toward the increasingly common association of "Arab" or "Muslim" with "terrorist." Religion and religiosity may also be apparent in clients' choice of words, as the Arabic language is full of everyday phrases and terms that are religion-influenced, such as *insha'Allah* (God willing). A client does not have to be a religious individual to use religious phrases, as some are simply colloquial norms (Nassar-McMillan, Gonzalez, & Mohamed, 2014). This is an example of how there may be complex differences between religious customs and cultural traditions.

Clinical Considerations in Counseling Psychology

In addition to the key values explored in the previous section, other issues that are important in establishing and carrying out the counseling process warrant further mention here. In most cases, such as in boundary setting, dual relationships, gender issues, and translation challenges, typical considerations for any counseling relationship need to be reassessed specifically in regard to working with Arab Americans.

Rapport Building and Boundary Setting

Erickson and Al-Timimi (2001) suggested that one of the most important factors in successful counseling for Arab American clients is the therapeutic relationship developed and maintained between counselors and clients. Through a review of the available literature, Haboush (2007) found that establishing therapeutic boundaries is something that will take place alongside developing rapport. For example, if meeting clients in their home, the gracious acceptance of food or beverage seems to be a useful adjunct in developing rapport with Arab Americans. Although this goes against traditional clinical training, it may be seen as an insult to refuse such hospitality. This also may apply to a similar situation in the counselor's office (Amri, Nassar-McMillan, Meisenhimer, & Bryan, 2013).

After the greeting and during the initial dialogue, Arab American clients may expect their counselors to answer personal questions. Counselors often try to understand why these personal questions are being asked in order to balance the need to answer adequately with the level of disclosure deemed appropriate. This often entails answering politely and without too much detail. Amri and colleagues (2013) recommended that if therapists are confronted with intrusive or overly personal questions (e.g. why they do not have children), they can appropriately respond with neutral replies such as "This is life" or "This is God's will."

Another consideration related to setting boundaries is punctuality. While punctuality is sometimes less valued by Arab cultures than in the U.S. (Al-Krenawi & Graham, 2000), it might become an important issue of education and negotiation between counselors and clients, particularly in settings where other clients may in fact arrive and expect to be seen on time, or where third-party billing is involved. Finally, with regard to gifts, Amri and colleagues (2013) explain that it is customary for Arab American clients to give a gift of appreciation to their counselors, especially at termination. Refusing such a gift could be insulting and could undo some of the progress that was achieved.

Dual Relationships

As with gift giving and other boundaries with which counselors may need to be flexible when interacting with Arab Americans, the notion of dual relationships in Western-based therapies should also be reviewed and reconciled. It may be appropriate in some instances for counselors to attend local community events or engage the support of local religious or community leaders in the counseling process. This can even be added to clients' treatment plans. These kinds of approach may necessitate continual assessment of clients' perceptions of their counselors within the community setting and how to maintain a balance between using this community role and stature as an advantage, without overstepping the bounds of confidentiality (Nassar-McMillan, Gonzalez, & Mohamed, 2014).

Because the Arab American community is tight-knit, a person with whom a client may be having an issue could hold many different relationships for the client. For example, the client may describe feeling overwhelmed by the demands of the workplace, yet the employer is also the brother-in-law. These types of dual relationships within the Arab American community create an additional need for counselors to be tactful and aware of all the underlying issues associated with the presenting problem.

Finally, there is the issue of dual relationships between counselors and clients. Arab American clients may initially look to the counselor as a professional and someone who is going to "fix" their problem; however, if rapport and trust are properly built, clients may also come to see the counselor as a friend. At that time, professional boundaries may become more blurred, and displaying respect when reaffirming boundaries may be important to not alienate clients.

Translation Issues

Language barriers can result in inadequate communication between counselor and client. Clients may not be able clearly to articulate presenting needs to counselors and, conversely, counselors may assume that their clients have a higher language proficiency than is actually the case (Graham et al., 2010). Gaps in communication, either noticed or unnoticed, can have detrimental effects on the effectiveness of the counseling intervention (Aboul-Enein & Aboul-Enein, 2010). When language deficits clearly pose a barrier, it is necessary to engage a professional translator or interpreter. If there is not such a person available within the counseling agency or setting in question, then the counselor may resort to seeking one out through community resources. It may be possible for clients to recommend someone with whom they have worked in the past in similar situations (e.g. healthcare, schools); however, there is some controversy about using cross-cultural interpreters for psychologically based services, suggesting that some of the true meaning of the client experience may be inadvertently lost or misinterpreted (Thomas, Bracken, Shabbir, & Yasmeen, 2010). Thus, selection of an appropriate interpreter needs to take into account not only technical language translation but also knowledge about client culture and associated language nuances.

Counselor Development and Cultural Competence

In recent years, scholars have increasingly paid attention to counselor development and cultural competence. In addition to pinpointing service accessibility and other institutional barriers (e.g. Graham et al., 2010), recent studies have focused on multicultural competence issues specific to Arab American populations. For example, Soheilian and Inman (2015) found that counselors-in-training who are people of color may have higher levels of both cultural competence and multicultural self-efficacy than their White counterparts with regard to Middle Eastern American clients. Graham and colleagues (2010) found in their Canadian study that social work professionals cited cultural insensitivity and cultural misunderstandings among key reasons for Muslim clients' underutilization of counseling services. Clearly, more research is needed that is specific to Arab American populations, yet these initial inquiries are compelling.

With regard to multicultural competence, Nassar-McMillan, Gonzalez, and Mohamed (2014) pointed out that building a positive working alliance with Arab American clients will involve both intellectual skills (e.g. understanding preferred approaches, learning about the individual and the group) and personal skills (e.g. monitoring internal prejudices, becoming empathic, finding ways to relate). Further, various helping professions cite aspects of multicultural competence within their professions' ethical codes. Moreover, some have developed guidelines and other best practice documents with the goal of creating greater multicultural awareness, sensitivity, and ultimately, competence, among psychologists, counselors, and other helping professionals.

For example, the American Psychological Association (APA), within its *Ethical Principles of Psychologists and Code of Conduct, Including 2010 Amendments* (2014), clearly reminds psychologists not to practice outside their respective scope of expertise, explicitly citing that they should work with populations with whom they have been trained. To that end, the APA developed *Guidelines on Multicultural Education, Training, Research, Practice, and Organizational Change for Psychologists* (2002), spanning attitudes that embrace diversity and commitment to cultural sensitivity, to diverse areas of professional practice. The Association for Multicultural Counseling and Development (AMCD), a division of the ACA, similarly published a set of Multicultural Counseling Competencies in 1991 (Sue, Arredondo, & McDavis, 1992), which is currently undergoing revision. These competencies cite the three areas of: (a) counselors' self-awareness, specifically of values and biases; (b) clients' worldviews; and (c) culturally appropriate counseling interventions. Within each of these three key areas, competencies are identified that address attitudes and beliefs, knowledge, and skills.

More recently, additional concepts of advocacy and social justice have been discussed in the counseling literature, often within the context of multicultural competence (Nassar-McMillan, 2014; Nassar-McMillan, Rezcallah, & Nour, 2014). These additional domains have been linked with various other professional competencies in efforts to extend the attitudinal, knowledge, and skill areas into action. Examples are: the ACA Advocacy Competencies (Lewis, Arnold, House, & Toporek, 2003); Competencies for Counseling with Transgender Clients (Association of Lesbian, Gay, Bisexual, and Transgender Issues in Counseling, 2009); and the Association for Specialists in Group Work's Multicultural and Social Justice Competence Principles for Small Group Work (Singh, Merchant, Skudrzyk, & Ingene, 2012).

Thus, in contemporary society it is critical for counselors to be culturally competent, and that competence increasingly calls upon psychologists and counselors to be aware of the ways in which their own cultural backgrounds and socialization processes impact their personal and professional development. Moreover, cultural competence depends on being open to learning about and understanding clients' perspectives and worldviews. Finally, all such awareness and knowledge should contribute to the development of culturally appropriate interventions. These interventions must increasingly attend to social justice issues and the need for advocacy at systemic levels, spanning familial life to schools, communities, and broader policies.

Case Example: Suhaila's Acculturation as an International Student

Suhaila Al-Mediene is a 22-year-old college student who emigrated with her family from Iraq to Saudi Arabia prior to the First Gulf War. Her family owns a chain of successful businesses in Saudi Arabia. The family is Muslim, and Suhaila wears a hijab, in part guided by her interpretation of Islamic tradition as well as her pride in Islamic culture. Suhaila moved to the U.S., where her maternal uncle lives, to attend university in the southeastern U.S. There she earned her bachelor's degree in biochemistry. She wished to pursue a master's degree in science as well, so she applied to another university in the same state. She was accepted onto the graduate program, but was not granted in-state tuition. Several of her friends from her undergraduate residence hall, who were out-of-state residents upon beginning their undergraduate degree programs, also applied to the same institution for graduate degrees and were accepted and granted in-state tuition, including another friend from the same city in Saudi Arabia but with an Anglicized name.

Despite the financial challenges of the out-of-state tuition rates, Suhaila's parents decided to commit to the financial requirements to support her educational and career goals. Suhaila moved to the city of the new institution and began the graduate program, but she continued to feel stress and anxiety over the financial situation, as well as a vague perception and concern about unfairness. She also felt guilty that she was burdening her family with this financial commitment. Upon the recommendation of one of her graduate instructors, she went to the university's counseling center for support.

Paula McFarland was the counselor at the counseling center assigned to work with Suhaila. Paula listened carefully during the intake session, as well as during the next few subsequent sessions, to ascertain the issues that emerged through Suhaila's narratives. Although Paula recognized the presenting issue as being related to the denial of Suhaila's residency request, she decided first to first establish rapport by exploring the feelings of "otherness," or being an outsider, that underlay Suhaila's anxiety. She facilitated exploration of the concrete dynamics of family and community support that Suhaila had had during her teenage years while living in Saudi Arabia, followed by the support she had perceived during her undergraduate years, and ending with the present circumstances at university where she felt disconnected from people. She had not yet established a social or peer network, and was beginning to feel resentment toward the institution. As rapport built, Suhaila became more aware and more verbal about her feelings in relation to these shifting dynamics of community and support.

Paula then moved into the arena of advocacy by helping Suhaila explore ways in which she could gather more specific information about the in-state residency application process and outcomes. Paula herself, after helping Suhaila gather more information, met with administrative personnel at the university to learn more about the procedures, as well as about possible strategies for helping to guide Suhaila through an appeal process. The appeal process ultimately yielded the same result – denial of in-state status. But their collective advocacy efforts led to further explorations by the administration into how to create an easier-to-use and more transparent process. Suhaila, although disappointed by the ultimate outcome, began to feel more supported, or at least heard, by her university and, having worked through some of her feelings of "otherness" and, correspondingly, loneliness, was feeling less anxious, happier, and more productive in her student role. Paula also helped connect Suhaila with a Muslim student group, through which Suhaila connected with some peers on campus. This helped her create a healthier balance of school and work, particularly to mediate the stressors that she had increasingly become aware of through the counseling relationship.

While Paula's more typical approach might have been initially to explore emotions, with Suhaila she chose a more concrete and cognitive-behavioral exploration that she thought might be more clearly aligned with the client's presenting issues and the need for validation of these issues within the counseling setting. This helped create a good vehicle for establishing rapport at the outset of their work together. She also sensed that while Suhaila seemed to be open to exploring the sources of her anxiety, she also expressed the need to identify and take concrete action steps to alleviate some of the issues related to her situation. Paula collaborated with Suhaila to learn about the administrative structure and systems in place at the university, and coached her in becoming her own advocate in the process of furthering her education. At the conclusion of their work together, Suhaila presented Paula with a gift – a beautiful, ornate copper necklace from Saudi Arabia. Paula talked to Suhaila about the mutual meaningfulness of the gift and asked Suhaila what she would think about having it displayed in one of the display cases in the hallway of the counseling center used to encase cultural artifacts of international and other university students. Suhaila indicated that she would be honored to have it presented in that way.

Critique

The research on clinical interventions and cultural competence with Arab Americans as presented in this chapter has spanned attitudinal studies on college campuses, surveys conducted with clinicians, and hypothetical views of clinicians or clinicians-in-training on working with Arab American clients. Some research has also reflected either qualitative or quantitative experiences of Arab Americans. The research agenda is beginning to build, and these preliminary studies set a strong foundation for future work.

As future research on Arab Americans is developed across the counseling settings described above, scholars need to be cautious about numerous limitations. Not unlike other research on counseling settings and issues, sample sizes are often small and research designs are quasi-experimental, at best. Arab Americans are not a protected class by the U.S. government and therefore data about this group is not as readily available as it would be otherwise, and there is a challenge in identifying prospective samples. Also, as with many other population research initiatives, sample selection can easily bias results. In researching Arab American populations, those who self-select as Arab American may tend to have higher Arab identities, and may not be as concerned about being stigmatized by presenting as such. It may be the very individuals whose study would be most illuminating who may be the most difficult to capture.

An additional caveat for counseling research and practice with this population relates to the rich intraethnic diversity that exists within the community nationally (Samhan, 2014). In addition to the numerous aspects of diversity across religion, ethnicity, gender, and the like, vast disparities among new immigrant groups – and those from later generations – in socioeconomics, education, and career achievements create challenges not only to research but in the dissemination of accurately representative results and conclusions. For example, the most prominent ethno-cultural characteristics may be found among the newest immigrant groups and thus can often not be accurately generalized to later generation groups of clients.

There is a need for empirically supported counseling approaches and other clinical interventions. For example, much of the "clinical considerations" literature presented in this chapter is based on anecdotal and clinical expertise, but not empirical study. In addition, research on career development and labor market participation are important areas within counseling psychology that warrant attention among Arab Americans, so that both the cultural influences on client career development and labor market navigation and the potential effects of discrimination in these same areas can be better understood. Multicultural counseling competency research that is empirically based is somewhat limited, but emerging quickly as a critical need within counseling psychology. With earlier models being currently revisited and revised, such as within the APA and the ACA, the newer models are likely to lend themselves more easily to empirical investigation and validation.

Conclusion

Arab American clients may seek counseling in a variety of settings – spanning schools, colleges, career centers, and settings focused on clinical mental health and couples and family issues. Due to multiple sociopolitical factors affecting Arab Americans, together with unique cultural characteristics and traditions, there is a need for counseling psychologists to be multiculturally competent. This competence involves being self-aware of attitudes and beliefs, as well as being aware of the worldviews of clients, leading to culturally appropriate counseling interventions. These culturally sensitive interventions ideally should be empirically based. Future research initiatives should, moreover, involve increased rigor in studying Arab Americans' presenting issues across settings. In particular, identity issues across the lifespan, such as bicultural and other complex identity paths, are emerging as particularly relevant to Arab Americans' wellbeing and mental health. Future Census and other government-sponsored research should include Arab ethnicity in its statistics, so that research questions and subsequent mental-health focused interventions can be more specifically attuned to the needs of Arab American clients.

References

Abdelhady, D. (2014). The sociopolitical history of Arabs in the United States: Assimilation, ethnicity, and global citizenship. In S. C. McMillan, K. J. Ajrouch, & J. Hakim-Larson (eds.), *Biopsychosocial perspectives on Arab Americans: Culture, development, and health* (pp. 17–43). New York: Springer. doi: 10.1007/978-1-4614-8238-3_2

Abouchedid, K. & Nasser, R. (2006). Info-bias mechanism and American college students' attitudes towards Arabs. *International Studies Perspectives* 7, 204–212. doi: 10.1111/j.1528-3585.2006.00240.x

Aboul-Enein, B. H. & Aboul-Enein, F. H. (2010). The cultural gap delivering health care services to Arab American population in the United States. *Journal of Cultural Diversity* 17, 20–23

Abudabbeh, N. (2005). Arab families: An overview. In M. McGoldrick, J. Giordano, & N. Garcia-Preto (eds.), *Ethnicity and family therapy* (3rd edn., pp. 423–436). New York: Guilford

Abu-Ras, W. & Abu-Bader, S. H. (2008). The impact of the September 11, 2001, attacks on the well-being of Arab Americans in New York City. *Journal of Muslim Mental Health* 3, 217–239. doi: 10.1080/15564900802487634

Ahmed, S., Kia-Keating, M., & Tsai, K. (2011). A structural model of racial discrimination, acculturative stress, and cultural resources among Arab American adolescents. *American Journal of Community Psychology* 48(3–4), 181–192. doi: 10.1007/s10464-011-9424-3

Ajrouch, K. J. (2004). Gender, race, and symbolic boundaries: Contested spaces of identity among Arab American adolescents. *Sociological Perspectives* 47, 371–391. doi: 10.1525/sop.2004.47.4.371

Al-Krenawi, A. & Graham, J. R. (2000). Culturally sensitive social work practice with Arab clients in mental health settings. *Health & Social Work* 25, 9–22. doi: 10.1093/hsw/25.1.9

Aloud, N. & Rathur, A. (2009). Factors affecting attitudes toward seeking and using formal mental health and psychological services among Arab Muslim populations. *Journal of Muslim Mental Health* 4, 79–103. doi: 10.1080/15564900802487675

Amer, M. & Hovey, J. D. (2007). Socio-demographic differences in acculturation and mental health for a sample of 2nd generation/early immigrant Arab Americans. *Journal of Immigrant and Minority Health* 9, 335–347. doi: 10.1007/s10903-007-9045-y

American-Arab Anti-Discrimination Committee. (2003). *Report on hate crimes and discrimination against Arab Americans: The post-September 11 backlash, September 11, 2001–October 11, 2002.* Washington, D.C.: American-Arab Anti-Discrimination Committee Research Institute.

American Psychological Association. (2002). *Guidelines on multicultural education: Training, research, practice, and organizational change for psychologists.* Retrieved from www.apa.org/pi/oema/resources/policy/multicultural-guidelines.aspx

American Psychological Association. (2014). *Ethical principles of psychologists and code of conduct, including 2010 amendments.* Retrieved from www.apa.org/ethics/code/principles.pdf

Amri, S. A., Nassar-McMillan, S. C., Meisenhimer, M., & Bryan, S. A. (2013). Counseling Arab Americans. In C. C. Lee (ed.), *Counseling for diversity* (3rd edn., pp. 135–147). Alexandria, VA: American Counseling Association.

Arab American Institute. (2014). *Demographics.* Retrieved from www.aaiusa.org/pages/demographics/

Arredondo, P., Toporek, M. S., Brown, S., Jones, J., Locke, D. C., Sanchez, J., & Stadler, H. (1996). *Operationalization of the multicultural counseling competencies.* Alexandria, VA: AMCD. Retrieved from www.counseling.org/docs/competencies/multcultural_competencies.pdf?sfvrsn=3

Association of Lesbian, Gay, Bisexual, and Transgender Issues in Counseling. (2009). *Competencies for counseling with transgender clients.* Alexandria, VA: Association of Lesbian, Gay, Bisexual, and Transgender Issues in Counseling. Retrieved from www.counseling.org/docs/competencies/algbtic_competencies.pdf?sfvrsn=3

Beitin, B. K. & Allen, K. R. (2005). Resilience in Arab American couples after September 11, 2001: A systems perspective. *Journal of Marital and Family Therapy* 31, 251–267. doi: 10.1111/j.1752-0606.2005.tb01567.x

Beitin, B. K. & Aprahamian, M. (2014). Family values and traditions. In S. C. Nassar-McMillan, K. K. Ajrouch, & J. Hakim-Larson (eds.), *Biopsychosocial perspectives on Arab Americans: Culture, development, and health* (pp. 67–88). New York: Springer. doi: 10.1007/978-1-4614-8238-3_4

Britto, P. R. (2008). Who am I? Ethnic identity formation of Arab Muslim children in contemporary U.S. society. *Journal of American Academy of Child and Adolescent Psychiatry* 47, 853–857.

Dávila, A. & Mora, M. T. (2005). Changes in the earnings of Arab men in the US between 2000 and 2002. *Journal of Population Economics* 18(4), 587–601. doi: 10.1007/s00148-005-0050-y

El-Islam, M. F. (2008). Arab culture and mental health care. *Transcultural Psychiatry* 45, 671–682. doi: 10.1177/1363461508100788

Erickson, C. D. & Al-Timimi, N. R. (2001). Providing mental health services to Arab Americans: Recommendations and considerations. *Cultural Diversity and Ethnic Minority Psychology* 7, 308–327. doi: 10.1037/1099-9809.7.4.308

Erikson, E. (1956). The problem of ego identity. *Journal of the American Psychoanalytic Association* 4, 56–121. doi: 10.1177/000306515600400104

Graham, J. R., Bradshaw, C., & Trew, J. L. (2010). Cultural considerations for social service agencies working with Muslim clients. *Social Work* 55, 337–346. doi: 10.1093/sw/55.4.337

Haboush, K. & Barakat, N. (2014). Education and employment among Arab Americans: Pathways to individual identity and community resilience. In S. C. Nassar-McMillan, K. J. Ajrouch, & J. Hakim-Larson (eds.), *Biopsychosocial perspectives on Arab Americans: Culture, development, and health* (pp. 229–255). New York: Springer. doi: 10.1007/978-1-4614-8238-3_11

Haboush, K. L. (2007). Working with Arab American families: Culturally competent practice for school psychologists. *Psychology in the Schools* 44(2), 183–198. doi: 10.1002/pits.20215

Haboush, K. L., Selman, J., & Sievering, K. (2008). Traumatized youth: New roles for school psychologists. In D. H. Molina (ed.), *School psychology: 21st century issues and challenges* (pp. 117–155). Hauppauge, NY: Nova Science Publishers.

Hassouneh, D. & Kulwicki, A. (2009). Family privacy as protection: A qualitative pilot study of mental illness in Arab-American Muslim women. *Research in the Social Scientific Study of Religion* 20, 195–215. doi: 10.1163/ej.9789004175624.i-334.67

Jamil, H., Farrag, M., Hakim-Larson, J., Kafaji, T., Abdulkhaleq, H., & Hammad, A. (2007). Mental health symptoms in Iraqi refugees: Posttraumatic stress disorder, anxiety, and depression. *Journal of Cultural Diversity* 14, 19–25.

Jamil, H., Nassar-McMillan, S. C., & Lambert, R. G. (2007). Immigration and attendant psychological sequalae: A comparison of three waves of Iraqi immigrants. *Journal of Orthopsychiatry* 77, 199–205. doi: 10.1037/0002-9432.77.2.199

Khan, Z. (2006). Attitudes toward counseling and alternative support among Muslims in Toledo, Ohio. *Journal of Muslim Mental Health* 1(1), 21–42. doi: 10.1080/15564900600654278

Kira, I., Lewandowski, L., Somers, C. L., Yoon, J. S., & Chiodo, L. (2012). The effects of trauma types, cumulative trauma, and PTSD on IQ in two highly traumatized adolescent groups. *Psychological Trauma: Theory, Research, Practice, and Policy* 4, 128–139. doi: 10.1037/a0022121

Kira, I. A., Amer, M., & Wrobel, N. (2014). Arab refugees: Trauma, resilience, and recovery. In S. C. Nassar-McMillan, K. J. Ajrouch, & J. Hakim-Larson (eds.), *Biopsychosocial perspectives on Arab Americans: Culture, development, and health* (pp. 229–255). New York: Springer. doi: 10.1007/978-1-4614-8238-3_9

Kira, I. A., Hammad, A., Lewandowski, L., Templin, T., Ramswamy, V., Ozkan, B., & Mohanesh, J. (2007). The physical and mental status of Iraqi refugees and its etiology. *Ethnicity & Disease* 17(S3), 79–82.

Lewis, J. A., Arnold, M. S., House, R., & Toporek, R. L. (2003). *Advocacy competencies.* American Counseling Association. Retrieved from www.counseling.org/docs/competencies/advocacy_competencies.pdf?sfvrsn=3

Marcia, J. E. (1966). Development and validation of ego identity status. *Journal of Personality and Social Psychology* 3, 551–558. doi: 10.1037/h0023281

Nassar-McMillan, S. C. (2010). *Counseling Arab Americans.* Belmont, CA: Brooks/Cole.

Nassar-McMillan, S. C. (2014). A framework for cultural competence, advocacy, and social justice: Applications for global multiculturalism and diversity. *International Journal for Educational and Vocational Guidance* 14, 103–118. doi: 10.1007/s10775-014-9265-3

Nassar-McMillan, S. C., Gonzalez, L., & Mohamed, R. (2014). Individuals and families of Arab descent. In D. G. Hays & B. T. Erford (eds.), *Developing multicultural competence: A systems approach* (2nd edn., pp. 245–277). Boston, MA: Pearson.

Nassar-McMillan, S. C., Lambert, R. G., & Hakim-Larson, J. (2011). Discrimination history, backlash fear, and ethnic identity among Arab Americans: Post 9–11 snapshots. *Journal of Multicultural Counseling and Development* 39, 38–47. doi: 10.1002/j.2161-1912.2011.tb00138.x

Nassar-McMillan, S. C., Rezcallah, A., & Nour, M. D. (2014). Arab American youth: Overcoming adversity. In M. T. Garrett (ed.), *Youth and adversity: Psychology and influences of child and adolescent resilience and coping* (pp.133–145). Hauppauge, NY: Nova Science Publishers.

Nassar-McMillan, S. C. & Tovar, L. Z. (2012). Career counseling with Americans of Arab descent. *Career Planning and Adult Development* 28, 72–87.

Padela, A. I. & Heisler, M. (2010). The association of perceived abuse and discrimination after Sept. 11, 2001, with psychological distress, level of happiness, and health status among Arab Americans. *American Journal of Public Health* 100, 284–291. doi: 10.2105/AJPH.2009.164954

Rasmi, S., Chuang, S. S., & Hennig, K. (2014). The acculturation gap-distress model: Extensions and application to Arab Canadian families. *Cultural Diversity and Ethnic Minority Psychology.* Advance online publication. doi: 10.1037/cdp0000014

Read, J. G. & Oselin, S. (2008). Gender and the education-employment paradox in ethnic and religious contexts: The case of Arab Americans. *American Sociological Review* 73, 296–313. doi: 10.1177/000312240807300206

Saigh, P. A., Yasik, A. E., Oberfield, R. A., Halamandaris, P. V., & Bremner, J. D. (2006). The intellectual performance of traumatized children and adolescents with or without posttraumatic stress disorder. *Journal of Abnormal Psychology* 115, 332–340. doi: 10.1037/0021-843X.115.2.332

Samhan, H. H. (2014). Intra-ethnic diversity and religion. In S. C. McMillan, K. J. Ajrouch, & J. Hakim-Larson (eds.), *Biopsychosocial perspectives on Arab Americans: Culture, development, and health* (pp. 45–65). New York: Springer. doi: 10.1007/978-1-4614-8238-3_3

Scull, N. C., Khullar, N., Al-Awadhi, N., & Erheim, R. (2014). A qualitative study of the perceptions of mental health care in Kuwait. *International Perspectives in Psychology: Research, Practice, Consultation* 3(4), 284–299. doi: 10.1037/ipp0000023

Shammas, D. S. (2009). Post-9/11 Arab and Muslim community college students: Ethno-religious enclaves and perceived discrimination. *Community College Journal of Research and Practice* 33, 283–308. doi: 10.1080/10668920802580507

Sheikh, M. F. (2009). *An exploratory study of the challenges of living in America as a Muslim adolescent attending public school* (Doctoral dissertation). Available from ProQuest Dissertations and Theses database (UMI No. 3402509).

Singh, A. A., Merchant, N., Skudrzyk, B., & Ingene, D. (2012). *Multicultural and Social Justice Competence Principles for Small Group Work.* Association for Specialists in Group Work. Retrieved from www.asgw.org/pdf/asgw_mc_sj_priniciples_final_asgw.pdf

Soheilian, S. S. & Inman, A. G. (2015). Competent counseling for Middle Eastern American Clients: Implications for trainees. *Journal of Multicultural Counseling and Development* 43(3), 173–190. doi: 10.1002/jmcd.12013

Sue, D. W. (2001). Multidimensional facets of cultural competence. *The Counseling Psychologist* 29, 790–821. doi: 10.1177/0011000001296002

Sue, D. W., Arredondo, P., & McDavis, R. (1992). Multicultural competencies and standards: A call to the profession. *Journal of Counseling & Development* 70, 477–486. doi: 10.1002/j.2161-1912.1992.tb00563.x

Thomas, P., Bracken, P., Shabbir, M, & Yasmeen, S. (2010). Language, culture, and mental health. *The Arab Journal of Psychiatry* 21, 2, 102–111.

Widner, D. & Chicoine, S. (2011). It's all in the name: Employment discrimination against Arab Americans. *Sociological Forum* 26, 806–823. doi: 10.1111/j.1573-7861.2011.01285.x

Wrobel, N. H. & Paterson, A. (2014). Mental health risks in Arab Americans across the lifespan. In S. C. McMillan, K. J. Ajrouch, & J. Hakim-Larson (eds.), *Biopsychosocial perspectives on Arab Americans: Culture, development, and health* (pp. 197–228). New York: Springer. doi: 10.1007/978-1-4614-8238-3_10

Youssef, J. & Deane, F. (2006). Factors influencing mental-health help-seeking in Arabic-speaking communities in Sydney, Australia. *Mental Health, Religion & Culture* 9(1), 43–66. doi: 10.1080/13674670512331335686

22

PSYCHOTHERAPY MODELS

Cultural Applications of Psychodynamic, Cognitive Behavior, Family Systems, and Culture-Specific Approaches

Fatimah El-Jamil and Sameera Ahmed

The utilization of psychological services by Arab Americans is a growing area of interest and concern (Martin, 2014; Rothermel, 2009) given the reported increase in immigration and acculturation stress that Arab Americans have been facing, particularly since 9/11 (Awad, 2010; Awad, Martinez, & Amer, 2013). Challenges have impacted Arab Americans' mental health and adaptation to American society, for both new immigrants and those born in the U.S. These include the struggle with value differences, social stigma, and the negative media representation of Arabs, as well as experiences of racism, discrimination, and war trauma (Abi-Hashem, 2008, 2011; Awad & Hall-Clark, 2009; Erickson & Al-Timimi, 2001; Hijazi et al., 2014; Ibish, 2003; Nobles & Sciarra, 2000; Pollara & Meleis, 1995).

Despite Arab Americans' increasing mental health needs, little has been written on the applicability of psychotherapy models to Arab American clients. While many suggestions and recommendations have been offered on how best to approach and counsel Arab Americans (e.g. Abi-Hashem, 2014; Abudabbeh & Nydell, 1993; Sayed, 2003b), there is little to no evidence for the efficacy of specific psychotherapy models or interventions with Arab Americans. The scarcity of empirical research on effective modalities when working with Arab Americans leaves great ambiguity about the appropriateness of Western-based psychotherapy for this population, and warrants increased attention on the use of relevant and culturally sensitive psychotherapy for this ethnic minority group.

The purpose of this chapter is to expand the discussion of culturally sensitive psychotherapy with ethnic minorities by offering a critical examination of current evidence-based psychotherapy models and their applicability to Arab American clients. The controversies, challenges, and strengths of these approaches for use with Arab American clients are addressed, and more recent culture-specific interventions applied with Arabs in the Middle East are also presented. A clinical case example of an Arab American client further serves to illustrate each model's cultural application. The chapter concludes with a critique that calls for greater psychotherapy effectiveness and efficacy research with the Arab American population.

Psychotherapy Models

When examining the appropriateness of a psychotherapy model for clients, research has demonstrated that factors such as clients' presenting problems, expectations, and levels of resistance each play a role in determining the most effective approach for a specific client (Norcross & Beutler, 2008). When working with ethnic minority groups such as Arab Americans, these factors must also be considered within the cultural and social contexts of that group and their interactions with the larger society (Abo-Zena & Ahmed, 2014). Immigration history, generation status, socioeconomic status, religion, religiosity, the degree of connection to their cultural community, and the degree of acculturation into American society are factors that may further influence Arab American clients' understandings of their presenting problems, levels of resistance, and expectations of treatment (see Abi-Hashem, 2011; Abudabbeh, 1996).

Psychotherapy models for examination in this chapter represent those most commonly discussed in publications on Arab Americans: psychodynamic, cognitive behavior, and family systems therapies. While scholarly work in the field of psychotherapy has traditionally focused on the four major psychotherapy models, including the humanistic/existential model, and despite their potential usefulness and suitability for Arab Americans, humanistic/existential models are not reviewed in this chapter due to lack of literature and scholarship on their use with Arab Americans. Moreover, the family systems therapy model, and not the group therapy model, was included in this examination due its pertinence to Arab American culture. The following sections present the major components or mechanisms of the psychodynamic, cognitive behavior, and family systems models, followed by a presentation of each model's relevance and cultural application to Arab American clients.

Psychodynamic Psychotherapy Model

In the little that has been written about the application of psychoanalytic or psychodynamic theory for Arab Americans, there exist discrepant views, some endorsing its use (Bushra, Khadivi, & Frewat-Nikowitz, 2007; Masalha, 1999; Shehadeh, 2008) and others describing psychoanalysis as theoretically and technically incongruent to Arab American culture (Abudabbeh & Hays, 2006; Dwairy, 1998, 2002). This discrepancy in the literature, however, may be explained by significant differences in the theoretical approaches to psychoanalysis.

Psychoanalytic theory has experienced a noteworthy paradigm shift from classical drive theory to a two-person relational theory, such that a greater emphasis is now placed on relationships rather than on repressed, sexual, and aggressive drives and fantasies (Wachtel, 2008). In the classical psychoanalytic paradigm, therapists work toward resolving unconscious, intrapsychic conflicts involving opposing sexual and aggressive drives. The analyst helps the individual recognize defense mechanisms that serve to protect him or her from threatening material and consequent anxiety, and gradually works through the individual's resistance in order to reveal hidden or repressed emotions or drives (Freud, 1926). The process allows the client to confront and manage these experiences rather than be controlled by them.

Contemporary psychodynamic therapy, on the other hand, places greater emphasis on early relationships, particularly between the child and his or her caregivers, and their effects on current relationships, including that between the therapist and client. Psychodynamic therapists argue that the internal representations of these early experiences organize current interpersonal relationships (Kohut, 1977). As such, exploring the client's relational and emotional experiences, and identifying relational patterns, embodies the approach of newer object relations, interpersonal, and self-psychology theories in the psychodynamic approach (Wachtel, 2008).

Psychodynamic models today involve a collaborative exploration of the client's experience. The "here and now," or experiential, aspect of psychodynamic work, through transference and countertransference interpretations, allows for a genuine exchange of emotions and insight between the client and therapist. Additionally, similar to the humanistic approaches, the empathic, accepting, and supportive therapeutic relationship gives the client permission to recognize parts of the self and emotions that had been previously avoided, allowing for new ways of perceiving the self and others, and new interpersonal behaviors both within the therapy room and outside (Luborsky, O'Reilly-Landry, & Arlow, 2008).

Cultural suitability to Arab American clients. Several scholars have warned against the use of psychoanalysis and other insight-oriented therapies with Arab Americans. The nondirective approach that characterizes the psychodynamic model has been raised as a concern. Sayed (2003a) described Arab clients viewing their doctors as an all-knowing authority and guide. As such, directive, problem-focused approaches have been recommended to accommodate their needs and expectations (Abudabbeh & Hays, 2006). Yet this recommendation has been debated in the literature. For example, Masalha (1999) noted that psychotherapy should strive to build the Arab client's sense of ownership, responsibility, and empowerment; and as such, the therapist should abstain from direct guidance.

From a more theoretical perspective, Dwairy (2002) explained that the intrapsychic conflicts central to psychoanalytic theory are not as relevant to Arab experience as intrafamilial conflicts, which more often define their core problems. Thus, he argued that psychodynamic theory may completely miss what is most essential and pertinent to the daily struggles of Arabs. Furthermore, Dwairy (1998, 2002) explained that the psychodynamic process requires clients to gradually expose their private experiences and emotions, and this intervention may generate intense shame or guilt that may change the nature of their interaction with family and thus may also destabilize their family support system. While the vulnerability of shame is intrinsic in the process of psychodynamic therapy as clients begin to expose their private layers (Ogden, 1985), for Arab Americans this feeling of shame may be particularly intense due to family values and expectations (Dwairy, 2002). Communication within the family is directed by values of respect (*ihtiram*) and fulfilling social/familial duties (*wajib*), which may make authentic self-expression of dissatisfaction or negative feelings toward a parent or authority figure particularly challenging (Dwairy, 2002).

On the other hand, some scholars have suggested favorable outcomes of psychodynamic therapy with Arab American clients, particularly with educated or financially secure individuals (Bushra et al., 2007) and even with Arab immigrants (Shehadeh, 2008). From a theoretical perspective, the relational basis of the psychodynamic model speaks to the essence of Arab American relational culture. The social fabric of Arab American culture results in the development of multiple, significant, self-other representations that make up the individual (Shehadeh, 2008). Understanding the impact of these internalizations becomes a valuable process of understanding the self and its resources. Furthermore, the relational emphasis of psychodynamic work can prove beneficial in providing Arab American immigrants an experience of relatedness after their loss of previous connectedness within their collective community in their country of origin. This may provide clients with a reduced sense of isolation and greater efficacy in being able to connect to others in their environment (Shehadeh, 2008).

The psychodynamic process, similar to other insight-oriented approaches such as humanistic, can also provide a protected space for Arab Americans to challenge beliefs and values of self and others, and to explore the meaning of these beliefs. For example, Arab Americans searching for greater autonomy and recognition of their needs and desires apart from family obligations may benefit from a safe space to explore such feelings and thoughts (Masalha, 1999). In addition, the safe space may empower individuals to acknowledge and accept long-held and hidden experiences and emotions that may be considered taboo or shameful within their subculture. The normalization process that is often a by-product of psychodynamic therapy allows clients to feel more integrated, empowered, and connected to their selves (Shehadeh, 2008).

Challenges may arise in the transference and countertransference experiences with Arab American clients, which are at times further complicated by the clients' complex relationship with the U.S. Arab Americans may be ambivalent toward America, glorifying it on the one hand for the safety and resources it provides, and loathing it on the other hand for perceived unjust foreign policies toward the Middle East (Dwairy & El-Jamil, 2016) and racial/ethnic profiling. Similarly, psychotherapists themselves may have conflicted sentiments about Arab Americans, due to stereotypes owing to the prejudicial media narratives of Arabs and the Middle East. Even in cases where the therapist is an Arab American, countertransference reactions can range from overidentification to feelings of rejection toward the client (Bushra et al., 2007). While an awareness of these reactions is essential in facilitating the therapeutic alliance and in understanding the interpersonal dyad, the exchange of these experiences may be particularly uncomfortable, alien, or even threatening to Arab American clients who do not receive adequate psychoeducation on the process.

Given the discrepant views in the literature on the relevance of the psychodynamic model for Arab Americans, Dwairy (2006) recommended a cultural assessment of the client prior to choosing the psychodynamic model or other insight-oriented models. Factors such as level of adherence to cultural traditions and values, desire for greater individuation and emotional expression, and the presence of internal and external resources to manage emerging feelings, beliefs, or changing behaviors should be carefully assessed for each client.

The Cognitive Behavior Therapy Models

Open expression of hidden emotions and vulnerabilities may be challenging for some Arab American clients; as such, behavior therapy offers a valuable alternative by emphasizing problem-solving skills and behavioral activation. Behavior therapy emerged as a treatment model for psychological disorders in the 1950s and has evolved considerably since then (Wilson, 2008). It began as a treatment approach that relied heavily on modern learning theory or the application of classical and operant conditioning models toward behavior change. However, a paradigm shift resulted in the inclusion of social learning theory, as described by Bandura (1986), and the integration of cognitive methods (Beck, 1967; Ellis, 1962), which led to the development of cognitive behavior therapy (CBT).

Abnormal behavior, according to behavior theory, is acquired in the same way that normal behavior is learned (Wilson, 2008). Thus, the behaviorist's primary aim is to support the client in learning new and more adaptive behaviors. Given that the primary mechanism of change associated with behavior theory is exposure, behavior therapy includes the encouragement of facing fears and taking risks, problem solving, and the reinforcement that comes from experiences of success (Lambert & Ogles, 2004). Exposure to feared stimuli, be they objects or experiences, underlies interventions such as exposure therapy, response prevention, behavioral rehearsal, and systematic desensitization.

Cognitive therapy also offers a directive, structured, and action-oriented approach that may appeal to Arab Americans. Cognitive therapy focuses on attending closely to the client's automatic thoughts in order to identify distortions of thought and beliefs that facilitate negative emotions as well as maladaptive behaviors (Beck, 1967). Automatic thoughts are generated from underlying core beliefs or assumptions that are contained in schemas, or perceptions of self and others stemming from one's past. These automatic thoughts can result in a rigid and inflexible repertoire of cognitions, emotions, and behaviors (Beck, 2011). Ellis (1962) also developed a cognitive method, known as rational emotive behavior therapy (REBT), which outlined a specific set of irrational beliefs that include demandingness, such as "shoulds" and "musts," and catastrophizing. The underlying assumption behind both REBT and cognitive therapy is that changing one's interpretation of negative events can alleviate distressing emotions and assist in changing maladaptive behaviors (Beck & Weishaar, 2008).

More recently, Hayes, Follette, and Linehan (2004) described what they call the "third wave" of behaviorism. This "third wave" emerged in the 1990s and involved an integration of the traditional emphasis on behavior change with an additional focus on acceptance. Two prominent forms of this "third wave" approach are dialectical behavior therapy (DBT; Linehan, 1993), and acceptance and commitment therapy (ACT; Hayes, Luorna, Bond, Masuda, & Lillis, 2006). Hayes and Smith (2005) explained that experiential avoidance, or the deliberate effort to avoid anything deemed aversive, is at the core of mental distress. Consequently, the process of acceptance – essential to DBT and ACT – is aimed at helping clients to choose to experience negative thoughts and feelings rather than feel controlled by them or struggling to avoid them.

Cultural suitability to Arab American clients. Behavior therapy with clear directives and objectives and an encouragement toward behavior change may be particularly attractive to Arab American clients who are new to the American way of life and may feel that achieving their goals without direct assistance would be quite overwhelming. CBT provides clients with a clear outcome and thus a sense of hopefulness in otherwise challenging circumstances. Cognitive therapy also provides a directive approach in educating clients on how to monitor and challenge thoughts. Arab Americans may value the concrete tools and strategies, as well as the structure associated with between-session assignments (Sayed, 2003a).

Scholars have described positive outcomes of CBT with Arab and Muslim Americans (Abudabbeh & Hays, 2006; Hamdan, 2008; Hodge & Nadir, 2008), and preliminary research has demonstrated positive results using narrative exposure therapy, which employs behavioral methods, with Arab refugees living in the U.S. (Hijazi et al., 2014). Additionally, positive outcomes may be increased when positive religious coping strategies are integrated into CBT with Arab Americans who report high religiousness and find faith as a source of comfort (Abu-Raiya & Pargament, 2010, 2011). Pargament, Koenig, and Perez (2000) defined positive religious coping as methods for coping with stressors that entail developing a safe and secure relationship with God, having a higher meaning to life, and enhancing a sense of spiritual connection to others. Moreover, ACT is an integrative approach that may have relevance to Arab American clients by indirectly addressing their cultural or religious values. Early in therapy, ACT involves the identification of the clients' personal values that give their lives meaning and purpose, which become the clients' guiding principles from which treatment goals are developed.

Like other models, CBT should be handled with an awareness of clients' cultural specificities. From a theoretical perspective, what is considered "rational" or "adaptive" may itself be embedded in cultural values (Amer & Jalal, 2012). For example, CBT's emphasis on assertiveness may not appeal to an individual who prefers more accommodating interpersonal communication. Furthermore, embedded in CBT interventions is the process of encouraging independent thinking; however, this also may be culturally incongruent at times. For example, assisting an adolescent toward greater autonomy by challenging a parent's irrational belief of demandingness (Ellis, 1962) may be seen as undermining the parent's authority in enforcing religious or cultural standards on his or her child. Similarly, challenging clients to examine their "shoulds" associated to family obligations, or *wajib*, can also create misunderstanding. Furthermore, depending on the communication style of the client, for some Arab Americans, the expression of intense emotions may be the most authentic way of expressing feelings such as despair (Amer & Jalal, 2012). If the cognitive technique of decatastrophizing is employed in such circumstances, clients may feel misunderstood or undermined. Arab Americans who may already feel marginalized by mainstream culture may reject a therapy that labels their language as irrational or distorted. As such, clients' thoughts must be examined in a culturally congruent way and without imposing the therapists' own beliefs (Abudabbeh & Hays, 2006).

Family Therapy Models

Intrafamilial interactions are often major sources of struggle in the personal lives of Arab Americans (Dwairy, 2002, 2006). Struggles can also arise between the family and the larger American cultural system. For example, Jordanian American mothers living in the U.S. expressed feelings of guilt, confusion, despair, and persistent worry primarily around raising their children within a different cultural context (Pollara & Meleis, 1995). Issues of identity and belonging to American society can also be stressful for adolescents, resulting in a tug-of-war between their longing for acceptance within American society and their loyalties to family and tradition (Nobles & Sciarra, 2000). Consequently, writers have argued that family therapy may in fact be the most relevant intervention for Arab Americans (Abudabbeh & Hays, 2006; Al-Krenawi and Graham, 2000), improving upon intrafamilial dynamics and communication, and bridging gaps between cultures and generations within a family (Sciarra, 2011).

The foundations of family therapy emerged in the 1940s with systems and communications theories. This was followed by numerous therapies, including Bowen's systems theory and strategic, structural, object relations, experiential, and social constructivism approaches. While these models emerged somewhat independently of one another, today family therapy approaches complement one another in their basic working concepts. The core of family therapy is its focus on context, complementarity, and circular causality. As such, each problem is viewed as based in a specific social context, in which each member of the system influences the other, and problems are maintained by an ongoing series of actions and reactions (Nichols, 2011). Family therapy removes blame from a single member of the family and shifts attention to a larger systemic problem that may lie within the family dynamics or between the family and other systems. Furthermore, family theory views families as unique cultures with particular characteristics that should be understood, including language, celebrations, rituals, behaviors, and communication styles (McGoldrick, Giordano, & Garcia-Preto, 2005). Therefore, inherent in the model is an appreciation of cultural diversity.

Several core concepts in family therapy include the importance of family subsystems and boundaries, feedback loops that maintain the problem, and the differentiation of self that separates self from other and promotes connectedness and harmony. Bowen's systems theory focuses on patterns and projected emotions transmitted across generations, with a particular emphasis on the levels of differentiation of individual family members (Bowen, 1966). Structural work in family therapy reorganizes the family subsystems, promoting healthier boundaries and ways of communicating (Minuchin, 1974), while strategic work aims to block and prevent negative interactional patterns or feedback loops (Jackson, 1965). Social constructionism added the subjective experience or perspective of the family (Gergen, 1985). As a result, therapeutic aims shifted toward helping families discover new perspectives to family behaviors, known as reframing, and toward constructing their own solutions by activating their own resources and strengths.

Cultural suitability to Arab American clients. For many people of Arab origin, family relationships have high priority, above any other relationship (Dwairy, 2006). As such, bringing family members into the therapy room may provide acknowledgment and respect to the family unit as a whole and to the important roles members play within the system. Moreover, specific family models may demonstrate congruence to Arab American family values. For example, the structural family model reinstates the importance of a family hierarchy whereby the parental subsystem may be empowered in the face of struggles with children or adolescents. Other models stemming from social constructivism, such as the solution-focused approach, offer families a value-free approach to problem solving, whereby family members are encouraged to identify their own strengths and build on preexisting abilities and interventions that have already worked for them in the past. These approaches offer a focus on empowerment and behavioral and structural shifts with minimal need for self-disclosure on the part of family members.

Many of Bowen's systems theory concepts may be meaningful to Arab Americans. For example, Bowen highlighted the important role of family of origin and extended family members, also fundamental to the Arab family system. Bowen described the family "triangle," which functions to shift anxiety away from an emotionally charged two-person relationship, such as the husband and wife, by triangulating a third person, such as a child, in an attempt to reestablish family equilibrium. While it may be natural for some families to have children involved in marital tensions, the triangulation often results in further problems and emotional burdens. Therefore "de-triangulation" and limited "boundary setting" can serve to reduce conflict and tension without compromising on values of loyalty and commitment to family needs.

However, in family theory there are also many value-laden constructs that may prove sensitive and challenging when applied to Arab American families. Depending on generation status and levels of acculturation, concepts such as "differentiation of self," "enmeshment," and "boundaries" may have different meanings and nuances to Arab Americans and their families. For example, what may be perceived as pathological enmeshment in the dominant American culture may be positively experienced as love, care, protection, and support in the Arab culture (Dwairy, 2006), and thus can be viewed as a healthy and adaptive interdependence. For some Arab Americans, boundaries among family members are often fluid. Some may view differentiation of self as distance, separation, or betrayal.

Practical obstacles may also exist in the application of family therapy with Arab Americans. In traditional Arab families, family concerns are expected to remain private within the family (Dwairy, 2002). The husband, in particular, may disconnect from any process that he perceives may undermine his authority, and the wife may also not wish to expose problems related to her marriage. Techniques taken from experiential or emotion-focused family therapy can be challenging because traditional Arab American parents may find emotional expression in front of children or spouses difficult or threatening to their roles (Sayed, 2003a). Similarly, the emotions of children may be considered secondary to family values and thus undermined by parents (Dwairy & El-Jamil, 2016), and expressed differences in religiosity and cultural identity among the children may also not be tolerated. Finally, multigenerational analyses or genograms may be more conducive to more acculturated Arab American families, as immigrants or less acculturated families may find such work to be too exposing or disloyal to past generations.

Culture-Specific Interventions

Western psychotherapy models may at times demonstrate theoretical or technical incongruence to Arab culture. This challenge has prompted the development of emic approaches to psychotherapy treatment, which base their interventions on an in-depth understanding of the culture group. The strength of emic approaches lies in the development of therapies with cultural specificities in mind, rather than a reliance on external, preexisting concepts.

Metaphor Therapy

The metaphor model proposed by Dwairy (2009, 2012, 2013) is an emic approach to treatment that emphasizes the adoption of metaphors and proverbs in the therapeutic dialogue with Arabs. Metaphor therapy is defined as attaining therapeutic outcomes through the use of figures of speech, images, or objects that represent meaning to clients (Dwairy, 2012). In employing metaphor therapy, clients use metaphors to represent their problems symbolically and innovatively find metaphoric solutions for them. Therapists who practice metaphor therapy may propose metaphors to their clients, whereas others either ask clients to provide the metaphors or else listen for them in their clients' dialogue (e.g. Grove & Panzer, 1989).

A metaphor has two components or layers: a concrete and an abstract layer. The concrete may be a verbal proverb or a nonverbal object, artistic work, or music that clients relate to their problems. The abstract layer is characterized by the creative interpretation of the verse or object, and triggers the emotional aspect for clients (Dwairy, 2009). For example, in the case of the use of an object, the client is asked to discuss the thoughts, emotions and memories associated with that object, and then to decide what to do physically with that object, as a metaphoric solution to the problem itself. Based on this model, once clients reach metaphoric solutions to their problems, these new images can generate real psychological, physiological, and social changes in their lives (Dwairy, 2009). According to Burns (2001), metaphor therapy is an interactive process that triggers creativity, circumvents defense mechanisms, inspires exploration, and prompts problem solving within cultures that commonly use metaphors in day-to-day language. It is an indirect method of addressing needs and thoughts that the client has difficulty confronting or coping with at the given moment.

Dwairy (2009) proposed metaphor therapy for clients whose language preference is Arabic, because the Arabic language contains a sufficient amount of metaphors that predisposes clients to express their own problems using metaphors. Less acculturated, first generation Arab Americans are more likely to benefit from the use of metaphor therapy because it allows for the development of meaning through the use of indirect rather than direct speech. A major limitation to the use of metaphor therapy, however, lies in the difficulty in translating metaphors from the Arabic language when therapists are speaking to their clients in English.

Culturanalysis

Dwairy (2009) proposed another culturally derived intervention for Arabs that circumvents the barriers of language, which he coined "culturanalysis." Culturanalysis pertains to the identification and specific use of values from clients' own belief systems that can more adaptively meet their needs, without threatening their predominant family, cultural, and religious beliefs. Dwairy proposed identifying conflicting values from within clients' culture or religion and bringing those values into awareness. Culturanalysis depends on the notion that every culture and religion has seemingly conflicting or contradictory values and beliefs, and this proposed intervention sheds light on values of which the client was not previously aware. The primary assumption of culturanalysis is that individuals assume some values of a culture or religion that are at times not compatible with their individual needs, and ignore or are unaware of other values that the culture holds, which may be a source of untapped strength or resource.

Culturanalysis can be understood from a humanistic perspective in its positive regard and empathy toward the culture (Dwairy & El-Jamil, 2016). It encourages clients to acquire a deeper understanding of their own religious or cultural values and become motivated to find alternative approaches and interpretations within their own belief systems. Arab Americans, being bicultural individuals, may feel forced to engage with seemingly contradictory values within themselves, between their collectivist heritage and individualistic environment, and between themselves and their families. Culturanalysis therefore becomes especially pertinent because of the shift from identifying the contradiction in individuals to identifying contradictions in the belief systems they uphold, which opens up new perspectives and possibilities of identification.

Case Example: Diverse Psychotherapy Approaches for Mariam, a Client With Obsessive-Compulsive Disorder

This section begins by highlighting the case of an Arab American client, Mariam, who seeks therapy for symptoms of obsessive-compulsive disorder (OCD). After she has presented the basic information about her case, four psychotherapy models (psychodynamic, CBT, family therapy, and culturanalysis) are used to highlight how the theory may be applied to her situation.

Mariam is a 30-year-old second generation Muslim Arab American, married to a Muslim European American male, and has recently given birth to a daughter. She struggles with symptoms of OCD. She reports obsessive concerns of physically or emotionally harming others due to her negligence, saying something wrong, or hurting others' feelings. She also reports obsessive concerns about religious impurity or *najasah*, resulting in ritualistic handwashing, bathing, cleaning rituals, and avoidance of objects viewed as "contaminated." This has resulted in skin damage, which was referred to a dermatologist for treatment. In addition, she engages in mental rituals, such as repetitive questioning of the validity of her prayers and feelings of guilt and responsibility, that have resulted in straining her social support network.

Symptoms first appeared when Mariam was 12 years old, which coincided with her nuclear family moving in with her paternal grandparents due to financial difficulties. The move resulted in increased conflict between her mother and grandmother, primarily because both had unusually controlling personalities. The tension resulted in prolonged stress experienced by all family members. Mariam and her parents moved out to their own house two years later. Since then, she has "channeled" her stress and anxiety by studying and working hard, resulting in academic success as well as promotions at work. Although the severities of her symptoms have fluctuated over the years, the current symptoms have increased following the birth of her daughter and subsequent visit from her mother.

Although she chose to stay home to raise her daughter, the financial strain of her decision on their family income and missing the positive affirmations she previously received at work have made her reconsider her decision.

Psychodynamic Application

The use of insight oriented, relational work may prove beneficial to Mariam due to the unexpected exacerbation of her symptoms during a period of interpersonal distress. With the return of Mariam's mother, Mariam is re-experiencing intrapsychic struggle and interpersonal conflict associated to her early life. From a psychodynamic perspective, Mariam appears to have experienced early childhood relational anxiety as a result of a mother-child relationship that lacked adequate mirroring and idealization. When Mariam was a child, her mother was demanding, controlling, and intrusive, which served to thwart her initial attempts at separation. Such experiences resulted in her feelings of anger and subsequent guilt, which she repressed over time because of the threatening nature of those feelings. As she got older, Mariam also engaged in sublimation by way of academic and professional achievement and may have attempted to individuate by marrying her European American husband. However, the birth of her daughter, coupled with her mother's extended visit and attempts to control the way Mariam cared for her daughter, resulted in the repetition of her childhood anxiety. Although she had successfully repressed those early experiences for many years and physically moved away from her parents, Mariam's current inability to channel her anxiety in the workplace has resulted in the resurfacing of OCD symptoms.

From a psychodynamic perspective, the obsessions may be viewed as an expression of Mariam's struggle and attempt to control her feelings of anger and sadness, as well as her need for control and autonomy. Her compulsions may be an attempt at resolving her feelings of guilt by way of undoing the "crime" of wanting to separate and individuate from her mother. Her guilt for having such desires stems from her belief that such feelings are an indication of a lack of respect for her mother and a betrayal or loss of cultural heritage and values. Therefore, in order to restrain her desires, she metaphorically and compulsively cleans and washes herself.

The safe space experienced in a therapeutic setting may allow the therapist to bring to Mariam's awareness the role of her early childhood relational experiences with her mother and its impact on her present behaviors. Through adequate mirroring, validation, and encouragement from the therapist, Mariam may have a corrective emotional experience, through which she can begin to experience and tolerate her unpleasant emotions and increase awareness and acceptance of her needs. Exploring her angry emotions and early disappointments will likely be difficult for Mariam, as she may emphasize thoughts over feelings, and may resist the exploration of her emotions toward her mother due to cultural values of respect toward parents and authority figures.

Transferentially, Mariam may also initially mistrust and resist the therapist, fearing judgment and control. The transference relationship can be used to help Mariam identify her sensitivity to fear of judgment and her reactive anxiety about being controlled. The therapist can further empower Mariam by encouraging her to voice experiences of anger or criticism toward the therapist and the therapeutic process, which can assist her in her ability to individuate and gain self-confidence. It is expected that the combination of bringing to awareness Mariam's early relationship with her mother, experiencing her emotions safely, and relating to others in new ways through practice in the therapeutic relationship, will result in greater understanding and control over her emotions, confidence in her autonomy, and the subsiding of her obsessive-compulsive symptoms without losing the important values of her cultural heritage.

Cognitive Behavior Application

A cognitive behavior conceptualization of Mariam's case would address her symptoms in a direct, short-term, and problem-focused way. It is likely that Mariam developed an erroneous belief system of responsibility and self-blame through feedback from her unusually controlling and authoritarian mother and grandmother. These mistaken beliefs led to erroneous perceptions of threat, which in turn provoked anxiety. The re-entry of her mother's control into her life – coupled with first-time parenting demands of a newborn – likely resulted in Mariam devaluing her abilities to adequately deal with such stressors, consequently leading to the re-emergence of obsessions and compulsions. The obsessive thoughts are likely associated with negative automatic thoughts that lead to emotional disturbances. Mariam experiences feelings of uncertainty, discomfort, and helplessness, and decreases these feelings through rituals that help reduce her responsibility and/or prevent blame.

In such a case, the therapist would begin by helping Mariam understand how OCD functions, helping her to separate herself from the emotional or moral implications of what the disorder seems to represent to her. This separation from herself will also help Mariam realize that engaging in her washing rituals is a result of choices that she makes and are not preprogrammed reflexive reactions. This reframing can help Mariam realize the control she exerts over her compulsions. The therapist would then focus on identifying objects or situations that Mariam avoids because they trigger anxiety, panic, or discomfort. The therapist would work with Mariam to identify the automatic thoughts that these experiences elicit. For example, Mariam struggles with feelings of incompetency and thoughts of not being good enough, resulting in questions of self-value. Using cognitive restructuring, the therapist would help Mariam develop alternative responses to her distressing thoughts, without the need to label the distortions of thought, as Mariam may feel judged by this experience. The therapist would further assist Mariam in reality testing by identifying examples of her experience as a valuable person.

Behaviorally, the therapist would teach Mariam relaxation techniques and thought-stopping strategies. Through the process of habituation, Mariam would also learn to become less emotionally responsive to her thoughts. Exposure situations can be selected collaboratively and arranged hierarchically (imaginal and/or in vivo) based on Mariam's self-appraisal of her ability to withstand the discomfort of evoking experiences. The combination of cognitive management and restructuring, hierarchal exposure to feared stimuli, and response prevention are expected to help decrease Mariam's obsessive-compulsive symptoms.

Family Therapy Application

The family therapy model provides an additionally relevant conceptualization of Mariam's presenting problem. Mariam's obsessions and compulsions may be seen as symptoms of an overall struggle with boundaries and control within her family of origin. Conflictual relationships, diffuse boundaries, and the struggle of differing cultural expectations can be identified through at least two generations (grandmother and mother). Mariam's family moving in with her paternal grandparents caused unexpected stress for her grandmother. Her grandmother channeled her stress by controlling family members, and Mariam's mother subsequently managed her stress and anxiety by attempting to control Mariam's behavior as a child. The overwhelming tension between Mariam's mother and grandmother brought about the triangulation of Mariam in order to reduce the overall anxiety experienced by the family system. As a result, Mariam was emotionally overburdened at a very young age. Triangulation can be seen as an attempt to maintain family homeostasis when external sources of stress (the grandmother's intrusiveness and the financial strain at the time) threatened the family cohesion.

Many Arab American families that maintain healthy interdependence and close relationships are marked with diffuse boundaries. However, in Mariam's case, her early struggle with individuation in the face of an unusually controlling and intrusive mother resulted in her rejection of those diffuse boundaries. Consequently, from a structural perspective, the boundary diffusion in this case would not be viewed as adaptive to the emotional needs of Mariam and her mother. From a Bowenian family therapy perspective, it appears that family fusion – or excess emotional reactivity between family members – represented a struggle of differentiation for these family members. As Mariam grew older, she made repeated attempts to differentiate by disengaging from her mother, becoming more acculturated into American society, and marrying a European American man. Yet, her mother's more recent re-entry into their lives and her attempts at controlling Mariam's parenting have resulted in the resurfacing of her struggles with differentiation and increased obsessive-compulsive symptoms. Moreover, an exploration of the relationship between Mariam and her husband would reveal Mariam's critical and controlling behavior with her husband, indicative of further struggles with differentiation of self in her own marital relationship.

Family therapy would ideally involve Mariam, her mother, and her husband, in order to assist the members in communicating their thoughts, feelings, and needs in a culturally respectful and meaningful manner. However, given that Mariam's mother is an immigrant and more culturally traditional, she may be uncomfortable with exposing private family interactions within the therapeutic context. Mariam's mother may also reject hearing about her daughter's need for separation and autonomy. In such cases, the family systems approach could respect the mother's position and still aim to improve Mariam's relationship with her mother. Communication skills involving healthier assertiveness of needs with more positive expression of emotions would serve to create safer boundaries and a decreased need for conflict. Moreover, Mariam's need for empowerment and support, in light of being a new mother, would be emphasized in order to reinstate the parental subsystem with her husband, and to prevent a repetition of the conflicting and controlling relationship that was seen between Mariam's mother and grandmother. The prevention of maladaptive family patterns, the establishment of safer boundaries and subsystems, and the communication and expression of feelings and needs, are expected to reduce Mariam's anxiety, which surfaced as obsessive-compulsive symptoms.

Culturanalysis Application

From a culturanalysis perspective, Mariam's case is conceptualized as the struggle between two seemingly opposing values: her desire to maintain the cultural and religious value of respecting elders, particularly mothers who are held in high esteem, and her desire for American cultural values of independence and freedom, as she sees in her husband's relationship with his family of origin. In addition, Mariam identifies her faith as an important source of support. As she begins the process of establishing her own nuclear family, she feels torn between honoring her ethnic/religious values and her American values, resulting in the presenting symptoms.

Through a culturanalysis approach and with the assistance of religious scholars, Mariam can be encouraged to explore religious texts to further her religious knowledge. Through this process, Mariam can discover verses in Islamic scripture, of which she was previously unaware, that promote experience and appreciation of different cultures. Such acknowledgment and appreciation of her bicultural identity may help Mariam balance her various needs, including her individual and familial rights and duties. Mariam may then become more confident about renegotiating her relationship with her mother, in order to establish comfortable boundaries for her nuclear family and integrate both cultures in her newly formed family. In addition, consulting with religious scholars can help Mariam address her anxiety related to religious impurity or *najasah*, which resulted in her ritualistic handwashing and avoidance. Through greater religious knowledge and awareness, the therapist can address Mariam's religious and cultural struggles and assist her in the reduction of stress and conflict, which can subsequently decrease her obsessive-compulsive symptoms.

Critique

With sound cultural competence, diverse psychotherapy models can be applied appropriately to Arab American clients and families, as demonstrated in Mariam's case narrative. This involves an awareness of Arab American culture and its heterogeneity, and a recognition of the specific features of each client. Several challenges may occur in the application of each of the major psychotherapy models, and yet, with flexibility and modification, these challenges need not compromise the meaning and relevance of the interventions.

Other psychotherapy models not addressed in this chapter may also be theoretically relevant and apply to the needs of Arab Americans. For example, humanistic/experiential models may be relevant to Arab Americans who may value an open, trusting space for self-exploration outside the potentially hostile, sociopolitical context in which they live (Amer & Jalal, 2012). With its rejection of pathology and dysfunction, and its emphasis on empathy, positive regard, and the importance of human achievement and growth potential (Moss, 2001), humanistic approaches are by definition culturally sensitive. For example, emotion-focused therapy (Greenberg, 2004), a contemporary form of humanistic therapy, focuses more specifically on emotional access, awareness, and regulation, and offers both the structure that some Arab Americans may find helpful, along with the space for emotional exploration and self-understanding. However, despite the emergence of directive and structured humanistic approaches, humanistic models have not, as of yet, received adequate attention in the literature on Arab Americans.

A valuable discussion is developing in the literature on Arab American culture and psychotherapy. Therapists have provided illuminating case descriptions and accounts of their experiences working with Arab Americans, offering helpful recommendations and suggestions. The dearth of treatment outcome research with ethnic minority groups (Miranda et al., 2005), particularly with stigmatized groups such as Arab Americans, however, is notable. Outcome studies are ultimately critical for establishing the efficacy or effectiveness of psychotherapy models with Arab Americans, and for resolving some of the ambiguity around the suitability of current evidence-based psychotherapy interventions. To date, there is only one preliminary, empirical study examining the efficacy of narrative exposure therapy for posttraumatic stress disorder in Iraqi refugees in the U.S. (Hijazi et al., 2014). With the increasing struggles that Arab Americans face, from war trauma to immigration stress and subsequent stigmatization, culture-specific psychotherapy interventions should also aim to address these most pertinent issues.

Conclusion

This chapter has provided a critical examination of three major psychotherapy models (psychodynamic, CBT, and family therapy), in addition to culture-specific approaches with Arab American clients. Each psychotherapy model was applied to the same clinical case example to demonstrate the value of each approach in conceptualizing the case and in addressing the various cultural values, needs, and beliefs of Arab American clients. The heterogeneity of Arab Americans further supports the notion that different psychotherapy models may be more favorable for different clients and families. Each therapeutic orientation or model poses potential challenges, and such difficulties, while they must be dealt with sensitively, can also be seen as opportunities for further growth on the part of therapists, clients, and families. There remains a pressing need for future research in establishing the efficacy or effectiveness of these psychotherapy models for Arab Americans.

Acknowledgment

The authors would like to acknowledge Shereen Eid, graduate assistant at the American University of Beirut, for her conscientiousness and contribution toward the research of this chapter.

References

Abi-Hashem, N. (2008). Arab Americans: Understanding their challenges, needs, and struggles. In A. J. Marsella, J. L. Johnson, P. Watson, & J. Gryczynski (eds.), *Ethnocultural perspectives on disaster and trauma* (pp. 115–173). New York: Springer. doi: 10.1007/978-0-387-73285-5_5

Abi-Hashem, N. (2011). Working with Middle Eastern immigrant families. In A. Zagelbaum & J. Carlson (eds.), *Working with immigrant families: A practical guide for counselors* (pp.151–180). New York: Routledge.

Abi-Hashem, N. (2014). Counseling Middle Eastern Arab-Americans. In D. A. Leeming (ed.), *Encyclopedia of psychology and religion* (pp. 402–407). New York: Springer. doi: 10.1007/978-1-4614-6086-2_9330

Abo-Zena, M. M. and Ahmed, S. (2014). Religion, spirituality, and emerging adults: Processing meaning through culture, context, and social position. In C. McNamara-Barry & M. Abo-Zena (eds.), *Emerging adults' religiousness and spirituality* (pp. 220–236). New York: Oxford University Press.

Abudabbeh, N. (1996). Arab families. In M. McGoldrick, J. Giordano, & N. Garcia-Preto (eds.), *Ethnicity and family therapy* (3rd edn., pp. 423–450). New York: Guilford.

Abudabbeh, N. & Hays, P. (2006). Cognitive-behavioral therapy with people of Arab heritage. In P. A. Hays & G. Y. Iwamasa (eds.), *Culturally responsive cognitive-behavioral therapy: Assessment, practice, and supervision* (pp.141–159). Washington, D.C.: American Psychological Association.

Abudabbeh, N. & Nydell, M. K. (1993). Transcultural counseling and Arab Americans. In J. McFadden (ed.), *Transcultural counseling: Bi-lateral and international perspectives* (pp. 261–284). Alexandria, VA: American Counseling Association.

Abu-Raiya, H. & Pargament, K. I. (2010). Religiously integrated psychotherapy with Muslim clients: From research to practice. *Professional Psychology: Research and Practice* 41, 181–188. doi: 10.1037/a0017988

Abu-Raiya, H. & Pargament, K. I. (2011). Empirically based psychology of Islam: Summary and critique of the literature. *Mental Health, Religion and Culture* 14(2), 93–115. doi: 10.1080/13674670903426482

Al-Krenawi, A. & Graham, J. R. (2000). Culturally sensitive social work practice with Arab clients in mental health settings. *Health Social Work* 25(1), 9–22. doi: 10.1093/hsw/25.1.9

Amer, M. M. & Jalal, B. (2012). Individual psychotherapy/counseling: Psychodynamic, cognitive-behavioral, and humanistic-experiential models. In S. Ahmed & M. M. Amer (eds.), *Counseling Muslims: Handbook of mental health issues and interventions* (pp. 87–118). New York: Routledge.

Awad, G. H. (2010). The impact of acculturation and religious identification on perceived discrimination for Arab/Middle Eastern Americans. *Cultural Diversity and Ethnic Minority Psychology* 16, 59–67. doi: 10.1037/a0016675

Awad, G. H. & Hall-Clark, B. N. (2009). Impact of religiosity and right wing authoritarianism on prejudice towards Middle Easterners. *Beliefs and Values: Understanding the Global Implications of Human Nature* 1(2), 183–192.

Awad, G. H., Martinez, M. S., & Amer, M. M. (2013). Considerations for psychotherapy with immigrant women of Arab/Middle Eastern descent. *Women & Therapy* 36(3–4), 163–175. doi: 10.1080/02703149.2013.797761

Bandura, A. (1986). *Social foundations of thought and action: A social cognitive theory*. Englewood Cliffs, NJ: Prentice Hill.

Beck, A. T. (1967). *Depression: Clinical, experimental, and theoretical aspects*. New York: Hoebet.

Beck, A. T. & Weishaar, M. E. (2008). Cognitive therapy. In R. J. Corsini & D. Wedding (eds.), *Current psychotherapies* (8th edn., pp. 263–294). Belmont, CA: Thomson Brooks/Cole.

Beck, J. S. (2011). *Cognitive behavior therapy*. New York: Guilford.

Bowen, M. (1966). The use of family theory in clinical practice. *Comprehensive Psychiatry* 7, 345–374. doi: 10.1016/S0010-440X(66)80065-2

Burns, G. W. (2001). *101 healing stories: Using metaphors in therapy*. New York: Wiley.

Bushra, A., Khadivi, A., & Frewat-Nikowitz, S. (2007). Dialogue 7: Multiple perspectives on the Middle Eastern identity in psychotherapy. In J. C. Muran (ed.), *Dialogues on difference: Studies of diversity in the therapeutic relationship* (pp. 219–235). Washington, D.C.: American Psychological Association.

Dwairy, M. (1998). *Cross-cultural counseling: The Arab-Palestinian case*. New York: Haworth.

Dwairy, M. (2002). Foundations of psychosocial dynamic personality theory of collective people. *Clinical Psychology Review* 22, 343–360. doi: 10.1016/S0272-7358(01)00100-3

Dwairy, M. (2006). *Counseling and psychotherapy with Arabs and Muslims: A culturally sensitive approach*. New York: Teachers College Press.

Dwairy, M. (2009). Culture analysis and metaphor psychotherapy with Arab-Muslim clients. *Journal of Clinical Psychology* 65, 199–209. doi: 10.1002/jclp.20568

Dwairy, M. (2012). Metaphor therapy. In S. Norbert (ed.), *Encyclopedia of the sciences of learning*, (vol. 7, pp. 2247–2251). New York: Springer. doi: 10.1007/978-1-4419-1428-6_677

Dwairy, M. (2013). A two-layers bio-psycho-social model of psychotherapy. *International Journal of Social and Behavioral Sciences* 1(4), 97–104.

Dwairy M. & El-Jamil, F. (2016). Counseling Arab and Muslim clients. In P. B. Pederson, W. J. Lonner, J. G. Draguns, J. E. Trimble, & M. R. Scharron-del Rio (eds.), *Counseling across cultures* (7th edn., pp. 185–203). Thousand Oaks, CA: Sage.

Ellis, A. (1962). *Reason and emotion in psychotherapy*. Secaucus, NJ: Citadel.

Erickson, C. D. & Al-Timimi, N. R. (2001). Providing mental health services to Arab Americans: Recommendations and considerations. *Cultural Diversity and Ethnic Minority Psychology* 7, 308–327. doi: 10.1037/1099-9809.7.4.308

Freud, S. (1926). Inhibitions, symptoms and anxiety. In J. Strachey (ed. and trans.), *The standard edition of the complete psychological works of Sigmund Freud* (vol. 20, pp. 77–178). London: Hogarth Press.

Gergen, K. (1985). The social constructionist movement in modern psychology. *American Psychologist* 40, 266–275. doi: 10.1037/0003-066X.40.3.266

Greenberg, L. S. (2004). Emotion-focused therapy. *Clinical Psychology and Psychotherapy* 11, 3–16. doi: 10.1002/cpp.388

Grove, D. J. & Panzer, B. (1989). *Resolving traumatic memories: Metaphors and symbols in psychotherapy.* New York: Irvington.

Hamdan, A. (2008). Cognitive restructuring: An Islamic perspective. *Journal of Muslim Mental Health* 3(1), 99–116. doi: 10.1080/15564900802035268

Hayes, S. C., Follette, V. M., & Linehan, M. M. (eds.) (2004). *Mindfulness and acceptance: Expanding the cognitive-behavioral tradition.* New York: Guilford.

Hayes, S. C., Luorna, J. B., Bond, F. W., Masuda, A., & Lillis, J. (2006). Acceptance and commitment therapy: Model, processes and outcomes. *Behaviour Research and Therapy* 44, 1–25. doi: 10.1016/j.brat.2005.06.006

Hayes, S. C. & Smith, S. (2005). *Get out of your mind and into your life: The new acceptance and commitment therapy.* Oakland, CA: New Harbinger Publications.

Hijazi, A. M., Lumley, M. A., Ziadni, M. S., Haddad, L., Rapport, L. J., & Arnetz, B. B. (2014). Brief narrative exposure therapy for posttraumatic stress in Iraqi refugees: A preliminary randomized clinical trial. *Journal of Traumatic Stress* 27, 314–322. doi: 10.1002/jts.21922

Hodge, D. & Nadir, A. (2008). Moving towards culturally competent practice with Muslims: Modifying cognitive therapy with Islamic tenants. *Social Work* 53, 31–41.

Ibish, I. (2003). *Report on hate crimes and discrimination against Arab Americans: The post-September 11th backlash, September 11, 2001–October 11, 2002.* Washington, D.C.: American-Arab Anti-Discrimination Committee.

Jackson, D. D. (1965). Family rules: The marital quid pro quo. *Archives of General Psychiatry* 12, 589–594. doi: 10.1001/archpsyc.1965.01720360061010

Kohut, H. (1977). *The restoration of the self.* New York: International University Press.

Lambert, M. J. & Ogles, B. M. (2004). The efficacy and effectiveness of psychotherapy. In M. J. Lambert (ed.), *Bergin and Garfield's handbook of psychotherapy and behavior change* (5th edn., pp. 139–193). New York: Wiley.

Linehan, M. M. (1993). *Skills training manual for treating borderline personality disorder: Diagnosis and treatment of mental disorders.* New York: Guilford.

Luborsky, E. B., O'Reilly-Landry, M., & Arlow, J. A. (2008). Psychoanalysis. In R. J. Corsini & D. Wedding (eds.), *Current psychotherapies* (8th edn., pp. 15–62). Belmont, CA: Thompson.

Martin, U. (2014). Psychotherapy with Arab Americans: An exploration of therapy-seeking and termination behaviors. *International Journal of Culture and Mental Health* 7, 162–167. doi: 10.1080/17542863.2012.742121

Masalha, S. (1999). Psychodynamic psychotherapy as applied in an Arab village clinic. *Clinical Psychology Review* 19(8), 987–997. doi: 10.1016/S0272-7358(99)00007-0

McGoldrick, M., Giordano, J., & Garcia-Preto, N. (eds.) (2005). *Ethnicity and family therapy* (3rd edn.). New York: Guilford.

Minuchin, S. (1974). *Families and family therapy.* Cambridge, MA: Harvard University Press.

Miranda, J., Bernal, G., Lau, A., Kohn, L., Hwang, W., & La Framboise, T. (2005). State of the science on psychosocial interventions for ethnic minorities. *Annual Review of Clinical Psychology* 1, 113–142. doi: 10.1146/annurev.clinpsy.1.102803.143822

Moss, D. (2001). The roots and genealogy of humanistic psychology. In K. J. Schneider, J. F. T. Bugental, & J. F. Pierson (eds.), *The handbook of humanistic psychology: Leading edges in theory, research, and practice* (pp. 5–20). Thousand Oaks, CA: Sage.

Nichols, M. P. (2011). *The essentials of family therapy* (5th edn.). Boston, MA: Pearson Education, Inc.

Nobles, A. Y. & Sciarra, D. T. (2000). Cultural determinants in the treatment of Arab Americans: A primer for mainstream therapists. *American Journal of Orthopsychiatry* 70(2), 182–191. doi: 10.1037/h0087734

Norcross, J. C. & Beutler, L. E. (2008). Integrative psychotherapies. In R. J. Corsini & D. Wedding (eds.), *Current psychotherapies* (8th edn., pp. 481–511). Belmont, CA: Thomson Brooks/Cole.

Ogden, T. H. (1985). On potential space. *The International Journal of Psychoanalysis* 66(2), 129–141.

Pargament, K. I., Koenig, H. G., & Perez, L. M. (2000). The many methods of religious coping: Development and initial validation of the RCOPE. *Journal of Clinical Psychology* 56, 519–543. doi: 10.1002/(SICI)1097–4679(200004)56:4<519::AID-JCLP6>3.0.CO;2-1

Pollara, M. H. & Meleis, A. I. (1995). The stress of immigration and the daily lived experiences of Jordanian immigrant women in the United States. *Western Journal of Nursing Research* 17, 521–539. doi: 10.1177/019394599501700505

Rothermel, P. C. (2009). *Arab American Muslims and psychotherapy: Perceptions affecting utilization of treatment* (Doctoral dissertation). Available from ProQuest Dissertations and Theses database (UMI No. 3374576).

Sayed, M. A. (2003a). Conceptualization of mental illness within Arab cultures: Meeting challenges in cross-cultural settings. *Social Behavior and Personality* 31, 333–342. doi: 10.2224/sbp.2003.31.4.333

Sayed, M. A. (2003b). Psychotherapy of Arab clients in the West: Uniqueness, empathy, and "otherness." *American Journal of Psychotherapy* 57, 445–459.

Sciarra, D. T. (2011). Intrafamilial separations in the immigrant family: Implications for cross-cultural counseling. *Journal of Multicultural Counseling and Development* 27, 31–41. doi: 10.1002/j.2161-1912.1999.tb00210.x

Shehadeh, S. (2008). *A psychoanalytic exploration into the Arab self and implications for therapy with Arabs in the United States* (Doctoral dissertation). Available from ProQuest Dissertations and Theses database (UMI No. 3370302).

Wachtel, P. L. (2008). *Relational theory and the practice of psychotherapy*. New York: Guilford.

Wilson, T. G. (2008). Behavior therapy. In R. J. Corsini & D. Wedding (eds.), *Current psychotherapies* (8th edn., pp. 223–262). California, CA: Thomson Brooks/Cole.

23

SCHOOL PSYCHOLOGY

Enhancing School Climate and School Connectedness

Karen L. Haboush and Hala Alyan

Education and academic achievement have traditionally been valued in Arab culture for girls and boys (Ajrouch, 2000; Al-Khatab, 1999; Haboush, 2007; Tabbah, 2011; Tabbah, Miranda, & Wheaton, 2012). Educational attainment enhances family honor by increasing prospects for employment and marriage, and therefore, financial security (Cainkar & Read, 2014). However, academic achievement is mediated by numerous variables, including the degree to which students feel connected to schools and experience school climate as supportive: stronger school connectedness is associated with higher academic achievement and social-emotional wellbeing (Eklund, Vaillancourt, & Pedley, 2013; Lehr & Christenson, 2002; Sulkowski, Demaray, & Lazarus, 2013).

Following 9/11, school climate has become less tolerant of Arab American students, as reflected by increased bullying and discrimination (Britto, 2008; El-Haj & Bonet, 2010; Fakhoury, 2012). Tabbah (2011) found that as many as 50% of Arab American students experienced bullying and discrimination or knew someone else who had. However, the extent to which changes in school climate have impacted Arab American students' academic achievement has received limited empirical investigation (Tabbah, 2011; Tabbah et al., 2012). Because statistics prior to 2010 demonstrated higher mean levels of educational attainment for many Arab Americans relative to the U.S. population as a whole, Arab American students have sometimes been referred to as "the invisible minority," and therefore have remained a relatively understudied population (Al-Khatab, 1999; Suleiman, 2001; Tabbah et al., 2012). Although academic achievement is mediated by many factors, school connectedness has been shown to be a predictive factor; thus raising questions about the degree to which changes in school climate impact Arab American students' experiences of school connectedness and, in turn, academic achievement (El-Haj & Bonet, 2010; Tindongan, 2011).

With roughly 29% of Arab Americans under the age of 18 and 41% under the age of 25, a sizable population of school-age Arab American youth exists (Asi & Beaulieu, 2013). These figures represent an increase from the 2000 Census, which reported that 25% were under age 18 (Brittingham & de la Cruz, 2005). Overall, the number of Americans claiming Arab ancestry rose by more than 72% between 1990 and 2010 (Arab American Institute, 2012; Asi & Beaulieu, 2013). Thus, the number of Arab American students attending U.S. public schools continues to rise. The growing Arab American population, including larger numbers of political refugees and immigrants with trauma histories, and generally higher birth rates among immigrant groups (Ruiz, Kabler, & Sugarman, 2011) increase the likelihood that school personnel will work with these students. However, many school staff continue to report they lack knowledge about Arab American students and Arab culture (Aburumuh, Smith, & Ratcliffe, 2009; Al-Qubbaj, 2003; Goforth, 2011; Wingfield & Karaman, 2014). As mentioned above, this has sometimes been attributed to Arab American students being considered an "invisible minority," owing to the generally average to above-average academic achievement for many Arab American youth prior to 9/11 (Aburumuh et al., 2009; Melhem & Chemali, 2014; Tabbah et al., 2012). This contrasts with other non-Asian ethnic minority groups, whose academic performance has frequently been below average in U.S. public schools (Merrell, Ervin, & Peacock, 2012; Sarroub, 2010), and, therefore, brought them under closer scrutiny.

During the 1990s, in response to growing recognition of the need for accurate information on Arab American students, literature on Arab Americans' schooling began to emerge, describing how political events involving Arabs resulted in increased discrimination in public schools (Ajrouch, 2000; Al-Khatab, 1999; Schwartz, 1999; Suleiman, 2001; Wingfield, 2006; Wingfield & Karaman, 2014). The aftermath of 9/11 witnessed an even greater proliferation of research and publications about Arab American and Muslim American youth (Ahmed, Kia-Keating, & Tsai, 2011; Amer & Bagasra, 2013). The visibility of Arab American students has greatly increased as widespread reports of anti-Arab bullying and harassment of students have been documented (Bonet, 2011; El-Haj, 2006; Fakhoury, 2012; Humphreys, 2010; Sarroub, 2010; Tabbah et al., 2012; Tindongan, 2011). Researchers have suggested that the academic performance of Arab American students suffers as a by-product of internalizing these negative messages (Bonet, 2011; El-Haj, 2006; Humphreys, 2010; Sarroub, 2010; Sulkowski et al., 2013; Tabbah, 2011). However, the effect of bias may be more complex, as other variables such as social support and school connectedness seemingly play a mediating role (Abassi-Zoabi, 2012; Fakhoury, 2012; Sarroub, 2010; Tabbah et al., 2012).

Despite a growing body of literature on anti-Arab discrimination in schools, the potential for schools to serve as a protective factor for Arab American youth by enhancing school connectedness has received limited scholarly attention to date (Haboush & Barakat, 2014). Culturally sensitive academic and social-emotional interventions that strengthen school climate and help to engage students within the school community can serve as protective factors and sources of resilience.

This chapter describes steps for enhancing school connectedness for Arab American school-age youth by establishing supportive classroom climates, utilizing culturally sensitive academic and social-emotional interventions, and providing a continuum of social-emotional services. The ecological model, which provides a framework for understanding school climate and school connectedness, is first presented. Next, an overview of the demographics of Arab American students along with specific features of U.S. public schools is presented, followed by a discussion of culturally sensitive academic and social-emotional resources and potential obstacles to systems-level implementation. It is noted that these systems-level interventions closely align with the role of the school psychologist (Cowan & Vaillancourt, 2013; Merrell et al., 2012); yet, their role in supporting Arab American students has received limited empirical attention (Goforth, 2011; Haboush, 2007). Therefore, this chapter also seeks to raise awareness of critical topics in school psychology that warrant empirical research on Arab American youth, including the representation of Arab American youth in special education and needs of Arabic-speaking English as a Second Language (ESL) students.

A Framework for Understanding School Connectedness, School Climate, and Resilience

Ecological Systems Model

School psychology practice is guided by application of an ecological framework (Merrell et al., 2012). Schools are socializing institutions that influence many features of youth identity development, including academic, gender, and ethnic identity (Aburumuh et al., 2009; Ajrouch, 2000; Alkhateeb, 2010; Britto, 2008; Sirin & Balsano, 2007). For youth, identity development is constructed through social relationships (Ajrouch, 2000, 2004; Britto, 2008; Tabbah et al., 2012). Bronfennbrenner's ecological systems model suggests schools are embedded within other systems (i.e. neighborhoods, cities, states) and thus reflect the societal messages promoted by those surrounding systems (Bonet, 2011; El-Haj & Bonet, 2010; Merrell et al., 2012; Sirin & Balsano, 2007). Because schools are open systems, they absorb societal messages of anti-Arab bias; over time, these negative messages may be internalized by Arab American youth as they consolidate educational and ethnic identity (Britto, 2008; Haboush, 2007; Tindongan, 2011) and impact Arab American students' educational achievement (Aburumuh et al, 2009; Al-Hazza & Bucher, 2008; Fakhoury, 2012; Tabbah, 2011).

For many Arab American youth, the consolidation of educational identity means navigating multiple, sometimes conflicting, cultural identities, including cultural and ethnic origins along with mainstream U.S. values (Britto, 2008; Tindongan, 2011). While identity formation is an inherently challenging developmental task, it is further complicated when one's reference group is the subject of fear, scrutiny, and derision (Sirin & Balsano, 2007). At present, empirical research aimed at identifying protective factors that strengthen Arab American youth's connectedness to schools remains limited.

School Connectedness and School Climate

Students' experiences of belonging, feeling cared about by school personnel, and degree of engagement in learning constitute their sense of connectedness to their school (Sulkowski et al., 2013). Higher levels of connectedness correlate with higher levels of academic achievement, as measured by standardized test scores and grades, and reflected in levels of educational attainment. Longitudinal research demonstrates that students who feel connected to their schools stay in school longer and are more likely to graduate (Sulkowski et al., 2013). Further, social-emotional wellbeing, including motivation, self-regulation, and student attitudes toward school, is also influenced by the degree of school connectedness (Sulkowski et al., 2013). Thus, connectedness is a protective factor against drop out (Eklund et al., 2013; Sulkowski et al., 2013). It promotes resilience, or the ability to persevere despite adverse conditions. The terms "school connectedness" and "school climate" are closely related as both refer to a school's atmosphere for learning (Lehr & Christenson, 2002; Sulkowski et al., 2013).

The extent to which school environments are supportive and students feel cared about is influenced by several factors. In general, culturally and linguistically diverse youth are at greater risk of feeling less connected: identification with negative messages about their culture reduces engagement in school out of a sense of alienation, hopelessness, and lowered expectations for their own performance (Merrell et al., 2012; Rossen & Cowan, 2012; Sulkowski et al., 2013). Although positive teacher-student and peer relationships can be protective factors, Arab Americans may experience difficulty bonding with educators, peers, and school psychologists from majority groups due to cultural and linguistic differences and the presence of racism in the school (El-Haj & Bonet, 2010). Further, the extent of students' acculturation to European American values versus Arab culture may also influence identity formation and, in turn, mediate the extent of school connectedness. The diversity of Arab Americans has implications for acculturation, as further illustrated by the demographics of this population discussed below.

Characteristics of Arab American Students

Beginning in the 1990s, immigration from Arab countries has tended to be politically motivated, with greater numbers seeking asylum or refugee status in the U.S. (Brittingham & de la Cruz, 2005; Office of Refugee Resettlement, 2013). Recent immigrants tend to be Muslim and arrive with less formal education and fewer financial resources, and may experience higher levels of trauma (Nassar-McMillan & Hakim-Larson, 2003).

Demographics of Arab Students in U.S. Schools and Colleges

Reliable data on levels of current educational attainment, or years of school completed, for Arab Americans is challenging to obtain. The American Community Survey (ACS; Asi & Beaulieu, 2013) provides estimates of Arab American educational levels based on the 2010 U.S. Census; however, these figures should be interpreted with caution, given that the U.S. Census is often believed to underrepresent the number of Arab Americans (Arab American Institute, 2012). Nevertheless, the available ACS estimates as presented by the Arab American Institute (2012) may suggest general trends worth further empirical investigation: Approximately 12% of Arab Americans attend preschool and kindergarten, 56% attend elementary and high school, and 32% are enrolled in college or graduate studies. Comparisons of levels of educational attainment relative to the U.S. population as a whole suggest 28.8% of Arab Americans have bachelor's degrees, compared to 18.4% of the general U.S. population, and 18.1% possess graduate or professional degrees, compared to the population as a whole at 11.2% (U.S. Census Bureau, 2013). It is unclear to what extent these figures reflect the fact that many newer immigrants are arriving in the U.S. with less formal education.

Recent Arab immigrants have more limited financial resources (Fakhoury, 2012). Poverty may impact academic achievement: According to the ACS (Asi & Beaulieu, 2013), poverty rates for families with Arab American children under the age of 18 (22%) are higher than the national mean (18%), thus suggesting that some Arab American children may experience poverty-related stressors that could impede their school performance. Financial pressures to work (Ajrouch, 2000) may also interfere with academic achievement among students missing school.

Trauma and Health Status

Children with refugee status and undocumented immigrants are at high risk for exposure to traumatic events (see Haboush, Selman, & Sievering, 2008; Ruiz et al., 2011). Trauma impacts learning through residual neurological effects on memory, attention, and emotional regulation. Changes in brain structure and neurotransmitter levels can impact cognitive functioning and emotional regulation. Furthermore, high levels of dissociation interfere with memory and retention of newly acquired material (De Bellis, Woolley, & Hooper, 2013; DePrince, Weinzierl, & Combs, 2009). In addition to neurological impacts on learning, trauma can also affect students' school connectedness. The school climate is less likely to be experienced as safe: The combination of increased hypervigilance on the part of Arab American youth with trauma histories, coupled with the present-day reality of anti-Arab discrimination and bullying, may limit students' academic engagement (Haboush et al., 2008).

Although refugees are eligible for public assistance, undocumented child immigrants are not and poor health can become another barrier to learning. Given the limited financial means for many Arab refugees and undocumented immigrants, the number of which is unknown (see Office of Refugee Resettlement, 2013), schools play an especially important role in helping children adapt. Schools serve as the main access point to treatment for medical and mental health problems since school-based health services are typically free (Rousseau & Guzder, 2008; Ruiz et al., 2011).

English and Arabic Language Fluency

Growing numbers of Arab American students speak Arabic as their native language, which may be reflective of the recent influx of immigrants and refugees (see Ryan, 2013). However, the number of teachers who speak Arabic is unknown, and frequently ESL classes are not staffed with Arabic-speaking teachers (Aburumuh et al., 2009), as described in accounts of Arab American students attending ESL classes conducted in Spanish (Aburumuh et al., 2009; Al-Qubbaj, 2003). When Arab American students do not receive adequate ESL instruction, this may affect their academic performance. Acquisition of conversational English facilitates greater interaction, engagement, and connection in school, with greater connectedness enhancing academic achievement.

The importance of adequate mastery of English for academic achievement has been documented (Palmer, El-Ashry, Leclere, & Chang, 2007) to prevent youth from being mistakenly identified as having learning disabilities (Merrell et al., 2012). Mastery of Arabic as a first language and subsequent difficulty in later mastering English tends to suggest problems with second language acquisition (Palmer et al., 2007), whereas difficulty with both languages is more consistent with learning disabilities or below-average cognitive ability. Best practices suggest that those students whose first language is Arabic and are ESL learners should be assessed in both Arabic and English to determine competence in both languages (Palmer et al., 2007). Assessment of reading and oral-language disabilities may be complicated by the fact that the spoken dialect of Arabic, which children learn first, is very different from the written form, known as Modern Standard Arabic (Palmer et al., 2007). Further, more than 20 Arabic language dialects exist (Aburumuh et al., 2009; Al-Qubbaj, 2003).

Some students report wanting to learn Arabic as consciously showing solidarity with their Arab heritage in the face of discrimination (Mango, 2011; Seymour-Jorn, 2004). Like wearing the hijab (see Zine, 2006), for some youth, these behaviors are a source of resilience. While the overall percentage of public schools offering Arabic language classes is still low (about 1%), the number is increasing at both the elementary and middle school levels (Al-Romi, 2000; Mango, 2011). For some youngsters, electing to learn Arabic maintains a connection with Arab and/or Islamic culture and thus promotes a more positive, affirming identity (Al-Romi, 2000).

Classroom Bias and Discrimination

Discussion of the above characteristics of Arab American students was intended to suggest some of the factors affecting Arab American students' ability to succeed in U.S. public schools. Another major factor that can negatively affect success is discrimination and bias. In line with an ecological framework, individual classrooms are viewed as a microcosm of the larger school system. Efforts can be made within classrooms to reduce such bias in three main areas: (a) instructional materials, (b) teacher instructional style, and (c) classroom climate (Al-Hazza & Bucher, 2008; Al-Khatab, 1999; Sabry & Bruna, 2007; Thomas-Brown, 2010; Wingfield, 2006). As such, they provide a starting point for addressing anti-Arab discrimination in both academic and social spheres.

Instructional Materials

The negative, inaccurate, and stereotyped portrayals of Arabs and Arab Americans in textbooks, along with the failure to accurately present Arab culture and history in instructional materials, have been well documented (Aburumuh et al., 2009; Al-Qubbaj, 2003; Wingfield, 2006; Wingfield & Karaman, 2014). Popular images of Arabs as terrorists, militants, and oil tycoons dominate print and video resources (Wingfield, 2006). Concerns about instructional materials extend beyond those expressly created for teaching purposes per se, such as textbooks, to include popular media (i.e. films, cartoons, videos, magazines, video games, and storybooks), which teachers may also incorporate into lessons and use during noninstructional times such as recess (Suleiman, 2001). Repeated exposure to such negative images in the classroom is believed to undermine academic self-concept for Arab American youth and to further reinforce negative stereotypes about Arabs among other students (El-Haj, 2006, 2009; Wingfield, 2006). At the same time, students often have little opportunity to learn about the positive aspects of Arab history and culture (Al-Hazza & Bucher, 2008, 2010; Wingfield, 2006). When it does occur, coverage in textbooks of Arab history and culture is often limited and superficial, and contains many errors (Al-Hazza & Bucher, 2008, 2010; David & Ayouby, 2005; Wingfield, 2006). This limits students' ability to see Arab culture portrayed in a positive light and, by extension, for Arab American youth to identify as competent in the academic and social spheres (Al-Hazza & Bucher, 2008, 2010; Wingfield & Karaman, 2014).

Recently, curriculum coverage of 9/11 has begun to come under scrutiny, as textbooks are increasingly discussing this topic (Saleem & Thomas, 2011). National educational standards, referred to as Common Core State Standards, include sections on discrimination and teaching tolerance, and may incorporate lessons on 9/11. In their review, Saleem & Thomas (2011) found textbook accounts of 9/11 contain some of the most recent examples of anti-Arab bias and stereotypes. Further, the political context leading up to 9/11 is often not adequately represented. Moreover, Moore (2006) noted many factual inaccuracies about Islam in the books he reviewed. For this reason, Sabry and Bruna (2007) recommended ongoing dialogue between schools and parents to further verify the appropriateness of instructional materials.

Consultation with schools and teachers to raise awareness of more culturally sensitive and factually accurate instructional resources can strengthen positive identity development and serve as a protective factor for Arab American students (Al-Hazza & Bucher, 2008, 2010; Wingfield & Karaman, 2014). Many recommendations regarding instructional resources, textbooks, and materials on Arab culture have been provided by previous writers, including Al-Hazza and Bucher (2008, 2010), Barlow (1994), and Wingfield (2006). The Arab American Institute's website has a page listing useful instructional materials, and Michigan State University's online Arab American Research Guide contains videos and books that may be utilized in teaching about Arabs. Furthermore, Hoot, Szecsi, and Moosa (2003) list reading resources for teaching about Islam.

Teachers' Instructional Style and Expectations

Teaching methods and instruction have been identified as a source of bias when teachers promote misinformation through inaccurate materials and set low expectations for students' performance based on their own biased beliefs about Arab Americans (Al-Hazza & Bucher, 2010). Although some overlap with instructional materials and classroom climate exists, this category is heavily influenced by teacher knowledge. Teacher expectations for students may derive from misinformation; for example, teachers often express a lack of training about Arab and Islamic culture (Al-Qubbaj, 2003; Al-Romi, 2000; Sabry & Bruna, 2007; Schwartz, 1999) and may inadvertently perpetuate misinformation through inaccurate and biased teaching materials (Hoot et al., 2003; Sabry & Bruna, 2007). Teachers may inadvertently perpetuate stereotypes, thereby reducing Arab American student engagement (Al-Hazza & Bucher, 2008; David & Ayouby, 2005; Thomas-Brown, 2010; Tindongan, 2011). In turn, students may set low expectations for their own performance based on a lack of positive cultural role models with which to identify, as well as low teacher expectations. Tabbah (2011) and Tabbah and co-authors (2012) reported that students judged by teachers as making limited progress had negative academic self-perceptions, whereas those judged by their teacher as being hard working had more positive self-perceptions.

In order to address inaccurate teacher expectations at the classroom level, consultation with teachers by school psychologists is recommended. Teachers and other school personnel can also examine academic publications and online resources to equip themselves with culturally competent knowledge, skills, and attitudes pertaining to instruction with and about Arab American youth.

Classroom Climate and Critical Discourse

A third critical aspect of classroom climate involves teachers' willingness to quickly confront bullying and create opportunities for open dialogue about Arab culture and critical analysis of related issues (Rossen & Cowan, 2012; Suleiman, 2001; Tindongan, 2011). A safe classroom environment sets the foundation for culturally sensitive instruction and students' active engagement. Teachers' ability to immediately confront bullying within the classroom sends a powerful message that bullying will not be tolerated (El-Haj & Bonet, 2010; Rossen & Cowan, 2012; Wingfield & Karaman, 2014). In a related vein, establishing an atmosphere that allows for critical discourse concerning topics such as the Middle East can allow for improved understanding among students and lessen discrimination (Bonet, 2011). For example, students need a safe atmosphere to discuss political and historical events that gave rise to the 9/11 attacks. Open dialogue that allows for critical analysis should not be mistaken for anti-U.S. or terrorist sentiments (El-Haj, 2006, 2009). As some teachers may lack the requisite classroom management skills and factual knowledge to manage these sensitive classroom discussions, consultation with the school psychologist might prove beneficial here.

To further counter negative stereotypes, discussion of Arab art and literature, cultural practices, traditions, and history is recommended to occur within the classroom and be infused throughout a wide range of learning activities. These practices can help to better enhance connectedness and integrate Arab youth into the classroom (Sabry & Bruna, 2007). For Arab Muslim youth in particular, consultation might extend to school psychologists educating staff about accommodations for prayer in school, halal dietary practices, modest dress during physical education classes, and the possible impact on schoolwork of fasting during religious holidays.

Additionally, some female Muslim students choose to wear the hijab, or headscarf, in order to protect female modesty and/or affirm religious identification. Following 9/11, there were many reports of female students being verbally harassed, derided, and having the hijab torn off by students and teachers (Bonet, 2011; Thomas-Brown, 2010; Tindongan, 2011; Wingfield, 2006; Zine, 2006). Although the hijab may be misunderstood by teachers and students as reflecting a female's subordinate position under Islam, among Muslim Arab Americans it can be seen as a source of protection and resilience that allows females to move about comfortably and signal pride in their religious identification (Bonet, 2011). School personnel are advised to respect the decision to wear the hijab – or not – as a matter of personal choice.

Psychological Services in Schools

The preceding sections illustrated some of the current stressors associated with the educational experience of Arab American students. These stressors may contribute to a range of academic and emotional problems and, relatedly, a need for mental health services. Schools are the largest provider of mental health services to children in the U.S. An estimated 70–80% of all children who receive mental health services within the U.S. receive them in schools, making school psychologists well poised to address the mental health needs of students (Eklund et al., 2013; Merrell et al., 2012), including Arab Americans. Providing school-based mental health services makes treatment and outreach accessible to students and also removes barriers associated with transportation and medical costs. This greatly enhances accessibility to services for immigrants as well as families living at or near the poverty level (Cowan & Vaillancourt, 2013; Rousseau & Guzder, 2008). Special education services, anti-bullying interventions, and outreach initiatives all constitute forms of psychological service delivery aimed at enhancing resilience and protective factors.

Special Education Services

Unlike other ethnic minorities, Arab American youth have often achieved at high academic levels and, as a result, have not been identified as at-risk for overrepresentation in special education categories. However, the potential for underrepresentation in special education is also of concern because of the prospect of denying children needed services (Merrell et al., 2012). The 2013 ACS estimates that roughly 3% of Arab American children under 18 years of age are institutionalized, presumably in hospitals and residential settings for children with disabilities (Asi & Beaulieu, 2013). Al Khateeb, Al Hadidi, & Al Khatib (2014) estimate roughly 23,400 Arab American children have disabilities, yet note that this figure may underrepresent the total population. Although these children may represent a portion of Arab American youth eligible for special education, this does not reveal how many Arab American children in total are receiving special education services under the federal Individuals with Disabilities Education Improvement Act (2004). Because Arab American youth are considered White/Caucasian, their numbers need to be teased apart from other White/Caucasian youth in trying to assess actual prevalence rates.

Although U.S. Federal law grants children with disabilities access to public school services provided parental consent is obtained, disabilities may still be a source of shame and confusion for some Arab American families. Religious beliefs, degree of acculturation, attitudes concerning disabilities in one's country of origin, degree of connectedness to the school, views regarding education, teachers' authority, and mental health all influence parental views regarding disabilities and their ability to advocate for their children with school personnel (Haboush, 2007; Hasnain, Shaikh, & Shanawani, 2008). Families in the Arab world may believe disabled youth should remain at home so as not to shame the family, and these beliefs and stigma may be held among recent immigrants (see Al Khateeb et al., 2014; Hadidi, 1998; Smadi & Sartawi, 1998). This may be especially true for cognitive and mental disabilities. A few Arabic words for disabilities connote "crazy" and "mad" (Hasnain et al., 2008), thus further reinforcing beliefs about stigma and the need for isolation. Traditional Arab attitudes concerning disabilities emphasize religious and supernatural explanations (Al Khateeb et al., 2014) such as evil spirits (*jinn*) and curses ("the evil eye"; Hasnain et al., 2008). These cultural differences position school psychologists to sensitively interface with families at various stages of acceptance regarding their child's disability (Goforth, 2011; Merrell et al., 2012).

Anti-Bullying Interventions

Bullying has received widespread attention in U.S. schools due to national policies and media coverage of several tragic deaths (Rossen & Cowan, 2012). While best practices recommend the use of empirically supported interventions at schools, there is difficulty finding examples of published evidence-based programs for Arab Americans. When implementing programs, the need for program fidelity should be balanced with cultural sensitivity. Rousseau and Guzder (2008) note that many empirically supported school-based prevention programs fail to address the cultural and migratory context, thereby limiting generalizability. Thus, while many anti-bullying programs exist, their efficacy with the Arab American student population remains largely unknown.

In coping with bullying, the extent to which Arab American youth turn to school staff for assistance warrants investigation. Although the sample size was small, it is noteworthy that female Arab American adolescents in Sheikh's (2009) study did not report feeling that they could turn to adults for support in coping with school-related stressors. Both Ajrouch (2000, 2004) and Sheikh (2009) found supportive peer networks appear to be a protective factor, especially for female Arab American adolescents, though some ambivalence was also noted due to increased anxiety about exposure.

Mental Health Outreach and Prevention

Arab American students who are faced with bullying or other stressors may develop mental health concerns that would lead them to benefit from school counseling or psychotherapy. However, traditional views of mental health treatment are characterized by a certain amount of stigma in Arab culture (Abdullah & Brown, 2011; Melhem & Chemali, 2014). In contrast to counseling, primary prevention and other forms of outreach initiatives may be less stigmatizing because they are delivered in a group format using lessons or programs. Such initiatives would also be a good fit with the collective emphasis that characterizes Arab culture and the ecological model. A classroom format may have greater potential for reducing shame because individual members are not singled out (Eklund et al., 2013; Rossen & Cowan, 2012; Sulkowski et al., 2013). Also, difficult topics such as sexual abuse might more comfortably be presented in this manner (Alyan, 2013; Haboush & Alyan, 2013).

Alternative School Settings: Arabic Heritage, Arabic Language, and Islamic Schools

Experiences of anti-Arab bias and discrimination in public schools may lead some Arab American parents to consider the alternative of placing their children in Arabic language and Arabic heritage schools. These schools have recently increased in popularity, based on a growing interest in maintaining a connection with Arab culture and language (Mango, 2011). They provide a relatively safe environment and may foster resilience as students' identity development consolidates around the internalization of positive messages about Arabs. Because Arabic is the language of the Qur'an, the majority of Arabic language/heritage schools are attached to religious institutions such as mosques.

Similar to Arabic language/heritage schools, the number of Islamic schools has also increased (Al-Romi, 2000; Mango, 2011). Data from 2011 suggest approximately 31,700 students attend Islamic schools (Mango, 2011). These schools allow for religious observance and practices, transmission of knowledge about the Qur'an, and a safe physical environment for Arab Muslim youth whose greater visibility (due to their attire and religious and dietary practices) renders them targets for harassment in public schools (Al-Romi, 2000). Islamic schools play a critical role in teaching accurate information about Islamic culture and history (Al-Romi, 2000). This is especially important because teachers frequently report they lack adequate training and knowledge about Islam (Al-Romi, 2000; Sabry & Bruna, 2007) and may inadvertently perpetuate negative stereotypes (Al-Hazza & Bucher, 2008; David & Ayouby, 2005).

Case Example: Dina Stays "Strong" and Navigates High School

Dina is a 16-year-old high school sophomore attending an urban New Jersey public high school. Her parents are Iraqi Christian immigrants. Born in Iraq, her family immigrated when Dina was six after her family was subject to anti-Christian violence. The community in which Dina's family resides has a sizable number of Arab immigrants, serviced by local stores, community organizations, churches, and mosques. English is Dina's second language. Upon beginning school in New Jersey, she was enrolled in an ESL class where instruction occurred in Spanish.

Dina first met the school psychologist in the Fall term, when she came in seeking support for instances of bullying and discrimination. Dina reported that she had been enduring increasing slurs by classmates about her physical appearance, and she expressed frustration about wearing long-sleeved clothing even in warm weather due to her parents "expecting me to dress modestly." Additionally, Dina shared that she feels her teachers "treat me differently," particularly when discussions around political situations in the Middle East arise in the classroom. She reported feeling uncomfortable around her peers because "I'm not accepted." As a result, Dina endorsed low mood, anhedonia, trouble concentrating, and feeling lonely. Dina's parents were supportive of her current struggles and were considering moving her to an Arabic ethnic heritage school to minimize bullying, particularly as her grades were slipping.

Upon meeting Dina, the school psychologist assessed acculturation by asking Dina about her family structure, reasons for immigrating, degree of religiosity, and community involvement. Addressing bullying was determined to be the most pressing concern in light of state anti-bullying laws. The school's zero-tolerance policies required the school psychologist to inform the principal, who immediately took disciplinary action with the suspected bullies, thus sending a strong message that anti-Arab bullying would not be tolerated. Consistent with an ecological framework, the school psychologist recognized that Dina's experiences also highlighted the need to consult with Dina's teachers. Consultation revealed a general lack of knowledge about Arab culture, which limited the teachers' ability to adequately counter negative stereotypes about Arabs and infuse more positive instructional content addressing Arab culture into lessons. As part of teacher consultation, the school psychologist shared culturally relevant and accurate instructional resources.

The school psychologist also viewed this as an opportunity for larger systems-level change and decided to approach a small group of Arab American parents and community leaders from a local church and mosque about the possibility of working together to develop some educational programs to highlight Arab culture and history in the school. As a result, representatives from different organizations were brought into the school for dance performances and other cultural events.

In terms of individualized interventions for Dina, the school psychologist met with Dina's parents in their home to provide education about the conflicts that may arise due to intergenerational differences in acculturation. Twice weekly, the school psychologist met with Dina to eat lunch with her and provide counseling. Eventually, Dina asked if two other Iraqi American students could join them. Recognizing the importance of peer support, the school psychologist agreed, with the result that the girls decided to name their group *Qawiya* (translated as "Strong"). The name reflected a sense of resilience and competence and, gradually, Dina began to assert herself with other students when they attempted to bully her.

In sum, the school psychologist's interventions with Dina included both individual and systems-level interventions aimed at addressing bias and discrimination and enhancing school connectedness. This included intervening with teachers, parents, and community leaders to foster a more inclusive school climate.

Critique

As Dina's case illustrates, school psychologists may employ a broad range of interventions to support Arab American students. However, empirical evidence for their effectiveness is often lacking, owing to a number of factors. The number of studies on Arab American youth, while increasing, is still minimal, due to the relatively small size of the overall population and specific challenges to establishing trust and recruiting Arab American participants post 9/11 (Amer & Bagasra, 2013; Melhem & Chemali, 2014; Sirin & Balsano, 2007). Generalizability of findings is limited due to non-random sampling, self-selection, small sample sizes, and need for parental consent. A good deal of research is qualitative (Sirin & Balsano, 2007) and includes unpublished dissertations (see, e.g. Abassi-Zoabi, 2012; Al-Qubbaj, 2003; Alyan, 2013; Fakhoury, 2012; Sheikh, 2009).

Numerous important topics related to the education of Arab American youth are in need of further research. The number of Arab American youth who access school-based services, including mental health counseling, is unknown and constitutes an area for future school psychology research. Critical topics related to school psychology services for ethnic minorities (see National Association of School Psychologists, 2013), including the representation of Arab American youth in special education, have yet to be examined in depth, thereby limiting recommendations about best practices for serving these youth. Research on related topics, such as the role of ESL for Arabic-speaking youth on academic achievement and nondiscriminatory assessment, is lacking. Additionally, although expert consensus has been utilized to develop instructional resources and bullying prevention programs, there is a lack of research on evidence-based interventions in both the academic and preventive spheres for Arab American students. The literature on evidence-based interventions clearly substantiates the need for specific identification of which programs work for which children in very specific circumstances (Rousseau & Guzder, 2008). The lack of such research for Arab American youth limits the development of effective recommendations. Finally, outcome data are needed that examine the educational outcomes of enhanced school connectedness.

Conclusion

This chapter summarized current features of the educational experience for many Arab American youth attending U.S. schools. Some of the risk factors affecting these youth – especially those who are recent immigrants and refugees – may include financial pressures, challenges with learning English, and history of trauma. Although the post-9/11 backlash has contributed to increased discrimination and bullying of students, many features of schooling can still serve as protective factors. Empirical investigation is encouraged to better understand the extent to which improving school connectedness can promote resilience among Arab American students and enhance academic achievement through evidence-based interventions. This includes the growing number of students attending

Islamic and Arabic heritage schools, for which school psychology research is nonexistent. Efforts are needed to expand school psychology research and interventions in order to better support Arab American students.

References

Abassi-Zoabi, M. J. (2012). *Discrimination, ethnic identity, and social support as predictors of self-efficacy in Arab American adolescents* (Doctoral dissertation). Available from ProQuest Dissertations and Theses database (UMI No. 3517889).

Abdullah, T. & Brown, T. L. (2011). Mental illness stigma and ethnocultural beliefs, values, and norms: An integrative review. *Clinical Psychology Review* 31, 934–948. doi: 10.1016/j.cpr.2011.05.003

Aburumuh, A. H., Smith, H. L., & Ratcliffe, L. G. (2009). Educator's cultural awareness and perceptions of Arab-American students: Breaking the cycle of ignorance. *The Journal of Multiculturalism in Education*, 4. Retrieved from www.wtamu.edu/webres/File/Journals/MCJ/Volume4/aburumuh.pdf

Ahmed, S., Kia-Keating, M., & Tsai, K. (2011). A structural model of racial discrimination, acculturative stress, and cultural resources among Arab American adolescents. *American Journal of Community Psychology* 48, 181–192. doi: 10.1007/s10464-011-9424-3

Ajrouch, K. J. (2000). Place, age, and culture: Community living and ethnic identity among Lebanese American adolescents. *Small Group Research* 31, 447–469. doi: 10.1177/104649640003100404

Ajrouch, K. J. (2004). Gender, race, and symbolic boundaries: Contested spaces of identity among Arab-American adolescents. *Sociological Perspectives* 47, 371–391. doi: 10.1525/sop.2004.47.4.371

Al Khateeb, J. M., Al Hadidi, M. S., & Al Khatib, A. J. (2014). Addressing the unique needs of Arab American children with disabilities. *Journal of Child & Family Studies*. Advance online publication. doi: 10.1007/s10826-014-0046-x

Al-Hazza, T. C. & Bucher, K. T. (2008). Building Arab Americans' cultural identity and acceptance with children's literature. *The Reading Teacher* 62, 210–219. doi: 10.1598/RT.62.3.3

Al-Hazza, T. C. & Bucher, K. T. (2010). Bridging a cultural divide with literature about Arabs and Arab Americans. *Middle School Journal* 41, 4–11. doi: 10.2307/23047567

Al-Khatab, A. (1999). In search of equity for Arab-American students in public schools of the United States. *Education* 120, 254–266.

Alkhateeb, H. M. (2010). Self concept in Lebanese and Arab-American pre-adolescents. *Psychological Reports* 106, 435–447. doi: 10.2466/pr0.106.2.435-447

Al-Qubbaj, K. (2003). *The process of acculturation among Arabic children and their families in the United States: Some educational considerations* (Doctoral dissertation). Available from ProQuest Dissertations and Theses database (UMI No. 3115660).

Al-Romi, N. H. (2000). Muslims as a minority in the United States. *International Journal of Educational Research* 33, 631–638. doi: 10.1016/S0883-0355(00)00041-0

Alyan, H. N. (2013). Experiences of Arab immigrant and Arab-American survivors of sexual violence: An exploratory study (Unpublished doctoral dissertation). Rutgers University, Piscataway, NJ.

Amer, M. M. & Bagasra, A. (2013). Psychological research with Muslim Americans in the age of Islamophobia. *American Psychologist* 68, 134–144. doi: 10.1037/a0032167

Arab American Institute. (2012). *Demographics*. Retrieved from www.aaiusa.org/pages/demographics

Asi, M. & Beaulieu, D. (2013). *Arab households in the United States: 2006–2010* (American Community Survey Brief ACSBR/10–20). Washington, D.C.: United States Census Bureau. Retrieved from www.census.gov/prod/2013pubs/acsbr10-20.pdf

Barlow, E. (ed.) (1994). *Evaluation of secondary-level textbooks for coverage of the Middle East and North Africa* (3rd edn.). Ann Arbor, MI/Tuscon, AZ: Middle East Studies Association/Middle East Outreach Council.

Bonet, S. W. (2011). Educating Muslim American youth in a post-9/11 era: A critical review of policy and practice. *The High School Journal* 95, 46–55. doi: 10.1353/hsj.2011.0013

Brittingham, A. & de la Cruz, G. P. (2005). *We the people of Arab ancestry in the United States* (Census 2000 special reports, CENSR-21). Washington, D.C.: U.S. Census Bureau. Retrieved from www.census.gov/prod/2005pubs/censr-21.pdf

Britto, P. R. (2008). Who am I? Ethnic identity formation of Arab Muslim children in contemporary U.S. society. *Journal of the American Academy of Child and Adolescent Psychiatry* 47, 853–857. doi: 10.1097/CHI.0b013e3181799fa6

Cainkar, L. & Read, J. G. (2014). Arab Americans and gender. In S. C. Nassar-McMillan, K. J. Ajrouch, & J. Hakim-Larson (eds.), *Biopsychosocial perspectives on Arab Americans: Culture, development, and health* (pp. 89–105). New York: Springer. doi: 10.1007/978-1-4614-8238-3_5

Cowan, K. C. & Vaillancourt, K. (2013). Advocating for safe schools, positive school climate, and comprehensive mental health services. *Communiqué* 41(6). Retrieved from www.nasponline.org/publications/cq/41/6/advocacy-in-action.aspx

David, G. C. & Ayouby, K. K. (2005). Studying the exotic other in the classroom: The portrayal of Arab Americans in educational source materials. *Multicultural Perspectives* 7, 11–20. doi: 10.1207/s15327892mcp0704_3

De Bellis, M. D., Woolley, D. P., & Hooper, S. R. (2013). Neuropsychological findings in pediatric maltreatment: Relationship of PTSD, dissociative symptoms, and abuse/neglect indices to neurocognitive outcomes. *Child Maltreatment* 18, 171–183. doi: 10.1177/1077559513497420

DePrince, A. P., Weinzierl, K. M., & Combs, M. D. (2009). Executive function performance and trauma exposure in a community sample of children. *Child Abuse & Neglect* 33, 353–361. doi: 10.1016/j.chiabu.2008.08.002

Eklund, K., Vaillancourt, K., & Pedley, T. (2013). Expanding the role of the school psychologist in the delivery of school-based mental health services. *Communiqué* 41(5). Retrieved from www.nasponline.org/publications/cq/41/5/advocacy-in-action.aspx

El-Haj, T. R. A. (2006). Race, politics, and Arab American youth: Shifting frameworks for conceptualizing educational equity. *Educational Policy* 20, 13–32. doi: 10.1177/0895904805285287

El-Haj, T. R. A. (2009). Imagining postnationalism: Arts, citizenship, education and Arab American youth. *Anthropology & Education Quarterly* 40, 1–19. doi: 10.1111/j.1548-1492.2009.01025.x

El-Haj, T. R. A. & Bonet, S. W. (2010). Education, citizenship, and the politics of belonging: Advocating for youth from Muslim transnational communities and the "War on Terror." *Review of Research in Education* 35, 29–59. doi: 10.3102/0091732X10383209

Fakhoury, N. (2012). *Academic achievement and attitudes of Arab-American immigrants* (Master's thesis). Available from ProQuest Dissertations and Theses database (UMI No. 1533342).

Goforth, A. N. (2011). Considerations for school psychologists working with Arab American children and families. *Communiqué* 39(6). Retrieved from www.nasponline.org/publications/cq/39/6/Multicultural-Affairs.aspx

Haboush, K. L. (2007). Working with Arab American families: Culturally competent practice for school psychologists. *Psychology in the Schools* 44, 183–198. doi: 10.1002/pits.20215

Haboush, K. L. & Alyan, H. (2013). "Who can you tell?" Features of Arab culture that influence conceptualization and treatment of childhood sexual abuse. *Journal of Child Sexual Abuse* 22, 499–518. doi: 10.1080/10538712.2013.800935

Haboush, K. L. & Barakat, N. (2014). Education and employment among Arab Americans: Pathways to individual identity and community resilience. In S. C. Nassar-McMillan, K. J. Ajrouch, & J. Hakim-Larson (eds.), *Biopsychosocial perspectives on Arab Americans: Culture, development and health* (pp. 229–255). New York: Springer. doi: 10.1007/978-1-4614-8238-3_11

Haboush, K. L., Selman, J. S., & Sievering, K. (2008). Traumatized youth: New roles for school psychologists. In D. H. Molina (ed.), *School psychology: 21st century issues and challenges* (pp. 117–155). New York: Nova Science.

Hadidi, M. S. Z. (1998). Educational services for visually impaired children in the Arab countries. *Journal of Visual Impairment and Blindness* 92, 535–539.

Hasnain, R., Shaikh, L. C., & Shanawani, H. (2008). *Disability and the Muslim perspective: An introduction for rehabilitation and health care providers.* GLADNET Collection. Retrieved from http://digitalcommons.ilr.cornell.edu/gladnetcollect/460

Hoot, J. L., Szecsi, T., & Moosa, S. (2003). What teachers of young children should know about Islam. *Early Childhood Education Journal* 31, 85–90. doi: 10.1023/B:ECEJ.0000005306.23082.7f

Humphreys, J. S. (2010). *"Why didn't they ask us?": Memories of Muslim young adults in public schools in the U.S. September 2001* (Doctoral dissertation). Available from ProQuest Dissertations and Theses database (UMI No. 3419753).

Lehr, C. A. & Christenson, S. L. (2002). Promoting a positive school climate. In A. Thomas & J. Grimes (eds.), *Best practices in school psychology IV* (pp. 977–991). Bethesda, MD: National Association of School Psychologists.

Mango, O. (2011). *Arabic heritage language schools in the United States.* Heritage Briefs. Washington, D.C.: Center for Applied Linguistics. Retrieved from www.cal.org/heritage/pdfs/briefs/arabic-heritage-language-schools-in-the-us.pdf

Melhem, I. & Chemali, Z. (2014). Mental health of Arab Americans: Cultural considerations for excellence of care. In R. Parekh (ed.), *The Massachusetts general hospital textbook on diversity and cultural sensitivity in mental health: Current clinical psychiatry* (pp. 3–30). New York: Humana Press.

Merrell, K. W., Ervin, R. A., & Peacock, G. G. (2012). *School psychology for the 21st century: Foundations and practices* (2nd edn.). New York: Guilford.

Moore, J. R. (2006). Teaching about Islam in secondary schools: Curricular and pedagogical considerations. *Equity & Excellence in Education* 39, 279–286. doi: 10.1080/10665680600788479

Nassar-McMillan, S. C. & Hakim-Larson, J. (2003). Counseling considerations among Arab Americans. *Journal of Counseling and Development* 81, 150–159. doi: 10.1002/j.1556-6678.2003.tb00236.x

National Association of School Psychologists. (2013). *Racial and ethnic disproportionality in education* (position statement). Bethesda, MD: National Association of School Psychologists. Retrieved from www.nasponline.org/about_nasp/positionpapers/Racial_Ethnic_Disproportionality.pdf

Office of Refugee Resettlement. (2013). *Fiscal year 2012 refugee arrivals.* U.S. Department of Health and Human Services. Retrieved from www.acf.hhs.gov/programs/orr/resource/fiscal-year-2012-refugee-arrivals

Palmer, B. C., El-Ashry, F., Leclere, J. T., & Chang, S. (2007). Learning from Abdallah: A case study of an Arabic-Speaking child in a U.S. school. *The Reading Teacher* 61, 8–17. doi: 10.1598/RT.61.1.2

Rossen, E. & Cowan, K. C. (2012). *A framework for school-wide bullying prevention and safety* (brief). Bethesda, MD: National Association of School Psychologists. Retrieved from www.nasponline.org/resources/bullying/Bullying_Brief_12.pdf

Rousseau, C. & Guzder, J. (2008). School-based prevention programs for refugee children. *Child and Adolescent Psychiatric Clinics of North America* 17, 533–549. doi: 10.1016/j.chc.2008.02.002

Ruiz, M., Kabler, B., & Sugarman, M. (2011). Understanding the plight of immigrant and refugee students. *Communiqué* 39(5), 23–25. Retrieved from www.nasponline.org/publications/cq/39/5/UnderstandingthePlight.aspx

Ryan, C. (2013). *Language use in the United States: 2011* (American Community Survey Reports, ACS-22). Retrieved from www.census.gov/prod/2013pubs/acs-22.pdf

Sabry, N. S. & Bruna, K. R. (2007). Learning from the experience of Muslim students in American schools: Towards a proactive model of school-community cooperation. *Multicultural Perspectives* 9, 44–50. doi: 10.1080/15210960701443730

Saleem, M. M. & Thomas, M. K. (2011). The reporting of the September 11th terrorist attacks in American social studies textbooks: A Muslim perspective. *The High School Journal* 95 15–33. doi: 10.2307/41236885

Sarroub, L. K. (2010). Discontinuities and differences among Muslim Arab-Americans: Making it at home and school. In M. L. Dantas & P. C. Manyak (eds.), *Home-school connections in a multicultural society: Learning from and with multiculturally and linguistically diverse families* (pp. 76–93). New York: Routledge/Taylor & Francis.

Schwartz, W. (1999). *Arab Amercian students in public schools* (ERIC Digest No.142). Retrieved from ERIC database (ED429144).

Seymour-Jorn, C. (2004). Arabic language learning among Arab immigrants in Milwaukee, Wisconsin: A study of attitudes and motivations. *Journal of Muslim Affairs* 24, 109–122. doi: 10.1080/1360200042000212205

Sheikh, M. F. (2009). *An exploratory study of the challenges of living in America as a Muslim adolescent attending public school* (Doctoral dissertation). Available from ProQuest Dissertations and Theses database (UMI No. 3402509).

Sirin, S. R. & Balsano, A. B. (2007). Editor's introduction: Pathways to identity and positive development among Muslim youth in the West. *Applied Development Science* 11, 109–111. doi: 10.1080/10888690701454534

Smadi, A. A. & Sartawi, A. A. (1998). The counseling needs of families with disabilities in the United Arab Emirates. *European Journal of Special Needs Education* 13, 200–207. doi: 10.1080/0885625980130206

Suleiman, M. F. (2001). *Image making of Arab Americans: Implications for teachers in diverse settings.* Retrieved from ERIC database (ED 452310).

Sulkowski, M. L., Demaray, M. K., & Lazarus, P. J. (2013). Connecting students to schools to support their emotional well-being and academic success. *Communiqué* 40(7), 1–22.

Tabbah, R. (2011). *Self-concept in Arab American adolescents: Implications of social support and experiences in the schools* (Doctoral dissertation). Available from ProQuest Dissertations and Theses database (UMI No. 3476922).

Tabbah, R., Miranda, A. H., & Wheaton, J. E. (2012). Self-concept in Arab American adolescents: Implications of social support and experiences in the schools. *Psychology in the Schools* 49, 817–827. doi: 10.1002/pits.21640

Thomas-Brown, K. (2010). Arab-American and Muslim-American diversity in a Dearborn public high school: A multicultural perspective. *The Journal of Multiculturalism in Education* 5. Retrieved from www.wtamu.edu/journal/volume-5-number-1.aspx

Tindongan, C. W. (2011). Negotiating Muslim youth identity in a post-9/11 world. *The High School Journal* 95, 72–87. doi: 10.1353/hsj.2011.0012

U.S. Census Bureau. (2013). *Selected population profile in the United States, 2013 American Community Survey 1-Year Estimates.* Retrieved from http://factfinder.census.gov/faces/tableservices/jsf/pages/productview.xhtml?pid=ACS_13_1YR_S0201&prodType=table

Wingfield, M. (2006). Arab Americans into the multicultural mainstream. *Equity & Excellence in Education* 39, 253–266. doi: 10.1080/10665680600788453

Wingfield, M. & Karaman, B. (2014). *Arab stereotypes and American educators.* Washington, D.C.: American-Arab Anti Discrimination Committee. Retrieved from www.adc.org/2009/11/arab-stereotypes-and-american-educators

Zine, J. (2006). Unveiled sentiments: Gendered Islamophobia and experiences of veiling among Muslim girls in a Canadian Islamic school. *Equity & Excellence in Education* 39, 239–252. doi: 10.1080/10665680600788503

24

HEALTH PSYCHOLOGY

The Interface Between Psychology and Medicine

Mark A. Lumley, Maisa S. Ziadni, Cynthia L. Arfken, and Adnan Hammad

Health psychology developed in the 1970s as the subfield of psychology that focuses on the intersection of psychosocial factors and people's physical health. Health psychology can be viewed as having four domains or foci of theory, research, and practice. The first examines stress and coping; that is, the processes by which stress is generated, experienced, and dealt with; and its effects on people's health. The second focus is health behaviors; that is, the factors that determine whether or not one engages in actions that are healthy or unhealthy as well as methods to increase healthy behaviors. The third domain examines patient-provider interactions, including the conditions under which people seek healthcare, their interactions with healthcare providers, and their behavior related to healthcare recommendations. The fourth area is adjustment to illness, which applies the above three domains to specific illnesses or clinical problems.

This chapter is organized around these four domains of health psychology as they apply to Arab Americans. These domains are not distinct, however, and important variables cut across them, influencing stress and coping, health behaviors, patient-provider interactions, and adjustment to illness. Thus, the chapter starts with an initial presentation of sociocultural variables or processes that are of particular relevance to Arab American health psychology. This is followed by a review of the literature on Arab Americans in the four domains of health psychology, each starting with a brief presentation of relevant theoretical models. Next, the authors discuss how the health of Arab Americans might be improved, and they present a case example of how a leading medical and social services center for Arab Americans is organized and operates. The chapter closes with a critique of the literature and makes suggestions for future health psychology theory and research with Arab Americans.

It should be noted that the relatively large health psychology literature has a substantial limitation – it has been developed primarily on European Americans. Although research on other ethnic minority groups has been ongoing for some years, the health psychology literature among Arab Americans is in its infancy. Thus, the authors, who are located in Southeast Michigan, home to one of the largest concentration of Arab Americans outside the Middle East (de la Cruz & Brittingham, 2003), have added observations from their extensive firsthand research and clinical experience with Arab Americans.

Important Factors in Arab American Health Psychology

What is "health" to Arab Americans? Interviews with Arab immigrants to the U.S. found that they endorsed a multidimensional concept that included physical and psychological health, as well as optimism to appreciate what they had (Abdulrahim & Ajrouch, 2010). This multidimensional concept was also found in an earlier health assessment of Arab Americans, in which the most frequently reported health problems were family stress, adjusting to the U.S., managing acute illness, coping with adolescents, and marital stress (Laffrey, Meleis, Lipson, Solomon, & Omidian, 1989). These findings suggest that Arab Americans hold a broader view of health than the biomedical perspective that dominates Western culture. The broader view is evident when one considers a number of sociocultural processes that are important for understanding the health psychology of Arab Americans.

Arab Americans have different countries of origin, which have different cultures, histories, and sociopolitical climates (Nydell, 2006). For example, Yemen has a largely poor, rural, and traditional population, which is very different from that of Lebanon, which is known for its cosmopolitan and progressive populace. Such differences may influence specific health behaviors and self-reported health. For example, one study of five Middle Eastern immigrant groups found that physical symptoms and positive morale differed by national origin (Meleis, Lipson, & Paul, 1992).

The type of migration process also matters. Immigrants often seek educational or economic opportunities or family unification, whereas refugees escape war, violence, or political threats. The process of migration, particularly if one is a refugee, may have health implications because it results in changes not only to one's living location, but also to one's social relationships, psychological status, health behaviors, and even physiology (Berry, 1992). In a Detroit area study examining Iraqi refugees and other Arab Americans who were obtaining mental health services, the refugees were more likely to report psychological symptoms and physical illnesses than other Arab Americans (Jamil et al., 2002).

Acculturation to American values and practices typically increases with time in the U.S. and each succeeding generation, and people's behavior and health status may be influenced by acculturation. For example, the population-based 2003 Detroit Arab American Study found that recent Arab immigrants reported worse health than those born in the U.S. (Abdulrahim & Baker, 2009). Other factors obviously influence self-rated health, such as education and connection with family (Ajrouch, 2007).

Arab Americans may experience violence and discrimination both before and after coming to the U.S. War, political oppression, and sectarian strife were experienced by some Arab Americans before arriving in the U.S., and stereotyping and discrimination may occur in the U.S., particularly after the events of 9/11 (Abdulrahim & Baker, 2009; Padela & Heisler, 2010). For other ethnicities, racism and discrimination harm health by increasing biological stress responses (Clark, Anderson, Clark, & Williams, 1999), and this likely occurs in Arab Americans as well.

Religious and cultural practices are integral factors in the health of Arab Americans. In the Arab world, Islam is the most commonly practiced religion. In the U.S., however, data on religious affiliation are more difficult to obtain. Although there are Arab Americans who are Muslim, a population-based survey in southeastern Michigan found the majority (58%) of Arab Americans were Christians (Detroit Arab American Study Team, 2009). Using the same survey data, Padela and Heisler (2010) found that Muslim Arab Americans reported more stress than Christian Arab Americans. Also, diet, modesty, gender relations, sexual behavior, and specific medical practices are influenced by religious and cultural beliefs and practices among Arab Americans (Hammoud, White, & Fetters, 2005; Kulwicki, Miller, & Schim, 2000; Yosef, 2008).

For some Arab Americans, Arabic is the preferred language for patient-provider interactions. Arabic-speaking immigrants report poorer health than English-speaking immigrants and those born in the U.S. (Abdulrahim & Baker, 2009). Limited English language proficiency is associated with increased likelihood of reporting a physical disability among Arab Americans (Dallo, Al Snih, & Ajrouch, 2008). In addition to the preferred language spoken, subtleties of communication style are important for patient-provider interactions and are related to health attitudes and behaviors (Berry, Kim, Minde, & Mok, 1987; Kulwicki et al., 2000).

Family and community cohesiveness are central to Arab culture (Awad, 2010) and play key roles in health and healthcare (Hammoud et al., 2005; Mulvaney-Day, Alegria, & Sribney, 2007; Navas et al., 2005). The family can be instrumental in deciding the nature of the health problem a member is facing and actions to be taken (El-Islam, 1982). Maintaining family honor and social status can influence the way Arab American patients communicate, the reasons that they seek care, and the health behaviors in which they engage (Erickson & Al-Timimi, 2001).

The community population size or density in which one resides is also relevant to health. Those who live in more densely populated communities of Arab Americans often have more access to Arab American healthcare providers and more community support than those living in areas with lower concentrations of Arab Americans, and may have better health as a result. For example, El-Sayed and Galea (2010) found that Arab American women residing in a city with a high density of Arab Americans (Dearborn, Michigan) were less likely to have low-birth-weight babies than Arab American women living elsewhere in Michigan.

Health-related resources also impact the healthcare of Arab Americans. Such resources include healthcare organizations specializing in the needs of this population, Arabic-speaking providers, social services such as language training, availability of higher education, and economic factors such as jobs and health insurance. These factors were highlighted in a survey in an Arab American community in Southwest Brooklyn (Sarsour, Tong, Jaber, Talbi, & Julliard, 2010) and are a central focus of the case example presented below. It should be noted that these factors are not independent of each other but rather operate jointly to influence the health of Arab Americans in each of the four domains of health psychology. The four areas and their relationship to Arab American health are examined next.

Theories and Research on Stress and Coping

Stress is a ubiquitous experience, and poor coping with stress is a well-recognized contributor to health problems. A model by Cohen and Rodriguez (1995) illustrates the pathways by which stress affects health. Excessive or prolonged stress can directly affect various physiological systems, impairing immune responses, altering endocrine systems, and increasing sympathetic nervous system activity. There is growing interest in the concept of allostatic load, in which stress disrupts a host of regulatory physiological processes that ideally remain in balance or homeostasis (Juster, McEwen, & Lupien, 2010). Stress can also promote unhealthy behaviors, such as poor diet, and interfere with adaptive management of chronic illness. Stress may also lead to negative mood and helplessness, which in turn can increase the focus on one's body and prompt people to seek care for stress-related physical symptoms.

Research in this domain also examines individual differences in personality, cognition, and social relationships to understand how they moderate or mediate the effects of stress. Several models of stress and coping have also been proposed, but a leading model is that of Lazarus and Folkman (1984), which posits that primary cognitive appraisals or interpretations of events can lead to a stress response, and then secondary appraisals determine how one copes with those events or stressful reactions. Clinical health psychologists are typically interested in reducing stress or helping people cope more adaptively, thereby preventing or treating health problems.

Several sources of stress and methods of coping are particularly relevant to Arab Americans. Some Arab Americans, especially refugees, experienced war, victimization, trauma, and other stressors prior to leaving their country of origin. For example, a study of 116 Iraqi refugees found that those who left after the Gulf War reported more stress-related medical conditions than those who left earlier, presumably because of the stress of living through that war (Hakim-Larson, Farrag, Kafaji, Jamil, & Hammad, 2005). Cumulative trauma and exposure to media reports of the war predicted a host of health problems among Iraqi immigrants, including neurological, cardiovascular, respiratory, digestive, musculoskeletal, and endocrine disorders (Kira et al., 2007).

Arab Americans, like most immigrant groups, also face the stress of acculturation. However, racial stereotypes of, and discrimination against, Arab Americans is particularly common (Rousseau, Hassan, Moreau, & Thombs, 2011). Potential differences in language, dress, and religious practices, and the tendency to equate "Arab" with "terrorist," may lead mainstream Americans to distance themselves emotionally from, or openly denigrate, Arab Americans (Panagopoulos, 2006). In addition, the Middle East has been a target of American military activity, which can lead Americans from other racial/ethnic backgrounds to view Arab Americans as the "enemy." All of these experiences may contribute to stress responses among Arab Americans. For example, the Detroit Arab American Study found that the experience of discrimination and abuse after 9/11 was associated with distress and poor perceived health among Arab Americans (Padela & Heisler, 2010).

Generational differences and acculturation issues, such as the conflicts between younger people who seek to adopt more liberal values, and their parents who hold more traditional values, are additional sources of potential stress. A study of 240 Arab American adolescents found that racial discrimination and acculturative stress strongly predicted psychological distress (Ahmed, Kia-Keating, & Tsai, 2011). A common conflict that the authors reported hearing from Arab American high school and college students was related to having boyfriends or girlfriends, which can create family discord, especially if these relationships are not with a person of the same religion or ethnicity. These relationships are often kept in secret, and secrecy itself is a substantial stressor. Sexual behavior, including loss of virginity among unmarried girls or women, can create substantial shame and fear of punishment (Abudabbeh & Nydell, 1993; Kulwicki et al., 2000).

Stress and accompanying negative emotions can lead to physiological changes, mood changes, and somatic symptoms. In a laboratory stress study, undergraduate students who self-identified as Arab American were compared to those who self-identified as White on their subjective and cardiovascular (heart rate, blood pressure) responses to mental arithmetic and stress-recall tasks (Chatkoff & Leonard, 2009). The Arab American subgroup reported greater subjective threat and stress than the White subgroup to both stressors. The two groups did not differ in cardiovascular reactivity to mental arithmetic; however, Arab Americans had less reactivity than the Whites to stress recall. The authors suggested that this reduced physiological stress response in Arab Americans may stem from habituation to the chronic stress of being an ethnic minority.

Both the experience of stress and its health effects are influenced by coping, which involves a range of cognitive, behavioral, emotional, and social processes. Whereas mainstream psychological views of coping emphasize cognition or emotion (Lazarus & Folkman, 1984), the coping of Arab Americans is also influenced by social factors and religious beliefs and practices. Coping and mental health are covered elsewhere in this book, but health behaviors, which are examined next, are both influenced by stress and sometimes serve as a form of coping.

Theories and Research on Health Behaviors

The health behaviors domain of health psychology focuses on the prevention of illness or disease by engaging in adaptive lifestyle behaviors, including screening for health problems. Various theoretical models have been developed to help explain and predict whether or not people engage in healthy behavior. For example, the health belief model (Rosenstock, 1974) posits that preventive action is determined by a person's appraisal of the threat that a health problem poses and the balance of the pros and cons of engaging in preventive behavior. The theory of planned behavior (Ajzen, 1991) suggests that a person's intentions are the best predictor of health-related behavior and that intentions are a product of three judgments: attitude about the behavior (whether or not it is a good thing to do), the subjective norm (others' opinions about the behavior and one's motivation to comply with those opinions), and perceived behavioral control (expectation of one's success in performing the behavior). An influential model of health behavior change is the transtheoretical model (Prochaska & Velicer, 1997), which accounts for a person's readiness to change behavior as a series of stages of increasing motivation: precontemplation, contemplation, preparation, action, and maintenance. These models are relevant not only for understanding or predicting whether or not people will engage in healthy behaviors, but also for targeting interventions to change behavior.

Much of the health behavior research among Arab Americans has been on the use and abuse of alcohol, tobacco, and other drugs, but these are examined in other chapters. Other health behaviors, such as eating a healthy diet, engaging in appropriate exercise, obtaining adequate sleep, getting recommended immunizations, reducing the risk of injury and violence, and avoiding unsafe behaviors, have rarely been examined in the Arab American literature. Thus, the authors offer several observations about diet, immunizations, cancer screenings, and sexual behavior based on the available literature and their own experience.

Obesity and problems related to obesity, such as type 2 diabetes, are increasing in Arab countries and among Arab Americans (Jaber, Brown, Hammad, Zhu, & Herman, 2003; Yosef, 2008). Obesity can become a problem in cultures where social interactions over meals are valued, and prosperity is expressed in food purchases (Brown, 1991), as it is in Arab culture. Traditional Arab diet includes high levels of vegetables and fruit but also sweets, which can negate the benefits of fruit and vegetables (Harb, 2007).

Immunizations are another health behavior of interest. It is believed that Arab American children usually obtain recommended immunizations, in part because Arab American parents appear to trust the medical establishment and prioritize protecting their children. The authors have observed, however, some problems reaching recent adult immigrants and low-income Arab Americans to inform them of new vaccines or annual flu shots. This is supported by a national study that found lower rates of vaccinations among foreign-born Middle Eastern men compared to U.S.-born White men (Dallo & Kindratt, 2015). Recent Iraqi refugees were more likely to get flu vaccinations if they had health insurance (Taylor et al., 2014).

Factors relevant to cancer screening have been examined in several studies. Barriers to mammography among both Arab immigrants and Arab women in the Middle East include perceived painfulness of the procedure (Soskolne, Marie, & Manor, 2007), embarrassment, and fear of detection of cancer (Azaiza & Cohen, 2006). These results are consistent with the health belief model, as is the finding that greater perceived seriousness of breast cancer and general health motivation were associated with having more frequent mammography screening among Arab American women (Schwartz, Fakhouri, Bartoces, Monsur, & Younis, 2008). The religious values of Muslim Americans, many of whom are Arab Americans, also influence breast cancer screening. In their study of Muslim women in Chicago (a third of whom were of Arab origin), Padela and colleagues (2015) found that higher levels of religiosity, more use of positive religious coping, and perceived religious discrimination in healthcare were associated with not having a mammogram in the past two years. Knowing someone with breast cancer was associated with having a mammogram.

Finally, the topic of safe sexual behavior, including the use of condoms to prevent sexually transmitted diseases or unintended pregnancies, is quite popular in the general health psychology literature. Among Arab Americans, however, there are cultural and religious prohibitions against homosexual relationships, premarital sex, and sexual behavior outside marriage. As a result, issues related to sexual behavior are generally not openly discussed and, therefore, are difficult to research; the authors could find no studies of these topics.

Theories and Research on Patient-Provider Interactions

One specific and important type of health-relevant behavior involves how people interact with the healthcare system and the factors that support or impede those interactions. The domain of patient-provider interactions covers processes such as obtaining healthcare, communication between providers and patients, and adherence to heathcare recommendations. Several theoretical models have been proposed to describe or explain these processes. For example, older models viewed patient nonadherence to medical recommendations as a function of patient resistance, but recent models broaden the view to take into account the disease or illness, the complexity of the regimen, the cultural and social context, and the quality of the relationship and communication between provider and patient

(DiMatteo & DiNicola, 1982). A leading model of provider decision-making is the evidence-based psychological practice model, which suggests that the provider's approach to the patient's problem should be based on the best available research evidence, as interpreted and applied by the provider's clinical expertise, while considering the patient's values, preferences, and culture (American Psychological Association, 2006).

The interaction between patients and providers has been one of the most frequently examined health psychology research topics related to Arab Americans. Although macroenvironmental factors such as insurance, cost of care, and transportation impact Arab Americans' use of healthcare services (Harb, 2007; Pinelli & Jaber, 2011), this section focuses on psychological and behavioral issues in the interactions between patients and providers.

There are many potential barriers to healthcare among Arab Americans, especially for recent immigrants and low-income Arab Americans. Language is particularly problematic (Kulwicki et al., 2000; Pinelli & Jaber, 2011; Torres, 1998; Yosef, 2008) and includes locating providers who are fluent in Arabic and who also understand the nuances of an Arab communication style. Also, U.S.-trained professionals typically maintain fairly rigid boundaries, but Arab Americans often have different social customs that call for more flexibility. For example, in one study Iraqi refugees often encouraged therapists to come to their homes and typically shared a beverage and pastry with them (Hijazi et al., 2014). Such cultural differences may influence not only Arab American patients' attitudes and perceptions of their providers, but also providers' behaviors toward Arab Americans, which can then impact adherence to providers' recommendations (Hammoud et al., 2005).

Modesty is prized by many Arab Americans and is a core practice of Islam (Yosef, 2008). The practice of modesty discourages exposing various body parts to the touch and perhaps sight of others, particularly of the opposite sex, but sometimes even same-sex strangers (Boulanouar, 2006). Even handshakes may be avoided. The degree of modesty practiced varies widely but may include requesting a same-sex provider (Hammoud et al., 2005; Yosef, 2008) and, for women, the presence of the husband or father in the examination room. Some women will not accept unnecessary exposure of their bodies and might refuse bed baths during hospital stays or breastfeed only in private (Hammoud et al., 2005). More subtly, a lack of eye contact, especially by women patients, may be viewed as avoidance or mistrust by non-Arab providers, but is actually a sign of modesty. More broadly, because of both modesty and the value of sexual chastity, patients may not easily discuss issues like sex and family planning with healthcare providers (Hammoud et al., 2005).

The long history of both overt and subtle racism against Arab Americans could negatively influence the behavior of some non-Arab American providers (Kulwicki et al., 2000), but few Arab American patients report problems with trust or confidence in medical providers (Inhorn & Fakih, 2006; Pinelli & Jaber, 2011). However, a small number of Arab American patients may be nonadherent with medications due to suspicions that medications might be poisonous or will interfere with sexual functioning (Harb, 2007). Also, observant Muslims may avoid certain medications because they contain alcohol, opioids, or pork products such as are found in the gelatin that is widely used in capsules (Hammoud et al., 2005; Lawrence & Rozmus, 2001). There are important considerations when providing medical care to Muslim Arab Americans who observe the holy month of Ramadan due to the expectation of fasting from food and drink during daylight hours. Islamic teaching influences a variety of medical requirements and procedures, as some patients want to fast despite their illness and recommendations of their physicians. Intravenous fluids or injections, parenteral nutrition, intramuscular injections, and blood transfusions can all invalidate a fast. Organ transplantation is allowed only if it saves a patient's life (Hammoud et al, 2005; Yosef, 2008).

The family plays a central role in both defining and managing illness (Hammoud et al., 2005; Yosef, 2008). This may lead to some conflict in obtaining informed consent or speaking only to the identified patient, as many U.S.-trained providers prefer to do, because an illness may be regarded as a family matter rather than an individual's problem. For example, a woman might prefer that a provider discuss her condition with her husband. Providers can also experience a challenge with patients' beliefs about future plans, and there are some cultural expectations about how serious diagnoses or "bad news" is delivered, such as the idea of informing the family rather than only the patient (Lipson & Meleis, 1983). There are also cultural notions of health and illness that can affect interactions of Arab Americans with the healthcare system (Yosef, 2008). In some Arab American communities, various folk practices that are outside contemporary Western medicine may be preferred, or at least tried first (Kulwicki, 1996; Kulwicki & Miller, 1999; Kulwicki et al., 2000; Yosef, 2008).

The communal nature of health among Arab Americans can be a great source of support, information, and comfort to patients. Arab Americans may prefer providers who are from a similar ethnic background; however, this may not be the case for some patients obtaining services related to highly stigmatized issues, such as mental health, substance abuse, or sexually transmitted disease, particularly when the provider is part of the same community as the patient. Patients may fear that such a provider might reveal information to others in the community or treat the patient or his/her family differently (Youssef & Deane, 2006). In such cases, it is possible that having providers who are not part of the Arab American community might facilitate accessing these services.

Theories and Research on Adjustment to Illness

Many health psychologists focus their research or clinical activities on specific clinical populations or health problems, such as cardiovascular disease, diabetes, cancer, chronic pain, or AIDS. Although there are specific theoretical models of adjustment that have been developed for certain health problems, theory and research from the three health psychology domains reviewed above provide general information about adjustment to a range of health conditions. That is, for each health problem they address, health psychologists examine stress and coping, health behavior, and patient-provider interactions. The goal of clinical practice is to treat or cure the condition when possible, but more often it is to help people function more adaptively while living with the illness, improving psychological status, enhancing quality of life, and increasing longevity. This section examines several specific health problems of concern to Arab Americans and notes the role of stress and coping, health behaviors, and patient-provider interactions, when relevant. However, the literature on these topics is minimal as most research on health conditions among Arab Americans has instead focused on epidemiology or sociocultural risk factors.

One disorder, type 2 diabetes mellitus, is a growing concern among Arab populations (Badran & Laher, 2012). In the U.S., one of the few studies that examined diet was surprised to find that consumption of a traditional diet was associated with a higher prevalence of diabetes (Jaber et al., 2003). This finding may be more related to how food is used and a greater tolerance of, or lack of knowledge on how to prevent, obesity than to actual nutritional components. Of concern is the quality of diabetes care among Arab Americans, which is less than that recommended by the American Diabetes Association (Berlie, Herman, Brown, Hammad, & Jaber, 2008). These problems are likely due, in part, to the lack of accessible, culturally appropriate healthcare and resources for patients (Berlie et al., 2008; Jaber et al., 2003) and limited knowledge and negative beliefs about diabetes (Pinelli & Jaber, 2011). A survey in 13 countries where Islam is a predominant religion found that fasting among diabetic patients (Salti, 2010) may interfere with diabetes management, and this practice may continue among Arab Americans in the U.S. These concerns have led to the development and implementation of a group lifestyle intervention diabetes prevention program for Arab Americans in a community setting (Jaber et al., 2003).

Sexually transmitted diseases, including HIV infection, occur among Arab Americans; however, the cultural and religious prohibitions against the behaviors that increase risk of these infections – multiple sexual partners, same-sex behaviors, and needle-based drug use – cause substantial stigma about these illnesses. As a result, Arab Americans show low levels of knowledge about AIDS, a high number of misconceptions related to how HIV is transmitted, and high levels of anxiety about HIV infection (Kulwicki & Cass, 1994). This dilemma has led to recommendations for changes at multiple levels, including having religious and community leaders speak about the disease, developing public service announcements that feature Arab role models such as celebrities, educating mothers to help raise awareness in their families, and speaking about HIV in schools (Reimann, Rodriguez-Reimann, Ghulan, & Beylouni, 2007).

Fertility and pregnancy-related concerns are emerging among Arab Americans. Generally, Arab cultures are pronatalist; children are a sign of social status (Inhorn & Fakih, 2006), so infertility adds an emotional burden beyond the disappointment of not having children. Although some Islamic scriptures consider infertility as a God-given condition and, therefore, not to be treated, other barriers to effective infertility care include economic constraints, as well as language and cultural barriers. Preterm births appear to be more prevalent among Arab Americans than among non-Arab women, and the determinants of preterm birth include lack of prenatal care visits and tobacco use (El-Sayed & Galea, 2009).

Improving the Health of Arab Americans

Researchers and clinicians have made many suggestions for improving the health of Arab Americans (Hammoud et al., 2005; Kulwicki et al., 2000; Lipson & Meleis, 1983; Reimann et al., 2007; Yosef, 2008). First, the elevated stress that contributes to symptoms, maladaptive behaviors, and illness among Arab Americans needs to be reduced. This should occur at multiple levels. Both the Arab American community and healthcare providers need to recognize that stressful life events and trauma, including torture, have occurred to some Arab Americans, particularly before their migration to the U.S. Such traumatic experiences retain their effects even though time has passed and the environment has changed, but this fact may be difficult to understand or appreciate. Medical providers should inquire about such earlier traumatic experiences and, when found, refer the patient to a mental health provider, ideally one who is integrated into, or at least co-located within, a medical clinic.

The experience of new stressors while living in the U.S. is also of concern. Part of this stress stems from the challenges of acculturation, assimilation, and shifting traditions that most immigrant groups experience. However, Arab Americans have unique stressors associated with stereotypes held by mainstream Americans, as noted above. Solutions to these sources of stress involve educating the population, which will need to stem from governmental, educational, and religious institutions, as well as from the Arab American community itself. Closer interactions between Arab and other Americans, including relationships at work, school, the community, and even religious institutions, will likely reduce such biases and stress. For example, after the attacks of 9/11, some churches had exchange programs with mosques to help Christians learn about Muslims, with the goal of building connections and trust.

There are various ways that patient-provider interactions for Arab Americans might be improved (Kulwicki et al., 2000). A personal approach and continuity of care by the same healthcare professional is helpful to bridge the gap between the cultures of Arab American patients and that of U.S.-trained providers (Hammoud et al., 2005; Lipson & Meleis, 1983). Increasing the cultural competence of the healthcare workforce is another crucial need (Kulwicki & Miller, 1999). Interestingly, cultural competence may be perceived differently by non-Arab providers and the Arab American community. U.S.-trained providers tend to value consistency in care, often following standardized protocols. Arab Americans, in contrast, view treatment that does not address their unique cultural practices or values as insensitive. For example, culturally competent care of immigrant Arab American women entails recognizing the experiences and cultural values associated with being a woman and being an immigrant, and developing ways to offer healthcare services that better match the immigrant women's situations (Meleis, 1991). For those Arab Americans who are religiously conservative, nurses and other providers may help patients by integrating religious teachings, when appropriate, into their interventions (Yosef, 2008). These advances can occur by improving the training and practice of non-Arab healthcare providers and incorporating Arab staff, including psychologists, in care settings. As suggested by focus groups conducted with Arab adults in New York City, developing partnerships with trusted community leaders can also enhance care (Shah, Ayash, Pharaon, & Gany, 2008).

Case Example: A Community-Based Model for Providing Integrated Health Services

To illustrate one approach to improving the health of Arab Americans, the authors describe the Arab Community Center for Economic and Social Services (ACCESS). This organization was developed over 40 years ago in southeastern Michigan, which is home to a substantial concentration of Arab Americans. The goal of ACCESS is to provide culturally sensitive health screening, prevention, and treatment, while conducting health research and education for the Arab American community. This organization improves health by attending to the four domains of health psychology: reducing stress, improving health behavior, enhancing patient-provider interactions, and facilitating adjustment to specific health problems.

Although ACCESS has a number of economic, social, and educational components, the Community Health and Research Center (CHRC) is the most relevant to health psychology. It is a fully integrated, community health, one-stop service center and also serves as a training site for medical residents, nurses, psychologists, and public health professionals. The CHRC administers more than 56 programs, which are organized into five services. The Medical Service provides primary care (internal medicine and family medicine), obstetrics and gynecology, and general surgery and oncology; and offers gender-specific medical providers, which obviates concerns some patients have about cross-gender exposure or touch. The Public Health Service offers a wide range of educational programs that focus on disease prevention and health promotion, such as breast cancer screening. Included here is a program for gay Arab American men, which includes education on safe sex behaviors and is led by a person who is not Arab American, thereby reducing fears that stigmatized information might be shared with others in the Arab American community. The Mental Health Service adopts a holistic, biopsychosocial counseling modality and includes individual and family counseling, and psychiatric services for children and adults, including a psychosocial rehabilitation and treatment center for victims of torture and refugees. The Environmental Program promotes the right of every person to live in a clean, safe, and healthy environment by engaging community members in outdoor programs to facilitate positive connections and stewardship for the environment – activities that also reduce stress and promote health. Finally, reflecting the fact that research on health is vital, there is a Research Program that seeks to gather and disseminate needed health information for the Arab American community by participating in collaborative studies.

Patient-provider interactions, communication, and understanding are improved by having the majority of staff members from the Arab American community. Arabic is regularly spoken by providers and staff, but other languages are spoken as well, which facilitates the provision of culturally and linguistically sensitive services to various minority communities in the region. Patients are screened through program intake forms to identify which services they are eligible to use. When making referrals, the patient's provider contacts the caseworker at the referred program to ensure that the service is provided as soon as possible. Many patients have limited transportation, so vans are provided to pick up and drop off patients. To further reduce barriers, improve care integration, detect chronic conditions in a timely manner, and reduce patient stress, ACCESS is building an electronic medical records system that will further streamline the process of cross-referral and ensure that all patients are assessed not only for their physical health, but also for the social determinants that impact their wellbeing.

Critique

There are several limitations with respect to Arab American health psychology theory and research. Regarding theory, there is a deficit in the applicability to Arab Americans of current health psychology theories, which tend to be highly individualistic and emphasize logical cognition. For example, the primary and secondary appraisal model of stress and coping, the transtheoretical model of motivation and readiness to change, and the theory of planned behavior were developed with an emphasis on individuals. Arab American health psychology, in contrast, highlights the influence of the community, family, and social systems rather than just the individual, and the vital role of religious beliefs and practices rather than solely rational analysis. Perhaps this lack of applicability of contemporary health psychology models explains why theory is rarely mentioned in research reports on Arab American health. Thus, scholars working in the Arab American communities are encouraged to consider current theoretical models in the field and determine when they are applicable to, and when they need revision for, this population.

Regarding research, studies have relied largely on surveys or interviews of Arab American community members and patients. Although these are valuable, it would be beneficial to see the perspectives of providers included in research. Furthermore, medical and objective data obtained from records, laboratory and biomarker measurements, and physical exams would add important data to patients' self-reports. Studies of processes over time, ranging from the use of daily diaries to longer-term prospective studies, would yield a more complete picture of the factors related to the health of Arab Americans. Tests of stress reduction and behavior change techniques among Arab Americans are also needed. Studies of the outcomes of trials to change stress, coping, health behavior, or patient-provider interactions are very rare. Small-scale studies on a series of patients as well as large-scale controlled clinical trials are needed.

A more basic issue regarding the health psychology of Arab Americans is whether and how this population differs from the population on which the larger body of health psychology knowledge has been developed. What is unique to Arab Americans, and what is common across people of very different backgrounds? It is not sufficient simply to assess and report certain variables or patterns in Arab Americans, without at least considering whether these are redundant in light of what is available on other populations. Ideally, research on Arab American health psychology would include comparison to non-Arab samples, as well as to other immigrant groups, to determine similarities and differences. Admittedly, this can be pragmatically difficult, so at a minimum, researchers should refer to research on other populations and discuss whether their own findings are similar or different. A final concern is that national surveys typically do not list "Arab American" or even "Middle Eastern" as a separate ethnicity, which prevents comparative analyses of this subpopulation. The federal government, the Institute of Medicine, and individual researchers should correct this omission in future surveys and studies.

Conclusion

Physical health is intimately tied to psychology, as the field of health psychology has well demonstrated. Research on Arab American health psychology is relatively new, but the available evidence reveals the importance of incorporating new observations from this population into the evolving body of knowledge. In particular, the role of social factors, culture, and religion stand out as key factors in Arab American health and healthcare. As the number and influence of Arab Americans increase in American society, it is vital to continue to study the factors that influence their health, to develop and test theoretical models of these factors, and to develop novels ways to enhance the health of this population.

References

Abdulrahim, S. & Ajrouch, K. (2010). Social and cultural meanings of self-rated health: Arab immigrants in the United States. *Qualitative Health Research* 20, 1229–1240. doi: 10.1177/1049732310371104

Abdulrahim, S. & Baker, W. (2009). Differences in self-rated health by immigrant status and language preference among Arab Americans in the Detroit Metropolitan Area. *Social Science and Medicine* 68, 2097–2103. doi: 10.1016/j.socscimed.2009.04.017

Abudabbeh, N. & Nydell, M. K. (1993). Transcultural counseling and Arab Americans. In J. McFadden (ed.), *Transcultural counseling: Bilateral and international perspectives* (pp. 261–284). Alexandria, VA: American Counseling Association.

Ahmed, S. R., Kia-Keating, M., & Tsai, K. H. (2011). A structural model of racial discrimination, acculturative stress, and cultural resources among Arab American adolescents. *American Journal of Community Psychology* 48, 181–192. doi: 10.1007/s10464-011-9424-3

Ajrouch, K. J. (2007). Health disparities and Arab-American elders: Does intergenerational support buffer the inequality-health link? *Journal of Social Issues* 63, 745–58. doi: 10.1111/j.1540-4560.2007.00534.x

Ajzen, I. (1991). The theory of planned behavior. *Organizational Behavior and Human Decision Processes* 50, 179–211. doi: 10.1016/0749-5978(91)90020-T

American Psychological Association. (2006). Evidence-based practice in psychology. *American Psychologist* 61, 271–285. doi: 10.1037/0003-066X.61.4.217

Awad, G. H. (2010). The impact of acculturation and religious identification on perceived discrimination for Arab/Middle Eastern Americans. *Cultural Diversity and Ethnic Minority Psychology* 16, 59–67. doi: 10.1037/a0016675

Azaiza, F. & Cohen, M. (2006). Health beliefs and rates of breast cancer screening among Arab women. *Journal of Women's Health* 15, 520–530. doi: 10.1089/jwh.2006.15.520

Badran, M. & Laher, I. (2012). Type II diabetes mellitus in Arabic-speaking countries. *International Journal of Endocrinology* (Article ID 902873), 1–11. doi: 10.1155/2012/902873

Berlie, H. D., Herman, W. H., Brown, M. B., Hammad, A., & Jaber, L. A. (2008). Quality of diabetes care in Arab Americans. *Diabetes Research and Clinical Practice* 79, 249–255. doi: 10.1016/j.diabres.2007.09.003

Berry, J. W. (1992). Acculturation and adaptation in a new society. *International Migration* 30, 69–85. doi: 10.1111/j.1468–2435.1992.tb00776.x

Berry, J. W., Kim, U., Minde, T., & Mok, D. (1987). Comparative studies of acculturative stress. *International Migration Review* 21, 491–511. doi: 10.1177/136346158802500203F

Boulanouar, A. W. (2006). The notion of modesty in Muslim women's clothing: An Islamic point of view. *New Zealand Journal of Asian Studies* 8, 134–156.

Brown, P. (1991). Culture and the evolution of obesity. *Human Nature* 2, 31–57.

Chatkoff, D. K. & Leonard, M. T. (2009). A preliminary investigation of cognitive appraisal and cardiovascular reactivity and recovery in Arab Americans. *Ethnicity and Dieases* 19, 258–264. Retrieved from http://txfvzgw.ishib.org/journal/19-3/ethn-19-03-258.pdf

Clark, R., Anderson, N. B., Clark, V. R., & Williams, D. R. (1999). Racism as a stressor for African Americans: A biopsychosocial model. *American Psychologist* 54, 805–816. doi: 10.1037/0003-066X.54.10.805

Cohen, S. & Rodriguez, M. S. (1995). Pathways linking affective disturbances and physical disorders. *Health Psychology* 14, 374–380. doi: 10.1037/0278-6133.14.5.374

Dallo, F. J., Al Snih, S., & Ajrouch, K. J. (2008). Prevalence of disability among US and foreign-born Arab Americans: Results from the 2000 US Census. *Gerontology* 55, 153–161. doi: 10.1159/000151538

Dallo, F. J. & Kindratt, T. B. (2015). Disparities in preventive health behaviors among non-Hispanic white men: Heterogeneity among foreign-born Arab and European Americans. *American Journal of Men's Health* 9(2), 124–131. doi: 10.1177/1557988314532285

de la Cruz, G. P. & Brittingham, A. (2003). The Arab population: 2000 (Census 2000 Brief, C2KBR-23). Washington, D.C.: U.S. Census Bureau. Retrieved from www.census.gov/prod/2003pubs/c2kbr-23.pdf

Detroit Arab American Study Team. (2009). *Citizenship and crisis: Arab Detroit after 9/11*. New York: Russell Sage Foundation.

DiMatteo, M. R. & DiNicola, D. D. (1982). *Achieving patient compliance*. New York: Pergamon Press.

El-Islam, M. F. (1982). Arabic cultural psychiatry. *Transcultural Psychiatry* 19, 5–24. doi: 10.1177/136346158201900101

El-Sayed, A. M. & Galea, S. (2009). The health of Arab Americans living in the United States: A systematic review of the literature. *BMC Public Health* 9(272). doi: 10.1186/1471-2458-9-272

El-Sayed, A. M. & Galea, S. (2010). Community context, acculturation and low-birth-weight risk among Arab Americans: Evidence from the Arab-American birth-outcomes study. *Journal of Epidemiology and Community Health* 64, 155–160. doi: 10.1136/jech.2008.084491

Erickson, C. D. & Al-Timimi, N. R. (2001). Providing mental health services to Arab Americans: Recommendations and considerations. *Cultural Diversity and Ethnic Minority Psychology* 7, 308–327. doi: 10.1037/1099-9809.7.4.308

Hakim-Larson, J., Farrag, M., Kafaji, T., Jamil, L. H., & Hammad, A. (2005). Medical complaints among Iraqi American refugees with mental disorders. *Journal of Immigrant Health* 7, 145–152. doi: 10.1007/s10903-005-3671-z

Hammoud, M. M., White, C. B., & Fetters, M. D. (2005). Opening cultural doors: Providing culturally sensitive healthcare to Arab American and American Muslim patients. *American Journal of Obstetrics and Gynecology* 193, 1307–1311. doi: 10.1016/j.ajog.2005.06.065

Harb, W. (2007). Health issues in the Arab American community. Managing cardiovascular risk barriers to optimal health outcomes in the Arab American patient. *Ethnicity and Disease* 17(S3), 28–30.

Hijazi, A. M., Lumley, M. A., Ziadni, M., Haddad, L., Rapport, L. J., & Arnetz, B. B. (2014). Brief narrative exposure therapy for posttraumatic stress in Iraqi refugees: A preliminary randomized clinical trial. *Journal of Traumatic Stress* 27, 314–322. doi: 10.1002/jts.21922

Inhorn, M. & Fakih, M. (2006). Arab Americans, African Americans, and infertility: Barriers to reproduction and medical care. *Fertility and Sterility* 85, 844–852. doi: 10.1016/j.fertnstert.2005.10.029

Jaber, L. A., Brown, M. B., Hammad, A., Zhu, Q., & Herman, W. H. (2003). Lack of acculturation is a risk factor for diabetes in Arab immigrants in the US. *Diabetes Care* 26, 2010–2014. doi: 10.2337/diacare.26.7.2010

Jamil, H., Hakim-Larson, J., Farrag, M., Kafaji, T., Duqum, I., & Jamil, L. H. (2002). A retrospective study of Arab American mental health clients: Trauma and the Iraqi refugees. *American Journal of Orthopsychiatry* 72, 355–361. doi: 10.1037//0002-9432.72.3.355

Juster, R. P., McEwen, B. S., & Lupien, S. J. (2010). Allostatic load biomarkers of chronic stress and impact on health and cognition. *Neuroscience and Biobehavioral Reviews* 35, 2–16. doi: 10.1016/j.neubiorev.2009.10.002

Kira, I., Hammad, A., Lewandowski, L., Templin, T., Ramaswamy, V., Ozkan, B., & Nohanesh, J. (2007). The physical and mental status of Iraqi refugees and its etiology. *Ethnicity and Disease* 17(S3), 79–82.

Kulwicki, A. D. (1996). Health issues among Arab Muslim families. In B. C. Aswad & B. Bilge (eds.), *Family and gender among American Muslims* (pp. 197–207). Philadelphia, PA: Temple University Press.

Kulwicki, A. D. & Cass, P. S. (1994). An assessment of Arab American knowledge, attitudes, and beliefs about AIDS. *Journal of Nursing Scholarship* 26, 13–17. doi: 10.1111/j.1547-5069.1994.tb00288.x

Kulwicki, A. D. & Miller, J. (1999). Domestic violence in the Arab American population: Transforming environmental conditions through community education. *Issues in Mental Health Nursing* 20, 199–215. doi: 10.1080/016128499248619

Kulwicki, A. D., Miller, J., & Schim, S. M. (2000). Collaborative partnership for culture care: Enhancing health services for the Arab community. *Journal of Transcultural Nursing* 11, 31–39. doi: 10.1177/104365960001100106

Laffrey, S. C., Meleis, A. I., Lipson, J. G., Solomon, M., & Omidian, P. A. (1989). Assessing Arab-American health care needs. *Social Science and Medicine* 29, 877–883. doi: 10.1016/0277-9536(89)90087-7

Lawrence, P. & Rozmus, C. (2001). Culturally sensitive care of the Muslim patient. *Journal of Transcultural Nursing* 12, 228–233. doi: 10.1177/104365960101200307

Lazarus, R. S. & Folkman, S. (1984). *Stress, appraisal, and coping.* New York: Springer.

Lipson, J. G. & Meleis, A. I. (1983). Issues in health care of Middle Eastern patients. *Western Journal of Medicine*, 139, 854–861.

Meleis, A. I. (1991). Between two cultures: Identity, roles, and health. *Health Care for Women International* 12, 365–377. doi: 10.1080/07399339109515961

Meleis, A. I., Lipson, J. G., & Paul, S. M. (1992). Ethnicity and health among five Middle Eastern immigrant groups. *Nursing Research* 41, 98–103. doi: 10.1097/00006199-199203000-00008

Mulvaney-Day, N. E., Alegria, M., & Sribney, W. (2007). Social cohesion, social support, and health among Latinos in the United States. *Social Science and Medicine* 64, 477–495. doi: 10.1016/j.socscimed.2006.08.030

Navas, M., García, M. C., Sánchez, J., Rojas, A. J., Pumares, P., & Fernández, J. S. (2005). Relative Acculturation Extended Model (RAEM): New contributions with regard to the study of acculturation. *International Journal of Intercultural Relations* 29, 21–37. doi: 10.1016/j.ijintrel.2005.04.001

Nydell, M. K. (2006). *Understanding Arabs: A guide for modern times* (4th edn.). Boston, MA: Intercultural Press.

Padela, A. I. & Heisler, M. (2010). The association of perceived abuse and discrimination after September 11, 2001, with psychological distress, level of happiness, and health status among Arab Americans. *American Journal of Public Health* 100, 284–291. doi: 10.2105/AJPH.2009.164954

Padela, A. I., Murrar, S., Adviento, B., Liao, C., Hosseinian, Z., Peek, M., & Curlin, F. (2015). Associations between religion-related factors and breast cancer screening among American Muslims. *Journal of Immigrant and Minority Health* 17, 660–669. doi: 10.1007/s10903-014-0014-y

Panagopoulos, C. (2006). The polls-trends: Arab and Muslim Americans and Islam in the aftermath of 9/11. *Public Opinion Quarterly* 70, 608–624. doi: 10.1093/poq/nfl029

Pinelli, N. R. & Jaber, L. A. (2011). Practices of Arab American patients with type 2 diabetes mellitus during Ramadan. *Journal of Pharmacy Practice* 24, 211–215. doi: 10.1177/0897190010367432

Prochaska, J. O. & Velicer, W. F. (1997). The transtheoretical model of health behavior change. *American Journal of Health Promotion* 12, 38–48. doi: 10.4278/0890-1171-12.1.38

Reimann, J. O., Rodriguez-Reimann, D. I., Ghulan, M., & Beylouni, M. F. (2007). Project Salaam: Assessing mental health needs among San Diego's Greater Middle Eastern and East African communities. *Ethnicity and Disease* 17(S3), 39–41.

Rosenstock, I. (1974). Historical origins of the health belief model. *Health Education Behavior* 2, 328–335. doi: 10.1177/109019817400200403

Rousseau, C., Hassan, G., Moreau, N., & Thombs, B. D. (2011). Perceived discrimination and its association with psychological distress among newly arrived immigrants before and after September 11, 2001. *American Journal of Public Health* 101, 909–915. doi: 10.2105/AJPH.2009.173062

Salti, I. S. (2010). Fasting the month of Ramadan in diabetic patients in the Muslim countries. *ACCESS Health,* 1, April, 23–24.

Sarsour, L., Tong, V.S., Jaber, O., Talbi, M., & Julliard, K. (2010). Health assessment of the Arab American community in Southwest Brooklyn. *Journal of Community Health* 35, 653–659. doi: 10.1007/s10900-010-9260-7

Schwartz, K., Fakhouri, M., Bartoces, M., Monsur, J., & Younis, A. (2008). Mammography screening among Arab American women in metropolitan Detroit. *Journal of Immigrant and Minority Health* 10, 541–549. doi: 10.1007/s10903-008-9140-8

Shah, S. M., Ayash, C., Pharaon, N. A., & Gany, F. M. (2008). Arab American immigrants in New York: Health care and cancer knowledge, attitudes, and beliefs. *Journal of Immigrant and Minority Health* 10, 429–436. doi: 10.1007/s10903-007-9106-2

Soskolne, V., Marie, S., & Manor, O. (2007). Beliefs, recommendations and intentions are important explanatory factors of mammography screening behavior among Muslim Arab women in Israel. *Health Education Research* 22, 665–676. doi: 10.1093/her/cyl132

Taylor, E. M., Yanni, E. A., Pezzi, C., Guterbock, M., Rothney, E., Harton, E., ... Burke, H. (2014). Physical and mental health status of Iraqi refugees resettled in the United States. *Journal of Immigrant Minority Health* 16, 1130–1137. doi: 10.1007/s10903-013-9893-6

Torres, R. E. (1998). The pervading role of language on health. *Journal of Health Care for the Poor and Underserved* 9, S21–S25. doi: 10.1353/hpu.2010.0716

Yosef, A. R. O. (2008). Health beliefs, practice, and priorities for health care of Arab Muslims in the United States: Implications for nursing care. *Journal of Transcultural Nursing* 19, 284–291. doi: 10.1177/1043659608317450

Youssef, J. & Deane, F. (2006). Factors influencing mental health help-seeking in Arabic-speaking communities in Sydney, Australia. *Mental Health, Religion, & Culture* 9, 43–66. doi: 10.1080/13674670512331335686

25
COMMUNITY-BASED PROGRAMS
Ethnic-Specific Approaches to Optimizing Wellness

Nadia S. Ansary and Raja Salloum

Arabs have been identified as an underrepresented population when considering utilization of traditional mental health treatment and social services in the West (Al-Krenawi, 2002; Youssef & Deane, 2006). Underutilization of such services in this population can be explained by a confluence of factors, including culturally entrenched stigma associated with mental illness, as well as immigration- and acculturation-related factors, to name a few (Erickson & Al-Timimi 2001; Nassar-McMillan & Hakim-Larson, 2003). Though these barriers to service utilization are well documented in the literature, there is a paucity of existing literature examining what factors do in fact promote service utilization for this group. In light of these issues, there is a growing need not only to understand the service barriers more clearly, but also, more importantly, to examine the alternative of ethnic-specific community-based programs. A review of existing community-based programs can give an insight into the services they provide and, potentially, the ways in which they have overcome the traditional service challenges to deliver culturally competent mental health and social services to Arab Americans.

This chapter discusses considerations for community-based programs targeting Arab Americans. First, an ecological model useful to understanding community programs is presented. The chapter next examines why traditional mainstream programs addressing the mental health and social service needs of Arab Americans have often failed. A case is made that, as for other immigrant groups, ethnic-specific community-based programming can be an effective option for addressing these outcomes. Insights are then gleaned from existing successful ethnic-specific community-based programs regarding key characteristics they share, including community input in program development, clear and holistic program philosophy, efforts toward adaptability and sustainability, and program evaluation. An overview is provided of community-based programs specifically designed to address the mental health and social service needs of the Arab American community. The chapter ends with a discussion of future directions and limitations of the existing literature concerning community-based prevention and intervention programs for Arab Americans.

Theoretical Framework for Culturally Sensitive Community-Based Programming

Social ecological theory, which places an emphasis on the dynamic role of social relationships functioning in various contexts, has been identified as a useful theory to ground community-based health promotion efforts (Stokols, 1996). A related but more comprehensive theory is Bronfenbrenner's bioecological model of human development (Bronfenbrenner & Morris, 2006), which emphasizes the transactional nature of gene-environment interactions that shape an individual's development. This theory also provides a more detailed emphasis of the dynamic interplay of the social contexts experienced in one's life (Bronfenbrenner & Morris, 2006). For instance, microsystem-level (e.g. school, family, and peers), mesosystem-level (e.g. interface between these proximal contexts such as family-school interactions), and exosystem-level (e.g. family location and neighborhood) influences are all levels that affect individuals, as well as their perceptions of mental health and treatment utilization. Importantly, though considered more distal, macrosystemic level factors, such as cultural influences (e.g. discrimination), are also important considerations in community-based models addressing mental health and social service needs.

Given the emphasis on the varied ecological contexts in which an individual is embedded, as well as the recognition of the interdependence of these contexts, the bioecological model has been extremely useful in explaining various aspects of community psychology. As such, there is a precedent in the literature for extension of this model from a strictly human development perspective to its application to inform community-based interventions (Kloos, Hill, Thomas, Wandersman, Elias, 2011; Trickett & Rowe, 2012). For example, the theory has been used to inform community outreach efforts concerning mental health and improving culturally competent service delivery to the Muslim American community (Ansary & Salloum, 2012).

Arab American Perceptions of Traditional Mental Health Services

Prior to delving into an evaluation of the literature on community-based programming addressing the mental health and social service needs of Arab Americans, it is first critical to provide a foundational understanding of the prevailing cultural views of mental health and treatment within this community. At the outset, it is also important to point out that not all Arab Americans share the same beliefs and practices when considering mental illness and treatment. Each individual possesses his or her unique amalgam of cultural and religious views (much like the distinctiveness of a fingerprint), which can influence the utilization of services. Accordingly, while there is a high degree of heterogeneity within the Arab American community on the one hand, on the other hand there are likely to be some salient cultural perceptions that are shared among many when mental illness and treatment are considered.

Due to the stigma associated with mental illness in the Arab culture, as well as concerns over shaming one's family if mental health services are sought, Arab Americans suffering from mental illness may commonly experience tensions related to treatment seeking (Aloud & Rathur, 2009). Furthermore, like many other immigrant groups, mainstream mental health services have typically failed to adequately address the unique needs of Arab Americans in the therapeutic context. In the following sections, perceptions of mental illness typically held by Arab Americans are examined, and the failure of mainstream mental health services to adequately address the mental health needs of this group is also explored.

Views of Mental Health Service Utilization

Shared by many Muslim and Christian Arabs is the notion that weak faith is a causal factor when considering mental illness, and consequently psychopathology may be attributed to supernatural forces or possession by an evil spirit (Youssef & Deane, 2006). As such, both Christian and Muslim Arab Americans may call on their religious leaders for assistance with mental health issues (Abu-Ras, Gheith, & Cournos, 2008; Nassar-McMillan & Hakim-Larson, 2003), as opposed to seeking out mainstream mental health services. Furthermore, due to the association between mental illness and religion, as well as concerns over family honor, many people from Arab cultures may restrain the expression of emotions and, similarly, withhold discussion of mental health issues (Al-Krenawi & Graham, 2000). Seeking and accessing mental health services is thus often perceived as an act that would bring shame to oneself and family for Arab Americans (Abu-Ras & Abu-Bader, 2008; Abu-Ras et al., 2008). Similarly, in an Australian sample of Arabs, shame and stigma were identified as the primary barriers to utilization of mental health services, reported by 97% of participants (Youssef & Deane, 2006).

Failure of Mainstream Programs to Effectively Address Community Needs

Without doubt, religious and cultural beliefs informing Arab Americans' views of mental health and social service utilization are significant factors underlying failure of mainstream services to adequately address the needs of this group. However, this is not unique to Arab Americans, since a considerable body of literature supports the fact that traditional services have poorly addressed the mental health needs of ethnic minorities in general, as is evidenced by inferior service utilization and retention, as well as poorer outcomes (Fernando, 2005; Griner & Smith, 2006; Sue, Cheng, Saad, & Chu, 2012). In all likelihood, this is because mainstream mental health and social service programs typically fail to recognize that "the experience of individuals is embedded in, and inextricably tied to, the historical, political, geographic, and social experiences of their broader communities" (Abe, 2012, p. 177). As Bronfenbrenner's theoretical framework suggests, mental health outcomes of individuals must necessarily be affected by the various contexts experienced by the individual.

The absence of a culturally relevant framework in mainstream service programs can be inferred from previous medical and behavioral health research on Arab Americans, which has documented barriers to service utilization. These barriers can be classified into six main categories:

1. limited time spent in the host country concomitant with acculturation-related stressors (Abu-Ras, 2007; Haboush, 2007; Nassar-McMillan & Hakim-Larson, 2003; Shah, Ayash, Pharaon, & Gany, 2008);
2. religious and cultural views perpetuating stigma concerning mental illness (Al-Krenawi & Graham, 2000; Erickson & Al-Timimi, 2001; Haboush, 2007);
3. anxiety over confidentiality (Abu-Ras, 2007; Nassar-McMillan & Hakim-Larson, 2003; Shah et al., 2008);
4. prior experience with service providers who lack cultural competency (Erickson & Al-Timimi, 2001; Haboush, 2007);
5. concern about discrimination and racism by providers (Abu-Ras, 2007; Erickson & Al-Timimi, 2001); and
6. lack of knowledge about available services (Abu-Ras, 2007; Aloud & Rathur, 2009).

Accordingly, it is no surprise that Aloud and Rathur (2009) found that Arab Americans typically rely on and potentially drain informal resources (e.g. family, friends, etc.) before seeking out more formal forms of treatment. It is important to note that these identified barriers to accessing services are not unique to Arab Americans, but have also been recognized among others, including Blacks and other ethnic minority groups in England (Fernando, 2005; Malik, Fateh, & Haque, 2009), as well as Asian communities in the U.S. (Fang & Chen, 2003), Canada (Lo & Chung, 2005), and England (Au & Tang, 2009). In light of this collective evidence pertaining to Arab Americans as well as other ethnic minority groups, it can be argued that community-based programs could better meet the needs of ethnic minority groups when they are specifically tailored to the ethnic culture. The sections that follow examine the evidence pertaining to the effectiveness of ethnic-specific community programs in addressing the mental health needs of these groups.

Ethnic-Specific Community-Based Programming

When exploring the usefulness of community-based prevention and intervention programs as a way to offer needed mental health and social service care, it is useful first to consider the question of whether these community initiatives should be developed specifically to target individual ethnic groups. Mixed evidence exists about the effectiveness of ethnic-specific approaches – those that provide services matching the clients' language as well as cultural beliefs and practices – as compared to traditional or mainstream mental health services. In support of ethnic-specific programming are findings suggesting that minorities are more likely to seek and utilize interventions that are consistent with their cultural beliefs and practices (Griner & Smith, 2006; Yeh, Takeuchi, & Sue, 1994). Furthermore, clients matched with their psychotherapists or counselors on language and ethnicity have been found to remain in therapy longer (Griner & Smith, 2006; Kumpfer, Alvarado, Smith, & Bellamy, 2002; Reese & Vera, 2007), although there is some evidence suggesting, to the contrary, that ethnic matching may not be associated with longer treatment length (Yeh et al., 1994). In terms of positive treatment outcomes, some evidence clearly favors ethnic-specific programs (Yeh et al., 1994; Lau & Zane, 2000), while other evidence suggests no difference when compared to mainstream services (Kumpfer et al., 2002; Zane, Hatanaka, Park, & Akutsu, 1994).

Perhaps the most compelling evidence in support of ethnic-specific mental health interventions is meta-analytic findings that demonstrate a moderate effect size for culturally adapted interventions (Griner & Smith, 2006). These findings suggest the following pattern of treatment outcomes vis-à-vis group ethnicity: Clients involved in a same-ethnic-group intervention report significantly higher positive outcomes than those in mixed-ethnic-group interventions, which, in turn, score significantly better on the same outcomes than minorities engaged in traditional services (Griner & Smith, 2006). These results concur with another meta-analysis (Smith, Rodríguez, & Bernal, 2011), as well as with the most comprehensive review to date (Huey, Tilley, Jones, & Smith, 2014), both of which document the broad benefits of culturally adapted interventions addressing mental health issues. Still, Huey and colleagues (2014) resolve that though there is support for the use of culturally-adapted interventions, inconsistent evidence exists regarding whether such interventions actually contribute to enhanced treatment effects.

In spite of the contradictions in the literature concerning the effectiveness of ethnic-specific mental health interventions, in the real world there exist many examples of successful, longstanding community-based programs that have met the mental health and social service needs of unique ethnic groups. Though such programs may not have published evidence substantiating their effectiveness, their ability to withstand the test of time is a testimony to their success. While the field awaits progress in the empirical evaluation of such programs, there is a good deal of practical evidence pointing to the benefits of such ethnic-specific community-based programming addressing mental health and social service utilization.

Insights From Existing Successful Ethnic-Specific Programs

This section examines common programmatic features of ethnic-specific community-based approaches to mental health treatment documented in the literature. Given the dearth of publications on programs for Arab Americans, literature pertaining to programs that specifically address the mental health needs of Asians living in the West are incorporated. The parallel between Arab and Asian communities in the U.S. is warranted given some similarities in cultural values that may influence mental health services, including: (a) collectivist culture, (b) patriarchal family, (c) emphasis on family honor, (d) perception that mental illness is shameful to the family, and (e) fear of sharing personal information (Durvasula & Mylvaganam, 1994; Yeh et al., 1994; Zane et al., 1994). It is important to note, however, that although Asian Americans were chosen as a comparison group, other ethnic groups may also share the aforementioned characteristics.

A search of the literature revealed very few publications that describe ethnic-specific programs addressing the mental health and social service needs of these two communities. This reflects a significant gap in the literature addressing community-based approaches to mental health and social service utilization for ethnic minorities (Griner & Smith, 2006; Reese & Vera, 2007). Of the publications that do address ethnic-specific community-based mental health programs, almost none provide empirical evidence documenting program effectiveness, including relevant outcomes such as reduced severity of mental illness and improved client functionality. Moreover, these publications also fail to identify or present data on what strategies were associated with improved outcomes (e.g. effectiveness of different types of intervention techniques).

Five ethnic-specific programs addressing mental health and social service needs of Arabs or Asians that were found in the literature, one for Arab Americans and four for Asians in North America or the U.K., are reviewed below to identify components of potentially effective programs. The one program targeting Arab Americans that was described in the literature is that run by the Arab Community Center for Economic and Social Services (ACCESS), which is considered by many as the forerunner of programs providing assistance with social service and mental health needs to the Arab American population. This program began as a grassroots effort in 1971 in Dearborn, Michigan, with the mission of assisting Arab immigrants to overcome the linguistic, cultural, and social barriers associated with acculturation (Aswad & Gray, 1996). Impressively, and as will be discussed later, to date ACCESS provides myriad services such as mental healthcare, psychoeducational workshops, assistance with employment services, and cultural sensitivity training for non-Arab professionals. It also publishes an online journal (ACCESS, n.d.; Dubaybo & Hammad, 2013).

With regard to programs designed to render services specifically to Asian communities in the West, four community-based programs were found documented in the literature. In the U.S., The Bridge Program was established in 1998 to address the mental health needs of the Chinese community residing in New York City (Fang & Chen, 2003). Similarly, The Hong Fook Mental Health Association, a community-based mental health program targeting Asians, was established in Toronto, Canada, in 1982 (Lo & Chung, 2005). Two programs exist in the literature that address the needs of Asians residing in the U.K.; namely, the Chinese Mental Health Association, whose doors opened in 1992 (Au & Tang, 2009), and the Marlborough Cultural Therapy Centre (Malik et al., 2009), which was established in 1996 to more broadly address the mental health needs of Black and minority ethnic groups (including a large Asian and Arab contingency).

Common features of the programs – gleaned from a review of the publications pertaining to each of them – were identified. Each has systematically addressed the following components in their program design and implementation, including: (1) at inception, community collaboration in program development (i.e. adoption of a community-based framework for shaping program design); (2) a clear program philosophy that adopts a holistic view of the individual, family, and community; (3) a process for addressing sustainability and flexibility of services; and (4) evaluation of program effectiveness. Accordingly, each of these core features is discussed below, and examples from the five programs are used to exemplify how the programs have implemented strategies derived from these essential elements.

Community Collaboration in Program Development

In their review of culturally adapted interventions addressing the mental health and social service needs of minority communities, Reese and Vera (2007) identify several critical steps that should be made at the inception of any program, most of which are derived from the central role of the community. First, a fundamental step is to develop a positive working relationship – including collaborations and partnerships – with the broader community. This promotes a shared community vision, builds social capital, and ensures that the community will be involved in all phases of program development.

Second, a community-based needs assessment is a critical step in the initial phases of program design and development. This can ensure that the program is tailored to the unique characteristics of the local community (e.g. immigration, socioeconomic status, etc.) and is sensitive to the existing mainstream service structures already in place. The importance of a community-based needs assessment was documented as an essential first step in the development of the Chinese Mental

Health Association (Au & Tang, 2009) as well as The Hong Fook Mental Health Association (Lo & Chung, 2005).

Third, and in parallel, program developers should also be familiar with the history of prior unsuccessful programs or initiatives in that community. Last, it is also imperative that community-based program development account for the complex sociopolitical factors that affect clients, staff, and community outcomes. This was noted as a critical factor for the Marlborough Cultural Therapy Centre (Malik et al., 2009). Across all publications pertaining to the five programs selected for review, each underscores the importance of community involvement throughout all phases of program development and implementation.

Clear Program Philosophy

A program's philosophy must represent a coordinated set of values that fully inform service delivery. Though tempting in the face of financial adversity, it is important that community-based programs do not sway too far to the whims of grant-funding opportunities that deviate from the core values set forth at the inception of the program (Lo & Chung, 2005). A fine example of such a coordinated program philosophy informing services offered is The Hong Fook Mental Health Association (Lo & Chung, 2005), which uses six core values underpinning program content: (1) social justice with regard to access to mental health, (2) importance of the community, (3) collaboration with key stakeholders, (4) educating mainstream professionals, (5) health promotion, and (6) a focus on client and family needs. Consistent with Bronfenbrenner's model, this longstanding program recognizes the dynamic interplay of the individual nested within families, communities, and cultures.

Likewise, the philosophical approach of ACCESS is consistent with both the ecological model and the core values identified by Lo & Chung (2005). To illustrate, Kira, Hammad, and Abou-Mediene (2007) state regarding the model employed by ACCESS: "integrated care is a new paradigm shift in how we view health and provide care; it changes the way we conduct research, develop programs and provide education and training to health and mental healthcare professionals" (p. 66). This foundational premise most certainly informs the types and delivery of services unique to the Arab American community, and also ensures a holistic view of the individual.

Holistic services approach. Consistent across many community-based programs addressing the mental health and social service needs of ethnic minority communities is a holistic orientation that emphasizes health and wellness. This often includes an integration of mental health with primary care services, as has been done in The Bridge Program (Fang & Chen, 2003), though many programs such as The Hong Fook Mental Health Association (Lo & Chung, 2005) and the Marlborough Cultural Therapy Centre (Malik et al., 2009) focus more on integration of mental health with the practical and social issues faced by the individual and family. Particular examples of services from these programs include efforts to share information such as raising awareness and destigmatizing mental health issues via the use of multimedia campaigns (Au & Tang, 2009; Fang & Chen, 2003), hosting conferences (Lo & Chung, 2005); and conducting psychoeducational workshops addressing parenting or stress reduction (Fang & Chen, 2003). There are also recreational and social support initiatives (Lo & Chung, 2005) such as a "befriending project" and social group development for at-risk individuals (Au & Tang, 2009, p.193). Some programs also offer cultural competency training for mainstream providers and students (Fang & Chen, 2003; Lo & Chung, 2005).

Similarly, a diverse range of services is also provided by ACCESS, such that Arab American clients can go to one central location for physical and mental health needs as well as for assistance with fiscal and social service amenities (Kira et al., 2007). The program spans 7 locations that house over 90 subprograms. Like the Asian-specific programs noted above, some examples of services offered by ACCESS include job training and employment assistance, social services, and youth education, as well as a community health and research center (ACCESS, n.d.).

Evidence-based approach. An evidence-based approach, which undergirds and ultimately informs current and new program content and service delivery, is an important feature of community-based programs. For this reason, an evidence-based approach is considered an important programmatic feature that should be considered at the program philosophy level. An example of an evidence-based approach has already been noted in terms of a community-based needs assessment in the prior section, and is discussed later in terms of evaluating program effectiveness.

Recognizing the relevance of an evidence-based approach in terms of informing a clear program philosophy is critical to the success of ethnic-specific community-based mental health programs. Generally speaking, "for each intervention that works, researchers need to know as much as possible about the range of youth, family, and community characteristics within which benefits accrue and outside of which benefits diminish" (Weisz, Sandler, Durlak, & Anton, 2005, p. 640). Though the empirical evidence is scarce about "what works" with regard to ethnic-specific programs addressing mental health outcomes, and many programs may use empirical evidence to inform program content and delivery, in the scholarly literature very few programs clearly state doing so. One exception with respect to the Asian-specific programs reviewed is the Chinese Mental Health Association, which explicitly notes using evidence from clients to develop and refine existing programs (Au & Tang, 2009). To illustrate, in that program, data were collected that identified emerging issues within the community – namely, marital difficulties and gambling. These findings were then utilized to craft new initiatives and services to tackle those issues community-wide.

Similarly, ACCESS documents their evidence-based approach to the provision of mental health and social services. Through the ACCESS Community Health and Research Center, regular publications and annual conferences are held detailing data gathered from the Arab American population, and these investigations regularly inform ACCESS's program content and service delivery. The topics investigated are diverse, including evidence garnered regarding mental health screening tools (Kira et al., 2007), prevalence and correlates of domestic violence (ACCESS Community Health & Research Center, n.d.), and tobacco and hookah use (Shafey & Elimam, 2010).

Recognition of the benefits and drawbacks of a community emphasis. As noted earlier, sustained community involvement is a critical facet of ethnic-specific community-based mental health and social service programs. This is reflected in the careful selection of program volunteers and board members that best represent the community of interest (Lo & Chung, 2005). Illustrative of the importance of community collaborations, the five ethnic-specific mental health community-based programs reviewed here emphasize the centrality of community partnerships.

Though there are many benefits to community involvement and collaboration, it is important to note unique challenges that may be faced in the ethnic-specific programming context. For instance, matching on ethnicity can be a double-edged sword, since oftentimes clients and staff share the same community. As documented by Malik and colleagues (2009), clients at the Marlborough Cultural Therapy Centre expressed concerns over their private mental health issues being leaked to community members. In order to allay client concerns, it is important that programs stress to clients that mental health professionals and staff members are ethically bound not to reveal confidential information (Malik et al., 2009). Another noteworthy challenge is that because program staff may oppose long-held cultural views about mental illness and treatment (e.g. mental illness stigma, indigenous healing methods, etc.), these mental health professionals may not be readily accepted by their community (Malik et al., 2009).

Sustainability and Flexibility of Services

While there are myriad operational issues to consider, the two areas that were most discussed in publications pertaining to the ethnic-specific community-based mental health programs highlighted here were funding and sustainability, and flexibility in the services offered. The literature related to these programs suggests that funding and a lack of resources is a formidable challenge facing such programs.

Accordingly, how community-based organizations navigate these issues necessarily shapes multiple aspects of the daily activity of the program from staffing, services provided, and ultimately, sustainability.

Funding and sustainability. Nearly all of the publications related to community-based programs addressing the mental health needs of minority ethnic groups note obstacles presented by limited funding, and consequently the sustainability of such programs. All too often many culturally adapted programs or initiatives within larger programs "suffer from 'short-termism' because they are project-based and often disappear as funding periods come to an end" (Malik et al., 2009, p. 176). Securing start-up funds, as well as operating with limited resources and staffing, means that a sustained financial commitment from that ethnic group is necessary for program survival. Funding-related challenges are documented for ACCESS (Aswad & Gray, 1996), The Bridge Program (Fang & Chen, 2003), and The Hong Fook Mental Health Association (Lo & Chung, 2005), as well as for the Chinese Mental Health Association (Au & Tang, 2009). Some discussed specific strategies for economic survival, such as how program content may be shaped by funding opportunities (Lo & Chung, 2005), as well as how funding should be secured for salaries for a core group of management professionals in order to ensure sustainability of the program (Au & Tang, 2009).

Adaptability of services. Just as long-term program sustainability is critical, so too is the ability of a program to render services in a flexible manner that matures to accommodate the evolving needs of the community it serves. The need for adaptability in the types of available service, as well as service delivery methods, is especially relevant to successful ethnic-specific community-based programming (Reese & Vera, 2007). In the five programs reviewed, each demonstrated that flexibility and adaptability in the types and delivery of services is fundamental. This also means that the definitions of what constitutes mental illness and what elements comprise wellbeing must also be malleable and ultimately framed by the client (Fernando, 2005). Adaptable services may take the shape of interventions in peoples' homes or in community settings (Malik et al., 2009). Alternatively, they may take on the form of the use of creative phrases in media campaigns, such as substituting the use of loaded terms such as "anxiety" with more acceptable phrases like "stress" (Fang & Chen, 2003).

Adaptability is also seen within an organization's ability to address emerging community needs. For example, Lo & Chung (2005) discuss the importance of creating services and hiring staff to address an influx of Vietnamese refugees seeking asylum in their community. Likewise, in response to community needs, ACCESS developed the Center for Psychosocial Rehabilitation of Torture Survivors (Farrag, Abdulkhaleq, Abdelkarim, Souidan, & Safo, 2007) to provide wraparound services for afflicted individuals. Thus, there are myriad facets of the community that can be in flux, and this necessitates that ethnic-specific community-based programs continuously monitor the mental health and social service needs of the current population they serve.

Evaluation of Program Effectiveness

Assessment of program effectiveness should extend beyond simply documenting service needs to implementing a comprehensive evaluation of the outcomes of services once delivered. There is a paucity of evidence documenting the effectiveness of ethnic-specific community-based programs addressing mental health treatment (Reese & Vera, 2007; Huey et al., 2014). As noted earlier, while many longstanding ethnic-specific community-based programs exist, very few have produced published empirical evidence of program effectiveness. In fact, none of the Asian-specific programs reviewed provide concrete outcome data. For example, success ofThe Bridge Program can be inferred from the continual increase in the number of intakes across the years, a rise in rates of successful referrals to off-site services, as well as positive client ratings (Chen, Kramer, & Chen, 2003). However, data on how well the mental healthcare services met their intended aims are not presented in any publication pertaining to the program. The Hong Fook Mental Health Association also documents a steady rise in intakes, as well as the expansion of services, as indicators of effectiveness (Lo & Chung, 2005); again, no data on service outcomes are presented.

On the other hand, the importance of empirical program evaluation, as well as of research on community-wide health issues, has been recognized by ACCESS. For instance, as noted earlier, the ACCESS Community Health and Research Center developed a program that provides wraparound services to Arab torture survivors. Using a pretest-posttest evaluation of that program, Farrag and colleagues (2007) found significant decreases in anxiety, depression, and posttraumatic stress disorder (PTSD) among participants. While this evidence is an important first step in establishing the effectiveness of that intervention, it is unclear which specific services were accessed by each of the 38 participants, which services rendered were associated with the greatest treatment effects, and whether any moderating factors (e.g. gender, acculturation levels) existed.

Case Examples: A Sampling of Existing Arab American Community-Based Programs

Though ACCESS is perhaps one of the most well known, there are many other Arab-specific community-based programs that provide mental health and social services in the U.S. Fortunately, from a practical perspective, these are generally distributed throughout the U.S. and can serve the diverse population of Arab Americans living in various states. Unfortunately, from a scholarly perspective, these programs have not received attention in the published literature and thus there are no data establishing what approaches are used in their services and how effective these are. The dearth of data should be interpreted as clear gaps in the research literature and should not be interpreted as indicating some defect in these programs, as they have provided and continue to provide extremely valuable services to their communities.

From the many Arab-specific programs addressing the mental health and social service needs of this community, 10 organizations were selected from across the U.S. to be highlighted here. The programs presented were identified based on consultation with colleagues in the field, in conjunction with an extensive Internet search. While there were far more than 10 organizations found, longstanding programs with the most informative websites were chosen for inclusion here. Information was gathered from their websites regarding the program features discussed earlier, namely: (1) community collaboration in program development, (2) a clear program philosophy, (3) sustainability and flexibility of services, and (4) evaluation of program effectiveness. Because none of the websites provided sufficient information on the last two issues (i.e. sustainability and flexibility of services, as well as program effectiveness) and there were no additional publications found regarding these programs, only the first two program elements are examined.

Table 25.1 presents a listing of the 10 organizations selected. They all have missions to support and provide comprehensive services addressing the needs of the Arab American community. In terms of involvement of the community in program development, all programs noted on their websites some degree of direct involvement of respected and influential members of their local Arab American community. Moreover, each of the organizations advertises its services through the use of media typically accessed by members of this community (e.g. Arabic television, newspapers, etc.). Perusal of the websites of these organizations demonstrates that organization board members are active and visible participants in media outlets in the community, as many appear on local radio shows, are featured in local and regional newspapers, and frequently put forth press releases.

In terms of program philosophy and operational issues for consideration, there are some commonalities shared across these programs. Consistent with the ethnic-specific programs reviewed above, as well as with the ecological framework, each of the programs espouses a holistic view of the individual. Most importantly, this is reflected in the diversity of services offered by the programs, ranging from crisis intervention and emergency services (e.g. shelter, assistance obtaining food) to psychoeducational workshops, as well as cultural sensitivity training offered to non-Arab professionals in the

Table 25.1 A Sample of Community-Based Programs Addressing Mental Health and Social Service Needs of Arab Americans

Name	*Est.*	*Location*	*Mission*
Arab Cultural and Community Center (ACCC)	1973	2 Plaza Street San Francisco, CA 94116 www.arabculturalcenter.org	"The Arab Cultural and Community Center of San Francisco is a nonprofit organization devoted to promoting Arab art and culture, and enriching the lives of the Arab American Community. [The ACCC] achieve[s] this by providing culturally focused social services, and promoting cross-cultural events to all residents of the Bay Area and beyond."
Arab American and Chaldean Council (ACC)	1979	28551 Southfield Road Lathrup Village, MI 48076 www.myacc.org	"ACC is the premier non-profit human service organization providing services to the Middle Eastern and mainstream communities in Southeast Michigan. As a bridge of understanding, ACC maximizes the skills, resources and expertise of the community to: Build cooperation and understanding; Raise the level of individuals' wellbeing; Increase cross-cultural understanding through education; Deliver human services, counseling and opportunities; Gear community members toward achievement; Empower through employment training and placement."
Arab American Community Center (AACC) of Florida	1990	4300 LB McLeod, Suite B Orlando, FL 32811 www.aaccflorida.org	"The AACC's main platform is to empower the community by providing services in health, employment, immigration, social services, cultural and political awareness, and charitable giving. The AACC has a special emphasis on programs directed at youth, women, and the business community. Our ultimate goal is to become a fully staffed professional organization dedicated to the growth of our community throughout the state."
Arab-American Family Support Center (AAFSC)	1994	150 Court Street, 3rd Floor Brooklyn, NY 11201 www.aafscny.org	"The Arab-American Family Support Center is a non-profit organization that empowers new immigrants with the tools they need to successfully acclimate to the world around them and become active participants in their communities."
Arab-American Cultural and Community Center (ACC)	1995	10555 Stancliff Road Houston, TX 77099 www.acchouston.org	"Since its inception in 1995, the ACC has been committed to fulfilling its mission of serving the Arab American community in Houston regardless of religion, nationality, ethnicity, gender or financial status. [The ACC's] goal is to serve the community through cultural programs, outreach and social services; promote Arab culture and heritage and foster a greater understanding of Arab culture amongst the Houston community at large by serving as a liaison and resource center."

Table 25.1 (cont.)

Name	*Est.*	*Location*	*Mission*
Arab American Action Network (AAAN)	1995	3148 West 63rd Street Chicago, IL 60629 www.aaan.org	"The Arab American Action Network (AAAN) strives to strengthen the Arab community in the Chicago area by building its capacity to be an active agent for positive social change. As a grassroots nonprofit, our strategies include community organizing, advocacy, education, providing social services, leadership development, cultural outreach and forging productive relationships with other communities."
Arab-American Community Development Corporation (AACDC)	1997	1501 Germantown Avenue Philadelphia, PA 19122 www.arabamericancdc.org	"The organization's mission is to empower the Arab-American community in the Philadelphia metropolitan area, promote its economic development, and combat racial, ethnic, and religious discrimination. The AACDC works to serve the complex needs of the estimated 30,000 to 50,000 Arab-Americans living in the five-county area (please refer to US Census 2010 results). The AACDC works closely with various organizations in Philadelphia to aid Arab-Americans with immigration issues, healthcare, English as a second language, citizenship learning and more."
Arab American Family Services (AAFS)	2001	9044 S. Octavia Avenue Bridgeview, IL 60455 www.aafsil.org	"AAFS is committed to empowering, educating, and supporting individuals, families, and organizations to foster and enhance economic wellbeing of Arab Americans. AAFS' mission is to change and impact the quality of life by serving and building stronger and healthier generations of Arab Americans in our communities."
Arab American Association of New York (AAANY)	2001	7111 5th Avenue, Brooklyn, NY 11209 www.arabamericanny.org	The Arab American Association of New York's mission is to "support and empower the Arab Immigrant and Arab American community by providing services to help them adjust to their new home and become active members of society. [AAANY's] aim is for families to achieve the ultimate goals of independence, productivity, and stability."
Wafa House	2004	New Jersey 1-800-930-WAFA (9232) www.wafahouse.org	"Wafa House Inc's objective is to maintain a facility that will strengthen and reinforce the family unit while emphasizing the value of human life through intervention and community awareness. The agency is dedicated to educating and empowering each member of the family, consequently cultivating a prosperous and healthy community."

community (e.g. law enforcement, educators, counselors) who wish to learn more about this group's cultural beliefs and practices. Despite differences between each of the organizations in terms of years in operation, size, location, and characteristics of the communities they serve, there is consistency in the services offered. This clearly speaks to the types of services sought by Arab Americans living in diverse communities across the U.S. Moreover, it is also a direct reflection of the need to provide integrated services under one roof.

As can be seen in Table 25.1, these case examples have in common one central objective: to support the Arab American individual, family, and community. All organizations appear to provide a wide menu of services that are quite similar to those found in ACCESS and the Asian-specific mental health programs reviewed earlier. In parallel, the programs highlighted in this section appear to provide services that are consistent with the theoretical framework discussed at the outset: targeting the various levels of Bronfenbrenner's model (e.g. microsystem, exosystem, etc.). Though there may be unique programmatic content, the programs highlighted in this section mirror in many ways, but on a smaller scale, the theoretical approaches and practical operations of ACCESS and the Asian-specific programs discussed earlier.

Critique

While tremendous progress has been made in the realm of community-based prevention and intervention programs addressing the mental health and social service needs of Arab Americans, there are still many strides to be made. There is scant empirical evidence at the intersection of mental health and community-based prevention and intervention programming that specifically addresses the challenges faced by Arab Americans. What evidence does exist is severely limited in utility, since extant studies consist mainly of findings related to qualitative data collected from small samples and the literature on outreach efforts has been drawn primarily from the fields of nursing and sociology, not psychology. Furthermore, though the literature is growing, the massive gap in the field with regard to ethnic-specific programming is very limiting. Importantly, this dearth of literature is not specific to Arab Americans alone, but is indicative of a much broader gap in the field concerning ethnic minorities in general (Griner & Smith, 2006; Reese & Vera, 2007).

The scholarly debate about the efficacy of culturally adapted interventions and, more specifically, ethnic-specific programming versus mainstream programming, has yet to fully resolve in the empirical literature. Sizable gaps in the literature remain regarding exactly what factors moderate the effects of treatment outcomes vis-à-vis cultural adaptations and ethnic-specific programming and, more specifically, what mechanisms underlie these associations. Clearly, the scarcity of outcome data documenting the overall effectiveness of such programs and, more specifically, which strategies work and which do not – as well as for *whom* these work – is a major omission in this literature.

While the paucity of literature examining community-based prevention and intervention programs addressing the mental health needs of Arab Americans is a serious impediment to progress, another related challenge is the scarcity of empirical evidence evaluating ethnic-specific risk and protective factors, which should inform prevention and intervention efforts (Sameroff, 2006). Risk factors (i.e. exogenous influences that exacerbate vulnerability to psychopathology and increase the likelihood of disorder onset) and protective factors (i.e. factors that buffer against psychopathology) can emerge from or be acutely influenced by culture. For instance, in terms of risk factors, some evidence has begun to emerge examining the influence of discrimination and acculturative stress on higher levels of anxiety and depression among Arab American adults (Amer & Hovey, 2007, 2012) and youth (Ahmed, Kia-Keating, & Tsai, 2011). Likewise, with respect to protective factors and depression, evidence has begun to mount in terms of the protective role of religiosity among Arab American adults (Amer & Hovey, 2007) as well as youth (Ahmed et al., 2011). This kind of evidence is promising and could inform programs designed to address the mental health and social service utilization for this group.

Another impediment to progress in the field is that – with the exception of work published by ACCESS – there have been no published empirical evaluations of the effectiveness of community-based programs addressing the needs of Arab Americans. Once program effectiveness can be shown, then empirically supported best practices can be identified and implemented in other programs. Unfortunately, the cycle of research informing intervention, and of intervention success or failure then in turn informing research, is still lacking.

Conclusion

Existing community-based prevention and intervention programs addressing the mental health and social service needs of Arab Americans have overcome myriad obstacles to provide valuable services to their community members. It is remarkable that the programs noted in the case examples generally offered a wide range of similar services despite differences in the number of years in operation, location, and characteristics of the Arab Americans served. Also noteworthy is the fact that there is a high degree of commonalty across the five Arab/Asian programs highlighted in this chapter, in that all placed an emphasis on community partnerships, held a clear program philosophy undergirding services offered, attempted to address sustainability and flexibility of services offered, and struggled with program evaluation.

Greater progress in scholarship examining Arab American ethnic-specific community programs would be a critical step toward promoting the growth of existing programs and the development of new ones. Furthermore, Arab American community programs may be more successful if they explicitly attempt to identify and reduce salient risk factors while emphasizing and supporting protective factors in the community. In turn, the evidence that emerges from these suggested directions will inevitably inform best practices to address barriers to service utilization so that programs of this sort may continue to do the good work they do.

References

Abe, J. (2012). A community ecology approach to cultural competence in mental health service delivery: The case of Asian Americans. *Asian American Journal of Psychology* 3(3), 168–180. doi: 10.1037/a0029842

Abu-Ras, W. (2007). Cultural beliefs and service utilization by battered Arab immigrant women. *Violence Against Women* 13, 1002–1028. doi: 10.1177/1077801207306019

Abu-Ras, W. & Abu-Bader, S. H. (2008). The impact of September 11, 2001, attacks on the well-being of Arab Americans in New York City. *Journal of Muslim Mental Health* 3, 217–239. doi: 10.1080/15564900802487634

Abu-Ras, W., Gheith, A., & Cournos, F. (2008). The imam's role in mental health promotion: A study of 22 mosques in New York City's Muslim community. *Journal of Muslim Mental Health* 3, 155–176. doi: 10.1080/15564900802487576

ACCESS Community Health & Research Center. (n.d.). *Domestic violence prevention survey assessment outcomes.* Retrieved from www.accesscommunity.org/sites/default/files/documents/access_dv_survey_assesment-narrative-final.pdf

Ahmed, S. R., Kia-Keating, M., & Tsai, K. H. (2011). A structural model of racial discrimination, acculturative stress, and cultural resources among Arab American adolescents. *American Journal of Community Psychology* 48, 181–192. doi: 10.1007/s10464-011-9424-3

Al-Krenawi, A. (2002). Mental health service utilization among the Arabs in Israel. *Social Work in Health Care* 35(1–2), 577–589. doi: 10.1300/J010v35n01_12

Al-Krenawi, A. & Graham, J. R. (2000). Culturally sensitive social work practice with Arab clients in mental health settings. *Health and Social Work*, 25, 9–22. doi: 10.1093/hsw/25.1.9

Aloud, N. & Rathur, A. (2009). Factors affecting attitudes toward seeking and using formal mental health and psychological services among Arab Muslim populations. *Journal of Muslim Mental Health* 4, 79–103. doi: 10.1080/15564900802487675

Amer, M. M. & Hovey, J. D. (2007). Socio-demographic differences in acculturation and mental health for a sample of 2nd generation/early immigrant Arab Americans. *Journal of Immigrant Minority Health* 9, 335–347. doi: 10.1007/s10903-007-9045-y

Amer, M. M. & Hovey, J. D. (2012). Anxiety and depression in a post-September 11 sample of Arabs in the USA. *Social Psychiatry and Psychiatric Epidemiology* 47, 409–418. doi: 10.1007/s00127-011-0341-4

Ansary, N. S. & Salloum, R. (2012). Community-based prevention and intervention. In S. Ahmed & M. Amer (eds.), *Counseling Muslims: Handbook of mental health issues and interventions* (pp. 161–180). New York: Routledge.

Arab Community Center for Economic and Social Services (ACCESS). (n.d.). About us. Retrieved from www.accesscommunity.org/site/PageServer?pagename=About_Us

Aswad, B. C. & Gray, N. A. (1996). Challenges to the Arab-American family and ACCESS. In B. C. Aswad & B. Bilgé (eds.), *Family and gender among American Muslims: Issues facing Middle Eastern immigrants and their descendants* (pp. 223–240). Philadelphia, PA: Temple University Press.

Au, S. & Tang, R. (2009). Mental health services for Chinese people. In S. Fernando & F. Keating (eds.), *Mental health in a multi-ethnic society: A multidisciplinary handbook* (2nd edn., pp. 187–195). London, UK: Routledge.

Bronfenbrenner, U. & Morris, P. A. (2006). The bioecological model of human development. In R. M. Lerner & W. Damon (eds.), *Handbook of child psychology: Vol. 1. Theoretical models of human development* (6th edn., pp. 793–828). Hoboken, NJ: Wiley.

Chen, H., Kramer, E. J., & Chen, T. (2003). The Bridge Program: A model for reaching Asian Americans. *Psychiatric Services* 54, 1411–1412. doi: 10.1176/appi.ps.54.10.1411-a

Dubaybo, B. A. & Hammad, A. (2013). ACCESS Health Journal: Investigating, educating, and improving health. *ACCESS Health Journal* 2, 1–2.

Durvasula, R. S. & Mylvaganam, G. A. (1994). Mental health of Asian Indians: Relevant issues and community implications. *Journal of Community Psychology* 22, 97–108. doi: 10.1002/1520-6629

Erickson, C. D. & Al-Timimi, N. (2001). Providing mental health services to Arab Americans: Recommendations and considerations. *Cultural Diversity and Ethnic Minority Psychology* 7, 308–327. doi: 10.1037/1099-9809.7.4.308

Fang, L. & Chen, T. (2003). Community outreach and education to deal with cultural resistance to mental health services. In N. B Webb (ed.), *Mass trauma and violence: Helping families and children cope* (pp. 234–255). New York: Guilford.

Farrag, M., Abdulkhaleq, H., Abdelkarim, G., Souidan, R., & Safo, H. (2007). The psychosocial rehabilitation approach in treating torture survivors. *Ethnicity & Disease* 17, 85–87.

Fernando, S. (2005). Multicultural mental health services: Projects for minority ethnic communities in England. *Transcultural Psychiatry* 42, 420–436. doi: 10.1177/1363461505055624

Griner, D. & Smith, T. B. (2006). Culturally adapted mental health interventions: A meta-analytic review. *Psychotherapy: Theory, Research, Practice, Training* 43, 531–548. doi: 10.1037/0033-3204.43.4.531

Haboush, K. L. (2007). Working with Arab American families: Culturally competent practice for school psychologists. *Psychology in the Schools* 44, 183–198. doi: 10.1002/pits.20215

Huey, S. J., Jr, Tilley, J. L., Jones, E. O., & Smith, C. A. (2014). The contribution of cultural competence to evidence-based care for ethnically diverse populations. *The Annual Review of Clinical Psychology* 10, 305–338. doi: 10.1146/annurev-clinpsy-032813-153729

Kira, I., Hammad, A., & Abou-Mediene, S. (2007). Models of health and mental health integration: ACCESS Community Health and Research Center model. *Ethnicity & Disease* 17, 66–69.

Kloos, B., Hill, J., Thomas, E., Wandersman, A., & Elias, M. (2011). *Community psychology: Linking individuals and communities*. New York: Cengage Learning.

Kumpfer, K. L., Alvarado, R., Smith, P., & Bellamy, N. (2002). Cultural sensitivity and adaptation in family-based prevention interventions. *Prevention Science* 3, 241–246. doi: 10.1023/A:1019902902119

Lau, A. & Zane, N. (2000). Examining the effects of ethnic-specific services: An analysis of cost-utilization and treatment outcome for Asian American clients. *Journal of Community Psychology* 28(1), 63–77. doi: 10.1002/(SICI)1520-6629(200001)28:1<63::AID-JCOP7>3.0.CO;2-Z

Lo, H. & Chung, R. C. Y. (2005). The Hong Fook experience: Working with ethnocultural communities in Toronto 1982–2002. *Transcultural Psychiatry* 42, 457–477. doi: 10.1177/1363461505055626

Malik, R., Fateh, R., & Haque, R. (2009). The Marlborough Cultural Therapy Centre. In S. Fernando & F. Keating (eds.), *Mental health in a multi-ethnic society: A multidisciplinary handbook* (2nd edn., pp. 174–186). London, UK: Routledge.

Nassar-McMillan, S. C. & Hakim-Larson, J. (2003). Counseling considerations among Arab Americans. *Journal of Counseling & Development* 81, 150–159. doi: 10.1002/j.1556-6678.2003.tb00236.x

Reese, L. E. & Vera, E. M. (2007). Culturally relevant prevention: The scientific and practical considerations of community-based programs. *The Counseling Psychologist* 35, 763–778. doi: 10.1177/0011000007304588

Sameroff, A. (2006). Identifying risk and protective factors for healthy child development. In A. Clarke-Stewart & J. Dunn (eds.), *Families count: Effects on child and adolescent development* (pp. 53–76). New York: Cambridge University Press.

Shafey, O. & Elimam, D. M. (2010). Tobacco use: Global perspective, Arab world, and Arab Americans. *ACCESS Health*, preliminary issue, April, 37–43.

Shah, S. M., Ayash, C., Pharaon, N. A., & Gany, F. M. (2008). Arab American immigrants in New York: Health care and cancer knowledge, attitudes, and beliefs. *Journal of Immigrant and Minority Health* 10(5), 429–436. doi: 10.1007/s10903-007-9106-2

Smith, T. B., Rodríguez, M. D., & Bernal, G. (2011). Culture. *Journal of Clinical Psychology* 67, 166–175. doi: 10.1002/jclp.20757

Stokols, D. (1996). Translating social ecological theory into guidelines for community health promotion. *American Journal of Health Promotion* 10, 282–298. doi: 10.4278/0890-1171-10.4.282

Sue, S., Cheng, J. K. Y., Saad, C. S., & Chu, J. P. (2012). Asian American mental health: A call to action. *American Psychologist* 67, 532–544. doi: 10.1037/a0028900

Trickett, E. J. & Rowe, H. L. (2012). Emerging ecological approaches to prevention, health promotion, and public health in the school context: Next steps from a community psychology perspective. *Journal of Educational & Psychological Consultation* 22(1), 125–140. doi: 10.1080/10474412.2011.649651

Weisz, J. R., Sandler, I. N., Durlak, J. A., & Anton, B. S. (2005). Promoting and protecting youth mental health through evidence-based prevention and treatment. *American Psychologist* 60, 628–648. doi: 10.1037/0003-066X.60.6.628

Yeh, M., Takeuchi, D. T., & Sue, S. (1994). Asian-American children treated in the mental health system: A comparison of parallel and mainstream outpatient service centers. *Journal of Clinical Child Psychology* 23, 5–12. doi: 10.1207/s15374424jccp2301_2

Youssef, J. & Deane, F. P. (2006). Factors influencing mental-health help-seeking in Arabic speaking communities in Sydney, Australia. *Mental Health, Religion & Culture* 9(1), 43–66. doi: 10.1080/13674670512331335686

Zane, N., Hatanaka, H., Park, S. S., & Akutsu, P. (1994). Ethnic-specific mental health services: Evaluation of the parallel approach for Asian-American clients. *Journal of Community Psychology* 22, 68–81. doi: 10.1002/1520–6629(199404)22:2<68::AID-JCOP2290220204>3.0.CO;2–5

PART VI

Methodology and Future Directions

26

RESEARCH MEASURES

Psychometric Methods and Challenges to Valid Assessment of Constructs

Nancy Howells Wrobel

Scientific literature on Arab Americans has been relatively sparse, to some extent due to the "invisibility" (Salari, 2002) of Arab Americans related to their identification as "White" in Census data and elsewhere. Attention to this population has increased, yet researchers may be humbled in their efforts to measure characteristics of individuals who have roots in 22 Arab countries. The diversity of education, language, and reasons for coming to the U.S. over many decades adds to the challenge of accurately capturing the Arab American experience. This makes the development and use of accurate and valid measurement tools particularly crucial to scholars.

This chapter reviews the current theories and methods of measure development from both cross-cultural and multicultural research that may be relevant to conducting research with Arab Americans. Issues related to translation, measurement equivalence, and different types of biases are discussed. The chapter provides a review of the progress in developing or adapting psychometrically sound measures that may aid in investigations with Arab American samples. A case example is provided to illustrate the chapter contents, and the literature is critiqued for challenges and directions for future research related to research measures for Arab Americans.

Cross-Cultural and Multicultural Theoretical Frameworks

Those engaged in cross-cultural and multicultural research have been sensitive to the complexity of measurement selection and interpretation. When judgments and cross-cultural comparisons are made using measures that were not specifically designed or adapted for all the groups examined, the results of cross-cultural comparisons can be "flawed" (Ferketich, Phillips, & Verran, 1993, p.227). Even when the instruments chosen are available in the languages of the groups examined, it cannot be assumed that the constructs contained will have the same relevance or meaning across cultures.

In a multicultural approach, research addresses the nature of ethnic groups within a country from both emic (inside the social group) and etic (outside the social group) perspectives, with characteristics measured in qualitative and/or quantitative ways. When utilizing quantitative measures, Awad and Cokley (2010) and Cokley and Awad (2008) noted the importance of ensuring equivalence of measures across these groups through typical examination of psychometric characteristics, such as adequate reliability and shared factor structure. Yet they recognized that even constructs that appear to replicate across groups may not fully capture the nature or depth of those constructs for a particular group. They stressed that constructs may not only vary due to distal factors, such as group membership, but also due to proximal factors, such as how acculturated or collectivist the individual or group may be. Among Arab Americans, for example, a construct such as "shame" may have a particular salience and meaning unique to those emigrating from more collectivist cultural environments (Wrobel & Paterson, 2014).

In addition to basic cross-cultural and multicultural research, much psychological research is aimed at the development and application of culturally appropriate tests and measures, which may enhance fair decision-making in hiring, school placement, admission to higher education, and mental health diagnosis (Geisinger & McCormick, 2013). Applied measurement involving Arab Americans also requires sensitivity to differences within the population, and unique aspects of communication about themselves. For example, while cross-cultural researchers advise against use of metaphorical language, the use of metaphor with Arab Americans may actually foster *more* valid self-disclosure of mental health symptoms, which are not as readily expressed in a direct fashion (Dwairy, 2009). Cokley and Awad (2008) noted that culturally competent research and application of measures include gaining awareness of and finding remedies for potential threats to validity. Essential practices in translation and back-translation, as well as the notions of equivalence of meaning, validity, and potential bias in assessing Arab Americans, are elaborated below.

Adapting and Developing Measures

The importance of appropriate adaptations of existing measures has led to the establishment of recommendations and standards for this type of work (Guillemin, Bombardier, & Beaton, 1993). If the language of the target group to be studied is the same as the group for whom the measure was developed, but cultural norms differ from the original normative group, adaptation may still be required. This may be the case for Arab American immigrants who have been in the U.S. long enough to master language, yet may differ in cultural practices such as the celebration of holidays or family traditions. For example, in their study in Michigan, Aroian, Hough, Templin, and Kaskiri (2008) removed items from a parenting measure developed in the U.S. that included social activities which, according to cultural informants, were not typical in Muslim Arab culture, such as a child having a friend sleep at their home. Similarly, utilization of measures developed in other Arabic-speaking countries may require modification even though there may be similarity in Arabic language proficiency.

Translation and Related Issues

In evaluation and research involving Arab Americans, translation of instruments may be a common first step. In addition, accents and dialects may impact understanding of Arabic versions of measures.

Choice of language for administration. When considering whether an instrument can be given in English, or requires translation, the length of time in the U.S., as well as the requisite number of years of language instruction, are important to determine (e.g. Geisinger & McMormick, 2013). There is a tendency not to translate measures when applied to samples of Arab American university students, or community samples that are expected to have a sufficient grasp of English, and thus participation in some of the studies reviewed in this chapter had specific requirements to assure the necessary level of English proficiency. For example, Henry, Biran, and Stiles (2006) measured perceived parental acculturation in English, but required that participants had lived in the country for at least five years.

Ideally, carefully translated, equivalent forms of measurement instruments should be available in Arabic when possible, and the examiner may need to determine which version (English or Arabic) would be best to administer. The researcher may make this determination using assessments of language skills or acculturation, or allow the respondent to select their preferred language (Guillemin et al., 1993). Second generation Arab Americans, for example, may be more proficient and comfortable addressing some issues in English. Yet, even when an individual is academically proficient in English, those who speak their language of origin at home may be better able to express psychological variables or emotions in their native language (Judd et al., 2009).

Initial translation. Translation of English measures into Arabic may be more complex and challenging than translation between languages within the same language family, such as English and German (Abdel-Khalek, 2003). Attempts to remain too close to the source language in the translation process may result in an instrument that does not read naturally in Arabic, and this may impact the way respondents react to the questions (Harkness & Schoua-Glusberg, 1998). Further, the educational background of Arab Americans varies greatly; thus, the language appropriate for a college or professional sample may not be appropriate for recent refugees.

In order to produce an Arabic translation that has equivalence to the original measure, the initial translation should be completed by at least two bilingual translators who are fluent in Arabic, yet representative of those who will be completing the instrument. The translators should have varied backgrounds, and both will translate the measure into Arabic. One translator should be familiar with the concepts being measured, with the aim of maintaining equivalence with the theoretical or clinical meaning of the original items. The second translator should be naïve to the constructs being measured. This translator will be more likely to produce a version that is closer to the common language of the population that will be sampled. In particular, this person may help identify items with ambiguous meaning or items that are used academically but not in common language (Beaton, Bombardier, Guillemin, & Ferraz, 2000). The two Arabic versions of the measure are then synthesized into one, with discrepancies identified and resolved.

Back-translation. Once a synthesized version of the two Arabic translations is established, the accuracy and validity of that version is commonly tested by means of back-translation (c.f. Beaton et al., 2000; Geisinger & McCormick, 2013). The back-translators need to be fluent in Arabic, but also be native speakers of the language of the original measure, without specific expertise in the concepts being evaluated or prior familiarity with the original measure. The back-translation is then compared with the original measure. A major concern is that the focus on how closely the back-translated version of an item is true to the meaning of that item in the original version does not really evaluate the meaning of the translated target item itself (Geisinger & McCormick, 2013). For example, even if the item "I feel blue" can be translated into Arabic and back while maintaining the literal meaning of individual words, that does not provide assurance that the Arabic language version of that item is equivalent to the original item in meaning. While this approach might assure a good match in translating a measure from an original English version to an Arabic version and back, it may yield an Arabic version that is awkward or lacking in meaning for the monolingual Arabic speaker.

Committee, decentering, and bilingual approaches. In a committee translation approach, several individuals prepare translations of the questionnaire independently. Translators meet to "reconcile" discrepancies in the translations and arrive at a final version that incorporates the best aspects of all translations (Harkness & Schoua-Glusberg, 1998). In a decentering approach, both the "source" measure in the original language and the translated measure are modified until there is a reasonably similar measure in the two languages (Sperber, Devellis, & Boehlecke, 1994). Elements of the original or source test that are too culturally specific are eliminated or altered. For example, when producing an Arabic version of an English measure of acculturative stress, which named certain specific holiday customs or practices (such as Halloween or Cinco de Mayo), care was taken to use more generic phrases, like "celebration" or "event" (Wrobel, Farrag, & Hymes, 2009). This same process may be useful even when surveying or testing Arab Americans who are able to complete a measure in English, but may not relate to certain concepts or events.

In research involving psychological constructs with existing valid measures, it may be necessary to keep as close as possible to the original version, without significant adaptation. To change the original language would make it difficult to apply the existing body of work related to reliability and validity of the measure, and interfere with use of existing normative data (Geisinger & McCormick, 2013). An alternative is a bilingual approach to validation, in which the source and translated versions of a measure are administered to bilingual individuals, and the consistency of results of both tests is evaluated. The one inherent flaw in this process is that those who are bilingual may also have some mastery of the concepts and attitudes of both cultures, and thus the results of this validation research may not generalize to other samples that are monolingual (Harkness & Schoua-Glusberg, 1998; Yang & Bond, 1980).

Equivalence of Measures: Types of Equivalence

Examining the equivalence of measures refers to determining whether the measures reflect comparable semantic meaning, experience, and concepts across languages and cultures. This process is essential to avoiding the validity threats described by previous authors (Beaton et al., 2000; Cokley & Awad, 2008). Authors van de Vijver and Leung (2011) organized forms of equivalency into four types: construct, structural, metric, and scalar.

Construct. Construct inequivalence occurs when a construct a researcher is attempting to measure is either uniquely distinct between cultures or, at an extreme, the construct is nonexistent or irrelevant in one culture. In this case, the translation of measures from one language to another and related cultural comparison is not viewed as possible (Geisinger & McCormick, 2013). As indicated earlier, the notion of shame may have a more profound meaning among immigrants of Arab descent and thus may be viewed as lacking in construct equivalence (Wrobel & Paterson, 2014).

Structural or functional. Structural or functional aspects of equivalence relate to the similarity of the psychometric aspects of measurement data across the source and target languages and/or cultures, allowing generalizability of test findings across groups. For example, exploratory or replicatory factor analysis has traditionally been utilized to see if the same number of factors and similar factor loadings emerge across translations and cultural groups (Geisinger & McCormick, 2013). This technique was applied by Amer, Awad, and Hovey (2014) in examining the application of the Center for Epidemiological Study of Depression (CES-D) scale to Arab Americans who were either second generation or had immigrated to the U.S. at a young age. For these individuals the factor structure of CES-D responses was more similar to immigrants than other non-Arab Americans, with presentation of symptoms similar to their heritage culture.

More recently, structural equation modeling, including confirmatory factor analysis (CFA), has been heralded as a more sophisticated technique, in which a goodness-of-fit statistic is applied as a means of establishing statistically whether the translated test measure shows consistent or equivalent constructs compared to the original measures (Hox, de Leeuw, & Brinkhuis, 2010). When this model has been applied to Arabic translations, some researchers have modified the test to acquire a better fit by removing or adapting items. For example, Aroian, Hough, and associates (2008) removed items from the Nurture-Disclosure scale of the Family Peer Relationship questionnaire that did not load well on its related factor. In this case, child disclosure of negative situations to the parent was associated with reported child behavioral problems rather than nurturance. Instead, substitution of items reflecting neutral or positive situations yielded a better fit. The authors concluded that dwelling on negative situations may not be the norm for immigrant families.

Metric and scalar. Metric and scalar forms of equivalence relate to the similarity of the units of measure and full score across translations or adaptations of measures, meaning that equivalent measures have the same interval or ratio scales, respectively, and so scores are seen as comparable. These forms of equivalence take on a particular significance in adapting measures where a specific cutoff score may be used for clinical diagnosis or academic placement, such as in the determination of depression, dementia, or mental impairment.

Equivalence of Measures: Establishing Equivalence of Items

Particularly in social science research, where use of single-item measures is common, Johnson (1998) and Mohler and Johnson (2010) stressed the need to address whether items serve as functionally equivalent. For example, when asked to relate the likelihood of going to a friend for help, does the description of who might be labeled as a "friend" vary across cultures? Johnson advised at least attending to the frequency of endorsement of an item across groups.

Pretesting, behavioral coding, and probes. Sometimes even a carefully translated and back-translated instrument may be problematic due to ambiguous concepts or differing social experiences of a group. Pretesting may be used to evaluate the psychometric qualities, but can also be used to assure face validity of the test items, assuring that the respondents will be able to respond to them without hesitation (Guillemin et al.,1993). When an interview format is used, behavioral coding can be used to detect behaviors that are indicative of difficulty understanding, such as asking for clarification, asking for an item to be repeated, or giving inadequate responses (Johnson, 1998; Thrasher et al., 2011). This approach appears to be more sensitive among some cultural groups than others. Participants in non-Western settings may be somewhat more acquiescent in the test setting (Yang, Harkness, Chin, & Villar, 2010), and thus this technique may be somewhat less sensitive to comprehension problems with those groups.

Probe techniques involve addressing the cognitive processes involved in the test response. In cognitive coding approaches, participants are specifically prompted to provide information about their responses. Such approaches have been applied in order to clarify responses among English- and Spanish-speaking participants. Ridolfo and Schoua-Glusberg (2011), for example, applied the question, "How do other people usually see you in this country?" The authors reported that while the respondents initially stated that they understood these questions as an appraisal of how others viewed them, coding of their responses during a discussion of the questions indicated that the questions were actually measuring how the individuals perceived their own racial identity. A similar technique may be useful to apply to Arab Americans in order to validate their responses to questions requiring self-identification of ethnicity.

Bilingual rating. In this technique a group of bilingual raters is asked to rate the similarity of items in the two languages. This method can identify discrepancies and determine whether there are limitations of the translated version within the target cultural context (Guillemin et al., 1993). Bilingual approaches have been utilized in translating many of the measures for Arab Americans reviewed below (e.g. Aroian, Kaskiri, & Templin, 2008; Kira et al., 2008; Wrobel et al., 2009). However, it is noteworthy that bilingual individuals who rate or translate items may not perform the same way on items as monolingual individuals who are study respondents.

Bias as a Challenge to Valid Assessment of Arab Americans

An instrument is viewed as biased if the meaning of scores differs across cultural groups (van de Vijver, 1998) due to measurement artifacts as opposed to actual distinctions between groups. There are several types of biases that can affect measure development including construct, method (which includes response styles), and item biases.

Construct Bias

Construct bias is a form of bias that occurs when a measured construct or its meaning does not perform similarly across cultures. A measure of "good parenting," for example, might differ if developed for use with European Americans versus Arab Americans raised in a country where more collectivist concerns are emphasized and authoritarian parenting may be viewed as more common (Dwairy & Achoui, 2006; Sorkhabi, 2005). Construct bias may be notable in assessing depression in Arab Americans, as the disorder may be more heavily represented by somatic symptoms, and feelings of guilt are not associated in the same way as might be expected in Western samples (Wrobel & Paterson, 2014). For example, in their psychometric evaluation of the Arabic language version of the Profile of Mood States, Aroian, Kulwicki, Kaskiri, Templin, and Wells (2007) dropped an item that referred to guilt because it did not load on the depression factor. In addition, the item "carefree" was eliminated as it was believed to have a negative connotation among Muslim mothers who are expected to be serious and therefore have "cares" regarding their role.

Method Bias

Method bias involves more procedural aspects of a study that may impact measurement as well as test results and comparisons. One type of method bias relates to instrument bias, which occurs when individuals in one cultural group consistently respond to an instrument or testing method in a way that is different than another. For example, second generation participants, who are more acculturated to the norms and taboos of the host society than first generation immigrants, may either include or edit out different types of information accordingly as they formulate a response (Morren, Gelissen, & Vermunt, 2012). Thus, response styles, such as social desirability, acquiescence, and extreme-range responding represent a potential instrument bias among Arab Americans.

Social desirability. The degree to which responses are impacted by social desirability varies along some relevant dimensions. Groups that view themselves as having less power, such as immigrants, may be more inclined to engage in positive impression management (Ross & Mirowsky, 1984). The degree to which individuals identify with an individualistic versus a collectivist society also has an impact. Those from individualistic cultures value being "honest" in their responses and they may be willing to reveal personal information to others from their own group as well as an outgroup. The collectivist approach favors responding in a socially desirable fashion, in order to save face as well as maintain group harmony (Triandis, 2001). Individuals from collectivist backgrounds may be less likely to disclose personal information to someone perceived as being from the outgroup (Johnson & van de Vijver, 2003). Among Arab immigrants the impact of cultural style may vary between those from more Westernized countries, such as Lebanon, and those from more traditionally collectivist cultures. For recent immigrants, it may be advisable for interview data to be collected from someone perceived as part of their "ingroup," as the degree of disclosure may be greater.

Social desirability can also be influenced by characteristics of the questions and the relationship between the interviewer and interviewee (Johnson & van de Vijver, 2003). Survey administration modes may impact responses to questions about matters such as substance abuse, mental and physical health, or disclosure of potentially illegal activities. It is well documented, for example, that ethnic groups such as African Americans may distrust both law enforcement agents as well as researchers due to a shared history of exploitation and unfair treatment, and thus may be reluctant to respond to questions about matters such as substance abuse. For Arab Americans, demonstrated fear of backlash following 9/11 or other world events (Ibish, 2003; Moradi & Hasan, 2004), as well as harsh treatment by authorities in their country of origin, may contribute to a similar reluctance to disclose such information.

Acquiescence. There is evidence for a greater level of acquiescent responses, which is a tendency to agree to questionnaire items, among those from more collectivist backgrounds (Yang et al., 2010). Consideration of the degree of collectivism may help predict when acquiescent responses may impact test or survey results. Using data from large international studies across 34 countries, Smith (2004) noted an interaction between family collectivism and uncertainty avoidance. Those with high collectivism who were from nations with greater levels of uncertainty avoidance were more likely to give responses that were biased by acquiescence when items were personally relevant. When uncertainty avoidance was low, acquiescence was higher on items that involved descriptions of others. These results have relevance, as the likelihood of high family connectedness is great among Arab American immigrants (Dwairy et al., 2006). Yet the degree of uncertainty avoidance may vary within the Arab American population, with those experiencing more uncertainty being less likely to self-disclose.

In assessing Arab Americans, it may be useful to single out the impact of education and socioeconomic status (SES) on response style. Acquiescence is higher among the minority elderly and those with lower SES and educational levels (Ross & Mirowsky, 1984; Yang et al., 2010). As such, response styles found among Arab American college students may not reflect characteristics of recently immigrated, less educated individuals. The degree of acquiescence may also vary with the mode of administration, such as whether the survey was administered in person. This is relevant given increased use of Internet data collection with Arab Americans.

Extreme or midrange responding. As with acquiescent response styles, extreme or midrange response styles have been related to culture. Individualism is associated with a more extreme response style, while midrange responses are favored among people from Asian countries, who favor cautious responses (Yang et al., 2010). In contrast, Arab Americans actually revealed a more extreme response style in response to questions of religious coping behavior (Amer, Hovey, Fox, & Rezcallah, 2008). Perhaps responses to questions about religious practices among those with a strong religious/ethnic conviction may be more extreme when responding to questions related to religion. Consistent with these results, the extremity of response styles varied depending upon the content of questions in a Chinese sample (Culpepper, Zhao, & Lowery, 2002).

Item Bias

Item bias occurs when a particular item or set of items does not relate to the construct measured in the same way across groups. A classic example of this issue can be seen in translation of the Mini-Mental State Examination (MMSE) for use as a measure of cognitive decline or dementia in the elderly. One of the phrases requiring repetition from memory is "no ifs and or buts." While this item is correlated with overall test performance in English-speaking people, failure to recall this item in an Arabic translation occurred frequently in those who were cognitively intact as well as those with identified cognitive decline (Wrobel & Farrag, 2007). Prior studies with other translations of the MMSE suggest that the lack of a comparable expression in the target language creates a lack of familiarity with the item for that group. A similar issue occurred in developing cutoff points for the Arabic version of the Hospital Anxiety and Depression (HAD) scale. Here, an item referring to "butterflies in my stomach" was not highly correlated with overall anxiety (El-Rufaie & Absood, 1995).

Avoidance of Bias

Careful translation and back-translation, as well as sensitivity to the possible need for an Arab American interviewer, are all ways potentially to avoid bias. When particular patterns of response are anticipated, such as an acquiescent style among immigrants, it may be wise to devise measures that either avoid or detect those responses. Research with Latino respondents, for example, favors a 10-point over a 5-point Likert scale (Hui & Triandis, 1989). For observable characteristics, such as mental health symptoms, use of external records or informant report can also help identify bias by comparing some external observation of a related behavior to reported attitudes. Use of family informants has been applied successfully in validating dementia and depression scales among elderly Arab Americans (e.g. Wrobel & Farrag, 2006, 2007). Details on item response theory techniques for sorting out bias from true group differences are provided by de Jong, Steenkamp, Fox, and Baumgartner (2008).

Summary of Measures Developed and Adapted for Use With Arab Americans

Over recent decades, increasing numbers of researchers have published works that explore the experiences and difficulties involved in the development, adaptation, or application of tests and survey measures for Arab Americans. Measures that were successfully developed are reviewed in this section, with attention to procedures utilized, techniques of translation, and validation. The accompanying three tables (found in the Appendix) summarize the use and psychometric qualities of scales related to acculturation and identity, social pressures and personal resources, and psychological wellbeing and health. Scales reviewed were selected from current literature addressing these concepts in Arab American samples. The measures reviewed are not necessarily inclusive of all measures, but represent commonly used measures with demonstrated validity. In cases where the measure was adapted or translated from a prior measure, the citation column in the tables lists the current citation, followed by a citation for the original measure.

Measures of Acculturation and Ethnic Identity

Table 26.1 lists measures of acculturation, ethnic identity, and related concepts. Acculturation scales were often applied to student groups with some English proficiency and so the tendency was to administer them in English rather than translate. Adaptations were applied in some cases to reflect Arab heritage culture (Britto & Amer, 2007; Rissel, 1997). Jadalla and Lee (2012) provided an Arabic version of the Acculturation Rating Scale of Arab Americans, using thorough procedures including translation, back-translations, and validation on a wide age range.

More thorough procedures were utilized on translations of scales measuring acculturative stress and demands. The Arabic language version of the Demands of Immigration Scale provided an appropriate model for employing individuals from the culture in translating and adapting a measure. Bilingual experts representing the countries of origin of examinees were used (Aroian, Kaskiri, and Templin, 2008). Arabic versions of the Multidimensional Acculturative Stress Inventory (Wrobel et al., 2009) and the Social Adjustment Measures (Kira et al., 2008, 2010) both reflected cautious translations and back-translations, with pilot testing in the latter case. The importance of further validation and piloting with primarily Arabic-speaking individuals was stressed, as the equivalence of measures may still be questionable given a reliance on bilingual translators.

Scales and measures that are not translated also require careful evaluation of their cross-cultural meaning and utility. Although not translated, Amer and Hovey's (2007) version of the Societal Attitudinal Familial and Environmental Acculturative Stress Scale was distinguished by use of a Rasch rating scale analysis as a guide to adaptation and removal of items. Aside from the Objective Measure of Ego Identity Status, translated by Dwairy (2004), the ethnic identity scales reviewed were primarily not translated. English versions of the remaining ethnic identity measures, primarily derived from the Male Arab Ethnic Identity Measure (Barry, 2005), demonstrated high levels of consistency as well as predictive, convergent, and discriminant validity (Amer & Hovey, 2007; Shammas, 2009).

Measures of Social Pressures and Personal Resources

The saliency of religious, social, political, and family life in Arab American communities suggests a need to have accurate assessments of these and related variables (see Table 26.2). Similarly, experiences of discrimination have been a focus of research since the events of 9/11 (Abu-Raiya, Pargament, & Mahoney, 2011; Ibish, 2003; Moradi & Hasan, 2004). Measures of perceived discrimination and racism reviewed for this chapter were either applied to young adult samples (often students), or required English fluency, so they were not translated. Adaptations were required as some instruments were initially developed for use with African Americans (e.g. Ahmed, Kia-Keating, & Tsai, 2011). The measures used with Arab

Americans have been sensitive to varied levels of discrimination across religious groups (Awad, 2010) and in some cases have predicted psychological distress (Ahmed et al., 2011; Moradi & Hasan, 2004).

Also represented in Table 26.2 are multiple measures of religiosity and religious coping, as well as sacred loss, which refers to violations of the sacred, such as desecrations. The measures reviewed displayed high internal consistency, and most had adequate construct validity as identified by statistical modeling techniques (Abu-Raiya, Pargament, Mahoney, & Stein, 2008; Amer et al., 2008). Although demonstrating construct validity through Rasch rating scale modeling, concept validation of the Brief Arab Religious Coping Scale (BARCS; Amer et al., 2008) was less successful. The authors noted that the complex relationship between identification as Muslim and higher levels of acculturative stressors may negate or cloud the impact of religious coping or decrease the impact of religious coping on such stressors. It is also possible that a restricted range of religious practices among those completing the BARCS in this study impacted results from participants recruited from college or community groups who may have had strong religious and ethnic identities.

Measures of family and social support are also summarized here. Perceived social support measures were thoroughly translated and adapted, with back-translation and committee review, by Aroian and associates (Aroian, Hough, et al., 2008; Aroian et al., 2007). For these measures, sensitivity to cultural differences in parenting and other social behaviors was particularly important. Research assistance by those who represented various Arab ethnicities contributed to a more useful set of measures. These authors applied a similar process in adapting and translating the Family Peer Relationship Questionnaire. Amer and Hovey's (2007) application of the McMaster Family Assessment device to an adult Arab American sample yielded internally consistent results that were predictive of acculturative stress and depression.

Measures of Psychological Wellbeing, Mental Health, and Health

The remaining measures reviewed for this chapter relate to self-esteem, mental health, and health (see Table 26.3). Just as notions of ethnic identity and discrimination were relevant for comprehending the experiences of Arab Americans, the self-esteem measures reviewed here addressed the role of more personal or individual concepts of self. Measures such as the Rosenberg Self-Esteem Scale (Rosenberg, as cited in Barry, 2005), Collective Self-Esteem (Luhtanen & Crocker, 1992), and Self-Construal Scale (Barry, Elliott, & Evans, 2000) demonstrated consistency in research and were sensitive to experiences of marginalization, separation, and assimilation. Unique to the self-construal measure was evidence that while interdependence was associated with strong Arab identity, independence appeared to be a separate construct, as it was not correlated with measures of male Arab identity.

Measures of current stressors and symptoms as well as pre-immigration trauma have been the focus of the many studies. For such measures, the notion of bias becomes particularly important as clinicians and researchers need to be cautious about either overdiagnosis within a population, or missing individuals who require intervention. As reviewed earlier, translation of colloquial expression of symptoms, such as having "butterflies" as a descriptor of anxiety (El-Rufaie & Absood, 1995) or unfamiliar content, such as English expressions or customs (Wrobel & Farrag, 2007), must be conducted with caution. Measures of posttraumatic stress disorder (PTSD) and related trauma represented by the work of Kira and associates (2008, 2010) are good examples of a thorough translation process, including back-translation, piloting, and demonstrated convergent validity. These measures are useful in identifying the impact of trauma experienced in the current life of refugees and other immigrants, as well as trauma experienced over a period of time. Trauma experiences unique to Arab Americans, such as trauma related to backlash following 9/11, are assessed with one of these measures, the Backlash Trauma Scale (Kira et al., 2008, 2010). Experiences unique to refugees and other recent immigrants need to be considered in evaluating data. For example, data from the Trauma History Questionnaire were highly skewed for female Arab immigrants who had experienced a significant level and frequency of traumatic events, as well as discrimination and acculturative stress, and thus a large proportion had very high scores on the trauma measure (Hassouneh & Kulwicki, 2007).

Establishing appropriate cutoff points for existing measures becomes an important issue with those used for diagnostic screening. Examination of both measures of psychiatric symptoms, such as the CES-D (Amer et al., 2014; Ghubash, Daradkeh, Al Naseri, Al Bloushi, & Al Daheri, 2000), and cognitive symptoms, such as the MMSE (Wrobel & Farrag, 2007), may require consideration of alternative cutoff scores when used for screening. In part, appropriate cutoffs may vary due to the performance of some items because of a possible lack of exposure to some content, as well as response styles that may be elicited by different item content. For example, content related to sex, appetite, and sleep negatively impacted the internal consistency of response to items within the Beck Depression Inventory–II when applied to students in Arab countries (Alansari, 2006).

The remaining scales reviewed were related to health. Arabic translations of both the 12-item Health Scale (Kira et al., 2008, 2010) and the Short Form Health Survey (SF-36; Jadalla & Lee, 2012) provided brief screenings of health-related problems, while the SF-36 addressed mental health as well. Both of these measures yielded consistent results upon translation, and were related to experiences such as acculturation and cumulative trauma. A translation of the Cornell Medical Index (Reizian & Meleis, 1987) has also been applied, and appeared to have some convergent validity, although details of translation were not as explicit as those provided for the other measures. The authors noted that in the Middle East the tendency is to downplay or underreport symptoms unless they significantly interfere with functional ability. Of importance is the notion that those who immigrated from different Middle Eastern countries had varying levels of reported symptoms, perhaps reflecting varying levels of modernization or degree of stress related to the nature of the immigration experience. In particular, refugees had higher levels of physical symptoms than those with other immigration statuses. While not included in this table, Maziak, Ward, Afifi Soweid, and Eissenberg (2005) discussed the need to adequately assess health-related behaviors common to those of Middle Eastern descent, such as waterpipe tobacco use. They suggested a set of standardized questions, with more consistent terminology that may allow for more comparison across samples.

Case Example: Communicating About Dementia and Mental Health

The following narrative illustrates the complexity of developing or adapting research methods and measures for use with Arab American populations. In preparation for recruitment of elderly participants for a study of the validity of Arabic translations of depression and dementia measures, the current author developed posters explaining the purpose of the study and engaged a bilingual scholar in Arabic studies as a translator. Back-translation of the poster was conducted by an instructor of the Arabic language who was unfamiliar with psychological constructs. As a student prepared to distribute posters in the community, her father, a physician, noted that the Arabic term for dementia used on the poster was an appropriate medical term, but not part of common language that would be readily understood by elderly Arabs. When the issue was raised with a group of Arab American counseling staff at a local community agency, it led to a spirited debate on the appropriate Arabic word to use on the poster. While ultimately a compromise was established among these professionals, it was not clear that this term for dementia represented the language that recent, fairly uneducated immigrants would use. Unfortunately, this concern was confirmed as few participants responded to the posters. Instead, face-to-face communication by individuals in the community was more successful.

Around this time, a public radio broadcast in the U.S. related a story about translating material into Arabic. It addressed the difficulty that news agencies around the world had in translating colloquial terms or phrases, such as "smoke 'em out," used in speeches by the American president at that time. In particular, they reported that there was often unresolvable disagreement regarding translation of these terms and phrases among the news staff at Aljazeera, the Arabic cable news channel, who were concerned with political implications of obscured meanings. These anecdotes reflect the notion that there is wide variation in dialect, as well as in cultural context, across diverse peoples in the Arab world, as well as among Arab Americans.

The lesson learned from these efforts to find shared meaning in the recruitment posters for a study of Arab American elderly, as well as from the reporting of news in the Arab world, has relevance to research and practice with Arab American samples. In applying survey and assessment techniques, for example, equivalence of meaning is not just necessary to establish between Arab Americans and others, but must also address multicultural aspects within the Arab Americans who are assessed. Ultimately, as noted, the best solution for recruitment of participants was to have individuals from the Arab American community serve as research assistants who could directly contact and solicit elderly individuals to participate in responding to the measures. This allowed an opportunity not only to explain unfamiliar terms, but also to assure a level of comfort in disclosing information to people with a familiar background. As a result, the research project yielded reliable and valid results from translations of the MMSE and the Informant Questionnaire for Cognitive Decline in the Elderly (Wrobel & Farrag, 2007), the Geriatric Depression Scale (Wrobel & Farrag, 2006), and the Multidimensional Acculturative Stress Inventory (Wrobel et al., 2009).

Critique

While researchers have made much progress in adapting and translating measures over the past few decades, there are still some challenges that remain particularly salient in studying Arab Americans. For example, in establishing equivalence of meaning in measures used, overreliance on bilingual translators and participants, who may not respond in the same way as monolingual study respondents, continues to be a concern. Perhaps one of the most consistent difficulties mentioned by authors of the works reviewed here has been the selection of participants. Recruitment and sampling of Arab Americans has been difficult not only because they are not clearly identified as a separate group in Census data, but also because of political and social experiences that may make these individuals more reluctant to provide personal information (Ibish, 2003). In order to facilitate participation, samples have been drawn through universities, recruited through trusted institutions, such as mosques, or attracted through electronic media. This has resulted in some confounding of variables, such as ethnicity and religion, and has also produced results that may not generalize across educational, age, and socioeconomic groups. Optimal progress will come with more sophisticated efforts at stratified sampling, and engagement of larger samples of participants. If circumstances preclude a truly random sample, then it is advisable to measure and control for potentially confounding variables (van deVijver, 1998) and to conduct careful evaluation of the impact of demographic characteristics on results.

An additional hurdle to overcome is response style, such as the tendency to respond in an acquiescent fashion or hesitance to self-disclose. This may take the form of more deliberate avoidance of self-disclosure with regard to certain information, such as acts of discrimination. As with other minority groups, it is possible that Arab Americans may be reluctant to appear to be perceived as "oversensitive." Yet it is also argued that perhaps some measures do not tap into subtle forms of discrimination that may have a cumulative impact. Shammas (2009) argued that it is the "moral responsibility" of the researcher to develop or restructure questions that are more sensitive to these experiences. Further research should also address and clarify the degree and nature of more subtle, culturally-based response styles among Arab Americans. Results of research with other immigrant groups from collectivist backgrounds suggest that Arab Americans may utilize a more acquiescent response style and/or more cautious responses to some items; however, Arab Americans have not always demonstrated patterns consistent with these predictions (Amer et al., 2008). As suggested above, the goal of future research should be to delineate true distinctions in the constructs or opinions measured versus response patterns that are characteristic of a group.

Conclusion

The Arab American experience is both complex and diverse; thus, it requires those who seek to capture and measure characteristics and attitudes of Arab Americans to fashion and apply measures with particular care. From selecting participants, through translation of measures, investigators need to be cognizant of the cultural meaning of constructs. Those applying "best practices" in the studies reviewed here not only utilized the recommended techniques of translation and back-translation, but also sought consultation and assistance from Arab Americans who resembled the target respondents in terms of demographics and countries of origin. Continued progress will require application of more sophisticated methodology to sort out the complexities of response style, to avoid bias, and to verify the equivalence of meaning of scale results. As noted, item response theory models can identify which items are "differentially useful" across groups in a more systematic fashion (de Jong et al., 2008). Structural equation modeling, including CFA, is advised as a means of establishing whether adapted and/or translated tests or surveys measure consistent equivalent constructs. Additionally, external validation of item responses continues to be a useful approach for measures tapping observable characteristics. Finally, the use of pretesting, probing, behavioral coding, and cognitive interviewing techniques can further contribute to the identification of translation and adaptation errors that may impede comprehension of measures in Arab American samples.

References

Abdel-Khalek, A. M. (2003). Adequacy of an English version of the Kuwait University Anxiety Scale based on back translation and testing bilingual subjects. *Psychological Reports* 93(3f), 1101–1104. doi: 10.2466/pr0.2003.93.3f.1101

Abu-Raiya, H., Pargament, K. I., & Mahoney, A. (2011). Examining coping methods with stressful interpersonal events experienced by Muslims living in the United States following the 9/11 attacks. *Psychology of Religion and Spirituality* 3, 1–14. doi: 10.1037/a0020034

Abu-Raiya, H., Pargament, K. I., Mahoney, A., & Stein, C. (2008). A psychological measure of Islamic religiousness: Development and evidence for reliability and validity. *The International Journal for the Psychology of Religion* 18, 291–315. doi: 10.1080/10508610802229270

Ahmed, S. R., Kia-Keating, M., & Tsai, K. H. (2011). A structural model of racial discrimination, acculturative stress, and cultural resources among Arab American adolescents. *American Journal of Community Psychology* 48(3–4), 181–192. doi: 10.1007/s10464-011-9424-3

Alansari, B. M. (2006). Internal consistency of an Arabic adaptation of the Beck Depression Inventory-II with college students in eighteen Arab countries. *Social Behavior and Personality: An International Journal* 34, 425–430. doi: 10.2224/sbp.2006.34.4.425

Amer, M. M., Awad, G. H., & Hovey, J. D. (2014). Evaluation of the CES-D Scale factor structure in a sample of second-generation Arab-Americans. *International Journal of Culture and Mental Health* 7, 46–58. doi: 10.1080/17542863.2012.693514

Amer, M. M. & Hovey, J. D. (2007). Socio-demographic differences in acculturation and mental health for a sample of 2nd generation/early immigrant Arab Americans. *Journal of Immigrant and Minority Health* 9, 335–347. doi: 10.1007/s10903-007-9045-y

Amer, M. M., Hovey, J. D., Fox, C. M., & Rezcallah, A. (2008). Initial development of the Brief Arab Religious Coping Scale (BARCS). *Journal of Muslim Mental Health* 3, 69–88. doi: 10.1080/15564900802156676

Aroian, K. J., Hough, E. S., Templin, T. N., & Kaskiri, E. A. (2008). Development and psychometric evaluation of an Arab version of the Family Peer Relationship Questionnaire. *Research in Nursing & Health* 31, 402–416. doi: 10.1002/nur.20277

Aroian, K. J., Kaskiri, E. A., & Templin, T. N. (2008). Psychometric evaluation of the Arabic language version of the Demands of Immigration Scale. *International Journal of Testing* 8(1), 2–13. doi: 10.1080/15305050701808490

Aroian, K. J., Kulwicki, A., Kaskiri, E. A., Templin, T. N., & Wells, C. L. (2007). Psychometric evaluation of the Arabic language version of the Profile of Mood States. *Research in Nursing & Health*, 30, 531–541. doi: 10.1002/nur.20211

Awad, G. H. (2010). The impact of acculturation and religious identification on perceived discrimination for Arab/Middle Eastern Americans. *Cultural Diversity and Ethnic Minority Psychology* 16, 59–67. doi: 10.1037/a0016675

Awad, G. H. & Cokley, K. O. (2010). Designing and interpreting quantitative research in multicultural counseling. In J. G. Ponterotto, J. Casas, L. A. Suzuki, & C. M. Alexander (eds.), *Handbook of multicultural counseling* (3rd edn., pp. 385–396). Thousand Oaks, CA: Sage.

Barry, D. T. (2005). Measuring acculturation among male Arab immigrants in the United States: An exploratory study. *Journal of Immigrant Health* 7, 179–184. doi: 10.1007/s10903-005-3674-9

Barry, D., Elliott, R., & Evans, E. M. (2000). Foreigners in a strange land: Self-construal and ethnic identity in male Arabic immigrants. *Journal of Immigrant Health* 2, 133–144. doi: 10.1023/A:1009508919598

Beaton, D. E., Bombardier, C., Guillemin, F., & Ferraz, M. B. (2000). Guidelines for the process of cross-cultural adaptation of self-report measures. *Spine* 25, 3186–3191. doi: 10.1097/00007632-200012150-00014

Britto, P. R. & Amer, M. M. (2007). An exploration of cultural identity patterns and the family context among Arab Muslim young adults in America. *Applied Development Science* 11(3), 137–150. doi: 10.1080/10888690701454633

Cokley, K. O. & Awad, G. H. (2008). Conceptual and methodological issues in multicultural research. In P. P. Heppner, D. M. Kivlighan, & B. E. Wampold (eds.), *Research design in counseling* (3rd edn., pp. 366–384). California: Wadsworth.

de Jong, M. G., Steenkamp, J. B. E., Fox, J. P., & Baumgartner, H. (2008). Using item response theory to measure extreme response style in marketing research: A global investigation. *Journal of Marketing Research* 45(1), 104–115. doi: 10.1509/jmkr.45.1.104

Culpepper, R. A., Zhao, L., & Lowery, C. (2002). Survey response bias among Chinese managers. *Academy of Management Proceedings* 2002, J1–J6. doi: 10.5465/apbpp.2002.7516876

Dwairy, M. (2004). Internal-structural validity of objective measure of ego identity status among Arab adolescents. *Identity* 4(2), 133–144. doi: 10.1207/s1532706xid0402_2

Dwairy, M. (2009). Culture analysis and metaphor psychotherapy with Arab-Muslim clients. *Journal of Clinical Psychology* 65, 199–209. doi: 10.1002/jclp.20568

Dwairy, M. & Achoui, M. (2006). Introduction to three cross-regional research studies on parenting styles, individuation, and mental health in Arab societies. *Journal of Cross-Cultural Psychology* 37, 221–229. doi: 10.1177/0022022106286921

Dwairy, M., Achoui, M., Abouserie, R., Farah, A., Sakhleh, A. A., Fayad, M., & Khan, H. K. (2006). Parenting styles in Arab societies: A first cross-regional research study. *Journal of Cross-Cultural Psychology* 37, 230–247. doi: 10.1177/0022022106286922

El-Rufaie, O. E. F. & Absood, G. H. (1995). Retesting the validity of the Arabic version of the Hospital Anxiety and Depression (HAD) scale in primary health care. *Social Psychiatry and Psychiatric Epidemiology* 30, 26–31. doi: 10.1007/BF00784431

Ferketich, S., Phillips, L., & Verran, J. (1993). Development and administration of a survey instrument for cross-cultural research. *Research in Nursing & Health* 16, 227–230. doi: 10.1002/nur.4770160310

Geisinger, K. F. & McCormick, C. (2013). Testing and assessment in cross-cultural psychology. In I. B. Weiner (ed.-in-chief), J. R. Graham, & J. Naglieri (vol. eds.), *Handbook of psychology: Vol. 10. Assessment psychology* (pp. 114–139). Hoboken, NJ: John Wiley & Sons.

Ghubash, R., Daradkeh, T. K., Al Naseri, K. S., Al Bloushi, N. B. A., & Al Daheri, A. M. (2000). The performance of the Center for Epidemiologic Study Depression Scale (CES-D) in an Arab female community. *International Journal of Social Psychiatry* 46(4), 241–249. doi: 10.1177/002076400004600402

Guillemin, F., Bombardier, C., & Beaton, D. (1993). Cross-cultural adaptation of health-related quality of life measures: Literature review and proposed guidelines. *Journal of Clinical Epidemiology* 46, 1417–1432. doi: 10. 1016/0895-4356(93)90142-N

Harkness, J. A. & Schoua-Glusberg, A. (1998). Questionnaires in translation. *ZUMA-Nachrichten Spezial* 3, 87–127.

Hassouneh, D. M. & Kulwicki, A. (2007). Mental health, discrimination, and trauma in Arab Muslim women living in the US: A pilot study. *Mental Health, Religion and Culture* 10, 257–262. doi: 10.1080/13694670600630556

Henry, H. M., Biran, M. W., & Stiles, W. B. (2006). Construction of the Perceived Parental Acculturation Behaviors Scale. *Journal of Clinical Psychology* 62, 293–297. doi: 10.1002/jclp.20228

Hox, J. J., de Leeuw, E. D., & Brinkhuis, M. J. (2010). Analysis models for comparative surveys. In J. A. Harkness, M. Braun, B. Edwards, T. P. Johnson, L. Lyberg, P. Ph. Mohler, … T. W. Smith (eds.), *Survey methods in multinational, multiregional, and multicultural contexts* (pp. 395–418). Hoboken, NJ: John Wiley and Sons, Inc. doi: 10.1002/9780470609927.ch21

Hui, C. H. & Triandis, H. C. (1989). Effects of culture and response format on extreme response style. *Journal of Cross-Cultural Psychology* 20, 296–309. doi: 10.1177/0022022189203004

Ibish, I. (2003). *Report on hate crimes and discrimination against Arab Americans.* Washington, D.C.: American-Arab Anti-Discrimination Committee.

Jadalla, A. & Lee, J. (2012). The relationship between acculturation and general health of Arab Americans. *Journal of Transcultural Nursing* 23, 159–165. doi: 10.1177/1043659611434058

Johnson, T. P. (1998). Approaches to equivalence in cross-cultural and cross-national survey research. *ZUMA-Nachrichten spezial* 3, 1–40.

Johnson, T. P. & van de Vijver, F. J. (2003). Social desirability in cross-cultural research. *Cross-Cultural Survey Methods* 325, 195–204.

Judd, T., Capetillo, D., Carrión-Baralt, J., Mármol, L. M., San Miguel-Montes, L., Navarrete, M. G., … the NAN Policy and Planning Committee. (2009). Professional considerations for improving the neuropsychological evaluation of Hispanics: A National Academy of Neuropsychology education paper. *Archives of Clinical Neuropsychology* 24(2), 127–135. doi: 10.1093/arclin/acp016

Kira, I. A., Lewandowski, L., Templin, T., Ramaswamy, V., Ozkan, B., & Mohanesh, J. (2008). Measuring cumulative trauma dose, types, and profiles using a development-based taxonomy of traumas. *Traumatology* 14(2), 62–87. doi: 10.1177/1534765608319324

Kira, I. A., Lewandowski, L., Templin, T., Ramaswamy, V., Ozkan, B., & Mohanesh, J. (2010). The effects of perceived discrimination and backlash on Iraqi refugees' mental and physical health. *Journal of Muslim Mental Health* 5, 59–81. doi: 10.1080/15564901003622110

Luhtanen, R. & Crocker, J. (1992). A collective self-esteem scale: Self-evaluation of one's social identity. *Personality and Social Psychology Bulletin* 18, 302–318. doi: 10.1177/0146167292183006

Maziak, W., Ward, K. D., Afifi Soweid, R. A., & Eissenberg, T. (2005). Standardizing questionnaire items for the assessment of waterpipe tobacco use in epidemiological studies. *Public Health* 119, 400–404. doi: 10.1016/j.puhe.2004.08.002

Mohler, P. P. & Johnson, T. P. (2010). Equivalence, comparability, and methodological progress. In J. A. Harkness, M. Braun, B. Edwards, T. P. Johnson, L. Lyberg, P. Ph. Mohler, … T. W. Smith (eds.), *Survey methods in multinational, multiregional, and multicultural contexts* (pp. 17–32). Hoboken, NJ: John Wiley & Sons, Inc. doi: 10.1002/9780470609927.ch2

Moradi, B. & Hasan, N. T. (2004). Arab American persons reported experiences of discrimination and mental health: The mediating role of personal control. *Journal of Counseling Psychology* 51, 418–428. doi: 10.1037/0022-0167.51.4.418

Morren, M., Gelissen, J. P., & Vermunt, J. K. (2012). Response strategies and response styles in cross-cultural surveys. *Cross-Cultural Research* 46, 255–279. doi: 10.1177/1069397112440939

Reizian, A. & Meleis, A. I. (1987). Symptoms reported by Arab-American patients on the Cornell Medical Index (CMI). *Western Journal of Nursing Research* 9, 368–384. doi: 10.1177/019394598700900308

Ridolfo, H. & Schoua-Glusberg, A. (2011). Analyzing cognitive interview data using the constant comparative method of analysis to understand cross-cultural patterns in survey data. *Field Methods* 23, 420–438. doi: 10.1177/1525822X11414835

Rissel, C. (1997). The development and application of a scale of acculturation. *Australian and New Zealand Journal of Public Health* 21, 606–613. doi: 10.1111/j.1467-842X.1997.tb01764.x

Ross, C. E. & Mirowsky, J. (1984). Socially-desirable response and acquiescence in a cross-cultural survey of mental health. *Journal of Health and Social Behavior* 25, 189–197. doi: 10.2307/2136668

Salari, S. (2002). Invisible in aging research: Arab Americans, Middle Eastern immigrants, and Muslims in the United States. *The Gerontologist* 42, 580–588. doi: 10.1093/geront/42.5.580

Shammas, D. S. (2009). Post-9/11 Arab and Muslim American community college students: Ethno-religious enclaves and perceived discrimination. *Community College Journal of Research and Practice* 33(3–4), 283–308. doi: 10.1080/10668920802580507

Smith, P. B. (2004). Acquiescent response bias as an aspect of cultural communication style. *Journal of Cross-Cultural Psychology* 35, 50–61. doi: 10.1177/0022022103260380

Sorkhabi, N. (2005). Applicability of Baumrind's parent typology to collective cultures: Analysis of cultural explanations of parent socialization effects. *International Journal of Behavioral Development* 29, 552–563. doi: 10.1177/01650250500172640

Sperber, A. D., Devellis, R. F., & Boehlecke, B. (1994). Cross-cultural translation: Methodology and validation. *Journal of Cross-Cultural Psychology* 25, 501–524. doi: 10.1177/0022022194254006

Thrasher, J. F., Quah, A. C., Dominick, G., Borland, R., Driezen, P., Awang, R., … Boado, M. (2011). Using cognitive interviewing and behavioral coding to determine measurement equivalence across linguistic and cultural groups: An example from the International Tobacco Control Policy Evaluation Project. *Field Methods* 23, 439–460. doi: 10.1177/1525822X11418176

Triandis, H. C. (2001). Individualism-collectivism and personality. *Journal of Personality* 69, 907–924. doi: 10.1111/1467–6494.696169

van de Vijver, F. J. & Leung, K. (2011). Equivalence and bias: A review of concepts, models, and data analytic procedures. In D. Matsumoto & F. J. R. van de Vijver (eds.), *Cross-cultural research methods in psychology* (pp. 17–45). New York: Cambridge University Press.

van de Vijver, F. J. R. (1998). Towards a theory of bias and equivalence. In J. A. Harkness (ed.), *Cross-cultural survey equivalence* (pp. 41–65). Mannheim: ZUMA-Nachrichten Spezial Band 3.

Wrobel, N. H. & Farrag, M. F. (2006). A preliminary report on the validation of the Geriatric Depression Scale in Arabic. *Clinical Gerontologist* 29(4), 33–46. doi: 10.1300/J018v29n04_03

Wrobel, N. H. & Farrag, M. F. (2007). Preliminary validation of an Arabic version of the MMSE in the elderly. *Clinical Gerontologist* 31(3), 75–93. doi: 10.1080/07317110802072223

Wrobel, N. H., Farrag, M. F., & Hymes, R. W. (2009). Acculturative stress and depression in an elderly Arabic sample. *Journal of Cross-Cultural Gerontology* 24, 273–290. doi: 10.1007/s10823-009-9096-8

Wrobel, N. H. & Paterson, A. (2014). Mental health risks in Arab Americans across the lifespan. In S. Nassar-McMillan, K. J. Ajrouch, & J. Hakim-Larson (eds.), *Biopsychosocial perspectives on Arab Americans: Culture, development, and health* (pp. 197–228). New York: Springer. doi: 10.1007/978-1-4614-8238-3_10

Yang, K. S. & Bond, M. H. (1980). Ethnic affirmation by Chinese bilinguals. *Journal of Cross-Cultural Psychology* 11, 411–425. doi: 10.1177/0022022180114002

Yang, Y., Harkness, J. A., Chin, T. Y., & Villar, A. (2010). Response styles and culture. In J. A. Harkness, M. Braun, B. Edwards, T. P. Johnson, L. Lyberg, P. Ph. Mohler, … T. W. Smith (eds.), *Survey methods in multinational, multiregional, and multicultural contexts* (pp. 203–223). Hoboken, N.J.: Wiley. doi: 10.1002/9780470609927.ch12

Appendix: Measures Developed or Adapted for Use with Arab Americans

Table 26.1 Measures of Acculturation, Ethnic Identity, and Related Concepts

Construct	*Length/Format*	*Citation**	*Population to Which Instrument Was Applied*		
			Gender/Religion	*Age*	*Immigration History*
Acculturation					
Acculturation, Habits, and Interests Multicultural Scale for Adolescents (AHIMSA)	8-item/ Self-report	Applied in Sirin & Fine (2007) and Sirin et al. (2008) Original Unger et al. (2002)	Mixed/Muslim (Largest groups were Arab and South Asian)	12–18; 18–28	Varied ethnic backgrounds; Most born in the U.S.; First and second generation immigrants
Acculturation Rating Scale of Arab Americans (ARSAA)	2-item/ Self-report rating	Jadalla & Lee (2012)	Mixed/No information on religion	18–86	First and second generation
Arab Acculturative Strategy Scale	2-item/ Self-report (based on identification with U.S. culture)	Amer & Hovey (2007) from Barry (1996)	Mixed/ Christian; Muslim	18–46	Second generation or immigrated at <5 years of age
Detroit Arab American Study Acculturation Items	Dichotomous items regarding language use, media use, and social relations	Aprahamian et al. (2011) from DAAS (Baker et al., 2003)	Mixed/Christian; Muslim	Over 18	279 were born in the U.S.; Majority immigrated between ages of 19 and 70
Identification with U.S. culture	2-item/ Self-report	Faragallah, Schumm, & Webb (1997); Schumm (1996)	Majority male/ 27 Christian; 12 Muslim	Adult	Households with >1 first generation immigrant; Majority Egyptian
Male Arab Acculturation Scale (MAAS)	8-item/ 7-point Likert; Self-report	Barry (2005)	Male/84% Muslim; 16% Christian	18–54	Immigrants from 12 countries; Students or college educated; 50% in U. S. for >5 years

Translation Adaptation	*Sample Size/Selection*	*Methods*	*Reported Reliability*	*Evidence of Validity*
None	N=70/Snowball sampling; N=97/Recruited with flyers from campus and community	Qualitative; Correlation	None reported; α=.65	Not explicitly; however, gender differences emerged in acculturation and discrimination patterns; Predicted measures of American and Muslim identification
Translation; Back-translation; Committee reviews & pilot	N=297/Convenience sample	Factor analysis; Multiple regression	α=.85–.89 for two subscales	Two independent subscales emerged; Scales predicted health-related behaviors and mental health outcomes
None	N=120/Convenience sample; Email solicitation to Arab leaders, individuals, & organizations	T-tests comparing religious groups; Correlation		Differed by religion; Predicted acculturation stress & depression
Professional translators and back-translators were hired; Choice of Arabic or English given; Bilingual examiners	N=1016/From Detroit Arab American Study, drawn from Arabic or Chaldean descent households in Detroit metro area	Multiple regression; Correlation	α=.83	Correlated with established Marin and Main Acculturation Scale in a smaller sample; Face and content validity established; Did not predict mental health
None	N=42/Recruited from Kansas, Coptic church, and other locations in U.S.	Correlation	α=.91	Differed by religion; Related to length of time in U.S., and other acculturation variables
None (new measure in English)	N=115/Recruited through electronic media, flyers, and university	Factor analysis; Correlation	α=.71–.73 for two subscales	Two independent subscales; Predicted ethnic identity, independence, and collective self-esteem

Table 26.1 (cont.)

Construct	*Length/Format*	*Citation**	*Population to Which Instrument Was Applied*		
			Gender/Religion	*Age*	*Immigration History*
Perceived Parental Acculturation Behaviors Scale (PPABS)	16-item/ Likert scales	Henry, Biran, & Stiles (2006)	Mixed/No information on religion	18–26	Second generation, or had been in U.S. for 5 years
Stephenson Multigroup Acculturation Scale	32-item/4-point Likert scale; Self-report	Awad (2010) from Stephenson (2000)	Mixed/Christian; Muslim	14–65	Majority citizens; Also permanent residents and student visa holders; Egyptian, Palestinian, and others
Vancouver Index of Acculturation – Modified Arab Version	20-item/ Adapted the 7-point scale to a 5-point scale; Self-report	Britto & Amer (2007) from Ryder, Alden, & Paulhus (2000)	Mixed, 2/3 female/Muslim	18–25	Second generation and early immigrants; Representing 12 Arab states
<u>Acculturative Stress/Adjustment</u>					
Arabic language version of Demands of Immigration Scale (DIS)	23-item/6-point Likert scale; Self-report, with verbal presentation provided in Arabic (97%) or English by choice of participant	Aroian, Kaskiri, & Templin (2008) from Aroian, Norris, Tran, & Schappler-Morris (1998)	Females with children aged 12–15/Muslim	Mean=40.9	Recent immigrants (within 9 years); Nearly 47.5% from Iraq and 36% from Lebanon
Multidimensional Acculturative Stress Inventory (MASI), Arabic version	36-item/5-point self-report rating; Items read by examiner if participant was not literate	Wrobel, Farrag, & Hymes (2009) from Rodriguez, Myers, Mira, Flores, & Garcia-Hemendez (2002)	Mixed/Mostly Muslim	60–92	Mostly citizens or permanent residents; Mainly from Iraq or Lebanon; Reside in metropolitan Detroit
SAFE Acculturation Stress Scale	24-item with 2 items added for this study/ Modified 4-point rating used	Amer & Hovey (2007) from Mena, Padilla, & Maldonado (1987)	Mixed/Christian; Muslim	18–46	Second generation or immigrated at <5 years of age

Translation Adaptation	*Sample Size/Selection*	*Methods*	*Reported Reliability*	*Evidence of Validity*
None (new measure in English)	N=44/Recruited by 3 students active in Arab American groups	Items were drafted, edited, & grouped logically; Inconsistent items were dropped	α=.89 for Openness; α=.81 for Preservation	Two subscales appeared independent and predicted number of years in U.S.
None; Fluency in English required	N=177/Paper and Internet surveys via snowball sampling	Hierarchical regression; ANOVA	α=.84 for Dominant Society Immersion; α=.78 for Ethnic Immersion	Predicted discrimination differentially for Muslims and Christians; Noted concerns that SMAS was not specifically designed for Arab Americans
Item adaptation to reflect Arab heritage culture	N=150/Internet survey study with electronic solicitation through individuals and organizations	Rasch rating scale analysis, Correlation; ANOVA; Chi-square	α=.86 for Arab subscale; α=.80 for American subscale	Acculturation groupings based on scales related to family variables
Translation; Back-translation; Committee review by bilingual experts representing countries of origin of sample	N=394/Written and verbal advertisements in metropolitan Detroit Arabic community; Individual recruitment	Confirmatory factor analysis; Correlation; T-tests	α=.79–.91 for 6 subscales	Fit of proposed CFA model was excellent and suggested unique factors; Positive correlations between subscales and measures of mood disturbance; Discriminated recent immigrants from others
Item adaptation; Translation by bilingual psychologist; Naïve back-translator; Third-party expert evaluation	N=200/Convenience; Recruited by Arab American interviewers individually and through mosques, social service agency, and senior residences	Correlation; Multiple regression; Factor analysis	α=.73–.94 for subscales and overall scale	Predicted English skills, years of education, proportion of time in U.S., and depression; Related to immigration status and country of origin
Adapted; Removed 3 items due to poor fit	N=120/Convenience; Email solicitation to Arab leaders, individuals, & organizations	Rasch rating scale analysis; T-tests; Correlation	α=.88	Predicted depression differentially for Muslims and Christians

Table 26.1 (cont.)

Construct	*Length/Format*	*Citation**	*Population to Which Instrument Was Applied*		
			Gender/Religion	*Age*	*Immigration History*
SAFE Acculturation Stress Scale	26-item/4-point Likert scale; Self-report	Ahmed, Kia-Keating, & Tsai (2011) from Mena, Padilla, & Maldonado (1987)	Mixed/Mainly Muslim	13–18	First and second generation; 1/3 had parents with refugee status
Sociocultural Adjustment Measure (SCA)	10-item/ Self-report	Kira, Lewandowski, Templin, et al. (2008, 2010)	Mixed/Over 97% Muslim	12–79	Iraqi refugees in Southeast Michigan
Ethnic Identity					
Arab Ethnic Identity Measure	33-item; Overall scale and 4 subscales/ Self-report	Amer & Hovey (2007) from MAEIM, Barry (2005)	Mixed/Christian; Muslim	18–46	Second generation or immigrated at <5 years of age
Ethnic Identity Measure	6-item/4-point scale; Self-report	Shammas (2009) from MEIM, Phinney (1992)	Mixed/Arab Christian; Muslim; non-Arab Muslim	Mean=20.3	44% first generation; 37% second generation
Male Arab Ethnic Identity Measure (MAEIM)	33-item; Overall scale and 4 subscales/ Self-report	Barry (2005)	Male/16% Christian; 84% Muslim	18–54	Immigrants from 12 Arab countries; Students or college educated; 50% in U. S. for >5 years
Multigroup Ethnic Identity Measure (MEIM)	12-item/4-point scales; Self-report	Awad (2010) from Phinney (1992)	Mixed/Christian; Muslim	14–65	Majority citizens; Also permanent residents and student visa holders; Egyptian, Palestinian, and others

Translation Adaptation	*Sample Size/Selection*	*Methods*	*Reported Reliability*	*Evidence of Validity*
None	N=240/Recruited using ads, school personnel, and organizations	Structural equation modeling	α=.93	Convergent validity; Predicted psychological distress
Translation by 3 bilingual mental health professionals; Consensus; Back-translation; Pilot testing on focus groups	N=501/Quota sample recruited using snowball technique	Factor analysis; Correlation	α=.73	Inversely related to trauma measures
None; Adapted MAEIM to include females	N=120/Convenience; Email solicitation to Arab leaders, individuals, & organizations	Rasch category functioning analysis; Eliminated 2 items	α=.64–.86 for two subscales	Differed by religion; Predicted acculturative stress
None	N=753/Community college sample recruited from ESL classes, places of worship, and Arab organizations	Factor analysis	α=.88	Convergent and discriminant validity
None (new measure in English)	N=115/Recruited through electronic media, flyers, and university	Correlation	Total α=.69–.89	Differed by acculturative strategy groups
None; Fluency in English required	N=177/Paper and Internet surveys via snowball sampling	Hierarchical regression	α=.88	Predicted ethnic society immersion and discrimination

Table 26.2 Measures of Social Pressures and Personal Resources

Construct	*Length/Format*	*Citation**	*Population to Which Instrument Was Applied*		
			Gender/Religion	*Age*	*Immigration History*
Discrimination					
Krieger & Sidney Checklist	4-item/5-point Likert scale	Sirin et al. (2008) from Krieger & Sidney (1996)	Mixed/Muslim Asian; Muslim Arab	18–25	First and second generation
Perceived Ethnic Discrimination Questionnaire	22-item/7-point Likert; Self-report	Awad (2010) from Contrada (2001)	Mixed/Christian; Muslim	14–65	Majority citizens; Also permanent residents and student visa holders; Egyptian, Palestinian, and others
Perceived Discrimination	9-item/5-point Likert scale	Shammas (2009)	Mixed/Arab Christian; Arab Muslim; non-Arab Muslim	Mean=20.3	44% first generation; 37% second generation
Perceived Racism Scale-Child (PRS-C)	10-item/Scales of Personal (Frequency) & Institutional Racism (5-point scale)	Ahmed, Kia-Keating, & Tsai (2011) from Nyborg (2000)	Mixed/ Mainly Muslim	13–18	First and second generation; 1/3 had parents with refugee status
Schedule of Racist Events (SRE)	18-item/6-point Likert scale; Self-report	Moradi & Hasan (2004) from Landrine & Klonoff (1996)	Mixed/ Christian; Muslim; Other	18–60	Majority students; First and second generation
Political Engagement					
Survey of Political Engagement	4-Item Political Consciousness; 6-Item Political Activity/ Self-report	Read (2007) from Zogby International (2004) and Georgetown U. Project MAPS	Mixed/Muslim	Mean=38.5; 45	Majority "foreign born," but in U.S. more than 10 years; High SES

Translation Adaptation	*Sample Size/Selection*	*Methods*	*Reported Reliability*	*Evidence of Validity*
None	N=97/Recruited with flyers from campus and community	Correlation	α=.89	Inverse relationship with American identity variables
None; Fluency in English required	N=177/Paper and Internet surveys via snowball sampling	Hierarchical regression	α=.96	Predicted by religious affiliation along with acculturation levels
None	N=753/Community college sample	Factor analysis	α=.83	Minimally significant predictions; Focus groups suggested reluctance to report discrimination
Adapted some items; Replacing "Black" with "Arab"	N=240/ Recruited using ads, school personnel, and organizations	Structural equation modeling	α=.85	Predicted psychological distress
Adapted but not translated; Participants reported proficiency in English	N=108/Recruited from student and community organizations; Personal contact; Snowball sampling	Correlation; Path analysis	α=.94	Discriminant and convergent validation; Scales did not relate to social desirability; Predicted discrimination experiences and outcomes
None noted	N=524 in 2001; N=642 in 2004/ Selected Arabic surnames from geographic areas with a mosque	Multiple regression	α=.698	Results reflected the high SES of samples; Interaction between gender and religious involvement on political engagement

Table 26.2 (cont.)

Construct	Length/Format	Citation*	Population to Which Instrument Was Applied		
			Gender/Religion	Age	Immigration History
<u>Religion-Related</u>					
Age Universal Intrinsic-Extrinsic Scale	9-item Intrinsic, 11-Item Extrinsic/ Self-report	Amer & Hovey (2007) from Gorsuch & Venable (1983)	Mixed/Christian; Muslim	18–46	Second generation or immigrated at <5 years of age
Brief Arab Religious Coping Scale (BARCS)	15-item/5-point rating; Self-report	Amer, Hovey, Fox, & Rezcallah (2008)	Mixed/Christian; Muslim	18–70; 18–81	Arab Americans of various heritage countries; First and second generation
Brief Religious Coping Measure	12-item scale/ Current study utilized only 6 positive items and the overall scale	Ahmed, Kia-Keating, & Tsai (2011) from Pargament (1998)	Mixed/Mainly Muslim	13–18	First and second generation; 1/3 had parents with refugee status
Political and Organizational Religious Identity	2 "dummy variables" for each construct (Political and Organizational)	Read (2007) from Zogby International (2004) and Georgetown U. Project MAPS	Mixed/Muslim	Mean= 38.5; 45	Majority "foreign born," but in U.S. more than 10 years; High SES
Psychological Measure of Islamic Religiousness (PMIR)	70-item; 2 scales of core Islamic and non-specific religious dimensions/3- and 5-point scale	Abu-Raiya, Pargament, Mahoney, & Stein (2013)	Mixed/Muslim	18–45	Reside in the United States, Europe, Asia, and Africa; Included Arab Americans
Religious Support Scale (RSS)	21-item/5-point Likert scale	Ahmed, Kia-Keating, & Tsai (2011) from Fiala et al. (2002)	Mixed/Mainly Muslim	13–18	First and second generation; 1/3 had parents with refugee status

Translation Adaptation	*Sample Size/Selection*	*Methods*	*Reported Reliability*	*Evidence of Validity*
None	N=120/Convenience sample; Email solicitation to Arab leaders, individuals, & organizations	T-tests comparing religious groups; Correlations	α=.88	Differed by religious group and marital status
None (new measure in English)	N=76/Initial pilot study; M=599/ validation sample	Rasch rating scale model; Category function analysis	Item reliability: .99; Person reliability: .89	Construct and convergent validation; Did not predict stress or depression
Adapted to include words: "Allah" and "mosque"	N=240/Recruited using ads, school personnel, and organizations	Structural equation modeling	α=.68	Negatively predicted psychological distress, along with other cultural resources
None noted	N=524 in 2001; N=642 in 2004/ Selected Arabic surnames from geographic areas with a mosque	Multiple regression	Not reported	Interaction between gender and religious involvement on political engagement
None (new measure in English)	N=138/Internet sample; Recruited from social media and university websites	Factor analysis; Hierarchical regression	α=.77–.97	Convergent, discriminant, predictive, and incremental validity demonstrated
Adapted to include words: "Allah" and "mosque"	N=240/Recruited using ads/school personnel, and organizations	Structural equation modeling	α=.93	Negatively predicted psychological distress, along with other cultural resources

Table 26.2 (cont.)

Construct	*Length/Format*	*Citation**	*Population to Which Instrument Was Applied*		
			Gender/Religion	*Age*	*Immigration History*
Sacred Loss	23-item/5-point scale; Subscales measure Sacred Loss and Desecration; Self-report	Abu-Raiya, Pargament, & Mahoney (2008) from Pargament, Magyar, Benore, & Mahoney (2008)	Mixed/Muslim	18–60	Reside in the U. S.
Subjective Religious Identity	3-item/Yes or no response	Read (2007) from Zogby International (2004) and Georgetown U. Project MAPS	Mixed/Muslim	Mean=38.5; 45	Majority "foreign born," but in U.S. more than 10 years; High SES
Family					
McMaster Family Assessment Device General Functioning subscale	12-Item/4-point Likert-type scale	Amer & Hovey (2007) from Epstein, Baldwin, & Bishop (1983)	Mixed/Christian; Muslim	18–46	Second generation or immigrated at <5 years of age
Family Peer Relationship Questionnaire (FPRQ)	55-item/ Self-report and parent informant report; Completed verbally; Majority of adults (97%) chose Arabic; Children chose English	Aroian, Hough, Templin, & Kaskiri (2008) from Ellison (1983, 1985)	Adult females; Children mixed gender/ Muslim	Mean=39; 12–15 years	Parents emigrated from the Middle East less than 15 years prior
Social Support					
Multi-Dimensional Scale of Perceived Social Support (MSPSS)	12-item/7-point Likert scale	Aroian, Kulwicki, Kaskiri, Templin, & Wells (2007) from Zimet et al. (1988)	Female/Muslim	Mean=40	Recent immigrants (within 9 years); Nearly 47.5% from Iraq; 36% from Lebanon
Multidimensional Scale of Perceived Social Support (MSPSS) Friends Subscale	Subscale contains 3 items/7-point Likert scale	Aroian, Hough, Templin, & Kaskiri (2008) from Zimet et al. (1988)	Mixed/Muslim	12–15	Children of parents who had emigrated from the Middle East <15 years prior

Translation Adaptation	*Sample Size/Selection*	*Methods*	*Reported Reliability*	*Evidence of Validity*
Adapted some items to reflect Islam	N=138/Randomly selected from Arab American Muslim community	Hierarchical regression; Mediation analysis	α=.94	Impact of loss on wellbeing mediated by religious coping
None noted	N=524 in 2001; N=642 in 2004/ Selected Arabic surnames from geographic areas with a mosque	Multiple regression	α=.709	Interaction between gender and religious involvement on political engagement
None	N=120/Convenience; Email solicitation to Arab leaders, individuals, & organizations	T-tests comparing religious groups; Correlations	α=.90	Predicted acculturative stress and depression
Adaptations suggested by Arab immigrants with social service experience; Translation; Back-translation; Committee review; Decentering	N=645/Mother-child dyads (402 primary; 243 cross-validation); Arab mother with children 12–15	Confirmatory factor analysis; Concurrent validity	α=.66–.81 for mothers; .69–.81 for children	Identified and replicated alternative factor structure; Predicted child internalizing & externalizing behaviors & social support from friends; Similar results from parent and child data
Translation; Back-translation; Committee review by bilingual experts representing countries of origin of sample	N=394/Written and verbal advertisements in metropolitan Detroit Arabic community and individual recruitment	Correlation	α=.75	Demonstrated convergent and discriminant validity
Translation; Back-translation; Committee review	N=645/Mother-child dyads (402 primary; 243 cross-validation); Arab mother with children 12–15	Concurrent validity	α=.72	Predicted other peer relations measure

Table 26.3 Measures of Psychological Wellbeing, Mental Health, and Health

Construct	*Length/Format*	*Citation**	*Population to Which Instrument Was Applied*		
			Gender/Religion	*Age*	*Immigration History*
Perceived Control					
Environmental Mastery	20-item/6-point Likert scale	Moradi & Hasan (2004) from Ryff (1989)	Mixed/Christian; Muslim; Other	18–60	Majority were students; First and second generation
Self-Esteem/Self Image					
Collective Self-Esteem	16-Item/7-point scale; Self-report	Barry (2005) from Luhtanen & Crocker (1992)	Male/84% Muslim; 16% Christian	18–54	Immigrants from 12 countries; Students or college educated; 50% in U. S. for >5 years
Rosenberg Self-Esteem Scale	10-item/4-point rating; Self-report	Moradi & Hasan (2004) from Rosenberg (1979)	Mixed/Christian; Muslim; Other	18–60	Majority were students; First and second generation
Rosenberg Self-Esteem Scale	10 Item/4-point rating; Self-report	Barry (2005) from Rosenberg (1979)	Male/84% Muslim; 16% Christian	18–54	Immigrants from 12 countries; Students or college educated; 50% in U. S. for >5 years
Self-Construal Scale	24-Item/7-point Likert; Self-report	Barry, Elliott, & Evans (2000) from Markus & Kitayama (1991)	Male/84% Muslim; 16% Christian	18–54	Immigrants from 12 countries; Students or college educated; 50% in U. S. for >5 years
Stressors					
Daily Hassles Scale (DHS)	117 short statements/3-point scale of severity	Aroian, Kulwicki, Kaskiri, Templin, & Wells (2007) from Kanner et al. (1981)	Female/Muslim	Mean=40	Immigrants mainly from Iraq and Lebanon; 53% refugees upon immigration; Median time in U.S.=9 years

Translation Adaptation	*Sample Size/Selection*	*Methods*	*Reported Reliability*	*Evidence of Validity*
None; Students reported proficiency in English	N=108/Recruited from student and community organizations; Personal contact; Snowball sampling	Correlation; Path analysis	α=.85	Convergent validation; Mediated self-esteem and psychological distress responses to events
None	N=115/Recruited through electronic media, flyers, and university	Correlation	α=.78–.83 for subscales	Predicted Separation/ Assimilation
None; Students reported proficiency in English	N=108/Recruited from student and community organizations; Personal contact; Snowball sampling	Correlation; Path analysis	α=.89	Convergent validation; Related to events and mediated by perception of self-control
None	N=115/Recruited through electronic media, flyers, and university	Correlation	α=.72–.92; Test-retest >.85	Predicted Integration/ Marginalization
None	N=115/Recruited through electronic media, flyers, and university	Correlation	α=.75 Independent; α=.78 Inter-dependent	Demonstrated predictive and discriminant validity; Two dimensions appear to be independent dimensions
Translation; Back-translation; Committee consensus; 97% chose Arabic version; Rest eliminated from analysis	N=537/Advertised; Face-to-face contact	Correlation	α=.94	Convergent validity; Predicted mood states

Table 26.3 (cont.)

Construct	*Length/Format*	*Citation**	*Population to Which Instrument Was Applied*		
			Gender/Religion	*Age*	*Immigration History*
General Mental Health					
Brief Symptom Inventory (BSI)	53-item/5-point Likert scale; Self-report	Moradi & Hasan (2004) from Derogatis (1993)	Mixed/Christian; Muslim; Other	18–60	Majority were students; First and second generation
Child Behavior Checklist (CBCL)	120-item/ 3-point rating; Parent-report	Aroian, Hough, Templin, & Kaskiri (2008) from Achenbach & Rescorla (2001)	Mixed/Muslim	12–15	Completed by parents who had emigrated from the Middle East <15 years prior, regarding their 12–15-year-old children
Kessler Psychological Distress Scale	10-item/ Self-report	Aprahamian et al. (2011) and Padela & Heisler (2010) from DAAS (Baker et al., 2003)	Mixed/Christian; Muslim	>18	279 were born in the U.S.; Majority immigrated between ages 19 and 70
Youth Self-Report (YSR)	112-item/ Self-report	Ahmed, Kia-Keating, & Tsai (2011) from Achenbach & Rescorla (2001)	Mixed/Mainly Muslim	13–18	First and second generation; 1/3 had parents with refugee status
Youth Self-Report (YSR)	112-item/3-point rating; Self-report	Aroian, Hough, Templin, & Kaskiri (2008) from Achenbach & Rescorla (2001)	Mixed/Muslim	12–15	Children of parents who had emigrated from the Middle East <15 years prior
Depression					
Center for the Epidemiologic Study of Depression Scale (CES-D)	20 symptoms/4-point frequency scale; Self-report	Amer, Awad, & Hovey (2014) from Radloff (1977)	Mixed/Christian; Muslim	18–46	Second generation or immigrated to U. S. at <5 years of age

Translation Adaptation	*Sample Size/Selection*	*Methods*	*Reported Reliability*	*Evidence of Validity*
None; Students reported proficiency in English	N=108/Recruited from student and community organizations; Personal contact; Snowball sampling	Correlation; Path analysis	α=.97	Convergent validity; Related to experiences of discrimination; Mediated by personal control
Translation; Back-translation; Committee review	N=645/Mother-child dyads (402 primary; 243 cross-validation); Arab mother with children 12–15	Correlation	α=.81–.90	Convergent; Low pathology predicted higher scores on Family Peer Relationship Scales
Professional translators and back-translators were hired; Choice of Arabic or English given; Bilingual examiners	N=1016/From Detroit Arab American Study, drawn from Arabic or Chaldean descent households in Detroit Metro area	Multiple regression; Correlation	α=.88	Scores were predicted by reported experiences of discrimination
None	N=240/Recruited using ads, school personnel, and organizations	Structural equation modeling	α=.92 for Internalizing and Externalizing scales	Scores were predicted by sociocultural adversity and negatively related to cultural resources
Translation; Back-translation; Committee review	N=645/Mother-child dyads (402 primary; 243 cross-validation); Arab mother with children 12–15	Correlation	α=.88–.86	Convergent validity; Low pathology predicted higher scores on Family Peer Relationship Scales
None	N=119/Convenience; Email solicitation to Arab leaders, individuals, & organizations in 20 states	T-tests; Factor analysis	α=.90	Factor structure reflected immigrant background; Need for a more accurate cutoff

Table 26.3 (cont.)

Construct	*Length/Format*	*Citation**	*Population to Which Instrument Was Applied*		
			Gender/Religion	*Age*	*Immigration History*
Geriatric Depression Scale (GDS) and GDS Collateral (GDSCOL), Arabic versions	30-item/ Self-report (GDS) and informant report (GDSCOL)	Wrobel & Farrag (2006) from Yesavage et al. (1983)	Mixed/Mostly Muslim	60–92	Varied, but mostly citizens or permanent residents; Mainly from Iraq or Lebanon; Reside in metropolitan Detroit
<u>Moods</u>					
Profile of Mood State (POMS) – Arabic Version, short form	6 Subscales reflecting affective mood states/5-point scales	Aroian, Kulwicki, Kaskiri, Templin, & Wells (2007) from McNair et al. (1971)	Female/Muslim	Mean=40	Immigrants mainly from Iraq and Lebanon; 53% refugees upon immigration; Median time in U.S.= 9 years
<u>Anxiety</u>					
State Trait Anxiety Inventory (STAI)	20-item/ Self-report; Utilized trait scale only	Ahmed, Kia-Keating, & Tsai (2011) from Spielberger (1983)	Mixed/Mainly Muslim	13–18	First and second generation; 1/3 had parents with refugee status
<u>PTSD/Trauma</u>					
Backlash Trauma Scale (BTS)	18-Item/5-point	Kira, Lewandowski, Templin, et al. (2010) from Loo and Associates (2001)	Mixed/Over 97% Muslim	12–79	Iraqi refugees in Southeast Michigan
Brief PTSD Instrument	13-item (original scale 17-item)/Yes or no format; 4-point Likert	Abu-Ras & Suarez (2009) from Foa et al. (1993)	Mixed/Muslim (>50% Arab)	18–68	Most in U.S. over 10 years; Mean time in U.S.= 19 years

Translation Adaptation	*Sample Size/Selection*	*Methods*	*Reported Reliability*	*Evidence of Validity*
Translation by bilingual psychologist; Naïve back-translator; Third-party expert evaluation by instructor of Arabic	N=200/Sample of convenience; Recruited by Arab-American interviewers individually and through mosques, social service agency, and senior residences	Factor analysis; Correlation; Multiple regression	α=.92 for both measures	Resulting factors similar to those derived cross-culturally; Sensitivity evident, but specificity unclear due to self-reported diagnosis; Self-report predicted informant report
Translation; Back-translation; Committee consensus; 97% chose Arabic version; Rest eliminated from analysis	N=537/Advertised and face-to-face contact	Confirmatory factor analysis; Cross-validation	α=.92	Short form was a better fit in confirmatory factor analysis, but high intercorrelation of factors; Good concurrent validity
None	N=240/Recruited using ads, school personnel, and organizations	Structural equation modeling	α=.87	Convergent and discriminant validity
Translation by 3 bilingual mental health professionals; Consensus; Back-translation; Pilot testing on focus groups	N=501/Quota sample recruited using snowball technique	Factor analysis; Multiple regression; Path analysis	α=.95; Subscales α=.77–.98	Demonstrated construct, convergent, divergent, and predictive validity; Predicted PTSD and cumulative trauma
None; English required for participation	N=102/Recruited through flyers at mosques in New York City	Multiple regression	α=.63	Viewed as more sensitive in non-Arabs; May not be sensitive to ongoing trauma

Table 26.3 (*cont.*)

Construct	*Length/Format*	*Citation**	*Population to Which Instrument Was Applied*		
			Gender/Religion	*Age*	*Immigration History*
Clinician Administered PTSD Measure (CAPS-2)	18-item measure/ Structured clinical interview	Kira, Lewandowski, Templin, et al. (2008, 2010) from Blake et al. (1990)	Mixed/Over 97% Muslim	12–79	Iraqi refugees in Southeast Michigan
Cumulative Trauma Measure (CT)	Lists 22 kinds of traumatic experience & their recurrence; 6 subscales	Kira, Lewandowski, Templin, et al. (2008, 2010)	Mixed/Over 97% Muslim	12–79	Iraqi refugees in Southeast Michigan
Cumulative Trauma Disorders Measure	15-item/ Measure of 13 symptoms	Kira, Lewandowski, Templin, et al. (2008, 2010)	Mixed/Over 97% Muslim	12–79	Iraqi refugees in Southeast Michigan
Impact of Events Scale	22-item/5-point Likert scale measuring degree of PTSD	Abu-Ras & Abu-Bader (2009) from Weiss & Marmar (1996)	Mixed, majority female/Arab American and non-Arab Muslim; 88% Muslim	18–77	Over half first generation from Arab countries; 9.5% second generation; Others from Africa or southern Asia
Posttraumatic Diagnostic Scale	Checklist of traumatic events & report of most bothersome event; 17-item/ 4-point scale of PTSD symptoms; 9-item/Yes or no scale of functioning	Norris & Aroian (2008a, 2008b) from Foa (1995)	Female/Muslim	Mean=40	Immigrants mainly from Iraq and Lebanon; 53% refugees upon immigration; Median time in U.S.=9 years

Translation Adaptation	*Sample Size/Selection*	*Methods*	*Reported Reliability*	*Evidence of Validity*
Translation by 3 bilingual mental health professionals; Consensus; Back-translation; Pilot testing on focus groups	N=501/Quota sample recruited using snowball technique	Correlation; Multiple regression	α=.97; Subscales α=.90–.93	Convergent validation predicted by cumulative and backlash trauma
Translation by 3 bilingual mental health professionals; Consensus; Back-translation; Pilot testing on focus groups	N=501/Quota sample recruited using snowball technique	Factor analysis; Multiple regression; Cluster analysis	α=.85; Subscales α=.65–.92	Demonstrated construct, convergent, divergent, and predictive validity
Translation by 3 bilingual mental health professionals; Consensus; Back-translation; Pilot testing on focus groups	N=501/Quota sample recruited using snowball technique	Exploratory factor analysis	α=.85–.98; 6-week test-re-test r=.76	Demonstrated convergent and divergent validity; Factor structure confirmed
None; however, group was highly educated and most in U.S. for over 10 years	N=350/Distributed 1200 surveys nationally through community-based organizations	Multiple regression	α=.92	Predicted by age, educational level, community support, and depression
Translation; Back-translation; Committee consensus; 97% completed in Arabic	N=546/Recruited by bilingual research assistants from ads and face-to-face contact	Confirmatory factor analysis for 17-item PTSD scale	Overall PTSD α=.93; Subscales α=.77–.91	Convergent and discriminant validity with experience and symptom measures; Avoidance symptoms presented less frequently; however, high avoidance symptoms predictive of other PTSD symptoms and functioning

Table 26.3 (cont.)

Construct	*Length/Format*	*Citation**	*Population to Which Instrument Was Applied*		
			Gender/Religion	*Age*	*Immigration History*
PTSD Checklist Military Version (PTSD-M)	17-item/5-point scale; Administered verbally as part of a larger interview process	Jamil, Nassar-McMillan, & Lambert (2007) from Weathers et al. (1993)	Mixed/Christian; Muslim	Means= 43–49	Primarily Iraqi immigrants and refugees
Trauma History Questionnaire	24-item; Based on high magnitude stressor questionnaire from DSM-IV PTSD field trials	Hassouneh & Kulwicki (2007) from Green (1996)	Female/Muslim	27–65	Immigrants from 5 Arab states
<u>Mental Status</u>					
Informant Questionnaire of Cognitive Decline in the Elderly (IQCODE), Arabic version	26-item/5-point rating of performance relative to 5 years ago; Informant report	Wrobel & Farrag (2008) from Jorm et al. (1991)	Mixed/Mostly Muslim	60–92	Varied, but most citizens or permanent residents; Mainly from Iraq or Lebanon; Reside in metropolitan Detroit
Mini-Mental Status Exam (MMSE), Arabic version	30-item/ Individually administered measure of cognitive ability and orientation	Wrobel & Farrag (2007) from Folstein et al. (1975)	Mixed/Mostly Muslim	60–92	Varied, but most citizens or permanent residents; Mainly from Iraq or Lebanon; Reside in metropolitan Detroit
<u>Health</u>					
Cornell Medical Index	195 questions; 2 forms, for Male and Female/ Self-report; Oral presentation	Reizian & Meleis (2013) from Broadman, Erdmann, Lorge, Gershensen, & Wolff (1949)	Mixed/Christian; Muslim	Adult	Mainly first generation from 9 Arab countries

Translation Adaptation	*Sample Size/Selection*	*Methods*	*Reported Reliability*	*Evidence of Validity*
Offered in Arabic or English; No details provided on translation	N=250/Recruited in Arab and Chaldean community through ads, flyers, and community centers	MANOVA	None reported	Discriminated immigrants arriving post-1990 from others
No formal translation or back-translation; Bilingual interviewer translated on the spot	N=30/Word of mouth and flyers	Correlation	Not reported	Not predictive of mental health symptoms; Data highly skewed due to high level of daily trauma in immigrants
Translation by bilingual psychologist; Naïve back-translator; Third-party expert evaluation	N=200/Convenience; Recruited by Arab-American interviewers individually and through mosques, social service agency, and senior residences	Correlation; Multiple regression	α=.96	Was predicted by performance on MMSE
Translation by bilingual psychologist; Naïve back-translator; Third-party expert evaluation	N=200/Convenience; Recruited by Arab-American interviewers individually and through mosques, social service agency, and senior residences	Correlation; Multiple regression; ROC analysis; Chi-square	α=.89	Subscales and overall score predicted informant report of decline; Specificity was better in high relative to low educated groups; Item performance also varied
Translated into Arabic; No details provided on translation; 5.8% completed in English	N=102/Patients seeking care at outpatient and inpatient healthcare facilities	T-tests; Correlation	Low α overall, but subscales range from α=.90–.91	Differentiated by country of origin and employment status

Table 26.3 (cont.)

Construct	*Length/Format*	*Citation**	*Population to Which Instrument Was Applied*		
			Gender/Religion	*Age*	*Immigration History*
Health Scale	12-Item/5-point scale; Self-rated health	Kira, Lewandowski, Templin, et al. (2008, 2010) from Kira et al. (2001)	Mixed/over 97% Muslim	12–79	Iraqi refugees in Southeast Michigan
Short Form Health Survey (SF-36)	36-item/Physical Composite Summary & Mental Composite Summary	Jadalla & Lee, (2012) from Ware & Shervourne (1992)	Mixed/No information on religion	18–86	First and second generation

* = Complete reference information for the citations can be obtained from the author at nwrobel@umich.edu.

Translation Adaptation	*Sample Size/Selection*	*Methods*	*Reported Reliability*	*Evidence of Validity*
Translation by 3 bilingual mental health professionals; Consensus; Back-translation; Pilot testing on focus groups	N=501/Quota sample recruited using snowball technique	Multiple regression	α=.75	Predicted by cumulative and backlash trauma
Arabic version obtained from Quality Metric, Inc	N=297/Convenience	Multiple regression	α=.94 (PCS); .89 (MCS)	Predicted by acculturation measures

27

RESEARCH CONSIDERATIONS

Minimizing Mistrust and Maximizing Participation

Karen J. Aroian

Many aspects of the research process, such as recruiting study participants, obtaining informed consent, and collecting data, warrant special consideration when Arab Americans are the study population. First, a climate of Arabs being under surveillance as suspected radical Islamists and terrorists (El-Haj, 2007; Naber, 2006) generates mistrust among Arab Americans and this mistrust may make them unwilling to participate in research (Kahan & Al-Tamimi, 2009). Second, as with any research about an ethnic group, it is important to incorporate the group's relevant cultural features so that the research process is culturally sensitive. Culturally sensitive research not only encourages study participation but also contributes to obtaining valid and meaningful study findings (Aroian, 2013).

Considering features of Arab culture that are relevant to the research process is complicated by the fact that Arab Americans are a diverse group with substantial intragroup variation (Suleiman, 2010). Although heritage from an Arabic-speaking country is what unites them, Arab Americans vary in terms of major religion (e.g. Muslim, Christian), have sects within each major religion, come from one of 22 different Arab countries, and are from varying historical waves of migration (Suleiman, 2010). Each of these variables affects how culture is interpreted and manifested by people with Arab heritage (Moghadam, 2004). Characteristics of the resettlement communities where Arab Americans live also affect cultural orientation. For example, living in a community with a dense co-ethnic population reinforces cultural norms and makes it likely that its inhabitants will be traditional or oriented toward the culture of origin (Birman, Trickett, & Buchanan, 2005; Logan, Zhang, & Alba, 2002). Individual factors also explain variation in cultural orientation among Arab Americans. Socioeconomic background, generation in the U.S., age at immigration, and personal preferences are but a few of these individual factors (Suleiman, 2010). Contributing factors are entangled, making it difficult to differentiate religious, country of origin, neighborhood, socioeconomic, generational, and other influences from one another.

Given this diversity among Arab Americans, it is crucial that researchers assess the degree to which the study population typifies or diverges from "so-called" Arab culture. Researchers also need to consider that culture is dynamic or changes over time. Research decisions must be based on contemporaneous Arab culture. Although published literature is informative, it may represent a different context or historical period. Relying solely on published literature may also inadvertently lead to stereotypes and simplistic assumptions that are not applicable to the specific study population. Thus, researchers will need to employ a theoretical framework about research methodology that will allow them to determine which cultural characteristics are important for a given study.

This chapter addresses research methods with Arab Americans, including how to minimize Arab Americans' potential mistrust and suspicion about participating in research and how to determine relevant features of Arab culture that should be addressed when conducting research with Arab Americans. Community Based Participatory Research (CBPR) is presented as a theoretical framework for adapting research strategies to minimize mistrust and conduct culturally sensitive research. A case example of a research study about mother-child adjustment in Muslim Arab American immigrant and refugee families is provided to illustrate the application of CBPR principles for three methodological challenges: diversity in language ability, inappropriate content in preexisting measures, and obtaining consent/assent in a group with traditional gender roles. Finally, the current state of research with Arab Americans is critiqued and recommendations for future studies are discussed.

The Community-Based Participatory Research Framework

Community-based participatory research (Minkler & Wallerstein, 2008) is an optimal theoretical framework for providing direction about the relevant features of Arab culture to address when conducting research with Arab Americans. Although it was developed for reducing health disparities, it can also be used in psychology. CBPR stresses the importance of being responsive to the study population, including determining which cultural values, beliefs, and behaviors are relevant. CBPR is also well suited to conducting research with vulnerable and hard-to-reach study populations, such as Arab Americans (Amer & Bagasra, 2013).

A defining feature of CBPR is that it fully engages insiders or members of the study population in a true partnership with community members (Minkler & Wallerstein, 2008). These insiders are people from the nonacademic community who are trusted by and knowledgeable about the study population. Their role is to inform and collaborate with the researcher on every aspect of the research process, including which research questions are important to their community and how to interpret and disseminate study findings. Engaging insiders and incorporating their perspectives reassures study participants that study findings will be interpreted in a manner that benefits Arab Americans rather than perpetuates negative and overly simplistic stereotypes. This reassurance also assists with gaining access to and recruiting Arab American study participants.

Sampling and Recruiting Arab American Study Participants

There are a variety of sampling methods that can be used to study Arab Americans, but each method has some challenges and limitations. Regardless of the method employed, researchers will also need to address Arab Americans' hesitancy to participate in research because of concerns about being under surveillance and portrayed negatively (Kahan & Al-Tamimi, 2009).

Sampling Methods

Arab Americans live in all 50 states and the District of Columbia (Arab American Institute, 2013). Thus, one method for obtaining a representative national sample is to randomly select Arab American study participants from the total U.S. population of Arab Americans. However, it is difficult to obtain a national sampling frame for random selection because the only means for obtaining data about the entire Arab American population is the U.S. Census American Community Survey (ACS). However, this method is not without sampling error and the data are limited to socio-demographic characteristics (Arab American Institute, 2013; Asi & Beaulieu, 2013). The few other national databases that provide a mechanism for identifying Arab Americans (e.g. data files from the Social Security Administration, cancer registries, the National Health Interview Survey) use country of birth as the identifier (Abdulrahim & Baker, 2009). This restricts the sample to foreign-born Arab Americans and confounds immigrant status with Arab ethnicity (El-Sayed & Galea, 2009).

The limited ability to delineate the total U.S. population of Arab Americans has prompted researchers to add questions to existing databases that ask more broadly about Arab heritage. For example, the Centers for Disease Control and Prevention's Behavioral Risk Factor Surveillance System (BRFSS) is a national survey that is administered yearly in all 50 states and the District of Columbia to randomly selected people. Because it is administered by individual states before results are combined across the nation, each state has the opportunity to add items of interest. In Michigan, which has the highest concentration of Arab Americans (Arab American Institute, 2013; Asi & Beaulieu, 2013), the BRFSS has an additional identifying question that asks if respondents are of Arab or Chaldean ancestry (Arfken, Arnetz, Fakhouri, Ventimiglia, & Jamil, 2011).

Similarly, the Detroit Arab American Study (DAAS), which is a companion to the Detroit Area Study, produces a sampling frame of the Detroit Metropolitan Area (DMA) that can be used to randomly select Arab American households for study participation. The DAAS uses Arab-dense Census tracts (i.e. Census tracts in the DMA in which 10% or more of persons self-classified as of Arab or Chaldean ancestry) combined with membership mailing lists from the major Arab and Chaldean organizations that serve the DMA (Abdulrahim & Baker, 2009). The membership lists allow Arab Americans to be located who are geographically dispersed and living in less Arab-dense Census tracts. However, a shortcoming of the use of membership lists is that they are biased toward Arab Americans who choose to join ethnic organizations.

Researchers using Michigan and DAAS databases for sampling have yielded informative findings (e.g. Jaber, Brown, Hammad, Zhu, and Herman, 2003; Padela, Rasheed, Warren, Choi, & Mathur, 2011; Rice & Kulwicki, 1992). Yet, Arab Americans living in Michigan are not representative of the national population of Arab Americans. Data suggest that the Michigan population of Arab Americans, on average, is less educated, has lower income, and contains fewer Egyptians than the national Arab American population (Aroian et al., 2009; El-Sayed & Galea, 2009). Arab Americans living in Dearborn, a city within the DMA known for its high concentration of Arab Americans, are also different from Arab Americans living in outlying DMA suburbs: Arab Americans living in Dearborn are, on average, less educated, of low income, recent immigrants, non-English speaking, traditional in cultural orientation, and Muslim (Arab American Institute, 2013; Asi & Beaulieu, 2013).

Another way to develop a sampling frame is to construct a list of Arab surnames from a combination of techniques, such as statistical manipulation of linguistic characteristics of Arab surnames and expert review of publically available databases, such as phone books, petition drives, and mailing lists (e.g. Lauderdale, 2006; Nasseri, 2007; Schwartz et al., 2004). However, it is important to note that a validation study of an Arab name algorithm for determining Arab ancestry found that the algorithm was only moderately sensitive. In addition, false positives and false negatives varied by gender and concentration of Arabs in the study location (El-Sayed, Lauderdale, & Galea, 2010).

Yet another sampling method, one that is used perhaps most often, is to rely on unifying mechanisms to recruit convenience samples of Arab Americans. Unifying mechanisms include advertising in Arab American local, regional, and national ethnic and religious institutions and blogs and Internet sites. Unifying mechanisms also include using social networks for snowball sampling and leveraging community members to identify and recruit Arab American study participants.

Unifying mechanisms can result in geographic diversity if a wide enough net is cast. For example, Read, Amick, and Donato (2005) obtained a national sample by using membership lists from the Arab American Institute and Zogby International, which are two organizations that maintain data about Arab Americans. Other researchers have successfully used the Internet and snowball methods to obtain geographically diverse Arab American study participants (Amer & Hovey, 2012; Barry, 2001). For instance, Internet and snowball sampling enabled Amer and Hovey to recruit participants for their study from 34 states and the District of Columbia.

However, sampling bias is a major problem that can result from using unifying mechanisms. Similar to membership in ethnic organizations, Arab American blogs and Internet sites are more apt to be used by people with a strong Arab identity. There is also some evidence, albeit limited, that Internet methods are biased toward reaching more highly educated Arab Americans and perhaps those who are more highly acculturated or oriented toward U.S. culture (Amer & Hovey, 2012; Barry, 2001; Kahan & Al-Tamimi, 2009). Social network/snowball methods can also produce samples that are biased by personal characteristics of the people who are doing the recruiting. One means for offsetting bias from recruiter personal characteristics is to use diverse sources. For example, Aroian and colleagues (2009) strategically selected a pool of 13 community-member recruiters who were representative of subgroups of Arab Americans in the community where the study took place.

With the exception of public records that mandate specifying country of birth, a challenge shared by all of the approaches mentioned above is that Arab Americans who prefer to avoid surveillance and anti-Arab sentiments can choose to hide their Arab ancestry. Anglicizing surnames and not responding to questions about Arab heritage are two examples of how to avoid surveillance. Similarly, gatekeepers of Arab organizations and interest groups may limit access to membership lists to protect their members from outsiders, including researchers. Lastly, even when lists or other identifying mechanisms are available, those invited to join a research study have the right to refuse study participation. Therefore, regardless of sampling method, researchers must address issues of mistrust when recruiting Arab Americans for research. As described below, a key feature of CBPR – using trusted insiders – is well suited for addressing issues of mistrust.

Recruitment Methods to Offset Mistrust

Much of the literature about recruiting Arab Americans for research mentions reluctance about study participation because of mistrust and concerns about ethnic profiling (Aroian, Katz, & Kulwicki, 2006; Barry, 2001; Jaber, 2003; Kahan & Al-Tamimi, 2009). For example, a study that used pedometers to measure physical activity (Kahan & Al-Tamimi, 2009) reported that some Arab Americans worried that the general public might construe the pedometer as threatening or a weapon. Mistrust generated additional reasons for nonparticipation, including fear of being under surveillance, possible repercussions from answering questions about language use or religiosity, and the belief that the study was a pretense for a negative motive toward people with Middle Eastern heritage. Even a study that was conducted before 9/11 mentioned concerns about ethnic profiling and mistrust (Barry, 2001), but these concerns were noted as intensifying post 9/11 in a study that spanned both pre and post 9/11 (Jaber, 2003).

An effective way to minimize mistrust is to use insiders or trusted members of the study population to endorse the study. For example, Aroian and colleagues (2009) obtained the endorsement of key imams from local mosques to advertise their study to Muslim Arab immigrant families in greater Detroit. Jaber (2003) obtained the endorsement of a local Arab community organization; used a 16-member advisory committee consisting of key leaders, religious institutions, and other gatekeepers; and capitalized on her own Arab ethnicity to publicize an epidemiological study of the prevalence of diabetes in Dearborn, Michigan.

Another common feature of successful recruitment efforts is the use of personal rather than impersonal contact to engage potential study participants. One study used Arab American community members (e.g. mothers, teachers, health and social service providers) whose ancestry matched the countries of origin of the study population to verbally advertise and recruit study participants face-to-face (Aroian et al., 2009). The same community members also collected the data from the people they recruited, further capitalizing on personal relationships that were established during recruitment (see Aroian et al., 2006, for a more in-depth discussion about using personal contact). Jaber (2003) also capitalized on personal contact by making phone calls to households selected by the DAAS method described above to personally address the concerns of people who were hesitant to participate. Barry (2001) and Amer and Hovey (2012), who contacted potential study participants by email, noted that participants appreciated the opportunity for personal contact with the researchers.

Although Barry's method of using the Internet for recruitment was reported as effective, it is worth noting that Barry obtained a participation rate of only 8.75%. In contrast, Jaber (2003), who was physically present in the community where the study was located, obtained an 87% participation rate in her study, but only after she capitalized on using insiders and personal contact as a remedy to address prior recruitment difficulties. Aroian and colleagues (2009) and Amer and Hovey (2012) did not document participation rates. However, Aroian and colleagues noted in a 2006 publication about recruitment for their study that their first approach, written advertisement in mosques and community centers, yielded no participants. In addition, their effort to use a single recruiter to obtain participants for others who would be collecting the data was not successful. Study participants clearly preferred personal contact by the person who would be their data collector rather than being referred to a data collector whom they had not yet met. This may have been because data collection occurred face-to-face in participants' homes. Even though this method of personal recruitment (as well as in-home data collection) was costly, it yielded a large sample of Arab American families who were willing to participate.

There is also some evidence that the importance of personal contact is variable. Kahan and Al-Tamimi (2009) found that different recruitment techniques appealed to different subgroups of Arab Americans based on religion and acculturation. More specifically, they tracked recruitment efforts for their study of physical activity in Arab Americans living in Southern California and found that snowball sampling and advertising through flyers and ethnic organizations were more successful with non-Muslims and highly acculturated Arab Americans. In contrast, face-to-face and personal methods were more successful with Muslims and those Arab Americans whose cultural orientation was primarily toward their Arab heritage.

Sample profiles obtained by other researchers are consistent with Kahan and Al-Tamimi's (2009) conclusion that various recruitment methods should be tailored to different subgroups of Arab Americans. For example, the Internet method employed by both Amer and Hovey (2012) and Barry (2001) yielded more highly educated and acculturated samples; 60% of the participants in the Amer and Hovey study had a minimum of a bachelor's degree and all of the participants in the Barry study had at least some college education. It is also possible that the participants in the Amer and Hovey study were at least somewhat acculturated, based on the fact that over half (55%) were second or later generations in the U.S. In contrast, the sample recruited through face-to-face personal contact by Aroian and colleagues (2009) was not highly educated. In this study, the majority of the women (64.8%) and slightly over half of their husbands (54.4%) had less than a high school education. Although Aroian and colleagues (2009) did not measure acculturation, it is likely that their sample was not highly acculturated; they were relatively recent immigrants who mostly spoke little to no English and lived in a community that was characterized as highly traditional by cultural informants. The importance of tailoring research procedures to specific subgroups of Arab Americans is discussed further in the next section on obtaining informed consent and collecting data.

Obtaining Informed Consent and Collecting Data

Like tailoring recruitment strategies for particular subgroups of Arab Americans, data collection may also need to be tailored to fit group variation. Salient dimensions of variability include language, language ability, and cultural orientation. The following discussion about these dimensions of group variation is based on generalities, and researchers are encouraged to use CBPR techniques (Minkler & Wallerstein, 2008) to assess their specific study population to determine if these generalities apply.

Language and Language Ability

Institutional review boards and scientific conditions for generating valid study findings require data collection materials that are easily understandable and not open to misinterpretation. These requirements include translation of informed consent forms and study measures into Arabic if study participants are not proficient in English. Different Arabic dialects also warrant consideration when translating study materials (Amer & Bagasra, 2013; Aroian, 2013; Asamarai, Solberg, & Solon, 2008). In addition, some Arab Americans may be illiterate (i.e. not able to read or write) in their spoken language, which requires alternatives to paper and pencil and Internet data collection. Each of these issues are particularly relevant whenever foreign-born Arab Americans are either exclusively or part of the study population.

Factors that relate to lack of proficiency in English for foreign-born Arab Americans in general include older age at immigration, shorter length of time in the receiving country, low education, and living in a community with a high density of co-ethnics (Remennick, 2004). Country of origin and gender are also relevant factors for foreign-born Arab Americans. Arab countries vary in their use of English as a second language. For example, English is a common second language in Egypt, Jordan, Yemen, Iraq, and Kuwait (Kulwicki & Ballout, 2013) and immigrants and refugees from these countries may possess a sufficient command of English. However, in some of these Arab countries women may be less likely to be bilingual than their male counterparts because of unequal access to life domains where English is used as a second language. More specifically, English use is likely limited to the public or work sphere, a sphere usually dominated by men in traditional Arab countries.

When literacy is low, researchers should consider potential effects from orally administering study materials. Oral administration is not only time-consuming but can also result in response bias because of the Arab cultural value on interpersonal harmony (Hodge, 2005). Arab Americans who highly value interpersonal harmony may be reluctant to exercise the right to refuse to answer study questions that they perceive as intrusive. Rather, they may employ a polite form of nondisclosure, such as giving socially desirable answers to questions about stigmatized, taboo, and culturally inappropriate topics (e.g. sexuality, mental illness).

Another problem with oral administration of study materials is that respondents may mishear certain questions. For example, a psychometric evaluation study of an Arabic language version of a measure of mood states that was administered orally found shared measurement error among items that were translated correctly to tap different mood states (Aroian, Kulwicki, Kaskiri, Templin, & Wells, 2007). Post hoc analysis revealed that the items in question were pronounced similarly in Arabic. Thus, a reasonable explanation for the shared measurement error is that respondents misheard similarly pronounced items and misinterpreted the items as asking about the same mood state.

Dialect differences can also be problematic when developing Arabic language versions of study materials. For example, Asamarai and colleagues (2008) discussed how dialect differences posed challenges when collecting data from North and South Somalis. Similarly, Aroian (2013) discussed challenges encountered when developing Arabic language versions of a battery of measures for Arab immigrants and refugees from 13 different Arab countries.

Arab Cultural Orientation

A number of scholars have identified cultural values and norms pertaining to interpersonal harmony and collectivism, gender role differentiation, and family honor as key features of Arab culture (Beitin & Aprahamian, 2014; Carolan, Bagherinia, Juhari, Himelright, & Mouton-Sanders, 2000; Hodge, 2005; Kulwicki & Ballout, 2013). These cultural values and norms have implications for obtaining consent and collecting data. Although each cultural feature is discussed below separately, they are interrelated. For example, differentiated gender roles in Arab families are structured to facilitate cooperation and interpersonal harmony, which are highly valued in collectivist societies (Beitin &

Aprahamian, 2014). In turn, family honor depends on complying with cultural norms about gender roles and appropriate behavior for men and women (Kulwicki & Ballout, 2013).

Interpersonal harmony and collectivism. In addition to the previously discussed potential for interpersonal harmony to result in response bias, the Arab cultural value on interpersonal harmony requires devoting time and paying attention to relational aspects of obtaining consent and collecting data. Many Arab Americans expect researchers to engage in social conversation and establish cordial relationships before getting down to the business of the research tasks. Often this means sharing a cup of tea or coffee during occasions such as data collection appointments (Kulwicki & Ballout, 2013). If the data collection appointment is in the study participant's home, the data collector is likely to be offered a selection of food choices. Also, impromptu guests may arrive and interrupt the data collection appointment. When this occurs, it is culturally appropriate to reschedule or delay the data collection rather than expect the study participant to shorten a visit with unexpected guests. Honor and reputation in the Arab culture are based on offering hospitality (Kulwicki & Ballout, 2013).

The collectivist nature of Arab society also has implications for obtaining informed consent. Arab families are embedded in a collectivist society whereby the "needs of the group" take precedence over the individual (Beitin & Aprahamian, 2014). Individual choice and autonomy are not what drive behavior in collectivist societies (Triandis, 1995), yet these are underlying principles of informed consent. Thus, Arab American individuals in collectively oriented families may not understand or accept the concept of individuals consenting to study participation. Rather, family members in authority may function as gatekeepers, deciding whether other family members should participate in a given study. As illustrated in the next section on gender norms, decisions about family member study participation is also a function of norms about gender roles.

Similarly, the collectivist nature of Arab societies has implications for maintaining confidentiality of research data. Confidentiality is an institutional review board requirement for protection of human participants, and individual privacy is a cornerstone of this principle. However, Arab American family members, particularly those in authority, may have a different notion of "protection." They may expect researchers to fully share information about individual family members who are participating in the study. For example, a parent might ask a researcher to disclose the child's answers to study questions, arguing that it is a parent's duty to monitor their child's activities and concerns.

Gender roles. Another important Arab cultural feature pertains to gender roles and gender expectations. In general, Arab Americans are oriented toward traditional gender roles, whereby gender relations are based upon respect rather than equality (Beitin & Aprahamian, 2014; Carolan et al., 2000). Men are typically the head of the household and, in this role, dictate permissible behaviors and activities for wives, female relatives, and children. Thus, Arab American men who are heads of households often expect to be consulted and grant permission for their family members' participation in research. Like individual choice, autonomy, and privacy, this gender role expectation may clash with principles of informed consent.

Family honor. Gender norms are closely aligned with family honor, which is another key cultural value for Arab Americans. Family honor is manifested, in part, by modesty and gender segregation (Carolan et al., 2000; Kulwicki & Ballout, 2013). Modesty and gender segregation mean that some Arab Americans will be more comfortable participating in the study if the gender of the data collector is matched to the gender of the study participant, particularly if data are collected face-to-face. Gender segregation may also be important when data are collected in a group setting, particularly when the study participants are women or girls. For example, a comparative study of the effects of same- and mixed-gender focus groups on self-disclosure in Arab Americans found that half of the women but none of the men found the mixed-gender focus group awkward and inhibited their responses (Sills, Jaber, & Pinelli, 2010).

Collecting data from Arab American women and girls in non-home settings, such as healthcare clinics or neighborhood centers, may also warrant consideration of transportation issues. Some Arab

American women without access to private transportation may be reluctant to take taxis or buses without being accompanied by a male family member. This issue was apparent in a study of discrimination against Arab American adolescents (Aroian, 2012). Fewer than anticipated adolescent girls arrived for a scheduled focus group, reportedly because of last-minute changes in family members' availability to drive them. In contrast, adolescent boys did not report transportation issues.

Family honor also colors consideration of how to approach certain topics of study. A number of researchers have noted that Arab Americans may be offended or hesitant to answer questions about topics that have implications for family honor, such as mental illness, substance abuse, domestic violence, and sexuality (Abu Raiya, Pargament, Stein, & Mahoney, 2007; Aloud & Rathur, 2009; Amer, Hovey, Fox, & Rezcallah, 2008; Aroian, 2013; Aroian et al., 2009). Thus, a number of studies about Arab Americans have engaged community experts to evaluate and adapt study materials for cultural appropriateness (Abu-Ras & Laird, 2011; Amer et al., 2008; Aroian, 2013; Kira et al., 2010; Sarsour, Tong, Jaber, Talbi, & Julliard, 2010).

There are a number of issues that can potentially result from adapting research measures for cultural appropriateness. On the one hand, removing questions about offending topics prohibits determining the true prevalence of certain problems and issues in Arab Americans. On the other hand, retaining offensive questions can alienate the entire study population, making it impossible to recruit study participants and conduct the study.

One means of resolving this dilemma is to avoid self-report and rely instead on participant observation and ethnographic methods to obtain a more accurate picture of hidden behavior. However, this approach is not consistent with principles of informed consent, and perpetuates Arab Americans' concerns about being under surveillance. Thus, an optimal approach would be to use CBPR, whereby community members define research problems of interest to the community and inform researchers about acceptable approaches to studying the identified problems.

Another issue to consider is that adapting research measures for cultural appropriateness can sacrifice content validity if the adaptation method shortcuts determining the full domain of content for the topic of interest (Aroian, 2013). For example, cultural experts were used in a study about Muslim Arab American families to identify and revise culturally inappropriate items in a measure of parent-child relationships (Aroian, Hough, Templin, & Kaskiri, 2008). One scale, the Togetherness Scale, which asks about the activities parents and children do together, needed substantial revision because it contained a number of activities that were not consistent with cultural experts' opinions about how mothers in the local study population behaved. Once identified, the cultural experts were asked to develop substitutions by modifying the wording slightly. For example, "Play a sport" was deemed inconsistent with local interpretations of modesty in women and revised to "Watch a sport." However, this approach of generating substitutive activities likely missed the full range of togetherness activities that were relevant to the study population. Interviewing the mothers and their children about the activities they do together would have been a more thorough approach to uncovering a more complete picture of their family life.

Case Example: The Arab Muslim Mother-Child Study

The study described in this case example was a National Institutes of Health-funded large-scale, longitudinal study of stress, coping, and psychological adjustment conducted in metropolitan Detroit with Muslim Arab immigrant and refugee mothers and their adolescent children (Aroian et al., 2009; Aroian, Templin, Hough, Ramaswamy, & Katz, 2011). Data were collected at three time points at approximately 18-month intervals to test a complex family-level structural equation model that included family, maternal, and child variables pertaining to socio-demographic risk, everyday hassles and immigration-related stressors, social support, coping, maternal distress, and child behavior problems. The quality of the mother-child relationship was the mediator between maternal distress and child behavior problems.

The sample was 635 Arab American mother-child dyads. Approximately three out of four of these dyads were retained for all three waves of data collection. A large battery of measures containing mostly fixed-choice questions was administered orally face-to-face by Arabic-speaking female data collectors in participants' homes, using participants' language of preference (English or Arabic). This study began after 9/11 in a location with a large concentration of relatively recent Muslim Arab immigrants.

Consistent with CBPR principles (Minkler & Wallerstein, 2008), the investigators relied heavily on community members for expert advice about designing the study procedures, adapting the study measures, implementing the study, and interpreting the study findings. The researchers used experts from the local community to provide information in advance about the local study population, including their cultural orientation and language ability. As described above in the section on sampling methods, a 13-member team of community members was also used to recruit and collect data from study participants as well as assist the researchers with interpreting study findings.

Three specific topics are illustrated next in this case example: (1) assessing and accommodating language ability, (2) balancing author, researcher, and ethnic group concerns about content in preexisting measures, and (3) obtaining consent/assent in a group with traditional gender roles. Study recruitment and the general process of adapting the measures for the study are published in more detail elsewhere (Aroian, 2013; Aroian et al., 2006). Study findings are also published elsewhere (Aroian et al., 2009; Aroian, Templin, & Hough, 2014; Aroian et al., 2011).

Assessing and Accommodating Language Ability

Community experts identified the need to develop Arabic language versions of the study materials for oral administration. The researchers followed these recommendations and proceeded to develop and pilot test the Arabic study materials with a small sample of 30 mother-adolescent dyads that was representative of the study population. A primary aim of the pilot study was to determine if the Arabic translation was comprehensible.

Items with low comprehensibility were identified and translation issues were resolved through further discussions with the translation team. These further discussions focused on dialect differences and removing colloquial expressions from the final Arabic language version of the study materials before they were used in the larger study (Aroian, 2013). Many of the adolescents also spontaneously offered that they would have preferred answering the study measures in English rather than Arabic.

Data collected from the larger study confirmed that it was necessary to have Arabic and English language versions of the study materials. More specifically, 97% of the mothers participated in Arabic, whereas 89.9% of the adolescents participated in English. Perhaps language differences were because all of the mothers were relatively recent immigrants or refugees, and the adolescents were either born in the U.S. (15.7%) or were, on average, relatively young when they immigrated (average age 6 years old; Aroian et al., 2009). Data about literacy also confirmed the need for orally administering the study materials. More specifically, 15.3% of the mothers reported not being able to read and write Arabic, perhaps because the majority of them had less than a high school education.

Culturally Appropriate Data Collection

Every item in every measure that was used in the study underwent extensive evaluation for cultural appropriateness by a panel of four cultural experts (Aroian et al., 2009). This process resulted in a number of adaptations in the original items. For example, some of the items from one of the measures of adolescent stress contained questions that pertained to dating, pregnancy, and alcohol and drug use. Although these behaviors do occur in some Muslim Arab adolescents from traditional families, the cultural experts advised that asking about these topics would alienate the study population and limit their interest in participating.

However, the author of one of the copyrighted measures, a measure of child internalizing and externalizing behavior problems, would not grant permission for his measure to be altered in any way. Both the cultural informants and the 13-member team of data collectors stated concern that seven of the items on the 113-item questionnaire would be very offensive to the study population (e.g. the child, "plays with own sex parts too much" and "thinks too much about sex"). This concern was validated when the entire 113-item questionnaire was pilot tested in Arabic: almost every participant refused to answer the seven offensive questions. In addition, when prompted, the study participants offered the opinion that many Muslim Arabs would refuse study participation if the offensive questions were retained. The author of the measure was contacted a second time to renegotiate his initial refusal to allow altering the measure. He eventually agreed, allowing researchers to not administer the seven items in question.

Informed Consent/Assent

As stated above, respondents for the study were Muslim Arab immigrant and refugee mothers and their adolescent children. Cultural informants were consulted prior to beginning the study about how to handle informed consent with this particular study population. Consistent with the literature about Arab culture (Kulwicki & Ballout, 2013), the cultural informants identified husbands as family gatekeepers who would likely expect wives and children to seek their permission for study participation. Yet, the institutional review board overseeing the study decided that informed consent from mothers and assent from children were sufficient. The cultural informants also introduced the possibility that some mothers would likely not want their husbands to know about their and their child's study participation, possibly because of wanting full control of the financial incentive for participating. (The financial incentive was $60 payable to the mother each time she and her child participated in one of the three data collection appointments.)

Study procedures were developed to fully respect mothers' wishes and accommodate either option, seeking permission or not disclosing. If a mother wished to seek permission from her husband, she was encouraged to do so. Upon request, data collectors also talked with husbands about potential concerns. Husbands were told that they could withdraw consent at any time if they had afterthoughts. Tracking strategies were also developed to document mothers' wishes and accommodate mothers who wished to keep study participation from their husbands. For this purpose, every mother participating in the study provided directions as to how she was to be contacted over the course of the study, including how personal phone calls could occur and whether messages and identifying information could be left on voicemail.

Only one instance occurred where a husband inadvertently learned about and become angry over his wife and child participating without his permission. In this instance, the data were destroyed and the family was dropped from further study participation. Limiting further study participation was due to concern about the safety of the involved study participants. Although how this incident was handled does not reflect the principle of individual autonomy that guides most Euro-American researchers and institutional review boards, it does reflect another principle of protecting human participants, which is minimizing risk and preventing adverse events from occurring as a result of study participation.

Critique

An obvious limitation of studies of Arab Americans, including the case example described above, is the focus on Arab Americans who live in ethnically dense geographic locations. As a consequence, many of the study findings about Arab Americans have limited generalizability (Amer & Bagasra, 2013; El-Sayed & Galea, 2009). For example, a systematic review of the last two decades of published studies about the health of Arab Americans revealed that 76% of these studies occurred in Michigan, with the majority occurring in metropolitan Detroit (El-Sayed & Galea, 2009). As previously discussed, these samples are not representative of the national Arab American population.

Given the challenges of obtaining representative samples and the likelihood that sampling methods with limited generalizability will continue to be used, researchers should provide sufficient background information about study participants and use this background information as the context for interpreting the study findings. By doing so, they will help consumers of research understand the diversity of the Arab American population and avoid using study findings to perpetuate stereotypes. Similarly, more intragroup comparative studies are needed to understand this diversity and how it affects phenomena of interest. Intragroup comparative studies should include variables that likely account for differences, such as acculturation, neighborhood ethnic density, years or generation in the U.S., religion, socioeconomic status, and so forth. In short, more research is needed with representative samples and comparisons that address intragroup differences to better understand Arab Americans.

Another limitation is that few studies mention evaluating the need for cultural adaptation of preexisting measures (i.e. measures that were originally developed for general populations). This omission may be for a number of reasons, such as: the materials were evaluated and it was determined that cultural adaptation was not needed for the study population in question; no such evaluation was conducted; or journal space limitations prevented describing the efforts undertaken. However, details about cultural considerations are essential so that consumers of research can consider sampling and measurement effects. Likewise, more research is needed to directly investigate sampling and measurement effects when data collection procedures and materials are adapted.

More culturally grounded studies of Arab Americans are also needed to discover nuances and explore how phenomena of interest are fully manifested in cultural contexts rather than trying to force Arab Americans to fit into existing psychological concepts and theories. Culturally grounded studies can employ qualitative, quantitative, or mixed methods. Qualitative methods, such as ethnography, grounded theory, and case studies, are well suited for inductively generating concepts and theories that are group-specific (Creswell, 2007) and therefore highly relevant to Arab Americans. With regard to quantitative culturally grounded studies, measures should be developed specifically for Arab Americans rather than adapting preexisting measures. As previously discussed, adapted measures are at risk for not addressing the full content domain of the constructs of interest (Aroian, 2013).

Yet another limitation of the current research about Arab Americans is that it relies on self-report. Arab cultural values about interpersonal harmony and family honor likely result in some response bias and underreporting, particularly when study participants are self-reporting about stigmatized topics. To minimize underreporting, researchers could use methods such as participant observation and reports from peers about other "anonymous" Arab Americans. However, to ensure that researchers are not violating Arab Americans' concerns about how they are portrayed, a "full" CBPR approach is crucial when using methods other than self-report. A full CBPR approach engages nonacademic members of the relevant community in every step of the research process from inception to interpretation of study findings (Minkler & Wallerstein, 2008). This full engagement includes having a central role determining the methods that will be employed for data collection.

Currently, there is a dearth of studies that use CBPR to engage Arab Americans in every step of the research process. The case example in this chapter used CBPR principles for adapting the study measures, developing culturally appropriate research procedures, and interpreting the study findings, but it was not a full CBPR approach. The case example sought advice from insiders from the community about designing the study procedures, adapting the study measures, implementing the study, and interpreting the study findings, but the insiders were not full partners in every aspect. For example, the study aims were developed in isolation by academic researchers, based on their understanding of the scientific literature about psychological adjustment in foreign-born mothers and their adolescent children. Nonacademic members of the local Arab American community were not involved in defining the phenomenon of interest and identifying the relevant research questions. For research findings to be truly meaningful to Arab Americans, Arab Americans must become key drivers in defining research questions and identifying the concepts that are important to them.

Conclusion

Psychological research on Arab Americans is still in its infancy. However, there is a growing body of literature that identifies issues and approaches to recruiting Arab Americans for research studies. There is also an emerging body of literature about making the research process culturally sensitive and meaningful to Arab Americans. Recommendations for how to conduct research with Arab Americans are complicated by the diversity of the Arab American population and growing appreciation that research strategies need to be tailored according to subgroup differences in language, cultural orientation, and a plethora of other factors, such as religion and generation in the U.S., that influence cultural orientation. A CBPR approach that engages community members from the Arab American population as full partners in the research process is a viable way to overcome many of the issues identified in this chapter.

References

Abdulrahim, S. & Baker, W. (2009). Differences in self-rated health by immigrant status and language preference among Arab Americans in the Detroit Metropolitan Area. *Social Science & Medicine* 68, 2097–2103. doi: 10.1016/j.socscimed.2009.04.017

Abu Raiya, H., Pargament, K. I., Stein, C., & Mahoney, A. (2007). Lessons learned and challenges faced in developing the Psychological Measure of Islamic Religiousness. *Journal of Muslim Mental Health* 2, 133–154. doi: 10.1080/15564900701613058

Abu-Ras, W. & Laird, L. (2011). How Muslim and non-Muslim chaplains serve Muslim patients? Does the interfaith chaplaincy model have room for Muslims' experiences? *Journal of Religion and Health* 50(1), 46–61. doi: 10.1007/s10943-010-9357-4

Aloud, N. & Rathur, A. (2009). Factors affecting attitudes toward seeking and using formal mental health and psychological services among Arab Muslim populations. *Journal of Muslim Mental Health* 4(2), 79–103. doi: 10.1080/15564900802487675

Amer, M. M. & Bagasra, A. (2013). Psychological research with Muslim Americans in the age of Islamophobia: Trends, challenges, and recommendations. *American Psychologist* 68, 134–144. doi: 10.1037/a0032167

Amer, M. M. & Hovey, J. D. (2012). Anxiety and depression in a post-September 11 sample of Arabs in the USA. *Social Psychiatry and Epidemiology* 47, 409–418. doi: 10.1007/s0012701103414

Amer, M. M., Hovey, J. D., Fox, C. M., & Rezcallah, A. (2008). Initial development of the Brief Arab Religious Coping Scale. *Journal of Muslim Mental Health* 3(1), 69–88. doi: 10.1080/15564900802156676

Arab American Institute. (2013). *Demographics.* Retrieved from www.aaiusa.org/arab-americans/22/demographics

Arfken, C. L., Arnetz, B. B., Fakhouri, M., Ventimiglia, M., & Jamil, H. (2011). Alcohol use among Arab Americans: What is the prevalence? *Journal of Immigrant Health*, 13, 713–718. doi: 10.1007/s10903-011-9447-8

Aroian, K. J., (2012). Discrimination against Muslim American Adolescents. *Journal of School Nursing* 48(3), 206–213. doi: 10.1177/1059840511432316

Aroian, K. J. (2013). Adapting a large battery of research measures for immigrants. *Journal of Immigrant and Minority Health* 15, 636–645. doi: 10.1007/s10903-012-9628-0

Aroian, K. J., Hough, E. S., Templin, T. N., & Kaskiri, E. A. (2008). Development and psychometric evaluation of an Arab version of the Family Peer Relationship Questionnaire. *Research in Nursing and Health* 31, 402–416. doi: 10.1002/nur.20277

Aroian, K. J., Hough, E. S., Templin, T. N., Kulwicki, A., Ramaswamy, V. & Katz, A. (2009). A model of mother-child adjustment in Arab Muslim immigrants to the US. *Social Science and Medicine* 69, 1377–1386. doi: 10.1016/jsocscimed.2009.08.027

Aroian, K. J., Katz, A., & Kulwicki, A. (2006). Recruiting and retaining Arab Muslim mothers and children for research. *Journal of Nursing Scholarship* 38(3), 255–261. doi: 10.1111/j.1547-5069.2006.00111.x

Aroian, K. J., Kulwicki, A., Kaskiri, E., Templin, T. N., & Wells, C. (2007). Psychometric evaluation of the Arabic language version of the Profile of Mood States. *Research in Nursing and Health* 30, 531–541. doi: 10.1002/nur.20211

Aroian, K. J., Templin, T. N., & Hough, E. E. (2014). Longitudinal study of daily hassles in adolescents in Arab Muslim immigrant families. *Journal of Immigrant and Minority Health* 16, 831–838. doi: 10.1007/s10903-013-9795-7

Aroian, K. J., Templin, T. N., Hough, E. E., Ramaswamy, V., & Katz, A. (2011). A longitudinal family-level model of Arab Muslim adolescent behavior problems. *Journal of Youth and Adolescence* 40, 996–1011. doi: 10.1007/s10964-010-9615-5

Asamarai, L. A., Solberg, K. B., & Solon, P. C. (2008). The role of religiosity in Muslim spouse selection and its influence on marital satisfaction. *Journal of Muslim Mental Health* 3, 37–52. doi: 10.108/15564900802006459

Asi, M. & Beaulieu, D. (2013). *Arab households in the U.S.: 2006–2010* (American Community Survey Brief, ACSBR/10–20). Washington, D.C.: U.S. Census Bureau. Retrieved from www.census.gov/prod/2013pubs/acsbr10-20.pdf

Barry, D. T. (2001). Assessing culture via the Internet: Methods and techniques for psychological research. *CyberPsychology and Behavior* 4(1), 17–21. doi: 10.1089/10949310151088334

Beitin, B. K. & Aprahamian, M. (2014). Family values and traditions. In S. C. Nassar-McMillan, K. J. Ajrouch, & J. Hakim-Larson (eds.), *Biopsychosocial perspectives on Arab Americans: Culture, development, and health* (pp. 67–88). New York: Springer. doi: 10.1007/978-1-4614-8238-3_4

Birman, D., Trickett, E., & Buchanan, R. M. (2005). A tale of two cities: Replication of a study on the acculturation and adaptation of immigrant adolescents from the former Soviet Union in a different community context. *American Journal of Community Psychology* 35(1/2), 83–101. doi: 10.1007/s10464-005-1891-y

Carolan, M., T., Bagherinia, G., Juhari, R., Himelright, J., & Mouton-Sanders, M. (2000). Contemporary Muslim families: Research and practice. *Contemporary Family Therapy* 22(1), 67–79. doi: 10.1023/A:1007770532624

Creswell, J. W. (2007). *Qualitative inquiry and research traditions* (2nd edn.). Thousand Oaks, CA: Sage.

El-Haj, T. (2007). "I was born here, but my home, it's not here": Educating for democratic citizenship in an era of transnational migration and global conflict. *Harvard Educational Review* 77(3), 285–316.

El-Sayed, A. M. & Galea, S. (2009). The health of Arab-Americans living in the United States: A systematic review of the literature. *BMC Public Health* 9, 272–289. doi: 10.1186/1471-2458-9-272

El-Sayed, A. M., Lauderdale, D. S., & Galea, S. (2010). Validation of an Arab name algorithm in the determination of an Arab ancestry for use in health research. *Ethnicity & Health* 15, 639–647. doi: 10.1080/13557858.2010.505979

Hodge, D. R. (2005). Social work and the house of Islam: Orienting practitioners to the beliefs and values of Muslims in the U.S. *Social Work* 50(2), 162–173. doi: 10.1093/sw/50.2.162

Jaber, L. A. (2003). Barriers and strategies for research in Arab Americans. *Diabetes Care* 26, 514–515. doi: 10.2337/diacare.26.2.514

Jaber, L. A., Brown, M. B., Hammad, A., Zhu, Q., & Herman, W. H. (2003). Lack of acculturation is a risk factor for diabetes in Arab immigrants in the U.S. *Diabetes Care* 26, 2010–2014. doi: 10.2337/diacare.26.7.2010

Kahan, D. & Al-Tamimi, A. (2009). Strategies for recruiting Middle Eastern-Americans for physical activity research: A case of snowballs and salaam. *Journal of Immigrant and Minority Health* 11, 380–390. doi: 10.1007/s10903-008-9117-7

Kira, I. A., Lewandowski, L., Templin, T., Ramaswamy, V., Ozkan, B., & Mohanesh, J. (2010). The effects of perceived discrimination and backlash on Iraqi refugees' mental and physical health. *Journal of Muslim Mental Health* 5, 59–81. doi: 10.1080/15564901003622110

Kulwicki, A. D. & Ballout, S. (2013). People of Arab heritage. In L. D. Purnell (ed.), *Transcultural health care* (pp. 159–177). Philadelphia, PA: FA Davis Company.

Lauderdale, D. S. (2006). Birth outcome for Arabic-named women in California before and after September 11. *Demography* 43, 185–201. doi: 10.1353/dem.2006.0008

Logan, J. R., Zhang, W., & Alba, R. D. (2002). Immigrant enclaves and ethnic communities in New York and Los Angeles. *American Sociological Review* 67, 299–322.

Minkler, M. & Wallerstein, N. (2008). *Community-based participatory research for health: From process to outcomes* (2nd edn.). San Francisco, CA: Jossey-Bass.

Moghadam, V. M. (2004). Patriarchy in transition: Women and the changing family in the Middle East. *Journal of Comparative Family Studies* 7(2), 137–163.

Naber, N. (2006). The rules of forced engagement: Race, gender, and the culture of fear among Arab immigrants in San Francisco post-9/11. *Cultural Dynamics* 18, 235–76. doi: 10.1177/0921374006071614

Nasseri, K. (2007). Construction and validation of a list of common Middle Eastern surnames for epidemiological research. *Cancer Detection & Prevention* 31, 424–429. doi: 10.1016/j.cdp.2007.10.006

Padela, A. I., Rasheed, S., Warren, G., Choi, H., & Mathur, A. K. (2011). Factors associated with positive attitudes toward organ donation in Arab Americans. *Clinical Transplantation* 25, 800–808. doi: 10.1111/j.1399-0012.2010.01382.x

Read, J. G., Amick, B., & Donato, K. M. (2005). Arab immigrants: A new case for ethnicity and health? *Social Science and Medicine* 61, 77–82. doi: 10.1016/j.socscimed.2004.11.054

Remennick, L. (2004). Language acquisition, ethnicity, and social integration among former Soviet immigrants of the 1990s in Israel. *Ethnicity and Racial Studies* 27, 431–454. doi: 10.1080/01491987042000189213

Rice, V. R. & Kulwicki, A. (1992). Cigarette use among Arab Americans in the Detroit Metropolitan Area. *Public Health Reports* 107, 589–594.

Sarsour, L., Tong, V. S., Jaber, O., Talbi, M., & Julliard, K. (2010). Health assessment of the Arab American community in Southwest Brooklyn. *Journal of Community Health* 35, 653–659. doi: 10.1007/s10900-0109260-7

Schwartz, K. L., Kulwicki, A., Weiss, L. K., Fakhouri, H., Sakr, W., Kau, G., and Severson, R. K. (2004). Cancer among Arab Americans in the metropolitan Detroit area. *Ethnicity and Disease* 14, 141–146.

Sills, S., Jaber, L. A., & Pinelli, N. R. (2010). Gender and self-disclosure: Methodological issues of mixed sex focus groups in Arab Americans. *Access Health* 1, 31–33.

Suleiman, M. W. (2010). The Arab community in the United States: A review and an assessment of the state of research and writing on Arab Americans. *British Journal of Middle Eastern Studies* 37, 39–55. doi: 10.1080/13530191003661112

Triandis, H. C. (1995). *Individualism and collectivism*. Boulder, Co: Westview.

28
RESEARCH SCHOLARSHIP
Critique of the Existing Literature and Visions for the Future

Mona M. Amer and Germine H. Awad

Scholars often refer to the late 1800s as the time when a significant stream of Arabs – mostly Christians from the region that now includes Syria and Lebanon – began to arrive in the U.S. (Naff, 1985). However, people from the Arab world have a much older bond with the U.S., having voyaged across the Atlantic to "discover" the New World before this claim was bestowed upon the Europeans (Suleiman, 2010). Although many of the earlier generations of Arabs melted into the fabric of American society, the Arab community in the U.S. has evolved into a distinct ethnic minority group, albeit one whose boundaries and characteristics (e.g. religion, national origin, language) are constantly changing.

The first academic publication on Arab Americans was by historian Philip Hitti in 1924, and since then many scholarly examinations of Arab Americans have been produced (Suleiman, 2010). Interest in studying this population budded during the 1960s and 1970s within the context of conflicts in the Middle East and greater attention to pluralism and ethnic politics in the U.S. (Aswad, 1974). A present-day perusal of book-selling websites reveals over 70 books related to Arab American culture, literature, immigration and settlement narratives, and post-9/11 experiences. However, overall Arab American studies pale in comparison to the volume of writings on other ethnic minority groups. Furthermore, much of the literature continues to concentrate on Arab Americans in Michigan (Bakalian & Bozorgmehr, 2011; Suleiman, 2010).

Writers from diverse disciplines have expressed both frustration and alarm at the juxtaposition between the little attention accorded to Arab Americans in academia and the relentless – feverish – concentration on Arabs and Muslims in the mainstream media. To complicate matters further, Arabs are swept into the folds of the "White/Caucasian" racial category while at the same time being yanked aside and targeted with prejudice and discrimination that is prototypical of an ethnic minority status. As Amer (2014, p. 153) stated, "Perhaps the most compelling acculturation paradox is that as an immigrant minority group, Arabs in America have the task of adapting to the host 'White' culture, of which they are already classified as being members!" These paradoxes have led numerous authors to describe Arab Americans as an "invisible" minority (e.g. Kadi, 1994; Naber, 2000; Salari, 2002).

The situation is particularly bleak with regard to psychological scholarship on Arab Americans. To explore the trends in publications over the past 20 years, a PsycINFO Boolean search was conducted for peer-reviewed journal articles that referred to Arab (e.g. Arab*, Middle East*, or any of the 22 Arab countries such as Syria*, Leban*, etc.) and American (e.g. U.S., USA, or America*) in the title. Up until the year 2001, zero to three articles were published annually (see Figure 28.1). However, after 2001 there was a steady increase in publications, with a range of 13 to 23 journal articles released annually over the five years to 2014. From the 185 relevant articles identified from 1995–2014, only

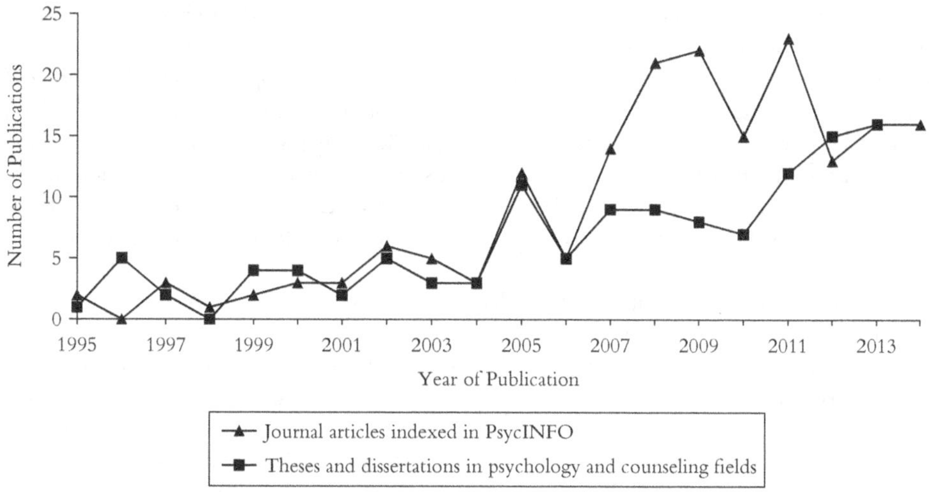

Figure 28.1 Trends in Psychological Research on Arabs in the U.S. and Canada
Note: The ProQuest Dissertations and Theses Global database was used for identifying theses and dissertations. The number of dissertations for 2013 may be underestimated due to a time lag in institutional indexing of dissertations.

28.6% were first-authored by a psychologist or counselor. Other disciplines that were represented by the first authors were public health (16.2%), nursing (12.4%), sociology (10.3%), and medicine (8.65%).

Of course, these numbers do not account for the total volume of psychological scholarship on Arab Americans. Not included were other types of research outputs (e.g. dissertations, books), relevant works that did not make reference to the Arab American population in their title, and psychology publications that are not indexed in PsycINFO. Nevertheless, three conclusions can be drawn from these search results. First, 9/11 was a turning point in catalyzing interest in psychology-related research on Arab Americans. Second, the bulk of this research has been produced by the health fields and not psychology. Third, the amount of psychological scholarship related to Arab Americans remains woefully inadequate and is a serious shortcoming in the field that needs to be rectified.

The aim of this chapter is to analyze the current state of the psychological academic literature related to Arab Americans and provide a vision for future scholarship. The chapter begins with a review of the subject matters that have captured the most attention in previous studies, as well as topics and subfields of psychology that have been virtually ignored. Next, the main themes that frequently emerge in scholarly writings are presented, based on an examination of the recurring arguments and salient issues raised throughout the *Handbook of Arab American Psychology*. Finally, the chapter looks toward the future, with suggestions for ways to enhance the quality of research, as well as practical strategies for promoting and developing the field of Arab American psychology.

Popular Topics of Investigation in the Arab American Psychological Literature

Multiple psychology-related topics have been addressed by previous scholars studying Arab Americans. There are some key areas, however, that have garnered the most attention, such as acculturation, post-9/11 discrimination, mental health status, mental health services, and human/family development. Health issues have also been represented, with a relatively large body of research on tobacco use. This section describes some of the most popular subject matters in previous publications and offers suggestions for important topics that have yet to be explored.

Research pertaining to the cultural adjustment of Arab immigrants and their children was historically dominated by scholars in sociology, anthropology, and ethnic studies. The era post 9/11, however, saw a boost in interest among psychologists. Most of these psychological studies have utilized Berry's model of acculturation (Berry, 1997, 2001) as a key theoretical framework guiding their work. Some studies have attempted to document socio-demographic predictors for acculturation and ethnic identity, whereas others have associated acculturation status with psychological outcomes such as mental health (for a review, see Amer, 2014). However, more complex modeling to examine multiple interacting variables has been utilized by only a few researchers (e.g. Ahmed, Kia-Keating, & Tsai, 2011; Amer, 2005).

The acculturation process for Arab Americans has been complicated by heightened stressors post 9/11, particularly discrimination. A relatively large volume of literature has focused on the increased prejudice and discrimination toward Arabs and Muslims in the U.S. This includes documenting prejudicial rhetoric and discrimination in different contexts (e.g. media, school curricula, policing, employment, and housing) and examining the mental health consequences of experiencing discrimination. Anti-Arab prejudice is the primary topic related to Arab Americans that has received attention from social and experimental psychologists, including experimental studies of implicit prejudice (e.g. Brown et al., 2013; Bushman & Bonacci, 2004; Lyons, Kenworthy, & Popan, 2010; Mange, Chun, Sharvit, & Belanger, 2012; Park, Felix, & Lee, 2007). In addition, studies have examined predictors of perceived discrimination for Arab Americans, which include factors such as acculturation, perceived control, ethnic identity, and religious identification (e.g. Ahmed et al., 2011; Awad, 2010; Moradi & Hasan, 2004). However, some topics related to discrimination have not yet been adequately addressed in the literature, such as the process of internalizing stigma, institutional discrimination, and physiological correlates.

Considering discrimination and other stressors, it is not surprising that psychological wellbeing is one of the key topics addressed in the literature on Arab Americans. Numerous studies conducted by psychologists, social workers, and healthcare professionals have examined the sociocultural correlates for mental health concerns such as anxiety, depression, and posttraumatic stress disorder. Trauma has been a central topic in the Arab refugee literature in particular. Overall, studies have shown disproportionately high rates of mental health concerns (e.g. Abu-Ras & Abu-Bader, 2009; Amer & Hovey, 2012; Jamil et al., 2008), with a focus on understanding risk or vulnerability. Very few studies (e.g. Ajrouch, 2007b; Beitin & Allen, 2005) have focused primarily on resilience and resources. Moreover, this literature has virtually ignored mental illnesses such as bipolar disorder and schizophrenia, as well as general indicators of wellbeing such as self-esteem and quality of life.

With regards to mental health interventions for Arab Americans, the literature has focused on two main threads: (a) cultural and institutional barriers toward seeking formal psychological supports; and (b) case descriptions and expert recommendations on culturally-sensitive service provision. Studies have only recently begun to address the issues of clinician cultural competence in serving Arab Americans (e.g. Sabbah, Dinsmore, & Hof, 2009; Soheilian & Inman, 2015). Moreover, treatment outcome studies are rare; only two journal articles were identified in the literature. Martin (2014) compared psychotherapy utilization among Arab Americans to non-Arab clients, including length of treatment, treatment satisfaction, and reason for discontinuing services. Other researchers reported on a randomized clinical trial evaluating narrative exposure therapy for Iraqi refugees (Hijazi et al., 2014).

While there are no studies yet from health psychology, there is a vibrant literature on Arab American health issues produced by medical, nursing, and public health specialists that may be of interest to psychologists. To date there are more than 100 published journal articles that report on Arab Americans' health, morbidity, and mortality. These include investigations related to prevalence of hypertension, heart disease, diabetes, cancer, asthma, maternal health, and infant mortality. A large portion of these reports showed racial/ethnic differences in these health conditions, with most researchers offering conjectures on potential factors (e.g. acculturation) that could explain the disparities but not actually measuring those hypothesized factors. Other studies examined predictors of disease for Arab Americans such as sociocultural, lifestyle, and health beliefs/behaviors. Some health-related publications also discussed health awareness, prevention, and intervention programs; barriers to health screening; and guidance for culturally sensitive healthcare.

One significant area of study related to health has been tobacco use. Given the high rates of smoking among Arab Americans (Haddad, El-Shahawy, Shishani, Madanat, & Alzyoud, 2012; Islam & Johnson, 2003; Rice et al., 2006), tobacco use was often measured in research on health conditions. Additionally, over 30 publications from nursing, public health, and psychology have focused exclusively on trends and interventions for tobacco use. The bulk of this literature was produced by a group of research collaborators in the Detroit-Dearborn area and focused on Arab American youth. The waterpipe (hookah) is a popular concern across studies on Arab American tobacco use. In general, the tobacco literature appeared to be the most advanced in regard to documenting recommendations and program evaluation results for community interventions targeting Arab Americans.

Aside from these areas of research concentration, some progress has been made in understanding issues related to developmental and family psychologies. There are numerous published articles that loosely focused on Arab American youth, although a cohesive narrative is missing. Topics related to identity development, gender double standards, intercultural gaps with parents, community pressures, peer relationships, and challenges at school. Almost all of these studies focused on adolescents, with minimal attention to younger children. There are also a few studies on family issues, particularly parenting. Contributions by sociologists dominate the literature focused on Arab American older adults. These studies tended to focus on risk and protective factors for the acculturation process.

In sum, there are many topics of investigation related to Arab Americans that have gained significant traction. However, some areas in psychology have been overlooked. For example, although psychological testing is a vital element of some psychological services, there have been no endeavors yet to evaluate the validity or applications of commonly-used clinical assessment instruments for Arab Americans. The literature related to forensic psychology is also virtually absent, despite the importance of understanding how Arab ethnic identity of crime victims or defendants may influence courtroom bias in a climate of anti-Arab prejudice post 9/11 (Clark et al., 2013). Suggestions for future areas of investigation are presented in Table 28.1.

Cross-Cutting Themes in the Existing Literature

Notwithstanding the varied topics that have been tackled in the literature on Arab Americans, a reading of the chapters in the *Handbook of Arab American Psychology* reveals several overarching themes that interconnect previous scholarly works. These themes provide an indication of the characteristics and issues that are salient to the Arab American community.

As described Part I of the *Handbook*, the racial/ethnic experience of what it means to be "Arab" has dynamically shifted over time, often in tension with public perceptions, institutional classifications, and Arab Americans' own self-identifications. As detailed in the chapters on race and community activism, since the early 1900s the status of Arabs in the U.S. has been repositioned from marginal whiteness to racialized minority, affecting the privileges that come with these classifications. The chapter on race points out that many Arab Americans today do not consider themselves White because they are not treated like other White ethnic groups. One of the outcomes of this racialization process is the popular view of Arab Americans as a monolithic and static group, a view that is fundamentally flawed and prejudiced.

Instead, Arab Americans form an incredibly diverse population. The main element that ties Arabs together – the Arabic language – is itself marked by an assortment of so many types and dialects that communication between two Arabs from different nations can be encumbered. As outlined in the opening chapter of the *Handbook*, the Arab world contains striking heterogeneity in geographies, socio-historical experiences, political systems, cultures and traditions, and religions. These diverse

Table 28.1 Recommended Areas for Future Empirical Research With Arab Americans

Specialization	*Topics*
Addiction	Cultural and psychosocial predictors for substance abuse; prevalence and predictors of khat drug use; effective tobacco prevention/cessation programs; culturally tailored drug addiction treatment; effectiveness of 12-step fellowships
Clinical, counseling	Cultural adaptation and validation of psychological tests; career counseling; humanistic approaches; group approaches; psychotherapy efficacy and effectiveness; effectiveness of integrating religion in treatment; intergenerational transmission of trauma; community trauma interventions; serious mental illness; effective clinician competence training
Community	Post-settlement refugee stressors; mental health awareness and stigma reduction; resources for resilience; community needs assessments; program evaluation results; community organizing and advocacy techniques
Cultural, multicultural	Empirical assessment of values and cultural characteristics; alternative models of acculturation; valid measures of acculturation; impact of host culture attitudes on acculturation strategies; role of technology in acculturation; experiences of sojourners; applicability of racial identity models and processes
Developmental	Experiences of preschool and elementary school children; developmental psychopathology; bicultural or multicultural skills and code-switching; leisure and after-school activities; effects of government welfare policies on older adults; support for caregivers of older adults; culturally tailored nursing/retirement homes
Family	Blended and nontraditional families; interethnic and interreligious couples; family conflict resolution techniques; male batterer interventions; alternative family violence interventions; refugee family dynamics; sexual minority experiences
Forensic	Cultural influences in divorce and custody disputes; impact of jury bias; immigration and documentation issues
Health	Alternatives to individualistic health psychology theories; acculturation and psychological correlates for health status; risky health behaviors; cultural/religious influences on treatment adherence; culturally sensitive healthcare strategies; effective strategies for patient-provider rapport; disclosure of taboo topics in patient-physician interactions; effective health awareness and prevention strategies
Industrial/Organizational	Effectiveness of employment diversity training; workplace experiences of Arab and Muslim employees and employers
Religion	Outcomes of group religious practices; multidimensional models of religiosity; tolerance and forgiveness; religion and prosocial behaviors
School/Educational	Effective anti-bullying interventions; mental health screening; impact of ethnic and religious schools on child development; correlates of academic achievement; adult education
Social	Consequences of nonnormative behavior within the Arab American community; intercultural peer relationships; psychological outcomes of overt vs. covert prejudice; effects of social media on prejudice and discrimination; intergroup conflict reduction; prejudice reduction interventions

characteristics are imported by those who arrive at the shores of North America, rendering sweeping statements about the characteristics of the community hard to come by. It is no wonder that the writers of many chapters struggle in trying to present a cohesive picture of Arab Americans to the reader.

Even attempts to create a profile of Arab Americans based on objective data can be misleading. For example, scholars and Arab American advocacy organizations have often embraced the conclusions from Census data that overall Arab Americans boast higher incomes and education levels compared to the U.S. population. This claim fails to appreciate the underlying nuances in the data, such as a rising poverty rate that exceeds the national average and lower-income and lower-education pockets among refugees, some recent immigrants, and persons from nations such as Iraq, Yemen, Morocco, and Somalia.

These socioeconomic disparities within the Arab American community can have important implications for psychologists studying this group. For example, the chapter on school psychology argues that the ongoing assumption that Arab Americans excel in education has muted the attention given to youth from less affluent backgrounds who face poverty-related stressors that can negatively impact their academic performance. The chapter on aging discusses how rising economic pressures disproportionately affect the wellbeing of older adults, especially later-life immigrants who are no longer able to benefit from government supplements due to changes in welfare policy. Likewise, the chapter on health disparities shows how health status reportedly worsens in parallel with lower income status, and therefore research with nonrepresentative samples in lower-income areas has distorted the ability to establish accurate prevalence rates for the Arab American community.

Other striking subgroup differences among Arab Americans are highlighted throughout the *Handbook*. For example, many of the issues discussed (e.g. acculturation, school achievement, health behaviors, tobacco use) are reported to differ depending on country of origin. Immigration status can have critical implications for acculturation stressors, academic achievement, trauma, mental health, and health status. For example, throughout the *Handbook* it is argued that refugees undergo a distinct migration and acculturation experience, facing many unique and arduous challenges to which voluntary immigrants may not be exposed.

Across the different subgroups of Arab Americans, there does seem, however, to be a set of cultural values that somewhat define the Arab American community, particularly among individuals and families that are more culturally traditional. For example, almost all of the *Handbook* authors refer to the central role of family in Arab American culture. A great deal of respect is accorded to family members, particularly authority figures, and interdependent family relations continue throughout the life cycle. The family is the main conduit for socializing youth into the ethnic culture and acceptable gender roles. It is also a primary source of emotional, financial, and social support, as shown in chapters that discuss the experiences of women and older adults. For all these reasons, family issues may be a focal subject in counseling and psychotherapy sessions. Family members can, moreover, be involved in providing valuable information for psychological assessments or in participating in psychotherapy sessions.

Given the value of family and a collectivist and tight-knit community structure, it is not surprising that honor is a central theme that is threaded throughout the *Handbook*. Violations of cultural norms and sanctioned behaviors may result in bringing shame to the family. This relates to monitoring gender and sexual relationships, child misbehavior, and spousal selection. It also influences psychological services, as one of the reasons that Arab Americans may avoid pursuing services is the associated stigma. Admitting to a mental health problem can negatively affect the reputation of the person and his or her family, and some clinical concerns (e.g. domestic violence, substance abuse) are particularly sensitive.

Religion is another value that is highlighted by many of the *Handbook* authors. As described in the chapter focused on religion, the Arab American community features diverse religious affiliations and practices. Although many Arab Americans may not be religious, as a whole religion may play a significant role in influencing individual, family, and community life. Many writers discuss how religiosity and religious coping can be potential protective factors for buffering stress and mental health concerns and preventing unhealthy behaviors such as smoking and substance abuse. At the same time, because religious beliefs and practices among Arab Americans may differ from the norms in mainstream society, particularly for Muslims, practicing religion may be met with challenges that contribute to acculturation stress.

The central role of acculturation in the lives of Arab Americans is underscored in almost all chapters. The authors of the acculturation chapter provide a detailed review of the acculturation, ethnic identity, and enculturation research related to Arab Americans, as well as a critique of the limitations of theoretical models of acculturation. Many authors argue that Arab Americans do not all display a single strategy or trend with respect to acculturation. Rather, the acculturation process itself can influence numerous aspects of Arab American life, including youth development, family relationships (e.g. intercultural tensions), gender roles, and health-related behaviors. Stressors faced during the acculturation process can compromise mental health. A person's acculturation level can also influence openness to seeking psychological services and the types of psychotherapy interventions that may be suitable to that person.

Contextual factors can have a powerful influence on the acculturation process. In the post-9/11 era, the environment has become increasingly hostile toward Arabs and Muslims, making acculturation more challenging. The chapter on discrimination discusses the underlying mechanisms and general experiences of discrimination for Arab Americans. Most *Handbook* authors note that Arab Americans face heightened discrimination across different ecological levels, including with peers, at school, in employment, in healthcare settings, in the media, and via government policies. The authors discuss the negative impacts of prejudice and discrimination on, for example, academic achievement, mental health, and health status. The increased targeting of Muslim Arab Americans in particular (compared to Christians) is noted in some chapters. Discrimination is conceptualized throughout the text as a key risk factor that can exacerbate the ongoing stressors that Arab Americans face in the U.S.

Despite ongoing pressures, Arab Americans show great adaptability and resilience, and connectedness with the Arab community appears to be a source of strength and psychological wellbeing. For many Arab Americans, ethnic culture – including foods, music, and other practices – is a source of pride. Ethnic identity is described by many *Handbook* authors as a source of psychological support. Living in Arab ethnic enclaves is discussed as a protective factor for youth and older adults, and as a buffer for health-related stressors. Moreover, community centers (including churches, mosques, and central meeting places) are described as venues where children are socialized into cultural norms and adults build essential networks. These community centers can also play an important role in supporting research endeavors and be a site for psychological interventions.

Enhancing the Quality of Psychological Research on Arab Americans

Prior to 9/11, psychological research on Arab Americans was in a nascent stage, where large data collection efforts were few and far between. For Arab American psychology to move forward, future studies must utilize better samples, more theory-driven research that appropriately defines constructs, and research methods that allow scholars to collect data that ensure the integrity of research participants and maximize the chance that hypotheses are appropriately tested.

The samples used in psychological research with ethnic minorities have a profound effect on the validity of the results. For example, external validity (i.e. the extent to which studies are generalizable across people, settings, and times) is compromised when researchers are not mindful in their sampling techniques and participant recruitment (Awad & Cokley, 2010). Because relatively few empirical studies exist that utilize Arab American samples, research that is conducted may have a disproportionate influence in determining what is believed about Arab Americans. Therefore, it is necessary that future studies with Arab Americans include more rigorous and representative samples.

The first step toward achieving this goal is to sufficiently define the Arab American sample in a given study. When sample sizes allow, researchers need to account for national differences within Arab Americans. For example, participants of Lebanese ancestry may be different from those of Libyan descent in their cultural traditions, mental health-related behaviors, and in other psychological constructs. Along those lines, attention should be paid to people from religious subgroups who may experience psychological phenomena differently. In addition, as previous research has shown, there is a pervasive flaw in the literature of conflating Arabs with Muslims. To combat this conflation, both demographic information (e.g. religious identification, ethnic identification) and deeper-level identity constructs (e.g. religious and ethnic identity levels, acculturation) could be measured to more accurately capture the sample of Arab Americans under study.

Relatedly, future studies should aim to utilize more rigorous sampling strategies. The major barrier to random or representative samples is the lack of recognition on the U.S. Census ethnicity and race demographic question. Currently, Arab Americans are classified under the White category. Even when they choose the "some other race" category, they are recoded by the Census as White. Currently, the only representation Arab Americans have on the Census is on the American Community Survey (ACS) through the ancestry question. The greatest limitation of the ACS is that it only samples 1% of the U.S. population and has disproportionately high error margins (Mather, Rivers, & Jacobsen, 2005). Only a minute proportion of the Arab American population (which may or may not be representative) is counted by the ACS. Therefore, compared to other ethnic minority groups, there is no population data from which to draw random samples, which severely hampers the external validity of findings.

The implications for not being represented on the Census are serious and far-reaching. The race and ethnicity questions on the Census are used as a standard for virtually every demographic form collected by U.S. institutions. These institutions range from government entities to neighborhood schools. Even when data are collected on Arab Americans (as they are by many institutions in Michigan), they are reaggregated into the White category when reported to government entities. In addition, because Arab Americans do not have their own category on demographic forms, sometimes researchers must guess if Arab Americans have chosen another non-White racial category. For example, in their study on youth waterpipe use in New Jersey based on representative state data, Jordan and Delnevo (2010) conjectured that the disproportionately high rate of waterpipe use among Asian Americans could be explained by Arab Americans who selected the Asian category in the absence of an Arab/Middle Eastern option. Without accurate ethnic identifiers by the Census, researchers are unable to collect vital information on health, education, discrimination, and other indicators for which there may be a disparate impact for Arab Americans.

The U.S. Census, in conjunction with the Office of Management and Budget (OMB), is working toward representing Arab Americans on the 2020 Census in a Middle Eastern/North African ethnicity category. The inclusion of such a category would greatly improve sample quality in Arab American research. In the meantime, it is important to encourage institutions and individuals who engage in data collection to include the Arab American ethnicity in their demographic forms so that systematic information about this group can be collected.

In addition to accurate ethnic identifiers on data collection forms, there needs to be better identification and selection procedures of Arab Americans recruited into research studies to limit the use of small convenience samples. Many of the studies that include large population-based samples are from places such as Michigan, which tends to be overrepresented in studies about Arab Americans. Future studies need to be more representative of the rest of the Arab American community in terms of religion, socioeconomic status, language, age, and generation status. Although researchers have used last name algorithms to obtain random samples of Arab Americans (e.g. El-Sayed, Lauderdale, & Galea, 2010), this procedure may contribute to the conflation of Arabs and Muslims since some names are both Muslim and Arab.

In addition to more rigorous sampling methods, Arab American research should aim to be more theory driven and less descriptive when possible. For research areas that are in their infancy (e.g. forensic psychology), more descriptive methods may be common. One possible way to frame studies that investigate a new phenomenon with Arab Americans is to ascertain if existing theories are applicable to this group. This process (see Cokley & Awad, 2008) would determine if existing theories are appropriate for Arab Americans and allow for theory building if found unsuitable. Even when there are theories that explain psychological phenomena for Arab Americans, the lack of theory testing may lead to misunderstandings about pertinent constructs. One such example is the conflation of the terms 'assimilation' and 'acculturation', which demonstrates a lack of understanding around the acculturation process for Arab Americans and how it relates to similar experiences shared by other ethnic minority groups. Relatedly, sometimes the measures of acculturation used in studies did not match the operationalization of this construct as chosen by the authors (e.g. using unidimensional scales to measure Berry's bidimensional model of acculturation).

Just as theoretical underpinnings can strengthen research designs, the research methodologies can themselves be improved to produce more accurate and useful information. The majority of research on Arab Americans has thus far focused on bivariate relationships to explore the intersections among variables such as acculturation, stress, family dynamics, and mental health. Future studies that use more advanced statistical modeling (such as structural equation modeling) can offer deeper and more complex understandings of the interrelations among variables. Additionally, longitudinal studies can better capture developmental perspectives when studying youth (Ahmed et al., 2011). To date, only one major longitudinal study – focusing on mother-child relationships and behavioral problems – has been conducted with Arab Americans (Aroian, Templin, Hough, Ramaswamy, & Katz, 2011). Furthermore, experimental and quasi-experimental designs can be used to test psychological interventions.

Given the numerous stressors and challenges faced by Arab Americans, it is important for psychologists to go beyond basic investigations and invest efforts in applied research that can have tangible impacts on improving the lives of Arabs living in North America. Such research can consist of conducting community needs assessments to identify key issues to target with interventions, and carrying out intervention research related to designing and evaluating programs and policies.

Community needs and assets assessments can be valuable in determining priorities for future research and interventions. For example, previous community assessments of health-related concerns were useful not only in identifying which health conditions were of most critical importance to Arab Americans, but also in discovering levels of health knowledge and awareness, service and intervention preferences, and cultural and institutional barriers to service access and utilization (e.g. Kulwicki & Cass, 1994; Laffrey, Meleis, Lipson, Solomon, & Omidian, 1989; Sarsour, Tong, Jaber, Talbi, & Julliard, 2010). Such information can be instrumental in improving community-based interventions, formal services, and even policy. Community assessments focused on social and psychological issues would be similarly useful in informing research and programming.

Research related to designing, implementing, and evaluating interventions is essential in establishing best practices and ensuring that programs and services are effective in meeting community needs. Previous authors have recommended that efforts be made to ease the acculturation and adjustment process for Arab international students (Alreshoud & Koeske, 1997), immigrants (Amer, 2014; Scuglik, Alarcón, Lapeyre, Williams, & Logan, 2007), and refugees (Gordon, Taylor, & Sarkisian, 2010; Yako & Biswas, 2014). As suggested by previous writers, programs can focus on reducing acculturative stressors (Gaudet, Clément, & Deuzeman, 2005; Yako & Biswas, 2014), combating prejudice and discrimination (Abouchedid & Nasser, 2006; Gaudet et al., 2005; Kira et al., 2010; Oswald, 2005), and enhancing resources for resilience such as strengthening ethnic identity, religious supports, and family/social supports (Ahmed et al., 2011; Ajrouch, 2007a; Amer, 2014; Yako & Biswas, 2014). Research on school-based interventions, counseling approaches, psychotherapy interventions, and other psychological services, such as mental health awareness and prevention programs, is also needed.

There is no doubt that many ethnic-specific community agencies have already established interventions related to these issues. For example, at the Arab Community Center for Economic and Social Services (ACCESS) in Dearborn, Michigan, programs have been developed to integrate mental health with physical healthcare services (Kira, Hammad, & Abou-Mediene, 2007) and provide comprehensive psychosocial and mental health services for families facing challenges or crises (Aswad & Gray, 1996). Unfortunately, only a few other psychological programs could be found documented in the literature, mostly focused on psychosocial services for refugees (e.g. Gordon et al., 2010), domestic violence campaigns (e.g. Kulwicki & Miller, 1999), or tobacco-related interventions (e.g. Al-Faouri et al., 2005; Rice, Weglicki, Templin, Jamil, & Hammad, 2010). Previous writings have mostly emphasized the program conceptualization and description of services and participants, without providing details on formal experimental and nonexperimental program evaluation results. Documenting such data is essential in order to ensure program effectiveness and encourage replicability of best practices.

When conducting applied research, whether focused on interventions or policy advocacy, participatory approaches can be instrumental in engaging community members in the process of research and producing more valid results that have greater impact on social change (Jason, Keys, Suarez-Balcazar, Taylor, & Davis, 2004). Examples are participatory action research (e.g. Fals-Borda & Rahman, 1991; Gaventa, 1988) and community-based participatory research (Israel, Eng, Schulz, & Parker, 2013; Minkler & Wallerstein, 2008). These research models acknowledge oppression affecting minority groups and empower community stakeholders, who have ownership over the research purpose, measurement tools, data collection procedures, interpretation of results, and dissemination or application of the findings. The time invested in these methods is worthwhile for building community trust, ensuring that the research is aligned to community interests, and improving validity and cultural sensitivity of the process and results.

Strategies for Promoting and Formalizing Arab American Psychology

The above-mentioned strategies for improving the quality of research on Arab Americans can only be realized if there is a healthy cadre of psychology students and professionals who are interested in and dedicated to studying this population. However, thus far there are only a few psychology researchers scattered across the nation who have made Arab Americans a priority for their work. Thus, efforts must be made to enhance not only interest in studying Arab Americans, but also the practical resources needed to facilitate the production of quality research.

At the level of psychology departments, graduate students can be encouraged to focus on Arab Americans for their master's or doctoral-level research, or at least include subsamples of Arabs in ethnically diverse participant groups. Students may avoid studying this population if there are no advisors in their departments that have expertise in Arab Americans or at least multicultural psychology. Therefore, efforts can be made to connect students with mentors and committee members external to their university. Over the past 20 years, over 200 theses or dissertations focused on Arab Americans were completed as part of psychology- or counseling-related degrees (see Figure 28.1 for years 1995–2013), the vast majority of which were never published as journal articles. Without publication, these items regrettably vanish from the landscape of Arab American psychology scholarship. Research can be conducted to determine the facilitators and barriers for publishing graduate-level research, with an eye toward establishing recommendations for encouraging student publication as well as supporting students in continuing their line of research through an academic career.

Students of Arab background may have a particular interest in contributing to the scholarship on Arab Americans. Considering that there is only a sparse number of Arab graduate students peppered across the nation, psychology programs could implement strategies for recruiting Arab students. Such strategies can be drawn from the many publications that provide recommendations for ethnic minority recruitment and retention (e.g. Hammond & Yung, 1993; Rogers & Molina, 2006; Suinn & Borrayo, 2008). It is important to note, however, that ethnic minority students may hesitate to concentrate on ethnic topics for fear of being marginalized from the mainstream research community, restricting themselves to topics that are less valued, or raising tensions with faculty (Padillo, 1994). Graduate programs should support Arab graduate students in finding mentors who can help them navigate such challenging dilemmas. Also, the American Psychological Association of Graduate Students, Committee on Ethnic Minority Affairs (2010) released a guidebook for ethnic minority students that can be of support to Arab Americans in their personal and professional development, including tips for conducting research and strategies for facing challenges in their graduate program such as microaggressions.

Needless to say, the existence of a formal network of Arab American psychologists could alleviate some of the above-mentioned concerns; for example, by offering mentoring support to graduate students. However, although the past decade has seen several roundtable discussions at the annual American Psychological Association (APA) convention aimed at formalizing an Arab/Middle Eastern working group, to date a formal psychological association for Arabs and Middle Easterners has not been established. In the last couple of years, those interested in Arab American psychology were offered space by the APA's Division 45 (Society for the Psychological Study of Culture, Ethnicity and Race) to network and discuss plans for a formal Arab American psychology association.

One of the challenges to establishing a formal organization is that currently Arab Americans are not recognized as an ethnic minority group within APA governance. A working group was formed in 2012 within the Committee of Ethnic Minority Affairs of APA to discuss the ethnic minority status of those with ancestry from the Middle East or North Africa. The support from this committee bodes well for the eventual recognition of Arab Americans as an ethnic group within the APA. Strides have already been made, however, at the level of APA divisions. For example, Division 45 has included an Arab/Middle Eastern American member-at-large slate to its executive committee.

Establishing an Arab American psychological association and being recognized as an ethnic minority group within the largest psychology professional organization will help strengthen research efforts concerning Arab Americans by enhancing opportunities for networking. Researchers who are currently working in their local communities can collaborate in larger research partnerships or coalitions, aimed at developing larger sample sizes and more sophisticated research designs. Creating an interactive web-based resource center for Arab American research would also be helpful. For example, one of the current frustrations faced by researchers is the paucity of culturally sensitive and validated measures. This website could offer summaries and access to available tools.

Finally, grant funding for graduate students and professional researchers is an important consideration for accomplishing research goals. However, limitations in the available funding for Arab American research relates once again to the issue of recognition of Arabs/Middle Easterners as an ethnic minority group. The lack of formal recognition as an ethnic minority group by the Census and the OMB signifies that Arab Americans are currently not protected by the U.S. government. Therefore, not only do Arab American researchers not qualify for ethnic minority investigator grants, but they also must justify studying health disparities with a non-protected group. Unfortunately, it is very difficult to obtain federal funding for studies that solely examine health or psychological phenomena with Arab Americans. The same restrictions may apply to state-level and private-funding streams focused on ethnic minority research. Thus, efforts should be made to advocate for the inclusion of Arab Americans as an ethnic minority group within relevant funding structures.

Conclusion

The psychological literature on Arab Americans is slowly burgeoning to include diverse areas of investigation. However, the volume of research has not sufficiently kept pace with the growing urgency to better understand and support this group in light of intensified pressures post 9/11. Greater efforts are needed to improve sampling and research methodologies used in research with Arab Americans. Official recognition as an ethnic minority group by the OMB, the Census Bureau, and the APA would certainly help improve research in this area. In the meantime, collaboration and networking among researchers, community stakeholders, students, and professionals can contribute to promoting further progress in the field of Arab American psychology.

Acknowledgment

The authors extend their appreciation to Reem Deif for supporting this chapter with her database search on theses and dissertations.

References

Abouchedid, K. & Nasser, R. (2006). Info-bias mechanism and American college students' attitudes towards Arabs. *International Studies Perspectives* 7, 204–212. doi: 10.1111/j.1528-3585.2006.00240.x

Abu-Ras, W. & Abu-Bader, S. H. (2009). Risk factors for depression and posttraumatic stress disorder (PTSD): The case of Arab and Muslim Americans post-9/11. *Journal of Immigrant & Refugee Studies* 7, 393–418. doi: 10.1080/15562940903379068

Ahmed, S. R., Kia-Keating, M., & Tsai, K. H. (2011). A structural model of racial discrimination, acculturative stress, and cultural resources among Arab American adolescents. *American Journal of Community Psychology* 48(3–4), 181–192. doi: 10.1007/s10464-011-9424-3

Ajrouch, K. J. (2007a). Health disparities and Arab-American elders: Does intergenerational support buffer the inequality–health link? *Journal of Social Issues* 63, 745–758. doi: 10.1111/j.1540-4560.2007.00534.x

Ajrouch, K. J. (2007b). Resources and well-being among Arab-American elders. *Journal of Cross-Cultural Gerontology* 22, 167–182. doi: 10.1007/s10823-006-9033-z

Al-Faouri, I., Rice, V. H., Weglicki, L., Kulwicki, A., Jamil, H., Baker, O., … Dakroub, M. (2005). Culturally sensitive smoking cessation intervention program redesign for Arab American youth. *Ethnicity & Disease* 15(Suppl. 1), 62–64.

Alreshoud, A. & Koeske, G. F. (1997). Arab students' attitudes toward and amount of social contact with Americans: A causal process analysis of cross-sectional data. *The Journal of Social Psychology* 137, 235–245. doi: 10.1080/00224549709595434

Amer, M. M. (2005). *Arab American mental health in the post September 11 era: Acculturation, stress, and coping* (Doctoral dissertation). Available from ProQuest Dissertations and Theses database (UMI No. 3171022).

Amer, M. M. (2014). Arab American acculturation and ethnic identity across the lifespan: Sociodemographic correlates and psychological outcomes. In S. C. Nassar-McMillan, K. J. Ajrouch, & J. Hakim-Larson (eds.), *Biopsychosocial perspectives on Arab Americans: Culture, development and health* (pp. 153–173). New York: Springer. doi: 10.1007/978-1-4614-8238-3_8

Amer, M. M. & Hovey, J. D. (2012). Anxiety and depression in a post-September 11 sample of Arabs in the USA. *Social Psychiatry and Psychiatric Epidemiology* 47, 409–418. doi: 10.1007/s00127-011-0341-4

American Psychological Association of Graduate Students' Committee on Ethnic Minority Affairs. (2010). *APAGS resource guide for ethnic minority graduate students* (2nd edn.). Washington, D.C.: American Psychological Association. Retrieved from www.apa.org/apags/resources/ethnic-minority-guide.pdf

Aroian, K. J., Templin, T. N., Hough, E. E., Ramaswamy, V., & Katz, A. (2011). A longitudinal family-level model of Arab Muslim adolescent behavior problems. *Journal of Youth and Adolescence* 40, 996–1011. doi: 10.1007/s10964-010-9615-5

Aswad, B. C. (1974). Arab-American studies. *Middle East Studies Association Bulletin* 8(3), 13–26.

Aswad, B. C. & Gray, N. A. (1996). Challenges to the Arab-American family and ACCESS. In B. C. Aswad & B. Bilgé (eds.), *Family and gender among American Muslims: Issues facing Middle Eastern immigrants and their descendants* (pp. 223–240). Philadelphia, PA: Temple University Press.

Awad, G. H. (2010). The impact of acculturation and religious identification on perceived discrimination for Arab/Middle Eastern Americans. *Cultural Diversity and Ethnic Minority Psychology* 16(1), 59–67. doi: 10.1037/a0016675

Awad, G. H. & Cokley, K. O. (2010). Designing and interpreting quantitative research in multicultural counseling. In J. G. Ponterotto, J. Casas, L. A. Suzuki, & C. M. Alexander (eds.), *Handbook of multicultural counseling* (3rd edn., pp. 385–396). Thousand Oaks, CA: Sage.

Bakalian, A. & Bozorgmehr, M. (2011). Middle Eastern and Muslim American studies since 9/11. *Sociological Forum* 26, 714–728. doi: 10.1111/j.1573-7861.2011.01273.x

Beitin, B. K. & Allen, K. R. (2005). Resilience in Arab American couples after September 11, 2001: A systems perspective. *Journal of Marital and Family Therapy* 31, 251–267. doi: 10.1111/j.1752-0606.2005.tb01567.x

Berry, J. W. (1997). Immigration, acculturation, and adaptation. *Applied Psychology: An International Review* 46, 5–68. doi: 10.1080/026999497378467

Berry, J. W. (2001). A psychology of immigration. *Journal of Social Issues* 57, 615–631. doi: 10.1111/0022-4537.00231

Brown, L. M., Awad, G. H., Preas, E. J., Allen, V., Kenney, J., Roberts, S., & Lusk, L. B. (2013). Investigating prejudice toward men perceived to be Muslim: Cues of foreignness versus phenotype. *Journal of Applied Social Psychology* 43(Suppl. 2), E237–E245. doi: 10.1111/jasp.12015

Bushman, B. J. & Bonacci, A. M. (2004). You've got mail: Using e-mail to examine the effect of prejudiced attitudes on discrimination against Arabs. *Journal of Experimental Social Psychology* 40, 753–759. doi: 10.1016/j.jesp.2004.02.001

Clark, J. W., Cramer, R. J., Percosky, A., Rufino, K. A., Miller, R. S., & Johnson, S. M. (2013). Juror perceptions of African American- and Arabic-named victims. *Psychiatry, Psychology and Law* 20, 781–794. doi: 10.1080/13218719.2012.736283

Cokley, K. O. & Awad, G. H. (2008). Conceptual and methodological issues in multicultural research. In P. P. Heppner, D. M. Kivlighan, & B. E. Wampold (eds.), *Research design in counseling* (3rd edn., pp. 366–384). California: Wadsworth.

El-Sayed, A. M., Lauderdale, D. S., & Galea, S. (2010). Validation of an Arab name algorithm in the determination of Arab ancestry for use in health research. *Ethnicity & Health* 15, 639–647. doi: 10.1080/13557858.2010.505979

Fals-Borda, O. & Rahman, M. A. (1991). *Action and knowledge: Breaking the monopoly with participatory action research.* New York: Apex Press.

Gaudet, S., Clément, R., & Deuzeman, K. (2005). Daily hassles, ethnic identity and psychological adjustment among Lebanese-Canadians. *International Journal of Psychology* 40(3), 157–168. doi: 10.1080/00207590444000267

Gaventa, J. (1988). Participatory research in North America. *Convergence: An International Journal of Adult Education* 21, 19–28.

Gordon, R. D., Taylor, R., & Sarkisian, G. V. (2010). Psychoeducational workshops as a practical tool to facilitate resettlement with Iraqi refugees and anchor relatives. *Journal of Muslim Mental Health* 5, 82–98. doi: 10.1080/15564901003605628

Haddad, L., El-Shahawy, O., Shishani, K., Madanat, H., & Alzyoud, S. (2012). Cigarette use attitudes and effects of acculturation among Arab immigrants in USA: A preliminary study. *Health* 4, 785–793. doi: 10.4236/health.2012.410122

Hammond, R. & Yung, B. (1993). Minority student recruitment and retention practices among schools of professional psychology: A national survey and analysis. *Professional Psychology: Research and Practice* 24, 3–12. doi: 10.1037/0735-7028.24.1.3

Hijazi, A. M., Lumley, M. A., Ziadni, M. S., Haddad, L., Rapport, L. J., & Arnetz, B. B. (2014). Brief narrative exposure therapy for posttraumatic stress in Iraqi refugees: A preliminary randomized clinical trial. *Journal of Traumatic Stress* 27, 314–322. doi: 10.1002/jts.21922

Islam, S. M. S. & Johnson, C. A. (2003). Correlates of smoking behavior among Muslim Arab-American adolescents. *Ethnicity & Health* 8, 319–337. doi: 10.1080/13557850310001631722

Israel, B. A., Eng, E., Schulz, A. J., & Parker, E. A. (2013). *Methods for community-based participatory research for health* (2nd edn.). San Francisco, CA: Jossey-Bass.

Jamil, H., Grzybowski, M., Hakim-Larson, J., Fakhouri, M., Sahutoglu, J., Khoury, R., & Fakhouri, H. (2008). Factors associated with self-reported depression in Arab, Chaldean, and African Americans. *Ethnicity & Disease* 18, 464–470.

Jason, L. A., Keys, C. B., Suarez-Balcazar, Y., Taylor, R. R., & Davis, M. I. (eds.) (2004). *Participatory community research: Theories and methods in action.* Washington, D.C.: American Psychological Association.

Jordan, H. M. & Delnevo, C. D. (2010). Emerging tobacco products: Hookah use among New Jersey youth. *Preventive Medicine* 51, 394–396. doi: 10.1016/j.ypmed.2010.08.016

Kadi, J. (ed.) (1994). *Food for our grandmothers: Writings by Arab-American and Arab-Canadian feminists.* Boston, MA: South End Press.

Kira, I., Hammad, A., & Abou-Mediene, S. (2007). Models of health and mental health integration: ACCESS Community Health and Research Center model. *Ethnicity & Disease* 17(Suppl. 3), 66–69.

Kira, I. A., Lewandowski, L., Templin, T., Ramaswamy, V., Ozkan, B., & Mohanesh, J. (2010). The effects of perceived discrimination and backlash on Iraqi refugees' physical and mental health. *Journal of Muslim Mental Health* 5(1), 59–81. doi: 10.1080/15564901003622110

Kulwicki, A. D. & Cass, P. S. (1994). An assessment of Arab American knowledge, attitudes, and beliefs about AIDS. *Image: The Journal of Nursing Scholarship* 26, 13–17. doi: 10.1111/j.1547-5069.1994.tb00288.x

Kulwicki, A. D. & Miller, J. (1999). Domestic violence in the Arab American population: Transforming environmental conditions through community education. *Issues in Mental Health Nursing* 20, 199–215. doi: 10.1080/016128499248619

Laffrey, S. C., Meleis, A. I., Lipson, J. G., Solomon, M., & Omidian, P. A. (1989). Assessing Arab-American health care needs. *Social Science and Medicine* 29, 877–883. doi: 10.1016/0277-9536(89)90087-7

Lyons, P. A., Kenworthy, J. B., & Popan, J. R. (2010). Ingroup identification and group-level narcissism as predictors of U.S. citizens' attitudes and behavior toward Arab immigrants. *Personality and Social Psychology Bulletin* 36, 1267–1280. doi: 10.1177/0146167210380604

Mange, J., Chun, W.Y., Sharvit, K., & Belanger, J. J. (2012). Thinking about Arabs and Muslims makes Americans shoot faster: Effects of category accessibility on aggressive responses in a shooter paradigm. *European Journal of Social Psychology* 42, 552–556. doi: 10.1002/ejsp.1883

Martin, U. (2014). Psychotherapy with Arab Americans: An exploration of therapy-seeking and termination behaviors. *International Journal of Culture and Mental Health* 7, 162–167. doi: 10.1080/17542863.2012.742121

Mather, M., Rivers, K. L., & Jacobsen, L. A. (2005). The American community survey. *Population Bulletin* 60(3), 3–20.

Minkler, M. & Wallerstein, N. (2008). *Community-based participatory research for health: From process to outcomes* (2nd edn.). San Francisco, CA: Jossey-Bass.

Moradi, B. & Hasan, N. T. (2004). Arab American persons' reported experiences of discrimination and mental health: The mediating role of personal control. *Journal of Counseling Psychology* 51, 418–428. doi: 10.1037/0022-0167.51.4.418

Naber, N. (2000). Ambiguous insiders: An investigation of Arab American invisibility. *Ethnic and Racial Studies* 23, 37–61. doi: 10.1080/014198700329123

Naff, A. (1985). *Becoming American: The early Arab immigrant experience.* Carbondale, IL: Southern Illinois University.

Oswald, D. L. (2005). Understanding anti-Arab reactions post–9/11: The role of threats, social categories, and personal ideologies. *Journal of Applied Social Psychology* 35, 1775–1799. doi: 10.1111/j.1559–1816.2005.tb02195.x

Padillo, A. M. (1994). Ethnic minority scholars, research, and mentoring: Current and future issues. *Educational Researcher* 23(4), 24–27.

Park, J., Felix, K., & Lee, G. (2007). Implicit attitudes toward Arab-Muslims and the moderating effects of social information. *Basic and Applied Social Psychology* 29, 35–45. doi: 10.1080/01973530701330942

Rice, V. H., Weglicki, L. S., Templin, T., Hammad, A., Jamil, H., & Kulwicki, A. (2006). Predictors of Arab American adolescent tobacco use. *Merrill-Palmer Quarterly* 52, 327–342. doi: 10.1353/mpq.2006.0020

Rice, V. H., Weglicki, L. S., Templin, T., Jamil, H., & Hammad, A. (2010). Intervention effects on tobacco use in Arab and non-Arab American adolescents. *Addictive Behaviors* 35, 46–48. doi: 10.1016/j.addbeh.2009.07.005

Rogers, M. R. & Molina, L. E. (2006). Exemplary efforts in psychology to recruit and retain graduate students of color. *American Psychologist* 61, 143–156. doi: 10.1037/0003-066X.61.2.143

Sabbah, M. F., Dinsmore, J. A., & Hof, D. D. (2009). A comparative study of the competence of counselors in the United States in counseling Arab Americans and other racial/ethnic groups. *International Journal of Psychology: A Biopsychosocial Approach* 4, 29–45.

Salari, S. (2002). Invisible in aging research: Arab Americans, Muslims and Middle Eastern immigrants in the United States. *The Gerontologist* 42, 580–588. doi: 10.1093/geront/42.5.580

Sarsour, L., Tong, V. S., Jaber, O., Talbi, M., & Julliard, K. (2010). Health assessment of the Arab American community in Southwest Brooklyn. *Journal of Community Health* 35, 653–659. doi: 10.1007/s10900-010-9260-7

Scuglik, D. L., Alarcón, R. D., Lapeyre, A. C., III, Williams, M. D., & Logan, K. M. (2007). When the poetry no longer rhymes: Mental health issues among Somali immigrants in the USA. *Transcultural Psychiatry* 44, 581–595. doi: 10.1177/1363461507083899

Soheilian, S. S. & Inman, A. G. (2015). Competent counseling for Middle Eastern American clients: Implications for trainees. *Journal of Multicultural Counseling and Development* 43(3), 173–190. doi: 10.1002/jmcd.12013

Suinn, R. M. & Borrayo, E. A. (2008). The ethnicity gap: The past, present, and future. *Professional Psychology: Research and Practice*, 39, 646–651. doi: 10.1037/0735-7028.39.6.646

Suleiman, M. W. (2010). The Arab community in the United States: A review and an assessment of the state of research and writing on Arab Americans. *British Journal of Middle Eastern Studies* 37, 39–55. doi: 10.1080/13530191003661112

Yako, R. M. & Biswas, B. (2014). "We came to this country for the future of our children. We have no future": Acculturative stress among Iraqi refugees in the United States. *International Journal of Intercultural Relations* 38, 133–141. doi: 10.1016/j.ijintrel.2013.08.003

INDEX

Note: Page numbers in **bold** indicate illustrations and tables.

Made in United States
Cleveland, OH
18 April 2025

16194132R00254